Distributed
Operating Systems
& Algorithms

Distributed
Operating Systems
& Algorithms

Randy Chow
Theodore Johnson

UNIVERSITY OF FLORIDA

 **ADDISON-WESLEY**

An imprint of Addison Wesley Longman, Inc.

Reading, Massachusetts • Harlow, England • Menlo Park, California • Berkeley, California
Don Mills, Ontario • Sydney • Bonn • Amsterdam • Tokyo • Mexico City

Senior Acquisitions Editor: J. Carter Shanklin
Editorial Assistant: Angela Buenning
Production Editor: Patricia A. O. Unubun
Text & Cover Designer: Loren Hilgenhurst Stevens
Cover Illustrator: Sheng-Wan Hu

The cover design was inspired by the "turtles all the way down" anecdote, which is believed to originate from William James and has been retold by many philosphers including Bertrand Russell and Steve Hawking. We added the stack of "gators" to show another layered-structured autonomous system. The artwork was contributed by Sheng-Wan Hu.

Access the latest information about Addison-Wesley titles from our World Wide Web site: http://www.awl.com/cseng

Many of the designations used by manufacturers and sellers to distinguish their products are claimed as trademarks. Where those designations appear in this book, and the publisher was aware of a trademark claim, the designations have been printed in initial caps or in all caps.

The programs and the applications presented in this book have been included for their instructional value. They have been tested with care but are not guaranteed for any particular purpose. Neither the publisher nor the authors offer any warranties or representations, nor do they accept any liabilities with respect to the programs or applications.

Library of Congress Cataloging-in-Publication Data

Chow, Randy.
    Distributed operating systems and algorithms / Randy Chow,
  Theodore Johnson.
       p.   cm.
    Includes bibliographical references and index.
    ISBN 0-201-49838-3
    1. Distributed operating systems (Computers)   2. Computer
  algorithms.   I. Johnson, Theodore. II. Title.
  QA76.76.063C459 1997   96-48480
  005.4'476--dc21   CIP

Reprinted with corrections, February 1998.

ISBN 0-201-49838-3
 2 3 4 5 6 7 8 9 10-MA-01009998

dedicated to:

Johna and Taiying

PREFACE

This book has developed from a set of lecture notes we used to teach a graduate two-course sequence on operating systems. We had difficulties finding a textbook that had balanced coverage of concepts and theories and sufficient detail for a graduate-level class. After using research papers and selected book chapters for several semesters (which students hate), we developed lecture notes for the students and then developed the notes into this book.

The key idea behind the book is to integrate the theory and practice of distributed operating systems. Many texts provide an overview of distributed systems with a vague description of the algorithms. It is difficult to teach an in-depth course from these books. Other texts focus on algorithms. However, it is hard to motivate students to study algorithms if they do not have a picture of what is needed in practice. For example, understanding the need for naming and directory services clarifies the need for causal message passing and update propagation.

The first part of the book (Chapters 1 through 8) is intended to be used for a core graduate course on operating systems. It provides a broad discussion of modern operating systems. Since we assume that the student readers already have taken an undergraduate course on operating systems, we do not include many topics, such as memory management, deadlocks, and device drivers, that are typically covered by undergraduate courses and that are well covered by existing texts. Instead, we concentrate on issues and implementations of modern operating systems for parallel systems, distributed systems, real-time systems, and computer networks. Major topics include concurrent programming, distributed process communication and coordination, distributed memory and file systems, and computer network security. The programming projects in this part concentrate on using tools, such as sockets, RPC, and threads.

The second part of the book (Chapters 9 through 13) is intended for an advanced course on distributed operating systems, focusing on algorithms for asynchronous distributed systems. The material provides a framework for thinking about distributed systems, precise algorithm descriptions, and an understanding of why the algorithms were developed and why they are correct. The underlying system assumption is a group of cooperating distributed processes with possible failures and data replications in the system. The theme behind much of the material presented in this part is providing the framework for implementing a replicated server — a prototype for implementing a fault-tolerant and highly available distributed system. The projects in this part use the tools presented in the first part to implement the algorithms.

The different focuses of the two parts of the book complement each other, with the first part supplying background and the second part supplying theory. While the book is intended for a two-course sequence, it also works well for a graduate operating system or an advanced distributed systems class alone. Although each of the two parts is self-contained, extensive cross-referencing allows the reader to emphasize either theory or implementation or to cover both elements of selected topics. With the widespread exposure of the Internet, we envision that the book could also be of interest to undergraduate students and can be tailored to undergraduate classes. Furthermore, the combined book with an extensive bibliography makes an excellent reference for the practitioner who has some working experience on operating systems.

BOOK ORGANIZATION

The book is structured to present the important concepts of distributed operating systems. We make many references to commercial and experimental systems to illustrate the concepts and the implementation issues. In addition, each chapter provides an extensive annotated bibliography that points the interested reader to recent developments in distributed computing theory, technology, and practice. In the following we give a brief description of the content of each chapter.

Part I of the textbook is a pragmatic presentation of the basic concepts and implementation issues of a distributed operating system. It is organized in three major components: fundamental concepts, distributed processes, and distributed resources.

Fundamental Concepts (Transparency, Service, and Coordination)

▪ Chapter 1 introduces a classification of centralized operating system, network operating system, distributed operating system, and cooperative autonomous systems, using the key characteristics of *virtuality, interoperability, transparency* and *autonomicity*, respectively, for each system. It illustrates the evolution that led to the development of modern distributed operating systems and explains the emerging need for distributed software and the importance of distributed coordination algorithms.

▪ Chapter 2 begins the discussion of distributed operating systems. It presents the concepts of *transparency* and *services*. Distributed systems and their underlying communication architectures are introduced. The chapter concludes with a list of major system design issues that establishes an order for the presentation of the subsequent chapters.

Distributed Processes (Synchronization, Communication, and Scheduling)

▪ Chapter 3 describes concurrent processes and programming. It defines processes and threads and shows how their interaction can be modeled by using some fundamental concepts such as a graph, a logical clock, and the client and server model. Both shared memory and message passing for synchronization and communication are addressed. They are presented along with the development of concurrent language constructs. A taxonomy of these language mechanisms and their implementation is given. This chapter presents an integrated view of synchronization and communication.

▪ Chapter 4 extends the discussion of process interaction from synchronization to communication and to distributed process coordination using message passing communication. Three communication models, message passing (socket), request/reply (RPC), and transaction communication, are presented. A special emphasis is placed on group communication and coordination. Two classical distributed coordination problems, mutual exclusion and leader election using message passing interprocess communication, are introduced. These problems are further studied in Chapters 10 and 11 in Part II of the textbook. The chapter also includes a presentation of name service, an essential facility for communication in distributed systems.

▪ Chapter 5 turns to the third process management issue, that of process scheduling. The effect of communication on both static and dynamic process scheduling is emphasized. The chapter describes distributed computation through dynamic redistribution of processes by using remote execution and process migration techniques. It also addresses several unique issues in real-time scheduling.

Distributed Resources (Files and Memory)

- Chapter 6 discusses the distributed implementation of file systems, the first of the two important distributed resources: files and memory. It demonstrates the use of the concept of transparency and service in the design of distributed file systems. Two major implementation issues, data caching and file replication, are discussed in this chapter. The chapter also covers distributed transactions as part of the file service. Since management of replicated data touches upon both data and communication, two central issues in distributed systems, it is further detailed in Chapter 12.

- Chapter 7 covers distributed shared memory systems that simulate a logical shared memory on a physically distributed memory system. The issues studied are coherence and consistency of data due to memory sharing. The chapter describes implementation strategies for different memory consistency requirements. It also shows the significance of the object-based data sharing models.

- Chapter 8 addresses unique security issues in network and distributed environments. These issues are divided into two areas: authorization and authentication. Authorization includes the study of distributed access and flow control models. Authentication covers cryptography and its applications for mutual authentication and key distribution protocols. Implementations of some security features in modern systems are illustrated.

Part II of the textbook discusses distributed algorithms. The discussion is pragmatic and is intended to give the reader a solid understanding of common problems and solution techniques. The topics are organized in five chapters.

Distributed Algorithms

- Chapter 9: introduces the concepts of time and global states in a distributed system. The fundamental problem of distributed algorithms is a lack of a global clock and a global state. Recent research on vector time and distributed predicates has developed unified models for thinking about distributed time and the distributed state. This chapter presents the concepts of causality, vector timestamps, and global states. The algorithms for implementing these concepts are presented. The connections between the different models are explored. Finally, a model for proving the correctness of distributed algorithms is presented.

- Chapter 10: covers distributed synchronization and distributed election. While the distributed synchronization algorithms are not considered pragmatic, they illustrate important algorithm design techniques. For example, voting algorithms for replicated data management are foreshadowed in Maekawa's algorithm, and the Chang-Singhal-Liu algorithm illustrates the ideas behind distributed shared memory (and distributed object) algorithms. The chapter concludes with algorithms for electing a computation leader. Election is a critical component of many systems. The invitation algorithm in particular is a prototype for handling failures in an asynchronous system and foreshadows the group view maintenance algorithms of Chapter 12.

■ Chapter 11 discusses the abstract distributed agreement problem. First, Byzantine agreement is discussed. Next, the Fischer–Lynch–Paterson (FLP) result that no algorithm solves distributed agreement problems in an asynchronous system is covered in detail. This is the appropriate point to introduce the FLP result, because the next chapter covers replicated data management and must solve distributed agreement in asynchronous systems. The FLP result leaves open three ways to achieve distributed agreement in an asynchronous system: hope that it happens, use relative agreement, or use a randomized algorithm. The chapter discusses these implications of the FLP result and concludes with some randomized agreement protocols.

■ Chapter 12 covers replicated data management. Since providing replicated servers reduces to replicating the state of the servers, this section also discusses the problems and concepts of replication. We cover three main approaches: the transaction approach, the reliable multicast approach, and the log propagation approach. The transaction approach includes discussion of two-phase commit, three-phase commit, one-copy serializability, voting, and dynamic voting protocols. The reliable multicast approach includes discussion of virtual synchrony, algorithms for implementing reliable and causal multicast, algorithms for totally ordered multicast, and consistent multicast group maintenance algorithms. The log propagation approach covers naive log propagation, epidemic, and causal log propagation. This chapter is the culmination of Part II of the text and draws together the results presented in previous chapters.

■ Chapter 13 covers distributed rollback and recovery. These techniques are critical for implementing fault-tolerant systems and are complimentary to the replicated data management techniques of the previous chapter. By using the theory developed in the previous chapters (especially Chapter 9), different rollback and recovery algorithms are presented in a unified manner and are related to algorithms discussed previously.

SUGGESTED COVERAGE

The book contains sufficient materials for a two-semester operating system (or distributed system) course sequence. To use the book for an one-semester course, we recommend the following two options for coverage with different orientations.

■ **Distributed Operating Systems:** This option covers the entire Part I with supplemental Sections 9.1, 9.2, 10.1.2, 10.1.3, 10.1.4, 10.2, 12.1, and 12.1.3 from Part II. The course will focus on the implementation issues of the major components in a distributed operating system. The supplemental sections in Part II extend the discussion of distributed coordination algorithms.

■ **Distributed Algorithms:** This option uses the entire Part II with Sections 4.1–4.4, 6.1–6.3, and 7.1–7.4 from Part I. The course will emphasize the design of distributed algorithms in distributed systems. The selected sections in Part I serve as the background and motivations for the discussion of distributed algorithms in Part II.

Solutions to exercise problems and program templates for projects will be provided to authorized instructors through the Web site of Addison Wesley Longman.

ACKNOWLEDGMENTS

The authors wish to acknowledge the COP5615 (Operating System Principles) and the COP6635 (Distributed Operating Systems) classes for allowing them to test preliminary versions of the book. Special thanks go to Anthony Bridgewater, Raja Chatterjee, William Chow, Roger Collins, Darin Davis, Carlos Guerra, Steve Greenwald, Vanja Josifovski, Eric Shaffer, and Shiby Thomas for finding errors in the examples and algorithms.

Several topics of discussion use the research work from theses and dissertations by students at the University of Florida. Frank Anger and J. J. Hwang contributed the multiprocessor scheduling models and algorithms. The LAM distributed shared memory system was given by Roger Denton. I-Lung Kao shared the discussion of the complex security policies. Lionel Maugis contributed the start of the bibliography and the total ordering algorithm from his thesis.

The comments and feedback from the reviewers were enormously valuable. We wish to show our appreciation to them for providing their expertise to improve the quality of the book. They are: Warren R. Carithers of Rochester Institute of Technology, Prasun Dewan of University of North Carolina, Peter G. Drexel of Plymouth State College, Gary Harkin of Montana State University, Eric H. Herrin, II of University of Kentucky, Mark A. Holliday of Western Carolina University, Michael A. Keenan of Columbus State University, William F. Klostermeyer of West Virginia University, Bruce Maggs of Carnegie-Mellon University, James Purtilo of University of Maryland, Gurdip Singh of Kansas State University, and Salih Yurttas of Texas A&M University.

The book cover design was inspired by the "turtles all the way down" anecdotes which is believed to originate from William James and has been retold by many philosophers including Bertrand Russell and Stephen Hawking. We added the stack of "gators" to show another layered-structured autonomous system. The artwork was contributed by Sheng-Wan Hu. Special thanks go to Michael Downes and S. Y. Cheng who helped to solve many LaTex technical problems.

We started writing the book when our wives complained that they did not have any book dedicated to them as many others do. We thank Johna and Taiying for giving us such great motivation to write the book. This book is dedicated to them.

Contents

Chapter 8

Distributed Computer Security 265

Distributed
Operating Systems
& Algorithms

I

Distributed Operating Systems

CHAPTER

Operating System Fundamentals

Advances in computer and communication technologies have revolutionalized our modern society. The use of computers in managing information and automation has become an integral part of our daily life. Systems with multiple computers connected through communication channels to facilitate information sharing and cooperative work are commonplace. Recently we have also experienced a significant growth of applications that require networking and distributed processing. As a result, various computer networks and distributed systems have been developed and put into practical use. The development of software technologies, both systems and applications, often falls behind advances in hardware. In this book we shall be concerned with the software issues in the design and implementation of modern computer systems, particularly the operating system and distributed algorithms that are essential in supporting networking and distributed processing. We assume that readers are familiar with the fundamentals of traditional operating systems.

The terms *distributed systems* and *distributed operating systems* have different meanings to different people. Further confusion arises when we are faced with a large variety of multiprocessor and network architectures. This chapter provides a clarification of these terms. In addition to a brief overview of traditional centralized operating systems, this chapter shows how modern operating systems have evolved, the relationship between distributed operating systems and distributed systems, and the roles that distributed algorithms play in these systems.

1.1 EVOLUTION OF MODERN OPERATING SYSTEMS

An operating system is a set of software modules that collectively serves as an interface between application programs and the system hardware, with the primary goal being to achieve an efficient, secure, and easy-to-use computer system. The specific functions of an operating system generally include multiplexing and scheduling of the processor (or processors), coordinating the execution of interacting processes, managing system resources (such as I/O, memory, and files), enforcing access control and protection, maintaining system integrity and performing error recovery, and providing an interface to the users. It is often desirable to structure these functions in two categories: **system services** and the **nucleus** (or **kernel**) of the operating system. The system services are high-level functions as seen by the application programs, and the kernel consists of only the essential functions that are dependent on the underlying architecture. Figure 1.1 depicts a simplified overall view of a layer-structured computer system. The placement of the system services in the figure is important. From the user's viewpoint, the operating system is really just an abstraction of the system presented by the system services, commonly referred to as an **extended machine**. The intent is to shield the users from the details of the system: hardware and software. From the system administrator's viewpoint, the system services and kernel behave like a **resource manager**. *Extended machine* and *resource manager* are two of the most commonly used terms for defining an operating system. Machine abstraction is the primary design goal, and resource management is the means for achieving the goal. The design of traditional operating systems often begins with a stronger emphasis on resource management, while modern operating systems focus more on machine abstraction. In the final analysis, what is most important is how users perceive the system.

The design and research issues for conventional **centralized operating systems**, which run on a single or multiprocessor system, are well understood. However the proliferation of personal workstations and local area networks has led to the development of new operating system concepts, namely, **network operating systems** and **distributed**

FIGURE 1.1   A layer-structured computer system.

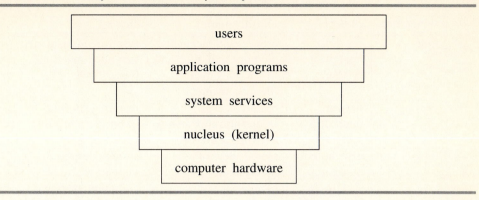

operating systems. Issues related to network and distributed operating systems are the main focus of this book. Another emerging concept is the development of **cooperative autonomous systems**, which emphasize the design of distributed applications for open system environments. An open system is concerned with the flexibility in integrating and porting heterogeneous system components to support large-scale cooperative work at the application level. This concept is broader than an operating system in the traditional sense.

It is always tempting to compare various system concepts. Figure 1.2 shows the relationship among the aforementioned four generations of systems based on the notion of **degree of coupling**. The degree of coupling is a rough measure of how a given system is centralized or decentralized. In terms of hardware architecture, we can describe a system as tightly coupled if its interprocessor communication overhead is relatively close to its intraprocessor communication time. A system is loosely coupled if its ratio of interprocessor communication to intraprocessor communication is high. A shared bus multiprocessor system is considered more tightly coupled in hardware than is a local area network. On the software side, we say a system is tightly coupled if its control software is centralized and uses global information. Otherwise it is classified as a loosely coupled system. The degree of coupling used in Figure 1.2 for classifying various systems combines both hardware and software coupling. Centralized operating systems are tightly

FIGURE 1.2   A spectrum of operating systems.

Decreasing Degree of Hardware and Software Coupling

1st	3rd	4th	2nd
centralized operating system	distributed operating system	cooperative autonomous system	network operating system

TABLE 1.1 A comparison of features in modern operating systems.

Generation	System	Characteristics	Goals
first	centralized operating system	process management memory management I/O management file management	resource management extended machine (virtuality)
second	network operating system	remote access information exchange network browsing	resource sharing (interoperability)
third	distributed operating system	global view of : file system, name space, time, security, computational power	single computer view of multiple computer system (transparency)
fourth	cooperative autonomous system	open and cooperative distributed applications	cooperative work (autonomicity)

coupled in hardware and software. Distributed operating systems (DOS, probably not a good acronym for the obvious reason) present a centralized logical view of the software system that runs under a loosely coupled multiple computer system. Network operating systems (NOS) are loosely coupled in both hardware and software. Finally the cooperative autonomous systems (CAS) relax the centralized logical view of the distributed operating systems and therefore fall between the DOS and NOS in the spectrum. The numbers in the figure show stages of evolution of the systems.

Another way to make a comparison is to identify each system with its unique objectives and characteristics. Table 1.1 provides such a comparison for the four different types of operating systems. It also shows how systems have evolved in time with added features and goals. Three additional goals, **interoperability**, **transparency**, and **autonomicity**, have become recent topics of interest. Interoperability refers to the system's ability to facilitate exchange of information among heterogeneous components in the system. It is the primary driving force for the design of network operating systems in a heterogeneous environment. The concept of transparency is similar to the **virtual** concept, such as a *virtual machine* or *virtual memory* in traditional operating systems. Both transparency and virtuality provide high-level abstractions of a system. However, there is a subtle difference. In a virtual system, users see what they like to see, while in a transparent system users do not see what they don't like to see. Combine the two concepts, and we have an ideal system where we see *only* what we like to see. Just as virtuality is an important concept in centralized operating systems, transparency is a key property and goal of a distributed operating system. Using the concept of transparency, we describe a distributed operating system as a system that provides a logical view of the system to the users, independent of the physical system. In particular, the users have a single computer view of a multiple computer system. The existence of the underlying network and details of the implementation of the system are transparent to the user.

Transparency seems to be a noble goal. However, it may not always be desirable since it implies some degree of centralized control. It is certainly possible that users might prefer to have their own view of the system. What the users need is an open system environment that does not necessarily require transparency as long as the system provides the *openness* for the users to modify, port, integrate, and expand their application software freely in a heterogeneous system. This is because the users are aware of the existence of multiple resources and other users, and users and systems are fully autonomous. In addition, software systems are constructed cooperatively by integrating services provided by autonomous units. This type of cooperative autonomous system behaves very much like a human society. The big question is whether software systems should also be built this way.

Interoperability, transparency, and autonomicity are all desirable properties. A user may not (and usually has no need to) distinguish whether a modern operating system is a network operating system, a distributed operating system, or an autonomous system. Modern operating systems will most likely be integrated systems. They are evolving from centralized, to networked, to distributed, and then to autonomous systems where users will be primarily concerned with constructing large cooperative applications using well-understood building blocks. We use the term *distributed operating system* as part of the title of this book since it has a broad meaning and covers mature concepts in the design of operating system software. To understand the evolution of these systems, it is helpful to find out the goals and issues for each of the four system types, as elaborated in the following sections.

1.2 CENTRALIZED OPERATING SYSTEM OVERVIEW

The traditional operating systems for single/multiprocessor architectures are centralized operating systems. These systems are tightly coupled in that all resources are shared internally and the interprocessor/interprocess communication is achieved through either memory sharing or direct process interrupts. The structure of centralized operating systems has evolved from a simple control program, responsible for providing a user interface and the control of I/O, to a full-blown multiuser/multitasking system that requires very complex management for processors, memory, files, and devices. This evolution is best illustrated in Table 1.2, which shows the management functions for each additional system requirement.

1.2.1 Operating System Structure

An operating system is a large piece of software ranging from thousands to millions of lines of code. When implementing such systems, it is necessary to structure the software in manageable modules. In addition, it is desirable to provide clearly defined interfaces between modules and to place constraints on how modules interact with one another. Two traditional approaches to partitioning the system modules, **vertical** and

TABLE 1.2 Major functions of a centralized operating system.

System Requirement	Management Functions
single user	user interface, I/O control, interrupt, device drivers
efficient I/O	virtual I/O, spooling
large program	virtual memory paging and segmentation
multiusers	multiprogramming and timesharing process scheduling access control and protection file sharing and concurrency control
multitasking	concurrent processing process synchronization, deadlock interprocess communication

horizontal, are often used. Vertical partitioning is a layering concept in which modules are grouped in different layers with the constraint that interactions are allowed only between adjacent layers. This provides a clean *one-in-one-out* (a structured programming or software engineering concept) interface between layers. Modules within each layer are again grouped (or partitioned horizontally) to form larger disjoint components. Each component may be further refined with the combination of vertical or horizontal partitionings. A module is typically a collection of instructions that performs a specific system service. In an object-oriented system, modules can be implemented as objects with well-defined operations on each object for a particular service. Modularization is based on objects rather than codes. All resources, including files and processes, can be abstracted as data objects with their physical representation hidden behind an abstract data structure. Module activation (execution) is confined to the set of operations and formal rules defined for the object. Object-oriented models offer several advantages. They provide uniformity for access and protection. Because of the uniformity, they are easier to modify and consequently increase the portability of the system.

Portability of operating systems can be further enhanced by separating the hardware-dependent codes from the system. A large part of the operating system software (i.e., system services) is hardware independent. Therefore the system should be structured in such a way that the machine-dependent part of the code is kept to a minimum and separated from the system services. This **minimal kernel** approach reduces the complexity of porting a system from one machine architecture to another since only the kernel needs to be rewritten. Typical functions implemented in a minimal kernel are multiplexing of processors with multiprogramming support, interrupt handling, device drivers, process synchronization primitives, and interprocess communication facilities. The structure of the kernel is usually *monolithic*, meaning that there is no horizontal or vertical partitioning used except the normal modularization of code. This structure occurs because the size of the kernel has been minimized. The design philosophy is that

FIGURE 1.3   Horizontal and vertical partitionings of the system.

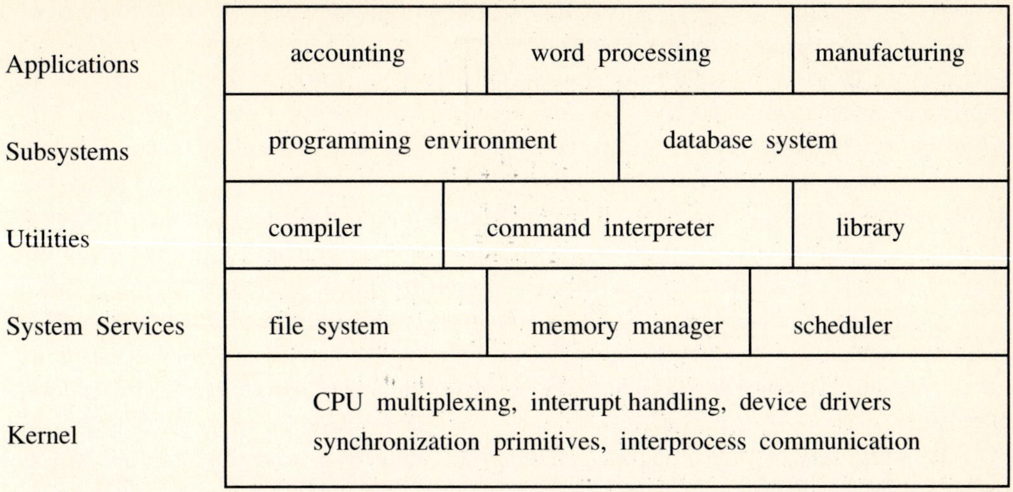

Applications	accounting	word processing	manufacturing
Subsystems	programming environment	database system	
Utilities	compiler	command interpreter	library
System Services	file system	memory manager	scheduler
Kernel	CPU multiplexing, interrupt handling, device drivers synchronization primitives, interprocess communication		

efficiency is more of a concern than the structure of the kernel. Figure 1.3 shows these modularization and structuring concepts, together with some examples of the system components in each layer of software.

The structure of an operating system can be further enhanced by using the **client/server** model. The client/server model is a programming paradigm. Using this model, system calls from application processes requesting system services from the operating system look like a direct client request to the server process. They are implemented indirectly through the operating system kernel. Different system calls share a uniform entry to the system. This mechanism simplifies the interface to the operating system and allows the system designer to move more system services to higher levels (in many cases to the user process space), resulting in a smaller and more manageable kernel. The client/server model is a natural way to describe the interactions between processes in distributed systems where *message passing* is the only means for data transfer among communicating entities. Message passing is an important subject and is discussed in later chapters.

The relationship between system and application programs is usually vague. Programs in the kernel and system services are system software (see Figure 1.3). Compiler writers may consider themselves to be system programmers. However, a compiler is an application program from the operating system viewpoint. Similarly, database software is an application program to a compiler or language and appears to be a system program to a database user. This hierarchy may go beyond several levels. Users see system as the *subsystem* characterized by the services provided to them. The relationship between system and application programming is relative. What is important is how subsystems can be built using the layering concept.

1.2.2 Subsystem and Microkernel

A universal minimal kernel on which standard operating system services can be implemented to support application-oriented subsystems is called a *microkernel.* A microkernel architecture consists of a hardware (platform) dependent minimal kernel and a set of hardware-independent executives (system services) with well-defined *Application Program Interfaces* (APIs). The significance of the microkernel concept is that it provides an environment with the *necessary* and *sufficient* conditions for constructing any tailored operating systems or subsystems with least effort. The kernel, although hardware dependent, is structured with hardware abstraction to ease the rewriting of the machine-dependent codes when porting to a different platform. This additional structure is called a *Hardware Abstraction Layer* (HAL) or *Service Provider Interface* (SPI) when used in a higher-level software module. As shown in Figure 1.4, the API provides *extensibility* for higher-level applications and the SPI (or HAL) enhances *portability* for lower-level platforms.

The system services are modular, generic, and complete so that they can be used as mechanisms to support a large class of applications. Software designers only have to know the standard interfaces to the executive service modules and can choose a subset of them as needed. The architecture is very attractive because of its modularity, portability, and marketing potential (executive modules can be licensed to other system vendors). There have been several industrial efforts for a common microkernel architecture, notably the IBM Microkernel and Microsoft Windows NT. We show the Windows NT in Figure 1.5 as an example of microkernel architecture. In this architecture, each client perceives the machine as a different computing environment (OS/2, Win32, POSIX) presented by the API in the subsystem. Each subsystem has its own logical address space and can be isolated and protected from other subsystems. The subsystems call on the system service API and thus can be implemented independently from the executives and the underlying kernel and hardware. Alternatively, a subsystem can interact with the system services indirectly through the Win32 subsystem, which supports window programming facilities. The architecture in the figure captures all system structuring concepts discussed thus far: modularization, layering, client/server model, object model, and minimal kernel.

FIGURE 1.4 API and SPI layers.

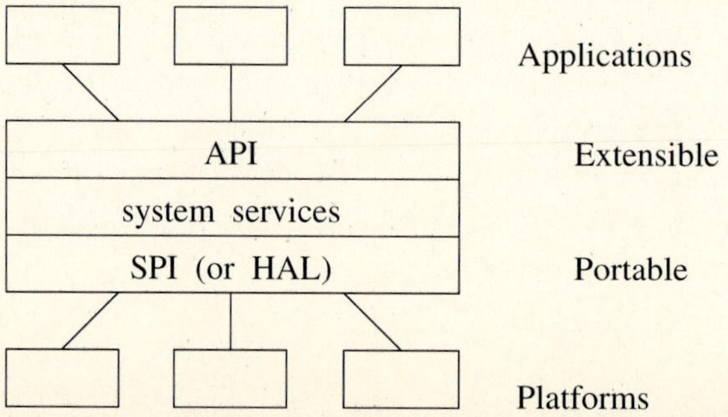

FIGURE 1.5   Windows NT system architecture.

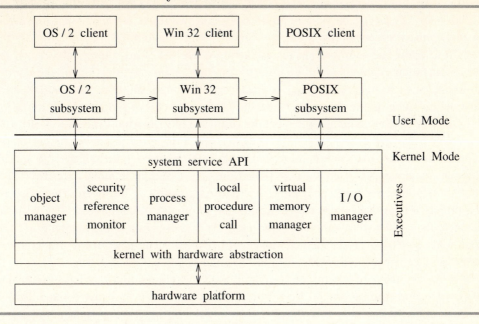

Most modern operating systems follow the same design philosophy with some minor differences in implementation details.

1.2.3 Management Functions

Coming back to the discussion of issues in a centralized operating system, we will take the view of the system as a resource manager. Resources in a computer system generally fall into one of the four categories: processors/processes, memory, I/O, and data/files. We shall briefly summarize the fundamental issues of a traditional centralized operating system. This terse summary will serve as background information for discussions of network operating systems, distributed operating systems, and cooperative autonomous systems.

The management of processors/processes at the lowest system level is provided by mapping (or scheduling) of processors to processes, or vice versa. To facilitate the efficient multiuser and multitasking features in a system, it is necessary to *space-multiplex* the memory (where processes reside) and to *time-multiplex* the processor (when processes execute). This multiplexing is implemented through the use of **multiprogramming** and **timesharing** with the support of an adequate interrupt-handling mechanism. At a higher level, the implementation is transparent to the *concurrent* executing processes. The users are only concerned with the coordination of interacting concurrent processes. The interaction of processes necessitates **process synchronization** and **interprocess communication**. During the last two decades, various process synchronization methods have been proposed to deal with the synchronization problems of **mutual exclusion** and **condition coordination**.

The most fundamental approach is the use of special system calls that operate on variables of a new type, called **semaphores**. Atomic operations (*atomic* means indivisible in this context) on semaphores with process-blocking capabilities are supported by the system to allow the coordination of interacting processes. Other approaches embed the synchronization capability in the language through either modification of the control structure (such as the **conditional critical region**) or the addition of new data type abstraction (such as the **monitor**). Yet another way to achieve process synchronization is by means of I/O commands such as **Communicating Sequential Processes (CSP)**. This approach is further generalized for procedure calls and led to the development of the **rendezvous** in the **Ada** programming language. Moving one step further, we can specify the control sequences of concurrent executions in a program without explicitly using synchronization primitives, as is done in a **path expression**. It has been shown that all the proposed approaches to the synchronization problem can be implemented, with the usual trade-offs between efficiency and expressive power for problem solving. (These traditional synchronization methods will be briefly revisited again in the discussion of language mechanisms for synchronization in Chapter 3.)

The development of interprocess communication facilities follows closely with that of process synchronization. In a centralized operating system, process communication through memory sharing would appear to be an easy solution. However, memory sharing violates the basic assumption that processes are asynchronous and generally do not share common address spaces. The alternative is to communicate via message passing. One advantage of message passing is that it is an intrinsic part of a distributed system and thus makes program development for centralized systems consistent with development for distributed systems.

It is worthwhile to note here that there is a strong relationship between process synchronization and process communication. Process communication requires some underlying assumptions of synchronization, such as synchronized sending and receiving of data. With process communication primitives, higher-level synchronization constructs can be implemented using only communication primitives. The introduction of synchronization and communication primitives also led to the development of concurrent languages: languages that allow the specification of concurrent processing, synchronization, and interprocess communication. Concurrent languages and synchronization/communication in distributed systems are discussed in Chapters 3 and 4, respectively.

In addition to process synchronization and process communication, process management also includes the function of **scheduling**. Processes in *ready* or *waiting queues* need to be rescheduled for execution when resources are available or when some condition has been met. Various strategies can be employed to achieve an objective function, such as minimizing the *turnaround time* or maximizing the *system throughput*. Task (or process) scheduling single and multiple processor systems is a classical operations research problem. Its application to distributed systems is complicated by the existence of multiple computers and the necessary communication overhead that must be accounted for when scheduling processes. There are two types of scheduling: static scheduling of processes modeled by process precedence relations and dynamic load sharing of processes modeled by process dependence relations. Precedence relations describe how processes must be synchronized, while dependence relations only indicate interactions between processes. These two types of scheduling represent different perceptions of process interaction in synchronization and communication. **Static process scheduling** and **dynamic load sharing** and **balancing** in distributed systems are discussed in Chapter 5.

Management of I/O devices is strictly the responsibility of the system to which the devices are physically attached. To reduce the complexity in system design due to machine dependency, the architecture of the processor is usually decoupled completely from the details of the I/O devices. The processor provides a general interface to all devices, and it is up to the manufacturers of I/O devices to develop the device controllers and software drivers for integration into the system. In an abstract sense I/O devices are just storage: Some are read and write (e.g., a disk drive), others only read (e.g., a keyboard), and some only write (e.g., a printer). From the operating system's standpoint, it is sometimes convenient to view all I/O devices as logical files. Logical files representing physical devices are called **virtual devices**. Processes then operate only on files, and the system is responsible for interpreting these files to the physical I/O devices.

Several techniques are often used to enhance I/O operations, notably the concepts of **spooling** and **buffering**. *Spooling* is a term that originally was an acronym for Simultaneous Peripheral Operation On-Line. While spooling facilitates sharing of I/O devices, buffering is primarily used for smoothing out the difference in speed between slow I/O devices and fast processors. Buffering can be implemented at various software levels such as file systems, device drivers, and in some cases, device controllers. Two of most important I/O devices are disk drives and terminals. High-speed and large-capacity (several gigabyte) disks are commonplace. High-capacity disks play a significant role in large software design. Memory-mapped terminals make it feasible to support **windows** on the terminal. Windows started out as a simple *virtual console*. With additional functions such as a graphical user interface and multiple interacting windows, windows have evolved into a full-blown interface for subsystems and have even become a *virtual machine* as in the case of the Windows 9x operating system.

An interesting problem that is related to I/O management is **deadlock**. Deadlock in systems occurs due to improper allocation of resources when multiple nonpreemptable processes, each holding resources and requesting more resources, create a cyclic waiting chain that cannot be broken. Resources may be physical devices or (more commonly) buffers and conditions. Deadlock prevention, avoidance, and detection have been widely studied. However, distributed deadlock detection and resolution still remains an open problem.

Memory management functions include allocation and deallocation of memory and mapping of logical program space to physical memory. The primary objective is to maintain a high utilization of memory and to provide **virtual memory** support for large programs, particularly for programs that exceed the physical memory size. Most of the modern computer systems use the **paging** and/or **segmentation** techniques to implement virtual memory. The implementation of virtual memory requires additional hardware, usually called the **memory management unit**. Both paging and segmentation are noncontiguous memory allocation schemes. The major difference between the two is that the partitioning of programs into modules for mapping to memory is physical with paging and logical with segmentation. Modern operating systems implement virtual memory using combined paging and segmentation. Since not all pages and segments reside in the physical memory simultaneously, it is necessary to replace some pages and segments to accommodate references to new data and instructions during the execution of programs. Various **page replacement** algorithms have been proposed to reduce the frequency of page faults. The performance of a page replacement strategy depends heavily on the behavior of the programs running at any given time interval. The *spatial* and *temporal* localities generally exhibited in programs have a significant impact on the choice of a replacement algorithm.

Virtual memory is a solution to solve the discrepancy in size and speed between the relatively slow disk storage and the faster primary memory. Similar problems exist when high-speed memory (cache) is used as a buffer between processors and primary memories. This buffering process, involving only the physical address mapping, is called **caching** and normally is considered as an architecture rather than operating system issue. The choice of page replacement algorithms, effect of page and memory sizes, impact of program localities, caching, and cache coherency are some of the basic issues in memory management.

In a centralized operating system, shared memory offers the advantage of simplicity for process communication and interaction. Many algorithms have been developed for shared memory. In a distributed environment, it may be desirable to simulate a shared memory system where no memory is physically shared. This **distributed shared memory** concept raises some questions about consistency and performance of data sharing that are similar to those about file sharing in a distributed file system. Chapter 7 addresses the topic of distributed shared memory.

Last, but not least, is the management of files in an operating system. Files are logical data entities that can be implemented by using any storage device including disk, memory, or even I/O. In the most abstract sense, any computation can be viewed as processes operating on files. If we were to remove the two basic terms, *processes* and *files*, there would be nothing to study in operating systems. Since we only have to deal with processes and files, all topics in the rest of the book are related to them. This is also why we exclude I/O and memory management from the book. Local management issues for I/O and memory are relevant only to centralized operating systems.

Files need to be structured and implemented before they can be manipulated. Once a general file structure and its interpretation have been decided, the fundamental functions for managing files are *file access* and *file sharing*. In addition to the efficiency objective, file access requires *protection* and *security* control mechanisms, and file sharing requires synchronization or *concurrency control*. Unlike the use with memory or I/O management, files are frequently distributed or replicated in a networked or distributed environment. File security and concurrency control for file operations become a more acute problem in the design of distributed operating systems than of centralized operating systems. Applying caching to file access is also complicated by the fact that files are cached on more than one computer. Several sections in this book discuss the implementation and control of distributed file systems.

Given this brief overview of a traditional centralized operating system, we are now ready to define some of its extensions, their goals, and the need for distributed algorithms for managing these systems.

1.3 NETWORK OPERATING SYSTEMS

We define a computer network as a loosely coupled multiple computer system where no direct hardware or software control of one workstation to another exists in the network, and the communication overhead among workstations (measured in time) is much higher than the internal data transfer within each workstation. The primary objective is to share resources (including programs and data) in the network. The only interaction in the system is the exchange of information among workstations via some form of external communication channel. We use the term *interoperability* to uniquely characterize the desired properties in a networked computer system. Interoperability provides flexibility in exchanging information among workstations in a heterogeneous computer network. Examples of mechanisms supporting interoperability include standard communication protocols and common interfaces to shared databases or file systems.

The function of information exchange may be hierarchically divided and implemented at various levels. At the hardware level, information exchange is the major responsibility of the *communication subnetwork*. At higher levels, the operating system provides data *transport services* and users use application-oriented *peer-to-peer* process communication protocols. Finer division of levels can be defined, such as the seven-layer OSI architecture of the International Standards Organization.

A network operating system can be regarded as a straightforward extension of a traditional operating system designed to facilitate resource sharing and information exchange. It is therefore convenient to describe a network operating system by illustrating its common network applications and the transport service that is needed to support these applications. The transport service serves as an interface between the network application processes and the physical communication network, and it implements the communication protocol between the peer operating systems. Figure 1.6 shows the integration of the transport service in an operating system for application processes that access a remote file system. This example is modeled after Sun's Network File System (NFS). Remote file accesses rely on the communicating network file systems and are then translated by the network system into data transfers between the peer transport services.

Most network operating systems use a high-level API, such as the *socket* and the *remote procedure call*, for transport service to support communication between operating systems in different network domains. A network operating system is characterized by the inclusion of a transport layer and the support for network applications that run on the transport service. Some unique classes of network applications are *remote login*, *file transfer*, *messaging*, *network browsing*, and *remote execution*. A brief description of each follows.

FIGURE 1.6 Integration of transport service.

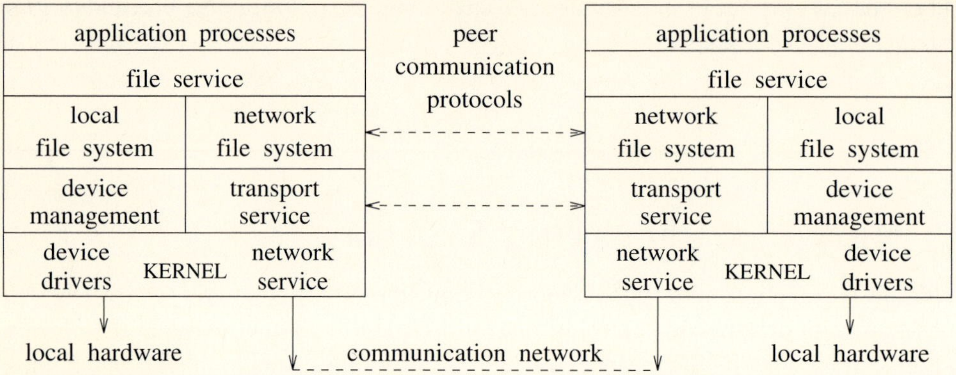

- **Remote login.** Remote login is a capability that turns a user's own station into a terminal logged into a remote workstation in the network, allowing direct sharing of the remote processor and its associated resources. For remote login the keyboard input must be converted into data packets that follow the network communication protocols. The opposite applies to the display output. Sometimes it is desirable to simulate various types of terminals (called *terminal emulation*). Thus, the negotiation of the terminal parameters is necessary before a connection is established. Service with these combined features is referred to as the *virtual terminal* support. A widely used network application with such features is **telnet**, a remote login service designed for scroll-mode asynchronous terminals. In Unix, **rlogin** is a similar service except that it does not support terminal emulation. In addition, rlogin assumes that the remote host is in the same homogeneous domain, and consequently, password verification is usually not a default option.

- **File transfer.** File transfer is the capability of transferring files or portions of files among different workstations in a network system. File transfer is not merely an exchange of data. Files consist of data, file structures, and file attributes. Thus, a file transfer protocol (e.g., Unix's **ftp**) must provide an interface to the local file systems and support the interactive commands of the user. Information about file attributes, data formats, data flow, and access controls must be exchanged and validated as part of the file transfer operation. Remote copy (**rcp**) in Unix is a restricted file transfer service for copying files between workstations, assuming the Unix file structure is in the same network domain (i.e., homogeneous).

- **Messaging.** Messaging systems allow network users to send and receive documents or messages without making a real-time connection. Two major messaging applications are the Electronic Data Interchange (EDI) for business transaction, and electronic mail (e-mail). EDI is a standard that specifies guidelines for transmitting business documents in specific formats among various computers running different operating systems. E-mail is a message facility for exchanging messages among network users. Different from file transfer, the messages in a mail system are uninterpreted except for the control messages embedded in the mail (this may not be strictly true anymore since some mail systems now have remote execution features). The structure, attributes, and access control of the mail data are not considered. The primary concern is the message handling and transferring and the user interface for manipulating the mail messages. Various standards, such as X.400 by CCITT (now ITU-T) and Simple Mail Transfer Protocol (SMTP) from the Department of Defense, have been proposed for implementing network mail systems. Many sophisticated e-mail systems have been built using these standards, which serve as translators to facilitate communication between different mail systems.

■ **Network browsing.** Network browsing is an information retrieval service for searching and presenting documents distributed among participating network sites. A *browser* is usually implemented as a client/server system where the browser program is a client accessing objects at remote file servers. The most widely used system today is the World Wide Web (WWW). WWW is a data model for linking hypermedia documents using pointers called Universal Resource Locators (URLs). Documents displayed by the browsers are usually hypertext and may contain pointers to other hypertext or hyper-media. A browser program such as Mosaic communicates with WWW servers using the HyperText Transport Protocol (http). Other protocols such as ftp and telnet can be used as well. Hypermedia documents are typically constructed by using the HyperText Markup Language (HTML) and are contributed by individual Web servers. Many other browsing systems with large distributed resources (databases) are available. At the time of this writing, Netscape is probably the most popular browsing system with its added efficiency and security features. Many references cited in the book were obtained from Web pages using Netscape.

■ **Remote execution.** Remote execution is the capability of sending a message to request a program execution at a remote site. Since executable programs are machine dependent and cannot be run on an arbitrary machine, remote executions are often done through interpreting (not compiling) a script file or machine-independent intermediate codes carried in the message. Remote execution is a very powerful but dangerous networking tool. Therefore it is usually restricted to some applications where confinement can be effectively enforced to prevent security threats and protection violations.

A good application of remote execution is the transport of multimedia data. Video or still image files require a tremendous amount of bandwidth if they are transmitted in raw pixel formats. They also suffer the problem of incompatibility in displaying output. Some common intermediate languages can be used to specify the raw data in a uniform and more compact format. At the receiving end, a corresponding interpreter is called upon to translate the data or execute the instructions in the intermediate language. The data conversion problem is solved and the load to the network is greatly reduced.

Many network applications use the concept of remote execution. For example, MIME, the Multipurpose Internet Mail Extensions, is an active mail system that supports the interchange of multimedia e-mail among different computer systems (e.g., a message can carry a special *type* for a particular display output). Depending on the type, a corresponding process is called upon to perform the task. Messages in a MIME mail are interpreted and have the same effect as program execution at a remote site.

A more general approach to remote execution can be found in the Java language and programming environment. Java is a general-purpose object-oriented language derived originally from C++. The Java compiler produces high-performance and compact machine-independent *bytecode* instructions that can be sent to and interpreted by any host with a Java interpreter. Bytecode programs are called **applets**. To support network and distributed applications, the Java programming environment provides a library of routines for incorporating Internet protocols such as *http* and *ftp*. A Java applet is an object which can be pointed at by a URL and may contain URLs to open other objects. An immediate application of applets in WWW is the use of the dynamic feature of applets to pull images, making animation easier in a browsing system. Newer versions of Netscape are implemented by using Java, and they support Java applets.

Due to the growing use of these network resource-sharing applications, they are commonly implemented as standard system servers (daemon processes) executing peer protocols on the underlying transport services and become a part of the network operating system.

1.4 DISTRIBUTED OPERATING SYSTEMS

The proliferation of powerful workstations and the advances in communication technologies have made it necessary and possible to extend resource sharing one step further: to include more general forms of cooperative activities among a collection of autonomous computer systems, connected by a communication network. Sharing of resources and coordination of distributed activities in this type of computational environment are the main goals in the design of a distributed operating system and are the main focus of this book.

What are the components in a loosely coupled distributed system that need to be distributed or decentralized? Physical resources are distributed by the inherent nature of a loosely coupled system. Information needs to be distributed by its nature or by organizational needs such as efficiency and security. Moreover, system performance can be enhanced by distributed computation. How these distributed resources and activities are to be managed and controlled is the primary responsibility of a distributed operating system. Should a distributed operating system itself be distributed? The answer is that a large part of it should be, again by its nature and by organizational needs. This raises the issue of the distributed implementation of the management and control functions of a distributed operating system, that is, the design of distributed algorithms. The need for distributed algorithms in distributed operating systems motivated us to integrate the two tightly related subjects into one book. Part I of the book addresses system design and implementation issues. Part II is devoted entirely to algorithms.

Given a distributed operating system for a distributed system, it is desirable to hide implementation details from the users of that system. The key distinction between a network operating system and a distributed operating system is the concept of *transparency*. The transparency concept is not new. In a centralized operating system, time-sharing users have *concurrency transparency* if they are not aware of the fact that others are sharing the same system. A program has *location transparency* if the mapping of the program onto the physical memory and/or processors is hidden. In a distributed operating system, the concept can be extended to a file's *location* and *access concurrency* if the file can reside anywhere in the storage system and its access is through a logical path rather than a physical one. For distributed processing we can achieve *parallelism* and *performance transparency* if processes can be executed on arbitrary processor(s) without users' awareness and without a noticeable difference in performance. Examples can go on and on. Should there be a limit? Whether a purely transparent system is possible or even desirable is a debatable question. In general, transparency is a good thing to have, and we will use it as a key feature of a distributed operating system.

Earlier we described a computation system as an abstract system consisting of processes and files. Now we add algorithms (or more precisely distributed control algorithms) that manage the execution of processes on files in distributed systems. Thus, a distributed operating system consists of three major components: coordination of distributed processes, management of distributed resources, and implementation of distributed algorithms. Topics in this book are organized according to these three components. Chapters 3 through 5, 6 through 8, and 9 through 13 describe distributed processes, distributed resources, and distributed algorithms, respectively.

1.5 COOPERATIVE AUTONOMOUS SYSTEMS

If we maintain some degree of transparency and abolish the notion of a single user view of a multiple computer system, we have a completely different view of a pure loosely coupled (both in software and hardware) system. Each user or process operates autonomously by exporting and requesting services. Group activities can be coordinated by exchanging services and requests. Higher-level services can be provided by composing them from lower-level services. Any software system can be formed freely by integrating various services with some agreed upon structures. This approach mimics the behavior of a human society. If human beings can form a sophisticated society, so can computer systems. This is the view of a cooperative autonomous system. In a computer system, we require a more orderly environment than human society has yet achieved. Figure 1.7 illustrates the fundamental difference between a distributed operating system and a cooperative autonomous system. Distributed systems are characterized by service decomposition, while cooperative autonomous systems emphasize service integration.

FIGURE 1.7   Service decomposition and integration.

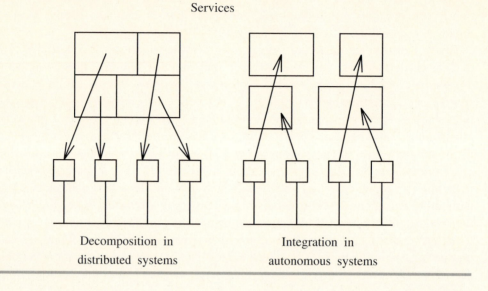

Services

Decomposition in
distributed systems

Integration in
autonomous systems

   A cooperative autonomous system is a high-level service-oriented software system that requires the support of communication mechanisms on which higher-level communication protocols are built. As an example, imagine how a real estate transaction can be accomplished in a cooperative autonomous system. The house buyer, which is a client process, can make a request to buy a house either directly from the house owner or indirectly through a real estate agent (both are considered server processes). The owner is a client process to the realtor. Realtors can form a real estate agency, a larger server that can refer a house buyer to an appropriate realtor server. The seller is a client to the real estate agency as well as a client to the realtor. The buyer can locate the real estate agency by looking it up in the Yellow Pages, which is a publicly known directory server process. If the house is to be sold by the owner directly, the owner has to advertise it somewhere using server processes with known addresses. Figure 1.8 shows the various client/server relationships of an example cooperative autonomous system application. Servers like the Yellow Pages and real estate agencies provide broker or trading services that locate services. The key concept in cooperative autonomous systems is the integration of services to form cooperative activities. Both hardware and software are completely decoupled and decentralized.

   The idea of a decentralized autonomous system may seem farfetched. However, it is simply an extension to the concept of Computer Supported Cooperative Work (CSCW). CSCW is a framework for supporting *groupware*, which is a large software application that encompasses cooperating users and distributed resources across a heterogeneous network. An example is *distributed conferencing*, where electronic meetings in a physi- cally distributed network can be managed. Contrary to the single-computer philosophy of distributed operating systems, the emphasis here is on how a logical group of dis-

FIGURE 1.8   An autonomous system through the integration of services.

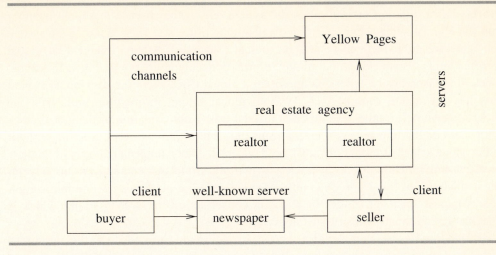

tributed users and resources can be constructed and administered, knowing explicitly the existence of multiple computers. The group users form their logical network domain with specific objectives and are responsible for access and protection control of the group. A decentralized autonomous system is a system that provides fundamental services for integrating higher-level cooperative services in a large network system. With the projected enormous number of networks and users, it seems to be a natural evolution from the older network and distributed operating systems.

The emerging need for cooperative autonomous system applications has triggered several standardization efforts for future development of distributed software, notably, the Open Distributed Processing (ODP) and the Common Object Request Broker Architecture (CORBA). ODP is a common system framework that supports distribution, interoperability, and portability for heterogeneous distributed processing both within and among autonomous organizations. CORBA follows the same philosophy and uses the object-oriented model to implement transparent service requests across an interconnected heterogeneous multiple object distributed system. Both ODP and CORBA use intelligent *trader* or *broker* services to facilitate interaction of cooperative autonomous systems. Yellow Pages and real estate agencies are like traders. They can be viewed as a *software bus* that connects client and server processes, and they serve as the *middleware* that supports distributed cooperative applications.

1.6 DISTRIBUTED ALGORITHMS

A significant part of this book is devoted to the design of distributed algorithms, which are required to support the implementation of distributed operating system services that coordinate the execution of concurrent processes. The algorithms are sometime referred to as **protocols** since their functions are to mainly establish orders or rules for interacting processes, rather than to perform computation. The inherent weakness or limitation of a distributed system is the lack of global system state information. Each process has a different perception of the system due to the absence of shared memory and the nonnegligible communication delay among processes. Their views of the system are therefore often incomplete and incoherent. The most essential element of global information is systemwide global timing information, commonly referred to as the global clock. It is theoretically impossible to obtain a global clock even in a distributed system that has a common central clock. Without global timing information, enforcing the order of event occurrences becomes a nontrivial task. Approximation of the global clock with some timing tolerance and mechanisms that achieve proper event ordering without using global clock information must be developed. Many implementations of higher-level control functions such as process synchronization and communication rely on the availability of these time-tolerant and event-ordering mechanisms. Communication delays impose great difficulties in reaching consensus on the system status, which is essential in coordinating distributed activities.

In addition to the complexities caused by communication delays, the design of distributed algorithms is further complicated because failures and unreliable sources of information are more commonplace in a distributed system than in a centralized one. *Fault tolerance* becomes a more critical issue for distributed algorithms. It is essential for the system to be able to recover from all kind of failures. Even though there are many centralized algorithms for process synchronization, scheduling, and concurrency control, they all must be reexamined for use in a distributed environment. Distributed algorithms can be classified into two categories: fully decentralized distributed algorithms and distributed algorithms with a fault-tolerant centralized coordinator. The latter is conceptually simpler, provided that efficient mechanisms exist for handling failures of the centralized controller and selecting a new leader.

The hardware architecture of distributed systems also plays an important role in the implementation of distributed algorithms. The methods for communication depend on whether the network topology is a complete connection, regular or irregular, and whether the data transfer is point-to-point or multipoint. The architecture may even have a changing topology, and failures of links and nodes may exist as well. On the software side, data are often replicated to allow for concurrent accesses and to achieve higher reliability. Data replication introduces data coherency problems. Replicated data management becomes another critical issue in the design of distributed systems.

Summarizing the above observations, the following list gives an overall view of the distributed algorithms of interest with respect to the unique problems of distributed systems. We discuss these topics in Chapters 9 through 13 of Part II of this book.

- **Message passing.** The consequence of not having shared memory implies that all coordination among concurrent processes must be accomplished by message passing. Therefore, algorithms for synchronization and deadlock handling need to be redesigned for the distributed environment. The distributed algorithms may be fully decentralized or centralized. In the latter case, a distributed election algorithm is usually required to establish and maintain a centralized controller.

■ **Lack of global information.** The effectiveness of a distributed algorithm depends on its knowledge about the state of the system. Since it is impossible to obtain the complete global state information due to network delays and unreliable system components, the interaction among processes must rely on *consensus* derived from some agreement protocols. The agreement protocols themselves are distributed algorithms.

■ **Data replication.** Replicated data management is a fundamental function for distributed file systems and databases. The primary goal of the protocols is to maintain data consistency. It will be seen in the later chapters that the problem is logically equivalent to that of *reliable broadcast*. A set of data replicas is similar to a group of broadcast members. The issues involved can be tackled from either the operating system or database point of view.

■ **Failures and recovery.** The reliability of a system can be enhanced by means of fault tolerance or recovery upon failures. The fault-tolerance approach uses redundancy such as replicated files or multiple servers. Recovery is a passive approach in which the state of the system is maintained and is used to roll back the execution to a predefined checkpoint. The recovery algorithms deal with the logging of the system state, checkpointing, and handling of orphan processes and messages.

1.7 SUMMARY

This chapter gives a brief summary of operating system structures, an overview of traditional operating systems, and an introduction to some of the evolving modern operating systems. The book will focus on the design and implementation of distributed operating systems and algorithms. The fundamental concepts of distributed operating systems and algorithms are introduced in Chapter 2. A discussion of system design and implementation issues begins in Chapter 3.

Based on the system goals of *virtuality, interoperability, transparency*, and *autonomicity*, we classify operating systems into four general categories: *centralized, networked, distributed*, and *autonomous* systems. We describe the evolution of these systems in terms of their characteristics and implementation requirements.

For background information, we give a terse overview of operating system structuring methodologies and of issues regarding the design of traditional centralized operating systems. An operating system is a large collection of software. Many software structuring methods such as *modularization, partitioning*, and *layering* are directly applicable to the implementation of operating systems. Furthermore, we add the concepts of the *client/server model, subsystem* and *microkernel*, which are essential in achieving better *extensibility* and *portability* of the system. The review of the traditional centralized operating systems is given in the context of *resource management*. However, the discussion of distributed operating systems in the later chapters will be based on the notion of an *extended machine*, which is more relevant from the user's perspective in terms of achieving transparency.

We define a network operating system as an extension of a traditional operating system with a *transport* service to support interoperability for network applications such as remote login, file transfer, messaging, network browsing, and remote execution. These network applications are oriented more toward *resource sharing*. A distributed operating system supports *distributed processing* in addition to resource sharing in the underlying computer network. Distributed processing requires the coordination of cooperative activities among processes executing on physically distributed processors and resources. It is desirable that the operating system provides transparencies to hide the physical dispersion of processors and resources. We will elaborate more on the concept of transparency in Chapter 2. Modern distributed systems often employ the *client/server* and *object-oriented* models. These service-oriented programming paradigms facilitate the development of cooperative autonomous systems. ODP and CORBA are two most notable efforts in this direction.

Part I of the book discusses the design and implementation of distributed operating systems. Part II addresses the fundamental algorithms for managing distributed systems. We concluded Chapter 1 by showing the need for distributed algorithms due to some unique problems in distributed systems. The complexities of the design of distributed algorithms are mainly caused by communication delay, lack of global information, data replication, and failures.

ANNOTATED BIBLIOGRAPHY

The review of traditional centralized operating systems serves as background information for the discussion of modern operating systems. Many excellent textbooks [Dei90, MOO87, SG94a, Sta92, Tan92] on the fundamentals of centralized operating systems have been widely used in classes. Readers are encouraged to review topics covered in these books.

Modern operating systems are evolving from centralized operating systems to network operating systems, distributed operating systems, and cooperative autonomous systems. We concentrate on the design of distributed operating systems since they have already employed many mature concepts, and yet many issues are still open. Several excellent textbooks [Gos91, SS94, CDK94, Tan95] on distributed operating systems can be found. They provide good cross-references. Other books [Mul93] that contain collections of papers on distributed systems are also available. They show the fundamental issues and future directions for distributed systems.

We distinguish our approach from the above books by broadening the scope of discussion to include topics such as concurrent programming and real-time scheduling and security and by emphasizing the importance of distributed algorithms. There is an enormous number of research papers on distributed algorithms. The areas that we select to integrate into the presentation are distributed computation model, distributed synchronization, consensus and agreement protocol, replica management, and failure and recovery. Books most relevant to our discussion of distributed algorithms are [Ray88, Lyn96].

A couple of common network and distributed system architectures and applications are quoted in this chapter. Windows 95 and Windows NT are products of MicroSoft [Cus93, Ric94]. Mosaic is a network browser developed at the National Center for Supercomputing Applications and copyrighted by the Board of Trustees of the University of Illinois. Netscape is a World Wide Web browser trademarked by the Netscape Communication Corporation. NFS and Java [AG96] are products of Sun Microsystems. ODP [ODP93] is an international standard draft for open distributed processing from ISO and ITU-T. CORBA [OMG91] is a standard for distributed object computing that is being developed by the OMG (Object Management Group), a consortium of computer vendors including DEC, HP, IBM, and Sun. Many of these industrial members of the consortium have implemented their versions of the CORBA architecture.

Distributed System Concepts and Architectures

We define a distributed operating system as an integration of system services, presenting a transparent view of a multiple computer system with distributed resources and control. The development of distributed systems and applications has been driven by the ever-increasing need to share resources and information, the rapidly decreasing cost of powerful workstations, the widespread use of networks, and the maturity of software technologies. The primary goal of the design of a distributed operating system that supports distributed applications is to provide a conceptually simple model leading to an efficient, flexible, consistent, and robust system. System implementation details need to be hidden as much as possible, and users must have maximal freedom in using the system. This chapter discusses the goals and the **transparency** and **service** concepts in a distributed system. It also presents some fundamental system architectures for which system services can be built and related to network concepts. The chapter concludes with a section on system design issues, which lead to the coverage of major topics in the subsequent chapters.

2.1 GOALS

The general goal for the design of a distributed operating system is no different from any other operating system. Both the users and the system providers are concerned with issues of the **efficiency, flexibility, consistency,** and **robustness** of the system. However, the underlying architecture of a distributed system raises the expectations and requirements of the system, and this causes the level of implementation complexity to consequently rise to achieve these objectives. The differences rest on the effect of distributed resources, nonnegligible communication overhead, and the higher likelihood of component failures in the system.

- **Efficiency** is more complex in distributed systems than in centralized systems due to the effect of communication delays. Communication through message passing in geographically distributed environments incurs delays ranging from microseconds to milliseconds and even seconds or more. This delay is caused by the data propagation, the overhead of communication protocols at various levels, and the load distribution of the system. There is nothing we can do about propagation delay. However, there should be effective communication primitives at the language or operating system levels and good communication protocols at the network levels. With respect to system load distribution, problems such as bottlenecks or congestion either in the physical networks or software components must be addressed. Applications (system or users) can take one further step by structuring distributed processes such that computation and communication can be balanced and overlapped whenever possible. An optimal schedule of tasks in a centralized system is not necessarily a good one when applied to a distributed system. Computation speed and system throughput can be enhanced through distributed processing and load sharing if the communication system is carefully designed.

- **Flexibility,** from the user's viewpoint, includes the *friendliness* of the system and his or her *freedom* in using the system. Friendliness has a very broad meaning. It primarily implies the ease of use of the system interface and the ability to relate the computation processes in the user's problem space to the system. The object-oriented approach is a commonly used strategy in achieving this goal. Friendliness is also tied to the properties of consistency and reliability. Inconsistent and unreliable systems are often viewed as unfriendly. Freedom lets the users decide how, where, and when to use the system without unreasonable restrictions. It should also provide an adequate environment from which additional tools or services can be easily built upon.

Flexibility from the system's view is the system's ability to evolve and migrate. The key properties include modularity, scalability, portability, and interoperability. In either case (system or user), these properties are of particular importance in distributed systems since most systems employ heterogeneous hardware and software components. On the one hand we want some autonomy with local authorities, but on the other hand we have to cooperate with others to form a coherent system, which eventually will place some restrictions on us. Flexibility is often caught in the middle.

■ **Consistency** is more difficult to achieve in a distributed system. The lack of global information, potential replication and partitioning of data, the possibility of component failures, and the complexity of interaction among modules all contribute to the problem of inconsistency in the system. A system is consistent from the user's perspective if there is uniformity in using the system and the system behavior is predictable. In addition, the system must be capable of maintaining its integrity with proper concurrency control mechanisms and failure handling and recovery procedures. Consistency control in data and files (or database in a transaction-oriented system) is a crucial issue in distributed file systems.

■ **Robustness** is obviously a more serious problem in distributed systems. Failures in communication links, processing nodes, and client/server processes are more frequent than in a centralized single computer system. What rules should the operating system follow when, for example, a request/reply message is lost or a processing node or server has crashed? Robustness with respect to fault tolerance means that the system is capable of reinitializing itself to a state where the integrity of the system is preserved with only some possible degradation of its performance. Even without explicit failures, to be robust, a system should be equipped to handle exceptional situations and errors, such as changes to the system topology, long message delays, or the inability to locate a server. Robustness should also be broadened to cover the aspect of security for users and the system. Reliability, protection, and access control are major responsibilities for a distributed operating system.

2.2 TRANSPARENCY

Perhaps the most frequently used property in distinguishing a distributed system from other systems is *transparency*. It is a goal motivated by the desire to hide all irrelevant system-dependent details from the users, whenever possible, and to create an illusion of the model they are supposed to see. This principle has been practiced in the design of computer systems for a long time. Transparency is a more important issue in distributed systems due to higher implementation complexities.

Shielding the system-dependent information from the users is basically a trade-off between simplicity and effectiveness. Unfortunately these two objectives often conflict with each other. Therefore it may not be wise to go to either extreme. A good distributed system tries to achieve as much transparency as possible but only to a certain extent. Analogous to the *virtual* concept in operating systems and the *abstraction* in programming languages, the objective of transparency is to provide a logical view of a physical system and at the same time reduce the effect and awareness of the physical system to a minimum (in particular, with respect to the physical separation of objects and control in the system). There are several different aspects of transparency:

- **Access transparency** refers to the ability to access both local and remote system objects in a uniform way. The physical separation of system objects is concealed from the user.
- **Location transparency** means that users have no awareness of object locations. Objects are mapped and referred to by logical names. This is sometimes called **name transparency**.
- **Migration transparency** is an added property of location transparency where an object is not only referred to by its logical name but can also be moved to a different physical location without changing the name. Migration transparency is also called **location independence**.
- **Concurrency transparency** allows the sharing of objects without interference. It is similar to the time-sharing concept in a broader sense.
- **Replication transparency** exhibits consistency of multiple instances (or partitioning) of files and data. It is closely related to concurrency transparency but is treated separately since files and data are special objects.
- **Parallelism transparency** permits parallel activities without users knowing how, where, and when these activities are carried out by the systems. The parallelism might not be explicitly specified by the users.
- **Failure transparency** provides fault tolerance such that failures in the system can be transformed into graceful system performance degradation rather than disruptions, and damage to the users is minimized.
- **Performance transparency** attempts to achieve a consistent and predictable (not necessary equal) performance level even with changes of the system structure or load distribution. In addition, the users should not experience excessive delays or variations in remote operations.
- **Size transparency** is related to modularity and scalability. It allows incremental growth of a system without the user's awareness. The size of the system has no effect on the user's perception of the system.
- **Revision transparency** refers to the vertical growth of systems as opposed to the horizontal growth in system size. Software revisions of the system are not visible to users.

To communicate with friends, we usually contact them by phone if they are nearby (local) and by letter if they are far away (remote). There is no access transparency since the access methods are not uniform. Even with a common access method by phone, if we have to specify the area codes and different local numbers when our friend (object) moves between two cities, we have neither location (area codes) nor migration (local numbers) transparency. The ideal transparent communication would be a system through which we can reach anybody by a universal name (symbolic or numerical) such as a social security number. The 800 number in the telephone system provides a step in that direction (the service was actually motivated by economic reasons rather than achieving transparency). Access, location, and migration transparencies are interrelated.

Parallelism, concurrency, and performance transparencies are designed to shield the management of concurrent activities from the users based on intrauser, interuser, and internodal relationships, respectively. Concurrencies are achieved at different levels of execution: within a user, among users, and among distributed nodes. Replication and failure transparencies are related to the maintenance of system integrity. Size and revision transparencies provide smooth transitions for system growth in hardware and software.

This list of desirable transparencies is by no means exhaustive. They are listed, however, according to their relevance to distributed systems. They can also be categorized with respect to the aforementioned goals. Concurrent and parallel transparencies provide efficiency. Access, location, migration, and system transparencies are related to flexibility. Consistency encompasses access, replication, and performance transparencies. And finally, failure, replication, and system transparencies have something to do with the robustness of the system. Table 2.1 characterizes the transparencies with respect to

TABLE 2.1   Categorization of transparencies based on system goals.

System Goals	Transparencies
efficiency	concurrency
	parallelism
	performance
flexibility	access
	location
	migration
	size
	revision
consistency	access
	replication
	performance
robustness	failure
	replication
	size
	revision

TABLE 2.2   Distributed system issues and transparencies.

Major Issues	Transparencies
communication synchronization distributed algorithms	interaction and control transparency
process scheduling deadlock handling load balancing	performance transparency
resource scheduling file sharing concurrency control	resource transparency
failure handling configuration redundancy	failure transparency

system goals. The implementation of a distributed operating system and its associated distributed control algorithms is largely concerned with achieving these transparencies. In summary, distributed systems provide physical separation of objects. Transparencies are intended to shield the effect of this physical separation. The end result is that a user views a multiple computer system as a logical single computer system.

The above discussion of transparencies is based on the desirable system properties from the viewpoint of users or systems. The major issues in distributed operating systems covered in this book also can be categorized by using the transparency concept, as shown in Table 2.2. In short, the goal of a distributed operating system is to provide a high-performance and robust computing environment with least awareness of the management and control of distributed system resources.

2.3 SERVICES

An operating system is a service provider. Since services can be built on top of existing services, there are different levels of services. The most fundamental services, called **system primitives**, are those that must be implemented in the kernel of each node in the system. Others can be implemented anywhere in the system and still perform functions basic to the operation of a distributed system. We will call these service providers **system servers**. Those that perform higher-level or special-purpose services (such as user applications) are **value-added servers**.

2.3.1 Primitive Services

In the earlier discussion of the *minimal kernel* approach for centralized operating systems, we identified three fundamental functions that the kernel must provide: *communication*, *synchronization*, and *processor multiplexing*. In a distributed system where process communication is done through message passing, a set of **send** and **receive** primitives must be defined and implemented. These primitives pass information in logical communication channels. Send and receive can be either synchronous or asynchronous (discussed in Chapter 4). Synchronous communication, in addition to serving communication purposes, carries the side benefit of achieving internode interprocess synchronization. If message passing is the only means of process interaction, process synchronization has to rely on communication, either by the synchronous semantics of communication itself or by some **synchronization servers** based on message passing.

Since we want to conceal physical dependencies in distributed systems, it is more appropriate to describe processor multiplexing as process serving. The **process server** manages creation, deletion, and tracking of processes by allocating the necessary resources such as memory and processing time. Whether the processors are local or remote and how many are available to the processes are transparent. The process server interacts with other process servers through remote communication and synchronization.

2.3.2 Services by System Servers

There are many services that need not reside in the kernel. We will describe some of them in the order of relevance to distributed systems. The first step in achieving transparency is to conceal physical objects with logical system names. This means a mechanism for mapping the logical names to the physical addresses must exist. The address of a process or location of a file can be obtained in an ad-hoc way, but it is commonly achieved by looking it up in a **name server** or **directory server**. Name servers are often used to locate users, processes, or machines, while directory servers are frequently used in conjunction with files and communication ports. Since a server that cannot be located is not useful, all services are preceded by name services. Thus, the name server is the most essential server in a distributed system. Addresses and locations obtained from the name server are system dependent and must be translated into **communication paths** before objects can be accessed. These translations, selection of paths, and actual routing of information are services provided by the **network server**. Network servers are transparent at the operating system level. However, broadcasting of messages in a network without efficient hardware support for broadcast will need a **broadcast** or **multicast server** in the operating system.

Another server of similar importance is the **time server**. Clocks (more generally timers) are used for synchronizing and scheduling of hardware and software activities in every computer system. Theoretically, it is impossible to obtain or agree on absolute global clock information. Even with the existence of a central clock (like Greenwich Mean Time), clock skew occurs due to time delay in receiving and recording the timing information. The skewing may be estimated and corrected. Most hardware designers build systems that can tolerate some deviation of timing. For distributed systems, this skewing will be enlarged due to longer communication delays between processes. At the operating system level, there are two typical ways of using timing information for synchronizing processes: one that requires a close approximation of time with respect to a real-time clock and one that uses artificial time only to preserve the causality of event ordering. They are referred to as **physical clocks** and **logical clocks**, respectively. The purpose of using physical clocks is to keep operations synchronized or to request that a certain operation be processed at a certain real time. Time must be agreed upon to a certain degree, but whether it is close to the real-world time is less important. Synchronization of processes using logical clocks is needed to maintain a total order of event occurrences to ensure the correctness of operations that depend upon each other. Time servers for physical clocks are based on a best approximation of "real" time. Solutions to achieve logical clock synchronization are possible and are best demonstrated by Lamport's **happens-before** logical clock (discussed in Chapter 3).

Name and time servers are information servers. Other basic system servers are usually involved in managing shared system resources. Familiar examples are **file servers** and **print servers**. Normally it is desirable to have location transparency for servers (with the exception of print services). File servers can be duplicated or partitioned if file consistency is maintained. A server can be hierarchically structured. For example, a file server may consist of **directory** and **security subservers** for access control and authentication purposes. To fully utilize the processing power of a distributed system, a process server can be supplemented to become a **migration server** that cooperates with process servers and facilitates the moving of processes from node to node. In a large distributed system where communicating processes may be mutually suspicious, a trusted **authentication** server is needed for authenticating process identities. System servers provide fundamental services for managing processes, files, and process communication.

2.3.3 Value-added Services

Value-added services are services that are not essential in the implementation of a distributed system but are useful in supporting distributed applications. From the user's viewpoint, use of a distributed application is motivated either by the desire to increase computational performance and enhance fault tolerance or by the need for cooperative activities. In either case there is the notion of **groups** of interacting processes. Computation groups are like social groups. They need to be managed. A **group server** manages the creation and termination of group activities. It is responsible for group addressing and communication. It also contain information such as membership, admission policies, and member's privileges. Group decisions or rules about joining or leaving the group can be set by group leaders or collectively by group members. Once a group is well defined, specific interest groups can be formed. The structure of groups varies in organization depending on applications. For example, network news groups, distributed conferencing groups, concurrent editing groups, and distributed computation groups range from loosely coupled to very tightly coupled groups with strict governing rules. When a group application becomes standardized, it can emerge as a new service. In that sense, the **distributed conferencing server** and the **concurrent editing server** would be good candidates. The **Web server** is another example of standardized value-added server. The service by server concept is attractive because of its simplicity, provided that the potential bottleneck and failure of servers can be properly dealt with.

2.4 ARCHITECTURE MODELS

Distributed services are described by functional specifications. Their implementations depend on the system architecture and the underlying communication network. In the upper level, system architecture is an abstract description of the major components and their relationships in a system. In the lower level, network architecture specifies the communication facilities. There are a wide variety of system and network architecture models. In the following sections we introduce some of the commonly used models. They illustrate software concepts.

2.4.1 Distributed System Architectures

In Chapter 1 we mentioned that, in the most abstract sense, the world of an operating system consists of only two types of entities: processes and files. With the assumption of a network, we must add a third component: the communication paths (or **ports**, to give the flavor of transparency). The visible hardware are workstations and the network. However, the users are not concerned with the physical components except for the cost, appearance, and performance of the system. User processes either request or provide services. Some workstations are dedicated for special services (for geographical or performance reasons). This is the **workstation-server** model as depicted in Figure 2.1.

In the workstation-server model, a workstation may serve as a stand-alone computer or as a part of an overall network. It provides both local processing capability and an interface to the network. Some workstations are diskless, and all file and boot services are supported by the network file system. The Sun workstation that was used to write this book has a disk, but it is for temporary scratch space only. The existence of the disk is transparent, except for the periodic noise of disk "chatter", which assures us that the computer is still alive. If processing can also be done remotely, the distinction between a

FIGURE 2.1   The workstation-server model.

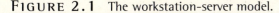

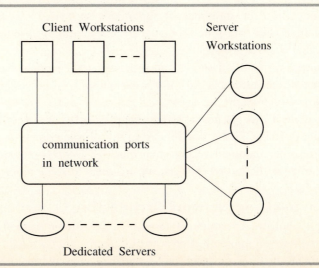

Dedicated Servers

FIGURE 2.2 The processor-pool model.

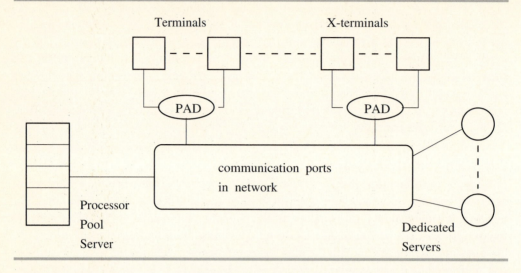

workstation and a terminal becomes blurred. Furthermore, most workstations are idling at any instance in time. This raises the question of whether we should collect all the processing power in one place and leave the users with only a terminal (one with good display hardware and software support). Processing power can be better utilized on a demand basis. This is the concept behind the **processor-pool model** shown in Figure 2.2. The major characteristic is the sharing of computation power in addition to the sharing of resources.

In the processor-pool model, users access a virtual single computer system with intelligent terminals, such as X-window terminals. The minimum intelligence must include remote booting, remote mounting of file systems, virtual terminal handling, and packet assembling and disassembling (PAD) capabilities for packet switching communication. PAD may be built into the terminals or standalone so that it can multiplex a larger number of terminals. File and processor allocation are done by the system. This model has an added parallelism transparency.

The two models, workstation-server and processor-pool models, can be combined to form an integrated hybrid model. An interesting question to ask is: Can the processors in a workstation-server model be used as a processor pool? There is no reason why this cannot be done if process migration can be efficiently implemented. Processes can migrate to idling or less loaded processors according to some load-sharing strategies. Of course, there are other implications. We may not like to see other people stealing our processing cycles even though we have no use for them at some moments.

2.4.2 Communication Network Architecture

The existence of multiple computer systems in a distributed system implies the need to interconnect these components. Hardware interconnections together with internode interprocess communication protocols are needed to support message passing in distributed systems. System components may be connected by point-to-point or multipoint communication channels. Point-to-point links are direct connections between pairs of computer nodes. Multipoint links allow the connection of nodes into a cluster and are usually implemented by using common buses or interconnection networks (switches). Accesses of communication media in common buses are timeshared, while switches provide both space and time multiplexing at a higher hardware cost and complexity. Bus-based communication networks are widely used for local area networks (LANs) because of their simplicity and matured technologies. The IEEE 802 LAN standards define several bus-based facilities including Ethernet, Token Bus, Token Ring, Fiber Distributed Data Interface (FDDI), and Distributed Queue Dual Buses (DQDB). Switched systems are more popular in the implementation of high-performance multiprocessor systems and for the interconnection of LANs through public communication service carriers. Typical private switches for multiprocessor systems are cross-bar and various multistage interconnection networks. Public switched services include the frame relay Integrated Services Digital Network (ISDN) and cell relay Switched Multimegabit Data Service (SMDS), and the emerging Asynchronous Transfer Mode (ATM). It is important to note here that in these public networks, the actual routing of data is performed by the switches, not by the network hosts. The switches assume some network-level functions.

Local area networks can be connected to form a metropolitan area network (MAN) or a wide area network (WAN). Networks are characterized by their capacity requirements and geographical distances. Most local area networks have a capacity ranging from 2 to 20 Mbps and an average distance of a few kilometers. They are normally governed under a single local organization. Wide area networks are characterized by their long propagation distance of several hundreds or thousands of kilometers and need to pass through several intermediate nodes for data transfer. In traditional low-speed wide area networks, data rates are limited to the kilobits-per-second (Kbps) range, due to line cost and the store-and-forward buffering requirement. Data rates of 56-Kbps and 1.544-Mbps T1 channels are typical. With the advances in optical fiber technologies, public carriers are upgrading their popular DS1 (1.5 Mbps) to DS3 (45 Mbps) and synchronous optical network protocol (SONET) (155 Mbps). High data rates lead to the development of high-speed wide area networks and metropolitan area networks. If local area networks are to be connected to form a larger networking environment covering a metropolitan area or the entire world, the communication subnetwork must be able to handle the aggregated data, including text, voice, and video generated by the local area networks. Metropolitan area networks and high-speed wide area networks using optical fiber communication are at least one order of magnitude larger in capacity and distance than that of a local area network. In addition to high-speed and longer distance communication channels, fast packet switching techniques must also be developed to route large volumes of data.

Capacity and distance play an important role in deciding the type of applications that can be supported by the network. Using the concept of coupling described in the last chapter, we can define a parameter, a, as the ratio of propagation delay to transmission delay. A LAN has a smaller value of a compared to a MAN or a high-speed WAN. Systems with smaller a values imply a greater "closeness" of the system components and are more suitable for distributed processing, which requires interactive exchanges of shorter

FIGURE 2.3   Examples of WAN and MAN connecting LANs.

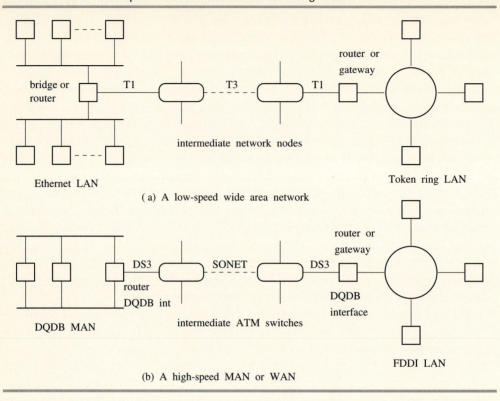

(a) A low-speed wide area network

(b) A high-speed MAN or WAN

messages. With a larger *a*, the system becomes more communication oriented. That is, in such a system, there is a large percentage of data or information in transit in the communication channels. This is contrary to our traditional perception of a system where the data resides only on computers. This issue is interesting to ponder when designing a distributed system under this type of network architecture, where the state of the communication network may be more significant than the state of the processors.

Figure 2.3 shows examples of a low-speed WAN and a high-speed WAN or MAN for connecting LANs to support distributed and network applications. Both examples show the point-to-point and multipoint connections of system components. Buses are used for LANs and MANs. Internetworked LANs use store-and-forward in the low-speed WAN and cell-relay ATM switches in the high-speed WAN. Optical fibers provide high-speed DS3 and SONET data services.

2.5 COMMUNICATION NETWORK PROTOCOLS

Given a network architecture, rules and standards must be set up to govern the communication. Communication protocols are sets of rules that regulate the exchange of messages to provide a reliable and orderly flow of information among communicating processes.

To communicate with a remote party in the ordinary world, we can make phone calls or send mail. Similarly, in a computer communication system, there are two categories of communication services: **connection-oriented** and **connectionless**. Connection-oriented protocols require an explicit set up of a connection before actual communication commences. Messages are delivered reliably and in sequence. Connectionless protocols operate more or less like the postal service. No initial connection establishment is necessary. Messages are delivered on a best-effort basis in timing and route and may arrive in arbitrary order. Choice of either protocol depends on the applications. For example, connection-oriented protocols are more suitable for file transfers, while broadcasting the local system status is more efficient using connectionless protocols. At the network level, we often refer these two services as **virtual circuit** and **datagram**. At the communication hardware level we call them **circuit switching** and **packet switching**. Connections in circuit switching are fixed physical connections. Virtual circuits are logical connections. A single physical link may carry several virtual circuits via multiplexing. By the same token, we can extend this abstraction to connection-oriented communication. That is, a connection-oriented communication can be implemented by using datagram services, and data are actually carried in a packet switching network as long as the system provides a reliable in-order delivery of messages and gives the users the illusion of a connection.

Communication occurs at different levels in a system. Users exchange messages between each other. Hosts communicate with other hosts. Networks also need to coordinate among themselves. These are peer-to-peer relationships: communication between entities at the same levels. The design of communication hardware and software within a computer system is a rather large undertaking. It is normally structured in layers. Each layer has a precise specification of its functions (or services). Adjacent layers have a clear interface and communication protocol between layers. A lower layer provides services to the layer immediately above it. Protocols between layers have a simpler and more uniform structure than the peer-to-peer protocols since they only need to address the information passed between layers. The decomposition of functions and the well-defined simple interface structure have the advantage of being used to set up an unambiguous network specification for implementation by different vendors. Standardized network specifications are called **network system architectures**. Layers for a standardized network architecture and the associated protocols are referred to as a **protocol suite**. In the following two sections we summarize two of the most popular network protocol suites: Open Systems Interconnection (**OSI**) from the International Standards Organization (**ISO**) and Transmission Control Protocol/Internet Protocol (**TCP/IP**) from the U.S. Department of Defense (**DoD**).

2.5.1 OSI Protocol Suite

OSI is a seven-layer protocol suite (see Figure 2.4). A process communicates with a remote process by passing data through the seven layers, then the physical network, and finally through the remote layers in reverse order. The details of the message transfer through the network are hidden from the communicating processes. Only the peer-to-peer protocol is observed by the processes. The data transparency between layers is achieved by an **encapsulation** process. Each layer receives a protocol data unit (**PDU**) from its upper layer and encapsulates it with **header** control information for its peer layer in the remote location. This combined message is treated as a new PDU for the layer below. Sometimes PDUs must be segmented due to a limitation on the PDU size at the next layer. The segmenting and reassembling should be transparent at the higher layer. At the receiving end, header information is stripped by the corresponding layers at the receiving node. A gateway or intermediate node only stores and forwards messages at the three lower network dependent layers. Each layer will be discussed, from the "bottom up."

FIGURE 2.4   The OSI seven-layer protocol suite.

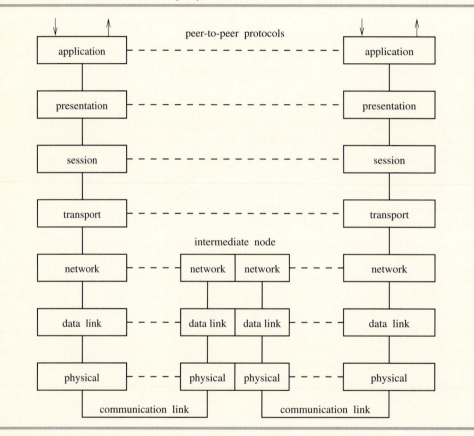

The Physical Layer

The physical layer specifies the electrical and mechanical characteristics of the physical communication link between a pair of nodes. Its major function is to provide a reliable logical *bit pipe* for the communication channel. Electrical or optical signals need to be converted to bits, and vice versa. Mapping of signals to bits requires *bit synchronization*: the detection of the beginning of a bit and a sequence of bits. Bit sequences may be *bit synchronous* or *character asynchronous*. Bit synchronous sequences are large blocks of bits transmitted at a regular rate. This method offers higher data transfer speed and better utilization of the link. Character asynchronous data are small fixed-size bit sequences transmitted asynchronously in the bit pipe. Low-speed character-oriented terminals usually use this mode for data transfer. The transmitting and receiving of logical bits require standardization of the electrical and mechanical properties such as the coding method, the modulation technique, and wire and connector specifications. RS232C and X.21 are two typical standards for point-to-point connections. In addition, modems may be used between a pair of RS232C ports and thus become part of a physical connection link. Therefore modems (both asynchronous and synchronous) must also be standardized. Finally, the sharing of common buses, such as the coaxial cables for Ethernet, necessitates interface standards for the medium access control in the data link layer.

The Data Link Layer

The Data Link Control (DLC) layer ensures the reliable data transfer of groups of bits, called **frames**. Data link protocols handle configuration setup, error controls, sequencing, and flow control of frames. Configuration performs the establishment and termination of a connection and determines whether a connection setup should be full- or half-duplex, synchronous or asynchronous. Errors include transmission errors and loss or replication of data frames. They are detected by using checksum or time-out mechanisms and are recovered from by retransmissions or forward error corrections. Sequencing control uses sequence numbers to maintain an orderly delivery of frames. Sequence numbers can also be used to detect missing or duplicate frames for error control and to assist in regulating the transmission of frames for flow control. Flow of data frames needs to be regulated if the receiver cannot keep pace with the sender, perhaps due to limited buffer space. Transmission of a frame is permitted only if it falls into an allowed window of buffers for the sender and the receiver. All these control functions contribute overhead bits that are added to the data frames as **headers** and **trailers**. As a consequence, each DLC protocol has a defined frame format so that bits in the control fields can be properly interpreted.

For multipoint configurations such as a common bus, the data link control layer is supplemented with a Medium Access Control (**MAC**) sublayer, which rests between the DLC sublayer and the physical layer. MAC resolves the access contention of the multiple access channel.

The Network Layer

In the first two layers, physical and data link control, we are concerned with only one link. The **network** layer addresses issues of sending **packets** across the network through several link segments. A packet is a basic unit of data transfer in the network layer. Its size is different from the data link frames, which are usually dependent on properties of the physical links. Packets to be forwarded by each node in the network may be transit packets from other nodes or may have originated from the same node. The immediate questions is: Based on the destination address of the packet, which link should be selected for forwarding the packet? This is the **routing** function of the network layer. Other functions such as error and flow controls are also performed by the network layer, at a higher level between nodes and through intermediate nodes. It is possible that a particular node is favored by the routing decisions and thus becomes a bottleneck in the network. Flow control that alleviates this problem is called **congestion** control. Routing decisions can be made at the time when a connection is requested and is being established. Or, routing decisions can be made on a packet-by-packet basis. The former case implies the assumption of a connection. Such a communication path is referred to as a **virtual circuit** and has the property of in-order delivery of packets. Packets delivered in the latter methods are called **datagrams** and require reassembly of packets into proper sequences. Routing decisions may be static or may adapt with the change of network status. The computation of routing decisions can be implemented by a central controller or can be distributed by some cooperating nodes. Network routing has been studied extensively.

Between every pair of source and destination nodes, there are a number of paths for routing packets. For some distributed applications, it is desirable to use **multiple path routing**. If a path is selected nondeterministically for each packet to be forwarded, the load of the system can be better balanced to avoid congestion. Of course, the packets may arrive out of sequence. Furthermore, multiple copies of a packet may be sent along different paths to enhance system performance. If we only accept the first successfully received packet, intuitively we would observe a shorter end-to-end delay and lower packet loss probability. Again this will require additional mechanisms to reassemble packets and discard duplicate ones. Applications that require high performance and reliability may be able to justify the overhead.

Finally, not all packets are data packets. Some control packets are used for network address resolution and status broadcasting. These protocols generally use datagram services since their packets are small in size and short lived.

The Transport Layer

From the operating system's view point, the **transport** layer is probably the most important layer in the seven-layer protocol suite since it serves as the only interface between the communication subnetwork (physical, data link, and network layers) and the higher network-independent layers (session, presentation, and application). The primary responsibility of the transport layer is to provide a reliable end-to-end communication between peer processes. All network-dependent faults or problems are to be shielded from the communicating processes. Process communication sessions are carried by transport connections. The transport layer breaks messages into packets and passes them to the network layer for transfer through the network. The receiving transport layer reassembles the packets back into messages. Several low rate sessions may be multiplexed onto a single transport connection to achieve better utilization of the connection, if they are destined to the same site. Similarly, the transport layer may allow a session to occupy multiple transport connections to increase the throughput of the session. The multiplexing and concentration of the transport service should be transparent to the sessions. Sessions are categorized by their requirements for error handling and multiplexing capabilities. OSI defines five classes (TP0 through TP4) of transport services to support sessions. The service class chosen depends on the application requirements and the quality of the underlying communication network. The most common TP4 transport service allows multiplexing of sessions, error detection, and retransmission. It is a reliable connection-oriented transport service for unreliable networks.

The Session, Presentation, and Application Layers

Layers above the transport layer are less essential to the implementation of the system and the communication network. They are simply added services to the system. So, we will briefly summarize them in this paragraph. The **session** layer adds additional dialog and synchronization services to transport layer. The dialog facilitates the establishment of sessions, and synchronization allows processes to insert checkpoints for efficient recovery from system crashes. The **presentation** layer provides data encryption, compression, and code conversion for messages that use different coding schemes. The standard for the **application** layer is completely left to the designer of the application. Example applications that have matured to become standardized include a variety of electronic mail and file transfer services.

2.5.2 TCP/IP Protocol Suite

The OSI specification covers a broad range of aspects. Given an underlying physical network, there are two major types of system interactions: interprocess and internode communications. From the system designer's point of view, we are only concerned with two basic questions: How is communication between a pair of processes maintained and how are messages routed through the network nodes? In other words, the transport and the network layers are most crucial to the design of the system. TCP/IP is a protocol suite that addresses these two issues in internetworking environments. TCP is a transport layer protocol equivalent to TP4 in OSI. IP is an Internet protocol that encompasses a little more than the network layer in OSI. The primary focus of the TCP/IP suite is interconnecting networks, while the OSI suite is about interconnecting computers.

Figure 2.5 shows the TCP/IP protocol suite for two networks connected through some gateways. The protocol actually contains only two layers; the others are shown in the figure for completeness. The application layer is unspecified. In fact, even the interface between TCP and the applications is left undefined for flexibility. The data link and physical layers are considered as a network interface where various standards are already in existence.

At the transport level we have the choice of either a connection-oriented or a connectionless service. This service can be implemented by a virtual circuit or a datagram in the network layer. Thus we have four combinations for achieving a desired process communication mechanism. Connection-oriented communication, by definition, has a more stringent requirement for correct and orderly delivery of messages than connectionless services. It is perhaps a more desirable service for most applications. However, a datagram (which is a connectionless communication) is easier and more efficient for implementation in the network layer, especially when the underlying network is unreliable. Combining the connection-oriented transport layer and a datagram network layer accommodates a large class of network applications. This is the philosophy of TCP/IP (connection-oriented TCP and datagram IP). We shift the burden of maintaining reliable communication from the network to the operating system level, where we have more

FIGURE 2.5 The TCP/IP protocol suite.

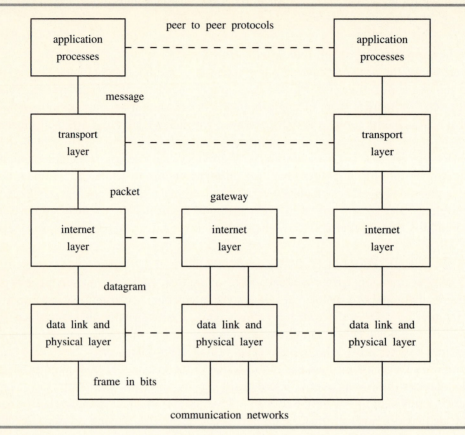

control of the host than we do in the network. For other data and control messages that only require connectionless services, a User Datagram Protocol (**UDP**) is also available at the transport level.

A process may communicate directly with its peer by using a *process id* as source and destination addresses. However, it is more convenient to use the concept of **ports** for interprocess communication endpoints. For example, a process may establish more than one communication path with another process by using multiple ports, and different processes may share a common destination port to achieve a multipoint connection. Ports are created and given an *id* by local operating systems. The port id is unique only within a local host. A nonambiguous networkwide endpoint can be obtained by concatenating the port id with host and network addresses. Figure 2.6 shows an IP address structure and a TCP connection between two endpoints. A connection endpoint is identified by a pair of Internet host addresses and a transport port.

A full Internet address consists of the network address and the host address within that network. If a network contains subnetworks, the network (also called **domain**) address is divided into two parts: the network and the subnetwork addresses. An Internet IP address is 32 bits (4 octets) long. The address of 128.227.176.62 identifies the University

FIGURE 2.6   TCP connections and IP addresses.

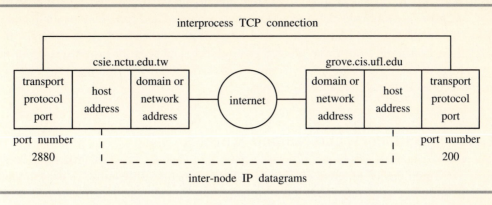

of Florida as a Class B domain (128.227), a subnet (176) in the CIS department, and the host computer (62). Its symbolic name is grove.cis.ufl.edu.

The transport layer in TCP/IP or UDP/IP provides ports for connection-oriented and connectionless services. It does not specify the interface to ports. The **socket** interface in Version 4 of BSD Unix developed at U.C. Berkeley is an example of an interface mechanism on which applications such as Unix **stream pipes** can be built. A socket is an abstraction of network I/O that allows standard *read* and *write* operations. A socket can be created by using the *socket* system call and can be given a *socket descriptor*, which is like a *file descriptor* for an opened file. The parameters in the system call specify the protocol family and the type of communication service to be established. For a TCP connection the socket must be bound to a destination transport port before *read* or *write* operations can commence. This is done through the *connect* system call, which associates a socket with a remote destination. The port number at the remote destination is chosen by its operating system. If the port number needs to be a well-known number, it can be assigned by the remote process using the *bind* system call that binds a socket to a specific local port. For connectionless data transfers, *sendto* and *recvfrom* system calls are used. Both require that the socket number and destination address be specified as parameters in the call. No prior *connect* is needed.

Since TCP/IP directly addresses the two most relevant layers for the design of distributed systems and communication networks, we often use it as a model for discussion in the later chapters. Sockets for interprocess communication are widely used in distributed system and network programming. We devote a special section to sockets in Chapter 4.

2.6 MAJOR DESIGN ISSUES

A distributed system consists of concurrent processes accessing distributed resources (which may be shared or replicated) through message passing in a network environment that may be unreliable and contain untrusted components. This sentence raises many design and implementation issues, in particular how to support transparency. First, we need to know how objects in the system are modeled and identified. Second, we have to find out how to coordinate the interaction among objects and how they communicate with each other. Third, if objects are shared or replicated, how can they be managed in a controlled fashion? Fourth, the protection of objects and security in the system must be addressed. These issues are briefly summarized in the following sections. They are the major focuses of discussion in later chapters.

2.6.1 Object Models and Naming Schemes

Objects in a computer system are processes, data files, memory, devices, processors, and networks. Traditionally, different object types are implemented differently. To keep in line with the spirit of transparency, it is tempting to assume that all objects can be represented in a uniform way. Since objects are meaningful only if they can be accessed, each object can be associated with some well-defined access operations to the object. Therefore, an object is represented abstractly by the allowable operations on the object. The physical details of the object are transparent to other objects. The process that manages the object becomes the object server. In other words, objects are encapsulated in servers and the only visible entities in the system are servers. Thus we have process servers, file servers, memory servers, etc. A client is a null server that accesses object servers.

To contact a server, the server must be identifiable. There are only three possible ways to identify a server:

- Identification by name;
- Identification by either physical or logical address;
- Identification by service that the servers provide.

Names used for identification purposes are generally assumed to be unique, while multiple addresses may exist for the same server and may have to be changed when the server moves. Names are more intuitive and transparent than addresses, but addresses contain structural information for locating servers. The name resolution for mapping names to logical addresses is the responsibility of name servers in the operating system. The address resolution of mapping logical addresses to physical addresses is a function of the network service. The *port* used in many systems is a logical address. Associating more than one port to a server allows multiple entry points to the server. Furthermore, multiple servers can share the same port. This approach is attractive for service identification in distributed systems. The third method (identification by services) is rather unconventional. The client is only interested in the requested service. Who provides the service is irrelevant. It is possible that multiple servers can provide the same service. This approach is critical to the implementation of autonomous systems discussed in Chapter 1. Naturally, a resolution protocol is necessary for translation of the services to servers.

Object models and naming are fundamental issues that must be decided early in the system design. The structure of the system, management of name space, name resolution, and access methods all depend on the naming scheme for system objects. These topics are covered in Chapters 3 and 4.

2.6.2 Distributed Coordination

Interacting concurrent processes require coordination to achieve synchronization. In general, there are three types of synchronization requirements:

- **Barrier synchronization:** A set of processes (or events) must reach a common synchronization point before they can continue.
- **Condition coordination:** A process (or event) must wait for a condition that will be set asynchronously by other interacting processes to maintain some ordering of execution.
- **Mutual exclusion:** Concurrent processes must have mutual exclusion when accessing a critical shared resource.

Synchronization implies the need for the knowledge of state information about other processes. Complete state information is difficult to obtain in distributed systems where there is no shared memory. State information may be conveyed by sending messages. However, it will be inaccurate or incomplete by the time messages are received due to the message transfer time delay in the network. The decision of whether a process can continue or not must rely on some message-based distributed resolution protocols. An alternative solution to the distributed coordination problem is to designate the responsibility of coordination to a centralized coordinator. The role of the centralized coordinator can be moved from one process to another so that the coordinator will not become the central point of failures. Using this approach, there must be provisions that allow a process to be chosen as the new coordinator if the original one has failed or has decided to relinquish its responsibility.

Another problem closely related to synchronization is the deadlock of processes. Interacting processes can be correctly run without violating any synchronization constraint, but this may lead to deadlock due to circular waiting for each other. Processes and resources in distributed systems are very diverse. Sometimes it is not practical to employ deadlock prevention or avoidance strategies for handling deadlocks. The only alternative is to detect a deadlock and try to recover from it if possible. Again, detection of deadlocks in a distributed system is a nontrivial problem because the global state of the system is not available. There are also questions about who should initiate the detection algorithm, how the algorithm can be implemented in a distributed fashion by message passing, who should be the victim in order to abort and resolve the deadlock, and how the victim can be recovered. The efficiency of the deadlock resolution and recovery strategies seems more important than detection in distributed systems.

Distributed solutions to the synchronization and deadlock problems attempt to assimilate partial global state information and use it for decision making. Many applications do not require absolute global state information as long as the involved processes agree on their perception of the system. Agreement protocols are message passing algorithms that achieve consensus in a distributed system that possibly has faulty components. Reaching agreement requires the exchange of local knowledge among the cooperating sites. It is not a difficult task unless some processors are prone to failures or are not trustworthy.

However, there is a sense in which achieving agreement is impossible in asynchronous distributed systems.

Distributed synchronization and deadlock handling are major process coordination tools for building distributed services. Chapters 4, 9, and 10 cover these topics. Chapter 11 presents theoretical material about the possibility and impossibility of distributed agreement.

2.6.3 Interprocess Communication

Communication is perhaps the single most essential issue in any distributed system design, since everything relies on it. In operating systems, interaction between processes and information flow between objects all depend on communication. At the lowest level, message passing is the only means of communication in distributed systems. Interprocess communication can be accomplished by using simple message passing primitives. However, it is desirable to have transparency in communication by providing higher-level logical communication methods that hide the physical details of message passing.

Two important concepts used to achieve this goal are the client/server model and Remote Procedure Call (**RPC**). The client/server model is a programming paradigm for structuring processes in distributed systems. In this model, all system interactions are viewed as a pair of message exchanges in which the client process sends a request message to a server and waits for the server to respond with a reply message. This request/reply message passing is analogous to the procedure-call concept in programming languages where a calling procedure passes parameters to a called procedure, and the called procedure returns the results to the calling procedure upon completion of the operation. The request/reply message exchange between client and server thus can be represented as a procedure call to a remote server. RPC communication built on top of the client/server model and message passing has been suggested as a standard interprocess communication mechanism for all future distributed systems. The client/server model and RPC communication are discussed further in Chapters 3 and 4.

The above discussion of message passing, the client/server model, and RPC assumes point-to-point communication (*unicast*). The notion of a *group* is intrinsic in distributed software. Processes cooperate in group activities. Group management and group communication (*multicast* or *broadcast*) are a necessity. Group communication in distributed systems is a logical multicast (perhaps without broadcasting hardware). Communication needs to go through several layers of protocols and be propagated to a number of physically distributed nodes. It is therefore more susceptible to failures in the system. Reliable and atomic group broadcast remains an open issue in distributed systems. Furthermore, group management, which is a cornerstone of CSCW, has not reached a matured stage yet due to the lack of experience in distributed software applications. Interprocess communication issues are fully explored in Chapter 4. Group management is addressed in Chapter 9.

2.6.4 Distributed Resources

Logically, the only resources needed for computation are data and processing capacity. Data may reside physically in distributed memory or secondary storage (e.g., as files). Processing capacity is the aggregate of the processing power of all processors. The ultimate goal of distributed processing is to achieve transparency in allocating processing capacity to processes or, inversely, distributing the processes (or load) to the processors. Static load distribution in distributed systems is referred to as *multiprocessor scheduling.* The objective is to minimize the completion time of a set of related processes. The main issue is the impact of communication overhead on the design of scheduling strategies. If load distribution (perhaps load redistribution is a better term) is done dynamically, it is called *load sharing.* The objective is to maximize the utilization of a set of processors. The primary issue is process migration and its strategy and mechanism. Aside from the desire for better performance and higher utilization, many distributed applications are constrained by time. In such cases scheduling of processes must satisfy some real-time requirements. Static and dynamic load distribution and real-time scheduling are topics of discussion in Chapter 5.

Transparency applied to distributed data is a more complex issue. If files are fundamental data entities, a transparent file system means that it presents a single file system view of dispersed files in a distributed environment. Distributed file systems are transparent file systems. We can extend the transparent data concept a little further by assuming that data granularity is smaller than files and that data reside in distributed memory modules. A transparent memory system is one that presents a single shared memory view of physically distributed memories. In essence, we can simulate a shared memory system, called *distributed shared memory*, if the communication overhead is tolerable.

The common issues central to a distributed file system and a distributed shared memory are sharing and replication of data. Both require protocols to maintain the consistency and coherency of the data so that the effect of sharing and the existence of replicas are transparent to the users. Although the problems are logically equivalent, there are some subtle differences in implementation between distributed file systems and distributed shared memory. Issues in distributed file systems are based on a file point of view, whereas the emphasis in distributed shared memory systems is more on a process perception of the system. Chapters 6 and 7 discuss distributed file systems and distributed shared memory, respectively. More advanced issues on replicated data management are covered in Chapter 12.

2.6.5 Fault Tolerance and Security

Distributed systems are vulnerable to failures and security threats because of their openness in the operating environment. Both can be considered system faults. Failures are faults due to unintentional intrusion, and security violations are faults due to intentional intrusion. A dependable distributed system is a fault-tolerant system in which system faults are transparent to the users.

The problem of failures can be alleviated if there is redundancy in the system. Redundancy is an inherent property in a distributed system since data and resources can be replicated. However, recovery from failures normally requires rolling back the execution of the failed process and possibly other processes affected by the failures. The execution state information must be kept for roll-back recovery, a difficult task in distributed systems. Chapter 13 addresses the important issue of checkpointing to support efficient process rollback and recovery.

Security has been a growing concern in network and distributed systems. From the operating system's standpoint, we are concerned with the trustworthiness of the communicating processes and the confidentiality and integrity of messages and data. The problems of authentication and authorization take on a unique quality in distributed systems. For authentication, clients and also servers and messages must be authenticated. For authorization, access control has to be performed across a physical network with heterogeneous components under different administrative units using different security models. Chapter 8 discusses models and techniques for distributed authentication and authorization applicable in a distributed environment.

2.7 DISTRIBUTED COMPUTING ENVIRONMENT (DCE)

It is instructive to conclude Chapters 1 and 2 by showing an overall picture of most of the issues discussed so far and their corresponding services. We will use the diagram in Figure 2.7 to describe a distributed computing system. The figure shows a slightly modified DCE architecture proposed by the Open Software Foundation (OSF). OSF is a joint venture by several U.S. computer companies with the goal of developing and standardizing an open Unix environment that is free from the influence of AT&T and Sun. Since most Unix implementations are already incorporating features to support distributed computing, the first major product from the OSF consortium is the DCE, which is an integrated package of software and tools for developing distributed applications on an existing operating system. DCE provides many key services, such as threads, RPC, security, and directory services, for ready integration into many Unix and non-Unix platforms. The placement of each individual service in the hierarchically layered architecture is important. At the heart of the system is the kernel and the transport service, which is an interface that provides communication services to processes on other hosts. Processes and threads are basic computational units supported by the kernel. Threads are a special type of processes (discussed in Chapter 3) that facilitate efficient implementation of concurrent servers. All other services reside in the user space and interact with each other by means of RPC and group communication. Time, name, and process services are examples of basic system services. With files as the primary objects in the system, higher-level services such as concurrency control and group management can be built on top of the distributed file service. Finally, security and management functions need to be integrated into all layers. The DCE approach is frequently quoted in the discussion of threads, RPC, time and name services, and security in the later chapters.

FIGURE 2.7   DCE architecture.

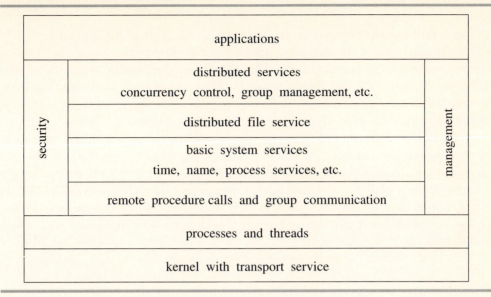

2.8 SUMMARY

This chapter presents the major goals for the design of distributed operating systems. It elaborates the *transparency* and the *service-oriented* concepts, two fundamental characteristics of distributed systems. The basic system architectures and the underlying network architectures are introduced. Distributed system architectures can be structured as a *workstation-server* or a *processor-pool* model. The underlying network architecture is a networking issue. We use the OSI and TCP/IP network architectures as the background for later discussions. The *transport* layer in these two network architecture is the most relevant component to distributed systems.

Given the system architectures, we summarize the important design and implementation issues. These issues include object models and naming schemes, interprocess communication and synchronization, data sharing and replication, and failure and recovery. These problems are unique to distributed systems. This summary and the DCE model serve as an outline for the chapters in the rest of the book.

ANNOTATED BIBLIOGRAPHY

Distributed systems are implemented on top of a communication network. We describe the basics of two popular network architectures, OSI and TCP/IP. OSI was proposed by ISO in 1978 to establish a framework for standardizing network development for open system network application. The seven-layer OSI/IEC 7498 became an international standard in 1983 [DZ83, Loh85, TS92]. The open network system concept was subsequently extended by ISO in 1987 to create the ODP Reference Model for open distributed processing. The

ODP reference model places a strong emphasis on transparency and the concept of a trader.

The TCP/IP model developed by the DoD was in use prior to the standardization of OSI. Its protocol suite is hierarchical as opposed to the layered structure of OSI. TCP/IP is oriented toward the interconnection of networks. The original description of the internet architecture based on TCP/IP can be found in [CL83, Enn83]. The books by Comer and Stevens [CS91] are good references for the internals of TCP/IP. Many other network books [Bla89, Tan90, Hal92, Sta94, Cyp91] are based on OSI and TCP/IP.

While ODP is a framework for open distributed processing, the DCE is an actual architecture implementation of distributed computing environment. We use the DCE architecture to describe basic services in a distributed operating system. DCE is a major software product of OSF. Its significance is that it provides software modules and an infrastructure which can be used readily to DCE*ize* (environmentize) an existing operating system. Information and software packages can be obtained from the Open Software Mall at OSF Web site, http://www.osf.org/mall/.

EXERCISES

1. Name a transparency concept that is significantly different from those described in the chapter.
2. Show an example of transparency that may not be desirable.
3. What are the advantages and disadvantages of using diskless workstations in a distributed system?
4. Why is a process pool an attractive model from the view point of distributed computation and transparency?
5. What hardware and software supports are needed in order to implement the processor-pool model?
6. What are the advantages and disadvantages of having standards for system architectures?
7. What are the differences between OSI and TCP/IP?
8. Why is medium access control (MAC) combined with the data link layer rather than the physical layer?
9. Why is UDP necessary when a connectionless IP already exists?
10. List some system design and implementation issues that are unique or more significant in distributed operating systems than in centralized operating systems.
11. Browse the World Wide Web for subjects on ODP, CORBA, and DCE. Show the fundamental philosophy behind each model and give examples of commercial implementation for each model.
12. Why is it that the security and management functions are not a single layer in the DCE architecture in Figure 2.7?

CHAPTER 3

Concurrent Processes and Programming

With the background information presented in Chapters 1 and 2, we are ready to discuss the most essential elements in the system, namely, *processes* and their variant, *threads*. Management functions for processes are categorized in three domains: communication, synchronization, and scheduling. These are not disjoint subject areas. There is a strong relationship between the issues of communication and synchronization in concepts and implementations, which are combined and presented in Chapters 3 and 4. Process scheduling is concerned with the order of process execution which achieves the best system performance. Ordering of process executions is tied to synchronization, while performance depends heavily on the underlying communication mechanism and communication delays. Since it is more distinct, process scheduling will be discussed separately in Chapter 5. Although communication, synchronization, and scheduling are also major issues in a centralized operating system, our discussion of process management in these three chapters will be oriented toward distributed systems.

This chapter begins with definitions and specifications of concurrent processes. It relates classical process synchronization solutions to distributed concepts and then leads to a more detailed discussion of communication, synchronization, and scheduling in Chapters 4 and 5.

3.1 PROCESSES AND THREADS

Processes are the basic computational units in an operating system. A process is a program in execution. A process is *sequential* if a single thread of control regulates its execution. We use the term *concurrent process* to describe simultaneous interacting sequential processes. Concurrent processes are asynchronous and each has its own logical address space. Between two processes, some components in the processes are disjoint and can be executed concurrently. Others need to communicate or have synchronization between them.

Allowing multiple threads of control in a process introduces a new level of concurrency in the system. A process may spawn new processes, thus creating multiple threads of execution. A special case of interest is when the process and subprocesses are grouped together to share a common address space, but each has its own local state. These processes are called **light-weight processes**, or **threads**. Figure 3.1 shows the two-level concurrency concept of a process and a thread. In the lower level, concurrent processes run asynchronously on a native operating system. Each concurrent process behaves like a virtual machine that supports concurrent execution of threads, forming the second level of concurrency. A process is simply a logical address space in which threads execute.

We use the term Process Control Block (PCB) to indicate the activation record of a process; it contains state information such as program counter, register contents, stack pointers, communication ports, and file descriptors. PCBs contain information necessary for context switching of processes and are managed by the native operating system. Threads are like processes in that they may have their own local procedures and stacks. The state information of each thread is represented by a Thread Control Block (TCB). TCBs are managed by the thread run-time library support, which serves as an interface between thread execution and the native operating system. The TCB is local to a thread, and a PCB is shared among interacting threads for synchronization and communication. Context switching of TCBs requires much less overhead than that of PCBs since only registers (program counter, stack pointers, and register set) need to be switched. Other per-process state information is maintained in a PCB. Thus, threads are called light-weight processes whereas conventional processes are called heavy-weight. In the user

FIGURE 3.1   Two-level concurrency of processes and threads.

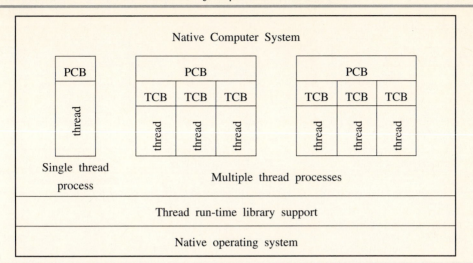

space thread implementation shown in Figure 3.1, only processes, not threads, are visible to the operating system. Alternatively, threads can be implemented in the kernel space and managed by the native operating system directly. Threads in a process may be created statically or dynamically by a control process or other threads.

3.1.1 Thread Applications

Threads have a number of interesting applications in distributed systems. They are useful when implementing a server process that provides similar or related services to multiple client processes, such as a terminal server or file server. When serving requests from client processes in a single-thread server process, the server process may need to suspend itself while it waits for some conditions or operations to be completed. However, suspending the server blocks new client requests from entering the server. To increase system throughput, multiple copies of the same server may be created to service different requests concurrently. Since the servers have similar codes and must interact with each other through shared global information, they can be grouped into the same address space, thus creating multiple threads in a single server. Client processes can be handled similarly. A client process may want to make concurrent requests to some servers without being blocked by any of the service requests.

Figure 3.2 shows three useful thread applications. The terminal server (a data multiplexer and concentrator) in Figure 3.2(a) multiplexes input from various terminals and sends the multiplexed data in a common buffer to a computer (or network). Without multiple threads, the terminal server needs to poll the terminal inputs using nonblocking receive primitives. Conceptually, it is simpler to structure the server in multiple threads, each of which is responsible for one particular input. The code for each thread would be identical and could be shared as a *reentrant code*, with each thread having its own local stack. Concurrent accesses to the common buffer shared by the threads need to be

FIGURE 3.2 Thread applications.

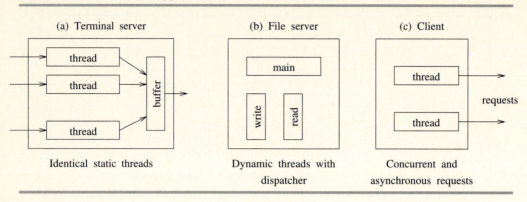

(a) Terminal server

thread

thread

thread

buffer

Identical static threads

(b) File server

main

write   read

Dynamic threads with
dispatcher

(c) Client

thread

thread

requests

Concurrent and
asynchronous requests

mutually exclusive. Mutual exclusion can easily be achieved by using shared-memory synchronization methods such as semaphores or monitors, since all threads share the same address space. Also thread synchronization can be more efficient because synchronization calls are local and can avoid kernel calls in some cases.

Threads in this terminal server example can be created statically and can run indefinitely. Essentially, they behave like a virtual interrupt handler. Figure 3.2(b) illustrates a different application scenario. The file server performs different file service operations upon request from a client. A thread can be created for each operation and control is returned to the main thread so it can accept new requests. If a thread blocks on some condition, another thread is scheduled for execution. A thread ceases to exist when its work is completed. The blocking and scheduling of threads are discussed in the next section. Notice in the file server example that there is a main thread that serves as a work dispatcher for concurrent file services and that thread creation and termination are dynamic. Thread creation and deletion are cheap because of the reuse of memory space. This is a common thread structure for most servers of this type.

The third thread example shown in Figure 3.2(c) is a client that is making multiple requests to different servers. The multiple threads in the client process make it possible to obtain services concurrently and *asynchronously* even when the request/reply communication is synchronous. A useful application of this structure is the concurrent update of replicated file copies managed by multiple file servers.

Threads are supported in modern operating systems largely so that application programmers can write concurrent programs efficiently. For example, a multiple thread Web browser application can initiate multiple file transfers, allowing slow file transfers in the Internet to overlap. Another example is multiple thread multiple-window applications. Coordination between window applications becomes easier if they are implemented in threads with a shared logical address space. For instance, one can perform an action in one window that results in an update in another. To effectively implement these types of applications, preemptable threads and multiprocessor supports may be required. We discuss two typical thread implementation approaches in the following.

3.1.2 User Space Thread Implementation

Thread support as an add-on package has been implemented on many systems including the DCE thread package from OSF and the Light Weight Processes (LWP) package from Sun. The key implementation issues are handling blocking system calls from a thread and scheduling threads for execution in a process. In the user space thread implementation, a process is assigned its share of processor time as is usually done in any operating system. This allocated time period is multiplexed among existing threads. Threads run on top of a run-time support library. It is the responsibility of the run-time procedure to perform context switching from one thread to another. A blocking system call from an executing thread is not trapped by the operating system but is routed to the run-time procedure. The run-time procedure simply saves the TCB of the calling thread and loads the TCB of a thread that it selects into the hardware registers (program counter, registers, and stack pointers), assuming that it is allowed to perform such privileged operations. In effect, no true blocking to the system has occurred, but a thread is blocked in a queue maintained by the run-time support, and the execution of the process continues with other threads.

The context switching of threads requires very little overhead since it involves saving and restoring only the program counter and stack pointers. Also because thread scheduling is performed by the run-time libraries, users have the option of assigning priorities to the created threads. Scheduling of a thread is normally nonpreemptive and on a first-come–first-served basis within a priority; it may be preemptive between different priorities when a thread is created that has a higher priority. Preemptive schemes such as round-robin execution of threads would be more difficult without the use of timer interrupts and are really not necessary at the thread level. If necessary, a thread can contain *sleep* or *yield* thread primitives that relinquish execution of one thread to another, making thread execution asynchronous. Thread primitives included in a typical thread package are:

- Thread management for thread creation, suspension, and termination;
- Assignment of priority and other thread attributes;
- Synchronization and communication support such as semaphore, monitor, and message passing.

3.1.3 Kernel Space Thread Implementation

Thread packages implemented as a software layer in the user space are straightforward and portable without kernel modification. Threads can also be implemented at the kernel level with some advantages. In the kernel space thread implementation, blocking and scheduling of threads are treated normally but there is greater flexibility and efficiency. For example, threads can be preempted easily, a thread issuing a system call can be blocked without blocking all other threads in the same process, and each thread can compete for processor cycles on an equal basis with processes. However, the nice two-level abstraction for concurrency becomes blurred, and the advantage of the lighter context switching overhead of the light-weight processes is lost. Portability and the two-level concurrency abstraction sometimes outweigh other disadvantages.

Like the client/server model and RPC, threads are a fundamental system design concept. Choosing either user or kernel space implementation is a critical system design factor. A combined user and kernel space implementation of threads, such as in Sun's **Solaris**, captures the advantages of both approaches. It also supports a multiple-thread kernel as illustrated in the following.

Traditional kernels are single-threaded. Often there is only one processor, and the structure of the kernel is monolithic and compact. Therefore, requests to the kernel service are run in a single thread without preemption. No synchronization is necessary for kernel operations. Recently, two important trends have emerged for modern systems. First, multiple processors in a single computer system have become commonplace. Second, the complexity of software requirements necessitates the inclusion of many new executive services in the kernel (see for example the microkernel architecture in Figure 1.4). The advantages of the user thread concept become equally applicable to the kernel structure. A multiple thread kernel to support concurrent kernel services may be justified.

Operations internal to the kernel and the services that the kernel provides for user space applications can be implemented as threads. Kernel space threads are multiplexed on the underlying multiprocessor system. Thread executions are truly parallel and can be preemptive. Synchronization between kernel threads becomes necessary and can be done by using shared memory. To incorporate both user space threads and kernel space threads in the same system, Solaris introduces the notion of an intermediate-level thread called a Light Weight Process (LWP) (termed to distinguish it from a regular thread). LWPs are created by the user processes and are managed by the thread run-time routines. They are recognized by the kernel as a basic unit that can be scheduled. User threads, which are not visible to the kernel, are also created and managed by the thread package. LWPs serve as a bridge interface between a user thread and a kernel thread. Figure 3.3 shows a preemptive multithreaded kernel with three levels of concurrency: user threads

FIGURE 3.3   Three-level concurrency of a preemptive multithreaded kernel.

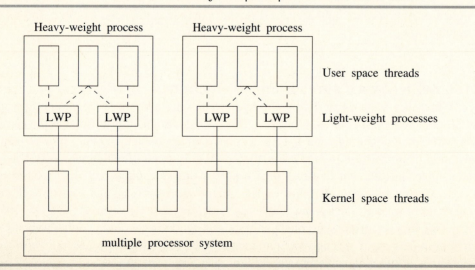

are multiplexed on the LWPs in the same process, LWPs are multiplexed on the kernel threads, and kernel threads are multiplexed on multiple processors.

A user thread can be scheduled to any of the LWPs created by the process. When attached to a LWP, it becomes executable using the time allocated to the LWP by the kernel. Each LWP is connected to a kernel thread. A blocking call from a user thread is trapped to the LWP. The LWP may, in turn, make a real system call to the kernel and become blocked. Blocking of an LWP does not block the entire process since the waiting threads can be scheduled to other LWPs in the same process. User threads are preemptive because LWPs can be preempted by the kernel. The combined hybrid implementation has the flexibility and efficiency of both user space and kernel space threads.

Many existing operating systems have thread support and numerous software packages use threads. Thread support has become an integral part of modern operating systems.

3.2 GRAPH MODELS FOR PROCESS REPRESENTATION

Having described processes and threads, we are now interested in how they are put together. Processes are related by their need for synchronization and/or communication. Synchronization means that the execution of some processes must be serialized in a certain order. A special example of synchronization is the precedence relationship between two processes when execution of one process must precede the other. In many cases, the precedence relationship or the ordering of processes is not always necessary for communicating processes as long as messages can be properly exchanged. Figure 3.4 uses graph models to illustrate these two different views of process interactions. The synchronous process graph in the Direct Acyclic Graph (DAG) model shows explicit precedence relationships and a partial ordering of a set of processes. The undirected edges in the asynchronous process graph indicate the existence of communication paths, and thus some dependency between processes.

The graphs in Figure 3.4 are too abstract to model any nontrivial system behavior. Yet they are not completely useless. For instance, we can use them to model the mapping between processes and processors in a distributed system. The synchronous process graph can be used to analyze the **makespan** (total completion time) of a set of cooperating processes, and the asynchronous communication graph can be used to study processor allocation for optimizing interprocessor communication overhead. A more detailed graph of distributed processes often makes analytical analysis more difficult and sometime even intractable. There is a trade-off between the expressive and analytical powers of the system model.

In Figure 3.4, the directed edges in the precedence graph can be interpreted as a synchronous communication of a sent or received message. Results produced by a process are passed to a successor process as input. The communication transaction happens and is synchronized only at the completion of a process and the beginning of its successor process(es). This communication is more precisely specified than in the asynchronous process graph, where nothing is said about how and when communication occurs except that there is a communication path between the processes.

FIGURE 3.4 Graph models for process interaction.

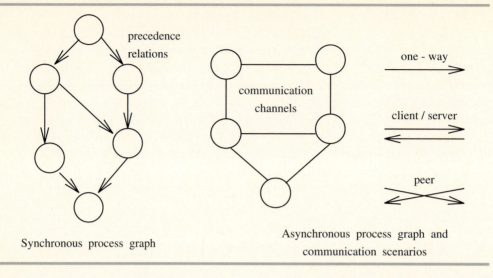

precedence relations

communication channels

one - way

client / server

peer

Synchronous process graph

Asynchronous process graph and
communication scenarios

Processes in the undirected graph live indefinitely, as opposed to the directed graph where processes have a finite lifetime. There are three types of communication scenarios for the asynchronous communication graph model: *one-way*, *client/server*, and *peer*. Using communication terminology, they correspond to *simplex*, *half-duplex*, and *full-duplex* communication, respectively. An application process in one-way communication sends messages and expects no reply. A good example is the broadcast of information. Client/server communication is two-way; it makes a request and receives a reply. Many communication applications use this assumption, which is a master/slave relationship. Peer communication is a symmetrical two-way exchange of messages. It is commonly used for coordination among peer processes.

Both synchronous and asynchronous process graph models are suitable for performance analysis but lack sufficient detail to describe the interaction among processes. Figure 3.5 shows the time-space model, a better representation of communication and precedence relations. The existence of communication paths and the precedence relations between the events and actual communications are explicit in the model. The corresponding precedence or communication graph can be derived easily from the time-space diagram. This model possesses more information for analyzing the instantaneous interactions among processes than for evaluating the overall system performance. All three models are used for various discussions in this book. The choice of models depends on the intended analysis.

Whether processes are represented by a precedence or communication graph, the interaction of processes must be expressed in a language or by some other formal mechanism. We can invent a new concurrent language for concurrent processing, but it is easier to take an existing sequential language and extend it with additional language constructs or operating system supports to provide for the creation, communication, and synchronization of processes. For example, we can introduce a *cobegin/coend*

FIGURE 3.5 A time-space model for interacting processes.

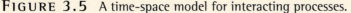

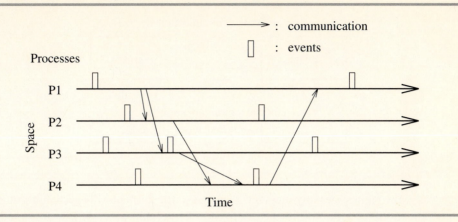

control structure or use *fork/join* system calls to create and synchronize concurrent processes. Processes created in this way are more tightly coupled since they have a *master/slave* or *parent/child* relationship and share some common attributes. They also work cooperatively toward a common goal and are normally implemented by a single individual or organization. This approach is suited to the implementation of the precedence process graph model. The other scenario for structuring processes is to assume a peer-to-peer relationship among processes. Processes interact with one another only through interprocess communication. No precedence relation exists between processes. In fact they may be created independently, executed asynchronously, and have different life spans. This is best modeled by a communication process graph. In this case, the specification and interaction of processes become an operating system issue rather than a language issue.

3.3 THE CLIENT/SERVER MODEL

Another way of describing process interaction is by how processes view each other. One popular approach is the client/server model (which is equally important as the transparency concept for distributed systems). The client/server model is a programming paradigm that represents the interactions between processes and structures of the system. Any process in a system either provides services for others or requests services from them. Processes that request services are clients, and those that provide services are servers. In any interaction a process is either a client or a server. In many cases, the same process plays the roles of both.

A client and a server interact through a sequence of requests and responses. A client requests a service from the server and blocks itself. The server receives the request, performs the operation, and returns a reply message to the client. The client then resumes its execution. The only underlying assumption is a synchronous request/reply exchange of information. Logically, the clients communicate directly with the servers.

FIGURE 3.6   Client/server model.

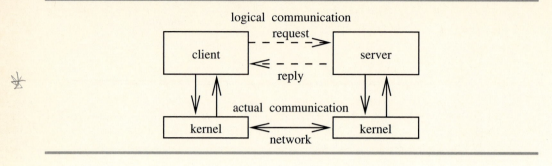

Physically, the request or reply message is passed to the kernel of the system, through the communication network, and to the destination kernel and process. The message is not interpreted by the system. Higher-level communication protocols between the client and the server can be built on top of the request and reply messages. Figure 3.6 illustrates the concept of the client/server model for process interactions.

The client/server model can also be considered as a service-oriented communication model. It is a higher-level abstraction of interprocess communication that can be supported by using either RPC or message passing communication, which in turn is implemented by either a connection-oriented or connectionless transport service in the network. Figure 3.7 shows the relationship among the three major concepts: the client/server model, RPC, and message passing. Services provided by a server may be connection-oriented or connectionless. A connection-oriented service can be built on top of a connectionless service. The opposite, however, is usually not logical. The client/server model achieves some degree of transparency for communication.

In Chapter 2 we grouped system services into three categories: primitive, system, and value-added. Primitive services are fundamental mechanisms that reside in the kernel. From the application point of view, only system and value-added services are visible to the users. To a user a program is a collection of clients and servers. If we implement system services as server processes and move them out of kernel space whenever possible, the size of the kernel can be greatly reduced. Clearly a minimized kernel is easier to port to different hardware platforms. A natural consequence of using the client/server model

FIGURE 3.7   Client/server communication model on RPC and message passing.

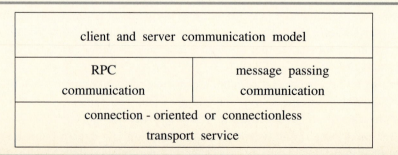

is that processes need only a single type of system call to the kernel (i.e., *send* and *receive* requests). There is no need for the kernel to parse the system calls and determine what needs to be done. Instead, it is the responsibility of the server process to interpret the message, as long as the kernel knows the basic message structure. The interface between processes and the kernel becomes simple and uniform.

Multiple servers can coexist to provide a similar service. They need to be identified either by their names or the functions that they perform. This requires servers that locate servers. These servers, called **binder** or **agent** servers, bind the client process and the selected server process together, and they sometimes may also need to be located. At the end, there should be a minimum number of servers with well-known names or addresses. Upon request from a client, the binder server can choose a server most suitable for the client or one that best balances the load of the servers. As an option, it can also perform authentication of clients for the servers.

Standard horizontal or vertical partitionings of modules can be applied to the structuring of servers. Horizontal partitions are used to group disjoint servers. Vertical partitionings are a layering concept; they allow servers to call on other servers that are sitting immediately below them. In addition, servers may be recursively structured, just like a process (i.e., a server may contain subservers and so forth).

3.4 TIME SERVICES

In the time-space model for process interaction, events are recorded with respect to each process' own clock time. In real life, clocks are used to represent *time* (a relative measure of a point in time) and a *timer* (an absolute measure of time interval) is used to describe the occurrences of events in three different ways:

- When an event occurs;
- How long it takes;
- Which event occurs first.

For computer applications we also need the notions of time and timer. For instance, we like to know when a file was last modified, how long a client should be given the privilege to access a server, and which update of a data object happened first. As long as the clock representing time is increased uniformly and monotonically, there is no ambiguity in answering these questions for events that occur within the same process. However, interacting processes on separate machines may have a different perception of the time. Without a global time consensus, it is difficult to coordinate distributed activities such as network garbage collection, file system backup scheduled at midnight each day, or validation of expiration time of a received message. This section describes two fundamental clock concepts, physical clock and logical clock, for specifying time in distributed systems. A physical clock is a close approximation of realtime that measures both a point and intervals of time. A logical clock preserves only the ordering of events. Both play an important role in distributed systems.

3.4.1 Physical Clocks

In every computer system, physical clocks are used to synchronize and schedule hardware activities. On the software side, it is necessary to simulate realtime or measure an interval of time. Software timers based on hardware clock interrupts keep track of software activities. In a distributed system, each clock runs at its own pace, and there is a nonnegligible communication delay in reporting clock time. Since timing information cannot be propagated and received instantaneously by all, an absolute global physical time is theoretically impossible to obtain. So, we have to settle for a close approximation of the global time. The challenge is for all machines to reach a consensus of time. It is sometimes desirable for this consensus to be as close to the realtime as possible. The former requires a clock synchronization algorithm, while the latter needs a universal realtime source. Figure 3.8 is a time service architecture that is similar to the Distributed Time Service (DTS) in DCE. A time clerk (TC) on each client machine may request time service by contacting one or more time servers (TS). Time servers are those that maintain up-to-date clock information and may have access to a universal realtime source. Time servers may exchange timing information so that their time services can be more consistent with that of their clients. There are two practical issues in implementing the time service. First, the delay in reporting time must be compensated. Second, the discrepancy among time sources must be calibrated.

Compensating Delay

Figure 3.8 shows three types of time access: time server to universal time source, client to time server, and time server to time server. Many standard Universal Coordinated Time (UTC) sources are available for computers and other time-critical applications. The National Institute of Standards and Technology (NIST) supports several UTC access methods at accuracy near 1 millisecond. The Automated Computer Time Service (ACTS) provides modem service to NIST time through telephone lines. ACTS is designed for applications that require only infrequent time service. A dial-up modem service may be too slow for synchronizing software activities. For frequent accesses, NIST operates a short wave radio station, WWV, which regularly broadcasts UTC signals. The message delay time to compensate the UTC can be calculated accurately if the distance to the radio station and the signal propagation speed are known. Unfortunately, short wave

FIGURE 3.8   A distributed time service architecture.

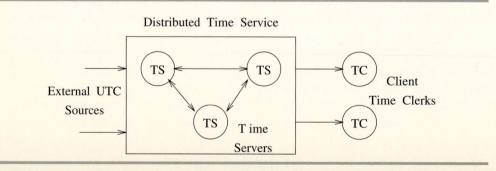

radio is susceptible to atmospheric interference. An alternative is to use the service of the Global Positioning System (GPS). However GPS satellites have a low orbit and are not geostationary, that is, their distances from Earth vary in time. Precise computation of delay (or distance) may require monitoring several GPS satellites. The cost of required receiver hardware and the associated computation is high. One can also rely on geostationary satellites to broadcast UTC information. The distance from a satellite to land computer stations is fixed, but the propagation delay is long (about 125 milliseconds). Many cable TV channels also carry in-band timing information. All these universal time sources have their pros and cons. Fortunately, not all time servers need to access UTC from these sources as long as one of the time servers can propagate its current UTC to other time servers timely and accurately.

The problem of delay in reporting or acquiring UTC from a client to a time server and between time servers is a different matter. In addition to signal propagation delay, there is the network communication delay. Network delay fluctuates and is several orders of magnitude higher than propagation delay. Let T_s and T_r denote the sending and receiving of a time service request from a client to a time server, respectively. Let t_p represent the time that the time server needs to process the request (determined in advance). The UTC returned from the time server to a client can be adjusted by adding half of the round-trip delay ($T_r - T_s - t_p$). This compensation of UTC is based on the assumption that the network traffic is symmetrical. If the local clock in the client is faster (higher) than the new UTC, its clock speed is slowed down (by software). Clock time cannot be set back abruptly since it may contradict the time of some earlier events. The problem with a slower clock is less serious, but it is still better to increase clock speed temporarily so that the clock time can catch up with the UTC gradually. For example, an abrupt advance of clock time may confuse processes that are waiting for a time-out and cause premature time-out.

Accessing UTC by clients from a time server is a *pull* (passive TS) service model. A time server can play a more active role by broadcasting its UTC to clients. This *push* (active TS) model has the advantage of maintaining a higher degree of clock consistency. Push is similar to the radio or satellite broadcast of UTC except that each client is expected to respond. Furthermore, the clients have no easy way to determine the network delay time. This drawback makes it suitable only for systems with multicast hardware where message delay time is shorter and more predictable. Both push and pull models can also be applied to the communication among time servers.

The problem of estimating network delay precisely, especially when the network traffic is high or congested, results in inconsistency among time servers. To improve consistency, time servers can calibrate their UTCs with each other. A client can also contact multiple time servers to calibrate the discrepancy between different UTCs.

Calibrating Discrepancy

Discrepancy among time servers can be reduced by requiring them to adjust their UTCs cooperatively. Time servers can periodically exchange UTCs with each other using either the push or pull model. After a number of UTCs have been collected, each time server attempts to reach a consensus on time by adjusting the UTC using previously agreed

FIGURE 3.9 Averaging UTC intervals.

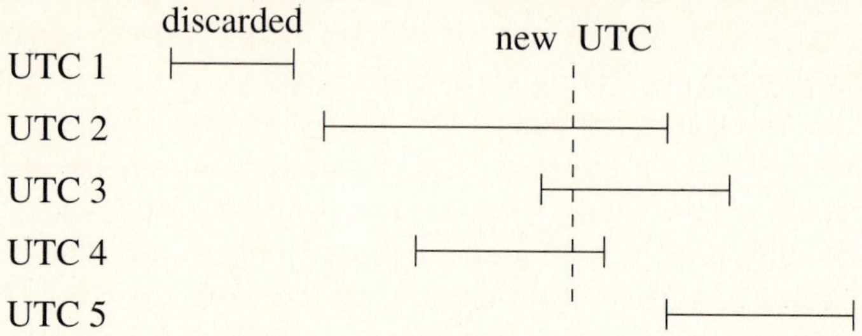

decision criteria. The decision may be based on the maximum, minimum, median, or average of the UTCs. The latter two are better choices for consistency purpose. If averaging is used, UTCs that are suspiciously small or large can be excluded from the computation.

There is always a small degree of uncertainty about the UTC that a time server possesses. The time server might report an interval of time, UTC $\pm \triangle I$, where $\triangle I$ is the statistical indicator of inaccuracy or interval of confidence. The inaccuracy indicator helps the clients to decide whether a time server can provide adequate precision for their application. The averaging of UTCs in a time interval can be modified as shown in Figure 3.9. UTC intervals that do not overlap with others are thrown away. The intersection that includes the most UTC sources is computed. The new UTC is set to the midpoint of the intersection.

Even with consistent time servers, clients' computation of UTC can still be inconsistent because of the unpredictable network delay. Inconsistency can be alleviated if clients follow the same strategy as the time server by contacting more than one time server and calibrating the UTC.

The physical clock is important for distributed software development because numerous software protocols rely on a *time-out* for handling exceptions. If a time-out set by one process is to be checked by another process on a different machine, the two physical clocks must be synchronized to a degree acceptable to both processes. A notable application is the use of the physical clock as a timestamp for secure internet communication. Physical timestamps are used to eliminate duplicated messages (thus avoiding *play back* attacks) and to check the expiration of privileges for access control.

3.4.2 Logical Clocks

A physical clock is a close approximation to the global real time. The time interval measurement is useful and can be derived directly from physical clocks. In general we can use physical clocks to tell whether an event happens before another unless they occur very closely. If the uncertainty of UTC is high or UTC intervals of events overlap with each other, it is not possible to determine the ordering of events. For many applications, events need not be scheduled or synchronized with respect to the real-time clock. It is only the ordering of event execution that is of concern. In such cases, logical clocks can be used to indicate the ordering information for events, particularly in distributed systems where it is difficult to maintain a common physical clock among all coordinating processes. Lamport's logical clock is a fundamental concept for ordering processes and events in distributed systems.

Each process P_i in the system maintains a logical clock C_i. Lamport defines the algebraic notation $\rightarrow$ as the *happens-before* relation to synchronize the logical clocks between two events. $a \rightarrow b$ means event a precedes event b. Within a process, if event a occurs before b, logical clocks $C(a)$ and $C(b)$ are assigned such that $C(a) < C(b)$. The logical clock in a process is always incremented by an arbitrary positive number when events in the process progress (i.e., time never goes back and is only a relative measure for logical clock). Processes interact with each other through a pair of *send* and *receive* operations. Sends and receives are considered to be events. A corresponding *send* and *receive* pair from process P_i to process P_j must have the property that $C_i(send) < C_j(receive)$ since a receive event cannot be completed until a corresponding send is done. This logical clock based on the *happens-before* relation is summarized in the two following rules:

1. If $a \rightarrow b$ within a same process then $C(a) < C(b)$.
2. If a is the sending event of P_i and b is the corresponding receiving event of P_j, then $C_i(a) < C_j(b)$.

Rule 1 can be easily implemented since events occur in the same process. Rule 2 can be enforced if the sending process *timestamps* its logical clock time in the message and the receiving process updates its logical clock by using the larger of its own clock time and the incremented timestamp. That is, $C(b) = C(a) + d$ and $C_j(b) = max(TS_a + d, C_j(b))$, where TS_a is the timestamp of the sending event and d is a positive number. The happens-before relation describes the **causality** between two events. It is *transitive*, that is, if $a \rightarrow b$ and $b \rightarrow c$, then $a \rightarrow c$. Two events, a and b, are said to be **disjoint** events and can be run **concurrently** if neither $a \rightarrow b$ nor $b \rightarrow a$ is true. The time-space diagram in Figure 3.10 shows examples of causally related events $[(a, e, c), (a, e, h)]$ and concurrent events $[(b, e), (f, h)]$. Logical clocks for concurrent events do not relate to each other.

FIGURE 3.10   The happens-before relation and assignments of logical clock time.

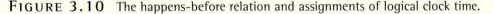
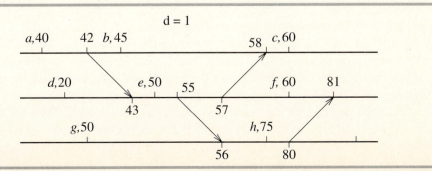

Partial and Total Ordering of Events

Using the happens-before relation and the above two rules, all causally related events are ordered by the logical clocks. This results only a **partially ordered** event graph. For two disjoint events, a and b, $C_i(a) < C_j(b)$ does not imply $a \rightarrow b$. Furthermore, it is possible that $C_i(a) = C_j(b)$. **Total ordering** of events may be achieved by assuming the following additional rule for disjoint events (causally related events are already ordered):

3. For all events a and b, $C(a) \neq C(b)$.

Disjoint events with identical logical clocks can be distinguished by concatenating their logical clock with a distinct process *id* number, thus ensuring systemwide unique logical clock times for all events. The ordering of disjoint events is irrelevant with respect to the correct execution of processes. A totally ordered set of events represents a feasible correct execution sequence of events. Many concurrency control algorithms use the property of total ordering of events based on logical clocks.

3.4.3 Vector Logical Clocks

Even with the total ordering of events using logical clocks as described, it is not possible to tell whether event a actually happened before event b if $C_i(a) < C_j(b)$ (i.e., they might be concurrent). This is where vector logical clock is used. In the vector logical clock method, each process P_i maintains a vector of logical clocks for each event. We denote the vector logical clock for event a at processor i as $VC_i(a) = [TS_1, TS_2, ..., C_i(a), ..., TS_n]$, where n is the number of cooperating processes. $C_i(a)$ (also represented as TS_i) is the logical clock time of event a in P_i, and TS_k (for $k = 1...n$, except i) is the best estimate of the logical clock time for process P_k. This best estimate of other process' logical clock times is obtained through the timestamp information carried by messages in the system.

The vector clocks are initialized to zero at the beginning of process execution. The logical clock within a process is incremented as in rule 1 for the basic logical clock approach. Rule 2 is modified as follow. When sending a message m from P_i (event a) to P_j, the logical timestamp of m, $VC_i(m)$ is sent along with m to P_j. Let b be the event of receiving m at P_j. P_j updates its logical clock vector $VC_j(b)$ such that $TS_k(b) = \max(TS_k(a), TS_k(b))$. That is, P_j takes the *pair-wise maximum* of the entries for every $k = 1...n$ and also increments its logical clock. Thus the most recent logical clock information is propagated to every process by sending timestamps TS_k in the messages.

It is obvious that if event a in P_i happened before event b in P_j, then $VC_i(a) < VC_j(b)$, meaning that $TS_k(a) \leq TS_k(b)$ for every k and also $TS_j(a) < TS_j(b)$. This is because there is a causal path from event a to event b, and event b should have a more up-to-date logical time information than event a since the timestamps are passed along the path and the update rule is based on the larger of the two timestamps. Furthermore, the logical clock of the successor event b has been incremented since event a; therefore $TS_j(b)$ must be greater than $TS_j(a)$. For disjoint events, it is not possible to have $VC_i(a) < VC_j(b)$ unless $a \rightarrow b$, since process P_i, which contains event a, should have a better update of its own time than any other process' estimate of the current clock time of P_i; that is, $C_i(a)$

FIGURE 3.11   Vector logical clocks.

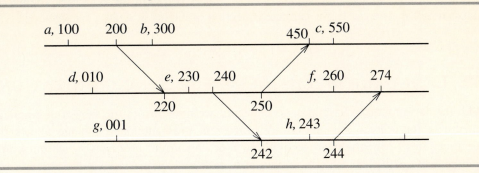

is greater or equal to the TS_i in other vectors. Similarly, $VC_j(b) < VC_i(a)$ is true only if $b \rightarrow a$. We can conclude that it is possible to tell whether two events are causally related or not by comparing the vector logical clocks of the two events. If $VC_i(a) < VC_j(b)$, then $a \rightarrow b$; otherwise a and b are concurrent. Figure 3.11 gives examples of the vector logical clocks using the time-space diagram from Figure 3.10. Events (a, e, h) are causally related and satisfy $VC_1(a) < VC_2(e) < VC_3(h)$. Disjoint events (b, f) can never satisfy $VC_1(b) < VC_2(f)$ or $VC_2(f) < VC_1(b)$.

3.4.4 Matrix Logical Clocks

The concept of a vector logical clock can be extended to matrix logical clocks. A matrix clock $MC_i[k, l]$ at process P_i is an n by n matrix that represents logical time by a vector of vector logical clocks. The ith row of the matrix $MC_i[i, 1...n]$ is the vector logical clock of P_i. The jth row of the matrix $MC_i[j, 1...n]$ indicates the knowledge process P_i has about the vector logical clock of process P_j. The updating rules for matrix logical clocks are similar to those for vector logical clocks. For each local event, a process increments its own clock time by setting

$$MC_i[i, i] = MC_i[i, i] + d$$

When sending a message from process P_i to process P_j, the entire matrix clock $MC_i[k, l]$ is timestamped as $TS_i[k, l]$ and piggybacked with the message to process P_j. P_j first updates its vector clock by using the same pair-wise maximum rule:

$$MC_j[j, l] = \max(MC_j[j, l], TS_i[j, l]) \quad : l = 1...n$$

Then P_j updates its entire matrix clock again by using the pair-wise maximum rule for the entire matrix:

$$MC_j[k, l] = \max(MC_j[k, l], TS_i[k, l]) \quad : k = 1...n, \; l = 1...n$$

The first update maintains the causal order of the events. The second update propagates the knowledge about other processes through message passing (this is similar to *gossip* in real life). We explore some applications of matrix clocks in the exercises. Chapter 12 makes use of matrix clocks for garbage collection problems in replica management.

3.5 LANGUAGE MECHANISMS FOR SYNCHRONIZATION

With the background in basic process concepts, we now turn to the subject of language constructs for process interactions. A concurrent programming language allows the specification of concurrent processing and how concurrent processes synchronize and communicate with each other. It is natural to take an existing sequential language and add additional language facilities to support concurrent processing. This approach is easier for people to learn since there are fewer new concepts to acquire. A concurrent language extended from a sequential language adds additional constructs to provide:

- Specification of concurrent activities;
- Synchronization of processes;
- Interprocess communication;
- Nondeterministic execution of processes.

Process synchronization has been widely studied for centralized operating systems. Process communication through message passing is a new issue when we consider distributed systems. This section summarizes some of the standard solutions for process synchronization, their relevance to distributed systems, and how they evolve into a communication issue in distributed systems. As we shall see, various approaches tackle the synchronization problem at different angles of a programming language. We will start with a brief description of language structures and see how they are extended for process synchronization.

3.5.1 Language Constructs

A common procedure-oriented language is generally defined by a complete specification of the syntactic structure and semantics of its major components. Typically these components can be categorized as follows:

- **Program structure** that specifies how programs and their subcomponents (procedures, blocks, statements, expression, terms, variables, constants, etc.) are composed. A sequential execution of program components is assumed unless explicitly altered by control statements.
- **Data structures** that are defined to represent objects in the program. Data type abstraction and its efficient implementation are primary goals.
- **Control structures** that regulate the flow of program execution. Most languages emphasize use of structured *one-in-one-out* control structures such as *if-then-else, while-do, repeat-until, etc.* Other implicit control structures include subroutine calls, returns, and exits.

- **Procedures and system calls** that activate special routines or system services. These calls imply change of execution flow and allow parameter passing.
- **Input and output** that receives input data and produces results of program execution. All programs contain at least some output operations. Input and output can be interpreted as a special case of message passing communication.
- **Assignments** that cause side effects for data objects. They are the primary operations that effect the state of program executions.

Table 3.1 shows examples of synchronization methods listed by their use of language facilities. The relationship between a synchronization method and its corresponding language facility is not precise. It is only used to demonstrate the evolution of the development of language constructs for process synchronization. These synchronization concepts are divided into two categories: The top five are shared variable synchronization methods and the bottom three are message passing approaches. In the following two sections, we discuss these synchronization mechanisms by solving the *concurrent readers/exclusive writer* problem using each method.

The reader/writer problems use the normal assumptions of reading and writing of data objects (i.e., reader processes may be concurrent and writer processes must be mutually exclusive from other readers and writers). These problems are generic enough to model synchronization and concurrency in many applications. The reader/writer problems have several variations. Since we will use them not only to show concurrent programming concepts, but also in several exercises and programming projects, we will define their variations more precisely. The **reader preference** version is defined as: *an arriving writer waits until there are no running readers*. Readers get higher priorities than writers and can cause writers to starve if readers continue to arrive before other readers complete. The **writer preference** version is defined as: *an arriving reader waits until there are no*

TABLE 3.1   Synchronization mechanisms and language facilities.

Synchronization Methods	Language Facilities
Shared-Variable Synchronization	
semaphore	shared variable and system call
monitor	data type abstraction
conditional critical region	control structure
serializer	data type and control structure
path expression	data type and program structure
Message Passing Synchronization	
communicating sequential processes	input and output
remote procedure call	procedure call
rendezvous	procedure call and communication

running and waiting writers. Similarly, readers may starve since waiting writers may block waiting readers indefinitely.

There is some ambiguity in the reader preference definition when both readers and writers are waiting for a running writer. The completing writer can turn the control to either a reader or a writer. We say a reader preference reader/writer problem is *strong* reader preference if a waiting reader is scheduled over the waiting writers upon the completion of the running writer. If the scheduling is implicit (doesn't care which is scheduled next), it is a *weak* reader preference problem. The remaining case is when the control is always turned to a waiting writer first. We can call this case a *weaker* reader preference problem. Such ambiguity does not exist for the writer preference problem since it is already taken care of by its definition that readers must also wait for the waiting writers. For clarity in comparing different synchronization approaches in the following discussion, we choose the simpler *weak reader preference* reader/writer version in which a writer must wait until there are no active readers or writer. No other constraint applies. Solution examples are simplified to show only the concepts and the algorithms. The syntax of the programs is informal.

3.5.2 Shared-variable Synchronization

Shared-variable synchronization mechanisms were developed for synchronizing concurrent processes in a centralized operating system. As the name implies, process coordination is achieved by sharing variables. Interprocess communication uses neither message passing nor client/server communication. Although they are centralized approaches, they still have their place in the design of distributed operating systems. For example, the threads and tasks using distributed shared memory continue to use shared memory synchronization. It may also be desirable to simulate shared-variable synchronization by message passing.

The following summary of shared memory synchronization mechanisms follows the order listed in Table 3.1. Capabilities and relationships with language facilities of the mechanisms are compared and their relevance to distributed systems is noted. The discussion leads to the conclusion of the structural requirements of a synchronization server, or more generally a resource server, in Section 3.6.

Semaphore: A Shared-variable and System Call Approach

Semaphores are a built-in system data type. A variable defined as a semaphore type is internally associated with a lock and a queue for process blocking purposes. Only two operations, P for acquiring the lock and V for releasing the lock, are allowed on semaphores for process synchronization. They are implemented as system calls to the operating system. The operating system maintains the indivisible property of the operations and is responsible for blocking and unblocking processes. The key characteristic of semaphores is that they provide only the most primitive locking mechanisms. Coordination of process activities to achieve correct synchronization is left entirely to the user processes. It is a shared memory concept and has virtually no transparency in hiding the synchronization details.

FIGURE 3.12   Semaphore solution to the weak reader preference problem.

var mutex, db: **semaphore**; rc: **integer**

reader processes	writer processes
P(mutex) rc := rc + 1 if rc = 1 **then** P(db) V(mutex)	P(db)
read database	write database
P(mutex) rc := rc −1 if rc = 0 **then** V(db) V(mutex)	V(db)

The semaphore solution in Figure 3.12 shows strong dependency between the reader and writer processes. The user processes are aware of the existence of other processes, which is an undesirable assumption for distributed systems. The shared variable rc is the reader count. The first and last readers lock and release the database, respectively. The semaphore *mutex* provides mutual exclusion for updating rc.

Extending the special built-in semaphore data type to a more general user-defined type leads to the development of the monitor concept, which uses higher-level data type abstraction.

Monitor: A Data Type Abstraction Approach

A monitor is an object model concept and has a syntactic structure similar to a user defined data type. A monitor consists of a declaration for its local variables, a set of allowable operations (or monitor procedures), and an initialization procedure that initializes the state of the monitor. The difference between a monitor and a regular user-defined data type is the semantic assumption that only one instantiation of a monitor object can be active at any time. This implicit assumption achieves the same mutual exclusion as a pair of P and V operations on a binary semaphore. However, the critical sections are fixed and predefined in the monitor procedures. Consequently, it is more structured than the semaphore approach. To coordinate activities once a process is in a monitor procedure, *conditional variables* with two standard operations, *wait* and *signal*, are used to suspend or resume execution of a process in the monitor. Because interleaving of monitor procedure activations is permitted, the implementation of monitors must ensure that no more than one process in the monitor is active at any time.

Since monitor procedures accept parameters, monitors provide process communication as well as synchronization. Clearly, shielding and shifting synchronization details from the user processes is a major step for the monitor approach toward providing transparency.

Figure 3.13 is a monitor solution to the same weak reader priority problem. The monitor serves as a controller that governs the rules for concurrent readers and writers. There is no direct interaction among reader and write processes. The monitor resembles a server and the reader and writer processes are clients. Unfortunately, even if the monitor is implemented by the system and assumes the responsibility of read/write control, the actual read and write operations are in the user processes. The monitor in this case is not a full-fledged resource server. In addition, the need for user processes to do a start/end of each read/write operation is not as transparent as a simple read/write.

Aside from its assumption of shared memory, the monitor concept is still far from ideal for adaptation in distributed systems. To provide transparent and concurrent reading/writing of the database, actual read and write operations must be performed

FIGURE 3.13   Monitor solution to the weak reader preference problem.

```
rw : monitor
var rc : integer; busy : boolean; toread, towrite : condition;


procedure startread              procedure endread
begin                            begin
if busy then toread.wait;
rc := rc + 1;                    rc := rc - 1;
toread.signal;                   if rc = 0 then towrite.signal;
end                              end


procedure startwrite             procedure endwrite
begin                            begin
if busy or rc ≠ 0
then towrite.wait;               busy := false;
busy := true;                    toread.signal or towrite.signal;
end                              end


begin rc := 0; busy := false end
-----------------------------------------------------------------
reader processes                 writer processes


rw.startread                     rw.startwrite
read database                    write database
rw.endread                       rw.endwrite
```

inside the monitor. However, multiple activations of the monitor procedures are not allowed. A multiple thread monitor seems a plausible solution. A thread is given to each activation of a monitor procedure without blocking the monitor. Threads are suspended upon *wait* on conditions, and they share variables by using semaphores. Unfortunately, we have lost the single most unique characteristic of the monitors, the single activation of a monitor procedure for mutual exclusion. It is no long a monitor. We observe the need for a monitor procedure to be sometimes exclusive and sometimes concurrent.

Conditional Critical Region: A Control Structure Approach

A Conditional Critical Region (CCR) is a structured version of the semaphore approach. Critical section codes are explicitly named and expressed by **region-begin-end**. Once in the critical region, a condition can be tested by the **when** predicate. If the condition is not met, the process is suspended and other processes are allowed to enter their critical regions.

Figure 3.14 shows the CCR solution to the weak reader preference reader/writer problem. This control structure approach assumes shared variables and requires compilation of the critical regions into synchronization primitives that are available from the operating system. The need for a common address space and the infeasibility of separate compilations make CCR an unlikely candidate for adaptation in distributed systems.

Serializer: A Combined Data Abstraction and Control Structure Approach

In the discussion of the monitor synchronization method, we see that it is necessary to allow concurrency in the monitor and at the same time maintain the atomicity of the operation of a monitor procedure. A *serializer* is an extension of the monitor concept to achieve just that. Serializers have structures that are similar to those of monitors. Processes invoke serializer procedures in the same way that they invoke monitor procedure calls. Like monitors, exclusive access to the serializer is assumed. However, a serializer procedure consists of two types of regions, one that requires mutual exclusion and the other that allows concurrent processes to be active in the region; the latter is called a *hollow* region. This is accomplished by a new control structure: **joincrowd-then-begin-end**. When a process enters a hollow region, it releases the serializer and joins a crowd

FIGURE 3.14   CCR solution to the weak reader preference problem.

---

var db: **shared**; rc: **integer**;

reader processes	writer processes
region db **begin** rc := rc + 1 **end**; read database **region** db **begin** rc := rc - 1 **end**;	**region** db **when** rc = 0 **begin** write database **end**

FIGURE 3.15 Serializer solution to the weak reader preference problem.

rw : serializer
var readq, writeq: queue; rcrowd, wcrowd: crowd;

procedure read
begin
enqueue(readq) until empty(wcrowd);
joincrowd(rcrowd) then begin read database end;
end

procedure write
begin
enqueue(writeq) until (empty(wcrowd) and empty(rcrowd));
joincrowd(wcrowd) then begin write database end;
end

of concurrent processes. The blocking of processes by *wait* on condition variables in monitors is replaced by an **enqueue** operation in the serializer. The removal of a queued process when its waiting condition has been changed is done implicitly by the system rather than by using explicit *signals* as in the monitor approach. The use of a queue and implicit signaling greatly improves the clarity of programs. We show the serializer solution in Figure 3.15 for comparison with previous examples. The serializer allows for mutual exclusion and concurrency in the serializer procedures. Of the mechanisms we have reviewed so far, the serializer best encapsulates the concurrent object and most resembles a resource server. Clients request accesses to the database using read and write serializer procedures directly and transparently.

Path Expression: A Data Abstraction and Program Structure Approach

The path expression concept is significantly different from all the previously discussed synchronization methods. Like the monitors, it is an abstraction of data type. However, the procedures defined in the abstract data type contain no explicit reference to any synchronization primitives. Only the order of procedure execution must follow the constraints set by the **path** expressions. Path expressions are a high-level language specification that describes how operations defined for a shared object can be invoked to satisfy the synchronization requirements. For this reason we refer to it as a program structure approach since it resembles the formal description of a program. The path expression solution to the weak reader preference problem is extremely elegant:

path 1:([read],write) end

The constant 1 constrains the number of simultaneous activities in the parentheses to one and thus specifies the exclusion between reader and writer. The square brackets indicate that readers may be concurrent. Although elegant in concept, path expressions must be sufficient in expressive power, and compilers must be available to translate path expressions into implementable synchronization primitives. Many extensions to the path expression concept have been explored to increase its capability in specifying concurrency and synchronization requirements. The most notable example is the inclusion of predicates in path expressions for condition coordination.

3.5.3 Message Passing Synchronization

Without shared memory, message passing is the only means for communication in distributed systems. Message passing is also a form of implicit synchronization since *messages can be received only after they have been sent.* For most applications, it is common to assume that receive is blocking, and send may be either blocking or nonblocking. We will call nonblocking send, blocking receive **asynchronous message passing** and blocking send, blocking receive **synchronous message passing**. This section describes how synchronization can be accomplished using the two different assumptions of message passing. Concepts relevant to message passing such as Communicating Sequential Processes (CSP), remote procedure calls, and rendezvous are discussed.

Asynchronous Message Passing

Although there is no sharing of variables in message passing, the communication channel is shared. Therefore, the blocking receive operation from a message channel is equivalent to a P operation on a semaphore, and the nonblocking send is analogous to a V operation. Asynchronous message passing is simply an extension of the semaphore concept to distributed systems. Note that asynchronous send operations assume that the channel has an unbounded buffer and so perhaps cannot be fully implemented. Asynchronous message passing synchronization is as useful as semaphores if communication channels can be specified in the language and supported by the operating system. Figure 3.16 demonstrates the use of asynchronous message passing for mutual exclusion. The **channel server** represents the operating system support of logical channels. It creates the logical channel solely for synchronization purposes and initializes the channel to contain one

FIGURE 3.16   Mutual exclusion using asynchronous message passing.

process P_i	channel server	process P_j
begin	begin	begin
receive(channel)	create channel	receive(channel)
critical section	send(channel)	critical section
send(channel)	manage channel	send(channel)
end	end	end

message. The message content in the channel is immaterial for this mutual exclusion example. The channel server also manages the queueing of messages and processes blocked on the channel. Good examples of asynchronous message passing are the **pipe** and **socket** facilities provided by many Unix systems. They will be discussed in greater detail in Chapter 4.

Synchronous Message Passing

Synchronous message passing assumes blocking send and blocking receive. This is necessary when there is no buffering of messages in the communication channel. A send must wait for the corresponding receive to occur, and a receive must wait for the corresponding send. In other words, whichever comes first must wait for the other, and the waiting is symmetrical. This mechanism allows two processes with a matching pair of send and receive to join and exchange data at a synchronization point and to continue their separate execution thereafter. This type of synchronization is called a **rendezvous** between send and receive. Rendezvous is a useful concept in computer systems, as well as in real life. Outside the stadium before the start of a football game, it is quite common to see people with their hands up either holding tickets to be sold or sticking up fingers to indicate how many tickets they need. Rendezvous of sellers and buyers take place asynchronously and symmetrically.

A mutual exclusion solution using synchronous message passing is shown in Figure 3.17. The semaphore server process first rendezvous with either P_i or P_j. Once it has done that, giving permission to a process to enter its critical section, the server notes the id of the process and expects to rendezvous only with that process to achieve the effect of a V operation. This completes a cycle of exclusive execution of the critical section, and the server loops back to accept another rendezvous. Again, the message content is immaterial. More importantly, the use of send and receive is irrelevant, too. All we need is a way of matching two rendezvous calls by using some procedure names. This leads to a more general definition of rendezvous that is not just limited to send and receive. The following describes three important synchronous message passing synchronization approaches.

FIGURE 3.17   Mutual exclusion using synchronous message passing.

process P_i	semaphore server	process P_j
begin	loop	begin
send(sem,msg)	receive(pid,msg)	send(sem,msg)
critical section	send(pid,msg)	critical section
receive(sem,msg)	end	receive(sem,msg)
end		end

Communicating Sequential Processes: An Input/Output Approach

Communicating Sequential Processes (CSP) was one of the first languages to address the synchronization problem in distributed systems. It uses input/output rendezvous to achieve synchronous message passing synchronization. Input/output is a form of message communication. A sender process P can issue an output command, $Q!exp$, to a receiver process Q with a corresponding input command, $P?var$. The rendezvous of the input and output commands is connected through explicit naming of each other's process names. The effect is equivalent to a remote *assignment* statement that assigns the value of *exp* in one process to the variable *var* of another remote process. The message exchanged between the input and the output processes is synchronous and thus achieves implicit synchronization between two processes.

The direct use of process names for communication in CSP has some drawbacks. This can be illustrated by the implementation of the reader/writer problem. First of all, it is not reasonable to require reader processes to send messages to the writer processes, or vice versa, since they are independently implemented and are not aware of each other's existence. Secondly, there is no need for them to communicate with each other. Therefore, we need a server process that receives requests from readers and writers and regulates the rules for concurrent reads and exclusive writes. In CSP, the readers and writers have only one form of output command for communicating with the server S (i.e., $S!req$, where S is the name of the server and *req* is the request message). The server performs the synchronous message exchange by using $R?msg$ or $W?msg$, where *msg* contains the received message, and R and W are readers and writers, respectively. To allow a nondeterministic rendezvous with either readers or writers, CSP introduces the **alternative** commands, which can consist of a number of **guarded** commands. A guarded command has a conditional part followed by a list of statements to be executed if the guarded command is chosen. Upon entering an alternative command, all conditions of the guarded commands are evaluated. Only one of the guarded commands that has a *true* condition is selected for execution. The selection of a guarded command within an alternative command is nondeterministic. The nondeterministic property of a sequential program is a very desirable feature for programming distributed systems. A CSP input statement is considered a condition that is evaluated to *true* if its corresponding output statement has been invoked.

For the reader/writer problem, the server will need an alternative command that allows it to rendezvous with either readers or writers. The first problem is that the server must know the names of all reader and writer processes at coding time for the controller process, which is an unrealistic assumption considering the nature of the problem. Secondly, due to the use of process names for communication, there is only one entry to invoke the server. The actual reading and writing operations cannot be performed by the user processes and must be encapsulated into the server codes. The encapsulation of the resource object in the resource server is a good idea because it provides more transparency. Concurrent reads can be implemented by using the CSP parallel statements, which create concurrent thread processes. However, synchronization among processes must still be established within the multiple thread server. This means that we are simply shifting the responsibility of synchronization to the thread processes in the server. The synchronous input/output statements only serve the purpose of request and reply communication. Without additional synchronization primitives for the threads, no elegant solution exists for the reader/writer problem in CSP. The problems in CSP can be alleviated if we extend the synchronous input/output to procedures. The concept basically leads to the development of the remote procedure call and Ada rendezvous.

Remote Procedure Call: A Procedure Call and Asymmetrical Communication Approach

The synchronous input/output in CSP provides blocking and exchange of data between the sender and receiver processes. Procedure calls have similar characteristics in that a caller is blocked until the called procedure completes and data can be passed between the caller and the called procedure. Remote communication thus can take the form of a conventional procedure call and is actually implemented by message passing. Using procedures instead of process names for communication has the advantage of distinguishing different communication points in a process. This type of remote procedure call also achieves transparency in communication since message passing communication is hidden from the users.

A remote procedure call is a client/server communication. Resource servers are represented by a set of procedures that can be invoked by remote clients using conventional procedure calls. Servers behave like a monitor. Both RPC and rendezvous use synchronous message passing. However, they differ in the way that the server interacts with its clients. Servers in RPC are passive. They export their services and sit back, waiting for clients to invoke server procedures. Servers in rendezvous, on the other hand, actively attempt to rendezvous with clients' requests. For this reason, we describe RPC and rendezvous as asymmetrical and symmetrical communications, respectively, between clients and servers. It seems that combining the two concepts, using RPC as the communication interface and rendezvous for synchronization, is a plausible approach to implement remote rendezvous in distributed systems. RPC implementation and examples will be discussed in Chapter 4.

Ada Rendezvous: A Procedure Call and Symmetrical Communication Approach

Although it is not designed for remote rendezvous in distributed network environments, Ada rendezvous is a good example of the use of the procedure call concept for rendezvous and provides a nondeterministic language construct for concurrent processes. Procedures in RPCs are static and need to be activated by the callers. To use procedures for rendezvous, they must also be able to express dynamically their readiness to accept callers. The Ada language introduces the **accept** statements for this purpose. An accept statement consists of an entry part followed by a list of statements that define the procedure. The entry part contains the entry name and formal parameters. An invocation of an entry can rendezvous with a corresponding accept statement that has the same procedure entry name. The blocking is symmetrical in that the first process to arrive (either caller) waits until its counterpart arrives. This rendezvous provides a synchronization point between two processes. The execution of the accept statement includes the exchange of parameters and is atomic. Codes that do not require mutual exclusion are placed outside the accept statements and can be executed concurrently.

FIGURE 3.18   Ada rendezvous solution to the weak reader preference problem.

```
task rw is
      entry startread;
      entry endread;
      entry startwrite;
      entry endwrite;
end

task body rw is
      rc: integer := 0;
      busy: boolean := false;
begin
loop
      select
            when busy = false →
            accept startread do rc := rc + 1 end;
      or
            →
            accept endread do rc := rc - 1 end;
      or
            when rc = 0 and busy = false →
            accept startwrite do busy = true end;
      or
            →
            accept endwrite do busy = false end;
end loop
end;
```

If processes are structured as client and server, the accept statements normally appear in the server process. The clients invoke services by calling the entry names in the server's accept statement directly. Since a server needs to rendezvous with multiple clients nondeterministically, a **select** statement, similar to the *alternative* command in CSP, is added to the Ada language. The *select alternatives* take the form of a *guarded* command by using **when** to indicate the condition for an accept statement. When a select statement is entered, all conditions in guards are evaluated and marked if they are evaluated to true. One of those marked statements that has a pending accept call is nondeterministically chosen to execute. Figure 3.18 demonstrates the use of accept and select statements in Ada for the weak reader preference problem. Note the similarity to the monitor solution (Figure 3.13). The *rw* task (server) rendezvous with readers and writers in a nonpredetermined order. Reader and writer processes interact with the server task by calling the task with appropriate entry points, just like an ordinary procedure call.

The combined use of the accept and select statements provides mutual exclusion and synchronization for the readers and writers. Actual reading and writing can also be embedded in the synchronization server. Concurrent reading can follow the accept-startread statement by forking another process (or thread) for actual reading operations. For distributed implementation, entry names can be exported, and rendezvous of procedures are accomplished by remote procedure calls.

3.6 OBJECT MODEL RESOURCE SERVERS

The need for synchronization arises from sharing of resources. Enforcing the rules that regulate the use of a resource should be the responsibility of the resource manager (server). Using the object-oriented concept for the resources provides resource transparency to the clients. A resource is a virtual object represented as a set of well-formed operations that can be called by the clients. Synchronization and concurrency control within the object server are transparent to the clients. Furthermore, the communication between clients and the object server can be made transparent by using the remote procedure calls. Concurrency in the server can be best implemented by using multiple threads to allow concurrent service of multiple client requests. Since threads share a common address space, shared-variable synchronization methods can be used for coordination among threads.

RPCs and rendezvous discussed so far assume synchronous message passing. For some applications, the clients may prefer to send requests asynchronously to the servers. A request without the need for a reply naturally should be asynchronous. Even if a reply is

FIGURE 3.19 Structure of an object model resource server.

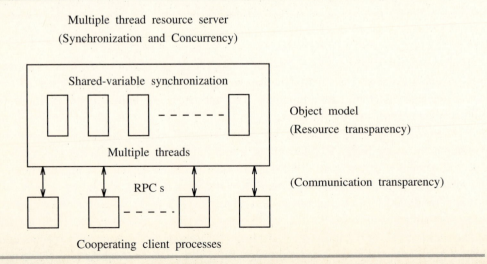

needed for a request, the client process can be made more efficient by performing other work if the request is not blocked. There are two ways to achieve asynchronous message communication with the server. One is to define a new asynchronous RPC; the other is to create a thread for each RPC in the client process. Either method requires a language mechanism by which a process can detect the completion (or abnormal exception) and obtain the results of pending RPCs.

Figure 3.19 summarizes the structure of a general resource server. It includes almost all the important keywords discussed in this chapter.

3.7 CONCURRENT PROGRAMMING LANGUAGES

Concurrent languages are programming systems that support the specification of concurrency, synchronization, and communication among interacting concurrent processes. The implementation of a concurrent language is more of an operating system issue in distributed systems than a compiler issue, as in the design of sequential languages. This is because concurrency, synchronization, and communication are run-time problems. A concurrent language can be implemented as an extension of an existing sequential language. This section summarizes some of these approaches using the language mechanisms described in the previous section. The discussion follows the taxonomy of synchronization mechanisms given in Figure 3.20.

A synchronization mechanism is classified as either shared-variable or message passing. A monitor is probably the most common choice as an add-on shared-variable synchronization concept for concurrent languages. The abstraction exhibited in the monitor concept makes it a suitable model for a data object and resource server. Classical languages that use monitors include Concurrent Pascal, Modula, and Turing Plus. Concurrent Pascal was the first concurrent language to support monitors. Modula was developed with a strong emphasis on modular programming. In addition to *interface modules* that support monitors, Modula uses *device modules* to implement abstract I/O, allowing more flexibility in interfacing with the kernel. Turing is a sequential language designed more for instructional purposes with a strong mathematical formalization. Turing Plus is an extension of Turing that supports monitors for concurrent programming. There are many monitor-based concurrent languages and their definitions of a monitor vary. The major differences are the semantics of the *signal* operation and nested monitor calls, and the scope rules of the variables.

Other notable concurrent languages that use shared-variable synchronization constructs include Path Pascal, various forms of CCR (Conditional Critical Region) in DP (Distributed Processes), and Argus. Path expressions are an elegant way of specifying the semantics of concurrent computations. However, simple path expressions are not sufficient in modeling process coordination that requires state information of the shared resources. Extended path expressions have been proposed for enhancing their modeling power, but this is at the expense of losing the original beauty of simplicity. CCRs are straightforward to implement. The evaluation of conditions for unblocking processes may

FIGURE 3.20   A taxonomy of synchronization and communication mechanisms.

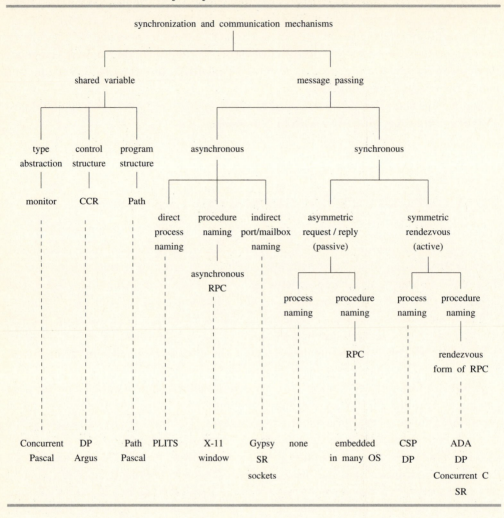

be expensive. This problem can be solved by explicit *wait* and *signal* on conditions that are similar to the *condition variables* in the monitor approach.

Both asynchronous and synchronous message passing synchronization methods are used in many concurrent languages. The sending and receiving of a message can be established by direct naming of the source and destination of a message. However, this method of naming is not practical, as explained in the previous sections. It is more flexible for processes to communicate indirectly through a named channel. *Ports* and *mailboxes* are named communication channels. Ports allow many-to-one communication, and mailboxes support many-to-many communication. The use of unbounded ports or mailboxes implies asynchronous message sending. Gypsy was one of the first high-level languages to use mailboxes for asynchronous message passing. PLITS is another example that uses asynchronous message passing, but it has direct naming of process modules.

The problems with direct naming in PLITS are alleviated by tagging messages with keys and by allowing the receive operation to leave out the source designation. A receiver process can receive messages from any source or any messages with certain tagged keys. It is therefore possible for the receiver to become a server serving multiple clients without knowing the clients' names. In addition, multiple communication channels between client and server can be established by using different keys for the messages. This approach is also used in Concurrent-C for asynchronous message passing synchronization. Channels can also be named by using high level language constructs such as procedure calls. This is called asynchronous RPC.

Synchronous message passing may be asymmetric or symmetric depending on the communication scenarios. Asymmetric synchronous message passing assumes that the two communication principals have a master/slave (primary/secondary) relationship. The primary makes a request, and the secondary responds with a reply message. When implemented in a client/server model, the server plays a passive role in accepting service invocations. Symmetrical synchronous message passing is the rendezvous concept where communicating processes are actively trying to synchronize with one another. Similarly, both synchronous request/reply and rendezvous require the establishment of a communication channel by process naming or procedure calls. Ports and mailboxes are not applicable here since they are used for asynchronous send. Conventional RPC uses asymmetric synchronous message passing and procedure calls and has been incorporated into several concurrent languages, such as DP, Argus, and Mesa. These languages also rely on additional shared-variable CCR or monitor synchronization. Since RPC is such an important communication method for distributed systems, it has been included as a software package in most modern operating systems.

Symmetric synchronous message passing uses rendezvous. The CSP discussed in the previous section uses the method of process naming for rendezvous. DP extends it to include procedure names in a process in which rendezvous can occur at different points. In effect, it is a rendezvous form of RPC, such as Ada. The Ada implementation of the RPC rendezvous is fairly complete. Its *select* statements support nondeterministic rendezvous calls (selective communication). Supplemented with the options for time-out and procedure entries to interrupt vectors in the *accept* statements, Ada becomes suitable for system and real-time programming. Figure 3.20 gives a taxonomy of the above description of concurrent language synchronization and communication. Many concurrent languages use a combination of available mechanisms. For example, the SR (Synchronizing Resources) language includes almost all the necessary constructs for concurrent programming. SR uses resource abstraction, asynchronous and rendezvous forms of RPC, selective communication, and hardware and interrupt modularization.

It is worthwhile to note some other concurrent language approaches that are beyond simple extension of sequential languages. The above discussion shows that concurrent process management, synchronization, and communication are really issues that are orthogonal to the computational aspects of a sequential language. What we truly need is a *coordination* language with a simple and efficient way to build concurrent programs by connecting some basic communicating entities together and providing them with the means to communicate and thus synchronize with each other. These communicating entities can represent processes, resources, a combination of both, or abstract objects. With the assumption of message passing for communication and synchronization, the only key issues would be how entities are modeled, how concurrent programs are composed, and how communication channels between entities are logically named and managed. A new concurrent language (or more precisely, a concurrent programming system) can be built based on the computation and communication models. In the following, we briefly introduce and compare three systems that were designed along these lines: Occam, SR, Linda.

Occam evolved from many ideas in CSP. It has been widely used for concurrent programming on Transputers and Digital Signal Processing (DSP) systems. Transputers and DSPs are single-chip computers with local memories and fast communication links. They can be configured to map concurrent processes for efficient parallel processing with frequent data communication between processors using the high-speed links. Since these single-chip processors have limited local memory, Occam assumes a small process granularity. Each imperative statement (assignment, input, and output) can be considered as a primitive process. Statements can be grouped together by using *constructors* to form a compound statement for one of the three types of execution: sequential execution of statements (by SEQ constructor); parallel execution of statements (by PAR constructor); and asynchronous and nondeterministic execution of statements (by ALT constructor), similar to the *alternative* statement in CSP. Two additional constructors, IF and WHILE, are needed to regulate sequential flow of constructor execution. A constructor is associated with some local variables and may be composed by other constructors. Although statements are executable primitive processes, constructors are the normal schedulable process units. There is no sharing of global variables between different constructors. The synchronization is accomplished by using the rendezvous concept of input/ouput statements in CSP, except that the naming of communication channels uses explicitly declared global channel names. The use of constructors in composing concurrent programs and global channels for communication between constructors make it very easy for the compiler to generate code for mapping processes to processors.

In SR, a concurrent program is a collection of resources, unlike Occam's process view. A resource is abstracted as a module that contains a declaration and a body. The declaration specifies import entries for other resources and export entries for the resource's own operations. The body consists of an initialization part, one or more processes, and a finalization code. Processes in a resource may be concurrent and interact by means of shared variables in the same resource. Between different resources, they interact by using *operations*, which are similar to Ada procedure entries. Operation entries represent either procedures or processes. An instance of a resource is invoked by the execution of a CREATE *resource-name* statement, which returns a *capability* for later communication with the resource operations. A resource operation is invoked by a synchronous CALL or asynchronous SEND to the resource using the resource capability. Capabilities are more flexible than the global channels in Occam. They are dynamically generated and may be passed as a variable. Moreover, capabilities may represent multiple instances of a resource and capture both notions of channel naming and access control. Rendezvous is specified by an input statement (*in*) with operation entry, which has an option (*and*) to support selective communication and (*by*) for scheduling pending invocations. SR uses data abstraction and supports almost all forms of message passing and shared variable synchronization.

Linda is quite different from Occam and SR. It is not a programming language but a unique *shared data* model that can be integrated with any programming language to support process coordination in parallel programming. Processes and shared data in the Linda model are uniformly represented as an unordered set of *tuples*, each with a format of $t = (``tag'', values)$, where *tag* is the symbolic name of a data tuple and *values* is a list of typed values associated with the tuple. Processes are active tuples, and data tuples are passive. The tuples form a *Tuple Space* (TS), which is a shared *content addressable* logical memory that can be distributed physically to represent distributed data structures in the problem space. Linda provides three basic primitives for accessing tuples. The *in*(*s*) and *out*(*s*) are blocking receive from and nonblocking send to the TS, where *s* is a template or *anti-tuple* with the format of $s = (``tag'', actuals, formals)$. An *in*(*s*) operation matches template *s* against tuples *t* with the tag and actuals. If a match is found, the formals in *s* are assigned with the corresponding values in *t*, and the calling process continues. Then the tuple is deleted from TS. In case of multiple matching, only one tuple is selected arbitrarily for the operation. The *in* operations are blocking, meaning that a calling process is suspended until a match is found. The *out* operations simply evaluate the expressions in *s* and put it in the TS. An update of a tuple is done by a matching *in* followed by an *out*. The third primitive *rd* is used to examine tuples. It is similar to the *in*, except that the matched tuple remains in the TS. The nonblocking versions of *in* and *rd* are also supported in Linda.

Processes in Linda are created by an additional primitive *eval*(*s*). An *eval* operation forks a new process that evaluates all expressions in *s*. Expressions typically contain procedures. *Eval* is similar to an *out*, except that *s* is put into the TS before its evaluation. When the process is completed (i.e., all expressions have been evaluated), *s* with the resulting values becomes a passive data tuple. Linda is the most abstract way of modeling process coordination. With only a few primitive operations, Linda can be embedded into a base language such as C. C-Linda is a realization of the Linda model in C.

FIGURE 3.21 Comparison of Occam, SR, and Linda.

	System	Object model	Channel naming
OCCAM	concurrent programming language	processes	static global channels
SR	concurrent programming language	resources	dynamic capabilities
LINDA	concurrent programming paradigm	distributed data structures	associative tags

Figure 3.21 shows the fundamental differences among Occam, SR, and Linda. They are compared with respect to the underlying system concept, the presumed data model, and how communication channels are named.

3.8 DISTRIBUTED AND NETWORK PROGRAMMING

Occam, SR, and Linda, described in the last section, are concurrent language or programming paradigms for tightly coupled systems. They are not adequate for loosely coupled distributed systems or computer networks where transparency and interoperability are the major concern. In a loosely coupled system, the implementation of concurrent programming systems requires support for handling reliable communication, partitioning objects, replicating data, and heterogeneous systems. In the following we introduce two programming languages, Orca and Java, that address these unique problems for distributed systems and network programming.

3.8.1 Orca

Orca is a concurrent programming language based on a logical shared-object model for loosely coupled distributed systems. It supports parallel execution of processes on different machines with concurrent access to shared data. Shared data objects are instances of user-defined abstract data types. They may be physically distributed or replicated to facilitate efficient local access, but they are made transparent to the application programs by the Orca implementation. Orca programs are procedure oriented with a syntax similar to Modula-2. Parallelism in Orca is created by explicit forking of processes, as in conventional systems.

Orca processes, once created, communicate through shared objects by using user-defined operations on these objects. The advantages of using shared objects for interprocess communication as opposed to message passing are quite obvious. Interprocessor communication is completely transparent and global information can be shared directly. Writing concurrent programs is closer to the conventional programming paradigm. Furthermore, if a complex data structure representing a data object is physically distributed, using explicit message passing to access portions of the data structure will be awkward, if not tedious.

The key concepts employed in the Orca system are the logical shared object and the abstract data type. We have seen the concept of a logical shared object (or data structure) in Linda and the concept of an abstract data type in SR. In Linda shared objects (which include data and processes) are tuples in the tuple-space. Access methods are associative (content addressable) but low level (primitive *in, out, rd*). Although conceptually simple and elegant, writing programs with complex data structures in Linda is not intuitive. Using an abstract data type in Orca allows for strong type checking and flexible operations on objects. SR is a strongly typed language and has data type abstraction like Orca. However, without the logical shared-object concept, SR must rely on a large set of synchronization and communication primitives (rendezvous, CALL, SEND, capability, and other shared variable synchronization). Although the language is rich for concurrent programming, process synchronization and communication are not as transparent. Orca seems to be a good compromise between Linda and SR, and it captures the best of the two extremes.

Concurrent processes in Orca are activated by spawning a new process on a specific machine by the **fork** statement:

fork process-name(parameters) [**on** (processor-number)];

The parameters passed from the parent process to a child process may be values, regular objects, or shared objects. Values and regular objects are local data to a process. Shared objects are global. They are replicated at each processor site and require an atomic update protocol to maintain the coherency of the replicas of the shared object.

Two types of synchronization on objects are supported by Orca: mutual exclusion and condition coordination. Orca assumes that all operations on objects are indivisible. Each object is associated with a lock for mutual exclusion. Locking is performed only at the object level and is limited to a single object. *Shared* locking is supported to allow for multiple read operations of an object. For condition coordination, Orca uses the guarded command, which is similar to that used in CSP:

operation op(parameters)
guard condition **do** statements;
guard condition **do** statements;

The statements in an operation are executed only if the condition in the guard is evaluated to true. Otherwise, the calling process is blocked. If more than one condition is true, only one guarded command is nonuniformly chosen to provide nondeterministic execution. Object operations in an Orca application program are compiled into **invoke** primitives:

invoke(object, operation, parameters)

The invoke primitives are trapped to the Orca Run Time System (RTS). The RTS checks to see whether the operation is read-only. If it is, RTS sets the shared-lock of the local copy, performs the read operation, and unlocks the object. Otherwise, RTS initiates a broadcast to all shared object sites, including itself, to update the object and blocks the process. On receiving a broadcast message to write the object, RTS sets the write-lock of the object, performs the write operation, and unlocks the object. If the broadcast message originated locally, it unblocks the process.

RTS assumes that the communication is reliable. It supports a reliable broadcast layer underneath the run-time system. The reliable broadcast layer can implement broadcast protocols with different semantic requirements. A desirable broadcast protocol guarantees that all object sites receive all broadcast messages and that all messages are delivered in the same order (i.e., the broadcast is *atomic*). Implementation of atomic broadcast protocols is discussed in next chapter. Here we outline a simple approach used by Orca to achieve atomic broadcast. When a broadcast is requested by the RTS, the kernel of RTS sends a point-to-point message to a special kernel called the *sequencer*. The sequencer assigns a sequence number to the request and broadcasts the message containing the sequence number to all replicated object sites. The sequence number is used by each kernel to determine the order of message delivery, to check for duplicated messages, and to request a message from the sequencer if some messages are missing.

Objects are fundamental units of data in Orca. Objects represented by data structures such as lists, trees, and graphs are often implemented by using pointers in conventional programming languages. Pointers are machine addresses. Passing machine addresses is meaningless and may causes protection violation in message passing distributed systems. A mechanism that allows implementation and passing of complex data structures must be available to make the shared-object model useful. Orca solves the problem by replacing pointers with *names*. For each object managed by the RTS, a *logical* array of structured data is maintained for the object. For example, a simple binary tree, t with three nodes (A, B, C) and respective left and right links, is represented as:

$$t[1] = 6, A, 8$$
$$t[6] = 0, B, 0$$
$$t[8] = 0, C, 0$$

Each node in the data structure is created dynamically by calling the RTS primitive **addnode**(t), which returns a name n for the node. n is used as an index to the array structure for naming a node (or a substructure) and as a link (pointer) to other nodes. Nodes can be deleted with a **deletenode**(t, n) primitive. References to a deleted node will cause a run-time error. Arrays for objects are only logical; their storage allocation and deallocation are dynamically managed by the RTS. Using node names to implement data structures achieves the effect of pointers without machine addresses. Passing complex data structures becomes possible but creates some overhead in the run-time system.

3.8.2 Java

The primary objective of Orca is to support concurrent programming in distributed systems. Its major implementation issues are distributing computation and making communication transparent to the coordinating processes. Java was introduced with a different perspective. It is a programming language and programming environment that achieves interoperability for network software development. We can envision a network application that consists of a set of software modules physically distributed over a heterogeneous wide area network. Each software module may be implemented and maintained by different individuals in separated network sites. Execution of the network application may need integration of several software modules transported to a single site. The interoperability of such an open system network application requires three fundamental system supports:

- Well-defined standard interfaces for integrating software modules
- Capability of running software modules on any machine
- Infrastructure for coordinating and transporting software modules

To facilitate software integration, Java adopts the object-oriented model, a programming paradigm that has been widely used for large-scale software development. The Java language is similar to the object-oriented C++. With the exception of a few basic types such as numbers and Booleans, all software entities are modeled as objects in Java. An object is an encapsulation of data and related procedures (or methods) on the object. It is created by the instantiation of a *class*. A class is a template that defines the variables and the methods which are common to all objects of a similar type. Class definitions usually consist of other class objects. They are the basic building blocks for Java programs. Commonly used class files are categorized and stored in class libraries called *packages*. Class packages can be loaded locally or remotely for the creation of objects. Network software development becomes more manageable since class libraries can be shared.

The approach taken by Java so that it can run any software module anywhere is the concept of the virtual machine. The Java system comes with a compiler and an interpreter. Java programs are first compiled into class files that contain intermediate bytecodes called *applets*. Applets are machine independent and can be interpreted by any host equipped with a Java interpreter. Interpretation of intermediate bytecodes is less efficient than execution of compiled machine codes. However, it has the great advantage that bytecodes can be transported as a message to any platform and executed directly without recompilation. A network application can bring in any bytecode file, on the fly, for execution. Since copies of bytecode files do not need to be kept locally, the problem of maintaining version update consistency for cooperative software development is eliminated.

Java is carefully constrained to ensure machine independence. Some common language features that may cause interoperability or security problems are excluded from the language. For example, Java does not support pointers, structure types, implicit type conversion, or multiple inheritance. The concept of header files in C is also excluded from Java. Furthermore, all methods and variables in a Java class file are referenced by name and resolved before execution. The delay of name resolution requires the support of a name service. It provides access and location transparency and added security.

The infrastructure for transporting Java applets is best illustrated by the integration of Java with the WWW browsing system. In many aspects, the Java philosophy is very much like a Web browser that uses transfer protocols such as the hypertext transfer protocol HTTP to transport HTML modules among heterogeneous network sites. HTML is a machine-independent markup language for specifying hypertext data. Similar to the class files in Java, HTML files are objects that may contain other HTML files and can be located or linked by using networkwide universal resource locator URLs. Java applets can be incorporated in an HTML file and interpreted by the Java interpreter, which is built into the browser. In this way the browser can display static hypertext data and can also execute active Java applets. The applications are numerous. With a multiple thread browser and multiple thread Java, the browser can concurrently display text and animated graphics and become interactive between the client and server of the application. Effectively, the Web page represented by an HTML file becomes the front-end of Java applets. The concept of online interpretive execution in Java is not new. For example, Postscript and Gif graphic data are also interpreted in the browser systems.

However, Java is a general-purpose language that has been carefully thought out for network programming.

One final note about Java is the consideration that was given to security in its design. Security is obviously a critical issue for open system network programming. In addition to strict language definition to guard against misuse of the language, Java is a strongly typed language, as is Orca. All objects must be explicitly typed. The compiler enforces static type checking. Since each machine only sees the foreign applets in the form of intermediate bytecodes, it is necessary to verify that bytecodes have not been forged or masqueraded. Type and other control information are embedded in every applet. Before the execution of an applet, its bytecodes are subjected to rigorous testing by a Java Verifier to check for violations of parameter passing, illegal type conversion, potential stack overflow and underflow, access protection, and masqueraded bytecodes generated by a suspicious compiler. Run-time checking is minimized to allow for efficient execution.

Another security problem unique to network programming is the spoofing of objects. The execution of an applet can call on other objects. The class file loaded for an object may be a genuine applet with the same name and appearance but may not be from a desired realm. For example, the class objects for the file system and I/O should come from the local realm. Each class file is associated with a protection realm. Protection realms are classified into at least three protection levels: local computer, local network domain, and global network, with the local computer having the highest protection level. When loading a class file, higher-protection-level classes take precedence over lower-protection-level classes. Furthermore, classes in one realm can only access methods of classes in the same realm. Methods of classes in other protection realms can be accessed only if they are explicitly declared as public. The class loading rules are enforced by the Java Class Loader, which can be defined by the Java programmers.

3.9 SUMMARY

Processes are the most fundamental entities in an operating system. Concurrent processes are asynchronous and interacting program executions, each with its own logical address space. To extend concurrency to within a process, many modern operating systems support the concept of *threads*. Threads are light-weight processes that share a common logical address space. This chapter begins with a discussion of the significance and the implementation of threads. *User-space* thread implementation is simple to add onto an existing system, but efficiency necessitates *kernel-space* thread implementation.

We show the significance of the *client/server* model and the *object* model for structuring concurrent processes in distributed systems. The interaction among concurrent processes and threads requires some means of interprocess communication and synchronization. We use the *synchronous* and the *asynchronous* graph models to represent two major classes of process interaction. These two graph models are simple and useful for modeling system performance. However, they are inadequate for analyzing time-dependent process interaction. Many later discussions of distributed algorithms and protocols require the use of the *time-space* model.

The time-space model gives greater details about event time ordering in the system. Time ordering implies the need for a time service. We discuss both *physical time* and *logical time* services. Logical times including *vector* and *matrix* clocks are used extensively throughout this book. Technological advances have made synchronization of physical clocks feasible for some applications. We will also see some applications of physical times in the later chapters.

Concurrent languages and/or concurrent programming systems are needed for specifying and implementing concurrent processes. It is tempting to extend an existing sequential language by incorporating new mechanisms for interprocess communication and synchronization. We show the evolution of such language mechanisms for concurrent programming languages. They are summarized in a simple taxonomy. The synchronization and communication mechanisms are divided into two major categories: *shared-variable* and *message passing.* For distributed systems, we are more interested in message passing mechanisms such as *rendezvous* and *RPC.* We point out two important observations. First, the issues of synchronization and communication are tightly coupled. That is, interprocess communication requires some underlying assumptions of synchronization, and higher-level synchronization can be accomplished by using interprocess communication mechanisms. Second, shared-variable communication and message passing communication are logically equivalent in that communication channels are also shared objects in message passing.

We also observed that concurrent programming and sequential programming are fundamentally different. Sequential languages represent the *computational* aspect of processes, while concurrent languages address the *coordination* among processes. Therefore, the design of concurrent languages should be tackled separately from sequential languages. We show three examples of such process coordination programming languages (or paradigms): Occam, SR, and Linda.

We conclude the chapter by showing two other important programming concepts: distributed and network programming systems. Distributed programming languages emphasize data sharing and replication. Network programming languages are more concerned with interoperability. The examples used are Orca and Java.

ANNOTATED BIBLIOGRAPHY

Threads are a revolutionary concept that extends concurrent programming, traditionally available only for system programming, to user applications. The examples we use are Sun's LWP and Solaris [SS92, EKB^{+}92, Pea92]. To analyze distributed process behavior in the later chapters, we introduce the time-space model, which captures process interactions with the notion of time and event ordering. Time services may be based on physical or logical clocks. The Distributed Time Service in DCE [OSF92, RKF92] is used to illustrate the synchronization of distributed physical clocks. The basic logical clock concept was developed by Lamport [Lam78]. It was extended to vector logical clocks by [Fid88, Mat89, SM94a]. The matrix clock [RS95] is a natural extension of the logical clock. An application of the matrix clock was first seen for efficient garbage collection in log management [WB84].

After discussing processes and their interaction, we show how sequential programming languages are supplemented with synchronization and communication primitives to support concurrent programming. We illustrate how shared memory synchronization approaches evolve into message passing interprocess communication, using a simple taxonomy. Concurrent programming for shared memory systems was an active research area in 1970s. The pioneer works are semaphore [Dij68], conditional critical region [Hoa72, BH73], monitor [BH73, Hoa74], serializer [HA79], and path expression [CH74, And79]. Examples of systems cited in this chapter are Concurrent Pascal [BH77], Modula [Wir77], and Turing Plus [HC88] for monitor; DP [BH78] and Argus [LS83, Lis88] for conditional critical region; and Path Pascal [CK79] for path expression.

We show that synchronization can be accomplished with the assumption of blocking send or blocking receive in a message passing system. Message passing synchronization for concurrent programming was an active research area in 1980s. We point out that a communication channel with nonblocking send and blocking receive is equivalent to a semaphore with V and P operations. Examples of this type of asynchronous message passing are used in PLITS [Fel79] with direct process naming, asynchronous RPC with procedure naming, and Gypsy [GCK79] and SR [And81] with indirect naming. We describe blocking send and blocking receive as a type of rendezvous. The synchronous message passing communication was introduced in CSP [Hoa78] and DP [BH78] with process naming, and incorporated into Ada, SR [And81], and Concurrent C with procedure naming.

It is noted that issues on the design of concurrent languages are more oriented toward coordination than the computational aspect of processes. Three such representative coordination languages are compared. The process model Occam was developed by the British computer firm INMOS [May83]. It is based on CSP. The object model SR was developed by [And81, And82]. SR supports all kinds of message passing communication and synchronization. The shared data structure model Linda developed by [Gel85] is significantly different from the other shared memory and message passing systems. It is more transparent and probably should be classified separately as a distributed shared-object model.

Orca and Java are programming systems that address some unique implementation problems in distributed systems and computer networks. Orca [BST89, BKT92] is also a distributed shared-object model. It addresses the atomicity and reliable multicast for parallel computation in a loosely coupled distributed system. Java was developed by Gosling at Sun [AG96]. It is a network programming language that supports interoperability for transporting and remote execution of software modules.

Interested readers are encouraged to read excellent survey papers [AS83, BST89] and books [And91] by Andrews on concurrent languages and [CM88] by Chandy and Mistra on concurrent programming.

EXERCISES

1. What is the significance of threads?

2. Compare the advantages and disadvantages of user- and kernel-space implementations of threads with respect to efficiency, portability, scheduling, and synchronization.

3. *Fork/Join* can be used to implement any precedence process graph. This is not necessarily true for *Cobegin/Coend*. Use the precedence graph in Figure 3.4 to show that the processes cannot be implemented by *Cobegin/Coend* without additional mechanism or loss of concurrency.

4. What are the significances and limitations of the client/server model?

5. What is the relationship between the client/server model and the object-based model?

6. What is the advantage of reporting physical time in intervals? How does the size of time intervals affect the time-averaging methods?

7. Show what other useful information can be derived from matrix logical clocks besides event ordering.

8. Two producer processes (P_1, P_2) and two consumer processes (C_1, C_2) share a common stack. The stack operations allowed for the processes are *PUSH* and *POP*, which require mutual exclusion to access the stack. Consumer P_i can only remove the top item from the stack if the item was produced by producer P_i. Write a semaphore solution to the problem.

9. Consider a binary tree with n leaves, one for each process. Each internal node (nonleaf) has an associated semaphore. A process desiring to enter its critical section performs P operations on successive semaphores from the leaf to the root of the tree, executes its critical section, and then performs V operations in the reverse order back down the tree. Show that the system can achieve mutual exclusion, and that it is deadlock and starvation free. What is the maximum number of processes that can be queued on each semaphore? How is a global queue distributedly implemented?

10. Write a monitor solution to implement the writer preference reader/writer problem. You may need an additional monitor procedure to keep track of the waiting writers.

11. Modify the conditional critical region solution in Figure 3.14 to solve the writer preference reader/writer problem. Compare it with the above monitor solution.

12. It is useful to add *predicates* to path expressions. Operations in a path expression can be conditioned on a predicate to achieve condition coordination. Predicates are Boolean expressions that contain variables. What kinds of variables would be meaningful and can be supported by the operating system with respect to synchronization?

13. What is the relationship between synchronization and message passing interprocess communication?

14. Why are communication links logically equivalent to semaphores?

15. Implement the writer preference reader/write problem using Ada rendezvous.

16. Implement semaphores *P* and *V* using Ada rendezvous.

17. The semaphore concept can be generalized to something called PV/chunk. In this synchronization method a semaphore is decremented or incremented by a positive integer constant *C*. That is, we have $P(S, C)$ and $V(S, C)$ operations on semaphore *S*. A process calling $P(S, C)$ is blocked if the current semaphore value is less than *C*. A $V(S, C)$ operation may wake up several processes if the newly incremented semaphore value can satisfy those processes. Show one synchronization problem that can be solved by using PV/chunk but not by using simple PV. Is it possible to implement PV/chunk by using Ada rendezvous?

18. Why there is no indirect naming category for the synchronous message passing in the taxonomy shown in Figure 3.20?

19. Give some example applications of the *capability* concept in Synchronous Resource (SR) other than for communication.

20. Use the *in, out, rd* Linda primitives to implement mutual exclusion and barrier synchronization.

21. Why is Orca distinguished from the other concurrent languages as a parallel language for distributed systems?

22. One of the unique features of the Java language is that it can be analyzed easily. Why is this property important for Java as a network programming language?

23. (Programming project) Unix supports semaphores and shared memory for interprocess communication. The code in Figure 3.12 for the weak reader preference problem has one shared variable and two semaphores. Implement and test the correctness of the algorithm. Your program should contain a coordinator process that creates the semaphores and shared variables and several instances of the reader and writer processes. The relevant Unix IPC utilities are: *semget, semctl, semop, shmget, shmctl, shmat, shmdt*. Use a Makefile to generate the executable codes. If you are running the Solaris system, you can use *sema_init, sema_wait*, and *sema_post* from the Solaris thread library to implement the project.

24. (Programming project) Unix supports Light Weight Processes (threads). Implement the same weak reader preference problem using threads and the monitor solution in Figure 3.13. Your program should be a single process that contains a definition of the monitor with four monitor procedures and several reader and writer threads. Readers and writers have no knowledge of the threading environment. They simply call the monitor procedures with various delays simulated by using *lwp-sleep*. Threads are nonpreemptive if your LWP is a user space implementation. To simulate the asynchronous behavior and concurrent execution of the reader and writer processes, you can add a *scheduler* thread that performs *preemptive* round-robin scheduling of the other threads. This can be done by assigning the *scheduler* thread a higher priority and requiring the readers and writers to voluntarily block their execution periodically. The actual reading and writing can also be simulated by delay (sleeping) in the critical section. Alternatively, you can use the preemptable LWPs in Solaris.

CHAPTER 4

Interprocess Communication and Coordination

Cooperating processes in a computer system must interact with each other using some forms of interprocess communication models to coordinate their execution. **Interprocess communication (IPC)** and **distributed process coordination** are the major topics of discussion in this chapter. In Chapter 3 we emphasized the importance of the client/server model for communication and the tight relationship between interprocess communication and synchronization. Interprocess communication plays a more significant role in distributed systems since the only method for exchanging data between processes is by message passing. Therefore, all higher-level interprocess communication models must be built on top of message passing communication. In addition, all distributed process coordinations must rely on message passing interprocess communication.

Interprocess communication is dependent on the ability to locate the communication entities. This is the role of the *name services* in distributed systems. This chapter presents three fundamental message passing communication models and a name service model. They are followed by an illustration of distributed process coordination that uses two classical problems of message passing interprocess communication, *distributed mutual exclusion* and *leader election.*

Interprocess communication can be viewed at different levels of abstraction. Table 4.1 outlines five levels of communication from network to transport system and to the application processes. With respect to distributed operating systems, we are primarily concerned with the top three levels for the transfer of messages among distributed processes. They are message passing, higher-level service-oriented communication models using request/reply communication, and transaction communication based on the request/reply model and message passing.

The table shows that message passing is the lowest level of communication between communicating processes. Request/reply communication is based on the client/server concept. When implemented as procedure calls in distributed programs, the communication model is referred to as a Remote Procedure Call (RPC). Naturally the request/reply, or RPC, requires the basic message passing facilities.

Transactions are sequences of request/reply communications that require communication atomicity. They form the basic units of communication for higher-level applications such as database systems. The concurrent execution of transactions needs to be synchronized to maintain the consistency of the system. Another communication method that is significantly different from the three message passing models is the concept of logically shared memory or data objects. In a system with only physically distributed memory, shared memory is simulated by message passing. The advantage of logically shared memory is the simplicity of programming, since communication is transparent. Transactions and distributed shared memory are covered in Chapters 6 and 7. This chapter starts with the basic message passing communication.

TABLE 4.1   Different levels of communication.

interprocess communication	transaction
	request/reply (RPC)
	message passing
network operating system	transport connection
communication network	packet switching

4.1 MESSAGE PASSING COMMUNICATION

Messages are collections of data objects, and their structures and interpretations are defined by the peer application processes. Data objects in a message are usually typed to facilitate conversion of data objects in a heterogeneous system. Messages have a header containing system-dependent control information, and a message body that can be of fixed or variable size. In a message passing system communicating processes pass composed messages to the system transport service, which provides connectivity for message transfer in the network. The interfaces to the transport service are explicit communication primitives, such as **send** and **receive**, or some variations of both. The semantics of these communication primitives need to be well defined. The major issues addressed in the following sections include whether the communication is direct or indirect, blocking or nonblocking, reliable or unreliable, and buffered or unbuffered.

4.1.1 Basic Communication Primitives

We use the following two generic message passing primitives as examples for sending and receiving messages. For application processes, it is sufficient to specify just the communication entity and the message to be transferred.

- **send**(destination, message)
- **receive**(source, message)

where source or destination = (**process name, link, mailbox,** or **port**).

An immediate question arising from the primitives is how the communication entities, *source* and *destination*, are to be addressed. We will discuss four commonly used options: process name, link, mailbox, and port. First, it is tempting to assume that communication entities can be addressed by using process names (i.e., global process identifiers). In a real implementation, a global process identifier can be made unique by concatenating the network host address with the locally generated process id. This scheme implies that only one *direct* logical communication path exists between any pair of sending and receiving processes, as shown in Figure 4.1(a). It is similar to the input/output communication used in CSP; we saw the drawback of this approach in Section 3.5.3. The addressing scheme is also referred to as symmetric addressing, since the corresponding sending and receiving processes must explicitly name each other in the communication primitives. For the receiving process, it is sometimes convenient to receive messages from unknown sources. In this case, the source address of the *receive* primitive is an input variable that is given the value of the process identifier of the process that sends the message (if one is received). The addressing between sender and the receiver becomes asymmetric because only the sender needs to indicate the recipient. Figure 4.1(b) shows the more general case of the receive primitive.

In the above schemes, we said that a *communication path* exists between a pair of processes. Actually, the communication path is completely transparent, and there is no notion of a *connection* in the message transfer. The concept is simple, but only one bidirectional communication path is possible between each pair of communicating

FIGURE 4.1   Direct send/receive communication primitives.

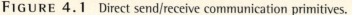

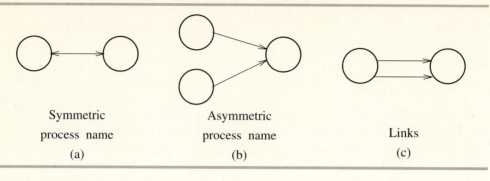

Symmetric	Asymmetric	
process name	process name	Links
(a)	(b)	(c)

processes. To allow for multiple data paths between processes and direct communication, we must be able to identify each path in the communication primitives. This requirement introduces the concept of *connections* or *links*. These are similar to the *virtual circuit* concept in communication networks. Messages can be sent along different virtual circuits. Thus, multiple communication points in a process can be identified by using different links, each pointing to an actual communication path. Like virtual circuits, links are created and released on request. They are managed locally by the system kernel and are unidirectional communication channels. Messages sent through a link are mapped to a network communication path and delivered to the remote host. The remote host maps the message to the input link in the receiving process. Figure 4.1(c) shows the possibility of maintaining two links between processes using two different link numbers. Readers should notice that links are analogous to the procedure entry names in a rendezvous (Section 3.5.3) in the sense that they both provide multiple communication points in a process. However data transfer by parameter passing in a rendezvous is bidirectional.

Using process names and link numbers for addressing communication points provides direct communication between peer processes. However, sometimes indirect communication is preferred. The sending processes are not particularly concerned with the identity of the receiving process as long as the message is received by a process. Similarly, receiving processes are interested only in the message itself, not in the identity of the sender. For example, multiple clients might request services from one of multiple servers (the identity of the client can be contained in the message itself). This communication scenario is cumbersome to implement using direct communication. The situation is common in our daily life, and we solve it by using shared *mailboxes*. Message passing using common mailboxes is an indirect communication scheme that offers the possibility of both multipoint and multipath communication. This scenario is illustrated in Figure 4.2.

Conceptually, mailboxes are global data structures shared by some *producer* (sender) and *consumer* (receiver) processes. The use of mailboxes requires proper synchronization across the network, which can be a difficult task. Since mailboxes are for communication, we might as well relate them to the underlying transport structure and implement them by using buffers and communication links. We can think of a *port* as a special example of a mailbox. A port is an abstraction of a finite-size first-in-first-out (FIFO) queue maintained by the kernel. Messages can be appended to or removed from the queue by

FIGURE 4.2   Indirect send/receive communication primitives.

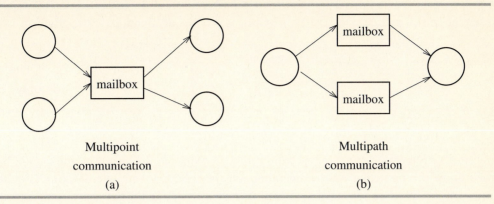

Multipoint
communication

(a)

Multipath
communication

(b)

send and receive operations through a communication path. Thus, ports are similar to links except that they are bidirectional and buffered. Process communication through ports is indirect. Ports are created by user processes with special system calls and can be associated with ownerships and capabilities. They are referenced by port numbers, which are not to be confused with the transport port addresses used in transport packets (transport port addresses are network ports and are transparent to user processes). In implementation, process ports are mapped to transport ports, and vice versa. A port or mailbox can be visualized as a communication and synchronization server, a concept discussed in Section 3.6. The terms *port* and *mailbox* are often used interchangeably in literature. So are *sockets* and *ports* in Unix systems. A socket is a higher-level interface that uses the concept of ports. Ports are owned by individual processes. Ports provide many-to-one communication. Mailboxes are shared objects and allow for many-to-many communication.

4.1.2 Message Synchronization and Buffering

Message passing communication depends on synchronization at several points. When sending a message to a remote destination, the message is passed to the sender's system kernel, which transmits it to the communication network. Eventually, the message reaches the remote system kernel, which delivers it to the destination process. The synchronization of a message transfer occurs between the user process and system kernel, kernel and kernel, and source and destination processes. Figure 4.3 shows different stages of message transfer in the system.

Send and receive primitives are said to be blocking primitives if the calling process needs to be blocked for the message delivery or receipt, respectively. Most systems allow the choice of blocking or nonblocking send/receive primitives. The common default is usually a nonblocking send and a blocking receive. This is because it is convenient to assume that message delivery is reliable and that the sender process can continue its useful work after the message has been composed and copied to the sender's kernel. The receiver, on the other hand, needs to wait for the message arrival to do its work. However, this is not always the case. For instance, a sender may want to synchronize with the

FIGURE 4.3   Message synchronization stages.

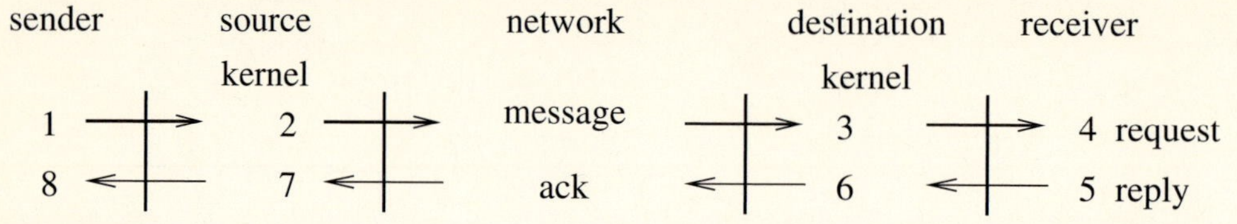

receiver or a receiver may be expecting messages from multiple senders and cannot be tied up with a particular receive operation. At the receiving side, the blocking is quite explicit; it is blocked for message arrival. The sender side is slightly more complicated. Should a sender wait for the receipt of the message by the source kernel, destination kernel, or receiver or even the completion of some operations by the receiving process? The following list shows five different options for the send primitive according to the diagram in Figure 4.3.

1. **Nonblocking send**, *1+8* : Sender process is released after message has been composed and copied into sender's kernel.
2. **Blocking send**, *1+2+7+8* : Sender process is released after message has been transmitted to the network.
3. **Reliable blocking send**, *1+2+3+6+7+8* : Sender process is released after message has been received by the receiver's kernel.
4. **Explicit blocking send**, *1+2+3+4+5+6+7+8* : Sender process is released after message has been received by the receiver process.
5. **Request and reply**, *1-4, service, 5-8* : Sender process is released after message has been processed by the receiver and response returned to the sender.

The first option is referred to as an asynchronous send, while the others are considered synchronous sends. The last one is explicitly called client/server communication. With the asynchronous send, a sender process is blocked if its kernel is not ready to accept the message, perhaps due to lack of buffer space. However, this is a minimum requirement since it is dangerous for the sender to continue working (perhaps creating another message) before its kernel assumes control of the message. When an asynchronous send or receive is assumed, it is desirable for the primitive to return a status code that indicates the success or failure of the operation.

Implicit in the diagram in Figure 4.3 is the existence of buffer space in the sender's kernel, the receiver's kernel, and the communication network. Buffer space in the system kernel allows messages be sent even if previous ones have not been delivered. Since senders and receivers run asynchronously, they generate and process messages at different rates. With buffer spaces, this discrepancy is smoothed out. In addition, the likelihood of a sender being blocked is reduced, and the overall message transfer throughput is increased. Buffer space is used for flow control in communication networks. In operating systems, buffer spaces are normally shared by multiple sender and receiver communications.

Efficient buffer management becomes an important issue. Improper buffer management can become a source of communication deadlocks.

Logically, we can combine the buffers in the sender kernel, the receiver kernel, and the network into one big buffer. The sender produces messages and inserts them in the buffer, while the receiver removes messages from the buffer and consumes them. If the buffer size is unbounded, an asynchronous send is never blocked. The other extreme case is when all components are bufferless (zero-buffer). In this case the sender and receiver must be synchronized to perform the message transfer (whichever arrives first has to wait for the other). This is the familiar *rendezvous* concept and is a type of explicit blocking send and receive.

4.1.3 Pipe and Socket APIs

As we have seen in the previous discussion, there is a large variety of message passing communication primitives with different concepts and assumptions. It is more convenient to the users and effective to the system if communication is achieved through a well-defined set of standard application program interfaces (APIs). User processes communicate using an API, independent of the underlying communication platform. The *pipe* and *socket* are two interprocess communication APIs that are widely used in both the Unix and Windows environments.

In Section 3.5.3 we said that shared communication channels are logically equivalent to shared variables. They are both shared objects. In reality, communication channels are implemented by shared storage, such as kernel space, memory, or files. On a single processor system supporting communicating processes, we can simulate a communication channel by forcing memory sharing in the kernel space. A user process sees the communication channel as presented by the API. The internal details and implementation, such as the capacity of the channel and synchronization of memory accesses, are managed by the kernel and are transparent to the users. Pipes are implemented with a finite-size, FIFO byte-stream buffer maintained by the kernel. Used by two communicating processes, a pipe serves as an unidirectional communication link so that one process can write data into the tail end of the pipe while another process may read from the head end of the pipe. A pipe is created by a *pipe* system call, which returns two pipe descriptors (similar to a file descriptor), one for reading and the other for writing. A typical scenario for piping between two processes is for one process to create the pipe, fork the other process, close the read end of the pipe for the parent process, and close the write end of the pipe for the child process. A one-way flow of data thus becomes available between the parent and child processes using ordinary write and read operations. Pipe descriptors are shared by the communicating processes. This implies that pipes are used only for related processes (i.e., processes that are created through fork operations). Under normal conditions, read and write processes are assumed to run concurrently for every created pipe. A pipe exists only for the time period when both reader and writer processes are active. Writes to a pipe without the corresponding read operations do not make sense since the pipe ceases to exist when the writer process terminates.

Data in pipes are uninterpreted byte sequences. This approach is chosen to coincide with the common assumption of the byte-oriented Unix file structure. Sometimes it is desirable to have structured data, such as variable-length messages, in the channel, so the pipe concept can be extended to include messages. This type of communication channel is referred to as a *message queue*. Message queues are also implemented in the kernel space memory. Many systems provide message queues as an IPC API.

For unrelated processes, there is a need to uniquely identify a pipe since pipe descriptors cannot be shared. One solution is to replace the kernel pipe data structure with a special FIFO file. Special FIFO files are uniquely identified by *path names*, just like ordinary files. Pipes with a path name are called *named pipes*. With a unique path name, named pipes can be shared among disjoint processes across different machines with a common file system. Since named pipes are files, the communicating processes need not exist concurrently. A writer process may have written data to a named pipe and terminated before any read operation to the special file occurs. Named pipes use the semantics of an ordinary file. They are created by an *open* statement before accesses can be made to the FIFO files.

Pipes and named pipes are realizations of the classical *producer and consumer* IPC problem. In the producer and consumer problem, the producer processes and the consumer processes interact through a common buffer to achieve interprocess communication. The synchronization issues are mutual exclusion for accessing the buffer and for the condition coordination when the buffer is full or empty. Buffer access is considered as a critical section that needs to be serialized. The full and empty conditions of the buffer are analogous to the blocking of the sender (producer) and receiver (consumer) with finite buffer. The implementation of pipes and named pipes merely ensures the atomicity of the shared kernel buffers and the special FIFO files and the blocking of the write and read operations when the shared storage is full or empty. Bytes written from multiple processes to a pipe are guaranteed never to be interleaved. Special care must be taken when writing partial data to the pipe before it becomes full. Either all bytes of a message should be written to a pipe, or none.

Use of named pipes is limited to a single domain within a common file system. To achieve interdomain process communication where neither data structures nor files can be uniquely named and shared, we need an IPC API running on top of the transport services. Two of the most widely used interdomain interprocess communication APIs are the Berkeley *socket* and the System V Transport Layer Interface (TLI). We will illustrate the communication API concept by using Berkeley socket examples.

It is not feasible to name a communication channel across heterogeneous domains. However a communication channel can be visualized as a pair of two communication endpoints. A socket is a communication endpoint of a communication link managed by the transport services. Similar to the use of pipes that follows the file I/O semantics for reading from and writing to pipes, sockets model network I/O based on conventional file I/O. The abstraction of network I/O as file I/O enhances access transparency in the system. A socket is created by making a *socket* system call that returns a socket descriptor for subsequent network I/O operations, including file-oriented *read/write* and communication-specific *send/receive*. The socket system call is also used to specify various network protocols such as the Internet TCP, UDP, and IP. TCP is a connection-oriented reliable stream transport protocol and UDP is a connectionless unreliable datagram

FIGURE 4.4 Connectionless socket communication.

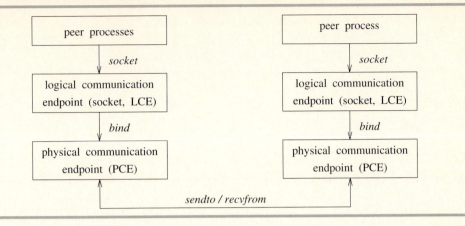

transport protocol. They represent two major transport services. IP is used to transmit raw data packets and is a connectionless network layer protocol in the Internet protocol suite. A socket descriptor is a logical communication endpoint (LCE) that is local to a process; it must be associated with a physical communication endpoint (PCE) for data transport. A physical communication endpoint is specified by a network host address and transport port pair. Network host addresses are global, while the transport port numbers are locally generated by the transport services. The association of a LCE with a PCE is done by the *bind* system call. Figure 4.4 shows an example of a connectionless peer communication using *socket, bind*, and *sendto/recvfrom* socket calls. Since the communication is connectionless, each *sendto/recvfrom* call must contain the local socket descriptor and the remote PCE.

In connectionless socket communication each peer process must know its remote PCE. The explicit naming of the remote PCE in the send/receive calls can be eliminated if a *connect* socket call, which binds a local LCE to its remote PCE, is performed before data transfer commences. After the connect operation, data transfer may simply use *send/recv* or *write/read* without specifying the remote PCE. The *connect* socket call is normally reserved for connection-oriented client/server communication. For client/server communication, a server is expected to have a well-known PCE. A server will need to communicate with multiple clients that have unknown PCEs. Clients issue a *connect* call to the server, which *rendezvous* with a client's request using an *accept* and effectively establishes a connection with the client. Conceptually, it is equivalent to the implementation of the Ada rendezvous concept for interdomain communication. Figure 4.5 illustrates a connection-oriented client/server socket communication. In the Unix implementation, the *listen* socket call is used to indicate that the server is willing to accept a connection and specifies how many pending requests can be queued. The *accept* calls rendezvous with *connect* calls accumulated in the *listen* queue. An *accept* call blocks if there is no pending *connect*. Otherwise it removes a connection request from the queue and returns a new socket descriptor, which is used for communication with the connected client. The old socket descriptor remains in service for other client requests. In a concurrent server

FIGURE 4.5   Connection-oriented client/server socket communication.

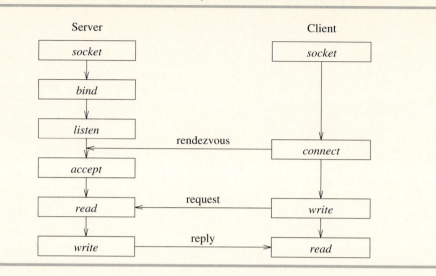

implementation, a child process (or thread) is forked for each connection using the new socket descriptor.

4.1.4 Secure Sockets

Sockets have become the most popular message passing API in the Internet community. Due to the widespread use of Windows applications, a standard Windows socket has been developed by the WinSock Standard Group, which comprises over 30 industrial members (including Microsoft). WinSock is a derivation of the Berkeley socket. It has an elaborate set of APIs and has been extended to provide complete transport transparency by using an abstract Service Provider Interface (SPI) that facilitates plug-in compatibility for almost all transport protocols. The most recent version also includes a Secure Socket Layer (SSL) in the specification.

The need for communication security on the Internet has prompted the development of the SSL by the Internet Engineering Task Force (IETF). The goal of SSL is to provide:

- **Privacy** in socket communication by using symmetric cryptographic data encryption;
- **Intergrity** in socket data by using message integrity check;
- **Authenticity** of servers and clients by using asymmetric public-key cryptography.

The heart of the SSL consists of two protocol layers: a Handshake protocol and a Record Layer protocol. The Handshake protocol is responsible for establishing the *write keys* (communication session keys for data privacy) and MAC (message authentication check for data integrity) secret and for validating the authenticity of clients and servers. The Handshake protocol is a client of the Record Layer protocol. The Record Layer protocol is responsible for fragmentation, compression/decompression, and encryption/decryption of message records. The end result of the Handshake protocol is a shared data structure

FIGURE 4.6   SSL Handshake protocol.

```
CLIENT                                                          SERVER

ClientHello             randomC, CipherSuites
                    ─────────────────────────────────▶

                        randomS, CipherSuite, session id
                    ◀─────────────────────────────────        ServerHello

                            server public key
                    ◀─────────────────────────────────        ServerKeyExchange

ClientKeyExchange       encrypted pre-mastersecret
                    ─────────────────────────────────▶

ChangeCipherSpec                                                ChangeCipherSpec

Finished                hashed message and secret
                    ─────────────────────────────────▶

                    ◀─────────────────────────────────        Finished

Socket Message            encrypted and signed
                    ◀─────────────────────────────────▶        Socket Message
```

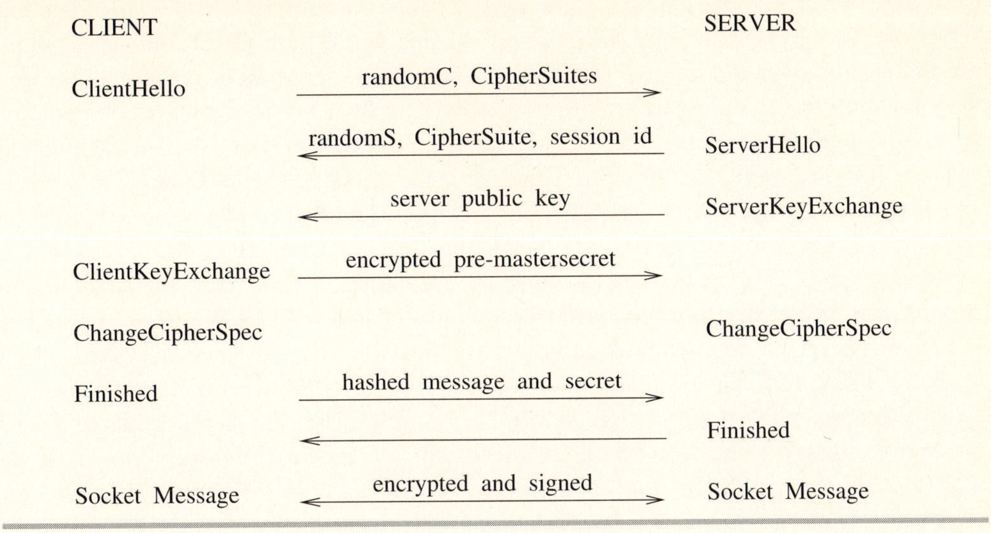

called the *mastersecret*, known only by the client and server, which can be converted into *write keys* and a *MAC secret* for secure communication by the Record Layer.

Figure 4.6 shows a simple scenario of the SSL Handshake protocol. A client wishing to communicate with a server sends a *ClientHello* message to the server. The major components of the message include a random number (*randomC*) and a set of cipher algorithms (*CipherSuites*). The random number is used in the final computation of the *mastersecret*. *CipherSuites* is a list of cryptographic options to be negotiated with and chosen by the server. The server returns a *ServerHello* message to the client; it contains a random number *randomS*, a selected *CipherSuite*, and a session identifier for the connection.

At this point, the server can prove its identity by sending a *certificate* to the client. A certificate for authentication is given by a third-party certification authority (CA). Certificates are *signed* by the certification authority using its secret key and thus cannot be easily forged. SSL uses X.509 certificates. The server can also request a certificate from the client to prove its authenticity. Each certificate carries the public key component of a pair of public and secret keys of a registered object (clients or servers). Clients need the server's public key to convey secret information to the server. Public key cryptography is discussed in Chapter 8. For the time being, we simply describe this dual-key (public and secret) method as a cryptographic algorithm. With it, a message encrypted by the public key can be decrypted by the corresponding secret key, and vice versa. The public key is registered public information while the secret key is known only to the object. For simplicity in illustrating the SSL Handshake protocol, we have left out the validation of certificates in Figure 4.6.

Without a certificate, an anonymous server can send its public key in a *ServerKey-Exchange* message to the client. This public key need not be a registered key. The public key is generated by the server for temporary one-time use by the requesting client.

The client responds with a *ClientKeyExchange* message, which carries a *pre-mastersecret* encrypted by the server's temporary public key. Only the server with the corresponding secret key can decrypt the *pre-mastersecret*. At this point, both client and server share the *pre-mastersecret* and the two random numbers. Both independently apply a one-way hash function to the shared information to derive the final *mastersecret*, which contains *write keys* and *MAC secret*. These keys and the *MAC secret* are used in conjunction with the just-negotiated cipher suite. They are made effective by the *ChangeCipherSpec*, which replaces the old cipher suite with the new one. The *finished* messages conclude the handshake. They are also used to verify whether the key exchange and authentication were successful. The verification is done by validating the *finished* message, which contains the hashed result of the *mastersecret* concatenated with all handshake messages.

Secure socket communication commences after the *finished* messages have been exchanged and verified. All subsequent socket messages are encrypted with the newly established cipher algorithm and secret *write keys*, until the session is renegotiated. Every message contains a message authenticity check, which is the hashed result of the message with a *MAC secret*. Without the *MAC secret* it is not possible to produce the *MAC* for a tampered message. The socket messages processed by the Record Layer become both confidential and tamper resistant. The concept of a secure socket protocol is expected to continue to evolve and improve.

4.1.5 Group Communication and Multicast

The communication models for message passing discussed thus far are all examples of point-to-point communication. This section describes the need for and implementation of multipoint group communication. The notion of a group is essential for the development of cooperative software in distributed or autonomous systems. The management of a group of processes or objects needs an efficient multicast communication mechanism for sending messages to members of the group. Generically, there are two types of multicast application scenarios. The first is when a client wants to solicit a service from any server who can perform the service. The second is when a client needs to request a service from all members of a group of servers.

In the former case, it is not necessary for all servers to respond as long as at least one does. The multicast is performed on a *best-effort* basis and can be repeated if necessary. The system needs only to guarantee the delivery of the multicast message to the reachable nonfaulty processes. This is called the **best-effort multicast**. In the latter case, it is often necessary to ensure that all servers have received the request so that consistency among the servers can be maintained. The multicast message should either be received by all of the servers or none of them (i.e., *all or none*); this is usually called **reliable multicast**. The all-or-none requirement implies that a received multicast message needs to be buffered before delivery to the application process. (In a virtually synchronous reliable multicast, messages can be delivered upon receipt. Virtual synchrony is discussed in Chapter 12.)

Another complication in implementation is caused by failures in the middle of an atomic multicast. Failures of the recipient processes or the communication links may be detected by the message originator using a time-out or acknowledgments. The originator can then abort the multicast or can continue by excluding the failed members from the group. Failure of the originator half-way through the multicast is trickier to deal with. It is difficult to determine that the originator has failed. In order to decide whether to abort or complete the partially completed multicast, one of the recipients must be chosen as the new originator. The usual technique also requires that the recipients buffer multicasts until messages become safe for delivery. Failures are handled by virtual synchrony. Multicasts without virtual synchrony are not really reliable; they are best-effort.

Orthogonal to the reliable delivery issue in multicast is the problem of message delivery ordering. When multiple messages are multicast to the same group, they may arrive at different members of the group in a different order (due to variable delays in the network). Figure 4.7 shows several group communication examples that require message ordering. G and s represent groups and message sources, respectively. Process s may be outside of the group or a member in the group. Ideally, multicast messages should be received and delivered instantaneously in the real-time order that they were sent. Programming groupware would be much simpler if this assumption were true. However, the assumption is unrealistic and meaningless since there is no global time, and message transfer in the network has a significant and varying communication delay. The semantics of the multicast can be defined so that messages received in different orders at different sites can be rearranged and delivered to the application processes with less restricted rules. The following multicast orderings are listed in increasing order of strictness:

- **FIFO order:** Multicast messages from a single source are delivered in the order that they were sent.
- **Causal order:** Causally related messages from multiple sources are delivered in their causal order.
- **Total order:** All messages multicast to a group are delivered to all members of the group in the same order. A reliable and total order multicast is called an **atomic multicast**.

At each site, a communication handler is responsible for message reception and ordered delivery to the application process. Readers are reminded to compare the consistency models with those of distributed file systems and distributed shared memory systems in the later chapters. These are similar problems with different perspectives.

The FIFO order, as shown in Figure 4.7(a), is easy to achieve. Because only those messages sent by the same originator need to be ordered, they can be assigned a message sequence number. The communication handler can delay messages or reject duplicates by using this sequence number. The message sequence numbers are local to each message source and therefore cannot be used to collate messages coming from different sources, as is shown in Figure 4.7(b). Causal and total ordering of multicast messages from multiple sources calls for more sophisticated solutions.

Two messages are causally related to each other if one message is generated after the receipt of the other. This message order may need to be preserved at all sites since the content of the second message may be affected by the result of processing the first message. As discussed in Chapter 3, this causality may span across several members in a group due to the transitiveness of the causality relationship. To implement the

FIGURE 4.7 Group communication and message ordering.

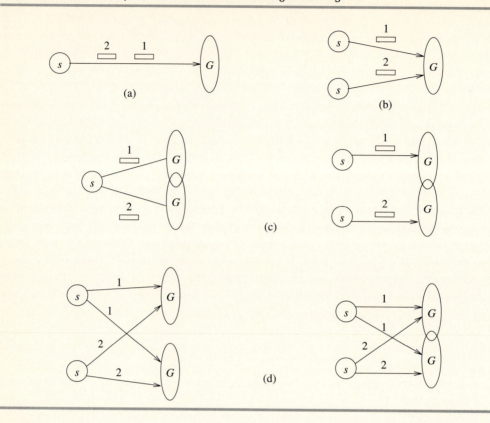

causal ordering of messages, we can extend the sequence number to a vector of sequence numbers, $S = (S_1, S_2, ..., S_n)$, maintained by each member. Each S_k represents the number of messages so far received from group member k. When member i multicasts a new message m, it increments S_i by 1 (indicating the total number of messages that i has multicast) and attaches the vector S to m. When receiving a message m with sequence vector $T = (T_1, T_2, ..., T_n)$ from member i, member j accepts or delays the delivery of m according to the following rules:

- Accept message m if $T_i = S_i + 1$ and $T_k \le S_k$ for all $k \ne i$. The first condition indicates that member j is expecting the next message in sequence from member i. The second condition verifies that member j has delivered all of the multicast messages that member i had delivered when it multicast m (and perhaps several more). So, j has already delivered all the messages that causally precede m.

- Delay message m if $T_i > S_i + 1$ or there exists a $k \ne i$ such that $T_k > S_k$. In the former case, some previous multicast messages from member i are missing and have not been received by member j. In the latter case, member i received more multicast messages from some other members of the group when it multicast m than member j did. In either case, the message must be delayed to preserve the causality.

■ Reject the message if $T_i \leq S_i$. Duplicated messages from member i are ignored or rejected by member j.

This causal order protocol assumes multicast in a closed group (i.e., the source of multicast is also a member of the group), and multicasts cannot span across groups. Chapter 12 gives a more detailed discussion of causal multicast and group management.

Total-order multicast is more expensive to implement. Intuitively, it requires that a multicast must be completed and the multicast messages must be ordered by the multicast completion time before delivery to the application processes. Thus, it makes sense to combine the atomic and total-order broadcasts into one protocol. This is the concept behind the *two-phase total-order* multicast, described as follows. In the first phase of the multicast protocol, the message originator broadcasts messages and collects acknowledgments with logical timestamps from all group members. During the second phase, after all acknowledgments have been collected, the originator sends a *commitment* message that carries the highest acknowledgment timestamp as the logical time for the commitment. Members of the group then decide whether a committed message should be buffered or delivered based on the global logical commitment times of the multicast messages.

The two-phase total-order multicast protocol is illustrated in Figure 4.8. In the figure, two messages, $m1$ and $m2$, from different sources have been broadcast to a group. For clarity, we only show the message transfer between the two sources ($s1, s2$) and two of the group members ($g1, g2$). Their initial logical clock times are shown in the circles. Solid and dashed lines represent multicast and acknowledgment messages, respectively. Each edge is labeled with a pair of numbers. The first number (from 1 to 8) shows the step of a particular order of occurrences, and the second number is the timestamp of the message. In the example, processor $s1$ multicasts $m1$. When all acknowledgments (steps 2 and 8) have been received by $s1$, the processor computes the commitment timestamp (9, the maximum of 6 and 9) and returns the commitment message to the group. The commitment multicast carrying the final completion time of the message broadcast is not shown in the figure. Similarly, $s2$ computes a commitment timestamp of 8 for its multicast $m2$. The table shows the buffer managed by the communication handler of the group member $g1$. This processor has acknowledged the two messages with timestamps 6 and 8. The commitment messages with timestamps 8 and 9 may come in any order, but the communication handler must wait for both before the delivery can be made. Multicast $m2$ is finally delivered before $m1$ since its commitment time is smaller. Message $m3$ (multicast by another source) need not be considered at this point because its commitment message will have a timestamp higher than 10, and therefore it must be delivered after $m1$ and $m2$. All future messages will also have a larger timestamp and consequently need not be considered.

The total message count in the two-phase total-order multicast protocol is high. Many systems (e.g., ISIS) simplify the solution to total message order by assuming the

FIGURE 4.8   Two-phase total-order multicast.

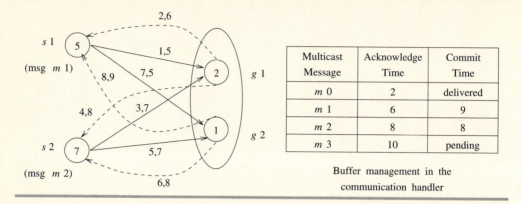

Multicast Message	Acknowledge Time	Commit Time
m 0	2	delivered
m 1	6	9
m 2	8	8
m 3	10	pending

Buffer management in the communication handler

existence of a global sequence number server. Every multicast message must receive a global sequence number from a *sequencer*, a processor that is a member of the group. When a processor receives a totally ordered multicast, the delivery of the message is delayed until a global sequence number has been received. The sequencer buffers the totally ordered multicasts it receives, assigns them global sequence numbers, and then multicasts these sequence numbers to the other members of the group (assigning many sequence numbers in a single message is an optimization that improves performance). Once sequence numbers for totally ordered multicasts are received, the processors deliver the multicasts in the order specified by the global sequence numbers. If the sequencer fails, a new sequencer is *elected* from among the members of the group. Chapter 10 discusses election algorithms. Also see Chapter 12 for more information about how ISIS implements reliable ordered multicast.

For many distributed applications, a process may belong to more than one group. Figure 4.7(c) shows two equivalent examples of multicast to overlapped groups. We have seen protocols for message ordering within a single group. However, the ordering may be different among disjoint groups even for the same multicast messages. With overlapping groups, some coordination among groups is necessary to maintain a consistent ordering of messages for the overlapped members. An example of where overlapping groups is useful is the implementation of replicated servers using atomic multicast. One group consists of only the servers. For each client, there is another group, consisting of the client and all of the servers. The clients might belong to other groups, perhaps obtaining other clients.

One solution to the problem of overlapping groups is to impose some agreed upon structures for the groups and to multicast messages using the structures. For example, the members of a group can be structured as a spanning tree (a spanning tree is a suitable representation for group membership in a computer network that does not support broadcast in hardware). The root of a tree serves as the leader of the group. The tree edges represent FIFO communication channels. A multicast message is first sent to the leader and then is sent to all members of the group by routing the message through

FIGURE 4.9   Tree representations of overlapped groups.

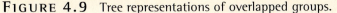

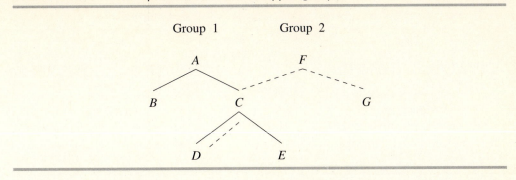

the edges in the tree. Overlapping members must be configured as a common subtree between two overlapping groups. The example in Figure 4.9 shows two groups, where group 1 contains members *A, B, C, D,* and *E* and group 2 contains members *C, D, F,* and *G.* The overlap set (*C, D*) appears as a common subtree between the two groups.

An additional degree of flexibility is acquired if a multicast to more than one group (see, for example, Figure 4.7(d)) is permitted. If we desire consistency between groups, we can define a new group that is a union of the two groups. The problem is then reduced to that of Figure 4.7(b) and (c).

4.2 REQUEST/REPLY COMMUNICATION

The next level of communication above basic message passing is service-oriented request/reply communication. The most widely used request/reply communication model is the Remote Procedure Call (RPC). RPC is a language-level abstraction of the request/reply communication mechanism based on message passing. We have previously described the roles of RPC in synchronization and communication in distributed systems. This section discusses the implementation issues of remote procedure calls.

4.2.1 RPC Operations

The operation of calling a conventional procedure and "waiting" for results is analogous to a pair of synchronous request and reply communications. This similarity between procedure call and communication is the primary motivation behind using procedure calls as a high-level abstraction for communication. A remote procedure call takes the form of a normal procedure call, with its associated input and output parameters. Since there is no distinction in syntax between an RPC and a local procedure call, the RPC provides access transparency to remote operations. However, its semantics are different because the execution of a remote procedure call involves delays and possibly even failures in the network operation. The user applications should be aware of the differences and their implications. Nevertheless, RPCs are a simple and elegant way of achieving communication transparency by shielding the low-level system calls, data conversion, and network communication from user applications. In Chapter 2, we

FIGURE 4.10 Flow of remote procedure calls.

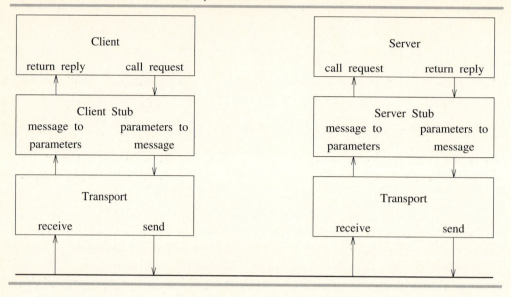

described the RPC support as a presentation service between the transport layer and the application layer. The RPC can be considered as an API for the transport service. The basic RPC operation in the client/server model is shown in Figure 4.10.

The implementation of the RPC will be discussed shortly. For now, we assume that information necessary for an RPC connection has been set up between client and server as in Figure 4.10. A remote procedure call is initiated by a client through a call request, which is iinked to a client stub procedure in the client stub. The client stub procedure is responsible for packing the call and its parameters into a message format for transfer (typically using the socket API) through the network by the transport service. This message is received by the server transport service, which passes it to the server stub. The server stub is the main entry point to the server. It unpacks the message into a call request with corresponding parameters and activates the procedure in the server. Upon completion of the service, the server procedure returns the reply to the server stub, which packs the parameters into a message and sends it to the transport service. The reverse process is performed at the client site, which finally gets the reply and resumes its execution. This basic RPC operation exposes a number of interesting problems and issues:

- **Parameter passing and data conversion**: What types of data can be passed and how is the data represented in messages?
- **Binding**: How does a client locate a server and how does a server register its services (making its services remotely visible)?
- **Compilation**: Where do the stub procedures come from and how are they linked to the clients and servers?

- **Exception and failures handling**: How are errors reported and what assumptions can be made about the failures in the system?
- **Security**: What can be said about secure RPC?

We will discuss the first three issues in this section and the others in the following sections.

Parameter Passing and Data Conversion

Rules for RPC parameter passing and data/message conversion are referred to as **parameter marshaling**. Parameter marshaling is the primary responsibility of the stub procedures. Numerous parameter passing semantics are available for procedure calls in existing high-level languages. They are *call-by-value, call-by-name, call-by-reference,* and *call-by-copy/restore.* Adoption of call-by-value in RPC is straightforward. A value passed to a procedure is copied to a local variable upon entry to the procedure. Modification to the local variable in the called procedure has no effect on the calling procedure. Call-by-name requires dynamic run-time evaluation of symbolic expressions, which is not easy to implement in a compilative environment. Call-by-reference passes pointer addresses, which are awkward if not meaningless in distributed systems where no memory is shared. Therefore, call-by-reference is not a favorite choice of parameter passing for RPC. Call-by-copy/restore is a combination of call-by-value and call-by-reference. It is a call-by-value at the entry of a procedure call and restricts the call-by-reference to the exit of the call. The results are copied back to the calling procedure at the completion of the called procedure without making any memory references during the execution of the procedure. This approach can be used to handle pointers to simple data structures such as arrays. Complex pointer structures, such as trees or graphs, would be difficult for an RPC implementation to handle without significant effort and overhead. Most RPC implementations assume that parameters are passed by call-by-value and call-by-copy/restore.

Data in high-level languages are usually typed with well-defined structures. Static type checking may be performed by the compiler when matching stub procedures with the clients or servers. Type checking across machines is more difficult, because the data is passed through interprogram messages. So, the question arises of whether or not data should carry type information for dynamic type checking. Moreover, each machine has its own internal representation of the data types. For example, integers may be represented by 32-bit 2's complement in one machine, but 16-bit sign-and-magnitude in others. Some systems may use ASCII code for text data while others use EBCDIC. These differences among heterogeneous system components make data conversion between communicating peers necessary. The situation is further complicated by the serial representation of bits and bytes in communication channels. In particular, different machines have different standards for whether the bits or bytes in a message are transmitted with the least or the most significant digit first.

Rules regarding transfer of messages in a network are called *transfer syntax.* Clearly some data conversion standards must be agreed upon in any system with heterogeneous data (or database) representations. If there are n data representations, $n * (n - 1)/2$

translators are required. A better solution is to invent an universal language or canonical data representation that each communicating process translates to its own native language or data representation. This reduces the total translations to $2 * n$ for n different systems. Unfortunately, using an universal language increases the packing and unpacking overhead. Thus, some manufacturers propose that the universal language be identical to the native language of the machines they manufacture. A common optimization is to avoid translations if the communicating processes can detect that they share the same native format. The three unique problems in conversion between data to message and message to data discussed above are *data typing, data representation,* and *data transfer syntax.*

One of the most important developments in standards for data typing and representation is Abstract Syntax Notation One (ASN.1). ASN.1 is a language that can be used to define data structures and it has been widely used for specifying formats of protocol data units in network communications. A transfer syntax and ASN.1 are the major facilities for building network presentation services. ASN.1 can be used directly in data representation for RPC implementations. Existing RPC implementations often use a subset of ASN.1. If RPC is supported in a single domain, the generation of client and server stubs is closely coordinated. Data types are checked during stub generation and compilation. There is no need to provide type information in messages (e.g., the *explicit* typing in ASN.1). In a homogeneous system, the problems related to transfer syntax are ignored. Examples of canonical data representations or description languages for RPC include Sun's XDR (eXternal Data Representation) and DCE's IDL (Interface Definition Language). Both are similar to ASN.1 but have simplifications for defining data structures and the procedure interface.

Binding

A server must exist before clients can make remote procedure calls to it. The services are specified by a server interface using an interface definition language such as XDR. A typical server interface specification has the format shown in Figure 4.11. This example specifies two procedures and is uniquely identified by its program and version numbers. Clients can locate the server by broadcasting a request of the service. However, it is more efficient to go through a separate name resolution server that has a well-known address, if one is available.

FIGURE 4.11   A server interface specification.

```
program   PROGRAMNAME {
        version   VERSIONNAME {
                long   PROCEDUREA (parameters)  = 1 ;        /* procedure number = 1      */
                string   PROCEDUREB (parameters)  = 2 ;      /* procedure number = 2      */
        } = 1 ;                                              /* version number = 1        */
} = 12345 ;                                                  /* program number = 12345    */
```

FIGURE 4.12   Binding between clients and server.

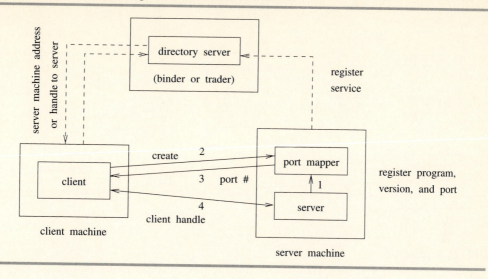

The binding between the clients and the server is illustrated in Figure 4.12 and is explained in the following steps:

1. When a server is started, it registers its communication endpoint by sending a request to the *port mapper*. This request contains the server's program and version numbers along with the port number that the server will be listening to. The port mapper manages the mapping between program numbers and port numbers. It is assumed that the port mapper is a daemon server process with a well-known port address.

2. Before making any remote procedure calls, a client process must contact the port mapper on the remote system to obtain a *handle* for accessing a server with a specific program and version numbers. This is done by calling an RPC run-time library routine *create*, which sends a message containing the server machine name, program and version numbers, and transport protocol (UDP or TCP) to the remote port mapper.

3. The port mapper, upon verifying the program and version numbers in its table, returns the port number of the server to the client system.

4. The client system builds a *client handle* for the client process for subsequent use in the remote procedure calls. The binding process establishes socket connections between clients and server.

In a more general case when the server machine is unknown, the clients will need to locate the server machine by contacting a directory server (sometimes called *binder*, *trader*, or *broker*) to locate the address of the server system. The dashed lines in Figure 4.12 represent this additional operation.

FIGURE 4.13   RPC program generation and compilation.

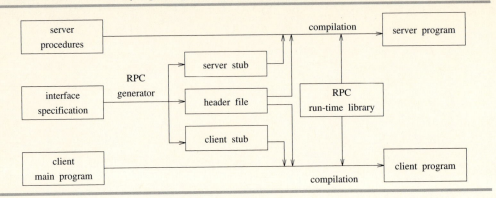

RPC Compilation

The compilation of RPC programs require three major components in the RPC package:

- An interface specification file;
- An RPC generator which takes the interface specification file as input and produces the client and server stub procedure source codes as output;
- A run-time library for the supporting execution of an RPC, including support for binding, data conversion, and communication.

Figure 4.13 shows the generation of stub procedures and the compilation of RPC programs. The RPC generator creates stub procedures and a header file for the independent compilation of the client and server programs. Since both client and server stub procedures come from the same interface specification file, they are syntactically matched. Code for registering a server is included in the server stub as the initialization part of the server process. System calls for binding a client to the server are in the client process. The system calls are executed for the first time when a client makes an RPC call to a server.

4.2.2 RPC Exception and Failure Handling

Although conceptually and syntactically similar, remote procedure calls differ from local procedure calls because of network limitations and failures. Two basic issues, exceptions and failures, need to be addressed for the implementation of RPC. Exceptions are abnormal conditions raised by the execution of stub and server procedures. Failures are problems caused by crashes of clients, servers, or the communication network.

Exception Handling

Exceptions in server procedures, such as overflow/underflow or protection violation in the execution of the procedure, must be reported to the clients. On the other side, a client or its stub procedures may have to stop the execution of a server procedure. The fundamental questions are:

- How does the server report status information to the clients?
- How does a client send control information to the server?

These problems are easily solved in conventional local procedure calls by using shared global variables and *signals*. For example, in Unix the global variable *errno* is used to report error status, and signals (or interrupts) can be used to exercise control over other processes. Neither shared variables nor interrupts are directly available on a computer network. The exchange of control and status information must rely on a data channel. This situation is analogous to the problem in data communication where a signaling channel must either find its place within the normal data channel (*in-band signaling*) or use a separate channel (*out-band signaling*). Many transport services provide an option to *flag* data as out-of-band information in the send primitives. We can also use a separate channel (socket connection) to eliminate the need to distinguish a signal from normal data. This approach is more flexible for RPCs because most system implementations already assume multiple ports for each process (for similar purposes such as communicating to the kernel). In either case, the sending and receiving of control and status information is implemented as part of the stub library support and should be transparent to the client processes.

Failure Handling

The possibility of failures is what makes the remote procedure calls different from local procedure calls. Failures are hard to hide and make transparent for the RPC users. One possible failure is that the client cannot locate the server when initiating the RPC call. This could be due to the nonexistence or the crash of the server. It is also possible that the client is using a outdated program or version number. This problem is more like an exception than a failure and can be reported as such. Once a server is located and a request message has been sent to the server, the message might be delayed or lost. Similarly, the response message might be delayed or lost. Lost messages are eventually detected by a time-out or by no response from the server. The delayed or lost message can be retransmitted.

Retransmission of requests can cause its own type of problem. If the request was not lost but merely delayed, the server will receive two requests from the client when only one request was intended. One solution to this problem is to make all requests **idempotent**, meaning that a request can be executed any number of times with the same effect. For example, the NFS file system provides only idempotent services (e.g., read a block, write a value into a block, but not append a block to a file). Not all services can be made idempotent (lock servers, for example). In this case, the client attaches a sequence number to each request so that a server can detect a duplicate or out-of-sequence request message. If the server receives a duplicate, it retransmits the result produced for the first request. Note that the server will need to keep track of the sequence number of the last request from each client and the result generated for that request. The sequence numbers for client RPC calls are not strictly necessary if the RPC is running on a reliable connection-oriented TCP transport service, which orders messages and eliminates duplicates.

Typical implementations of an RPC do not use sequence numbers. The server doesn't care who is, and how many clients are, making requests as long as it has a way of detecting duplicates. For example, the UDP protocol for Sun's implementation of RPC uses a unique random number *xid*, called the transaction id or **nonce** (number used only once), for each request message (transaction). The *xid* is used to relate requests and replies. The RPC server maintains a cache table indexed by the program and version numbers, procedure number, client's UDP address, and the *xid* for each completed transaction. The previous execution result is returned to the caller if the new request is already in the cache. If a reply message is duplicated for any reason, the *xid* is used by the client to eliminate the duplicate or even wrong replies.

A crash of a server is a more critical problem. Even with a reliable TCP connection, a duplicate request may be delivered to the server. This problem can occur if the client times out waiting for a response to its request (i.e., on top of TCP time-outs). The client will attempt to reestablish a connection. When the connection is reestablished (perhaps after the server recovers from a failure), the client retransmits its request. Note that the failure of a TCP connection does not necessarily mean that the server has crashed, because TCP connections sometimes break due to network problems, buffer overflows, etc. Whether or not the server failed, it might or might not have performed the service. If the TCP connection broke but the server did not crash, an examination of the cache table will determine whether or not the request is a duplicate. If the server did crash, the cache table will be lost. In this case, the server may choose to raise an exception at the client process, and the client process may either wait for the server to recover or give up immediately. This leads us to three possible assumptions for the RPC call semantics in the presence of failures:

- The server raises an exception, and the client retries the operation when the server recovers. Since the operation will be performed at least once, these are **at least once** semantics. These semantics are acceptable for idempotent operations.
- The server raises an exception and the client gives up immediately. Since the requested operation may have been performed by the server before the crash, these are **at most once** semantics.
- The server does not report any error, and the client resubmits its request until it gets a response or gives up. These are **maybe** semantics, since the operation might have been executed any number of times (including no times at all).

Naturally, the most desirable RPC semantics are **exactly once**. It is difficult to achieve exactly once without significant effort. Since the problem lies in the loss of the cache table, the solution is to use the *at least once* semantics and to *log* the cache table to stable storage. When the server recovers, it reloads the cache table from its log. However, for proper operation each service must be executed as a *transaction* at the server. This implies more overhead than is necessary for many applications.

Finally, if a client process crashes (or otherwise terminates prematurely) before the server completes the client's request, the server has an *orphan* computation and its reply is undeliverable. There is no easy way for the server to detect the disappearance of clients except by using a time-out or by waiting for the failed client to reboot and announce its new presence. Orphan computations consume server resources (e.g., memory space, locks) and may also confuse the client with invalid replies from previous connections. Orphan computation can be eliminated in the following ways:

- By client: Upon reboot of a failed client, the client explicitly cleans up all of its previous orphan computations. This requires the client to have the knowledge of its past unfinished procedure call activities and the ability to locate them.
- By server: The server occasionally tries to locate the owners of its remote operations and abort those whose owners cannot be found. This solution requires a reversal of the roles of client and server, which can complicate an otherwise simple design.
- By expiration: Each remote operation is given a maximum lifetime. An operation is killed when it reaches its expiration time (unless the client explicitly asks for additional time).

4.2.3 Secure RPC

Security is extremely important for RPC for two reasons:

- RPC is a form of remote execution that allows programs or commands to be executed on other systems. It is a powerful facility for distributed system implementations and applications. However, RPC introduces vulnerability because it also opens doors for attacks from unfriendly remote users.

- RPC has become the cornerstone of client/server computation. All security features of a computer system will have to be built on top of a secure RPC.

RPC is based on a request/reply message exchange between clients and servers. The primary security issues are the authentication of client and server processes, authenticity and confidentiality of messages, and access control authorization from client to server. The general distributed computer security problems are discussed in Chapter 8. Here we only present some relevant concepts on authentication with respect to RPC. An authentication protocol for RPC should establish the following:

- **Mutual authentication**: The identities of client and server are verified. The request message is truly generated by the client and is intended for the server. The reply message is truly generated by the server and is intended for the client. Authenticity must be assured for messages and the communicating processes.

- **Message integrity, confidentiality, and originality**: Request/reply messages have not been tampered with (integrity), their contents are not revealed (confidentiality), and the same message has not appeared more than once (originality).

The design of a secure authentication protocol is a fairly complex matter. The complexity of a protocol depends on how strong the security goals are, what possible attacks to the system are presumed, and some inherent limitations of the system. A highly

FIGURE 4.14   Sun's Secure RPC.

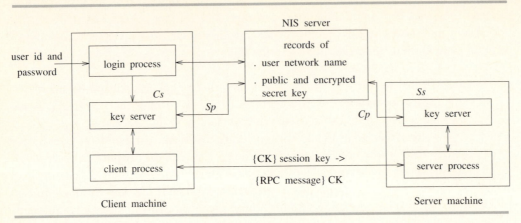

secure system is likely to involve many fundamental changes in the operating system. For a short-term solution, it is desirable to have some additional security features that can be easily added on to an existing system. The following discussion of the Sun secure RPC is an example of a security feature that can be incorporated into an existing system easily.

Sun's Secure RPC is built into Sun's basic RPC system. It assumes that there is a trusted Network Information Service (NIS) in place of an authentication server, which is commonly used in most authentication protocols. However, the NIS in Sun's Secure RPC does not perform authentication functions. It is simply a place to keep a database that contains records of a user's network name and public and secret keys. The keys are not for encryption/decryption as they are normally used in cryptography. Instead, they are used for generating a true cryptographical *session* key for communication, as we shall see shortly. The public keys are public information, while the secret keys are made secret by encrypting them using the Data Encryption System (DES) encryption algorithm with the users' passwords as the encryption keys. When a user logs into a workstation running Secure RPC, the login program contacts the NIS to obtain the key record for the user. The login program then prompts the user for a password, uses it to decrypt the encrypted secret key, and discards the password immediately afterward. This is shown in the user login phase of Figure 4.14. Notice that passwords are *not* transmitted in the network.

Upon a successful login, the client process, working on behalf of the user, attempts to establish a communication session with the server process as follows. The login program deposits the client's secret key C_s in the *key server*'s memory. A similar procedure previously occurred at the server site. The key server processes in the client and server are responsible for generating a common *session* key between the client and the server. This is done by **exponential key exchange**. First, a pair of secret and public keys are assigned (or registered) for every client (C_s, C_p) and server (S_s, S_p) in the system. These keys are generated in the following way:

- C_s and S_s are 128-bit random numbers.

- $C_p = \alpha^{C_s} \bmod M$, and $S_p = \alpha^{S_s} \bmod M$, where α and M are known constants.

Although public keys are derived from secret keys, the reverse operation of evaluating discrete logarithms is computationally expensive. Users cannot infer the secret key easily from its corresponding public key even if the algorithm is known. At the client site, the session key, SK_{cs} is computed by using its secret key C_s and the server's public key S_p as

$$SK_{cs} = S_p^{C_s} = (\alpha^{S_s})^{C_s} = \alpha^{S_s * C_s}$$

Symmetrically and independently, the server computes the session key SK_{sc} by using its secret key S_s and the client's public key C_p as

$$SK_{sc} = C_p^{S_s} = (\alpha^{C_s})^{S_s} = \alpha^{C_s * S_s}$$

It can be seen that $SK_{cs} = SK_{sc} = SK$. The session key is computed with module M (the *mod* operations are omitted for clarity). Once the session key is generated, the secret keys are erased from the key servers' memory. The agreed upon session key establishes mutual authenticity of the client and server since it can only be derived from the secret keys, which represent the true identity of the communicating principals.

Each RPC message is authenticated by a *conversation key CK*, which is a 56-bit random number generated by the client and conveyed to the server by using the session key. The conversation key is kept in the key server and is used for the entire session between client and server. The session key is used only briefly in the network, when the conversation key is transmitted. The possibility of being compromised is minimized. The reason for using the conversation key for the subsequent RPC messages is that it is not derived from the secret keys and therefore is safer to use for a longer period. It is also different for each session.

An RPC message may contain more information, including a *timestamp*, a *nonce*, and a *message digest*. Timestamps are used to check the expiration of messages. Nonces are used to protect against the replay of a message. A message digest is a hashed value of the message data, used for detecting any tampering. Encryption of this information by a conversation key provides both authenticity and secrecy of the messages.

The Sun implementation of secure RPC is very simple. It uses the existing NIS rather than a separate authentication server. The secret information passed to the network or contained in the client and server machines is kept to a minimum.

4.3 TRANSACTION COMMUNICATION

The service-oriented request/reply communication and multicast described in the previous sections can be combined to form a new level of communication called *transaction communication*. A transaction is more commonly known as a fundamental unit of interaction between client and server processes in a database system. A database transaction is represented by a *sequence* of *synchronous* request/reply operations that satisfy the atomicity, consistency, isolation, and durability (ACID) properties (to be described later). Transactions in communication are similar to transactions in databases except they are defined as a *set* of *asynchronous* request/reply communications that also have the ACID properties but are without the sequential constraint of the operations in a database transaction. A communication transaction may involve the multicast of the same message to *replicated* servers and different requests to *partitioned* servers. Transaction services and concurrency control for database transactions are discussed in Chapters 6 and 12. Here we only address the communication aspect of transactions.

4.3.1 The ACID Properties

The ACID properties are primarily concerned with achieving the *concurrency* transparency goal of a distributed system. In Section 2.2 we described concurrency transparency as a property that allows sharing of objects without interference. In a sense, the execution of a transaction appears to take place in a critical section. However, operations from different transactions are interleaved (in some "safe" way) to gain more concurrency. In addition, transactions have additional properties:

- **Atomicity**: Either all of the operations in a transaction are performed or none of them are, in spite of failures.
- **Consistency**: The execution of interleaved transactions is equivalent to a serial execution of the transactions in some order.
- **Isolation**: Partial results of an incomplete transaction are not visible to others before the transaction is successfully committed.
- **Durability**: The system guarantees that the results of a committed transaction will be made permanent even if a failure occurs after the commitment.

Since all four properties are related to *consistency*, sometimes it is preferable to call the second property **serializability** to differentiate it from the others. Atomicity refers to the consistency of replicated or partitioned objects. Violation of isolation is seeing something that has never occurred, and violation of durability is not seeing something that has actually occurred. Both are inconsistent perceptions of the system state.

Ensuring the ACID properties requires that the participating processors coordinate their execution of a transaction. We name the processor that initiates the transaction the *coordinator*, and we name the remaining processors the *participants*. A transaction begins with a multicast of requests from the coordinator to all the participants. The transaction ends with a final decision to *commit* or to *abort* the transaction, depending on whether or not the ACID properties can be satisfied. All participants must agree on the final decision. One solution to the atomicity requirement of a transaction is for each participant to defer making its operation permanent until being assured or informed that all other participants are also ready to do so. This technique is similar to the two stages, message receipt and delivery, that we saw in the two-phase protocol for total-order multicast in

Section 4.1.5. The following section describes how atomicity, isolation, and durability properties are achieved by the two-phase commit protocol for atomic transactions.

4.3.2 The Two-phase Commit Protocol

The two-phase commit (2PC) protocol is analogous to a real-life unanimous voting scheme. Voting is initiated by the coordinator of a transaction. All participants in the distributed transaction must come to an agreement about whether to commit or abort the transaction and must wait for the announcement of the decision. Before a participant can vote to commit a transaction, it must be prepared to perform the commit. A transaction is committed only if all participants agree and are ready to commit.

Each participant (including the coordinator) maintains a private work space for keeping track of updated data objects. Each update contains the old and new value of a data object. Updates will not be made permanent until the transaction is finally committed, to ensure the isolation semantics of the transactions. To cope with failures, it is necessary to flush the updates to a stable storage. The updates recorded in the stable storage are an *activity log* of a transaction. Each participating site has an activity log. The activity log can be replayed upon the recovery of a failure to facilitate either the *redo* of committed transactions or the *undo* of uncommitted transactions. A stable activity log is necessary for the durability or permanence of a committed transaction.

Figure 4.15 illustrates the execution flow of a two-phase commit atomic transaction. There are two synchronization points, *precommit* and *commit*, for each participating site. The coordinator begins a transaction by writing a *precommit* record into its activity log. The coordinator must be prepared to commit the transaction before writing the precommit record (i.e., updates have been flushed to stable log, resources are available to perform the commit, etc.). Writing the pre-commit record into the activity log tells the coordinator the status of the transaction if a failure occurs; the transaction has finished execution but is not yet committed. A vote request is then multicast to all participants. When a participant receives the vote request, it tests whether the transaction can be committed (the updates have been flushed to the activity log, serializability is ensured, resources are available, etc.). If the test is positive, the participant writes a *precommit* into the log and sends a YES reply to the coordinator. Otherwise, the participant aborts the transaction and sends a NO reply to the coordinator.

If the coordinator is able to collect all YES replies within a time-out interval, it commits the transaction by writing a commit record in the log and multicasting a *commit* message to all participants. Otherwise the coordinator aborts the transaction and multicasts an *abort* message. On receiving the *commit* message, each participant commits the transaction by writing a commit record into the activity log and releasing the transaction's resources. Finally, any response is returned to the coordinator. If the received message was an *abort*, the participant writes an abort record into the log, aborts the transaction, and releases the transaction's resources.

When used with an activity log, the two-phase commit protocol is highly resilient to processor failures. Figure 4.16 shows the time-lines of the protocol for the coordinator and a participant. Since writing *precommit* and *commit* to the activity log flushes all updates before these synchronization points, proper actions upon recovery from failures

FIGURE 4.15 Two-phase commit atomic transaction protocol.

COORDINATOR   PARTICIPANT

Phase 1

- precommit the transaction

- send request to all participants   —request→   - received request message

                                                   - if ready

                                                        then precommit and send YES

- collect all replies   ←reply—   else abort transaction and send NO

Phase 2

- if all votes are unanimous YES

     then commit and send COMMIT

     else abort and send ABORT   —decision→   - receive decision

                                                - if COMMIT then commit

                                                - if ABORT then abort

- received response   ←result—   - send response

can rely on the replay of the log at least up to the synchronization points. Thus recovery actions can be categorized into three types: failures before a precommit, failures after a precommit but before a commit, and failures after a commit. A processor (either the coordinator or a participant) can simply abort the transaction if it discovers from the log that the failure occurred before a precommit. This is equivalent to voting NO for the transaction. The coordinator can also abort the transaction if it crashes between precommit and commit, but it is more efficient to attempt to commit the transaction by remulticasting the request messages (if duplicates can be detected by the participants).

FIGURE 4.16 Failures and recovery actions for the 2PC protocol.

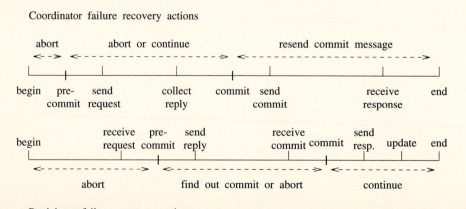

Coordinator failure recovery actions

abort   abort or continue   resend commit message
←--→ ←-------------------------→ ←------------------------------→

begin   pre-   send   collect   commit send   receive   end
        commit request   reply   commit   response

begin   receive pre-   send   receive   send
            request commit reply   commit commit resp. update   end

      ←-------------→ ←----------------------→ ←-------------→
         abort   find out commit or abort   continue

Participant failure recovery actions

Similarly, it is safe to resend the commit messages if the coordinator crashes after writing the commit record to its log. The recovery action is slightly more complicated if a participant crashes between precommit and commit. The recovering participant must determine whether the transaction was committed or aborted by contacting the coordinator or the other participants. Finally if a participant recovers from a failure after a commit record has been written to the log, the participant simply makes the transaction's updates permanent. With stable storage, the recovery mechanisms ensure the durability of the commitments.

Section 12.1.1 contains a more formal description of the two-phase commit protocol and its enhancement: the three-phase commit protocol. Chapter 13 is devoted to failure and recovery handling.

4.4 NAME AND DIRECTORY SERVICES

A discussion of communication is not complete without considering naming and addressing issues. Making a request to a service or accessing an object by means of interprocess communication requires that one must first locate the service or object. Services are abstractions of objects. They are usually represented by processes with a service access point. Objects may be users, computers, communication links, or other resources such as files. Services and objects are normally identified by textual names. Alternatively, if names are unknown, service or object entities can be described by using *attributes* associated with them. Although services and objects have distinct meanings, their naming issues are similar. For clarity, we will use the term *object entity* to represent both services and objects in the discussion of name and directory services.

4.4.1 Name and Address Resolution

Name and directory services, in a narrow sense, are *look-up* operations. Given the name or some attributes of an object entity, more attribute information is obtained. The terms *name service* and *directory service* are often used interchangeably. A name service is a generic way of describing how a named object can be addressed and subsequently located by using its address. The term *directory service* is sometimes used to describe a special name service, such as the directory service of a file system. Other times, it is used to represent a very general name service for all kinds of attribute look-ups on different object types, not just limited to address information. X.500, defined by CCITT, is an example of such a directory service. Higher-level name services can be built on top of a standard directory service.

Any object entity in a system must be named (or be identifiable) and located before it can be used. The operation of locating an object, called a *resolution* process, may require a number of look-up (or mapping) operations. Each object entity has a logical address in the operating system and a physical location in the network. The resolution process involves two stages: a *name resolution* that maps names to logical addresses and an *address resolution* that maps logical addresses to network routes.

- **Name resolution**: Names are application-oriented denotations of objects. Addresses are object representations that carry some structural information relevant to the operating system for managing and locating an object. The name resolution process maps names to addresses. A name represents who the object is, and its address tells where it can be found. Names are usually unique, but the same name may have multiple addresses. The mapping of a server name to its port addresses is an example of name resolution.

- **Address resolution**: Address resolution maps addresses to routes that show how an object can be physically located. The difference between an address and a route is that routes are the lowest level of location information and cannot be reduced any further. Addresses consist of intermediate object identification information between names and routes. The mapping of a server port to its Ethernet port is an example of address resolution.

Name resolution is a fundamental function of distributed operating systems, while address resolution is a network problem. We will focus only on name resolution, a mapping of names to standard addresses in operating systems. A name service is implemented by one or more name servers. It is important to emphasize here that a name resolution is normally iterative and involves several name servers.

4.4.2 Object Attributes and Name Structures

An object entity is characterized by its attributes. For example, a user object may have an affiliation attribute, and a file object may be associated with a version number and a creation date, among other attributes. In the context of name resolution, we are particularly interested in two special object attributes, *name* and *address*. Names are attributes with a unique value for the purpose of identification. Addresses are attributes, too, except they are the output of the name resolution process. The collection of names, recognized by a name service, with their corresponding attributes and addresses, is called a **name space**. A large name space containing different object classes may be structured with respect to its unique *types*. For examples, objects may be categorized separately as users, computers, or files. These object types are attributes for organizing the name space.

The name of an object entity can be a simple attribute or can consist of several attributes, with or without an internal structure among the attributes. A name structure that uses only a single attribute for the names is called a *flat* naming structure. A flat structure name is a symbolic attribute. The only requirement for flat structure naming is that the names must be unique across systems. Flat structure naming is conceptually simple and has the desirable properties of being location transparent and independent. The major disadvantage is that unique naming is difficult to achieve without global coordination. On top of that, it is difficult to resolve names and manage the name space without structural information in the names.

If a name is partitioned into several attributes, an ordering of attributes may be imposed. For instance, a user with a name attribute $< chow >$, an organization attribute $< ufl >$, and a country attribute $< us >$ may form a new compound attribute $< chow.ufl.us >$ as the name attribute. In this popular scheme [used by the Internet

FIGURE 4.17   Object attributes and name structures.

Service /object Attributes	Name Structures	Attribute Partitioning

< attributes >
 	
< name, attributes, address >
 	
< name, type, attributes, address >
	flat structure
	hierarchical structure name-based resolution
	  (e.g., white pages)
	structure-free attribute-based resolution
	  (e.g., yellow pages)
		physical
		
		organizational
		
		functional

Domain Name Service (DNS)] the names are hierarchically structured attributes. In a more general case without an ordering of the attributes, an object can still be referred to or located by specifying a collection of attributes, such as $< (U = chow, C = us, O = ufl) >$. Here U, C, and O stand for types of attributes for users, countries, and organizations, respectively. The name service address look-up operation can be based on names of concatenated attributes (**hierarchical structure name-based resolution**) or only on collections of attributes (**structure-free attribute-based resolution**). These two types of name resolution are analogous to the *white* and *yellow pages*, respectively, in a telephone directory.

The partitioning of attributes for an object name may be *physical, organizational,* or *functional.* A physically partitioned name structure carries explicit location information about the object. A name such as $< user.host.network >$ is location dependent and requires no name resolution, only address resolution. An organizationally partitioned name structure is based on an administrative structure. A name such as $< user.department.organization >$ is location transparent and offers better autonomicity for unique naming than does physical naming. Both physical and organizational partitionings are hierarchical, meaning that there is a containment relationship among attributes. For example, *hosts* are contained in *networks* and *departments* are contained in *organizations*. The use of hierarchical names for name-based resolution protocols is effective in resolving names and managing name spaces. Some name attributes are not strictly hierarchical. For example, the attributes profession = $< professor >$ and specialty = $< computer science >$ cannot be conveniently incorporated into a name to reflect either physical or organizational property of the objects. This naming is functional and is more suitable for structure-free attribute-based name resolution. Figure 4.17 shows various ways of using attributes to characterize object entities and to represent name structures.

4.4.3 Name Space and Information Base

The name space and its object information in a distributed system potentially could be enormous. For efficient name resolution and management, there is a need for an information model to serve as a basis of the name space database implementation. Using X.500 terminology, the conceptual data model for storing and representing object information is called the Directory Information Base (DIB). The Directory Service (DS) of the CCITT X.500 standard provides structural and syntactic rules for specifying a DIB in a hierarchical Directory Information Tree (DIT). Figure 4.18 is an example of a DIT. Each object entry in the DIB is represented by a node in the DIT. The attributes corresponding to an object entry are the set of attributes from the node to the root of the tree. Use of the tree structure is advantageous since every node in a tree has an unique path to the root. A path can be used to uniquely identify a structure-free named object for attribute-based resolution. Attributes used for naming purposes are called *distinguished attributes*. If distinguished attributes of the same type are grouped for each level of the tree, the concatenation of the distinguished attributes along a path becomes a structured name of the object. Figure 4.18 shows a directory information tree with a hierarchical grouping of distinguished attribute types (*country, organization, user*). The hierarchical tree structure is suitable for name-based resolution.

A large name space and its corresponding DIT can be decomposed and distributed into **naming domains** and **naming contexts**. A naming domain is a subname space for which there is a single administrative authority for name management. A naming context is a partial subtree of the DIT. Figure 4.18 shows five naming contexts (A, B, C, D, E) in dashed-line boxes. Naming contexts are the basic units for distributing the information base to Directory Service Agents (DSAs), which are the servers for the name service. There are three DSAs in solid-line boxes in Figure 4.18 that manage five naming contexts. The naming contexts also form a tree. Each DSA maintains links to other cooperating DSAs of the name service.

A name resolution process is initiated by a Directory User Agent (DUA), working on behalf of a user process. The resolution request is sent from one DSA to another until the object is found in the DIT and returned to the DUA. Whether the resolution scheme is structured and name-based or structure-free and attribute-based, the interaction among DSAs can be in one of the four modes shown in Figure 4.19.

FIGURE 4.18   Distribution of a DIT.

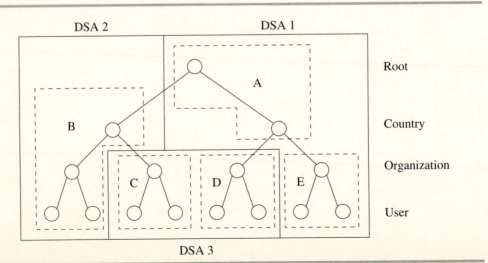

FIGURE 4.19   Name resolution interaction modes.

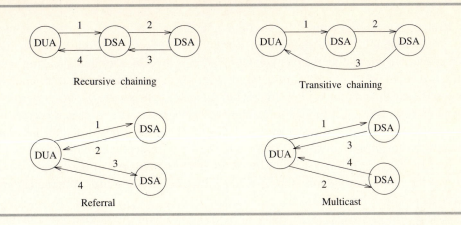

In the *chaining* mode, a request is forwarded from DSA to DSA until the name can be resolved. The result can be sent back along the original path (*recursive chaining*) or directly (*transitive chaining*) to the DUA. Recursive chaining is a normal mode for structured name resolution. Transitive chaining requires fewer messages, but each message needs to carry the source DUA address. The major drawback of transitive chaining is that it does not follow the RPC and client/server programming paradigm. In the *referral* mode, a DSA that cannot resolve the requesting name from a DUA makes a best suggestion of another DSA to the DUA. The referral mode can be used for both name and attribute-based resolutions. In the *multicast* mode, a resolution request is replicated and sent to multiple DSAs concurrently. One of the valid responses is chosen by the DUA. Multicast is suitable when structural information is not available. It is possible to combine different modes of operation. For example, some chaining stages may be followed by referrals.

There are two common techniques, *caching* and *replication*, that enhance the performance of name resolution. Recently used names and their addresses can be kept in a cache to reduce the need for name resolution. Naming contexts can also be duplicated in different DSAs to shorten the resolution path. In either case, the problem of consistency in data copies arises. However, inconsistency is not considered a serious problem since updates in a directory information base are not frequent. Finally, object entries in a directory may be an *alias* or a *group*. Aliases and groups are pointers to other object names and are leaf-nodes in the DIT. Alias and group names add flexibility in naming for users of the name/directory services.

A name service is a key component in every distributed system. The name service in DCE is a good example of supporting a large class of naming schemes. For cooperative autonomous systems, the name service must be extended to support a communication infrastructure for identifying and locating all autonomous objects in the system and managing connection and delivery of data between objects. The Object Request Broker (ORB) is such a central facility in the CORBA architecture for cooperative autonomous systems.

4.5 DISTRIBUTED MUTUAL EXCLUSION

In Chapter 3 we described three major communication scenarios: one-way, client/server, and peer communication. Applications using one-way communication usually don't need synchronization. Client/server communication is for multiple clients making service requests to a shared server. If coordination is required among the clients, it is handled by the server and there is no explicit interaction among client processes. But, interprocess communication is not just limited to making service requests. Oftentimes, processes need to exchange information to reach some conclusion about the system or some agreement among the cooperating processes. These activities require peer communication; there is no shared object or centralized controller. The remaining sections of the chapter address some of the distributed coordination problems that occur when peer communication is used.

We start our discussion of distributed coordination with distributed versions of the classical mutual exclusion synchronization problem. Then we discuss another important class of distributed coordination problem, distributed leader election. The primary purpose of these sections is to show the fundamental concepts and issues in distributed coordination. An in-depth study of the implementation of distributed synchronization and election algorithms is presented in Chapter 10. The generalization of distributed synchronization algorithms into agreement protocols is discussed in Chapter 11.

Mutual exclusion ensures that concurrent processes make a serialized access to shared resources or data (e.g., updating a database or sending control signals to an I/O device). A distributed mutual exclusion algorithm achieves mutual exclusion (and some fairness and progress properties) using only peer communication. The problem can be solved by using either a *contention-based* or a *controlled* approach. A contention-based approach means that each process freely and equally competes for the right to use the shared resource by using a request resolution criteria. The resolution criteria may be based on the times of the requests, priorities of the requesters, or voting. In the controlled approach, a logical token representing the access right to the shared objects is passed in a regulated fashion among the competing processes. Whoever holds the token is allowed to enter its critical section.

Processes may need to contend for a mutual exclusion token in a controlled approach algorithm. In a contentionless controlled approach, the control token is distributed in an orderly, effective, and fair manner. It is worthwhile to point out the analogy between distributed mutual exclusion in operating systems and medium access control in local area networks. Here, the shared resource is the broadcast right. Ethernet in a LAN is a contention-based mutual exclusion access protocol for the communication channel, while Token Bus is a controlled approach with no contention.

4.5.1 Contention-based Mutual Exclusion

Contention for the critical section can be resolved by any criteria for breaking ties when simultaneous requests occur. The fairest way is to grant the request to the process which asked first (in logical time) or the process which got the most votes from the other processes. We will call these two different approaches *timestamp prioritized* and *voting* schemes.

Timestamp Prioritized Schemes

In timestamp prioritized schemes, we can use Lamport's logical clock concept to totally order the requests for entering a critical section. Lamport's distributed mutual exclusion algorithm works as follows. A process requests the critical section by broadcasting a (Lamport) timestamped $REQUEST$ message to all other processes (including itself). Each process maintains a queue of pending $REQUEST$ messages arranged in the ascending timestamp order. On receiving a $REQUEST$ message, a process inserts the message in its request queue and sends a $REPLY$ message to the requesting process. A process is allowed to enter its critical section only if it has gathered all the $REPLY$ messages and its request message is at the top of the request queue. When exiting the critical section, a process broadcasts a $RELEASE$ message to every process. On receiving a $RELEASE$ message, a process removes the completed request from its request queue. At that moment, if the process' own request is at the top of the request queue, it enters its critical section provided that all $REPLY$ messages have been received. Lamport's algorithm achieves mutual exclusion since all requests are serialized with respect to the logical timestamps of the request messages. The total message count per completion of a critical section is $3 * (N - 1)$, where N is the number of cooperating processes.

The message complexity of Lamport's algorithm is reduced by Ricart and Agrawala, who observe that deferred reply messages can block a processor from entering the critical section. If a process receives a $REQUEST$ message when it is in its critical section, or has made a request and its timestamp is smaller than that of the arriving $REQUEST$ message, the process delays sending a $REPLY$ message. A requesting process is allowed to enter as soon as it has collected all of the $REPLY$ messages. Note that a requesting process will obtain these messages only when it becomes the highest-priority requesting process. In essence, the $REPLY$ and the $RELEASE$ messages are combined. The message complexity is reduced to $2 * (N - 1)$.

The timestamp prioritized algorithms are simple to implement. The logical clock in each process is advanced on the arrival of a message, which establishes an order between the sending and receiving processes and consequently, a total ordering of all requests. The algorithms achieve mutual exclusion and progress without indefinite postponement of any requesting process.

Voting Schemes

With the Lamport (or Ricart and Agrawala) algorithm, if a single processor is unavailable, the lock becomes unavailable. We would like to have a scheme by which a processor does not need the permission of every other processor to enter the critical section. In civil society, we hold elections to select our public officials. The winner of a political race can often be determined before the last vote is counted; as soon as a candidate has a majority of the votes, we know that the candidate will win the election.

We can apply the idea of voting to distributed mutual exclusion. When a process receives a $REQUEST$ message, it sends a $REPLY$ (i.e., a *vote*) only if the process has not voted for any other *candidate* (requesting processor). Once a process has voted, it is not allowed to send any more *REPLY* messages until its vote has been returned (e.g., by a *RELEASE* message). A candidate wins the election (obtains permission to enter the critical section) when it has received a majority of the votes. Since only one candidate can get a majority of votes at one time, mutual exclusion is assured.

A problem with this voting scheme is **deadlock**. If there are three candidates, each one can win a third of the votes. One can envision a scheme in which the candidate with the most votes wins the election. However, this scheme becomes more complicated and requires global communication to break ties.

Alternatively, a processor can change its vote when it receives a request from a "more attractive" candidate. Each processor maintains a Lamport timestamp and attaches the timestamp to its *REQUEST* messages. If a processor that has already voted receives a *REQUEST* with a lower timestamp than that of the candidate it voted for, the processor will try to retrieve its vote by sending an *INQUIRE* message to the candidate. If the candidate has not yet entered the critical section, it returns the vote to the inquirer with a *RELINQUISH* message (otherwise the candidate returns the vote with a *RELEASE* message when it exits the critical section). When the processor gets its vote back, it votes for the candidate with the lowest timestamp. Eventually some candidate enters the critical section because one of the candidates will have the lowest timestamp.

The majority rule for voting requires $O(N)$ messages per critical section entry (and perhaps some more messages for deadlock avoidance). We can reduce the messaging overhead by reducing the number of votes required to enter the critical section. Each process i has a *request set* S_i, and a processor needs the votes from every member of its request set to enter the critical section. To ensure mutual exclusion, every request set must intersect (i.e., $S_i \cap S_j \neq null$ for every pair of request sets). Request sets suitable for mutual exclusion are commonly referred to as **quorums**, and sets of request sets are referred to as **coteries**. There are other conditions for quorums and coteries that are not directly related to correctness but are desirable for performance. If no one quorum is a proper subset of another, the coterie is *minimal*. If each quorum is the same size, the coterie requires *equal effort* and *equal responsibility* of all the processors.

Given a set of desirable conditions, the problem is to determine a coterie that satisfies the properties such that each quorum is of minimal size. It is possible for each quorum to be of $O(\sqrt{N})$ size. (Chapter 10 discusses this topic further.) Such small quorums must remove all redundancies, so if a single processor becomes unavailable, some (but not all) of the processors will not be able to enter the critical section. Many alternative schemes for generating coteries have been proposed, with various trade-offs between efficiency, equal effort, and fault tolerance. Chapters 6 and 10 have more material on distributed mutual exclusion.

4.5.2 Token-based Mutual Exclusion

Although contention-based distributed mutual exclusion algorithms can have attractive properties, their messaging overhead is high. An alternative to contention-based algorithms is to use an explicit control token, possession of which grants access to the critical section. If there is only one token, mutual exclusion is assured. Different methods for requesting and passing the token give different performance and fairness properties. To ensure that a request gets routed to the token holder and the token routed to the requester, algorithms impose a logical structure on the processes. We will illustrate the token-based algorithms using three typical topologies: *ring, tree,* and *broadcast* structures.

Ring Structure

The processes are connected in a logical ring structure where a token circulates in the ring. A process possessing the token is allowed to execute its critical section. When the process has finished the critical section (if any), it passes the token to the successor node in the ring. The logical ring structure is attractive because it is simple, deadlock-free, and fair. However, the token needs to circulate in the ring even if no process wants to enter its critical section, resulting in unnecessary network traffic. In addition, a process that wishes to enter the critical section must wait until the token arrives. This wait can be large, even if no other process enters the critical section, when the token must travel a large portion of the ring to reach the requesting processor. If the request load is high, the logical ring algorithm will work well because the token will usually make only a few hops between processes that wish to enter the critical section.

One of the most significant advantages of the token-based approach over the contention-based methods is that the token can be used to carry state information. For example, a priority scheme can be implemented by embedding priority information in the token. A process can claim the token only if it has received the token and its priority is higher than that indicated in the token. The priority may be user-defined or a timestamp. The Token Bus (IEEE 802.4) and Token Ring (IEEE 802.5) standards for local area networks make use of these ideas. These standard LAN protocols specify procedures for forming rings, and handling of priorities and system failures. The major difference is the assumption of network architecture. The Token Bus and Token Ring standards use hardware bus and ring architectures, while our mutual exclusion concern is an application-level problem where no assumption is made about the underlying network. Protocol functions that require capabilities such as bus monitoring in Token Bus cannot be implemented in the application levels. Nevertheless, using a token to carry information among cooperating nodes may help to facilitate distributed coordination.

Tree Structure

A problem with the ring structure approach is that the idle token is passed along the ring when no process is competing for it. An alternative is require a process to explicitly request the token and to only move the token if it knows of a pending request. Since the request must find the token, we risk the danger of indefinite postponement and deadlock. We also observed that the ring structure is not the best way to acquire a token because the paths may be long (for the request or for the token). The worst case is one node less than a complete circle. We will show how we can solve these problems by using a logical tree structure. The algorithm we present is due to Raymond.

Figure 4.20 shows an example of a logical tree where the token always resides at the root of the tree. Note that the arrows point towards the root, which is the opposite of conventional tree notation. Each node of the tree represents the current logical position

FIGURE 4.20   Tree-structured token passing.

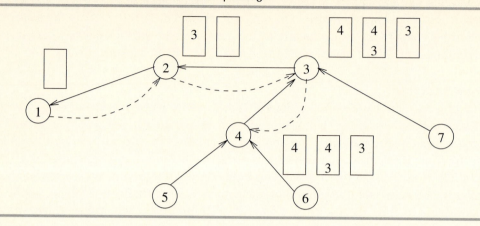

of a process. When a process wishes to acquire the token, a request is sent from the node along the path to the root. When successfully acquired, the token migrates to the requesting node, forming a new tree rooted at the new node. The algorithm is fully analyzed in Chapter 10. Here we only present the fundamental concept.

Each process maintains a FIFO request queue and a pointer to its immediate predecessor (the node to which the outgoing edge points). When a process receives a request, it appends the request to the FIFO queue. If the FIFO queue is empty and the process does not have the token, the process must take an action to obtain the token, so it requests the token from its predecessor in the tree. Otherwise, the process has or will soon get the token, so no further action is taken. A process requests a token by generating a local request and performing the above processing.

If a process has the token, but is not using it, and has a nonempty FIFO queue, the process removes the first entry from the FIFO queue and sends the token to that process. The triggering condition can occur when a request arrives, when the token arrives, or when the process releases the token. Since the process no longer holds the token, it changes its pointer to the process to which it sent the token. If the FIFO queue is not empty, the process will need to reobtain the token, so it sends a request to the new token holder. An exception occurs if the process is the first entry in the FIFO list. In this case, the process enters the critical section.

Figure 4.20 shows how the tree structure changes dynamically. The token initially resides in node 1. Node 4 attempts to claim the token first. Node 3 follows after it has forwarded the request from node 4 to node 2. The token migrates from node 1 to node 4 via nodes 2 and 3. Node 3 passes the token and sends a request to node 4 since node 3's request queue is not empty. This request establishes the link between node 4 and pending requests known by node 3. The dashed lines in the figure are the pointer changes showing token migration and the numbers in the boxes indicate contents of the request queues in steps.

The algorithm is a *distributed implementation of a global FIFO queue.* Local FIFO queues are linked to form a global FIFO using the logical tree topology. The acyclic nature of a tree structure makes it impossible to form a cyclic waiting list, removing the possiblity of deadlock. Each node representing a subtree sends a single request to the predecessor node, requesting the token for the entire subtree. The request queue on each node prioritizes the requests from its successor subtrees in FIFO order to ensure fairness and freedom from indefinite postponement. The logical tree can also dynamically change its topology, potentially improving performance. The *path compression* approach for improving performance in tree topologies is discussed further in Chapter 10.

Broadcast Structure

Imposing a logical topology improves efficiency but makes the algorithm implementation more complex, since the topology must be initiated and maintained. It is more transparent and thus desirable to use group communication without being aware of topology. The contention-based mutual exclusion algorithms discussed in the previous section use broadcast and resolve contention with timestamps or votes. If we use a broadcast to contend for a token, it appears that we do not really change the nature of the problem since contention still exists. However, there is a significant advantage in using a token. A token can carry global information that can be useful for process coordination. The control token for mutual exclusion is centralized and can be used to serialize requests to critical sections. This is the the basis for Suzuki/Kasami's broadcast algorithm.

The control token in the Suzuki/Kasami algorithm is associated with a data structure, which consists of a token vector T and a request queue Q. Entries in T are indexed by process numbers and represent the accumulated number of completions of a critical section by the corresponding process. Each process keeps a local sequence number, which counts the number of times the process has requested the critical section. This sequence number is attached to all $REQUEST$ messages that the process broadcasts. Every process p also maintains a sequence vector S, which contains the highest sequence number of every process that p has heard of. The request queue in the token is a list of pending requests in FIFO order.

The algorithm works as follows. A process i requests the critical section by broadcasting a $REQUEST$ message with its incremented sequence number seq attached to the message. A process j, receiving a $REQUEST$ message from i, updates its sequence vector by $S_j[i] = max(S_j[i], seq)$. If process j is holding an idle token (a token with an empty Q), it sends the token to process i if $S_j[i] = T[i] + 1$. A process can enter the critical section when it has received the token. The request queue in the token may contain a nonempty Q if the token is passed by a process that has modified Q. Upon completion of the critical section, process i updates the token by setting $T[i]$ equal to $S_i[i]$. The completing process also compares its S against T and appends all processes with $S_i[k] = T_i[k] + 1$, where $k \neq i$, to Q if they are not already in the request queue. After the update of Q, process i removes the top entry from the request queue and sends the token to the process indicated by the removed top entry. If Q is empty, the token stays with process i.

Figure 4.21 shows an example of the broadcast algorithm with four cooperating processes. Initially, process 1 holds the token and has just completed its critical section. The other three processes requested the token. Some request messages are received late

FIGURE 4.21   Token-based broadcast algorithm.

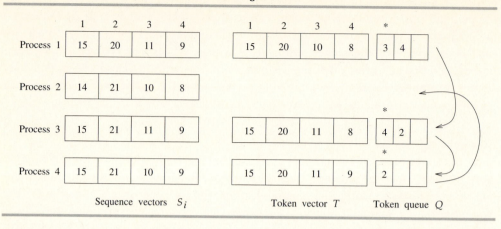

due to network delays. Process 1 recognizes the requests from processes 3 and 4. It appends the requests on the request queue and sends the token to process 3. The top entry in the request queue is deleted (shown with an asterisk) before the token is sent to process 3. After process 3 has finished, it appends process 2's request to the token queue and sends the token to process 4. Finally, process 4 forwards the token to process 2 and the token stays with process 2 (since no more requests are detected).

The token-based broadcast algorithm is simple and effective, particularly if the system has an efficient broadcasting facility. While the Suzuki/Kasami algorithm is not fully distributed, as the contention-based approaches are, there is no central controller and the management of the shared token is distributed. Only the contention for mutual exclusion is centrally serialized by the FIFO token queue. The algorithm incurs no deadlock or starvation.

4.6 LEADER ELECTION

The existence of a centralized controller greatly simplifies process synchronization. However, the centralized controller is a single point of failure and can limit service availability. The problem can be alleviated if a new controller (the leader) can be chosen upon failure of the existing controller. Leader election is concerned with the election of a unique leader process, known to all other processes in the group. Leader elections occur during the initiation of a system of processes or when an existing leader fails. A leader election process should be activated when a failure is detected or suspected. The detection of failures is normally based on a time-out. A process that gets no response from the leader for a predefined time-out interval suspects a failure of the leader and initiates the election process. Note that false alarms can occur, and the leader election algorithms must be aware of this possibility. False alarms should be rare if the time-out interval is properly chosen. In the token-based synchronization algorithms, the process holding the token can be considered the leader of the system. In this case, the leadership role rotates among processes, and a process does not need to know the identity of the current leader. The loss of the token is equivalent to failure of the leader.

There are two basic election criteria. First, a leader election can be based on a global priority. This type of election is called *extrema finding.* Second, processes in the group can vote for a leader based on a personal preference (e.g., locality, reliability estimation, etc.). This class of voting schemes is called a *preference-based* leader election algorithm. Voting is more general than extrema finding. For example, one voter can carry more weight than the others or can cast multiple votes, resulting in more complex decisionmaking and a less predictable outcome.

In many aspects, leader election and distributed mutual exclusion are the same; they both try to reach an agreement for identifying a unique process. However, there are some interesting differences. For leader elections, a process may yield to others and return to its normal execution as long as one leader is elected, while in mutual exclusion, a process competes until it succeeds. A mutual exclusion algorithm must ensure that no process is starved, while a leader election algorithm is more concerned with the fast and successful termination of the election process. Another distinction is that the result of a leader election needs to be announced to all processes. For mutual exclusion, a process does not care which other process is currently in a critical section as long as it eventually enters it. Like distributed mutual exclusion algorithms, the design of a leader election algorithm also depends on the topological structure assumption of the group of processes. Three common topologies, complete, ring, and tree, are described in the following sections.

4.6.1 Complete Topology

In a complete topology, each process in the group can reach any other process in the same group in one message hop. Election messages are sent point-to-point from one process to another. So our first assumption of the operating environment is that all process ids are unique and known to every process. Since a leader election process is initiated upon detection of failures, we must also make some assumptions of the failure model and detection mechanism. To simplify the discussion, we assume the most naive failure model (as follows). Our second assumption is that the communication network is reliable and only the communicating processes may fail. A reliable communication network means that messages are never lost, corrupted, or duplicated and are always orderly delivered in a known finite time. The third assumption concerns failures of a process. A process takes a known finite amount of time to handle a message. Failure of a process halts the computation and does not generate erroneous messages to confuse the system. Furthermore, when a process recovers, it knows that it experienced a failure. The second and third assumptions make it possible to detect a failure and for a failed node to rejoin the group. A failure is reliably detected by setting the time-out interval to be a little larger than the sum of round-trip message delay and message processing time. A failed process can rejoin the group by forcing an election upon its recovery. Alternatively, a failed process can rely on the coordinator to poll periodically for recovered processes to be rejoined to the group. Given these assumptions, we are ready to discuss the **bully** leader election algorithm, introduced by Garcia-Molina.

The bully algorithm is an extrema-finding algorithm. Each process has a global priority (one possibility is to use processor ids), and the highest-priority processor is elected leader. A process starts a leader election if it suspects that the coordinator has failed (e.g., by detection of a time-out) or when it recovers from a failure. The process first sends an inquiry message ($Are - You - Up$) to all nodes that have a higher priority, to check the liveness of the higher-priority processes. If there is any response from the inquiries, the process gives up the election attempt and waits for a higher-priority node to elect itself leader. If there is no response from the higher-priority processes, the process attempts to establish itself as the leader by sending a request message ($Enter - Election$) to all processes with lower priorities. The $Enter - Election$ message informs the lower-priority processes that an election is in progress, and that they should prepare to accept the processor that contacted them as the new leader. The election is not completed until the result is sent and received by all active nodes that have a lower priority.

It is possible that several processors attempt to elect themselves the leader simultaneously. For example, a high-priority failed process might recover while an election is being held. To ensure consistency, the processes enter a transient state upon receiving the $Enter - Election$ message. The initiator of the election will declare itself the new leader only after receiving a response to the $Enter - Election$ message, or timing-out on the response, from every lower-priority process. Now every process is either failed, executing a recovery procedure, or in a transient state. Thus it is safe for the initiator to declare itself leader, since no other processor can think that there is a different leader. Finally, the initiator distributes the new state and tells all other processes that it is the leader of the new computation. The complete bully election algorithm and a discussion of its correctness are given in Chapter 10.

4.6.2 Logical Ring Topology

Leader election algorithms can be greatly simplified if a fixed topology connecting all cooperating processes is assumed. Since the topology is only used to facilitate communication, we might as well assume the simplest one, a logical ring topology. A logical ring is easy to construct and offers the unique property that a message initiated by any node will return to the node, indicating completion of a round of operation or broadcast, without the need for acknowledgments. To find the highest-priority process in a logical ring, an initiator process can start circulating a message with priorities (or ids) appended to the message by each node along the ring. When the message comes back to the initiator, it chooses the highest-priority process in the message and broadcasts the identity of the new leader to all nodes, again, along the ring. The algorithm can be improved in two ways. First, it is not necessary to collect all ids into a single message. To find the maximal id, each node can simply forward the larger of its id and the received value, on the fly, to the successor node. In that way the maximal id will eventually *bubble* through the ring and end up at the leader node. Second, a node that is already involved in the election process does not need to forward a message unless the message contains a value higher than the node's own id. This enhanced ring election algorithm was developed by Chang and Roberts and is illustrated in Figure 4.22.

FIGURE 4.22   Chang and Roberts' ring election algorithm.

The initiator node sets partcipating = true and
send (id) to its successor node;

For each process node ,

    receive (value);

    case

        value > id : participating := true,   **send** (value);

        value < id and participating == false : participating := true,   **send** (id);

        value == id : announce leader;

    end case

Every process has a local variable, *participating*, initially set to *false*, that indicates whether it has been involved in an election process. An initiator asynchronously starts the election by sending an election message containing its id. Each process receiving an election message compares its id with the value in the message. The larger of the two is forwarded to the next node and the process sets *participating = true*. If a process is already participating in the election and receives an election message with an id value less than its own, there is no need to forward the message. A leader is found when the message carrying the maximal value takes a full circle and returns to the highest id node. At that moment, the leader sends its id through the ring, informing all nodes about the new coordinator and setting their *participating* variables to *false*.

In the normal situation when there is only one initiator, the Chang and Roberts algorithm takes an average of $N/2$ messages to reach the maximal node and from there another N messages for the message to return. Both time and message complexities are $O(N)$. Message complexity can be higher in the extreme case when all nodes initiate the leader election at the same time. If no optimizations are made, N simultaneous election initiations take $O(N)$ messages each, so a total of $O(N^2)$ messages are sent. It can be seen that the best and worst cases for the ring algorithm are $O(N)$ and $O(N^2)$, respectively, depending upon whether nodes in the ring are arranged in ascending or descending order of the nodes' ids.

Several ring leader election algorithms with message complexities bounded by $O(N\log N)$ have been proposed. The idea is to disable some elections initiated by lower-priority nodes as much as possible, irrespective of the topological order of nodes. This can be done by comparing a node's id with those of its left and right neighbors. An initiator node remains active only if its id is higher than both neighbors'. Otherwise, it becomes passive and only relays messages. This effectively eliminates at least half of the nodes in each round of message exchanges, yielding the factor of $\log(N)$. This approach requires a bidirectional ring. For a unidirectional ring, the equivalent effect of comparing three nodes can be achieved by buffering two consecutive messages before a node is determined to be in an active or passive mode.

4.6.3 Tree Topologies

In the previous discussion of ring-based leader election algorithms, we did not address the issue of ring management, in particular, how a ring is first formed and how the ring topology is maintained in the face of node failures. Construction and management of a logical ring are easier if the underlying network has a shared communication channel where hardware broadcast facilities are available. A failed ring can be detected and reconfigured effectively by monitoring and broadcasting messages in the channel. In a more general network with irregular network topology, broadcasts are simulated by multiple point-to-point unicasts. In this section, we present some methods for constructing a logical topology in an irregular network. The benefit of having a logical topology is obvious. It defines and connects a group of processes, facilitates the process of leader election, and can be used effectively to communicate between the leader and the subordinates.

We use spanning trees as a representative topological structure for connecting member nodes in a process group. A network of N nodes can be represented in a graph with E edges connecting the nodes. Each node is considered an autonomous entity that exchanges messages with adjacent nodes. The communication costs from a node to its adjacent nodes, represented by weights of the outgoing edges, are known to the node. A spanning tree of size N is a tree that covers a network of N nodes with $N - 1$ edges. A minimum-weight spanning tree (MST) is a spanning tree with the least sum of its edge weights. A spanning tree is an acyclic graph. Any node in a tree can be considered the root of the tree and therefore the leader of the tree of nodes. Each node has a unique path to the root for making requests to the leader. The leader can broadcast effectively to all nodes by using the tree structure. Consequently, the tree structure can also be used to elect a new leader. Distributed algorithms for construction of minimum spanning trees in a network are one of the most intensively studied problems in distributed computing. The problem of leader election and that of constructing minimum spanning trees can be reduced to each other easily. An efficient distributed algorithm for one can be transformed into an algorithm for the other with only minor modifications.

The pioneering work on distributed minimum spanning tree algorithms was done by Gallager, Humbelt, and Spira. Their algorithm is based on *searching* and *combining*. It works by merging fragments, starting from each node being a zero-level fragment. The fragments are merged level by level in a bottom-up fashion until a final fragment, which is made of the edges of a minimum spanning tree, results. Fragments are minimum-weight subtrees of the final MST. Each fragment, asynchronously and independently, finds its minimum-weight outgoing edge of the fragment and uses it to join with a node in a different fragment node, forming a larger fragment of the MST. A tree obtained by merging two minimum-weight subtrees, using a minimum edge, yields another minimum-weight tree. For the purpose of leader election, it seems that any spanning tree will suffice. The weights of edges have no bearing on finding the best leader, so whether the tree has a minimum cost or not is irrelevant. However, the algorithm is distributed, so the final spanning tree must be unique to be agreed upon at the completion of the algorithm. Otherwise, the algorithm may not terminate or may even deadlock. This is why we need to find an MST, and the algorithm works only if the MST is unique. It has been shown that if all edges in a connected graph have unique weights, a unique MST exists. For leader election, we can assume that outgoing edges from a node are uniquely labeled and concatenated with the node's id. If node ids are unique across the system, edge weights are also unique.

A leader can be designated as the last node that merges and yields to the final MST. We can also elect a leader after an MST has been constructed. An initiator broadcasts a *Campaign-For-Leader* (CFL) message, which carries a logical timestamp, to all nodes along the spanning tree. When the broadcast message reaches a leaf node, the node replies with a *Voting* (V) message to its parent node. A voting message is merely a short acknowledgment of a CFL. The need for acknowledgments is the primary difference between tree and ring topologies. A parent node will send its voting message to its parent after all its children's voting messages have been collected. A child does not vote directly for a CFL; the vote is delegated to the parent. Once a node finishes its reply, its part is done. The node then waits for the announcement of the new leader and accepts no further CFL messages. Since there are usually several initiators during this stage, two or more CFL messages may collide at a node. In this case the receiving node will choose as its parent the sender node whose CFL has the lowest timestamp. A tie is broken by the order of the initiators' ids. Note that a node's parent may change several times before it makes a final commitment by sending a reply V that carries all the votes in its subtree. The algorithm allows the node that initiates the leader election first (with the smallest logical timestamp) to become the leader. It is the only node that will be successful in getting all votes from its children.

In a network with frequent failures and configuration changes, it is not realistic to assume that a topology already exists for leader elections. However, a spanning tree can be constructed for any irregular network by *message flooding*. Message flooding is a broadcast mechanism in which every node repeats a received message (which has not been seen yet) to all neighboring nodes, except the node that sent the message. Eventually every node in the network will be reached and a spanning tree is formed. Using this scheme, the initiators *flood* the system with CFL messages. As messages are flooding, a spanning forest with each tree rooted at an initiator is built up. Reply messages (Vs) are sent by backtracking the path from leaf nodes to the root. In the process, each node dynamically changes its parent node to the node that sent the lowest timestamped CFL message. The winner in a flood is the CFL message with the lowest timestamp, and it is the message that is allowed to spread. The winning flood takes over the ground of the losing floods and at the same time tracks down the children that have not replied. When a lower timestamp arrives at an initiator, this initiator is conquered and becomes an ordinary node with a parent. At the end, only the spanning tree with the lowest timestamp will prevail. Since the algorithm uses flooding and does not presume a fixed tree topology before initiation of the leader election, it is very robust in failure-prone networks.

4.7 SUMMARY

This chapter discusses communication models and the name service support for inter-process communication in distributed systems, and it illustrates how message passing interprocess communication affects the implementation of distributed coordination al-gorithms. The primary objective is to show how interprocess communication can be effectively implemented, how process synchronization can be achieved by interprocess communication, and what basic synchronization mechanisms are needed for distributed processing.

We categorize interprocess communication models by three levels of abstraction: basic message passing, request/reply RPC, and transaction communication. Message passing is the lowest level of interprocess communication. The examples of message passing communication illustrated in the chapter are *pipe* and *socket*. The request/reply RPC communication can be built on top of message passing communication. The significance of RPC is that it provides higher-level abstraction for interprocess communication. Due to its communication transparency property, RPC has become a central component in most distributed systems. We have addressed several RPC implementation issues, including security. The transaction and the group communications both require *atomicity* in the operation. We briefly introduce the concepts of *atomic transaction* and *atomic multicast* in this chapter, but leave the detail discussion of these two subjects to Chapters 6 and 12.

Interprocess communication in distributed systems relies on the support of a *name service*. We use the X.500 directory standard to show various approaches for name structure and name resolution. The example shown for the structure of a directory information base also demonstrates a typical implementation of service by multiple cooperating servers in distributed systems.

We conclude the chapter by illustrating two essential distributed coordination problems using message passing communication, *mutual exclusion* and *leader election*. Some basic algorithms for mutual exclusion and leader election are presented in this chapter for completeness of the discussion of process communication. They are covered in greater detail in Chapter 10.

ANNOTATED BIBLIOGRAPHY

The two major issues addressed for the basic message passing are the concept of socket for interdomain process communication and the notion of group and multicast for distributed coordination. Socket is a mature concept and has been widely used in the Internet environment. We use the Berkeley socket and WinSock [Win96] as examples in the discussion. Since socket has become the most fundamental tool for building network software, there is a great need for secure socket facilities. The SSL [Int96] has been proposed for secure socket communication. Many Unix-based network programming books [Ste91, LMKQ89, San91] are available. They are helpful for the socket and RPC programming projects in the exercises. Multicast for group management is still an active research area. We introduce the concept of atomic multicast using simple examples based on research work done by the Cornell ISIS project [BJ87, BSS91, Bir93a]. More references on atomic multicast are cited in Chapter 12. The multicast tree example for message ordering is due to [CL96].

Sockets are a network programming tool while RPC is a communication facility for distributed systems. RPC provides communication transparency by shielding the underlying low-level details of message passing from the users. RPC was first introduced in the Xerox network system [MMS79, Xer81]. It has been explored in many research projects such as Cedar [BN84] at University of Illinois, Argus [Lis88] at MIT, and Mach [DJT89] at CMU. Most commercial systems have implemented RPC, including the one from Sun that we use as an example in this chapter. Services provided by RPC are identified by names. The RPC concept can be extended to cooperative autonomous systems if requested services can be described by using attributes. Attribute-based service models are the future direction of client/server distributed systems.

We describe the transaction communication as a special case of database transaction [EGLT76] where a message needs to be atomically multicast to a group of replicated or partitioned servers. The all-or-none atomicity of multicast can be accomplished with a two-phase commit protocol [Gra78, LS76]. The protocol illustrates how failures are dealt with to achieve an atomic commit for multicast communication in distributed systems. We will revisit atomic multicast, along with reliable multicast, in Chapter 12. For general database transactions, there is the issue of serializability, in addition to atomicity. Since serializability is commonly perceived from the data point of view, we delay the discussion of transactions to Chapter 6.

Name and directory service is the most essential component in distributed systems since all network communication and access operations rely on the service. The Domain Name Service [Moc87] for Internet uses a name-based organizationally partitioned hierarchical name structure. It is primarily used for resolving network host names and addresses. X.500 [CCI88] supports both name-based and a more flexible structure-free attribute-based resolution. It provides a directory schema for all objects in the network. DNS and X.500 are the prevailing standards for name and directory service. The name-based hierarchical structure of DNS and the attribute-based structure of X.500 have been incorporated in the DCE name service [OSF92, RKF92].

Distributed mutual exclusion and leader election using message passing interprocess communication are two classical distributed coordination problems. They have been studied extensively. The problem of distributed mutual exclusion can be tackled by using either a contention- or token-based approach. For the contention-based, approach we present the timestamp prioritized schemes by [Lam78, RA81] and a voting scheme by [Tho79, Mae85]. The complexity of the contention-based algorithms can be greatly reduced if an unique control token is available in the system for the purpose of arbitration. Token passing assumes a given logical topology. Examples of token-based mutual exclusion algorithms are due to [Ray88, Ray89b] for ring and tree topologies and to [SK85] for the broadcast topology.

Many similarities exist between the mutual exclusion and leader election issues. A logical topology helps to eliminate contention and to facilitate communication. Leader election algorithms are categorized with respect to the topological assumptions. The bully algorithm [GM82] uses a complete topology. Extrema-finding algorithms for ring topology with various assumptions [CR79, Pet82, HS80, DKR82, Fra82] can be found in the literature. Examples of leader election using the concept of spanning trees are due to [GHS83, Gaf85, CT85, CLNW92]. The significance of the tree topology is that logical spanning trees can be constructed by using flooding without a presumption of the network topology. Therefore it is practical for systems with an unknown or changing topology.

An in-depth study of distributed mutual exclusion and leader election continues in Chapter 10. Chapter 11 extends the distributed coordination problems to a more general and fundamental problem: distributed agreement. It addresses the issue of how to reach consensus in distributed systems that possibly have faulty processes and processors.

EXERCISES

1. In a system that supports only blocking receive primitives, how can user programs accomplish message passing communication that is effectively equivalent to using nonblocking receives?

2. Is there any advantage if a receive primitive allows user processes to retrieve messages with a certain key? Should this primitive be blocking or nonblocking? How should source and destination addresses be identified? Relate this receive primitive to the two-producer and two-consumer problem in Chapter 3 Exercises.

3. In a network system, why is using a port more desirable than using a process identifier or mailbox as message destination? What advantages can we gain if communication can be addressed to a group of ports?

4. Ports are unidirectional communication channels with a data structure implemented and managed by the kernel. What information needs to be contained in a port data structure?

5. Write a pseudo code semaphore solution for the producer/consumer problem implementing pipes.

6. How are certified and anonymous servers handled differently in the handshake protocol for the SSL (Secure Socket Layer)?

7. In the sequence vector causal order multicast protocol, what is the effect on the protocol's correctness and performance if some messages are not received by all members of the group? This could happen if messages are lost or sent point to point. Why is the protocol limited to multicast in a single group?

8. In the two-phase total-order multicast protocol, is it possible for commitment messages to carry a same logical timestamp? How does it effect the protocol if group members have very different logical clocks?

9. In the Figure 4.23 time/space diagram, three messages are broadcast to a group. Using the sequence vector causal order multicast protocol, show which message(s) must be buffered before delivery to ensure causal ordering.

10. Give an example of an RPC operation that is idempotent and another example that is not idempotent.

FIGURE 4.23 A multicast group.

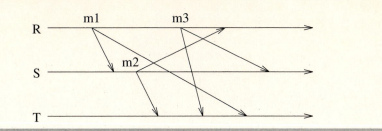

11. Some variations of RPC are of interest. Show why the following RPCs could be useful:
    a. Asynchronous RPC: nonblocking RPC calls
    b. Light-weight RPC: RPC calls within the same host computer
    c. Null RPC: RPC calls with no parameter passing and null execution
12. Does it make sense to have a *multicast* RPC?
13. Orphan computation caused by client crashes can be cleaned up by the recovering clients or the server, or by expiration of RPC operations. Show the advantages and disadvantages of each approach.
14. How are authenticity, confidentiality, integrity, and originality achieved in Sun's secure RPC?
15. Show how the isolation and durability of the ACID properties could have an effect on the atomicity and consistency of the transaction communication.
16. The two-phase atomic commit protocol consists of a voting phase and a commitment phase. Is atomic commit achievable in one phase? Outline a one-phase solution and show its limitation.
17. In the two-phase atomic commit protocol, each client has an uncertainty period after it has voted YES for a request and is waiting for the final decision from the coordinator. What could prolong this uncertainty period? Can the client time out and unilaterally abort the transaction? What can be done to shorten the delay?
18. What are the major differences between DNS and X.500?
19. Frequently used names and their attributes can be cached at a client or at intermediate name servers to eliminate or reduce the need for name resolution. Show that caches also improve fault tolerance.
20. When do caches for name service need to be invalidated? Propose a scheme for cache invalidation.
21. Alias and group names offer flexibility in naming. Are there potential problems in implementing them?
22. Derive the nonempty intersecting request sets for a system of seven and nine processes, respectively. Show a scenario of a deadlock sequence in each system.
23. An instance of the logical tree structure for the token-based mutual exclusion protocol is shown in Figure 4.24. All request queues are empty and the token is at node 1. At this moment, requests to claim the token come every one unit time apart in the order of (7,6,5,4,3,2,1). Assume that the communication delay between each pair of nodes is also one-unit time. Show the distribution of the requests in the

FIGURE 4.24   A logical tree topology.

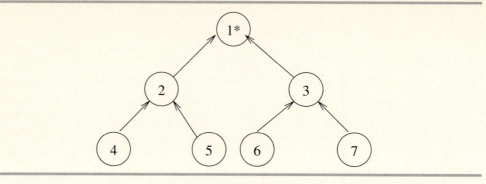

request queue at each node after node 7 has claimed the token and has been in its critical section for five units of time. How are the request queues linked to form a global FIFO queue? What is the order of execution sequence?

24. Use the Chang and Roberts ring election algorithm and assume that all nodes initiate the election simultaneously. Show that the best- and worst-case message complexities are $O(N)$ and $O(N^2)$, respectively.

25. What are the time and message complexities of leader election using tree topologies?

26. (Programming project) Use the socket facilities to write a concurrent time server. The time server accepts concurrent time accesses from *reader processes* and exclusive time updates from *writer processes*. Since currency of time is more important, we assume that writers have priority over readers (the writer preference problem). Time update must be monotonically increasing. Run the server on a machine with a well-known host address and port number. Multiple instances of the reader and writer processes should run on different machines asynchronously and concurrently.

27. (Programming project) Implement the same time service as in Exercise 26, but use an RPC package instead of sockets. Modify the stub procedures generated by the RPC generator if necessary. Compare the advantages and the disadvantages of socket and RPC implementations of the time server.

CHAPTER

Distributed Process Scheduling

Communication and synchronization facilities are essential system components for supporting concurrent execution of interacting processes. Before execution, processes need to be scheduled and allocated with resources. The primary objective of scheduling is to enhance overall system performance metrics such as process completion time and processor utilization. The existence of multiple processing nodes in distributed systems presents a challenging problem for scheduling processes onto processors, and vice versa. Scheduling not only is performed locally on each node but also globally across the system. Distributed processes may be executed on remote processing nodes and may migrate from node to node to redistribute the work load to improve performance. The secondary objective of scheduling is to achieve location and performance transparencies by distributed process scheduling.

The issue of process (or job) scheduling has been studied extensively in operations research. Many theoretical results on the complexity of multiprocessor scheduling are available. However, process scheduling in distributed systems touches upon several practical considerations that are often omitted in the traditional multiprocessor scheduling analyses. In distributed systems, communication overhead is nonnegligible, the effect of the underlying architecture cannot be ignored, and the dynamic behavior of the system must be addressed. These practical implications contribute to the complexity of distributed process scheduling.

This chapter presents a model for capturing the effect of communication and system architectures on scheduling. The discussion of distributed process scheduling is organized into two areas: static process scheduling and dynamic load sharing and balancing. The implementation of distributed scheduling algorithms requires remote execution and/or process migration capabilities in the system. Some implementation issues for remote execution and process migration are discussed. The chapter concludes with an introduction of distributed real-time systems, where scheduling is time critical and merits special consideration.

5.1 A System Performance Model

Parallel and distributed algorithms are represented by sets of multiple processes governed by rules that regulate the interactions among processes. Mapping an algorithm onto an architecture may be considered as part of the algorithm design or may be treated separately as a scheduling problem for a given algorithm and a given system architecture. In Chapter 3 we used graph models to describe process communication. Let us look again at how process interactions are generally represented in terms of mapping. Figure 5.1 shows a simple example of a program computation consisting of four processes mapped to a two-processor multiple computer system. Process interaction is expressed differently in each of the three models.

In the **precedence process model** shown in Figure 5.1(a), processes are represented by a **Directed Acyclic Graph** (DAG). The directed edges denote the precedence relationships between processes and may incur communication overhead if the processes connected by an edge are mapped to two different processors. This model is best applied to the concurrent processes generated by concurrent language constructs such as *cobegin/coend* or *fork/join*. A useful measure for scheduling such a set of processes is to minimize the total completion time of the task, which includes both computation and communication times. The **communication process model** in Figure 5.1(b) depicts a different scenario, where processes are created to coexist and communicate asynchronously. The undirected edges in the communication process model only represent the need for communication

FIGURE 5.1   Partitioning of processes.

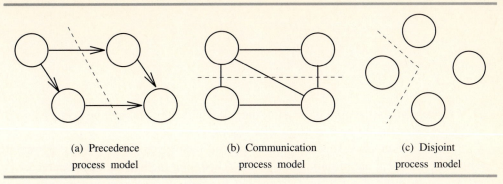

| (a) Precedence | (b) Communication | (c) Disjoint |
| process model | process model | process model |

between processes. Since execution time is not explicit in the model, the goal of scheduling may be to optimize the total cost of communication and computation. The task is partitioned in such a way that minimizes the interprocessor communication and computation costs of processes on processors. Precedence and communication process models are **interacting process models.**

For the **disjoint process model** in Figure 5.1(c), process interaction is implicit, and we assume that processes can be run independently and completed in finite time. Processes are mapped to the processors to maximize the utilization of the processors and minimize the **turnaround time** of the processes. Turnaround time is defined as the sum of service and queueing times due to waiting for other processes. In the dynamic case we allow processes to migrate between processors to achieve the effect of load sharing and balancing. If processes are allowed to migrate from a heavily loaded node to a lightly loaded site, the initial placement of processes is not critical. Furthermore, the performance can be significantly improved since scheduling of processes becomes adaptive to the change of system load. Load sharing and balancing are not limited to disjoint processes. If the processes do communicate with one another, the migration strategy should consider the trade-off between the change in interprocessor communication requirements due to the switching of processors and the gain from load sharing.

Partitioning a task into multiple processes for execution can result in a **speedup** of the total task completion time. Speedup as a performance measure is a focus of interest in the design of parallel and distributed algorithms. Computational speedup is a function of the algorithm design and the efficiency of the scheduling algorithm that maps the algorithm onto an underlying system architecture. A speedup model that describes and analyzes the interrelationship of the algorithm, system, and scheduling is given below. In the model, the speedup factor S, which is a function of the parallel algorithm, system architecture, and schedule of execution, is denoted by:

$$S = F(Algorithm, System, Schedule)$$

S can be written as:

$$S = \frac{OSPT}{CPT} = \frac{OSPT}{OCPT_{ideal}} \times \frac{OCPT_{ideal}}{CPT} = S_i \times S_d$$

where

- $OSPT$ = optimal sequential processing time; the best time that can be achieved on a single processor using the best sequential algorithm.
- CPT = concurrent processing time; the actual time achieved on an n-processor system with the concurrent algorithm and a specific scheduling method being considered.
- $OCPT_{ideal}$ = optimal concurrent processing time on an ideal system; the best time that can be achieved with the concurrent algorithm being considered on an ideal n-processor system (a system with no interprocessor communication overhead) and scheduled by an optimal scheduling policy.
- S_i = the ideal speedup obtained by using a multiple processor system over the best sequential time.
- S_d = the degradation of the system due to actual implementation compared to an ideal system.

In order to distinguish the role of algorithm, system, and scheduling, the formula for speedup is further refined. S_i can be rewritten as:

$$S_i = \frac{RC}{RP} \times n$$

where

$$RP = \frac{\sum_{i=1}^{m} P_i}{OSPT}$$

and

$$RC = \frac{\sum_{i=1}^{m} P_i}{OCPT_{ideal} \times n}$$

and n is the number of processors. The term $\sum_{i=1}^{m} P_i$ is the total computation of the concurrent algorithm where m is the number of tasks in the algorithm. It is normally greater than $OSPT$ since additional codes may be needed when converting the sequential algorithm to the concurrent algorithm. S_d can be rewritten as:

$$S_d = \frac{1}{1 + \rho}$$

where

$$\rho = \frac{CPT - OCPT_{ideal}}{OCPT_{ideal}}$$

In the expression for S_i, RP is the **Relative Processing** requirement, which is the ratio of the total computation time needed for the parallel algorithm to the processing time of the optimal sequential algorithm. It shows how much loss of speedup is due to the substitution of the best sequential algorithm by an algorithm better adapted for concurrent implementation but which may have a greater total processing need. RP is different from S_d in that RP is a loss of parallelism due to algorithm conversion, while S_d is a degradation of parallelism due to algorithm implementation.

RC is the **Relative Concurrency**, which measures how far from optimal the usage of the n-processor is. It reflects how well adapted the given problem and its algorithm are to the ideal n-processor system. $RC = 1$ corresponds to the best use of the processors. A good concurrent algorithm is one that minimizes RP and maximizes RC. The final expression for the speedup S is

$$S = \frac{RC}{RP} \times \frac{1}{1 + \rho} \times n$$

In short, the speed up factor S is a function of RC (theoretical loss of parallelism), RP (increase in total computation requirement), ρ (loss of parallelism when implemented on a real machine), and n (number of processors utilized).

The term ρ is called the *efficiency loss*, which is defined as the ratio of the real system overhead due to all causes to the ideal optimal processing time. It is a function of scheduling and the system architecture. It would be useful to decompose ρ into two independent terms: $\rho = \rho_{sched} + \rho_{syst}$, the efficiency loss due to scheduling and the system, respectively. However, this is not easy to do since scheduling and the system are so intertwined. Communication overhead can sometimes be hidden and overlapped with other computations by scheduling, and therefore may not contribute to the loss of efficiency. This is a major point for scheduling processes with interprocessor communication overhead. A good schedule is the best possible schedule on a given system that hides the communication overhead as much as possible. The following paragraph attempts to illustrate the interdependence between scheduling and system factors and decomposes the two factors in a limited way.

Let X represent a multiple computer system under investigation and Y' represent a scheduling policy that is extended for system X from a scheduling policy Y on the corresponding ideal system. $CPT(X, Y')$ and $CPT(X, Y)$ are the concurrent processing times for the given machine X under scheduling strategies Y' and Y, respectively. The efficiency loss ρ can be expressed as

$$
\begin{aligned}
\rho \quad &= \quad \frac{CPT(X, Y') - OCPT_{ideal}}{OCPT_{ideal}} \\[2mm]
&= \quad \frac{CPT(X, Y') - CPT_{ideal}(Y)}{OCPT_{ideal}} + \frac{CPT_{ideal}(Y) - OCPT_{ideal}}{OCPT_{ideal}} \\[2mm]
&= \quad \rho_{syst} + \rho'_{sched}
\end{aligned}
$$

FIGURE 5.2   Efficiency loss due to scheduling and communication.

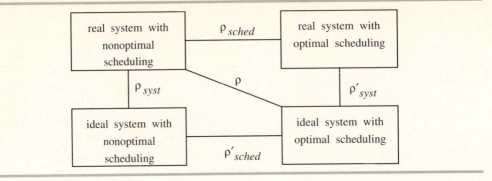

Similarly, we can reverse the decomposition process by analyzing the efficiency loss due to nonoptimal scheduling before analyzing the effect of nonideal system. That is,

$$
\begin{aligned}
\rho &= \frac{CPT(X, Z) - OCPT_{ideal}}{OCPT_{ideal}} \\
&= \frac{CPT(X, Z) - OCPT(X)}{OCPT_{ideal}} + \frac{OCPT(X) - OCPT_{ideal}}{OCPT_{ideal}} \\
&= \rho_{sched} + \rho'_{syst}
\end{aligned}
$$

Figure 5.2 demonstrates this decomposition of efficiency loss due to scheduling and system communication. The significance of the impact of communication on system performance must be carefully addressed in the design of distributed scheduling algorithms.

The **unified speedup model** integrates three major components, algorithm development, system architecture, and scheduling policy, with the objective of minimizing the total completion time (**makespan**) of a set of interacting processes. If processes are not constrained by precedence relations and are free to be redistributed or moved around among processors in the system, performance can be further improved by sharing the workload. That is, processes can be moved from heavily loaded nodes to idle nodes (if they exist). One can go a step further to distribute the workload among all nodes as evenly as possible, either statically or dynamically. Static workload distribution is referred to as **load sharing**, and dynamic workload distribution is called **load balancing**. The benefits of workload distribution are increased utilization of processors and improved turnaround time for processes. Migration of processes attempts to reduce queueing time, at the cost of additional communication overhead.

The desirability of sharing the workload in distributed systems is quite obvious. It is almost universally true that in any computer installation that consists of multiple loosely coupled processing nodes, there are always some heavily loaded and some lightly loaded nodes, but a large percentage of them are simply idle. To achieve a higher utilization of the processing power, processes can be dispatched to the idle processors statically upon arrival (corresponding to the processor pool model) or can migrate dynamically from heavily loaded processors to lightly loaded processors (corresponding to the workstation

FIGURE 5.3   Processor-pool and workstation queueing models.

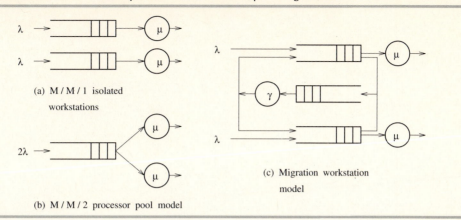

(a) M / M / 1 isolated
    workstations

(b) M / M / 2 processor pool model

(c) Migration workstation
    model

model). Turnaround time of a process can also be improved. Figure 5.3 shows two simple queueing models for the processor pool and workstation distributed environment, compared with a baseline isolated workstations system. For clarity, only two processing nodes are shown in the models. For the processor pool model, a process is dispatched to an available processor and remains there statically throughout the entirety of its execution.

The performance of systems described as queueing models can be computed using a branch of mathematics known as **queuing theory**. The standard notation for describing the stochastic properties of a queue is **Kendall's notation**. An $X/Y/c$ queue is one with an arrival process X, a service time distribution of Y, and c servers. For example, we can describe the processor pool as an M/M/2 queue. The M stands for a *Markovian distribution*, which is analytically tractable. The two servers model a system in which a waiting job can be serviced by either processor. More generally, we can model a processor pool as an M/M/k queue.

In the **migration workstation model**, processes are allowed to move from one workstation to the other. The decision of when, where, and how to migrate processes is discussed later and is not explicitly shown in the figure. Migration of a process incurs some communication delay, which is modeled by a communication queue serviced by the communication channel. The migration rate γ is a function of the channel bandwidth, process migration protocol, and more importantly, context and state information of the process being transferred.

Figure 5.4 shows the benefit of load distribution (or redistribution) in the processor pool and workstation models. The upper and lower bounds of average process turnaround time are represented by the two equations for M/M/1 and M/M/2 models:

$$TT_1 = \frac{1}{\mu - \lambda}$$

$$TT_2 = \frac{\mu}{(\mu + \lambda)(\mu - \lambda)}$$

FIGURE 5.4   Comparison of performance for workload sharing.

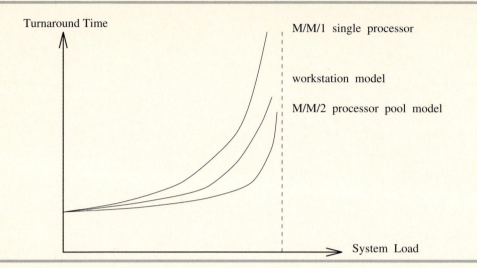

TT_i is the average turnaround time and λ and μ are the arrival and service rates of each processing node. The closed-form formulas can be found in classical queueing theory books. The performance of the workstation model with communication overhead falls between M/M/1, where no sharing of the workload is attempted, and M/M/2, an ideal processor pool model with negligible communication overhead. The process migration rate γ varies from zero to infinity, which asymptotically approaches the performance of M/M/1 and M/M/2, respectively.

5.2 STATIC PROCESS SCHEDULING

Static process scheduling (or deterministic scheduling theory) has been studied extensively. The problem is defined as scheduling a set of partially ordered tasks on a nonpreemptive multiprocessor system of identical processors to minimize the overall finishing time (makespan). Many excellent review articles exist, including those by Coffman and Graham. Research in this area has shown that except for some very restricted cases (such as scheduling tasks with unit execution time or two-processor models), scheduling to optimize makespan are NP-complete. Therefore, most research is oriented toward using approximate or heuristic methods to obtain a *near optimal* solution to the problem. The underlying computing system of the classical problem assumes no interprocessor overhead due to communication or memory contention. This assumption may be reasonable for some multiprocessor architectures. However, it is no longer valid for message passing distributed systems or computer networks in which interprocessor communication is not only nonnegligible but is also an important characteristic of the system. Since the problem is hard enough without the consideration of communication, for systems with nonnegligible communication overhead we concentrate on finding *good* but easy-to-implement heuristic approaches for scheduling processes in distributed systems.

A good heuristic distributed scheduling algorithm is one that can best balance and overlap computation and communication. Consider the two extreme schedules, one where we schedule all processes on a single processor and the other where a processor is assigned to each process. The former has no communication overhead but enjoys no concurrency. The latter has maximal concurrency but incurs the most communication overhead. Our scheduling objective is to strike a compromise by absorbing or hiding communication as much as possible and at the same time achieving higher concurrency.

In static scheduling, the mapping of processes to processors is determined before the execution of the processes. Once a process is started, it stays at the processor until completion. That is, it is never preempted to move to another processor. A scheduling algorithm must have good knowledge about process behavior such as process execution time, precedence relationships and communication patterns between processes. This information might be available from a compiler of a concurrent language. The scheduling decision is centralized and nonadaptive. These are some of the drawbacks of static scheduling.

In the following two sections we illustrate the impact of communication in static scheduling, using the precedence and communication process models.

5.2.1 Precedence Process Model

Precedence process models in Figure 5.1(a) were used for static multiprocessor scheduling where the primary objective is to minimize overall makespan. In the precedence process model, a program is represented by a DAG. Each node in the graph denotes a task with a known execution time. An edge represents a precedence relationship between two tasks and is labeled with a weight showing message units to be transferred to the successor task upon completion of a task. Figure 5.5(a) is an example of a DAG program that consists of seven tasks (A through G) with given task execution times and message units between related tasks. The underlying architecture, on which the tasks are to be mapped, can be characterized by a communication system model showing unit communication delays between processors. Figure 5.5(b) is an example of a communication system model with three processors (P1, P2, P3). The unit communication costs are nonnegligible for interprocessor communication and negligible (zero weight on the internal edge) for intraprocessor communication. The model is very simple. It captures the communication without showing the detail of the hardware architecture. The communication cost between two tasks is computed by multiplying the unit communication cost in the communication system graph and the message units in the precedence process graph. For example, if tasks A and E in Figure 5.5 are scheduled on processors P1 and P3, respectively, the communication cost is $8 = 2 \times 4$. Rayward-Smith considered a similar but more restricted model in which all processes have unit computation and communication times. Even with such a simple assumption, it was shown that finding the minimum makespan is NP-complete. So we will rely on heuristic algorithms for finding a good mapping of the process model to the system model.

FIGURE 5.5 Precedence process and communication system models.

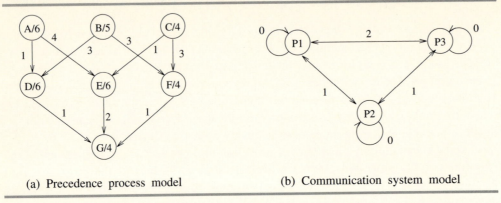

(a) Precedence process model   (b) Communication system model

Without considering communication overhead, we can consider a simple greedy heuristic, the **List Scheduling** (LS) strategy: No processor remains idle if there are some tasks available that it could process. For the DAG in Figure 5.5(a), the resulting schedule is shown in Figure 5.6(a). The total completion time is 16 units. For precedence process graphs, the notion of a **critical path** is useful. A critical path is the longest execution path in the DAG, which is the lower bound of the makespan. The critical path is a very important concept for scheduling. It is frequently used to analyze the performance of a heuristic algorithm. The critical path for the graph in Figure 5.5(a) is (ADG or AEG) of length $16 = 6 + 6 + 4$. Therefore, the LS in Figure 5.6(a) (the makespan happens to be 16, too) is optimal even though the algorithm is heuristic. Many heuristic scheduling algorithms also rely on a critical path in deriving priorities for scheduling tasks. A simple heuristic scheduling strategy is to map all tasks in a critical path onto a single processor. For the example in Figure 5.5(a), tasks A, D, and G on the critical path are mapped to process P1.

With communication overhead, we can extend the List Scheduling directly. The Extended List Scheduling (ELS) first allocates tasks to processors by applying LS as if the system were free of communication overhead. It then adds the necessary communication delays to the schedule obtained by LS. The communication delays are computed by multiplying the unit communication cost and message units. The result of ELS for the same scheduling problem has a makespan of 28 units, as shown in Figure 5.6(b). Dashed-lines in the figure represent waiting for communication (unit communication cost multiplied by number of message units).

The ELS strategy is far from optimal. The basic problem is that its scheduling decision is made without anticipating the communication. The algorithm can be improved if we delay the decision as long as possible until we know more about the system. Following this greedy strategy, we have an Earliest Task First[1] (ETF) scheduling: the earliest schedulable task is scheduled first. Using the strategy in the same example, we would delay scheduling task F because task E will become schedulable first if communication

---

[1] The material on the Earliest Task First scheduling algorithm and the speedup model is from the dissertation research by J. J. Hwang (National Chiao Tung University) and Frank Anger (NSF) at the University of Florida.

FIGURE 5.6   Makespan calculations for LS, ELS, and ETF.

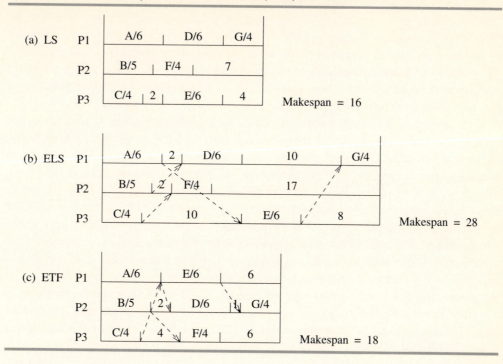

delay is also included in the calculation. The ETF scheduling in Figure 5.6(c) gives a better result of an 18-unit makespan.

The process and system models are fairly general for modeling the problem of scheduling processes in a DAG onto a system with communication delays. The example shows that an optimal schedule for one system is not necessarily a good schedule on another system with different communication architecture. A better schedule can be obtained by overlapping communication with computation, and therefore effectively *hiding* much of the communication overhead. The concept of critical path can be used to assist communication hiding (absorb communication overhead in the critical path). Any computation path that is shorter than the critical path can afford to absorb some communication overhead by overlapping with other computation without affecting the overall makespan.

5.2.2 Communication Process Model

The precedence graph representation of processes discussed in the previous section is a computational model. Programs expressed in a DAG are typically user applications, where precedence constraints among tasks in a program are explicitly specified by the users. The primary objective of task scheduling is to achieve maximal concurrency for task execution within a program. Minimizing task communication is only secondary, although it has a significant impact on the major performance index, makespan.

Process scheduling for many system applications has a very different perspective, since processes in a system application may be created independently. There are no precedence constraints except the need for communication among processes. Processes do not have an explicit completion time as in the case of the precedence process model. The purposes of process scheduling are to maximize resource utilization and to minimize interprocess communication. These applications are best modeled by the communication process model, as shown in Figure 5.1(b).

A communication process model is modeled as a undirected graph G with node and edge sets V and E, where nodes represent processes and the weight on an edge is the amount of interaction between two connected processes. The assumptions of process execution and communication are similar to but slightly different from those of the precedence process model. The process execution and communication are represented in *cost*. Process execution cost is a function of the processor to which a process is assigned for execution. The implication is that the processors are not identical (different in speed and hardware). We use the notation $e_j(p_i)$ to denote the execution cost of process j on p_i, where p_i is the processor allocated to process j. The communication cost $c_{i,j}(p_i, p_j)$ between two processes i and j, allocated to two different processors p_i and p_j, is proportional to the weight of an edge connecting i and j. The communication cost is considered negligible (zero cost) if $i = j$. The problem of finding an optimal assignment of m process modules to P processors with respect to the following objective function is called the **Module Allocation** problem.

$$Cost(G, P) = \sum_{j \in V(G)} e_j(p_i) + \sum_{(i,j) \in E(G)} c_{i,j}(p_i, p_j)$$

The module allocation problem was first formulated by Stone and has been studied extensively since. Like most graph applications, the general module allocation problems are NP-complete except for a few restricted cases. For $P = 2$, Stone suggested an efficient polynomial-time solution using Ford–Fulkerson's maximum-flow algorithm. Polynomial-time algorithms were also developed by Bokhari and Towsley for some special graph topologies such as trees or serial-parallel graphs. In the following example we will illustrate the concept by using Stone's two-processor commodity model for partitioning a communication process graph to achieve minimum total execution and communication cost.

Consider a program consisting of six processes to be allocated to two processors, A and B, for minimizing the total computation and communication cost. The execution time of each process on either processor is shown in Figure 5.7(a). Figure 5.7(b) is a graph showing interprocess communication among the six processes. The two processors are not identical. For example, process 1 takes 5 units of cost to run on processor A but 10 units on processor B, and process 2 can only be allocated to processor A. The label assigned to an edge in the communication graph is the communication cost if the two adjoining processes are allocated to different processors. To map processes on the processors, we can partition the graph by drawing a line that cuts through some edges. The partition results in two disjoint graphs, one for each processor. The set of edges removed by the

FIGURE 5.7   Computation cost and communication graphs.

Process	Cost on A	Cost on B
1	5	10
2	2	infinity
3	4	4
4	6	3
5	5	2
6	infinity	4

(a) Computation cost

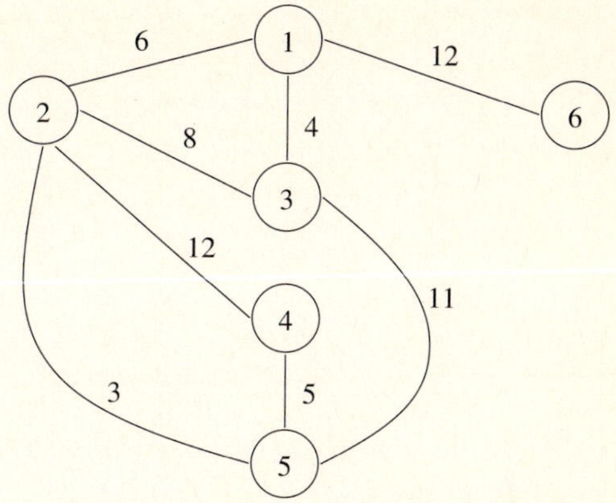

(b) Communication cost

cut is called a *cut set*. The cost of a cut set is the sum of weights of the edges, which represents the total interprocess communication cost between two processors.

The optimization problem would be trivial if we only had to minimize the communication cost, since we could map all processes onto a single processor and eliminate all interprocessor communication. The optimization is meaningless unless we can also satisfy some other computation or implementation constraints. The condition that restricts some processes to run only on certain processors in Figure 5.7(a) is a good example of a computational constraint. Some implementations may require that no more than k processes are allocated to each processor or, that processes are allocated to all processors evenly.

Figure 5.8 shows the minimum-cost cut set for the problem in Figure 5.7 using the cost function $Cost(G, P)$. In the diagram, two new nodes representing processors A and B are added to the communication graph, along with dashed-line edges between a processor to every process node. The weight assigned to an edge between processor A and process i is the cost to execute process i on processor B. This weight assignment makes sense, because a cut through the dashed-line edge assigns the process to execute on processor B. We will only consider cuts that separate the processor nodes (A, B). The sum of the weights of the edges in the cut is the sum of the communication and computation costs.

Computing the minimum-cost cut set for the above model is equivalent to finding the *maximum flow* and *minimum cut* in a commodity-flow network. The graph in Figure 5.8 can be interpreted as a network of highways (edges) connecting cities (nodes) together. The weight on an edge is the capacity of that segment of highway. Nodes A and B are source and destination cities to which commodities are to flow. Given a commodity graph, the optimization problem is to find the *maximum flow* from source to destination. Ford and Fulkerson show a labeling algorithm that is a systematic search for a *flow augmenting path* from source to destination (this algorithm can be found in most algorithm textbooks).

FIGURE 5.8 Minimum-cost cut.

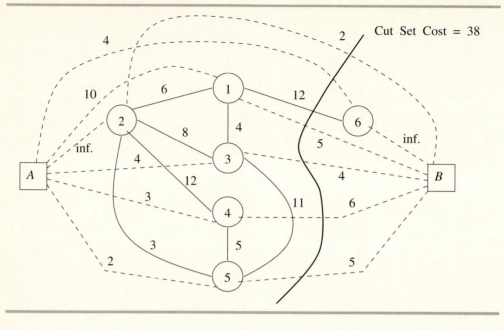

They also prove that the *maximum flow* for a network is equal to the *minimum cut* set that separates the source and destination in the graph. The maximum-flow algorithm and the maximum-flow minimum-cut theorem match perfectly with the optimization of the two-processor module allocation (process scheduling) problem.

To generalize the problem beyond two processors, Stone outlines a solution to the three-processor system and suggests a repetitive approach using the two-processor algorithm to solve n-processor problems. To find a module allocation of m processes to n processors, the maximum-flow minimum-cut algorithm can be applied to a processor p_i and an imaginary super processor P that consists of the remaining processors. After some processes have been scheduled to p_i, the same procedure is repeated iteratively on the super processor until all processes are assigned.

The module allocation problem is complex because the optimization objectives of minimizing computation and communication costs are often conflicting. The problem is important enough to justify heuristic solutions. One approach is to separate the optimization of computation and communication into two independent phases. In a network where communication cost may be more significant than computation cost, we can merge processes with higher interprocess interaction into clusters of processes. Processes in each cluster are then assigned to the processor that minimizes the computation cost. Merging processes eliminates interprocessor communication but may impose a higher computation burden on the processor and thus reduce concurrency. A simple heuristic approach is to merge only processes with communication costs higher than a certain threshold C. In addition, the number of processes in a cluster is constrained. For example, the total execution cost of the processes in a single cluster cannot exceed another threshold X.

Using the example in Figure 5.7 and an estimated average communication cost $C = 9$ as the threshold, three clusters, (2,4), (1,6), (3,5), can be found. Obviously clusters (2,4) and (1,6) must be mapped to processors A and B, respectively. Cluster (3,5) can be assigned to either A or B. Assigning them to B has a lower computation cost but incurs a much higher communication cost. So they are assigned to A, resulting in a computation cost of 17 on A and 14 on B and a communication cost of 10 between A and B. The total cost is 41, which is slightly higher than the optimal cost of 38 derived from the minimum cut algorithm. The threshold value X can be used to balance the execution load on processors. Using an appropriate X to distribute the workload evenly will also force the assignment of (3,5) to processor A in the same example.

The complexity of optimal static scheduling is high. Simple heuristic algorithms are attractive. Also, heuristic solutions make more sense if we only have approximate information about computation and communication costs. Moreover, the performance of initial process assignment is not critical if processes can be moved after they have been assigned. This is one of the motivations for the dynamic process scheduling presented in the following section.

5.3 DYNAMIC LOAD SHARING AND BALANCING

The two scheduling examples shown in the previous section are *static* scheduling. Once a process is assigned to a processing site, it remains there until its execution has been completed. Both examples require prior knowledge of the execution times and the communication behaviors of the processes. For the precedence process model, the primary objective of scheduling is to minimize the overall completion time, while the communication process model tries to minimize the communication overhead and at the same time satisfy some computational constraints. Nice mathematical models and algorithms are available for the computation of the schedules. However, the computation is *centralized* and occurs at a fixed point in time.

The assumption of prior knowledge of processes is not realistic for most distributed applications. Without knowing the computation and communication requirements, we have to rely on an ad hoc scheduling strategy that is adaptive (*dynamic*) and allows its assignment decision to be made locally (*decentralized*). In this section we will use the disjoint process model in Figure 5.1(c) to show some dynamic scheduling strategies. The use of the disjoint process model does not imply that all processes considered are disjoint. Since we do not know how these processes interact with each other, we might as well schedule them assuming that they are disjoint. This means that we are ignoring the effect of the interdependency among processes. Under this model, the objective of scheduling will have to be different from that of the precedence and communication process models. The most intuitive performance goals for scheduling that we can target are the *utilization* of the system and the *fairness* to the user processes. Utilization of processors has a direct bearing on the performance measures such as throughput and completion time. Fairness is difficult to define and its effect on performance is not clear. Let us demonstrate how utilization and fairness can be used as an objective function for the scheduling of disjoint processes in a distributed system.

A simple heuristic strategy to achieve higher utilization of a system is to avoid having idle processors as much as possible. Let us assume that we can designate a controller process that maintains the information about the queue size of each processor. Processes arrive and depart from the system asynchronously. An arriving process makes a request to the controller for the assignment to a processor. The controller schedules the process to the processor that has the shortest waiting queue. To update the queue size information, each processor must inform the controller whenever a process completes and departs from the processing site. Joining the shortest queue is a static **load sharing** scheduling strategy that attempts to reduce processor idling and to equalize queue sizes (**load balancing**) among processors. Load balancing is a stronger requirement than load sharing. It improves utilization and achieves a sort of fairness in terms of equal workload for each processor. Load balancing has the effect of reducing the overall average turnaround time of the processes. This strategy can be made adaptive by allowing processes to migrate from a longer queue to a shorter queue dynamically. Its queueing model was presented in Figure 5.3(c), the workstation model. Utilization and fairness are further improved by dynamic **load redistribution** (or **process migration**).

The fairness described above is not very meaningful since it is based on the system's rather than the user's perspective. Processes are generated by users on each local site. A fair system from the user's viewpoint is a system that gives priority to a user's process if the user has a lesser share of the computation resources. Using this criteria, the controller can keep track of the number of processors that are currently allocated to the processes generated by a particular user. Whenever a processor becomes available, the controller allocates that processor to a waiting process at a user site that has the least share of the processor pool. Utilization is maintained by trying to allocate every available processor. The criteria may be adjusted to take into account the queue size, which reflects local workload, and therefore also achieves limited load balancing. Comparing with the join-to-the-shortest-queue scheduling, we notice that this strategy has a better fairness definition, the scheduling is initiated by a process' departure instead of arrival, and it is more suitable for the processor pool model in Figure 5.3(b).

A discussion of any distributed system problem is never complete unless we can justify the use of a centralized controller or do away with it. If we abolish the centralized controller for transferring a process from one site (sender) to the other (receiver), the process transfer must be initiated either by a sender or receiver or both. The following two subsections discuss the **sender-** and **receiver-initiated** algorithms for process migration to achieve load sharing and balancing.

5.3.1 Sender-initiated Algorithms

A **sender-initiated algorithm**, as the name implies, is activated by a sender process that wishes to off-load some of its computation. The load distribution (or redistribution) algorithm facilitates migration of process(es) from a heavily loaded sender to a lightly loaded receiver. The transfer of a process from a sender to a receiver requires three basic decisions.

- **Transfer policy**: When does a node become the sender?
- **Selection policy**: How does the sender choose a process for transfer?
- **Location policy**: Which node should be the target receiver?

If queue sizes are the only indicator of the workload, a sender can use a transfer policy that initiates the algorithm when detecting that its queue length has exceeded a certain threshold upon the arrival of a new process. The newly arrived process would be a natural candidate for the selection policy since no preemption is necessary for removing the process. The location policy is more difficult to decide because it requires some knowledge to locate a suitable receiver. Without knowledge of load distribution, the sender can choose a receiver node randomly. However, this may cause a chain effect of process transfers if the chosen receiver node is already heavily loaded. Unless some global information about the load distribution is maintained, a sender must probe other nodes to decide on a suitable receiver. A simple probing strategy is to poll a certain number of nodes (defined as the *probe limit*) one at a time and select the node with the smallest queue length as the target receiver, provided that the queue length of the target receiver will be less than or equal to the queue length of the sender after the transfer. Naturally, the probing process can be terminated earlier if an idle node is found before the probing limit is reached. Alternatively, multicast can be used instead of probing if group communication facilities exist.

Figure 5.9 shows the flow diagram of the sender-initiated algorithm just described. SQ, ST, and PL are the sender's queue length, threshold, and probe limit, respectively. RQ is the queue length of a polled receiver. Probing of receivers and migration of processes between senders and receivers incurs additional communication overhead, which increases the actual load to the system. In an already heavily loaded system the problem could be worsened by the possibility of a *ping-pong* effect among senders trying to off-load processes fruitlessly if all nodes are initiating the algorithm simultaneously.

FIGURE 5.9   Flow-chart of a sender-initiated algorithm.

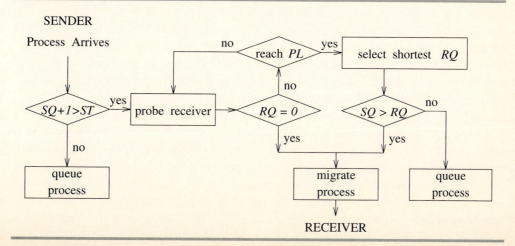

The sender-initiated algorithm, however, performs very well in a lightly loaded system. When the load is not heavy, it is easy to find a receiver, and the communication overhead has little effect on the system performance. (As can be seen in Figure 5.4, a slight load increase under a high system load has a much greater impact on the average turnaround time than that of the same change under low system load.) The choices of ST and PL for various probing strategies have been studied extensively. We include an exercise problem on the subject.

5.3.2 Receiver-initiated Algorithms

Sender-initiated load sharing algorithms are *push* models, where processes are pushed from one processing site to the others. Symmetrically, a receiver can *pull* a process from others to its site for execution. These are the **receiver-initiated algorithm**. A receiver-initiated algorithm can use a similar transfer policy, which activates the pull operation when its queue length falls below a certain threshold (RT) upon the departure of a process. A probing strategy can also be used to implement the location policy that identifies a heavily loaded sender. However, the selection policy will require preemption since the processes at the sender site have already started their execution. The decision about which process to remove is not as obvious as in the sender-initiated algorithms. The benefit of load sharing must outweigh the preemption and migration communication overhead.

The receiver-initiated algorithms are more stable than the sender-initiated algorithms. At high system load, process migrations are few and a sender can be found easily. Load sharing is effectively accomplished with little overhead. When the system load is low, although there will be many migration initiations, degradation of performance due to the additional network traffic is not significant. On average, the receiver-initiated algorithms perform better than the sender-initiated algorithms. This is to be expected since generous (receiver-initiated) individuals tend to contribute more toward the well-being of the society than the self-centered (sender-initiated) ones.

It seems logical to combine the two algorithms into one. For example, a processing node can activate the sender-initiated algorithm when its queue size exceeds the threshold ST and can enable the receiver-initiated algorithm when its queue size falls below the threshold RT. Alternatively, the decision of which algorithm to use can be based on the estimated system load information. The former is a static and symmetrical sender/receiver-initiated algorithm, while the latter is an adaptive algorithm. In both cases, each node may dynamically play the role of either a sender or a receiver. Senders *rendezvous* (not in the sense of synchronization) with receivers. For practical implementation of this rendezvous, a registration service can be used to match a sender with a receiver. Probing thus becomes unnecessary. The registration server can even perform the function of a trader that matches the highest bidder (sender) to the lowest offerer (receiver) if a price can be associated with the execution of each process. This is a concept that we have known for a long time, since well before the invention of computers and their operating systems, for example, in the operation of the New York Stock Exchange. Casual stock owners usually refrain from selling when the market is down heavily and from buying when the up volume is high. These people may not be successful in investment, but they

FIGURE 5.10   Performance comparison of dynamic load-sharing algorithms.

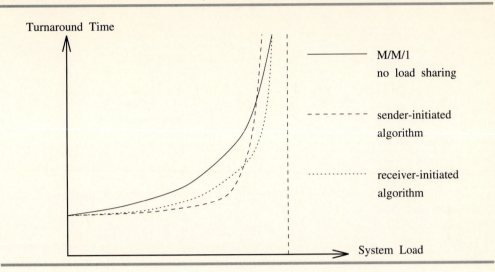

are a major stabilizing force of the stock market. For load sharing, good "citizens" should disable the sender-initiated part of the algorithm when they sense that the system load is high and enable only the receiver-initiated part; the opposite applies when the system load is low. The algorithm becomes adaptive to the change of the system.

Figure 5.10 compares the performance of dynamic load-sharing algorithms. The turnaround time of the M/M/1 system with no load sharing is the baseline for comparison. The sender-initiated algorithm performs well at light system load but becomes unstable at heavy system load due to high communication overhead. The receiver-initiated algorithm does not suffer from the unstable problem since the algorithm becomes inactive when the system load is high. Many research papers on dynamic load sharing and balancing are cited in the annotated bibliograph.

5.4 DISTRIBUTED PROCESS IMPLEMENTATION

Both static and dynamic load sharing require the activation of process execution at a remote site. The creation of a remote process can be implemented by using the client/server model, which is similar to the implementation of RPC. Figure 5.11 assumes that there are front-end stub processes that facilitate the creation of and communication between processes on different machines. A local process on a client machine first makes the request for a remote operation to its front-end stub process, which contacts the stub at the server site on behalf of the local process. If the request is successfully validated and the required resources are met, the server stub creates the requested process on the server machine. All subsequent communication between the local and remote processes is supported indirectly through the stub processes. The stub processes serve as a logical link, making the physical boundary between the local and remote processes transparent.

FIGURE 5.11   Logical model of local and remote processes.

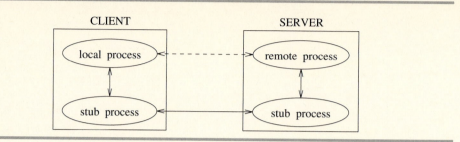

Depending on how request messages are interpreted, there are three significant application scenarios:

- **Remote service**: The message is interpreted as a request for a known service at the remote site.
- **Remote execution**: The messages contain a program to be executed at the remote site.
- **Process migration**: The messages represent a process being migrated to the remote site for continuing execution.

Each of the three applications requires a different treatment. They are discussed in the following subsections.

5.4.1 Remote Service

Remote service is a familiar concept. Its primary application is resource sharing in distributed systems. By allowing remote access operations, multiple clients on different machines can share some common resources such as file systems, peripherals, and processing capabilities. A request message for remote service can be generated at three different software levels:

- As remote procedure calls at the language level
- As remote commands at the operating system level
- As interpretive messages at the application level

At the language level, the remote procedure call seems to be the most suitable model for remote service requests. It is service oriented and provides both access and location transparency. We addressed many implementation issues for RPCs in the previous chapter. At the operating system level there are some frequently used commands that need to invoke remote objects. These commands can be built in as part of the command shell and recognized by the local operating system. For example, a command such as *rcp* in Unix, which copies a remote file, is useful. The idea can be extended to other commands by introducing a remote shell command that allows users to run an arbitrary shell command on a remote system. For example, a *rsh host -l user ls* in Unix can list the home directory files of the user, *user*, on a remote host machine, *host*. The *rsh* is a single remote command. We can extend it again by having an *rsh* in a script file to allow multiple remote commands. However, it is probably more manageable to use a remote login, *rlogin* (or a simple *rsh* with no command parameter), to initiate a session of remote commands. Remote command facilities are available on most modern machines to support network operations.

Remote commands are limited only to shell commands. The concept can be generalized to process messages. A user may want to send a message to a remote host and invoke some user-defined operations at the remote host, based on the content of the message. It is equivalent to doing an RPC at the operating system level. In this case a stub process at the server site has the capability of interpreting messages sent from the client stubs and invoking respective operations. The rules for governing the transfer and interpretation of messages become the application communication protocol between the client and the server. A good example is the file transfer protocol *ftp*. The stubs are the *ftp* daemon processes. They interpret messages such as *get* and *put* for downloading and uploading files. Some common messaging facilities such as mail systems can be used to build application level remote services. Mail messages are interpreted by user-defined daemon processes. Using daemon processes is a popular technique for network programming.

Remote operations initiated by remote procedure calls, remote commands, or interpretive messages are constrained only to services that are supported at the remote host. The primary implementation issues are I/O redirection and security. For redirection, the client stub copies the client process' standard input to the remote command, and the server stub copies the standard output and error of the remote command to the client process. If the client machine is not trusted, the server stub may authenticate the client process. Accesses to the remote resources are also subjected to access authorization.

5.4.2 Remote Execution

We differentiate remote execution from remote service by assuming that the remote operation initiated by a client is created by the client. The message sent from a client to a server is a client program to be executed at the server. In essence it is the spawning of a process at a remote host. The selected host may be a system with specific resources for resource sharing or any system simply for the purpose of load sharing. The former is a more general case of remote service. The latter is a *processor-pool* model for distributed computation; we refer to it as remote execution or dynamic task placement.

The most significant difference in implementation between remote service and remote execution is the assumption of the computation environment. Since the purpose of remote service is to access the remote resources, the view of the remote process is that of the remote host. For example, the file system used is the remote file system instead of the root of the originating client process, whereas for the remote execution, the remote process maintains the view of its originating system. Remote hosts are only used to off-load computation. The complexity of implementing remote execution increases significantly since multiple interacting remote processes may be created concurrently to perform a distributed computation. Some additional implementation issues are:

- Load sharing algorithms
- Location independence
- System heterogeneity
- Protection and security

Let us describe these issues. To facilitate remote execution we assume that a *process(or) server* exists in every participating machine. Process servers are responsible for maintaining the load information, negotiating a remote host, invoking a remote operation, and creating the stub processes for linking clients and servers. A remote execution may be initiated explicitly by a process or implicitly by the local process server. Thus, processes may carry a parent/child relationship or may be disjoint (noninteracting). In either case a remote host must be selected first. Among process servers, a sender-initiated load-sharing algorithm similar to those discussed in Section 5.3.1 can be employed. For practical implementation, each process server can maintain a list of registered hosts that are willing to honor remote execution. Registering and deregistering services can be implemented by broadcasting. Alternatively, the selection process can go through a centralized broker process. Once a remote host is selected, the negotiation process begins. The client process server indicates the resource requirements to the process server at the remote site. If the client is authenticated and its resource requirements can be met, the server grants permission for remote execution. The transfer of code image follows, and the server creates the remote process and the stub. Finally, the client initializes the process forked at the remote site.

Location independence for remote execution is a stronger requirement than the simple I/O redirection for remote service. Since processes created by remote execution may require coordination to accomplish a common task, it is necessary to support a logical view for the processes as though they are all running on a single machine. Each remote process is represented by an agent process at the originating host. The parent/child relationship is preserved. All interprocess communication mechanisms, including *signals*, are location transparent. Typically the file system of the originating process is used to provide a common logical computer view for the processes.

Normally, remote execution assumes a homogeneous environment in which machines have compatible hardware and software configuration. If a remote execution is to be invoked on a heterogeneous host, it is necessary to recompile the program. The overhead may be too high to justify remote execution. One solution to the problem is to use a canonical machine-independent intermediate language for program execution. Such an approach is used in the Java system to facilitate network programming. Java programs are compiled into machine-independent *bytecodes* that can be interpreted by any remote host equipped with a bytecode interpreter. Network objects can be uniquely addressed by Java programs using Universal Resource Locators (URLs). Code compatibility is not the only problem in heterogeneous systems. Data transfer between heterogeneous sites must be translated. Again a universal data representation such as External Data Representation (XDR) needs to be integrated into the remote execution facility.

Remote execution is a double-edge sword. It is powerful but invites abuse of the system. A foreign code image can be a Trojan horse. From the protection and security viewpoint, it is safer to accept only remote execution in source or intermediate codes. The language used to describe a remote execution could be restricted to exclude potential problems such as the use of pointers and multiple inheritance. If intermediate codes are used, they must be verified to ensure that they are indeed generated by a real source program. Other run-time checking of parameters and stack overflow is also necessary to protect the integrity of the remote hosts. Protection and security issues for remote execution in distributed systems are subjects of ongoing research.

5.4.3 Process Migration

The remote execution discussed above assumes that once a remote operation starts at a remote host, it remains at the same remote host until completion of the execution. We can extend the load-sharing model further to allow a remote execution to be preempted and moved to another remote host. In effect, a process can migrate from host to host dynamically. Process migration is a subject of great interest. A system with transparent migration facility is the ultimate goal of distributed processing.

Similar to remote execution, a process migration facility needs to locate and negotiate a remote host, transfer the code image, and initialize the remote operation. Since the target process for migration is preempted, its state information must be transferred also. The state information of a process in a distributed system consists of two parts: computation state and communication state. The computation state is the information necessary to save and restore a process at the remote site; this is similar to the conventional context switching. The communication state is the status of the process communication links and the messages in transit. The transfer of the communication state is a new issue for the implementation of process migration.

Link Redirection and Message Forwarding

Processes are associated with communication links for interprocess communication. They are implemented by using a link table maintained by the kernel. A link table contains pointers to the communication endpoints (host network address concatenated with port number) of the peer processes. To migrate a process, the link tables of those processes that have an out-going link to the migrating process must be updated so that communication links can remain intact after the migration. We have seen many examples of solutions to problems in computer systems that can be found in real life. Link redirection is analogous to changing an address when moving to a new residence. We normally inform our closest friends about the new address before we move, and casual friends after the move. Others that we don't care about will have to find out by some other means. Likewise link redirection can be performed at different stages of a process migration, before or after the move (context transfer), as shown in Figure 5.12. First, the migrating process is suspended (or *frozen*) after a remote host has been selected and successfully negotiated. When the remote host is ready, the next major task is to transfer the state and context (code image) of the process to the remote host before execution can be resumed there. Link redirection can be done explicitly by making link update requests to the communicating processes. The time of the link update affects how messages that arrive during the migration period are forwarded. Messages that arrive before the link update are buffered and may be

FIGURE 5.12 Link redirection and message forwarding.

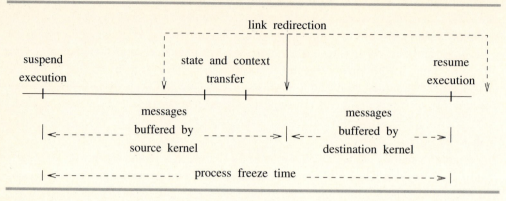

transferred together with the context or forwarded later by the source kernel. After link update, messages may arrive before the process resumes execution at the remote host. They are buffered by the destination kernel for the process. An earlier link update reduces the *residual* work of handling messages at the source kernel. Ideally, after a process has been migrated, its trace at the original host should be kept at a minimum and cleaned up as soon as possible. Otherwise, it defeats the purpose of off-loading the computation.

Even with earlier link updates, after a process has been migrated, messages may still arrive at the source host due to network delays or messages sent by processes which do not know about the migration. To prevent loss of messages, it is necessary for the source kernel to continue forwarding messages to the already migrated process. Theoretically, this period could be indefinite. Practically, we need to put a limit similar to the six-month mail forwarding service provided by the postal service. During the grace period messages are forwarded to the destination kernel, from which the migrated process might have migrated again, causing cascaded forwarding. As an option, when forwarding a message, the source kernel may also inform the sender about the new location of the migrated process to reduce indirect message transfer. (This service is typically not provided by the postal service.) Reporting the new location to the senders can be done only if the sender information is known (e.g., when using the connectionless datagram messages). In connection-oriented communication the sender information is generally not contained in the messages. (The telephone company does provide this service but not automatic forwarding. Phone calls are connection-oriented but they are circuit-switched. So the source information is available.) Messages arriving after the grace period are ignored and presumed lost. It is the responsibility of the application process to deal with message loss.

State and Context Transfer

The time between suspension and resumption of a process is called the *freeze time*. It is an overhead for process migration. To reduce the overhead, context transfer, link redirection, and message forwarding can proceed concurrently. In fact, link redirection and message forwarding can wait until the process resumes execution at the new location. The only necessary condition for the migrated process to resume execution is the transfer of the computation state information and some initial codes. That is, to minimize freeze time, the point of resume execution in Figure 5.12 can be moved backward to overlap with context transfer. If the process code image is large, the transfer can be processed in batches of blocks (or pages). The remote process can begin execution immediately after its state and initial code blocks have been transferred and before migration is fully completed. Other code blocks can be copied over on demand (**copy-on-reference**); this is similar to a demand paging system. Although freeze time can be greatly reduced, it leaves much *residual computation dependency* on the source host. The concept, however, fits very well with distributed shared memory systems (discussed in Chapter 7). A distributed shared memory system simulates a logical shared global memory on physically distributed memory modules. The location of physical memory blocks that are mapped to the logical address space of a process is transparent to the process. In such a system, only the state information needs to be transferred. Context transfer is a null issue to the process migration facility. It is hidden in the underlying mechanism that implements distributed shared memory. Whether blocks referenced by a process are copied or not (or even replicated) is transparent to the process. Residual dependency is not necessarily an evil. It enhances transparency and may improve performance.

5.5 REAL-TIME SCHEDULING

The problem of process scheduling has a very different flavor when timing constraints are imposed. In many applications, the operating system must ensure that certain actions are taken within specified time constraints. These systems are called *real-time systems*, because they have real-time deadline constraints. Examples of real-time systems include avionics computers, automobile control computers, factory automation systems, and stock trading systems.

Real-time services are carried out by a set of real-time *tasks*. Each task τ is described by

$$\tau_i = (S_i, C_i, D_i)$$

where S_i is the earliest possible start time of task τ_i, C_i is the worst-case execution time of τ_i, and D_i is τ_i's deadline. A *real-time task set* V is a collection of real-time tasks:

$$V = \{\tau_i \mid i = 1, \ldots, n\}$$

If the real-time computer controls safety-related or otherwise critical equipment, every task must complete before its deadline or a disaster might occur. These systems are called *hard real-time* systems and are only judged to be correct if every task is guaranteed to meet its deadline. Other systems (such as multimedia systems) have deadlines but are judged to be in working order as long as they do not miss too many deadlines. These systems are called *soft real-time* systems. In a soft real-time system, a task is executed to completion even if it has missed its deadline. A *firm real-time* system is similar to a soft real-time system, but tasks that have missed their deadlines are discarded. For example, a factory automation computer should not trigger a mechanical action if the deadline is missed, to prevent the equipment from damaging itself.

If tasks arrive into a system at arbitrary times, the real-time task set is *aperiodic*. In many real-time systems, task arrival times, execution times, and deadlines are very predictable. Such task sets are called *periodic*. For example, an engine control computer must compute the fuel to be injected and the spark timing for every engine revolution.

We can simplify the description of a periodic real-time task set. Each task executes one of *n jobs*. A request to execute job *i* occurs once every T_i seconds. The previous execution of the job must be completed before the new job execution is requested. That is, the start time of the new task is the deadline of the old task. Since only one instance of a job is executing at a time, we will label the task executing job J_i as τ_i. A description of the task set reduces to a description of the period and execution times of the *n* jobs:

$$V = \{J_i = (C_i, T_i) \mid 1 \le i \le n\}$$

We are interested in scheduling the tasks for execution in such a way that all tasks meet their deadlines. We will be concerned with uniprocessor scheduling only (we give some references to multiprocessor real-time scheduling in the Annotated Bibliography). A *schedule* is an assignment of the CPU to the real-time tasks such that at most one task is assigned the CPU at any given moment. More precisely, a schedule is a set A of execution intervals, described as

$$A = \{(s_i, f_i, t_i) \mid i = 1, \ldots, n\}$$

where s_i is the start time of the interval, f_i is the finish time of the interval, and t_i is the task executed during the interval. The schedule is valid if:

1. For every $i = 1, \ldots, s_i < f_i$.
2. For every $i = 1, \ldots, f_i \le s_{i+1}$.
3. If $t_i = k$, then $S_k \le s_i$ and $f_i \le D_k$.

Condition 1 requires that execution intervals are really intervals. Condition 2 requires that the intervals be time ordered. Condition 3 requires that a task only be executed between its release time and its deadline. A task set is *feasible* if every task τ_k receives at least C_k seconds of CPU execution in the schedule. More precisely, let

$$A(\tau_k) = \{a = (s_i, f_i, t_i) \mid a \in A \text{ and } t_i = k\}$$

Then, the schedule is feasible if for every $\tau_k \in V$,

$$\sum_{(s_i, f_i, k) \in A(\tau_k)} f_i - s_i \ge C_k$$

A set of tasks is *feasible* if there is a feasible schedule for the tasks. The goal of real-time scheduling algorithms is to find a feasible schedule whenever one exists. In this section, we present algorithms for scheduling a set of real-time tasks under assumptions of varying complexity. We discuss hard real-time scheduling only. In the Bibliography, we list some references to subjects not covered in this book, such as parallel and distributed real-time scheduling.

5.5.1 Rate Monotonic

In the simplest type of real-time scheduling, we make the following assumptions:

1. Tasks are periodic and T_i is the period for task τ_i.
2. Tasks do not communicate with each other.
3. Tasks are scheduled according to priority, and task priorities are fixed (*static priority scheduling*).

The fact that task priorities are fixed greatly simplifies the implementation of a scheduler. In a static priority scheduler, the scheduler only needs to find the highest-priority task that is ready for execution. In *dynamic priority* scheduling, the scheduler must reevaluate task priorities on the fly. Although more task sets are feasible with dynamic priority scheduling, the simple implementation of static priority scheduling makes it of great practical interest.

Because we are restricting our attention to static priority scheduling, we might come across a task set that is feasible, but not by using any static priority scheduler. If a task set does have a feasible schedule that can be created by a static priority scheduler, we will say that the task set has a *feasible static priority assignment*. The goal of this section is to find the feasible static priority assignment, if it exists.

If task τ_i is requested at time t, τ_i can meet its deadline if the time spent executing higher-priority tasks during the time interval $(t, t + D_i)$ is $D_i - C_i$ or less. When a task execution is requested (i.e., at the start of its period), the task might or might not be able to complete its execution before its deadline, depending on the CPU service demands of the higher-priority tasks. However, we can identify a worst-case situation. The *critical instant* for task τ_i occurs when task τ_i and all higher-priority tasks are scheduled simultaneously. The critical instant for task τ_5 is illustrated in Figure 5.13 (shaded areas are task executions, dashed line boxes are task waiting times). If τ_i can meet its deadline when it is scheduled at a critical instant, τ_i can always meet its deadline.

The reason is illustrated in Figure 5.13. Let us consider what can happen to the schedulability of τ_l if we move the request time of higher-priority task τ_h slightly forward or backward. If we move the request time of τ_h forward to $t + \epsilon$, we might reduce the time spent executing τ_h in the interval $(t, t + D_{\tau_l})$ by up to ϵ. However, we won't increase the amount of time spent executing τ_h in $(t, t + D_{\tau_l})$. Similarly, moving the request time of τ_h backward to $t - \epsilon$ can only decrease the amount of time spent executing τ_h. So, at the critical instant, the amount of time spent executing higher-priority tasks is maximized.

As a result, we can determine if a priority assignment results in a feasible schedule by simulating the execution of the tasks at the critical instant of the lowest priority task. If

FIGURE 5.13   The critical instant of a task.

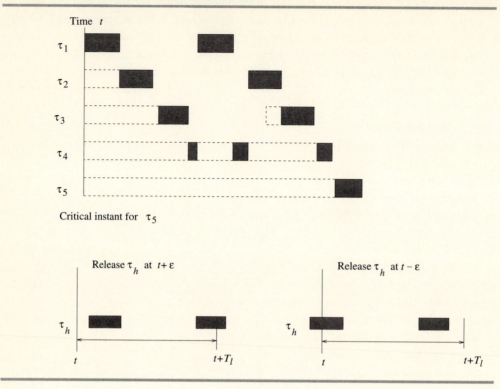

Critical instant for τ_5

the lowest-priority task can meet its deadline starting from its critical instant, all tasks can always meet their deadlines. Tasks with short periods have less time in which to complete their execution than tasks with long deadlines. Intuitively, it is better to give high priority to tasks with small periods than to tasks with large periods.

Let PR_h be the priority assigned to task τ_h. We assume that if $PR_h > PR_l$, the CPU is assigned to τ_h in preference to τ_l (i.e., higher values of PR_l correspond to higher priorities). Then, the rule for assigning priorities to tasks is the *Rate Monotonic* (RM) priority assignment:

Rate Monotonic Priority Assignment

$$\text{If } T_h < T_l \text{ then } PR_h > PR_l$$

Rate monotonic priority assignment is easy to implement; just sort the tasks by the lengths of their periods. Rate monotonic also makes very good priority assignments. It has been shown that if there is a feasible static priority assignment for a set of periodic tasks, then rate monotonic priority assignment produces a feasible static priority assignment.

In short, rate monotonic is an optimal priority assignment algorithm, in the following sense: If there is a static priority assignment such that any resulting schedule is feasible, the rate monotonic priority assignment will produce feasible schedules.

To understand this property of RM assignment, let us suppose that there is a non-RM priority assignment A that always produces feasible schedules. We can list the tasks in order of priority so that τ_1 has the highest priority and τ_n has the lowest. Because the priority assignment is non-RM, there must be a pair of tasks τ_i and τ_{i+1} such that $T_i > T_{i+1}$. Suppose we exchanged the priorities of τ_i and τ_{i+1}. Are all possible schedules still feasible?

Recall that we only need to see if τ_i and τ_{i+1} can meet their deadlines at the critical instant. Let us consider what happens at the critical instant under priority assignment A (see Figure 5.14). In the time interval $(0, T_{i+1})$ after the critical instant, tasks τ_1 through τ_{i-1} take H seconds. Since task τ_{i+1} can meet its deadline, we know that

$$H + C_i + C_{i+1} \le T_{i+1}$$

Next, let us exchange the priorities of τ_i and τ_{i+1}. Task τ_{i+1} can certainly meet its deadline, because we increased its priority. Task τ_i will also meet its deadline, because it will complete within $T_{i+1} < T_i$ seconds. So, the modified priority assignment also produces feasible schedules.

If we repeat the priority exchange for long enough, we will create a rate monotonic priority assignment. Therefore, if a set of periodic tasks has a feasible static priority assignment, RM is a feasible static priority assignment.

Timing Analysis of Rate Monotonic

To ensure that all real-time tasks can meet their deadlines, we might be forced to leave the CPU idle for some periods of time (these idle periods can be used to execute noncritical tasks). We need to ensure that our scheduling algorithms make good use of the CPU (i.e., the required idle periods are not too long).

We define the *load L* of the real time tasks to be the fraction of time that they use the CPU.

$$L = \sum_{i=1}^{n} \frac{C_i}{T_i}$$

Studies have shown that the sufficient condition for RM to be a feasible priority assignment is $L \le n(2^{1/n} - 1)$. That is, if the load of the real-time tasks is low enough, RM is a feasible priority assignment for them. The proof of this property is complex but not instructive, so we omit it. However, we note that $n(2^{1/n} - 1)$ approaches 69 percent from above as n becomes large. So, RM never wastes more than 31 percent of the CPU.

The $n(2^{1/n} - 1)$ bound on the load can be very pessimistic (i.e., it is a sufficient but not a necessary condition). For example, the task set $V = \{(1, 2), (1, 3), (1, 6)\}$ has a feasible RM priority assignment and a 100 percent load.

FIGURE 5.14   Example of swapping tasks.

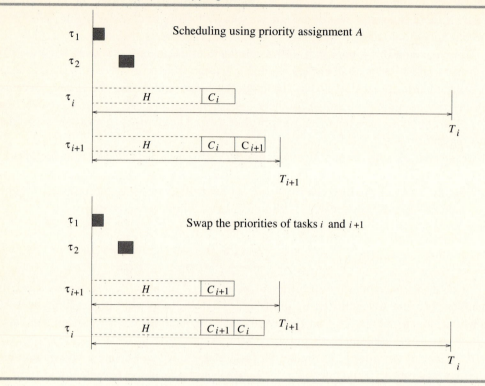

We can find a necessary condition for determining if the task set has a feasible priority assignment by simulating the execution of the tasks at the critical instant. Let us list the tasks in order of their priority so that τ_1 has the highest priority and τ_n has the lowest. Let r_i be the *response time* of task τ_i at the critical instant. That is, τ_i will complete its execution r_i seconds after the critical instant. During this time, a higher-priority task τ_h will request service $\lceil r_i/T_h \rceil$ times and will require C_h seconds of CPU service for each request. Therefore, r_i satisfies the following equation:

$$r_i = C_i + \sum_{h=1}^{i-1} \lceil \tfrac{r_i}{T_h} \rceil C_h$$

Since r_i appears on both sides of the equation, it is very hard to solve directly. But, we can solve it iteratively. First, assume that τ_i does not wait for any higher-priority tasks (i.e., set $r_i(0) = C_i$). Put the value of r_i into the right-hand side of the equation to compute a new, larger value of r_i that accounts for higher-priority task service during the first C_i seconds after the critical instant. During the revised response time, more executions of the higher-priority tasks might be invoked. Put the new value of r_i into the right-hand side of the equation to get another value of r_i and continue until you find a stable value. That is, solve the recurrence equation

$$r_i(0) = C_i$$
$$r_i(k+1) = C_i + \sum_{h=1}^{i-1} \lceil \frac{r_i(k)}{T_h} \rceil C_h \qquad (5.1)$$

until $r_i(k) = r_i(k+1)$. If on some iteration $r_i(k) > T_i$, the task set does not have a feasible priority assignment.

5.5.2 Deadline Monotonic

Some tasks in a real-time system might need to complete execution a short time after being requested. We can account for this new task model by modifying our model of periodic tasks. Let:

$$V = \{J_i = (C_i, T_i, D_i) \mid 1 \le i \le n\}$$

be a description of the jobs that execute in the system. As before, we label a task that runs program i as τ_i. A task τ_i is requested once every T_i seconds and requires C_i seconds of CPU execution. If τ_i is requested at time t, it must complete its execution by time $t + D_i$ or τ_i misses its deadline.

The optimal static priority assignment for this model is the *Deadline Monotonic* (DM) algorithm:

Deadline Monotonic Priority Assignment

$$\text{If } D_h < D_l \text{ then } PR_h > PR_l$$

The reason for DM's optimality is the same as the reason for RM's optimality. Analyzing DM is a little harder than analyzing RM because there is no formula based on the load that guarantees feasible schedules. Fortunately, we can use the response time Equation 5.1 without any change. The task set is feasible if $r_i \le D_i$ for $i = 1, \ldots, n$.

5.5.3 Earliest Deadline First

If we are willing to build a more complex scheduler, we can obtain a much higher CPU utilization than if we are restricted to static priority scheduling. A general purpose scheduler uses *dynamic priority scheduling*. That is, the relative priorities of the real-time tasks can vary during the system's execution. Task priorities are reevaluated when important events occur, such as task arrivals, task completions, and task synchronization.

Let $\tau_k(i)$ be the ith instantiation of job J_k, and let $d_k(i)$ be its real-time deadline. Similarly, let $PR_k(i)$ be the priority assigned to $\tau_k(i)$. An optimal dynamic scheduling algorithm is *Earliest Deadline First* (EDF):

Earliest Deadline First Priority Assignment

$$\text{If } d_h(i) < d_l(j) \text{ then } PR_h(i) > PR_l(j)$$

We can show that EDF is optimal the same way that we show that RM or DM is optimal. Suppose there is a non-EDF feasible schedule. Then, there is a $\tau_h(i)$ and a $\tau_l(j)$ such that $d_h(i) < d_l(j)$, but $PR_h(i) > PR_l(j)$. It must be the case that the schedule is still feasible if we exchange the priorities of $\tau_h(i)$ and $\tau_l(j)$. (Why?) Repeat the priority exchange until the schedule is EDF.

In the exercises, we show that if $D_i = T_i$ for a set of periodic tasks, then the task set has a feasible EDF priority assignment as long as $L \leq 1$.

Note that EDF uses the deadlines of the instantiation of the tasks to determine priorities, not any information about the program that the task instantiates. Therefore, EDF is applicable to scheduling aperiodic real-time tasks. Since the proof that EDF is optimal only uses the deadlines of the task instantiations, EDF is an optimal algorithm for scheduling aperiodic real-time tasks.

5.5.4 Real-time Synchronization

In the previous task models, we assumed that each task is independent. However, a set of tasks that cooperate to achieve a goal will need to share information and otherwise synchronize with each other. In addition, the tasks might need to reserve physical resources (memory, communications channels, etc.). Synchronization among the real-time tasks can be generally called acquiring and releasing semaphores. Unfortunately, blocking due to synchronization can cause subtle timing problems.

Consider a real-time system that contains tasks τ_1, τ_2, and τ_3, arranged in order of decreasing priority, and semaphore S, as shown in Figure 5.15. Suppose that τ_3 has locked S when τ_1 is requested. Since τ_1 is the highest-priority task, τ_3 is preempted and τ_1 is executed. If τ_1 attempts to lock S, it blocks and must wait for τ_3 to release S (this is the normal and expected behavior). However, τ_3 can be preempted by τ_2 (or, if τ_2 was already in the ready queue). In this case, τ_3 will not complete its execution to release S until τ_2 finishes its execution (or blocks). Therefore, τ_2 executes at the expense of τ_1. This phenomenon is called *priority inversion* because τ_2 effectively has a higher priority than τ_1 for a period of time. Another subtlety is *chain blocking*. Suppose that τ_1 locks semaphore R, τ_2 locks R and then S, and τ_3 locks S. Then, τ_1 might be blocked by τ_3 even though τ_1 does not lock S.

Real-time synchronization protocols interact with the scheduler to reduce priority inversions to a small and predictable level. The interaction is accomplished by adjusting the priorities of the real-time tasks and by selectively granting access to the semaphores.

A task τ_i will access a set of c_i critical sections, $\{z_i(k) \mid 1 \leq k \leq c_i\}$. The critical sections can overlap within the same task to allow access to multiple resources simultaneously. However, overlapping critical sections must be properly *nested*. That is, if $z_i(1)$ and $z_i(2)$ overlap and $z_i(1)$ starts before $z_i(2)$, $z_i(2)$ must end before $z_i(1)$ ends.

Task τ_h is *blocked* by critical section $z_l(k)$ of lower-priority task τ_l if τ_h must wait for τ_l to exit $z_l(k)$ before resuming execution. Task τ_h might be blocked by $z_l(k)$ by indirect

FIGURE 5.15   Priority inversion and chain blocking.

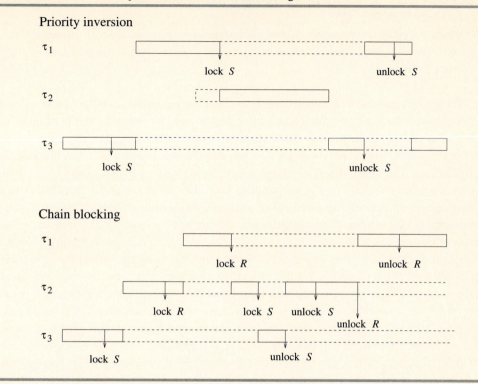

mechanisms, such as chain blocking or by artifacts of the real-time synchronization protocols. If $z_l(k)$ is protected by semaphore S, τ_h is *blocked through* S.

Priority Inheritance Protocol

In our example of priority inversion, the blocking of task τ_1 occurs for an unpredictably long time because τ_2 preempts τ_3 while τ_3 blocks τ_1. Intuitively, τ_3 should execute in preference to τ_2 while τ_3 blocks τ_1. That is, τ_3 should *inherit* τ_1's priority. This idea is expressed in the *Priority Inheritance Protocol* (PIP), whose rules are:

1. A task is assigned its normal (RM) priority when it is requested.
2. The CPU is assigned to the highest-priority ready process.
3. Before a task can enter a critical section, it must first acquire a lock on the semaphore that guards the critical section.
4. If task τ_h is blocked through semaphore S, which is held by lower priority task τ_l, τ_h is removed from the ready list, and PR_l is assigned PR_h (i.e., τ_l inherits the priority of τ_h).

5. Priority inheritance is transitive. That is, if τ_2 blocks τ_1, and τ_3 blocks τ_2, both τ_2 and τ_3 inherit PR_1.

6. When τ_l releases semaphore S, the highest-priority process blocked through S is put on the ready queue. Task τ_l releases any priority it inherited through S and resumes a lower priority.

The priority inheritance protocol limits the time during which a task is blocked (i.e., the time during which a low-priority task executes). If we can compute the maximum time that τ_i can be blocked, we can modify our previous calculations to determine if a task set has a feasible schedule. There are two ways that a low-priority task can block a high-priority task. The first is *direct blocking*, which occurs when a high-priority task attempts to lock a semaphore held by a low-priority task. The second type of blocking is newly introduced with the priority inheritance protocol. *Push-through* blocking occurs when a low-priority task inherits a high priority and executes at the expense of a medium-priority task. In this case, it is the medium-priority task that experiences push-through blocking, while the high-priority task experiences direct blocking. Note that when the low-priority task releases the semaphore, the high-priority task executes, and the medium-priority task must wait. The high-priority task is not blocking the medium-priority task because the tasks are executing in priority order (which we have analyzed). For example, in Figure 5.16 when τ_h requests a lock on S, τ_h experiences direct blocking by τ_l through S, and τ_m experiences push-through blocking by τ_l through S.

A high-priority task τ_h can be blocked by a low-priority task τ_l only if τ_l was executing in a critical section when τ_h was requested. This occurs because once τ_h is submitted, τ_l can execute only if τ_h is blocked by τ_l (since there is no other way for τ_l to increase its priority high enough).

We can make a further observation that lets us compute maximum blocking times. It is possible that task τ_l can block task τ_h on two different occasions. For example, suppose that τ_l locks R and then S before τ_h is requested. While τ_h is executing, two higher-priority tasks, τ_1 and τ_2, are requested, in that order. Suppose that τ_1 attempts to lock S. Then, τ_l inherits PR_1 until it releases S. Later, τ_2 attempts to lock R, so τ_l inserts PR_2 until it releases R. But, the push-through blocking of τ_h by τ_1 is not important, because the same duration of blocking would have occurred if only τ_2 was requested.

FIGURE 5.16 Direct and push-through blocking.

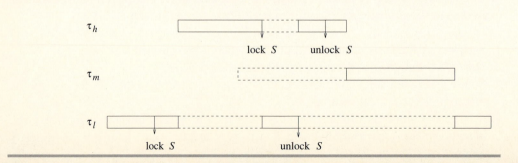

A low-priority task τ_l can block τ_h only while τ_l is in a critical section. Since we assume that critical sections are properly nested, we can look at the longest single critical section during which τ_l can block τ_h. Let $B_h(l)$ be the set of all critical sections of τ_l that can block τ_h ($B_h(l)$ is empty if $PR_l > PR_h$). Since blocking can be either direct or push-through, we must analyze the set of all tasks that lock a semaphore S.

Let $ceiling(S)$ be the priority of the highest-priority task that can be blocked by S. Then, a critical section $z_l(j)$ of τ_l blocks τ_h if $z_l(j)$ is protected by S and $ceiling(S) \geq PR_h$. If there are no nested critical sections, $ceiling(S)$ is the priority of the highest priority task that locks S. If some critical sections are nested, *chain blocking* might be possible, as shown in Figure 5.16. In this case, a more sophisticated analysis is needed (see the exercises).

Let $E_h(l)$ be the maximum execution time of any critical section in $Bl_h(l)$. Let B_h be the maximum time that task τ_h will be blocked. Then,

$$B_h \leq \sum_{\{l \mid PR_l < PR_h\}} E_h(l) \tag{5.2}$$

There is another way to compute B_h that might give a better bound. Instead of looking at blocking due to tasks, we can look at blocking due to critical sections. Suppose that τ_h is blocked through semaphore S. Then, S is held by lower-priority task τ_l, and the blocking is finished when τ_l releases S. After τ_l releases S, no other low-priority task can acquire S until after τ_h completes its execution. That is, τ_h can be blocked through S at most once.

Let $E_h(S)$ be the longest execution of a critical section protected by semaphore S by a task with priority lower than PR_h (or zero if there is no such task). Then,

$$B_h \leq \sum_{\{S \mid ceiling(S) \geq PR_h\}} E_h(S) \tag{5.3}$$

We can incorporate the maximum blocking time B_h into the schedulability formula with only minor modifications. The key observation is that while the blocking period increases the time until task τ_h completes its execution, the CPU is not wasted during this period. The sufficient condition for feasible RM assignment in the previous section can be extended as follows for $h = 1...n$.

$$\sum_{j=1}^{h} \frac{C_j}{T_j} + \frac{B_h}{T_h} \leq h(2^{1/h} - 1)$$

where $PR_h > PR_{h-1}$ for $h = 2...n$.

For a more precise analysis, we can modify the response time calculations of Equation 5.1, as follows:

$$r_i(0) = \qquad C_i + B_i$$
$$r_i(k+1) = \quad C_i + B_i + \sum_{h=1}^{i-1} \lceil \tfrac{r_i(k)}{T_h} \rceil C_h \qquad (5.4)$$

As with rate monotonic or deadline monotonic, the task set is feasible if the response time is always less than or equal to the tasks' deadline.

5.5.5 Priority Ceiling Protocol

While the priority inheritance protocol bounds blocking, the blocking periods B_h can still be rather long. The priority ceiling protocol (PCP) can ensure that B_h is limited to the duration of one critical section. To accomplish this, PCP will impose seemingly draconian restrictions on when a task can acquire a critical section. However, the restrictions make sense from a global point of view.

When task τ_h is requested (using PIP), there might be several low-priority tasks τ_l that hold locks on semaphores that can block τ_h. We would like to ensure that when τ_h is requested, at most one low-priority task holds a lock on a semaphore that can block τ_h. This requirement suggests a simple rule: A task can acquire a lock on semaphore S only if no other task holds a lock on a semaphore R such that a high-priority task τ_h can be blocked through both S and R.

Implementing the locking rule efficiently requires a simple method to determine which tasks a semaphore can block. Fortunately, we have already seen such a method. Recall that $ceiling(S)$ is the priority of the highest-priority task that can be blocked through S. Then, τ_h can be blocked through S if and only if $ceiling(S) \geq PR_h$. We call $ceiling(S)$ the *priority ceiling* of S.

When τ_i attempts to lock S, it checks the priority ceiling of all locked semaphores R. If the priority ceiling of R is less than PR_i, R cannot block a task that τ_i could block through S. Otherwise, it is possible that a high-priority task τ_h could be blocked through both S and R.

An example of using the PCP rule is shown in Figure 5.17. In the execution at the top of the figure, task τ_m is blocked from acquiring semaphore S because task τ_l holds R, and $ceiling(R) \geq PR_m$. If τ_m was permitted to acquire S, τ_h might be blocked for the duration of two critical section executions. Even though τ_m is blocked by a lock that it never attempts to acquire, PCP guarantees that it is blocked at most once. In the execution at the bottom of the figure, $ceiling(R) < PR_m$, so τ_m can safely acquire S without the danger of blocking τ_h twice.

At this point, we have almost completely specified the *priority ceiling protocol*. All that remains is to account for a few details. The additional rules are:

1. Each semaphore S has an associated priority ceiling $ceiling(S)$.
2. When task τ_i attempts to set a lock on semaphore S, the lock is granted only if PR_i is larger than $ceiling(R)$ for every semaphore R locked by a different task. Otherwise τ_i is blocked.

FIGURE 5.17   Example execution of the priority ceiling protocol.

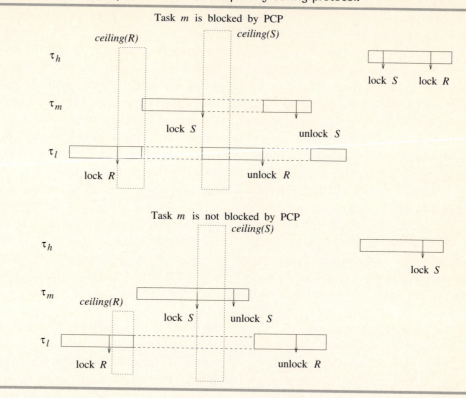

3. If task τ_h is blocked through semaphore S, which is held by task τ_l, then τ_l inherits the priority PR_h. Priority inheritance is transitive.

4. When τ_i releases S, τ_i releases any priority it had inherited through S. The highest-priority task that was blocked on S is put in the ready queue.

If we compute the maximum blocking time for each task, we can apply Equation 5.4 to determine if the task set has a feasible schedule using a static priority assignment. Since a task can be blocked by at most one task and through at most one semaphore (see the exercises), we can calculate

$$B_h \leq \max\{E_h(S) \mid ceiling(S) \geq PR_h\} \tag{5.5}$$

5.6 SUMMARY

Distributed process scheduling is one of the most diverse and widely studied research areas in distributed systems. This chapter attempts to give an overall view of both theoretical issues and practical implementations of scheduling processes on multiple computer systems. A desirable scheduling strategy depends on the nature of application processes, the performance objectives, and the underlying computing system. We can model process interactions using one of the three graph models: the *precedence process* model, the *communication process* model, and the *disjoint process* model. The unique factor that distinguishes distributed scheduling from the traditional multiprocessor scheduling is the communication overhead that must be accounted for when scheduling in distributed systems. We show how the factor communication overhead can be integrated into the design and analysis of scheduling algorithms for each of the three models.

The scheduling strategies discussed in this chapter are classified as either *static* or *dynamic* (where a scheduled process can be preempted and resumes execution on a different processor). Two examples of static scheduling are illustrated, the ETF scheduling for the precedence process model and the *module allocation* algorithm for the communication process model. In both cases, we emphasize the importance of using heuristic approaches.

The assumption of prior knowledge about processes and the system in static scheduling is not realistic for distributed systems. The problem can be alleviated if processes are scheduled dynamically. *Load-sharing* and *load-balancing* algorithm are dynamic scheduling strategies that improve process turnaround time and system utilization. We discuss the basic *sender-initiated* and *receiver-initiated* algorithms for dynamic load sharing.

The implementation of dynamic load sharing requires the support of *remote execution* and *process migration* facilities in the system. We address many practical implementation problems such as how remote processes are created, how process state is transferred, how messages and communication links are redirected, and how security can be enhanced. Remote execution and process migration facilities have become a necessity for modern network and distributed programming.

The chapter concludes with the presentation of another unique and important scheduling problem, *real-time scheduling*. The fundamental real-time scheduling algorithms discussed are *rate monotonic, deadline monotonic* and *earliest deadline first* scheduling. The *priority ceiling* and the *priority inheritance* protocols show an interesting problem of how real-time priority scheduling is affected by process synchronization.

ANNOTATED BIBLIOGRAPHY

The integrated *speedup model* showing the interplay among three major factors (algorithm parallelization, distributed scheduling, and system architecture) that affect the performance of distributed processing on a given network architecture is described in [HCA88]. To study the problem of distributed scheduling we represent process interaction in one of three types of graph model: the precedence, the communication, and the disjoint process models.

The precedence process graph model (DAG) has long been used to analyze static multiprocessor scheduling [Ram72, CL75, Cof76]. Almost all nontrivial multiprocessor scheduling problems have been shown to be NP-complete [Ull75]. Many heuristic approaches [SH86, SWP90] exist for practical implementation. Extending multiprocessor scheduling to include communication for distributed systems was studied in [RS87]. The complexity of multiprocessor scheduling is further complicated when interprocess communication must be accounted for. Simple heuristic scheduling algorithms are needed. We show some examples of such algorithms from [LHCA88, HCAL89]. A more formal model for multiprocessor scheduling with communication can be found in [VLL90].

The communication graph model has also been used extensively to study the problem of mapping process modules to system architectures, with consideration of both computation and communication cost. It is called the module allocation or task assignment problem. We illustrate the problem by using Stone's [Sto77] application of the maximum-flow minimum-cut commodity flow control [FF62, Hu70, EK72] for multiprocessor scheduling with communication. Extension of the communication graph models can be found in [Bok79, Bok81, Tow86]. Many heuristic algorithms are also available [Lo88, FB89, BS84, BNG92].

The precedence and communication graph models are used for static process scheduling. We use the disjoint process model to show the concept of dynamic process scheduling for load sharing and balancing. Research papers in this area are abundant. Various sender- and receiver-initiated algorithms have been proposed and analyzed [WM85, ELZ86, Rom91, SKS92]. A fairly complete taxonomy of all scheduling problems, both static and dynamic, is given in [CK88]. Some recent research on distributed scheduling can be found in the *Journal of Parallel and Distributed Computing* special issue edited by Shirazi and Hurson [SH92], and the book by [SHK95].

Many remote execution and process migration facilities to support distributed process scheduling have been experimented with on recently developed distributed operating systems. [Esk89] describes fundamental design issues such as transparency, state and context transfer, separation of policy and mechanism, message redirection, and residual dependency. Various system designs (DEMOS/MP at Berkeley [PM83], V-System at Stanford [TLC85], LOCUS at UCLA [PW85], SPICE at CMU [Zay87], Charlotte at Wisconsin [AF89]) are compared with respect to these issues. Some queueing models are used in this chapter to demonstrate performance analysis. For more information about queuing models, see [Kle75, Kan92]

The first rate monotonic and earliest deadline algorithms are found in the classic paper of Liu and Layland [LL72]. The deadline monotonic algorithm is attributed to Leung and Whitehead [LW82]. The response time equation is given by Joseph and Pandya [JP86]. Extensions to the response time equations that account for release jitter, among other issues, is given by Tindell, Burns, and Wellings[TBW94]. The priority ceiling and the priority inheritance protocols are from a paper by Sha, Rajkumar, and Lehoczky [SRL90]. The real-time synchronization protocols have been extended to handle multiple processors, dynamic priorities, and multiple resource instances [Bak90, TN91, FP88, CL90, Raj90].

EXERCISES

1. In classical multiprocessor scheduling, the problem of minimizing the makespan is trivial if there are more processors than tasks to be scheduled. This is not true in distributed systems where communication delays are present.

   a. Draw a DAG in which there are four tasks (T_1, T_2, T_3, T_4), each with unit execution time. Tasks T_2 and T_3 must wait for the completion of T_1. Task T_4 must wait for the completion of T_2 and T_3.

   b. What is the optimal schedule when the interprocess communication delays are 0, 0.5, and 1.5, respectively?

   c. Can you find a better schedule if task T_1 is replicated?

2. Use the problem in Figure 5.5. A possible process assignment for processors P1, P2, and P3, is (A, E, G), (B, D), and (C, F). Give a good justification for this particular assignment. What is the total makespan?

3. Use the example in Figure 5.7. Compare and justify the heuristic algorithm with threshold $C = 11$ against the optimal assignment. Also compare the costs if the cluster (3,5) is mapped to B.

4. Assume a homogeneous system of n processors. Each processor is modeled as a M/M/1 system with load ρ. Given $p_0 = 1 - \rho$ as the probability that a processor is idling and $p_1 = \rho * p_0$ as the probability that a processor has exactly one job in the queue, derive a formula S for the success of load sharing. S is defined as the probability that the system has at least one processor idling and at least one processor has more than one job in the queue. Plot S as a function of ρ (0.0 to 1.0) for $n = 5, 10, 15, 20$. Give an intuitive explanation for the results.

5. The threshold queue length used for the transfer policy of the sender-initiated algorithm plays an important role in improving the average job turnaround time. Studies have shown that the optimal value of the threshold is usually small. Draw a figure that shows the average turnaround time as a function of load ρ for threshold values of 2, 3, and 4. Use M/M/1 as the baseline for comparison. Justify your figure.

6. The probe limit is the number of inquiries sent out to select a target processor for process migration. Its optimal value is also shown to be small (3 to 5). Give an intuitive explanation. If the system is heterogeneous in the sense that each processor has a very different load factor, should the probe limit be increased or decreased? Why?

7. Figure 5.10 shows only the comparison between sender- and receiver-initiated algorithms. Conjecture how the static symmetrical or the adaptive combined sender- and receiver-initiated algorithms should fit in the figure.

8. Show some of examples of daemon processes on your machine that support remote services.

9. Some recent literatures describe *mobile agents* as agent processes that travel from one host to another. How is this mobile agent concept different from the process migration discussed in this chapter?

10. If two processes connected by a communication channel are migrated simultaneously, what potential problems could result?

11. In real life we often rely on a *home address* for communication. Show how the home address concept can be used to facilitate process migration with respect to communication and transparency.

12. Consider the task set $\{(1, 4), (2, 5), (1.5, 6)\}$.
    a. Compute the response time of each task under RM scheduling. Does the task set have a feasible static priority assignment?
    b. Compute the load of the task set.
    c. Show the EDF schedule of the task set at the critical instant of the task set.

13. Repeat Exercise 12 using the task set $\{(1, 4), (2, 5), (3, 12)\}$.

14. Show that deadline monotonic is an optimal scheduling algorithm.

15. Show that earliest deadline first is an optimal scheduling algorithm.

16. Consider real-time tasks τ_1, τ_2, and τ_3 (in decreasing order of priority).
    a. Task T1's execution is: execute 1 second, P(T), 1 sec., P(S), 1 sec., V(S), 1 sec., V(T), 1 sec., end
    b. Task T2's execution is: execute 2 seconds, P(S), 2 sec., V(S), 2 sec., end
    c. Task T3's execution is: execute 1 sec, P(T), 3 sec, V(T), 1 sec, end
    Suppose that τ_3 arrives at time 0, τ_2 arrives at time 2, and τ_1 arrives at time 5. What are the completion times of τ_1, τ_2, and τ_3 if
    a. No priority inheritance is used
    b. The priority inheritance protocol is used
    c. The priority ceiling protocol is used

17. In actual systems, one must account for context switching overhead. Suppose that the worst-case time to perform a context switch is CS seconds. Modify response time Equation 5.1 to account for context switching overhead.

18. Modify response time Equation 5.4 to account for context switching overhead.

19. In actual systems, a high-priority task is not executed as soon as it is requested. The scheduler can notice the ready high-priority task at a clock interrupt. The difference between the ready time of a task and when the scheduler can determine that the task is ready is called the *release jitter*, j. Modify Equation 5.1 to account for release jitter.

20. Modify response time equation 5.4 to account for release jitter.

21. Give an algorithm to compute *ceiling*(S) in the presence of nested critical sections.

22. Show that a task will be blocked at most once under PCP.

23. Show that PCP prevents deadlocks.

CHAPTER

Distributed File Systems

A computing system is a collection of processes operating on data objects. *Persistant* data objects need to be stored on a long-term basis for later retrieval. They must be named and saved on a nonvolatile storage device, such as a magnetic disk. Named data objects are called **files**. We assume that files are basic data objects, and their internal structure and interpretation are left as system-specific implementation issues. A file system, which is a major component in an operating system, is responsible for the naming, creation, deletion, retrieval, modification, and protection of all files in the system. Files need to be shared to facilitate cooperative work and may be distributed over a number of distinct sites in a distributed system.

A **Distributed File System** (DFS) is an implementation of a file system that consists of physically dispersed storage sites but which provides a traditional centralized file system view for users. That is, the existence of files crossing system boundaries is transparent to the users. Many important concepts in distributed system design can be demonstrated by the implementation of a distributed file system. First, DFSs employ many aspects of the notion of transparency. Second, the **directory** service in a DFS is a good example of a **name** service, a key component in all distributed systems. Third, the performance and availability require the use of caching and replication, leading to problems of cache coherence and replica management. Fourth, access control and protection for DFSs opens many problems in distributed system security. This chapter introduces these issues and provides references to other chapters where certain aspects are investigated in greater detail.

6.1 CHARACTERISTICS OF A DFS

Two key characteristics of a DFS are the *dispersion* and *multiplicity* of users and files. That is, multiple clients in dispersed locations may access dispersed files, which are often replicated. Our design goal is to hide the dispersion and multiplicity from the users. A transparent DFS should exhibit the following transparency properties:

- **Dispersed clients**: A user can log in at any host (assuming that the user has the privilege to use that host) in the system with a uniform login procedure and perceive a uniform view of the file system, independent of the host. This property is called *login transparency*. Once on a host, the client processes running on the host have a uniform mechanism to access all files in the system, regardless of whether the files are on the local or a remote host. This property is referred to as *access transparency*.

- **Dispersed files**: The names used to refer to files need not contain information about the physical location of the files; the files are *location transparent* to the clients. Furthermore, files can be moved from one physical location to another without changing their names. This property is called *location independence* and is a stronger property than location transparency.

- **Multiplicity of users**: Files can be shared by multiple concurrent users. An update to a file by one process should not have an adverse effect on the correct execution of other processes that are concurrently sharing the file. This property is called *concurrency transparency*. Transaction-based applications require that the application appears to access the file in isolation (in spite of interleaved file accesses by several applications). The problem of ensuring the concurrent execution of a transaction is referred to as *concurrency control* in database systems. It is desirable for a DFS to support concurrency transparency at the transaction level.

■ **Multiplicity of files:** Files in a DFS may be replicated to provide redundancy for availability and also to permit concurrent accesses for efficiency. A DFS with *replication transparency* performs atomic updates on the replicas, and clients are not aware that more than one copy of the file exists.

The various transparency properties described above are important requirements for the design of a DFS. Other desirable characteristics relevant to transparency include fault tolerance, scalability, and heterogeneity of the system. Failures, such as the crash of a server or client process, loss of messages, and partition of network, are not perceived by the users except as a minor degradation of system performance. Incremental file system growth and updates should not interrupt the normal operation of the file system. These transparency issues are not restricted to distributed file systems but are applicable to distributed system in general.

6.2 DFS Design and Implementation

We will first present some basic concepts of files and file systems. The unique problems in the design and implementation of a distributed file system are due to the need for sharing and replication of files. Protocols for achieving transparency in sharing and replication are the main focus of this chapter.

6.2.1 Files and File Systems

To the users, a file consists of three logical components:

file name	file attributes	data units

Files created by users are associated with a symbolic name. When accessing a file, its symbolic name is mapped to an unique file id (*ufid* or *file handle*) that can locate the physical file. This is the primary function of the *directory service* in the file system. File attributes typically contain information about ownership, type, size, timestamps, and access authorization of the file.

Data units can be organized as a *flat* structure of a stream of bytes or sequence of blocks or, alternatively, as a *hierarchical* structure of indexed records. Depending on the underlying file structure, file accesses are generally in one of the three modes: *sequential access, direct access,* and *indexed sequential access.* In the sequential access mode, a *file position* pointer is maintained by the system for each *opened* file, to indicate the position of the next data unit to be accessed. The file position pointer is *not* part of the file attributes; rather it is part of the process state (although the file pointer usually can be shared among related processes). Opening a file initializes the file pointer and starts a *session* of subsequent file accesses, which last until the file is closed. A session is similar to a connection in connection-oriented network communication.

Unlike the the sequential access methods, where the position of a data unit for read/write is implicit, direct access methods explicitly reference fixed-size data units by their block numbers. Each read/write operation contains complete addressing information and is independent of other read/write operations. File accesses are similar to connection-less network communication. Opening the file is not strictly necessary unless the session semantics (discussed further in Section 6.2.5) are desired for file sharing. In addition to defining a session, most file systems also use the *open* system call to achieve a one-time mapping of the symbolic file name to an internal machine representation for later file accesses and to gain access authorization of the files. For direct file access methods, the *open* operation functions more like a file location *look-up*.

Alternatively, data units can be addressed directly by using an index (or key) associated with each data block. Indexed file access requires the maintenance of an search index on the file, which must be searched to locate a block address for each access. Due to the storage and time overhead, indexed access is usually used only by large file systems in mainframe computers. To reduce the size of the search index, a two-level scheme is often used, the *indexed sequential access method*. A sequence of key/object pairs is stored in a large data block. A key/object pair is located by using the search index to locate the block in which the pair resides, and then accessing the data in the block until the key/object pair is found. This two-level operation combines the direct and sequential access methods in a way similar to finding information through the index in a textbook. It is commonly used for large data files, where the data records are kept on secondary storage devices and the index table is maintained in primary memory for efficient searching.

Flat file structures have gained more popularity recently due to their simplicity and their resemblance to the storage devices that implement files. For example, Unix assumes that files are streams of characters for application programs and sequences of logical fixed-size blocks for file systems. Both sequential and direct access methods are supported. Other access methods can be built on top of the flat file structures.

A file system organizes and provides access and protection services for a collection of files. Functionally, it consists of four major components: directory, authorization, file service, and system services. File systems that support transactions further divide the file service into the transaction and the basic file service. Transaction service has its unique implementation problems, discussed in Section 6.3.3. Figure 6.1 shows some examples of functions provided by each service. The organization of data files in a file system can be

FIGURE 6.1   Major components in a file system.

directory service		name resolution, add and deletion of files
authorization service		capability and / or access control list
file service	transaction	concurrency and replication management
	basic	read / write files and get / set attributes
system service		device, cache, and block management

FIGURE 6.2   Hierarchical structure of a file system.

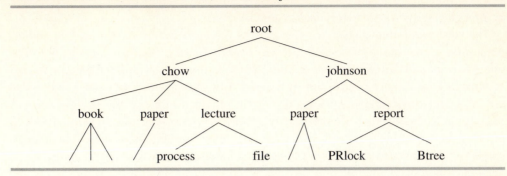

either flat or hierarchical, similar to the choice of an internal structure of an individual file. However, it is more natural to organize files in multilevel categories, resulting in a hierarchical directory and naming structure. Files are named and accessed using a hierarchical path name such as /chow/lecture/file, as shown in Figure 6.2.

Accesses to a file must first use a directory service to locate the file. Mapping textual names to addresses by the directory service is quite independent from actual file operations. It is therefore a common practice to separate directory service from file service to facilitate modularity and portability. A major advantage of this separation of services is that different directory structures can be supported by a common file service. Directories are files that contain names and addresses of other files and subdirectories. Operations on directory files include look-up, addition, and deletion of directory entries in the files. Thus directory servers are clients of the file service that performs file updates.

File access must be regulated to ensure security. This is the role of an authorization service. A logical placement of the authorization service should be between the directory and file services for protection of files or on top of the directory service for protection of the directory also. In an actual implementation, it could be merged either with the file service or with the directory service. In the former case, the file servers maintain access control information. The directory service merely performs name resolution that provides a file handle for locating the requested file in a file server. Each file operation is checked to ensure that the client is authorized to submit the operation. In the latter case, the directory service performs access control verification in addition to name resolution. The directory service maintains file (and directory) access control information. If the client authorization to open a file is verified, the client is issued a file handle and a nonforgeable *capability*, which represents the client's file-using privileges. For subsequent accesses to the file service, only the capability is validated by the file servers. The identification of the client is irrelevant to the file servers, since the capability implies the authenticity of the client. The role of access authorization is discussed in greater detail in Chapter 8.

The basic file operations provided by the file service are the read/write of data blocks and get/set of file attributes. Since a file must be created before it can be used and deleted when it is no longer needed, the file service should also support creation and deletion operations for a file. The creation and deletion of a file involve more than just adding and deleting entries in the directory by the directory service. They interact with system services underneath to allocate and deallocate buffer and file spaces. The file service becomes a client of the directory and system services.

The most interesting file service operation is the open operation. An open operation implies the initialization of a session of file operations on a file. It is analogous to the establishment of a connection between the client and the file server. The directory service is consulted by the open operation only once. The subsequent read/write requests are sent to the file service directly using a file handle obtained from the directory service and kept by the client's kernel. The kernel keeps track of the connection, including the file position pointer for the next read/write operation. Many systems also assume that an open operation will create a new file if the file does not already exist. Therefore, implicitly, the open operation plays the role of a file creation operation. The close operation indicates the end of an opened session. Open operations are not strictly necessary if the client and server relationship is *connectionless*. In this case, read and write are one-shot operations. Each request from clients to a file server contains all the necessary information for the file access.

Directory, authorization, and file services are user interfaces to a file system. System services are a file system's interface to the hardware and are transparent to users of the file system. The major functions provided by system services include mapping of logical to physical block addresses, interfacing to services at the device level for file space allocation/deallocation, and actual read/write file operations. System services are supported by system calls to the kernel. Finally, files in a file system may be cached for performance enhancement and replicated to improve reliability. It is important to note that management of cache and replicas is another essential system service of a file system. Caching and replication are further complicated by file sharing in a distributed system. This chapter addresses these two important issues in the design of distributed file systems.

6.2.2 Services and Servers

It is necessary to distinguish between services and servers. Servers are processes that implement services. A service may be implemented by a particular server or by a number of coordinating servers. Large file systems distribute the managed files among many file servers. A server may also provide multiple services, such as in the case of a directory server that performs both directory and authorization services.

The client/server relationship is relative. To access a file, a user process first becomes a client process of the directory server. The directory service may request file services and thus become a client of the file server. Access authorization makes the file or directory server a client of the authorization server. The authorization server may in turn require services of the file server. File services rely on the system services for low-level functions provided by the kernel. Figure 6.3 shows an example of the interaction among the four services in a DFS. The dashed lines in the figure indicate that the authorization service can be merged either with the directory server or the file server.

Servers normally are associated with the machines that have the resource that the servers manage. Many large centralized file systems use dedicated machines as file servers for performance and administrative reasons. These systems clearly differentiate server

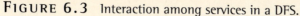

FIGURE 6.3   Interaction among services in a DFS.

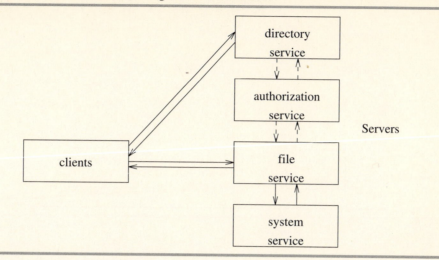

machines from client machines. However, in a distributed environment where files are dispersed among several machines, it is more cost effective for each machine to assume both client and server roles. Each machine wishing to provide file services is allowed to do so by exporting all or parts of its file system for remote file accesses. These exported files can be *mounted* on a client's directory structure.

To keep the spirit of the client/server model and the division of responsibilities in distributed systems, servers in a DFS are usually structured to provide directory, authorization, file, and system services separately.

6.2.3 File Mounting and Server Registration

We assume that directories are hierarchically structured. Mounting files is a useful concept for constructing a large file system from various file servers and storage devices. A mounting operation from a client attaches a remote named file system to the client's file system hierarchy at the position pointed to by a path name. The mounting point is usually a leaf of the directory tree that contains only an empty subdirectory. The named file system to be mounted is identified by a remote host or a local device followed by a path name to the file system. Figure 6.4 shows a file system that is formed by mounting local and remote file systems. In the figure, a remote file server exports a subfile system *OS*, which contains three files, *DFS, DSM,* and *Security*. This subfile system is mounted to a client's subdirectory, *book*, through the use of a mounting protocol.

Once files are mounted, they are accessed by using the concatenated logical path names without referencing either the remote hosts or local devices. Location transparency of the files is achieved. The linkage information (usually called *mount table* for access redirection) for the remote file systems is maintained by the host file system until they are unmounted. Using this mounting mechanism, it is possible that different clients may perceive a different file system view since remote files can be mounted on different subdirectories of each client. If a uniform global file system view is desirable, the system

FIGURE 6.4 Mounting of file systems.

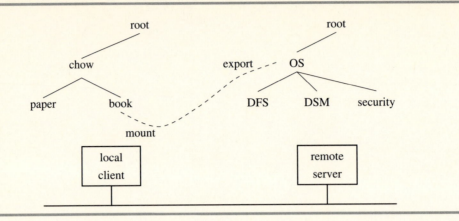

administrator can enforce mounting rules. For example, shared system files must be mounted at some agreed upon positions in the directory hierarchy, separate from the local file systems. For security reasons, a file server normally restricts the mounting of all or part of its file system to a predefined set of hosts. This information is contained in the server's *export* file. File system mountings are privileged operations and can be done in three different instances:

- **Explicit mounting**: Clients make explicit mounting system calls whenever one is desired.
- **Boot mounting**: A set of file servers is prescribed and all mountings are performed at the client's booting time.
- **Automounting**: Mounting of the servers is implicitly done on demand when a file is first opened by a client.

Explicit mounting of each file system is flexible but less manageable than boot mounting, where a uniform configuration of the file system can be enforced at boot time. Using boot mounting, a client has a static but complete file system view for the entire computing session. Naturally, boot mounting has the disadvantage of wasting work in mounting unnecessary servers. Automounting is a combination of explicit mounting and boot mounting and has the advantages of both. It is dynamic, like explicit mounting (actually more so since files are mounted only when they are to be accessed), and transparent, like boot mounting without explicit mounting calls. When a file is opened, the kernel selects a server from a prescribed set and mounts the requested file system. The automounting in Sun's Network File System (NFS) carries this one step further. It allows clients to specify a number of servers that can support the same file service. The operating system broadcasts the request and mounts the first server that responds to the request.

File mounting is a convenient way of achieving file access location transparency. However, the initial mounting requires knowledge of the location of file servers; that is, the mounting protocol is not transparent. In a system in which multiple file servers can provide the same file service, the location information becomes irrelevant to the clients. A file server can be located in two different ways:

- File servers register their services with a registration service, and clients consult with the registration server before mounting.
- Clients broadcast mounting requests, and file servers respond to clients' requests.

Both approaches are essentially a name or address resolution protocol. For a DFS, the registration service offers the additional advantage of a performance gain. A registration server can assign the best file server, or one that balances the system load, to a client's request based on the registration server's knowledge of the system. The registration server behaves like an intelligent *trader*, a concept found in the decentralized cooperative autonomous systems discussed in Chapters 1 and 2. A client can also choose one of the responses that it receives from a broadcast using any reasonable policy. Furthermore, the linkage information residing in the client's kernel can be treated as a cache. If a file server moved to a different host, a file access to the server would result in a cache miss. Either one of the two resolution protocols can be activated to find the new location of the server without client intervention. Effectively, we have achieved file location independence.

Mountings of remote file systems are often cascaded. A mounted file system may have some of its subdirectories mounted from other file servers. In this case traversing a path name requires going through multiple mount tables across machine boundaries. It is possible that the destination file server is available for access, but problems in the intermediate file servers prevent the client from reaching the file. A solution is to allow direct access to a file once the file is located. This information can be kept in a cache for all opened remote files. Address resolution relies on the network routing rather than on the file system.

6.2.4 Stateful and Stateless File Servers

We have described a session of file operations as a *connection* for a sequence of *requests* and *responses* between a client and the file server. A connection intrinsically requires the establishment and termination of the communication session. Furthermore, there is state information associated with each file session (connection). Some examples of state information are listed below:

- Opened files and their clients
- File descriptors and file handles
- Current file position pointers
- Mounting information
- Lock status
- Session keys
- Cache or buffer

This state information is maintained dynamically when files are being used. They are different from file attributes, which are static properties of files. We will see why and where state information is needed. Starting from the top of the list, the state must contain information about what files are being opened by which clients. This information may reside either in the client or the server system or both. Next, to avoid going through the directory server repeatedly for each file access, a file descriptor and its file handle are given to each opened file and kept by the client's kernel. For sequential accesses, an implicit file position pointer must be associated with each opened file session. When a shared file is opened by multiple clients, each opened file session has its own current file position pointer, except in the cases of inheritance. In such cases, clients inherit files from their parents, and the file position pointers are shared between the parent and child processes. File position pointers naturally should be kept with the opened file information. Next on the list is file mounting information. Files on file servers are mounted by clients for remote accesses. The client's kernel must maintain the linkage information to the remote files. The servers do not need to be aware of which files are being mounted by which clients once their files are mounted.

To coordinate sharing of files, it is often desirable to allow clients to have the capability of locking a file. Since a lock is global information shared by some clients, it seems most suitable for the file server to manage this information. Another example of information sharing is the session key for communication. The concept of using session keys for secure communication between clients and file servers is discussed in Chapter 8. To discuss the state of a connection between clients and file server, we will simply assume that session keys are an agreed upon secret between a file server and its clients, and thus are state information. Some secure communication protocols exist that use one-time session keys. In those cases, there is no need to store the keys as part of state information. Finally, caches or buffers may be used either in the client or in the server to reduce access delay. Caching and buffering are useful when access requests exhibit localities. Data in the cache and buffer are state information of the connection.

It is clear that the state information of a file session may be distributed between the communicating client and file server. How state information is divided greatly affects the performance and management of the distributed file system. Obviously, the requesting client must maintain much of the information. What the file server should assume for an opened session needs to be determined. A file server is called **stateful** if it maintains internally some of the state information and **stateless** if it maintains none at all. Clearly the more that is known about a connection, the more flexibility there is in exercising control over it. However, the notion of state is something to avoid as much as possible in the design of a distributed system. A stateless server is much easier to implement and is more fault-tolerant upon client or server failures than one that has to keep track of state information. The trade-off is between flexibility and simplicity. Since failures are more frequent in distributed systems, many DFS implementations chose to implement stateless file servers. Client failures have no effect on the file server. Crashes of a stateless file server are easy to recover from and are perceived by other clients as a delay in response (or no response) without disrupting their sessions. For a stateless file server, each file request to the server must be contain full information about the file handle, position pointer, session key, and other necessary information. The implementation of a stateless file server must address the following issues:

- **Idempotency requirement:** How does a file server deal with possible repeated client requests caused by the previous failures (nonresponsiveness) of the server? Is it practical to structure all file accesses as idempotent operations?

- **File locking mechanism:** How can sharing clients implement a file locking mechanism on top of stateless file servers? Should locking mechanisms be integrated into the transaction service?

- **Session key management:** How is the session key generated and maintained between the communicating client and stateless file server? Can a one-time session key be used for each file access?

- **Cache consistency:** Is the file server responsible for controlling cache consistency among clients? What sharing semantics are to be supported?

The above discussion indicates that while the concept of a stateless file server is simple and attractive, for practical implementations some minimal state information may have to be maintained by the servers. The idempotency requirement and the problem with shared session keys were addressed in Chapter 4 in the discussion of an RPC implementation. These solutions are applicable to file servers if remote procedure calls are used for invoking file services. File locking and cache consistency are left as exercises.

6.2.5 File Access and Semantics of Sharing

The complexity of implementing concurrent accesses to a remote shared file depends on how files are shared and the semantics of file sharing as defined by the users.

File Access

File sharing means multiple clients can access the same file at the same time. Such sharing may result from either overlapping or interleaving access operations.

Overlapping accesses implies that there are multiple copies of the same file, and concurrency is achieved by *space* multiplexing of the file. An example of where file data could be replicated is the use of a cache. It is advantageous to bring parts of a remote file into a local cache for fast access. Similarly, it is sometimes necessary to maintain a working copy of a file before permanent changes are made to it. In both cases, replicated copies of a shared data file exist and simultaneous accesses to the file become possible. Each site that has a copy of the replicated file may see a different view of the data. Managing accesses to the replicas, to provide a coherent view of the shared file, is called *coherency control.*

Interleaving accesses are due to multiple granularities of data access operations. Some file accesses are simple read/write operations. Others involve sequences of interrelated operations spanning across a user-defined time interval, such as a transaction or a session. The interleaving execution of these sequences on the same files also creates an

FIGURE 6.5 Space and time concurrencies of file accesses.

time \ space	remote access	cache access	down/up load access
simple RW	no true sharing	coherency control	coherency control
transaction	concurrency control	coherency and concurrency	coherency and concurrency
session	not applicable	not applicable	ignore sharing

illusion of simultaneous file sharing. Concurrency is achieved by *time* multiplexing of the files. The management issues here are primarily how to prevent one execution sequence from interfering with the others when they are interleaved and how to avoid inconsistent or erroneous results. This problem is commonly referred to as *concurrency control*.

Figure 6.5 shows the space and time multiplexings that achieve the effect of concurrent accesses to shared files. The entries in the table are the management functions required for each sharing assumption. In the space domain, read and write accesses to a remote file can be implemented in one of the following ways, depending on how file data is staged for accesses:

- **Remote access**: No file data is kept in the client machine. Each access request is transmitted directly to the remote file server through the underlying network.
- **Cache access**: A small part of the file data is maintained in a local cache. A write operation or cache miss results a remote access and update of the cache.
- **Download/upload access**: The entire file is downloaded for local accesses. A remote access or upload is performed when updating the remote file.

The first approach is a single-level access model, while the others are a two-level hierarchical storage representation of the data. The implementation of the single-level remote access model is straightforward since only one copy of the data file exists, and all access requests can be serialized by the file server. The primary drawbacks are the long network access delay and limited concurrency. The cache and download/upload models allow concurrent accesses and reduce access delay by keeping some or all accesses locally. However, these approaches introduce the file coherency problem. Since file data are replicated and may be shared by several concurrent users, a shared file may appear differently to different simultaneous clients. Coherency control for replicated data is a nontrivial problem. Coherency of replicated data can be interpreted in many different ways. The following interpretations (or definitions) are listed in the order of stringency:

1. All replicas are identical at all times.
2. Replicas are perceived as identical only at some points in time.
3. Users always read the "most recent" data in the replicas.
4. Write operations are always performed "immediately" and their results are propagated in a best-effort fashion.

The first definition of coherency is ideal but is impossible to achieve in distributed systems due to nonnegligible communication delays. Therefore, we accept the fact that not all copies are identical at all times. The second definition is a compromise, but it is difficult to determine the good synchronization points. The currency of data is meaningful only at the time when they are read. Thus the third definition seems logical. The trouble is the vagueness of the term, *most recent* (or *latest*). The relative order of write operations should be based on their "completion" times, which are the times when the effect of a write operation has been reflected in all copies. A protocol is needed such that a read operation is always returned with the result of the most recent write. The last definition is just a coarse attempt to approximate the third definition.

The file coherency problem is due to the existence of replicated data and the client's delayed updates to the replicas. Coherence is a more serious problem in distributed systems since network delays are longer and less predictable. Compounding the delay problem is the fact that failures (clients, servers, or communication) happen more frequently in distributed systems. Failures during the update of a file may put the file in an inconsistent state. It is highly desirable for a system to guarantee the **atomicity** of updates, such that each update operation is either successfully completed or has no effect. For multiple copies of the same data file, an update to the file is atomic if all or none of the copies are updated. An atomic update requires that the system be *recoverable* (i.e., capable of *undoing* a partial update and restoring the system to the state before the partial update). An *undo* operation implies the use of *stable* storage that can be used to restore the system state in the face of all system failures. The atomicity property of the atomic update of replicas was introduced in the context of atomic multicast communication in Chapter 4. It is revisited in the latter sections of this chapter from the data point of view and will be discussed again in Chapter 12, with topics on replica management protocols.

In the time domain, related file operations can be grouped in different time intervals according to their application requirements. Interleaved read and write operations from different processes result in concurrent file accesses. Some file access assumptions are:

- **Simple RW**: Each read and write operation is an independent request/response access to the file server.

- **Transaction**: A sequence of read and write operations is treated as a fundamental unit of file access (with some additional semantic requirements for the transaction). Syntactically, a transaction is expressed by a *begin transaction* that is followed by several file accesses and ends with a *end transaction*. A transaction here is defined in a narrow sense that read and write operations are accesses to the same file.

■ **Session:** A session consists of a sequence of transactions and simple RW operations, with additional semantics associated with the session as defined by the applications. Typically, a session is encapsulated with a pair of open and close operations.

Simple RW access and sessions are familiar concepts in all operating systems. A transaction is a high-level synchronization concept. The transaction's data accesses are enclosed by a *begin transaction/end transaction* pair. This sequence of accesses (including updates) is atomic or *indivisible*, meaning that the sequence of operations be performed without interference from other clients. The result of an interleaved execution of accesses by many clients is equivalent to a serial execution of the sequence, taking the data from one consistent state to another consistent state. If the atomicity, consistency, isolation, and durability (ACID) properties are satisfied (see Chapter 4), the data access is made in an *atomic transaction*. The concept of an atomic transaction is very common for business applications. The function of enforcing atomicity and consistency in a file server is called the **transaction service**, discussed in the next section.

Semantics of Sharing

Sharing of files using space and time multiplexed accesses raises coherency and concurrency control problems. Solutions to the problems depend on the semantics of sharing required by applications. Ideally, we like updates of a file to be completed instantaneously and their results to be visible to other sharing processes immediately. Practically, this semantic is hard to achieve and consequently is often relaxed. Write delays are unavoidable in distributed systems, since the effect of a write operation can be delayed by the network or by the system services that enforce coherency and consistency. Using the notion of space and time in Figure 6.5, we list three popular semantic models that have different objectives for file sharing:

■ **Unix semantics:** The result of a write is propagated to the file and its copies immediately so that reads will return the "latest" value of the file. No delay of a write is imposed except unavoidable network delays. Subsequent accesses from the client that has issued the write must wait for the write to complete. The primary objective is to maintain currency of the data.

■ **Transaction semantics:** The results of writes are tentatively stored in working storage and committed permanently only when some consistency constraints are met at the end of a transaction. The primary objective is to maintain consistency of the data.

■ **Session semantics:** Writes to a file are performed on a working copy, and the result is made permanent only at the close of the session. The primary objective is to maintain efficiency of data accesses.

The major difference between Unix semantics and the other two is the delay of write operations. Unix semantics attempt to make the effect of writes visible immediately, while transaction and session semantics use delayed writes. Unix semantics are easy to implement in a single processor system, where data are cached on a *per file* (**server**

6.3 TRANSACTIONS AND CONCURRENCY CONTROL

Transaction processing was developed for database management, but we can apply the ideas and techniques to distributed file system management. The motivation is to make use of the clean and powerful atomic transaction semantics (i.e., the ACID properties introduced in Section 4.3). In this section, we discuss how transactions can be implemented in a distributed system, in the specific context of implementing distributed file systems.

6.3.1 Transaction Services

Figure 6.6 shows a simple architecture for a distributed transaction processing system. Clients at each distributed site issue their transaction service requests to the local transaction processing system (TPS), which consists of three major components: a transaction manager (TM), a scheduler (SCH), and an object manager (OM). A transaction may invoke operations on remote objects. These operations are represented as subtransactions and sent to the remote TPSs. The transaction manager works in concert with other TMs to oversee the correct execution of both the local transactions and the remote subtransactions. The primary responsibility of the scheduler is to schedule operations to objects to avoid conflicts. The object managers ensure the coherency of replicas and caches and provide an interface to the file system. We will use this simple architecture for distributed transaction services to address three atomicity requirements:

- The execution of the collection of operations in each transaction is *all or none.*
- The execution of a transaction that is interleaved with the execution of other transactions appears to be *indivisible.*
- The update of a replicated object is *atomic.*

Atomicity is the primary goal of atomic transactions. Isolation and durability are secondary in the sense that they are needed only to support atomicity. The responsibilities

FIGURE 6.6   A distributed transaction processing system.

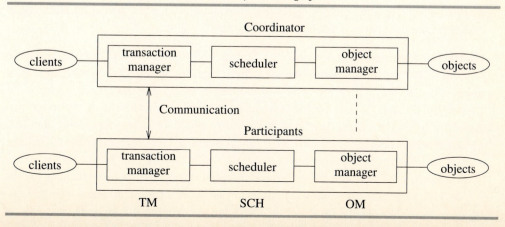

of enforcing the three different atomicity requirements fall naturally on the three transaction service managers: TM, SCH, and OM, respectively.

In Chapter 4 (Figure 4.15) we saw how a two-phase commit protocol can be used to achieve *all or none* atomicity. Using the same approach for transaction processing, a transaction manager serves as the coordinator, with the remote transaction managers being the participants in the two-phase commit protocol. Similarly, the protocol can be applied to the atomic update of replicated objects. The object manager where an update is requested initiates the two-phase commit protocol in conjunction with other object managers that are holding a replica of the object. The consistency problem of the replication of objects is the responsibility of the object managers and should be transparent to the transaction managers and schedulers. Various protocols less restricted than the two-phase commit have been proposed for more efficient management of replicated objects. The basic concepts of replicated data management will be discussed in Section 6.4 and advanced topics will be discussed later in Chapter 12 after we have addressed the concurrency control issue for achieving *indivisible* atomicity.

Protocols for implementing *all or none* and *indivisible* distributed transactions are often integrated. We can use the diagram in Figure 6.6 to outline such a solution approach. The following summarizes the functions performed by each of the four entities (client process, transaction manager, scheduler, object manager) in Figure 6.6 and the interactions among them.

Transaction Processing System

- **Client process:** A client process initiates the start of a transaction by issuing a *begin transaction* to its local transaction manager (TM). Upon receiving the initiation request, the TM generates a transaction id and a work space to be used by the client for subsequent *read/write* operations. The client is at liberty to abort its transaction at any time before issuing the *end transaction* by informing the TM of the abort. An *end transaction* from a client to the TM indicates that the client is ready to commit the transaction and expects the TM to return the status of the atomic commit at all TMs involved in this transaction, as either successfully *committed* or *aborted*. The protocols used for atomicity and consistency by the transaction manager, scheduler, and object managers are completely transparent to the client.

- **Transaction manager:** The TM creates a transaction id and a work space in response to a client's *begin transaction*. Following the initiation, each access request to a data object (by the TM acting on behalf of a client's *read/write* operation), carries the transaction id and is sent to the scheduler. Access results in the work space are visible only to the client. This is the *execution phase* of a transaction at the TM. The transaction manager has knowledge of all pending local transactions and remote subtransactions invoked at the site.

  Access requests from the TM are either accepted or rejected by the scheduler (SCH). An accepted operation changes the state of the work space and acknowledges the completion to the client. To maintain the *none* part of the *all or none* property, a rejected operation causes the TM to abort the transaction by sending an *abort* to the client and all other transaction managers involved in that transaction. If everything goes well (no aborts), the client reaches the *end transaction*, signaling the TM to do the *all* part of the transaction. The transaction manager concludes the *execution phase* of read/write operations and enters the *commit phase* of the transaction to decide whether the transaction should be committed or aborted. The commit operation must be atomic (i.e., the TM must get unanimous votes from all involved TMs before making any update permanent). Again, this can be accomplished by a two-phase commit protocol. If the final two-phase commit is successful, updates are committed at all OMs and a *committed* status is reported to the client. Otherwise the transaction manager aborts the transaction and informs other TMs to clean up all traces left by the transaction.

■ **Scheduler:** The SCH chooses a concurrency control protocol to ensure the consistency of concurrent execution of transactions at distributed sites. There are three general approaches to the concurrency control problem. Inconsistency can be *prevented* or *avoided* or consistency can be *validated*. In the first approach, all access requests in a transaction are constrained in a certain format such that interference among conflict operations can be prevented. It is the responsibility of the TM to transform client's transactions into the restrictive form. Typically, locks are used in this approach. Schedulers assume the lock management functions. In the second approach each individual access operation is checked by the scheduler and a decision of whether the operation should be accepted, tentatively accepted, or rejected to avoid conflicts is made by the scheduler. The most common criteria implemented for this decision makes use of timestamps. Schedulers perform the scheduling of operations based on timestamp ordering. In the third approach conflicts are completely ignored during the execution phase of a transaction. The consistency is validated at the end of the execution phase. Only transactions that can be globally validated are allowed to commit. Schedulers become validation managers. An example of each of the three different approaches is given in the next section. They are the two-phase locking, timestamp ordering, and optimistic concurrency control protocols.

■ **Object manager:** The OM is responsible for interfacing with the underlying file service for actual operations on an object. It provides cache management for efficiency and participates in failure recovery protocols to support durability. If objects are replicated, the OMs manage the consistency of the replicas using a replica management protocol.

For clarity, we isolate the issue of concurrency control for the SCHs in the above discussion of distributed transaction processing systems. Concurrency control protocols are based on the concept of serializability. Serializability is an extensively studied subject in distributed transaction systems. The following sections use a simple example to illustrate the concept of serializability and to motivate three popular concurrency control approaches: two-phase locking, timestamp ordering, and optimistic concurrency control protocols.

6.3.2 Serializability

The concept of transactions is extremely useful for data integrity in a multiuser file sharing distributed system. The ACID properties ensure that no adverse interference can be caused by other transactions and failures in the system. Programmers write sequential transaction-based applications that may be executed concurrently with other transactions but appear to be serial. The concurrency transparency allows users to develop fault-tolerant database applications independently from others.

Each transaction in a database system consists of a sequence of operations that may read from or write to some data objects. To avoid race conditions, we assume that data objects must be locked before being read or written to. Moreover, to differentiate between concurrent reads and an exclusive write, a *shared* lock is used for concurrent reading, and an *exclusive* lock is used for writing. All locks must be released after the operations and before the end of a transaction. If locks are not used, writes can only be made tentatively. A transaction is *well formed* if it follows this convention for every read/write access to a shared data object. Operations in different transactions are said to be in *conflict* with each other if they *write-write*, *write-read*, or *read-write* on a shared object.

All operations in a set of transactions are interleaved to form a *schedule* for execution. A *legal* schedule is one that observes the internal ordering of operations for each transaction and in which no transactions hold conflicting locks simultaneously (if the protocol is a locking algorithm). Obviously, not all legal schedules will yield consistent results or even complete (a deadlock may occur due to cyclic hold-and-wait of locks). We are interested only in those schedules that can be successfully completed with consistent results. A schedule is called *serializable* if the result of its execution is equivalent to that of a *serial* schedule. A serial schedule is a special legal schedule that is formed by a strict sequential execution (no interleaving operations) of the transactions in some order. Of course, we assume that each transaction in this serial schedule satisfies the ACID properties. The *serializability* of serial schedules ensures the consistency requirement, meaning that the database is transferred from one consistent state to another consistent state as the transactions execute.

Enforcing consistency requirements is the primary responsibility of the transaction manager and the scheduler. It is desirable to find the necessary and sufficient conditions for serializability so that a transaction manager can use them to derive a serializable schedule or to validate the consistent execution of a transaction. We use the following example to illustrate the concept of serializability.

Assume that there are three transactions: t_0, t_1, and t_2. Transaction t_0 has already been committed. Transactions t_1 and t_2 are presented to two different transaction managers for concurrent execution.

t_0 : **bt** Write A=100, Write B=20 **et**
t_1 : **bt** Read A, Read B, 1: Write sum in C, 2: Write diff in D **et**
t_2 : **bt** Read A, Read B, 3: Write diff in C, 4: Write sum in D **et**

These three transactions share data objects A, B, C, and D, located in different sites in a transaction processing system like the one shown in Figure 6.6. Acquiring and releasing the locks for each of the data objects are omitted in the transactions for clarity. They are actually inserted by the transaction managers and issued to the object managers. Operations in the transactions relevant to the following discussion are numbered from 1 to 4. Operation pairs (1, 3) and (2, 4) have *write-write* conflicts to objects C and D. All other operations are nonconflicting. There are six possible interleavings of operations 1 through 4, as shown in Table 6.1 (24 combinations for the permutation of four objects but the internal order of (1, 2) and (3, 4) must be observed). If transactions t_1 and t_2 are executed serially, the consistent outcome of objects (C,D) should be either (80, 120) or (120, 80). The notation W_i, in object sites C and D, is the write update from transaction t_i. Updates are buffered and written to a log at each local site. Updates are made permanent only if the execution of the transactions satisfies the serializability requirement and is successfully committed.

In the table we notice that schedules 1 through 4 are consistent and schedules 5 and 6 yield inconsistent results. The consistent schedules all have conflicting operations executed in the same order in both C and D, while the order is reversed in the inconsistent schedules. It is intuitive that *if the interleaved execution of transactions is to be equivalent to a serial execution in some order, then all conflicting operations in the interleaved serializable schedule must also be executed in the same order at all object sites.* This is the sufficient condition for the serializability of the transactions.

Readers may have observed the similarity between serializability and the two-phase total-order message multicast discussed in Chapter 4 (Figure 4.8). Applying the two-phase total-order multicast protocol for serializability, each transaction can be interpreted as a source of multicast and the object sites are multicast group members. Each local site follows the protocol and delivers the messages (for conflicting operations) in the same order. The analogy seems plausible except that there is one significant difference between a multicast and a transaction. A transaction is a sequence of operations, unlike

TABLE 6.1 Interleaving schedules.

Sched	Interleave	Log in C	Log in D	Result (C,D)	2PL	Timestamp
1	1, 2, 3, 4	$W_1 = 120$ $W_2 = 80$	$W_1 = 80$ $W_2 = 120$	(80, 120) consistent	feasible	feasible
2	3, 4, 1, 2	$W_2 = 80$ $W_1 = 120$	$W_2 = 120$ $W_1 = 80$	(120, 80) consistent	feasible	t_1 aborts and restarts
3	1, 3, 2, 4	$W_1 = 120$ $W_2 = 80$	$W_1 = 80$ $W_2 = 120$	(80, 120) consistent	not feasible	feasible
4	3, 1, 4, 2	$W_2 = 80$ $W_1 = 120$	$W_2 = 120$ $W_1 = 80$	(120, 80) consistent	not feasible	t_1 aborts and restarts
5	1, 3, 4, 2	$W_1 = 120$ $W_2 = 80$	$W_2 = 120$ $W_1 = 80$	(80, 80) inconsistent	not feasible	cascade aborts
6	3, 1, 2, 4	$W_2 = 80$ $W_1 = 120$	$W_1 = 80$ $W_2 = 120$	(120, 120) inconsistent	not feasible	t_1 aborts and restarts

a multicast, which is logically a single operation. Messages in the two-phase multicast protocol are ordered by multicast completion time. If we were to use the same strategy for transactions, updates would have to be ordered by transaction completion time. This means that transactions are processed in batches. The delay of one transaction will tie up the others, making the protocol impractical for transactions.

We have illustrated the concept of serializability by using a simple two-transaction example. For systems with a larger number of interacting transactions, a more precise model for serializability is needed. Chapter 12 presents the *serialization graph* model to address general serialization problems.

6.3.3 Concurrency Control Protocols

There are three general approaches to the concurrency control problem, whereby inconsistency can be *prevented* or *avoided* or consistency can be *validated*. In this section, we discuss two-phase locking, timestamp ordering, and optimistic concurrency control, which are examples of these approaches.

Two-phase Locking

Using the locking approach, all shared objects in a well-formed transaction must be locked before they can be accessed and must be released before the end of the transaction. The two-phase locking (2PL) protocol adds an additional requirement that a new lock cannot be acquired after the first release of a lock. A transaction is divided into two phases: a growing phase of locking and a shrinking phase of releasing the objects. An extreme case of a 2PL transaction is one that locks all required objects at the beginning of the transaction and releases all of them at the same time at the end of the transaction. Serialization is trivial because the only possible schedules are serial schedules. This method is used by some simple database applications but is not generally acceptable since it completely ignores sharing and concurrency. One can increase concurrency by releasing locks as soon as possible. However, typical practice is to release locks at the commit point, discussed shortly.

Two-phase locking produces serializable transactions, as can be seen from the above example. If transaction t_1 has acquired object C in operation 1, it will not release the object until after operation 2 has been completed. This will make it impossible for operation 3 in transaction t_2 to occur between operations 1 and 2. Similarly, if transaction t_2 obtains the lock on C first, operation 1 in transaction t_1 cannot be scheduled between operations 3 and 4. Updates to D are forced to have the same order as updates to C. This means that schedules 3, 4, 5, and 6 in Table 6.1 are not feasible if t_1 and t_2 are 2PL transactions. The resulting schedules are limited to schedules 1 and 2. Thus, two-phase locking sacrifices concurrency for serializability.

Locking a resource and waiting for another is a source of potential deadlocks in any system. If operations 3 and 4 are reversed in transaction t_2, it is possible that transaction t_1 may be holding C and waiting for D while transaction t_2 is holding D and waiting for C. The result is a circular hold-and-wait deadlock.

It would seem that the TM should attempt to release locks as soon as possible; as soon as it knows that the last lock has been obtained and a data item will not be accessed by the transaction again. However, there are several difficult problems with this approach. First, we may encounter *rolling aborts*. Suppose that transaction t_1 updates data item C, and then releases the lock on C. Suppose next that transaction t_2 reads the value in C. If transaction t_1 aborts, t_2 must abort also, because t_2 has read *dirty data*. The abort of t_2 might cause the abort of another transaction t_3, and so on. Since t_2 can commit only if t_1 can commit, t_2 has a *commit dependence* on t_1. The commit dependencies must be tracked, and the commit of t_2 must be delayed until after the commit of t_1.

The problems of rolling aborts and commit dependence tracking can be solved by using *strict two-phase locking*. A transaction only releases its locks at its commit or abort point. It is difficult to implement two-phase locking systems that are not strict, since the TM does not know when the last lock has been requested. Strict two-phase locking sacrifices some concurrency but has the benefit of greatly simplifying the implementation.

Timestamp Ordering

Two-phase locking orders conflicting operations by the time a shared object is first locked. Previously we have seen many applications of logical timestamps for event ordering. Conflicting operations in interleaved transactions can be ordered by timestamps as well. If every object manager follows the transaction timestamp order to perform its invoked operations, the execution of transactions satisfies the serializability conditions.

Let us assume that t_0, t_1, and t_2 in the previous example are unique logical timestamps representing the three transactions, such that $t_0 < t_1 < t_2$. (We are using t_i to represent both the transaction and its timestamp.) When an operation on a shared object is invoked, the object records the timestamp of the invoking transaction. Suppose that later, a different transaction invokes a conflicting operation on the object. If the transaction has a larger timestamp than the one recorded by the object, we let the operation proceed (and record the new timestamp). If the transaction has a smaller timestamp, we must abort it; otherwise the transaction will execute out of order. The aborted transaction restarts and samples a larger timestamp.

Allowing a conflicting operation to proceed means that the operation is permitted to wait for its turn at the object site (i.e., an implicit lock). Younger (larger timestamp) transactions *wait* for older (smaller timestamp) transactions and older transactions *die and restart* when they confront with a younger transaction. Deadlocks are not possible because the execution of transactions based on the increasing order of transaction timestamps excludes the possibility of a circular hold-and-wait condition. Using this timestamp ordering approach, schedules 1 and 3 in Table 6.1 are feasible schedules and satisfy the consistency constraint. For schedules 2, 4, and 6, transaction t_1 arrives too late at object C. Transaction t_1 is aborted before it accesses object D. It will return with a larger timestamp, and will be executed in a schedule similar to that of 1 and 3.

The situation for schedule 5 is slightly more complicated. Operations 1, 3, and 4 execute without a problem, but operation 2 on object D in transaction t_1 sees a larger timestamp written by transaction t_2 in object D. To abort transaction t_1, we must also nullify its operation on C. In this particular example, object C, written by t_1, is simply rewritten by t_2's operation 3, causing no effect on t_2. However, if operation 3 were a read operation, t_2 would have read some data that is not supposed to be visible to it.

Consequently t_2 should be aborted too. To avoid violation of the isolation property, read operations must be distinguished from write operations and write operations can only be made *tentative* before a transaction commits to ensure the isolation property. The tentative writes are maintained by the scheduler SCH.

To implement the protocol with tentative writes, each object is associated with a pair of logical timestamps (RD and WR), indicating the transaction commitment times for the last read and write operations and a list of tentative times (T_s) for the pending transactions with a write operation to the object. Let us assume that these tentative times are sorted in an ascending order and T_{min} is the minimum of all. There is no need for tentative reads, but each object must keep track of the read transactions so that when a transaction commits, the latest time can be recorded as the new RD.

Figure 6.7 shows a typical event sequence of object invocations. The timestamp ordering two-phase commit protocol is described by the proper actions taken by the scheduler upon receiving a *read, write, abort,* or *commit* message from a transaction manager.

- **Read:** A read operation does not conflict with other reads. Thus, its timestamp is compared only with WR and T_{min}. The operation is aborted to maintain increasing timestamp order if its timestamp is smaller than WR. It is allowed to proceed if its timestamp is greater than WR but less than T_{min}. The read result is put into the TM's work space and returned to the client. An object may already have some tentative write operations pending when a read operation arrives (i.e., the timestamp of the read

FIGURE 6.7 Timestamp ordering concurrency control.

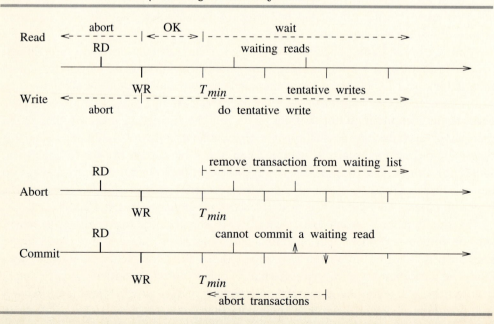

transaction is larger than T_{min}). The read operation finds its place in the tentative list and waits for the write operations that precede it to commit.

- **Write:** A write operation conflicts with both read and write. Thus, it is allowed to proceed tentatively only if its timestamp is greater than both RD and WR. The operation is marked tentative and inserted in the tentative list. The transaction manager is informed of the success or failure of the prewrite operation.

- **Abort:** An abort of a read operation has no effect on other transactions. The OM simply discards the waiting read. If a tentative write is aborted it is removed from the tentative list. If a waiting read reaches the head of the list as a result of the abort, the read operation is performed.

- **Commit:** A commit is issued only after the successful completion of the atomic commit phase in TM. A commit for a transaction waiting to read can never happen, since the transaction is blocked. For commitment of a transaction that has involved only completed read operations, OM records the larger of the transaction's timestamp and the object's RD as the new RD. If the committed transaction has done a tentative write, SCH aborts all pending transactions (both waiting reads and tentative writes) ahead of the committed transaction, makes the update permanent, and removes it from the tentative list. Removal of the transaction may allow a waiting read to proceed. The permanent update calls a replication manager if replicas of the object exist.

One final note on the timestamp ordering concurrency control is about the potential complication due to more than one transaction running the atomic commit phase at the same time. The atomic commit protocol used in this example is a unanimous voting scheme that can cause deadlocks when no TM can get all the needed votes from other TMs. In Chapter 4 we described how deadlocks in the unanimous voting scheme can be avoided by using vote return strategies. A transaction manager can withdraw its solicitation of votes if it has been rejected by some remote TMs. However, an uncoordinated vote return strategy may lead to indefinite postponement. Timestamps can be used to resolve the ties for transaction commitments.

Optimistic Concurrency Control

Two-phase locking concurrency control is a pessimistic approach; it prevents serialization problems from occurring. Timestamp ordering is less pessimistic and often allows transactions to proceed freely. The price of less blocking is more aborts, since conflicts sometimes occur and need to be resolved. We can extend this strategy one step further to allow an entire transaction to complete and then validate the transaction before making its effect permanent. This assumes that a private work space that contains *shadow copies* of the shared objects is available at each transaction site. Since this approach assumes that conflicts are less likely and can be temporarily ignored, it is called an *optimistic concurrency control*.

In the 2PL and timestamp ordering concurrency control, actions performed by each transaction manager are divided into two stages: the *execution phase* and the *commit phase.* The transaction processing system enforces or resolves consistency in the execution phase and enforces atomicity in the commit phase. For the optimistic concurrency control, no validation of consistency is performed in the execution phase until the *end transaction* is reached. At that time the TM begins its *validation phase.* A transaction is globally validated among TMs using a two-phase commit protocol. After the consistency of the transaction is validated, the TM enters the *update phase* to make changes permanent in the persistent memory. Since it is pointless to throw away a completed and validated transaction, we assume that once a transaction is validated, it is guaranteed to be committed. This means that all commitments must follow the order of validation time. Thus, the update phase of the commitment must also be atomic.

The optimistic concurrency control protocol is described in the following by the actions that a TM performs at each of the three phases: execution, validation, and update. Each transaction t_i is assigned a timestamp TS_i at the start of the transaction and a timestamp TV_i at the beginning of its validation phase. Every object O_j records its commitment time for the last read and write operations as RD_j and WR_j, respectively. WR_j is called the *version number* of O_j. The set of data objects read by a transaction t_i during its execution phase is denoted by R_i (*read set*). The corresponding *write set* of data objects by the same transaction is represented by W_i. The transactions are to be serialized with respect to the timestamps TV_s of the validated transactions.

- **Execution phase**: Begins at a TM when it receives a *begin transaction* from a local client. A private work space is created for each transaction. For simplicity, we will assume that the work space is managed locally at the TM site rather than being distributed at the object sites. Shadow copies of objects with their version numbers are read into the work space, where updates are performed locally, in a way similar to the session semantics of files. An abort from the client is handled by deleting the transaction and its work space. Otherwise the *end transaction* from the client signals the request for commit. The transaction manager moves to the validation phase.

- **Validation phase**: The transaction manager must validate the mutual consistency between the requested transaction and other distributed transactions being performed at remote TPS sites, to ensure serializability. To validate mutual consistency, TM initiates the two-phase validation protocol with itself as the coordinator. The validation request, which carries R_i, W_i, and TV_i, for transaction t_i, is sent to all participating TMs for validation. The validation request is not exactly a solicitation of a vote because a participant can respond with a positive validation to more than one validation request. Each TM has knowledge of all outstanding transactions t_k at its local site. The validation of mutual consistency between t_i and t_k is checked by the following steps:

  1. Validation of transaction t_i is rejected if $TV_i < TV_k$. All transactions must be serialized with respect to TV.
  2. Validation of transaction t_i is accepted if it does not overlap with any t_k. t_i is already serialized with respect to t_k.
  3. The execution phase of t_i overlaps with the update phase of t_k, and t_k completes its update phase before TV_i. Validation of t_i is accepted if $R_i \cap W_k = \phi$.

4. The execution phase of t_i overlaps with the validation and update phases of t_k, and t_k completes its execution phase before TS_i. Validation of t_i is accepted if $R_i \cap W_k = \phi$ and $W_i \cap W_k = \phi$.

The four cases are mutually exclusive and are illustrated in Figure 6.8. Since TV_i must be greater than TV_k and t_k must be completed before t_i, if both are validated, conflicts need only be checked against the write set W_k of t_k. Case 3 says that t_k has been promised that it can complete. If the intersection of the read set of t_i and the write set of t_k is not empty, t_i may have read some stale data that are being updated by t_k. This conflict must also be checked in case 4 since t_k may be successful in its validation. In addition, the intersection of the write set of t_i and the write set of t_k must be empty. Otherwise the update of t_k might effect the update of t_i. Accepted validations are made ready for commitment in the stable storage.

Validations involve only short computations. For implementation it is simpler to assume that each transaction site performs only one validation at a time. If a validation request comes to the transaction manager while it is in the process of validation, a *busy* response is returned to the requesting TM. The requesting TM withdraws its validation from all participating TMs and tries again later. An accepted validation carries the current version number of the shared remote object. It is compared with the TV_i for work-space consistency. All WR_s must be smaller than TV_i for transaction t_i. The transaction moves to the update phase once it has gathered an accepted validation from all participating TMs and the state of the work space is consistent.

- **Update phase:** An accepted validation in the optimistic concurrency control protocol is equivalent to a tentative prewrite in the timestamp ordering approach. The update phase is also similar to the commit phase in timestamp ordering except for one major difference. Tentative writes can be aborted (Figure 6.7), while validation cannot be denied once it is given. Updates must be committed in the TV order for those validated transactions. It is neither desirable nor necessary for a completed and validated transaction to wait for its turn to complete the update. Since validated transactions are already ordered and efficient storage management techniques are available for making shadow copies permanent, the problem can be alleviated by assuming a shared update manager that can be called to serialize the updates by all TMs.

FIGURE 6.8   Optimistic concurrency control protocol.

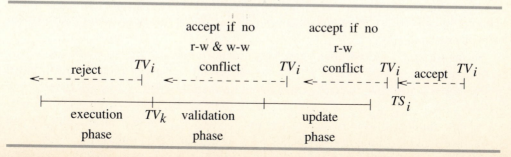

The optimistic concurrency control protocol requires a very elaborate validation and commitment scheme for *every* transaction. It seems to contradict the protocol assumption for applications that conflict among transactions is unlikely. Among the three concurrency control protocols, 2PL is still the most popular choice due to its simplicity.

6.4 DATA AND FILE REPLICATION

Data objects and files are often replicated to increase system performance and availability. With replication, higher performance is achieved by allowing concurrent accesses to the replicas, and higher availability can be obtained by exploiting the redundancy of the data objects. These are parallelism and failure transparencies, which are desirable in a distributed system. However, they are useless unless we can also provide replication and concurrency transparencies. Replication transparency means that clients are not aware of the existence of replicas. A condition of concurrency transparency is that interference among sharing clients must be avoided.

In the discussion of distributed transactions, we have addressed two atomicity issues. First, the operations on distributed sites requested by a transaction should be *all or none*. This property can be achieved by using a locking or two-phase atomic commit protocol. Second, the concurrent execution of object sharing transactions should be equivalent to a serial execution of the transactions. We showed several different approaches for concurrency control in the previous section. If data objects are replicated, we need to add a third desirable atomicity requirement: Updates to all replicas must also be atomic. The object managers assume the responsibility of replica management to ensure the replication transparency, such that clients perceive only a single copy of objects and the execution of transactions on replicated objects has results that are equivalent to the execution on nonreplicated objects. The combined atomic transaction and atomic update property is commonly called **one-copy serializability** for distributed transaction services.

Atomic updates are not just limited to transaction services. It is a generic management function for data replication in any file system. Obviously, atomic update can be considered and implemented as a transaction. However, data objects in a file system are replicated for different purposes. For some applications performance and availability issues may be more important than data consistency. Thus, the consistency requirements for managing replicated data are often less stringent than those required by transactions. This section discusses atomic update and some of its variations for efficient management of replicated data.

So far we have touched upon three very similar problems, *atomic multicast*, *atomic transaction*, and *atomic update*, all due to the use of the *group* notion in distributed systems. It is worthwhile to clarify them based on their differences in application:

■ **Atomic multicast:** Multicast messages are reliably delivered to all nonfaulty group members and the order of message delivery must obey a total ordering.

- **Atomic transaction:** Operations in every transaction are performed on an *all or none* basis and conflicting operations among concurrent transactions are executed in the same order.
- **Atomic update:** Updates are propagated to all replicated objects and are serialized.

For message multicast our primary concern is the order of message delivery if the underlying transport service (such as TCP) is reliable. Depending on the required semantics of multicast, the order can be relaxed from *total* to *causal* or *FIFO*. An atomic multicast is a special transaction where every message representing an operation conflicts with every other. Similarly, we have noted that atomic update is very much like a transaction where every update is a conflicting operation. The atomic update requirement for management of replicas can be relaxed for many applications. For example, failures of replicas may be allowed as long as at least one copy is available for client access, and a client may not be interested in the global coherency of the replicas as long as it can read the most recently written data. It seems that management of replicated data can be tackled from either the group multicast or the transaction point of view. We will show how multicast and transaction protocols can be tailored more practically for management of replicas.

6.4.1 Architecture for Management of Replicas

We assume the generic system architecture shown in Figure 6.9 for management of replicated data. Clients may choose one or more file service agents (FSAs) for accessing data objects. File service agents serve as a front end to the replica managers (RMs) to provide replication transparency for the clients. An FSA may contact one or more RMs for the actual reading and updating of data objects. Depending on how replica management protocols are to be implemented, the responsibility of replica management may be divided between the FSAs and the RMs. The architecture is a client/server model, which is different from the peer architecture (shown in Figure 6.6) that we used to demonstrate distributed transaction services. If each replica manager is merged with a file service agent, we have a special application where a group of peer client processes participate in *concurrent editing* of an identical but fully replicated object (document).

Object access operations may be *read* or *update*. An update operation can be further refined as either an *overwrite* or *read-modify* write. In the following we use write and

FIGURE 6.9 An architecture for replica management.

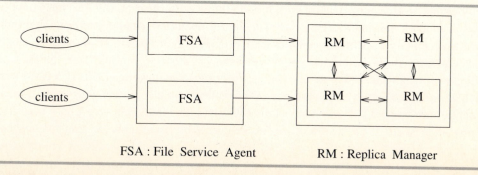

FSA : File Service Agent   RM : Replica Manager

update interchangeably. From the client's view point, a read operation needs to be addressed to only one of the replicas. However, replicas are transparent to the clients, and the file service invoked by a client may be required by the replication manager protocol to contact more than one replica manager to ensure that the data read is the most recent. There are three options for read operations.

- **Read-one-primary**: FSA can only read from a primary RM to enforce consistency.
- **Read-one**: FSA may read from any RM to gain concurrency.
- **Read-quorum**: FSA must read from a quorum of RMs to decide the currency of data.

Similarly from the system's view point, a write operation should be addressed to all replicas atomically. However, the applications may not need to enforce such a strong consistency requirement as long as updates can be propagated to some or all of the replicas in a timely fashion. The possible scenarios for write operations are:

- **Write-one-primary**: All write operations are addressed to one primary replica. The primary replica manager propagates the updates to all other secondary RMs.
- **Write-all**: Updates to all RMs by a write operation are atomic. Subsequent write operations must wait until the previous write has been atomically committed.
- **Write-all-available**: The atomic update is applied only to the available (non-faulty) RMs. Upon recovery of a failure, the replica manager restores its state to a consistent state before making its replica available for accesses.
- **Write-quorum**: The atomic update is applied only to a quorum of replica managers.
- **Write-gossip**: Updates can be directed to any RM and are *lazily* propagated to other neighboring RMs.

The following sections describe some combinations of the above read and write operations for managing replicas.

6.4.2 One-copy Serializability

If both read and write operations must be directed to the primary replica manager (*read-one-primary/write-one-primary*), the issue of replication does not exist. All operations can be serialized by the primary RM. The secondary RMs only supply redundancy in case of primary failures. Consistency is easy to achieve, but concurrency is completely ignored. To provide concurrency, read operations should be performed at any RM site. However, this introduces the coherency problem since the propagation of updates from the primary RM to secondary RMs incurs communication delay. The propagation of updates must be made atomic. If an atomic update protocol is available, we can allow an update to be initiated at any RM, preferably one that is closer to the requesting client. This is the *read-one/write-all* strategy. The consistency of the replicas can be enforced by using a standard concurrency control protocol such as the two-phase locking or the two-phase timestamp ordering protocol. If the read/write operations are subtransactions, the *read-one/write-all* protocols achieve *one-copy serializability*; the execution of transactions on replicated objects is equivalent to the execution of the same transactions on nonreplicated objects.

The assumption of *write-all* is not realistic for replica management. Data objects are replicated to tolerate failures. Requiring all replicas to participate in the atomic update contradicts the purpose of replication. Therefore, the atomic update should be performed only on all of the available (nonfaulty) replicas. A *read-one/write-all-available* protocol seems more appropriate. However, this approach slightly complicates the one-copy serializability property. We will use a simple example to illustrate the problem. We use three transactions:

t_0 : **bt** $W(X)$ $W(Y)$ **et**

t_1 : **bt** $R(X)$ $W(Y)$ **et**

t_2 : **bt** $R(Y)$ $W(X)$ **et**

Transaction t_0 initializes X and Y with write (W) operations. It is followed by two concurrent transactions t_1 and t_2. Each has a read (R) and a write operation on the shared objects X and Y. The *correct* execution of the two transactions is when t_1 and t_2 are executed serially. That is, either t_1 reads X written by t_2 or t_2 reads Y written by t_1. It can be seen that there is no equivalent serializable schedule for the two transactions except for the serial schedules. Now suppose that we replicate X to X_a and X_b and Y to Y_c and Y_d, and failures occur to X_a and Y_d. The two transactions become:

t_1 : **bt** $R(X_a)$ $(Y_d$ fails$)$ $W(Y_c)$ **et**

t_2 : **bt** $R(Y_d)$ $(X_a$ fails$)$ $W(X_b)$ **et**

After the failures of X_a and Y_d, the available replicas to X and Y are only X_b and Y_c, respectively. If we use the *read-one/write-all-available*, transactions t_1 and t_2 are serializable since there is no conflict in the read and write operations. The execution of the transactions is not equivalent to the one-copy system because neither t_1 nor t_2 sees the object written by the other. That is, the execution is not one-copy serializable. Additional constraints must be added to ensure the one-copy serializable property for *read-one/write-all-available* with failures. This topic is explored further in Chapter 12.

From the example, we see that failures and their recoveries must also be serialized with respect to transactions. It is incorrect for t_2 to read Y_d if Y_d fails before t_2 completes its transaction. The failure of Y_d in t_1 ideally should force t_2 to abort and roll back its read operation on Y_d. In other words, the failure should appear before the start of a transaction. When t_2 restarts, it will have to contact Y_c since Y_d has already failed. The conflict between $W(Y_c)$ in t_1 and $R(Y_c)$ in t_2 becomes visible.

We also observe in the above example that the conflict between t_1 and t_2 in accessing Y is not accounted for because the available replica for $W(Y)$ (which is only Y_c) in t_1 does not include Y_d read by t_2. We can solve the problem by requiring t_2 to read both Y_c and Y_d when accessing Y. Conflicts can be preserved if the read set of replicas of one transaction overlaps with the write set of another transaction. This observation motivates the *read-quorum/write-quorum* approach to replica management, which is discussed in the next section.

6.4.3 Quorum Voting

Read-quorum/write-quorum requires that each read operation to a replicated data object d must obtain a read quorum $R(d)$ of replica managers to perform the read. Similarly, each write operation needs a write quorum $W(d)$ to complete the write. This is a special case of the *semi-unanimous quorum voting* scheme for synchronization described in Chapter 4. Using the two quorums, conflicts between access operations on replicated data objects may be implicitly represented by an overlapping of the quorums. Let $V(d)$ be the total number of copies (votes) of object d. The overlapping rules for read and write are:

1. **Write-write conflict:** $2 * W(d) > V(d)$.
2. **Read-write conflict :** $R(d) + W(d) > V(d)$.

Once conflicts can be expressed, a standard two-phase locking or timestamp ordering protocol can be used to enforce one-copy serializability. To ensure that clients read the most recently *completed* update of data, a version number can be associated with each replicated data object. A read operation queries all $R(d)$ replicas. The value in the replica with the highest version number is chosen to be returned to the client. A write operation queries $W(d)$ replicas and adds 1 to the highest version number found: this is the new version number for writing to the replicas. Since the read and write quorums overlap with each other, a read is always returned with the most updated write. An example is shown in Figure 6.10, where $V(d)$ is 9 and both $R(d)$ and $W(d)$ are set to 5.

For most applications $R(d)$ is chosen to be smaller than $W(d)$. The special case of $R(d) = 1$ and $W(d) = V(d)$ represents the *read-one/write-all* protocol. If $W(d) < V(d)$, failures can be tolerated such as the *write-all-available*, but $R(d)$ must be larger than one. The *read-quorum/write-quorum* protocol is a good compromise between *read-one/write-all* and *read-one/write-all-available*. If $W(d)$ is much larger than $R(d)$, the data storage overhead for replicating data may be high. To reduce the storage requirement, the write-quorum may be extended to include *witnesses* (or *ghosts*). A witness does not carry a full replication of data. It maintains only the necessary information such as the version number and object identifier to participate in the write quorum. Two witnesses are shown in dash-line circles in Figure 6.10. The highest version number is 8.

FIGURE 6.10 A read-quorum/write-quorum with witnesses.

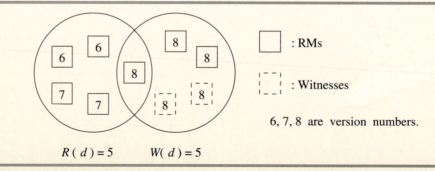

$R(d) = 5$ $W(d) = 5$

The quorum voting example shown assumes one vote per replica manager. Many generalized quorum voting schemes with variable vote weights have been proposed for different applications of replicated data. For example, heavier weights can be assigned to some preferred replica managers to enhance either performance or availability. Other issues about quorum voting are detailed in Chapter 12.

6.4.4 Gossip Update Propagation

Many applications of data replication do not need as strong consistency as the one-copy serializability in *read-one/write-all-available* or the most recent update in the *read-quorum/write-quorum* protocol. If updates are less frequent than reads and ordering of updates can be relaxed, updates can be propagated *lazily* among replicas, which is similar to the dissemination of information by gossip in real life. This *read-one/write-gossip* approach is called a *gossip update propagation* protocol. In the gossip architecture, both read and update operations are directed by a file service agent (FSA) to any replica manager (RM). The FSA shields the replication details from the clients. Replica managers bring their data up to date by exchanging gossip information among themselves. The primary purpose of gossip architectures is to support high availability in an environment where failures of replicas are likely and reliable multicast of updates is impractical.

We will use the architecture illustrated in Figure 6.11 to demonstrate two simple implementations of the gossip update propagation protocol. The first assumes *overwrite* updates. The second uses *read-modify* updates, which depend on the current state of the data object. In the latter case an *update log* is used to record the history of updates so that data dependency can be observed. In the simplest implementation each RM i is associated with a timestamp TS_i which represents the last update of the data object. Each FSA also maintains a timestamp TS_f, which indicates the timestamp of its last successful access operation. Updates are *overwrite* and the group is not definitive, so no update log is necessary. The implementation can be described by actions taken by the FSA and RM when *read, update*, and *gossip* messages are presented to them.

Basic Gossip Protocol

- **Read:** TS_f of the FSA is compared with TS_i of the RM contacted. If $TS_f \leq TS_i$, the RM has more recent data, so its value is returned to the FSA and TS_f is set to TS_i. Otherwise, the FSA waits until the RM has been brought up to date through gossip. Alternatively, the FSA can try other RMs for more recent results.

- **Update:** The FSA increments TS_f. If $TS_f > TS_i$, the update is executed. TS_i is set to TS_f to reflect the new update. The RM can propagate the new knowledge at its own convenience by way of gossip. If $TS_f \leq TS_i$, the update has come too late or concurrent updates are being processed. Depending on the application, the FSA can either perform the overwrite (ignore the missing updates) or become more up to date by performing a read followed by the update. In either case timestamps must be advanced.

FIGURE 6.11   A gossip architecture.

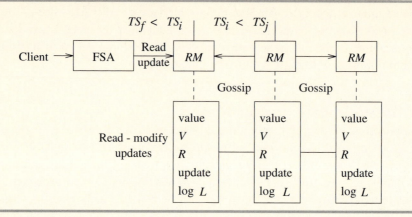

■ **Gossip:** A gossip message carrying a data value from replica manager j to replica manager i is accepted if $TS_j > TS_i$. The RM can repeat the gossip if so desired.

If the group is definitive so that all replica managers are known, vector timestamps can be used instead of single timestamps. The use of vector timestamps has a number of advantages that we will explain shortly. Since we are concerned only with updates of data objects, a vector timestamp can be composed of sequence numbers (or version numbers) representing the number of updates executed at each replica manager site. For example, the vector timestamp $TS_i = < 2, 3, 4 >$ shows that two, three, and four updates have occurred at RM_1, RM_2, and RM_3, respectively. A read operation with vector timestamp $TS_f = < 2, 2, 2 >$ pairwise and equal or less than TS_i is allowed to proceed. A TS_f of $< 2, 5, 5 >$ will need to wait, but we know more recent updates can be found at RM_2 and RM_3.

We used the concept of vector timestamps to implement causal order multicast in Section 4.1.5. Maintaining causal order is necessary for gossip propagation if updates are *read-modify*. The result of data multiplied by 2 and incremented by 1 is different from that when the order is reversed or an operation is missed. Read-modify updates are shorter messages. They are more efficient than using pairs of read and overwrite. Causal order gossip can be implemented by using vector timestamps and a buffering mechanism for orderly delivery of updates.

As shown in Figures 6.11 and 6.12, each replica manager is associated with two vector timestamps, V and R, and an update log L. V carries the timestamp of the current value of the object. R represents the replica manager's knowledge of update requests in the group. For example, $R = < 2, 3, 4 >$ at RM_1 indicates that exactly two updates originated from RM_1 and to the best of its knowledge three and four updates were initiated at RM_2 and RM_3, respectively. This estimated information is obtained through gossip. It is computed by *merging* (pairwise maximum) two Rs when exchanging gossip. The update log L is a list of update records collected by the RM. Each record in the log consists of a unique identifier r for the update u, in addition to other essential information such as the operation type and value. Record r and update u are denoted by vector timestamps. u is the timestamp issued by the FSA for an update operation. r is made unique for update u by RM_i by taking the corresponding u and replacing the ith component of the vector timestamp u with the ith component of R. We summarize the causal order gossip protocol as follows:

Causal Order Gossip Protocol

- **Read:** The FSA assigns its vector timestamp TS_f to the query q. If $q \leq V$, the RM returns the stable object value to the FSA. The FSA advances its timestamp by merging q with V. Otherwise the FSA either waits for the object to become up to date or contacts other RMs.

- **Update:** The FSA assigns its vector timestamp TS_f to the update u. It is compared with the current timestamp V of the object. If $u < V$, the update comes too late and is rejected by the RM since causal order needs to be enforced. The FSA contacted is out of touch. A read should have preceded the update. Under the normal situation, u is either greater than or equal to V or concurrent with V, meaning that neither $u < V$ nor $u > V$ (using vector comparison discussed in Section 3.4.3). In any case, the update is accepted. The replica manager RM_i increments the ith component of R by 1 indicating one more update has been processed at the replica site. A unique identifier r is generated and placed with the update operation u in the log L. If $u = V$, the update operation is executed. The timestamp V is advanced by merging with r. As a result of this execution, some records in the log may become *stable*, meaning that they satisfy the stable condition, $u \leq V$, and are ready to be executed. The stable condition implies that all operations that are supposed to *happen before* u have been committed. If more than one record satisfies this condition, their execution must be performed in causal order. This is easy to do because their vector timestamps reflect causal ordering. Other update operations wait in the log for the stable condition, which will be changed when the RM receives gossip that may contain executable updates. Updates that have been executed are marked so that they will not be repeated. Executed updates are not deleted immediately since they need to be propagated to other RMs.

- **Gossip:** A gossip message from RM_j to RM_i carries RM_j's vector timestamp R_j and log L_j. R_j is merged with the vector timestamp R_i in RM_i. The log L_i in RM_i is joined with L_j except for those update records with $r \leq V_i$. Records with $r \leq V_i$ must have been accounted for by RM_i. The aggregate of logs is a *true* gossip in that it contains not only the knowledge of one RM but also that of many others.

Figure 6.12 illustrates the execution of three update operations using update logs for causal ordering. All vector timestamps are initialized to $< 0, 0, 0 >$. Update $u_1 = < 0, 0, 0 >$ is directed to RM_1. It is accepted since u_1 is not less than V_1. R_1 is incremented to $< 1, 0, 0 >$. An update record of r_1 and u_1 is generated and placed in log L_1. It is executed and V_1 is updated to $< 1, 0, 0 >$. Meanwhile, L_1 which contains one executed update, is gossiped to RM_2. Updates u_2 and u_3 come to RM_2 and RM_3 separately.

FIGURE 6.12   A causal order gossip scenario.

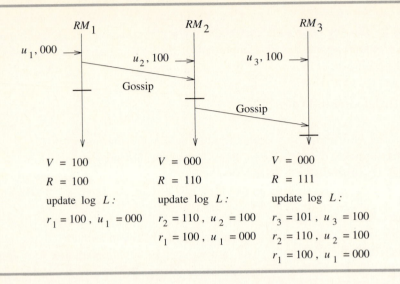

They must have read data from RM_1 earlier since they have the timestamp $< 1, 0, 0 >$. u_2 arrives at RM_2 before the gossip. Its timestamp is larger than $V_2 = < 0, 0, 0 >$, so it is placed in log L_2 after R_2 has been updated to $< 0, 1, 0 >$ and r_2 has been assigned $< 1, 1, 0 >$. The arrival of the gossip from RM_1 adds r_1 to L_2 and advances R_2 to $< 1, 1, 0 >$. Similarly, u_3 is accepted by RM_3. A record of $r_3 = < 1, 0, 1 >$ and $u_3 = < 1, 0, 0 >$ is put into L_3. When the gossip arrives from RM_2, r_2 and r_1 are added to log L_3. R_3 merges with R_2 to become $< 1, 1, 1 >$. At the instance shown in the diagram, r_1 in L_2 becomes stable and is ready for execution. The execution of r_1, in turn, makes r_2 ready. Following the same procedure, the causal execution sequence will be r_1, r_2, and r_3 at RM_3. The same execution sequence will be observed by all three RMs when RM_3 sends gossip to RM_1 and RM_3.

The example shows the basic gossip update propagation concept. Other issues such as garbage collection of the logs and optimization of message count are presented in Chapter 12.

6.5 SUMMARY

This chapter presents the fundamental concepts and design issues for the implementation of distributed file systems. A distributed file system is characterized by how dispersion and multiplicity of files and users are made *transparent*, how *caching* and *replication* are supported to enhance performance and availability, what *file sharing semantics* is assumed, and whether the system is *scalable* and *fault tolerant*.

We show how file access and location transparencies can be achieved by using a hierarchical file naming structure and a file system mounting protocol. A distributed file system consists of a set of file servers that collectively perform transparent file services. A critical design factor of a DFS is whether the file servers should be *stateless* or *stateful*. Stateless file servers are robust and simple to implement. However, many file applications require management of the state information.

File sharing is a result of *overlapping* (space multiplexing) and/or *interleaving* (time multiplexing) file access operations to the same files. We describe two unique cases of file sharing due to overlapping: use of *client caches* to enhance file access time and *replication* of files to improve file availability. In both cases, data replicas exist and the primary implementation issue is the maintenance of data consistency for achieving replication transparency. We also show two unique examples of file sharing due to interleaving: *session* and *transaction* file accesses. Both access methods involve interleaved read and write operations to the same files. The main implementation consideration is to prevent interference among the sharing processes to achieve concurrency transparency.

Based on different objectives for file sharing, we discuss three common file sharing semantics models: *Unix*, *session*, and *transaction* semantics models. The Unix semantics model and its variations can be implemented by using the *write-through*, *write-back*, *write-invalidate*, and *write-update* cache coherence protocols. The choice of a cache coherence protocol is a trade-off between the implementation efficiency and the consistency requirement of the protocol. The session semantics model assumes that file sharing is infrequent for some applications. Thus, the model ignores the problems of sharing within a session and shifts the burden of coordinating file sharing between sessions to the application users.

For other applications (particularly database applications), file sharing is essential and also frequent. The transaction semantics model for these applications requires a concurrency control protocol to maintain the ACID semantics for concurrent transactions. We illustrate three common approaches for concurrency control in the context of a distributed transaction processing system. *Two-phase locking* is a pessimistic concurrency control protocol that achieves serializability by restricting the operations in a transaction. The *timestamp ordering* approach is a less pessimistic approach that allows operations in a transaction to proceed freely and resolves the serializability using timestamps only when conflicts exist. The *optimistic* concurrency control protocol ignores conflicts completely during the execution phase of a transaction. The result of the execution is committed only if consistency can be validated in the validation phase. We outline and discuss the pros and cons of each of the three concurrency control approaches.

Files can be replicated to allow for concurrent accesses and to tolerate failures. For many applications, a strong consistency requirement of the replicas is not necessary as long as data can be updated orderly. We show three replicated data management protocols for such applications, the *primary copy*, *quorum voting*, and the *gossip update* protocols. Since data replication implies the use of the notion of a *group*, we will revisit the topic of replicated data management in the context of group communication in Chapter 12.

ANNOTATED BIBLIOGRAPHY

An excellent survey of distributed file systems can be found in [LS90] by Levy and Silberschatz. Many distributed system research projects have proposed an implementation of DFS. The most widely quoted DFSs are NFS [SGK+85] of Sun, Andrew [MSC+86, HKM+88] of CMU, Locus [PW85, SP86] of UCLA, and Sprite [Hil86, OCD+88] of UC Berkeley. Locus and Coda [SKK+90], an extension of Andrew, incorporate many features in dealing with atomic replica management, network failure and partition, and concurrent transaction services.

Transaction service is a higher-level file service. It is an integral part of a modern distributed file system. Concurrency control for distributed transaction systems is an extensively studied subject in database and operating systems. The fundamental issues of distributed concurrency control are applicable to both database and distributed systems from the management of data and communication points of view. The chapter gives an overview of concurrency control for distributed systems. The first survey on concurrency control can be found in [BG81] by Bernstein and Goodman, and in their book [BHG87]. Other books and book chapters that address this subject include [Bha87, OV91, CDK94, Gos91, Bac93]. Another more recent survey is by Barghouti and Kaiser [BK91], which addresses advanced applications with multilevel and cooperating transactions using the group concept.

The problem of replica management has been dealt with from various perspectives: database approach, group management, and update propagation. The examples given in this chapter are: primary copy [AD76, Sto79], quorum voting [Mae85, GMB85], and update propagation [FM82, WB84, LLSG92]. Since replication involves management of both *data* and *communication*, two of the most important subjects in distributed systems, we devote a full chapter, Chapter 12, to replica management. Advanced topics and thorough references are given in that chapter.

EXERCISES

1. The authorization service can be merged with the directory service or the file service, or it can stand alone. Discuss the pros and cons of each approach.
2. Each file in the Unix system is represented by an i-node, which is separated from the directory structure. An i-node contains file attributes and data block information. An entry in the directory is just a file name and pointer pair to an i-node. What is the advantage of this separation? Compare this approach with the DOS (MicroSoft) file and directory structure if you are familiar with the DOS operating system.
3. When a file is opened, its i-node structure is loaded into the kernel space. What additional information needs to be maintained by the kernel for the opened files?
4. What file sharing semantics is used in your network or distributed file system?
5. Propose a file mounting strategy such that all users in the same domain have a uniform view of the file system. Discuss its advantages and disadvantages.

6. What is an appropriate action to perform if a file system is mounted on a nonempty subdirectory?

7. Sun's Netwok File System (NFS) allows automounting of a file system from any of a list of identical file servers. Why is automounting in NFS limited to read-only file systems? Automounting is transparent to the client users. What would be a good strategy for unmounting file systems?

8. NFS is considered stateless. Find out how file locking is supported in the system. Choose an equivalent network file system that you have access to for the exercise if you do not use NFS.

9. If a file is shared by multiple clients and client cache is used, there is the potential of cache inconsistency. Consistency can be improved by timely invalidation of cache. Cache invalidation can be initiated either by the server (a *push* model) or by the clients (a *pull* model). Propose an approach for both models by showing when and how cache should be invalidated. Discuss their pros and cons.

10. Both file caching and file replication result in multiple copies of the same data. How do they differ from each other in requirement and implementation?

11. The architecture in Figure 6.6 shows that the transaction services (TM, SCH, OM) reside at the client hosts. Why are they not located in the object sites?

12. Assume the following two transactions:

   t_1 : **bt** 1: Read A, 2: Write A+1 to B **et**
   t_2 : **bt** 3: Read B, 4: Write B+2 to A **et**

   Both A and B have an initial value of 1.

   a. Show all possible legal schedules.
   b. What are the results of consistent execution of the transactions?

13. Use the two-phase locking concurrency control protocol for the above transactions.
   a. What are the feasible schedules?
   b. What are the deadlock schedules?

14. Assume that t_1 has a smaller timestamp than t_2. Use the timestamp ordering concurrency control and Figure 6.7.
   a. What are the consistent schedules?
   b. Which schedule(s) will result in the roll-back of t_1?
   c. Which schedule(s) will result in the roll-back of t_2?

15. Using the optimistic concurrency control protocol and Figure 6.8 for the transactions in Exercise 14, show under what condition the execution of the transaction will be validated successfully.

16. Show formally that there is no serializable schedule for t_1 and t_2.

17. Compare the differences between the quorum voting for replica management and the Maekawa's algorithm for distributed mutual exclusion (Chapter 4).

18. In the gossip protocol using vector timestamps, an update u is rejected if $u < V$. Why is it possible that there are updates in the update log L where u is less than or equal to V (the stable condition)?

19. In the protocol in Exercise 18, we use r to uniquely identify an update operation u. Why is r unique while u is not?

20. Executed updates in the gossip architecture are not deleted immediately since they need to be propagated to other replica managers. Show how matrix clocks (Chapter 3) can be used to eliminate obsolete update records r in L (garbage collection) and to expedite gossip.

CHAPTER

Distributed
Shared
Memory

The use of message passing as a process communication paradigm for programming is a natural consequence of the physical separation of objects in distributed systems. In message-passing communication, processes exchange information by interpreting the data transferred in the underlying communication network. Two other process communication paradigms, *shared memory* and *remote procedure call* (RPC), were discussed in the previous chapters. Shared memory provides direct communication in a tightly coupled system in which information can be shared and accessed through memory attached to a common bus or interconnection network. RPC achieves the effect of interprocess communication by using a higher-level language abstraction of parameter passing, which can be implemented by message passing mechanisms in distributed systems.

The high-level abstraction in RPC provides communication transparency. However, true sharing of information cannot be easily obtained due to the pass-by-data-value limitation, imposed because remote memory cannot be directly accessed in the system. For example, a large complex data structure with pointers cannot be passed in RPC without significant effort. The difficulty lies in the difference between data passing and information sharing. Data passing is an indirect way of conveying information.

The dilemma is also common in our daily life. We often say, "I don't know how to describe it to you verbally; I wish you could read my mind." It is not easy to read someone's mind, but it is certainly feasible to read a remote computer's memory if the overhead can be reduced to a tolerable level. Along with other potential benefits, direct information sharing is the primary motivation behind the concept of the Distributed Shared Memory (DSM). DSM simulates a logical shared memory address space over a set of physically distributed local memory systems to achieve direct information sharing among coordinating systems. As a result, the conventional shared memory programming paradigm for multiprocessor systems can be extended to the distributed system environment. The implementation of DSM relies on message passing, which is made transparent by a layer of mapping and management software between DSM and message passing communication.

Many issues in the design and implementation of DSM are similar to those of the traditional research in multiprocessor caches and distributed database systems. One common feature of these systems is the nonuniformity of memory accesses. Since memory and data may be physically distributed, the access mechanisms are different (i.e., nonuniform), depending on whether the desired information is local to or remote from the processor. In a large-scale multiprocessor system, it is desirable to distribute the shared memory so that frequently accessed locations are closer to some processors, while others are distant from the processors. Multiprocessor architectures with this type of multilevel memory access hierarchy are referred to as **Nonuniform Memory Access (NUMA)** systems.

Figure 7.1 shows the generic architecture of a NUMA system. The connection among local modules may be buses, interconnection networks, or a communication subnetwork. The granularity of memory accesses may be a word, a cache line of words, a page, or a segment. Choosing the size of granularity is an important system consideration. Without loss of generality, we will use *blocks* to denote the basic units for memory sharing in the discussion of system implementation.

To facilitate efficient memory accesses, pages of shared memory may be migrated from one local node to another or replicated in several local nodes. Replication of shared memory pages in a distributed system requires that **memory coherence** be maintained. Memory coherence (or consistency) control is a major issue in the design of DSM. This chapter presents two special cases of NUMA architectures, multiprocessor cache and

FIGURE 7.1   A generic NUMA architecture.

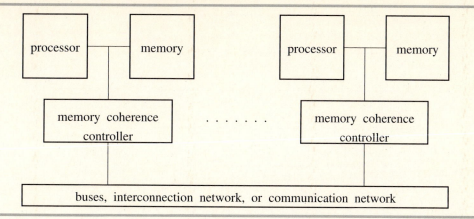

DSM, and discusses some memory coherence models and their implementation in these systems. Multiprocessor cache architecture is an extensively studied topic. We choose to include a discussion of multiprocessor cache architecture in this chapter since many of its design issues are directly related to the design of DSMs. The chapter concludes with the demonstration of a simple user-level implementation of DSM.

7.1 NONUNIFORM MEMORY ACCESS ARCHITECTURES

Multiprocessor cache and DSM are two practical configurations of the NUMA architecture. It is interesting to see the contrast between them. Figure 7.2 shows the general structure of the two systems. The memory coherence components are omitted from the figures. For the multiprocessor cache system, local caches on each processor are used to reduce memory access latencies and access traffic to the global shared memory, which is often a source of congestion in the system. In a real implementation, the global memory may be a collection of memory modules, and the bus may be multiple buses or a scalable interconnection network for achieving higher memory access bandwidth. For the DSM system there is no physical global memory. Instead, a virtual global memory is created by mapping all or parts of the local memory into a global address space shared by all nodes. Furthermore, processors in a DSM are connected through a loosely coupled LAN (or WAN).

The key difference between the two architectures is the delay time in accessing shared information. Since DSMs are loosely coupled systems, the time incurred for remote (or global) accesses for DSMs is several orders of magnitude higher than that of multiprocessor cache systems. Another important distinction that affects the design of the memory management system is the connection of modules. Multipoint connections in multiprocessor cache systems allow for easy broadcast and monitoring of bus activities (memory accesses), which is not feasible in DSMs.

FIGURE 7.2   Multiprocessor cache and DSM architectures.

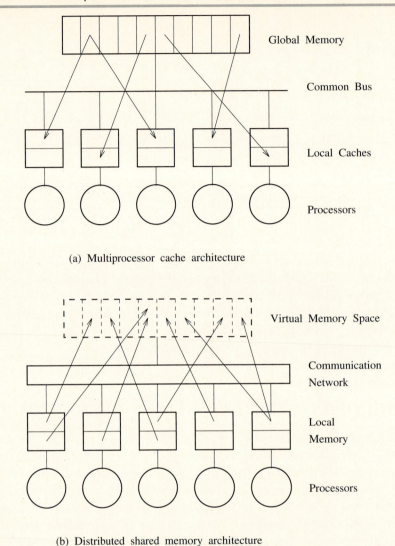

(a) Multiprocessor cache architecture

(b) Distributed shared memory architecture

Blocks (or pages) are the basic units for mapping between local memory (or cache) and the global address space (physical or virtual) in a NUMA system. The granularity (size of the block) is chosen to optimize data sharing and system overhead. Local caches in multiprocessor systems and local memory in DSM systems benefit from the locality of references if frequently used data are kept in local sites. Concurrent access to shared data introduces the need for data replication. In multiprocessor cache systems, an image of a global memory block may exist in multiple caches, as shown in Figure 7.2(a). Replication of data is a direct result of data sharing when using caches. For DSM systems, a shared data block in one local node may be copied (replicated) to another node, as shown in Figure 7.2(b), to facilitate simultaneous access. In both cases, allowing concurrent accesses to replicated data blocks implies the need for an access protocol to maintain coherency among data copies.

7.1.1 Performance and Transparency

The primary concern in the development of multiprocessor cache systems is improving the memory access, while the design of distributed shared memory systems is motivated mainly by the desire to achieve transparency.

Caches in multiprocessor systems are used to exploit memory referencing that exhibits *temporal* and *spatial* locality properties in application programs. Each processor maintains copies of a portion of main memory to facilitate faster local accesses of frequently referenced or physically nearby memory locations. If a large fraction of memory references can be satisfied from the local cache, the effective average memory access time can be significantly improved. Caches are widely used in uniprocessor systems to reduce the difference in speed between processor and memory modules. In a multiprocessor system, local caches also reduce bus contention caused by competing processors.

Since distributed applications require sharing of information, the activity in the shared bus could be significant. The shared bus will eventually become a bottleneck when the number of processors increases in the system. *Scalability* must be dealt with if the performance of the system is to be further enhanced. There are two common approaches for alleviating congestion problems in the shared bus. A hardware solution is to increase the memory access bandwidth by utilizing multiple buses or scalable interconnection networks. A software solution is to replicate the shared information in local caches to reduce global accesses. The latter raises the complexity of managing cache coherence problems. In a distributed shared memory system running on a loosely coupled network, software solutions seem to be the only plausible approaches.

From the viewpoint of application programmers, the major advantage of the DSM model over traditional message passing models is information sharing transparency. Information sharing in DSM is implemented by data movement through message passing, but DSM is a higher-level communication abstraction than message passing. Users of DSM are not aware of the data movement, which must be explicitly specified in a message passing system. With shared memory, complexities associated with message passing, such as data conversion, parameter marshaling, and protocol handling, become irrelevant. Complex data structures and objects are shared in their original representations. This effect is also referred to as communication transparency.

There are many other advantages of using DSM systems. The shared memory programming paradigm exhibited in DSM is considered easier to understand and more efficient in coding. Most programmers are familiar with shared-memory concepts for process communication and synchronization. There is a wealth of shared-memory software developed for both single and multiprocessor systems. These programs are readily adaptable for DSM distributed systems. Scalability is also an attractive feature of DSM. The application programmers need no notion of the communication network. Increasing the number of local nodes only makes available a larger memory space without any need to modify either the hardware or software. The memory access traffic load is less sensitive to the size of the network due to the existence of local memory. All these arguments contribute to the justification of using the DSM model in distributed systems.

7.1.2 Data Placement, Migration, and Replication

To reduce the effective average memory access time, as much data as possible must be placed in the local caches in multiprocessor cache systems or in the local memory modules in DSM systems. The objective is to maximize the hit ratio of local to remote accesses. It is intuitive that a larger cache or local memory will result in higher cache or local memory hit ratio. Moreover, there are two other size considerations that affect the hit ratio. They are the size of basic organizational units for data sharing (blocks, cache lines, or pages) and the size of data that must be fetched upon a cache or local memory miss. These two sizes need not be the same, but for clarity of discussion and ease of implementation, we will assume they are and will call them **blocks**.

The effect of block size on hit ratio is similar to the effect of page size in conventional paging systems. A larger block size may improve the hit ratio since it can cover a larger locality of references. However, this is true only to a certain extent. When a block becomes too large, it will contain too much irrelevant data that replaces other useful information and thus reduce the hit ratio. Aside from the hit ratio, another implementation consideration is the system overhead. To keep track of copies of blocks, a table or directory structure must be maintained. A smaller block size requires a larger storage overhead for the directory structure but less communication overhead for the data movement to service a fault.

Upon the miss of a memory reference, either the desired data can be accessed remotely or the block that contains the data can be moved to the local site for future local accesses. A distinction is made here when a block is actually "moved" or just copied (**block migration** and **block replication**, respectively). Block migration becomes necessary when, during a period of time, a threshold of remote to local accesses is crossed, indicating that it is more beneficial to move the data blocks to the local site. Analogous to the *demand* and *anticipatory* strategies in the paging systems, a block in NUMA systems may be *pulled* or *pushed* when it needs to migrate from one processor to the other. Push-based strategies are policies in which a processor moves its local blocks to another processor in the hope that those blocks will be used by the other processor in the near future. Existing migration policies are usually pull-based, where a processor pulls a block from a remote processor into its own local memory, on demand or when needed. Blocks are sometimes identified with an **owner**. The notion of owner is used to keep track of the original and current owners of the shared blocks.

Block migration suffers from *block-bouncing* (or page-bouncing), which is similar to the *thrashing* problem in a demand-paging system. Block-bouncing occurs when a migrated block is immediately requested by another processor and is then continuously migrated from one node to another in a *ping-pong* fashion. This problem can be solved by making duplicate copies of the shared block (i.e., block replication). However, block replication has a more important purpose, that is, to support concurrent accesses of the same data. But, there is a high cost associated with replication, namely, the need for memory coherence control, which is discussed in the subsequent sections. For the implementation of memory coherence control, it is sometimes convenient to designate one of the replicated copies as the *master* copy. An update of replicate copies can commence from the master copy and propagate to all copies in an orderly fashion.

Finally there is the problem of **false-sharing**, which complicates both block migration and replication. False-sharing is due to our earlier assumption that blocks are the basic units of migration or replication. An entire block is moved, although only a small part of it is shared and needs to be fetched. Consider an example where the first byte of a block is used by one processor and the last byte of the same block is used by another processor. The memory management system treats the block as a shared block when in fact there is no data sharing at all. The phenomenon of block bouncing could be worsened by false sharing. The problem of false sharing can be alleviated if we use objects (or data structures) as the logical sharable units. Sharing of data is explicit and is recognizable by the memory management systems. The concurrent programming systems, Orca and Linda described in Chapter 3, are examples of distributed shared memory systems that are based on distributed objects or data structures. They are high-level abstractions of distributed shared memory systems. We will call them **object-based** DSMs as opposed to the **page-based** DSM structure discussed thus far and shown in Figure 7.2(b).

7.2 MEMORY CONSISTENCY MODELS

In the previous chapters we addressed the coherence problem in the context of multicast communication and distributed file systems. The coherence problem in these systems is based on the data point of view. Processes interact with each other only indirectly through shared data that are *external* to the processes. For DSM systems, the interaction is through shared memory, where the processes also reside. This means that inconsistency in memory not only affects shared data but also the integrity of the execution of processes. For example, processes may not be properly synchronized or may even crash, if shared synchronization variables are inconsistent. The coherence problem is based more on the viewpoint of processes than that of data. Clearly the coherence control problem in DSM systems requires a more thorough investigation. This section discusses several memory coherence (consistency) models on which coherence control schemes can be built.

7.2.1 Coherence and Consistency

In order to improve performance through concurrent accesses, replicated copies of shared memory are maintained by the system. Due to access delays in distributed systems, an update of a data item may not be reflected instantaneously in all copies. It is possible that copies of cache or local memory may contain different values at the same time. In the execution of a program with competing memory accesses from multiple processes, a *read* operation may obtain a stale value. To further complicate the matter, non-over-lapping *write* operations may be observed in a different order by each processor. Thus, interacting processes may have an inconsistent or erroneous perception of the state of the system. Without knowing the intention of the competing accesses, the system cannot determine whether a particular ordering of events will yield a "correct" result. Instead, the system can only guarantee that the memory state is coherent or consistent according to some predefined model of coherence or consistency. From the programmers' viewpoint, the most desirable definition of coherence is that a *read* operation always returns the value given by the latest *write* to the same shared variable. However, the notion of "latest" is vague and not meaningful since no true global time exists in distributed systems. One can relax the coherence definition by requiring that all replicated copies eventually contain the same information when all *write* operations are completed at some point in time. The memory is in a consistent state only at some synchronization points. The terms *coherence* and *consistency* are often used interchangeably. Here we assume coherence is the most strict requirement for consistency and consistency models have a less restrictive view of the time ordering of events, as perceived by the processors and presented to the application programs.

The choice of a consistency model is a trade-off between system concurrency and ease of programming. A restrictive consistency model gives more assurance about memory consistency to the users. Therefore, it makes programming tasks easier but at the expense of potential gain for pipelined or overlapping operations, which can be more fully exploited by the system using a less restrictive model. Once a consistency model is chosen for a system, the implementation of the model requires either hardware (**hardware-based DSM**) or software (**software-based DSM**) support for the memory management system to enforce the model. The module for the enforcement of memory coherence is referred to as the coherence controller. Memory coherence models that have a more complex semantics usually require a higher implementation complexity.

So far we have mentioned only two types of memory accesses: *read* and *write*. They are general memory access operations performed on user-defined variables. All variables can be shared in a DSM system. However, some variables are truly shared by interacting processes, and others are not. We will call the accesses to a truly shared variable *competing* accesses and the others, *noncompeting* accesses. Only competing accesses are to be synchronized.

If we are interested in memory consistency only at certain synchronization points, we can express the synchronization points by using a synchronization access operation *synch(S)*, which accesses a certain synchronization variable S. Synchronization variables are distinguished from general variables. They are synchronization type-specific variables similar to a semaphore. The required synchronization may be mutual exclusion, barrier, or condition synchronization. It is obvious that the burden of the coherence controller in the memory management system can be greatly reduced if consistency constraints are applied only to the synchronization accesses.

Sometimes a synchronization point may involve more than just a simple memory access. In this case we can indicate the beginning and ending of a synchronization period by using two additional synchronization access operations, *acquire(S)* and *release(S)*. Competing access operations are enclosed between an acquire and release pair. The exact semantics of the *synch, acquire*, and *release* are different and need to be defined for each consistency model. However, they share a common characteristic in that they are all synchronization access operations to a synchronization type-specific variable.

The following two subsections present a list of common memory consistency models in the order of restrictiveness. These consistency models are grouped into two categories: models based on general *read/write* accesses and models based on synchronization type-specific *synch/acquire/release* accesses. In the first category, consistency models can be made less restrictive by relaxing the requirement of the ordering of *write* operations with respect to either processors (**processor relative weakening**) or memory locations (**location relative weakening**). Models in the second category limit coherence requirements only to synchronization accesses (**access type weakening**). Consistency requirements in these models are weakened by different assumptions of the synchronization access operations.

7.2.2 General Access Consistency Models

In a general *read/write* access consistency model, the consistency enforcement is applied to all read/write access operations in the system. We use the notations $R(X)v$ and $W(X)v$ to represent *read* and *write* operations to variable X with value v. P_i denotes the ith processor. The examples used for the following consistency models are due to Hutto, Ahmad, and Mosberger.

Atomic Consistency

This model requires that the distributed shared memory system behave exactly like a centralized shared memory system with no replication of data. It is therefore the most strict consistency model and thus is also called strict consistency. All *read* and *write* operations must appear to be executed atomically and sequentially. Furthermore, all processors observe the same ordering of event execution, and the order coincides with the real-time occurrence of all non-over-lapping events. The model achieves the coherence definition that each *read* operation receives the "latest" value and all *write* operations are completed before subsequent *read* operations to the same variables. The complexity of implementing atomic consistency is high. Usually the atomic consistency model is used only as a baseline to evaluate the performance of other consistency models.

Sequential Consistency

This model was first presented by Lamport. A memory system is sequentially consistent if "the result of any execution is the same as if the operations of all the processors were executed in some sequential order, and the operations of each individual processor appear in this sequence in the order specified by its program." The real-time ordering of non-over-lapping events is not required. This relaxation of consistency is to accommodate the unique characteristic in DSMs that different access operations may experience different access delays and thus may effectively appear commuted when observed by the processors. The following shows an example of sequential consistency.

$$
\begin{array}{lllll}
P_1: & W(X)1 \\
P_2: & & W(Y)2 \\
P_3: & & & R(Y)2 & R(X)0 & R(X)1
\end{array}
$$

In this example, $W(Y)2$ was *performed*[2] before $W(X)1$, as observed by P_3 and all other processors. The commuted *write* operations from different processors are legal executions for sequential consistency models but illegal for atomic consistency. The sequential consistency model assumes that all processors observe the same order, including $P1$ and $P2$. Therefore, $W(X)1$ should not be visible to $P1$ until its effect has been propagated to all other processors (i.e., until it has been performed). This is also true for the $W(Y)2$ operation.

Causal Consistency

In the sequential consistency model, multiple *write* operations from different processors may be commuted but must be observed in the same order by all processors. For the causal consistency model, we relax this requirement such that only *writes* that might be causally related must be observed in the same order by all processors. Therefore, processors may have a different global view of the system. This relaxation of consistency allows disjoint *writes* to be pipelined or overlapped by the memory management system to improve concurrency. In this model, a *write* is interpreted as a message-send event and a *read* is considered as a message-receive event. The memory is said to be consistent if all processors agree on the order of causally related events. The following example is causally consistent but not sequentially consistent.

$$
\begin{array}{lllll}
P_1: & W(X)1 & & W(X)3 & \\
P_2: & R(X)1 & W(X)2 & & \\
P_3: & R(X)1 & & R(X)3 & R(X)2 \\
P_4: & R(X)1 & & R(X)2 & R(X)3 \\
\end{array}
$$

Here $W(X)1$ and $W(X)2$ are causally related since P_2 received the result from P_1 before issuing $W(X)2$. P_3 and P_4 observe the same processing order for $R(X)1$ and $R(X)2$. $W(X)2$ and $W(X)3$ are not causally related and are observed in a different order by P_3 and P_4. Naturally the effect of $W(X)1$ and $W(X)3$ must be observed in order since they are issued by the same processor and thus are causally related.

Processor Consistency

This model gives the greatest flexibility in the ordering constraints for *writes*; it ignores part of the causality requirement in the causal consistency model. *Writes* from the same processor are still performed and observed in the order in which they were issued, while *writes* from different processors can be observed in any order. Since only the *write* operations issued by the same processor need to be maintained in order, the processor consistency model is the most general form of processor relative weakening of memory consistency. The example below shows two *writes* issued by P_1 and P_2 that were perceived in a different order by P_3 and P_4. It is consistent in the processor consistency

---

[2] We distinguish when an access operation is being issued from when it has been performed. A *write* operation is considered to have been performed (or completed) when all subsequent *read* operations return the result written by the *write*. Similarly, a *read* is said to have been performed when no subsequent *write* can change the value returned by the *read*. These definitions of performed access operations are protocol independent.

model but not in the sequential or causal consistency models as $W(X)1$ and $W(X)2$ are causally related.

P_1 : $W(X)1$
P_2 : $R(X)1$ $W(X)2$
P_3 : $R(X)1$ $R(X)2$
P_4 : $R(X)2$ $R(X)1$

The processor consistency model also allows a *read* access to bypass a *write* access if the two accesses by the same processor are made to different locations, which is a violation in the sequential consistency model. Processor consistency is easy to implement. It gives no assurance of event ordering of operations issued by different processors and leaves most of the burden of synchronization to the application programs.

Slow Memory Consistency

This is an extreme case of the *read/write* consistency model. It is a location-relative weakening of the processor consistency model in that only *writes* to a same location issued by the same processor must be observed in order. *Writes* are immediately visible locally and propagated slowly (thus the name slow memory) throughout the system. The model provides no synchronization except for the basic form of interprocessor communication that uses *write* as a nonblocking send. In the following slow memory consistency example, $W(Y)2$ is issued immediately after $W(X)1$ is visible to $P1$ to improve overlapped execution. $W(X)3$ must stall for the completion of $W(X)1$ since they are *writes* to the same location. Thus $P2$ may observe $R(Y)2$ followed by $R(X)1$ and $R(X)3$. This is an illegal sequence in all previous consistency models. If an operation after $R(Y)2$ in $P2$ relies on both Y and X, execution of the program in $P2$ will give incorrect results. Care must be taken in using the interprocessor communication in the slow memory model for synchronization.

P_1 : $W(X)1$ $W(Y)2$ $W(X)3$
P_2 : $R(Y)2$ $R(X)1$ $R(X)3$

The slow memory model is very relevant to distributed shared memory systems where protocols that implement write updates are actually very slow. For performance purpose, it is desirable to make local updates visible before the global update is completed.

7.2.3 Synchronization Access Consistency Models

In the previous discussion, we recognized that weakening the consistency model complicates the programming model as seen by the users. On the other hand, if the users can provide more information about how and why data are to be used, particularly with respect to synchronization, the supporting consistency model can be further relaxed. For example, if a program uses semaphore synchronization variables to achieve mutual exclusion in executing a critical section, only the memory accesses to the semaphores need to be coherent as long as the data and control dependencies within the critical section are preserved, which is an assumption we made in all consistency models. Synchronization of the competing memory accesses within the critical section is explicitly controlled by the semaphores. Codes outside the critical section are noncompeting accesses and do not require synchronization. Consistency is maintained only at synchronization points. For this reason, we separate memory accesses into two categories: general competing *read/write* accesses to shared variables and synchronization accesses. Synchronization accesses are read/write operations to synchronization variables only. They can be identified with special instructions and recognized by the memory coherence controller, which applies different rules for enforcing consistency.

Weak Consistency

This model assumes that not all memory accesses need to be sequentially consistent. Only synchronization accesses require sequential consistency since they are explicitly used for coordinating interaction among multiple processors. Other memory accesses are either noncompeting accesses or nonsynchronization accesses that do not support synchronization purposes. This consistency assumption is called *weak* ordering as opposed to the *strong* ordering of all memory accesses in the sequential consistency model. The weakening of the consistency requirement is based on access type rather than whether accesses are relative to processors or locations. Stated formally, in the definition of the weak consistency model, a memory system is consistent if:

- Accesses to synchronization variables are sequentially consistent
- No access to a synchronization variable is issued by a processor before all previous *read/write* data accesses have been performed
- No *read/write* data access is issued by a processor before a previous access to a synchronization variable has been performed

A synchronization access ($synch(S)$) serves as the synchronization point that ensures that all previous accesses have been performed before a synchronization access is issued, and no future access is issued until all previous synchronization accesses have been performed. In other words, synchronization accesses work like a *barrier* and are visible to the memory management system for enforcing sequential consistency. A *performed synchronization access* is similar to a performed read or performed write, depending upon whether the synchronization access is a read or write operation. A synchronization access forces the system to complete all pending accesses to reach a consistent system state. If the synchronization accesses are sequentially consistent, a read access immediately following a synchronization access will return the most recent written value. The weak consistency model is shown in Figure 7.3(a).

Release Consistency

The synchronization access ($synch(S)$) in the weak consistency model can be refined as a pair of *acquire*(S) and *release*(S) accesses. The release consistency model uses the acquire and release operations to exploit further potential for overlapping operations. An acquire synchronization access is equivalent to a *lock* operation that stalls on a certain

FIGURE 7.3 Weak, release, and entry consistency models.

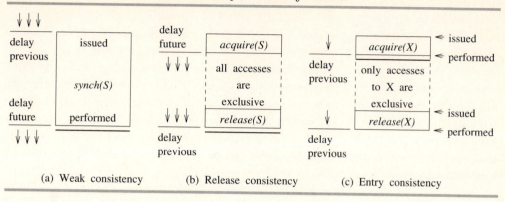

(a) Weak consistency   (b) Release consistency   (c) Entry consistency

condition to gain access to some shared variables. It is a *read* or *read-modify-write* synchronization access. Similarly, a release works like an *unlock* operation that signals the completion of the critical section codes between acquire and release. It is a *write* synchronization access.

The assumption of an acquire operation is that no future access can be performed until the acquire operation is completed. And for a release operation, all previous operations must have been performed before the completion of the release operation. Thus, additional concurrency can be achieved by not requiring an acquire to delay its previous accesses and a release to delay its future accesses, as in the weak consistency model. Therefore, the release consistency model allows some limited overlapping operations in the critical section that are not possible in the weak consistency model.

Ordering of synchronization accesses follows the processor consistency model, with *acquire* and *release* corresponding to *read* and *write*, respectively. The model is called release consistency since the shared variables in the critical section are made consistent when the release operation is performed.

Figure 7.3(b) contrasts the release consistency model with the weak consistency model in Figure 7.3(a). The dark solid lines indicate the point when shared variables are in a consistent state. The release consistency model is of course more general and flexible than the weak consistency model. In fact, the barrier in the weak consistency model is just an acquire and release pair with a null operation in between.

Entry Consistency

In the effort to weaken consistency requirements for improving concurrency, the entry consistency model was proposed to further relax the release consistency model. In the release consistency model, an *acquire* and *release* pair is used on a synchronization variable to provide mutual exclusion for a critical section. The system is not concerned about whether the critical section involves *read* or *write* operations or how many variables are actually shared with respect to other critical sections. The entry consistency model attempts to achieve more concurrency even in the critical section by reducing the granularity of the critical section to the access of a single shared variable (this could be extended to an exclusive object or data structure).

Each shared variable X, as specified by the program, is associated with an implicit synchronization variable. The synchronization variable serves as a lock for the shared variable. A critical section, which may contain both noncompeting and competing accesses, is enclosed with an *acquire*(X) and *release*(X) pair. A successfully performed *acquire*(X) operation will lock the shared variable X for the subsequent exclusive operations on X until X is unlocked by a *release*(X). Since operations on X are exclusive, the critical section may be interleaved with others for pipelined or overlapped execution. Furthermore, the *acquire* access can be extended to include both exclusive lock and shared lock acquisitions to add more concurrency.

The entry consistency model uses the locking of objects rather than the locking of critical sections for mutual exclusion synchronization. It is logical to assume that a locked object should be in a consistent state. Therefore, the acquire operation should have the semantics that all accesses to the requested variable must have been performed before the completion of the acquire operation. The model is called entry consistency because the shared variable is consistent at the entry of the critical section. The memory management system only ensures the consistency of the shared variables. Figure 7.3(c) contrasts the

FIGURE 7.4 A taxonomy of consistency models.

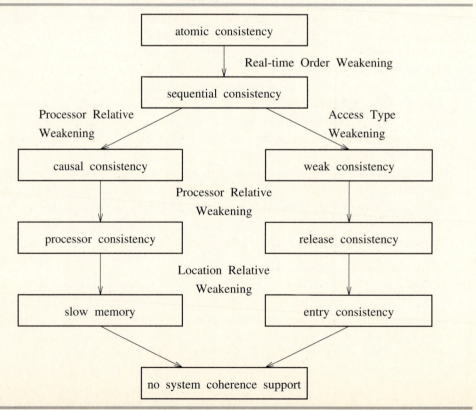

entry consistency model with the release consistency model in Figure 7.3(b). The entry consistency model is a location relative weakening scheme since synchronization is performed with respect to each variable.

Figure 7.4 gives a taxonomy of all the consistency models discussed in this section. The models are compared in the relative degree of strictness with respect to real-time ordering, access type, processor- and location- relative weakening of the coherence requirements.

7.3 MULTIPROCESSOR CACHE SYSTEMS

To identify the design issues in DSM systems, it is useful to understand some of the fundamental problems in multiprocessor cache systems, which were developed before DSM. As shown in Figure 7.2, the two systems are similar in structure but the implementation is different. The memory manager in multiprocessor cache systems manages the mapping and data transfer on the common bus, which is replaced by a loosely coupled communication network in DSM systems.

7.3.1 Cache Structures

To manage the memory coherence problem for replicated shared cache blocks, we assume a conceptual model, as shown in Figure 7.5. There is the notion of a *master copy* of the replicated blocks, which could reside in a local processor or in a separate global memory module shared by all processors. Each replicated block has a couple of bits representing the state of the shared block. At a minimum, the state must indicate whether the replicated block in a local site is *valid* or *invalid* and *shared-read-only* or *exclusive*. The invalid state means that the block contains stale data, and a read to it will force a cache miss. The exclusive state indicates that the block is the only valid copy and a processor is free to write to the exclusive copy. The shared-read-only state prevents writing to the block

FIGURE 7.5   Replicated cache block structure.

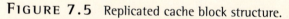

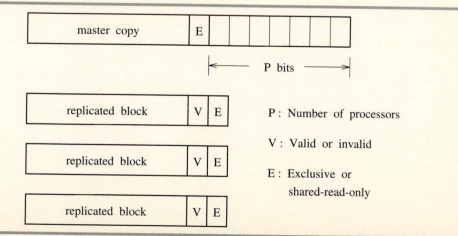

until an exclusive access has been obtained and the block is changed to the exclusive state. Furthermore, for each memory block, there is a vector of P-bits, where the ith bit in the vector represents the presence of a copy in the ith processor. Additionally, an E-bit, when set, indicates the exclusive copy of the block. This bit is actually redundant since it is equivalent to a single bit set in the P-bits vector. It is clearer to use a separate E-bit to indicate the lock status of the block. The collective information on P-bits vectors for some memory blocks is called a **directory**.

Other control bits may be used in implementing the cache structure. For example, a bit may be used to indicate whether a block is shared or private. For clarity, it is omitted in the figure since we are only concerned with the shared blocks. Some cache systems also use a *dirty* bit to facilitate *write-back* if there are two levels of memory in a local processor. It is also excluded in the following discussion of cache coherence protocols.

7.3.2 Cache Coherence Protocols

Using the simple cache structure in Figure 7.5, we can outline a cache coherence protocol that maintains block consistency. Cache coherence protocols are generally classified as either *write-invalidate* or *write-update*. When a *write* operation occurs, the write-invalidate strategies signal the holders of the shared block to invalidate its copy. The invalidation forces a cache miss the next time the block is referenced. The write-update approaches propagate the new block to all other copy holders. The following illustrates the actions taken by a typical write-invalidate protocol.

■ **Read hit:** The processor reads the data block and continues.

■ **Read miss:** A read miss occurs if the processor does not hold the block or the block is marked invalid. A consultation is made to the directory to transfer the block from the memory of one of the copy holders. The corresponding P- and valid-bits are set. If the processor is the sole holder of the block, it sets the exclusive bit. If the block is exclusive, the exclusive bit in the directory is cleared and the exclusive-bit in the block is set to shared-read-only to reflect that there are two copies of the shared block.

■ **Write hit:** A write hit to an exclusive cache block is allowed to proceed and the processor continues. If the cache block is in the shared-read-only state, permission must be obtained before the write access. A message is sent to the directory that invalidates all cache copies according to its P-bits vector. Upon the completion of the invalidations, the processor writes data and sets the exclusive bit. In effect, the processor becomes the sole owner of the cache block until other read accesses arrive from other processors. At that moment the block changes to the shared-read-only state.

■ **Write miss:** Actions required for a write miss are similar to that of a write hit except a block copy is transferred to the faulting processor by the directory server after the invalidation. The block is then updated and set to exclusive.

The write-invalidate protocol sends the invalidation signals to the other sharing processors. The updated data block is copied only when necessary. The write-update protocol, on the other hand, propagates the update to all shared copies whether the new data will be needed or not. The traffic generated by the write-update protocols could be significant. The write-invalidate protocols are easy to implement. They have precise and dynamic information about the number of copies being shared. Every write operation results in a single exclusive copy, and the number of shared copies is the number of processors accessing the block between consecutive writes. The protocol is efficient when there are multiple writes between reads. Under this circumstance, the writes will be either exclusive or will require invalidation by only a few processors. However, the write-invalidation protocol has a higher read–miss ratio. The invalidations cause additional cache misses when a block is shared and frequently accessed by many processors. A block has to be copied back immediately after every invalidation. There is a trade-off between miss rate and cache coherence enforcement overhead. This leads to a hybrid approach that dynamically chooses either the write-invalidate or write-update protocol depending on the changing memory access pattern. Most directory-based multiprocessor cache systems use the write-invalidate protocol. The write-update protocol is hard to implement unless special hardware is available. The argument is left as an exercise.

7.3.3 Snooping Cache and Strong Consistency

We mentioned earlier that the choice of a consistency model is a system design trade-off between the degree of consistency as seen by the programmers and the potential for achieving higher concurrency as desired by the system. The concurrency, which can be obtained by overlapping accesses, is a more critical issue in systems that require a higher overhead in enforcing coherence. For a system with lower latency in performing global access operations, a strong consistency model can be implemented without significant loss of concurrency. Multiprocessor cache systems are usually implemented on a high-speed common bus or interconnection network. This type of hardware provides the capability for broadcasting and monitoring communication accesses, which makes it possible to implement write-invalidate or write-update efficiently. Consequently, many multiprocessor cache systems support sequential consistency.

There are two general classes for the implementation of memory coherence control mechanisms: **directory-based** and **snooping cache**. In the previous discussion of coherence control mechanisms, we assumed a generic directory-based system. The directory maintains the state of each memory block and is responsible for the invalidations and updates. Its implementation can be either centralized or distributed. Snooping cache with broadcast is a hardware implementation of a fully distributed directory. With a common bus, each cache controller can monitor all memory accesses on the bus. As a processor *snoops* on other processors' memory references, it can detect whether a cache block is being shared or (more importantly) being updated by other processors. Since all data and control are broadcast on the bus, each processor can invalidate or update its own cache blocks to maintain data currency for future references. The write-update with broadcast is referred to as *write-broadcast*. Because of the hardware bus arbitration and predictable

FIGURE 7.6 Implementation of the processor consistency model.

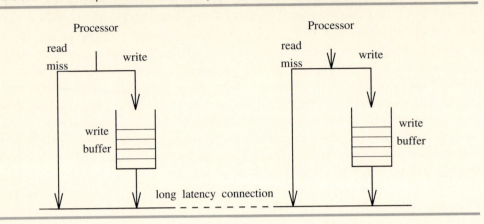

access latency, it is easy to enforce strong ordering such as atomic (strict) or sequential consistency.

Like all centralized control, the shared common bus in a multiprocessor cache system that supports strong consistency eventually becomes a potential bottleneck and even worse, a single point of failure. Various approaches have been proposed to alleviate the problem. Some solutions are:

- Coherence control traffic such as updating and invalidation is separated from regular data accesses using multiple buses.
- Processors are clustered on segmented buses and coherence is maintained at two different levels: local clusters and intercluster coherence control.
- Bus contention is reduced by using special bus topologies or interconnection networks.

The last two approaches increase the access bandwidth at the expense of longer access latency and thus require more complex coherence protocols. Alternatively, one can relax the consistency requirement to weak consistency or processor consistency. Figure 7.6 shows a simple implementation of the processor consistency model. Write operations issued from different processors are overlapped and may be observed in different orders due to long and nondeterministic access latency. Write operations issued by the same processor will appear in order through the FIFO write buffer. Read misses normally stall on the write buffer but may bypass the write buffer to achieve higher concurrency as long as the internal data dependency between read and write operations originating from the same process is observed.

7.4 DISTRIBUTED SHARED MEMORY

Distributed shared memory systems differ from multiprocessor cache systems in that their memory modules are strictly local and physically separated by communication links with access latency several orders of magnitude higher than internal memory accesses. Simulating shared memory in distributed systems requires that remote accesses be implemented by message passing. It is no longer feasible to make updates immediately visible so that read operations can observe the most recent result as in the multiprocessor cache systems with broadcast hardware. Efficient memory management algorithms and coherence protocols are the main issues in the design of DSMs.

7.4.1 Memory Management Algorithms

In a page-based DSM system, it is convenient to assume that the basic units of data sharing, blocks, coincide in size with pages in each processor's own memory space. Each processor sees a virtual memory with its working pages distributed among some local and remote blocks. A block may appear in more than one virtual space and, in effect, becomes shared. There are three options for a processor to access a remote block.

- A remote access is performed remotely at a remote node.
- A remote block is migrated to the local node. Future accesses to the block become local. Effective average access time can be greatly reduced if the memory accesses exhibit strong locality.
- A remote block is replicated at the local node. Concurrent accesses to the same block become possible. Concurrency of the system can be enhanced.

With two different types of accesses, read and write, there are a total of nine different combinations in managing remote accesses. Of the nine combinations, illustrated in Figure 7.7, four are more meaningful than the others for use as a memory management strategy. We will discuss these four models in the following.

Read-remote-write-remote
The shared block is neither migrated nor replicated. A remote access can be implemented as a request sent to a centralized server, and the server responds with returned data for

FIGURE 7.7   Memory management strategies.

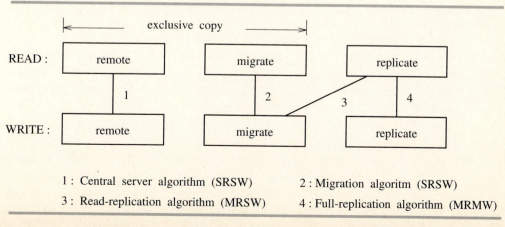

reads and an acknowledgment for writes. The remote access strategy is called the **central server algorithm**. However, this request and response protocol need not be centralized. Multiple memory servers may perform the same service. We can also partition the service so that each server is associated only with the memory blocks on a processor on which the server resides. The central server algorithm is essentially a brute force implementation of a DSM. No performance improvement is attempted. The servers are potential bottlenecks. One positive aspect of this algorithm is that the memory coherence problem is trivial. The system is always sequentially consistent if the server serializes the request and response services.

Read-migrate-write-migrate

Upon an access to a remote block, the block is always migrated to the requesting processor, where it is kept for future reference. The data block in the requested processor is marked invalid. This access strategy is called the **migration algorithm**. Since there is no replication of the block, reads and writes to the block are exclusive. It is a Single Reader Single Writer (SRSW) protocol. The algorithm is akin to the central server algorithm except the owner processor (or server) of a shared block changes dynamically. Migration of a block requires each processor to update its *virtual-page-to-physical-block* mapping table. This can be accomplished by broadcasting the new block location to all processors for every migration. Alternatively, a central location server can be designated to keep track of the block locations.

The migration algorithm achieves better performance by exploiting program localities. However, it suffers the *ping-pong* or *thrashing* effect between competing processors. The problem can be further complicated if *false-sharing* (see Section 7.1.2) exists among processors. The problem of thrashing can be alleviated by replicating the shared block or reducing the block size. Another solution to the problem is to have limited migration. For example, not allowing a block to migrate until it has resided in a local site for a certain time interval or some number of references. The algorithm becomes a combination of remote access and migration. Similar to the central server algorithm, the coherence control for the migration algorithm is straightforward since there is no replication of data.

Read-replicate-write-migrate

This is the same algorithm that we used to describe the write-invalidate protocol for the multiprocessor cache systems. Blocks for read accesses are replicated for concurrent read operations. Write blocks are made exclusive to avoid inconsistency. The strategy is a Multiple Readers Single Writer (MRSW) protocol called the **read-replication algorithm**. Shared blocks are classified as either shared-read-only or exclusive write. A read access to a remote block activates transferring of the block, and all copies of the block are marked shared-read-only. Subsequent reads from the shared-read-only blocks by different processors may proceed simultaneously. Writes to a shared-read-only block use the write-invalidate protocol, which invalidates all shared copies and then updates the local block. The updated block becomes an exclusive copy of the shared data with the processor as its new owner. In effect, the write block migrates from one processor to the other. Subsequent writes to the block by the new owner processor are always permissible since the block is guaranteed to be the only copy. Writes to the block by other processors will force a write-miss as a result of the invalidation.

The read-replication algorithm together with the write-invalidate protocol are a popular choice for the implementation of many DSM systems. The semantics of multiple-read/exclusive-write is widely accepted. The system achieves strong consistency because each read operation receives the value returned by the most recent write operation. The write-invalidate protocol for coherence enforcement is simple to implement. Reads are concurrent, and thrashing occurs only for some write operations. The system performs well when read accesses dominate write accesses, which is the case for most applications.

Invalidation of shared blocks is slightly more complex in DSMs than in multiprocessor cache systems, where efficient broadcast hardware is available. For DSMs, it is necessary to keep track of the copies of a shared block so that invalidation of each copy may be performed by sending an invalidation message to the processor holding that copy. Typically a linked list or table is used to represent the current state of sharing. An important implementation issue is deciding who should be responsible for this data structure and the actual invalidation operations. It is natural to use the notion of a **block owner**. The owner of a block assumes this responsibility. The ownership may be static (the original owner) or dynamic (the current owner resulted from write-migration). The number of the read-replicate increases by 1 each time there is a read-miss. However, it will be reset to one upon a write to the shared block. The number of shared copies is a measure of read-misses between consecutive writes.

Read-replicate-write-replicate

This algorithm assumes that all shared blocks are fully replicated, and write operations are allowed to perform concurrently on replicated blocks as with the read-replication algorithm. It models Multiple Readers Multiple Writers (MRMW) applications and is called the **full-replication algorithm**. Allowing concurrent writes make it more difficult to achieve strong consistency in DSMs unless write operations can be properly sequenced. Write results must be timely and atomically propagated by the write-update protocol. Unlike multiprocessor cache systems where strong consistency relies on the write-broadcast common bus hardware, DSMs must depend on software solutions for implementing atomic broadcast protocols. A write is interpreted as a broadcast of a message, and all messages must be received and delivered (updated) in the same order to maintain sequential consistency. Protocols such as the *two-phase commit* and *sequencer* discussed in Chapter 4 can be used for the full-replication model. These protocols assume a definitive group of members (i.e., the **copy set** of the shared data blocks is known).

Since concurrency is a fundamental requirement for any distributed system, virtually all DSM systems employ block replication. Among them read-replication is more widely used than full replication due to its simplicity. Factors that affect performance of the algorithms include:

- Granularity or size of a block
- Block transfer communication overhead

- Read/write ratio
- Program locality
- Number of interacting nodes and type of interaction

In message passing, a fixed header is normally associated with each block transfer. A larger block size has a better channel utilization but requires a longer transfer time, which must be amortized over a larger number of local references (thus a higher hit ratio or a lower fault rate) to be cost effective. The fault rate (read or write misses) is a function of block size, program locality, and the read/write ratio for each process. A higher read/write ratio yields good performance for both read replication and full replication. For systems with a low read/write ratio, read replication may suffer from thrashing, and full replication will cause traffic congestion in the system. The number of interacting nodes contributes to the degree of sharing and the number of replicates that need to be managed. Its effect is more critical for the full-replication algorithms than for the read-replication algorithms since updates incur more overhead than invalidations.

7.4.2 Block Owner and Copy List

Without the capability of hardware broadcast, the memory coherence managers (MCMs) in a DSM must maintain some data structures to perform two essential tasks:

- To locate the current owner of a data block after several migrations
- To identify all replicated copies for invalidation or update

When making a remote reference to a data object, each processor consults its page map table, which points to a remote processor and the page number within the processor's address space. The remote processor may be the true owner of the block if it is still holding the block or the previous owner of the object if the block has been migrated to another node. In the latter case, the requested processor can forward the request on behalf of the originating processor, and this procedure is repeated until the current owner is found. Alternatively, the requested processor can inform the originating processor about the probable new owner and let the originating processor contact the probable new owner directly. Block transfer is activated after the current block owner is located. Figure 7.8 illustrates the two different approaches using solid and dashed lines, respectively. The operation is similar to the name resolution service provided by a name server, as discussed in Chapter 4. In this case, the difference is that the owner information is only a best estimate, unlike a name server where the resolution process is more structured. Nonetheless, the estimation of the probable owner for each block can be improved whenever a processor participates in a block transfer, observes an invalidation, or forwards a page fault request. Strategies for updating the probable block owner are left as an exercise.

The notion of ownership of an exclusive write-block for the write-invalidate protocol is not ambiguous. The owner is the sole owner of the block. For replicated shared-read-only blocks, the owner may be interpreted as a processor that is holding a valid copy of the block. One of the copies may be designated as the master copy. However, a read-miss

FIGURE 7.8   Locating the owner of a data block.

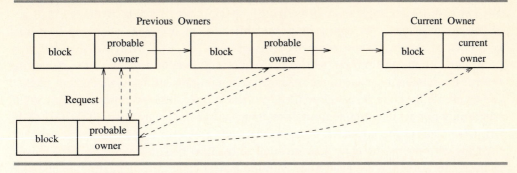

to a shared-read-only block can get a copy from any of the owners. For replicated shared-read-write blocks in the write-update protocol, it is desirable to update the master copy first. In either case, it is necessary to use a *copy list* (or *copy set*) for each shared block to keep track of the replicas. This information structure can be distributed among all sharing nodes.

Each processor maintains a set of pointers for every shared block known to it. The *From* pointer points to the processor from which the block was copied, and the *To* pointers point to the processor to which a copy was sent. As blocks are replicated, a spanning tree that covers all the participating nodes is constructed. Figure 7.9(a) shows an example of such a spanning tree representing a copy set. After a write operation to a replicated

FIGURE 7.9   Data structures for copy set.

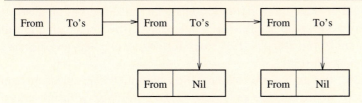

(a) Spanning tree representation of copy set

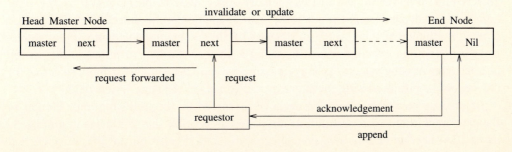

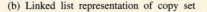

(b) Linked list representation of copy set

block, the processor broadcasts invalidation or update messages along the spanning tree. The tree reverts to a single node if the write-invalidation protocol is used.

One drawback of this approach is the difficulty in deciding when the broadcast is completed. Some acknowledgment schemes must be used. Acknowledgments may propagate bottom-up from the leaf to the requesting node or directly to the requesting node if the number of replications is known. A more efficient acknowledgment method can be used if the copy set is represented by a linear linked list, as shown in Figure 7.9(b) where only one acknowledgment needs to come back from the processor at the end of the list. To implement the linked list distributedly, each processor keeps two pointers, one to the node with the master copy and the other to the next node in the list. A write request is always forwarded to the head node with the master copy for propagating invalidation or update through the list. The end node acknowledges the completion to the requesting node. A read request can be made to any owner of the block copy. The requesting node is appended to the end of the list after replication. This approach is simpler than using a spanning tree (it is actually a special case of the spanning tree).

7.4.3 Object-based DSM Systems

We have argued that DSM is an attractive programming concept because it offers direct information sharing (like reading someone's mind). Page-based DSM is implemented as a global virtual memory shared by all interacting processes using the same address space. Mapping of a virtual address to the physical address is handled by the kernel using pages as a basic sharable data unit. This type of sharing is probably an overkill solution to many distributed applications. Consider the human mind analogy. We often say, "a penny for your thoughts" (not a page of brain cells). Furthermore, even if we could read people's minds, we would be reluctant to let people write to our mind directly. It seems that information sharing should be done by using logical sharable units, such as an abstract object. From the application viewpoint, only objects are shared. The implementation of shared objects is transparent to the users. A DSM space formed by a collection of shared objects is called an **object-based DSM**.

In an object-based DSM, the granularity of the coherence unit is an object or data structure. An object can be defined as an encapsulated data structure with prescribed *methods* or *operations*. Since objects can be recognized by the software system, information sharing is explicit. There are several advantages. First, only the declared shared objects that form the logical shared memory space need to be managed by the DSM kernels. Second, synchronization accesses can be applied at the object level. Third, false sharing is eliminated. And lastly, object-based DSM can be implemented without significant change to an existing system by using a layer of library routines running on top of a message passing system. Message passing by run-time support is more selective for objects than message passing for pages by the kernels in the page-based DSM.

Objects are created and may be declared as shared by the user programs. Similar to the page migration and replication in the page-based DSM, shared objects in an object-based DSM need to be migrated or replicated to facilitate efficient local and concurrent accesses. Synchronization accesses may be specified explicitly by using the *acquire*(X) and *release*(X) operations on an object X or implicitly by using the methods defined on the object. In either case, locking (and unlocking) of a potentially replicated object is required. Locking can be supported by a lock manager in the run-time system.

Since synchronization accesses are invoked through the run-time system, it is easy to implement synchronization type-specific consistency models. For example, to implement the entry consistency, the run-time routine $acquire(X)$ can send a message to the object copy holders to *pull-in* the variables of object X when a lock has been obtained for X. Similarly for the release consistency, updates of the object variables can be *pushed-out* to all copies of X before the $release(X)$ operation is completed.

The Orca programming system discussed in Chapter 3 is a good example of an object-based DSM system. Shared objects in Orca are passed through process creation as parameters and are replicated at each site at which the process resides. The invocation of a method on a shared object is assumed to be indivisible for facilitating mutual exclusion of shared objects. Like a monitor procedure, the locking of an object for method invocation is implicit. Orca assumes that high-bandwidth local area networks are common. This assumption and the fact that the size of an object is normally small compared with the size of a page make it justifiable to use the write-update protocol for memory consistency. Since the Orca run-time system maintains the object space, an atomic broadcast protocol can be used to serialize the updates. Sequential consistency for the shared object is easily accomplished.

Another interesting programming paradigm that is suitable for an object-based DSM system is Linda (also discussed in Chapter 3). The notion of tuple space in Linda fits nicely with the concept of a shared-object pool. However, Linda is quite unconventional. Linda does not have a *write* operation. Linda data structures are "immutable" in the sense that to modify data one must perform an *in* operation followed by an *out* operation on the same data. Furthermore, multiple data may have the same *tag*, which is used to identify data associatively. An *in* operation may return different data nondeterministically. The distinction between multiple data and replicated data is blurred. Many implementations of distributed and replicated tuple space have been proposed for distributed Linda systems. We leave some of the interesting Linda implementation issues for the exercises.

7.5 IMPLEMENTATION OF DSM SYSTEMS

In the past one primary factor in the choice between DSM and message passing (MP) models was the underlying communication hardware. MP systems made few assumptions regarding the support hardware. In contrast, the performance of a DSM system is directly related to the performance of the underlying hardware. This factor led to performance being listed as one of the primary advantage of MP over DSM systems. This also led to DSM systems being built on top of an MP interface/hardware. Recently, the parameters of performance have changed. Commercially available communication mechanisms routinely exceed 1 Gb/s in speed and, in addition, support mapping of the interconnect hardware into the address space of the process participating in the DSM systems. As a result, many DSM systems based on either hardware or software or a combination of both have been proposed. This section describes a classification of DSM systems and presents a sample implementation to illustrate the concepts discussed in this chapter.

7.5.1 DSM Classification

Over the last decade extensive research has been done in the area of DSM, with a large number of systems being built in both the research and commercial community. It is instructive to show a classification of these systems in terms of their characteristics and capabilities. The following parameters are due to Protic, Tomasevic, and Multinovic.

- **Implementation level:** This is the first and most important characteristic of the implementation of DSM. A DSM system can be implemented entirely in hardware. The DASH system developed at Stanford University is a good example of a hardware DSM system. A software DSM system assumes no hardware support. A classical software DSM system is the Munin system developed at Rice University. The software support for a software DSM can be implemented as an operating system service on the participating system or as a library for accessing the DSM. Alternatively, the software DSM system can use compiler-inserted primitives for control and/or synchronization in the application programs.

  Hybrid implementations of DSM using both hardware and software components are becoming more prevalent. Hybrid DSM systems are appealing because of the opportunity of performing operations that are common or time critical in hardware and implementing the remaining logic in software; as we have all noticed, software is considerably easier to update than hardware. The SHRIMP DSM system developed at Princeton University implements DSM using a hybrid approach.

- **Architecture configuration:** The architecture configuration describes the system and the interconnect mechanism on which the DSM is running. These characteristics are interesting in that they significantly affect the DSM design decisions. Local nodes may consist of clusters of processors such that one or more processors can be dedicated to servicing DSM requests. Processors or clusters are connected through an interconnect network (bus hierarchy, ring, mesh, hypercube, LAN, or WAN).

- **Shared data organization:** The shared data organization supported by the DSM systems is generally a function of whether the DSM system is implemented in hardware or software or as a hybrid. Shared data organization can use either structured or nonstructured data. Structured data are objects or language types. In the case of language types, compiler-inserted primitives and programmer-inserted directives typically support DSM operations. Software and hybrid DSM systems commonly use structured data (at least the size is known). Hardware DSM systems generally have no knowledge of the use or structure of the data and therefore manage unstructured data as a series of independent shared-memory locations.

- **Granularity of coherence unit:** The granularity of the coherence unit determines the size of the object on which coherence is maintained. This may or may not equal the fundamental size of the shared data object. Typical coherence units are word, cache block, page, or data structure (or object).

- **DSM algorithm**: DSM algorithms are the distributed memory management strategies described in the previous section. They are classified as SRSW, MRSW, and MRMW.

- **Management responsibility**: Management of the DSM system may be centralized or distributed. If it is distributed among multiple processes, the management responsibility can be fixed (static) at the initialization time or may vary (dynamic) over the lifetime of the execution.

- **Consistency model**: The choice of a consistency model is one of the most fundamental design decisions in the development of a DSM system. Several consistency models are defined and compared in Section 7.2.

- **Coherence control protocol**: The write-invalidate and write-update coherence control protocols are derived from classical cache coherence models and applied to DSM systems.

Given the above classification, we outline the design of a hybrid DSM system, LAM,[3] in the following two sections.

7.5.2 LAM Architecture Environment

LAM is an implementation of a coherent distributed shared-memory system. It was designed to be scalable and provide an intuitive interface to the programmer. LAM is a hybrid implementation of DSM and is similar to SHRIMP in that they both use memory-mapped interconnect to reduce the overhead due to message passing network protocols. In terms of the DSM classification, LAM has the following characteristics:

- **Implementation level**: *hybrid with library routines*. LAM's hybrid implementation uses the combination of a Reflective Memory (RM)[4] and a small collection of library routines. LAM uses RM hardware as the interconnect media. The library routines are linked into the application and allow the programmer to allocate and synchronize shared memory from RM space.

- **Architecture configuration**: *interconnected clusters of processors*. The architecture of LAM is an eight-node network with a four-processor cluster on each node.

- **Shared data organization**: *data structure*. LAM allows the programmer to allocate and share data structures of any size that fits within the available memory.

- **Granularity of coherence unit**: *data structure*. In fact, LAM has no knowledge of the content or structure of the data; it only knows the size of the data structure, and the structure is imposed by the application. Each allocated data structure is guaranteed to be consistent using LAM primitives. Maximum parallelism can be obtained by defining

---

[3] The LAM hybrid DSM system was developed, as a Masters thesis at the University of Florida, by Roger Denton of Encore Computer Corporation. Roger contributed the materials in these sections.

[4] RM is a trademark of Encore Computer Corporation.

the size and content of the data structures to maximize data availability and minimize synchronization events.

- **DSM algorithm employed**: *multiple reader, multiple writer.* Any cooperating process on any participating node may initiate a read or write operation at any time.

- **Responsibility for DSM management**: *distributed.* Each node has access to all control information.

- **Consistency model**: *entry consistency.* LAM uses acquire and release primitives to achieve memory consistency. The shared data structure is guaranteed to be coherent and available for exclusive update after the acquire call to LAM has completed.

- **Coherence policy**: *write-update.* RM is responsible for this portion of coherence management. As each RM location is updated locally, it is staged for transmission (assuming they are shared locations) on the RM network to update the local RM space of the participating nodes.

Figure 7.10 shows the architecture of a four-processor cluster node connected to the interconnect hardware using the RM. The interconnect is similar to a Token ring network. Only write operations transmit data to the ring. These data are appended in a FIFO order and forwarded to every RM on the ring. Each RM contains a fully replicated copy of the shared data structures. The coherence of the RM is kept up by the updates propagated in the ring. Updates at a local RM are reflected (thus, it is called Reflective Memory) at all other nodes in an orderly fashion.

At each node the user's virtual memory address space is mapped to the physical memory in the local RM. This support is provided by standard Unix system calls (*shmget* and *shmat*). RM pages that are mapped into the process virtual address space are protected (but not paged or replaced) by the same virtual memory support that protects local pages.

FIGURE 7.10   The LAM DSM system architecture.

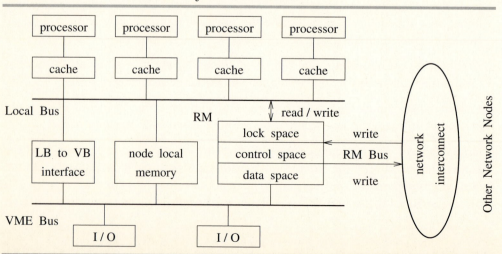

Each RM controller has three ports connected to two buses and the interconnection network. Local processes use the local bus to read and write RM. Read and write accesses to the RM are *not* cached. The RM controller uses the VME bus for I/O accesses and the third port for writing to the network.

Even though the updates are ordered in a ring, the RMs are not sequentially consistent. However, since the RM controller has the knowledge of read accesses to the shared data structures, the write operations are causally ordered. The processor consistency is automatic in the LAM system. The entry consistency of the LAM is achieved by using the consistency property exhibited in the RM network together with a distributed locking mechanism managed by the LAM run-time support as described in the following.

7.5.3 Consistency Implementation

Although the RM network is causally ordered, strict consistency of memory at each processor is not guaranteed because of asynchronous, noninstantaneous communication. In LAM, mutual exclusion and entry consistency are implemented utilizing properties of the RM hardware.

RM allows mapping transmit (write) and receive (read) operations to different addresses. Additionally, the RM network arbitration logic guarantees that RM network traffic is causally ordered with respect to the nodes attached. This allows for an efficient implementation of distributed locks, as described below.

A distributed lock is associated with each LAM data structure. By convention, the process owning the lock owns the LAM data structure. The LAM allocates an area of RM for locks. This area is configured to have the receive/transmit locations at different addresses. A node bids for an *apparently* available lock by setting a word associated with its node id in the lock structure. (A processor test-and-set instruction first acquires a node local guard lock to achieve efficient local node mutual exclusion.) When this transmission appears in the receive address, the lock word is checked for competing bids. RM ordering ensures that all bids that were present at the time this process made a bid are visible at the time this check is made. If no other nodes have bid for the lock, the bidding processor has acquired the lock and may enter the mutual exclusion region. If other nodes have bid for the lock, the competing nodes enter a prioritized retry algorithm (each node clears its bid and retries in a few microseconds; the number of microseconds is based on the node identification number, and in a four-node system will be less than 5 microseconds) until one node successfully acquires the lock. RM locks are released by clearing the RM bid word and then the processor local guard lock.

LAM uses such locks (transparent to the programmer) as part of the *acquire* and *release* code. A user cannot acquire a lock until the lock owner resets its lock bit. The owner's writes are processor consistent and precede the reset of the lock bit. Since writes are causally ordered on the RM network, if a node is able to obtain a lock, it must also be true that writes to the shared data structure preceding the acquisition of the lock must have been stored in the local copy of the shared data structure. Again, due to write ordering on the RM network, once the lock is acquired, this also guarantees that the associated LAM shared data structure is globally consistent. Therefore, the LAM system achieves entry consistency.

7.5.4 LAM Software Environment

LAM consists of a run-time support for managing the RM and a library for external interface. The RM is partitioned into three chunks of memory space: data, control, and lock space.

Lock pages contain the node local and distributed locks used to maintain shared data structure consistency. One lock is required for each LAM shared data structure. The automatic back off spin-locking is similar to the bus arbitration of Ethernet Carrier Sense Medium Access with Collision Detection (CSMA/CD) medium access control.

Control pages contain information related to allocating, locating, and updating LAM shared data structures. The process allocating a shared structure provides an integer tag that uniquely identifies the shared data structure. This tag is used by other processes to attach to the shared structure. One control entry is required for each LAM shared data structure.

Data pages contain the shared data. LAM has no knowledge of the structure or content of the shared data. LAM structures may cross page (and window) boundaries, and no particular byte alignment is required. LAM simply manages the allocation and deallocation of the data pages.

Since the lock and control pages must be shared across nodes, they reside in RM space. RM spinlocks protect these LAM control areas to maintain consistency.

One of the design goals was to produce an intuitive, programmer friendly external interface. The set of library routines is extremely simple and minimized. Each library routine entry point is listed in the following:

- lam_init() --- initialize the LAM system. Called once by each participating process.
- lam_alloc() --- allocate a LAM shared data structure.
- lam_acquire() --- obtain exclusive access to a LAM shared data structure.
- lam_release() --- relinquish exclusive access to a LAM shared data structure.
- lam_free() --- remove a LAM shared data structure from the global pool.
- lam_retire() --- withdraw this process from the LAM system.

The use of these routines is self-explanatory. It is not even necessary to show an application program. Only *acquire* and *release* are relevant to the user programs. LAM access time is directly proportional to the number of bytes accessed and is unrelated to the size of the data structure being accessed. Performance analysis shows that the overhead for each write access to RM is about 15 microseconds for a 145-MB/s RM bus.

7.6 SUMMARY

With the advances of communication technologies, efficient distributed processing in high-bandwidth networks has become not only desirable but also feasible. Distributed shared memory is an innovative approach that supports transparent distributed processing in network systems. A distributed shared memory system simulates a shared *virtual* address (or object) space on a collection of physically separated memory modules. Conventional shared-memory programming paradigms can be applied directly and transparently in distributed shared-memory systems.

Since there are at least two levels (local and remote) of memory access in DSM systems, *migration* and *replication* of data to local memory become necessary to improve access performance. Sharing and replication of data in memory introduce the *memory coherence* problem. The memory coherence problem is more critical in DSMs than the data coherence problem is in distributed file systems because cooperating distributed processes in DSMs are more tightly coupled. Performance and memory coherence are the two most importance issues in the design of distributed shared memory systems.

DSM and multiprocessor cache are dual system architectures that belong to NUMA machines. This chapter begins with an introduction to multiprocessor cache architectures, describing the memory consistency models and coherence control protocols, then shows how these models and protocols are related to the DSM systems. The key difference between cache and DSM architectures lies in the implementation of the systems, in particular, the choice of consistency model and the underlying hardware/software support.

In the discussion of memory coherency, we give a complete taxonomy of the existing consistency models. The memory consistency models are categorized as those that apply to all memory accesses (*general read/write*) and those that apply only to synchronization accesses (*type-specific*). Within each category, the consistency requirement can be further relaxed with respect to processors or memory locations. We give examples showing the relationships among the consistency models.

The *write-invalidate* and *write-update* memory coherency protocols are used to illustrate how consistency models can be implemented in a multiprocessor system. Multiprocessor systems can rely on some special hardware to implement the *directory* or the *snooping cache* to enforce a chosen consistency model. To implement the distributed shared memory in a loosely coupled computer network, we need to define a memory management algorithm and to simulate the directory in software. The chapter describes four memory management algorithms based on migration and replication of memory blocks. Among the four algorithms, the *read replication* (MRSW) and the *full replication* (MRMW) algorithms are more interesting since they allow concurrent accesses. We also show how the directory of a DSM can be maintained by using a block *owner list* and a block *copy list*.

We point out that it is more meaningful to share data objects than to share memory locations. There are many advantages to the *object-based* DSM systems. First, the problem of false sharing is eliminated. Second, synchronization needs to be applied only to objects. Many concurrent programming systems such as Orca and Linda fit very well with the object-based DSM systems and can be built into an existing system with a run-time software library layer.

Finally, we show that much special hardware is now available to support DSM in a high-bandwidth local area network. The *hybrid* (hardware and software) approach seems to be the current trend for implementing DSMs. We demonstrate this concept by using the LAM system to conclude the chapter.

Annotated Bibliography

We use the NUMA architecture [RN91, LE91, LEH92] to discuss the performance and transparency issues in multiprocessor and multicomputer systems. The memory consistency requirements for these systems are illustrated by using examples from [Lam79, Mos93, HA90, CF78, HW90]. The synchronization type-specific consistency models have attracted more attention recently because they are directly related to the operating system. Examples such as the weak, release, and entry consistency models were described in [DSB86, GLL+90, GGH91, BZ91].

Cache coherence is an extensively studied subject in the computer architecture research arena. Multiprocessor multilevel caches are even available on personal computers. A good survey paper on cache coherence by Lilja can be found in [Lil93]. The use of a snooping cache makes it easier to support stronger consistency. Archibald and Baer [AB86] gives a good summary of some existing snooping cache architectures and their coherence protocols. Implementation of cache coherence control protocol for supporting strong consistency requirements may add a significant traffic load to the common bus. Various hardware approaches such as special buses or an interconnection network have been proposed to alleviate the bus congestion problem [GW88, Arc88].

Data migration and replication can be applied to either read or write operations. We describe four common distributed memory management algorithms (central server, migration, read replication, full replication). A thorough performance comparison of these DSM algorithms can be found in [SZ90].

Due to the importance of DSM for distributed processing, a large number of DSM systems have been proposed and built. We use the parameters by Protic, Tomasevic, and Multinovic [PTM95] to characterize various DSM systems. We quoted only three representative systems in the chapter: the Stanford DASH [LLG+92] hardware DSM, the Rice Munin [CBZ91] software DSM, and the Princeton SHRIMP [BLA+94, BDLM95] hybrid DSM. The DASH project is followed by a hybrid DSM system, FLASH [KOH+94]. Other notable DSM systems include Agora [BF88], Alewife [ABC+95], Amber [CAL+89], Clouds [DLA88, RAK88], IVY [Li88, LH89a], Midway [BZS93], PLUS [BR90], S3.mp [NAB+95], and SCI [Gas92]. The last one is a standard scalable coherence interface developed by IEEE to promote heterogeneous interconnect. A detailed survey of DSM systems is available in [NL91] and [PTM95]. An extensive bibliography of DSM systems and related work can be found in [Esk96].

The chapter is concluded by showing a simple implementation of an entry consistency DSM system using existing hardware RM. A full description of the system can be found in [DeJo95].

Exercises

1. A NUMA system has two levels of memory access. The local and remote memory access times are l and r, respectively. Assume that all pages of a program reside in remote memory. A page with a hit ratio h is brought into the cache for local access.

What is the average memory access time? If it takes c time to copy the page, for how many memory references will it take to amortize the cost of copying the page?

2. What is the difference between the unit of replication and the granularity of coherence? What are the advantages of having small granularity?

3. What are the similarities and dissimilarities between the serializability in transaction systems and the sequential consistency in DSMs?

4. The atomic Test-Set-Lock (TSL) instruction exists in most machines. It is often used for mutual exclusion. Explain how this instruction can cause problems in multiple processor shared-memory systems. Suggest an approach for implementing the instruction efficiently.

5. Why is it difficult to implement the causal memory consistency model for DSM systems?

6. Which of the following is a stronger definition of a performed write? Why?
   a. The result of write has been propagated to all sites.
   b. All subsequent reads at any site return the value written by the write.

7. In the release consistency model, *acquire* and *release* operations only need to be processor consistent. Why is this a sufficient condition for the shared variables to be sequentially consistent?

8. Why is it difficult to implement the write-update protocol for the directory-based multiprocessor cache systems where hardware for monitoring and broadcasting does not exist?

9. Describe how the probable block owner information can be estimated distributedly in a DSM system with migration and replication of data blocks.

10. Show the sequence of changes for the copy set data structures in Figure 7.9 when a processor makes a request to write, using the write-invalidate coherence protocol.

11. In Section 7.4.3 we said that an object-based DSM can be implemented by using a layer of software routines running on top of a message passing system. How is object-based DSM different from a message passing system?

12. Is there a need to migrate objects in the Orca system?

13. What are the advantages and disadvantages of using *tag* to identify data objects in Linda?

14. Assume that the tuple space in Linda is fully replicated at each site. Using the *in* and *out* operations in Linda, propose a scheme similar to the write-invalidate or write-update protocol for the coherence of tuple spaces.

15. Why are the Reflective Memories in the LAM architecture not cached?

CHAPTER 8

Distributed Computer Security

Computer security and fault tolerance are subjects that everyone considers important, and yet very few are willing to invest in them when designing a computer system. This is because in our society we are often pressured into making things work first and worrying about the consequences later, when exceptional problems occur or new requirements are added. This chapter is motivated by several implications of the increasing popularity of network usage and the recent developments of secure distributed systems. Computer security and fault tolerance problems are more critical in distributed systems because of the openness of the application environment. Solutions to the problems are closely related to many of the fundamental issues in the design of distributed systems. Furthermore, since many prototype distributed operating systems have been started from scratch, to experiment with new innovative distributed concepts, we might as well incorporate distributed security and fault tolerance mechanisms in the new systems during the initial design phases.

A *secure* (or more generally, *dependable*) computer and communication system is a robust system that exhibits the characteristics of **secrecy, integrity, availability, reliability,** and **safety** in the operation of the system. Secrecy (*privacy* or *confidentiality*) refers to the protection from unauthorized disclosure of system objects such as data and resources. Integrity means that system objects can be modified only by authorized users. Modification may include changing, deleting, and creating objects. Availability means that an authorized user should not be prevented from accessing objects to which he or she has a legitimate right of access. Such a *denial of service* may result from intentional intrusions or unintentional system faults. Computer security, in a narrow sense, is concerned about the violation of the first three characteristics: secrecy, integrity, and availability, due to intentional intrusions. In a broader sense, reliability and safety are also desired. Reliability and safety are fault-tolerant features for unintentional system and user faults. A *fault-tolerant* and *secure* computer system is a **dependable** computer system.

Distributed systems and computer networks are inherently more vulnerable to security threats than single computer systems on account of their open architecture and need for interactions across a wide range of autonomous and heterogeneous systems over open communication links. Application processes share resources and require communication to achieve their goals. Resources are managed by different authorities, and users are administered by different administrative units. Under these circumstances, resource access control and user authentication become extremely difficult to coordinate among distributed nodes.

Message passing interprocess communication through a communication network also opens several fronts of security risk. Communication not only requires confidentiality, but the communicating processes and the messages they use must be authenticated to protect against *spoofing* and *forging*. Information flow needs to be regulated to provide secure communication. In addition, networks and distributed systems are prone to failures and contain possibly untrustworthy components. The correctness of algorithms and communication protocols is often hard to prove in a system that has unpredictable behavior. A careful study of the security issues in distributed systems is warranted.

The key characteristic in a distributed system is *transparency* and in a computer network, it is *interoperability*. In addition to basic security concepts and models, this chapter addresses new security issues resulting from the implementation of these two features.

8.1 FUNDAMENTALS OF COMPUTER SECURITY

The world of a computer system may be represented abstractly as a collection of *subjects* and *objects*. Subjects are active entities that access objects. Objects are passive entities whose security attributes must be protected. Subjects and objects have a master/slave relationship between them. A security policy that describes how objects are to be accessed by subjects is an **access control policy**. Alternatively, we can treat all subjects and objects uniformly as one type of entity, with only information flow between entities. A security policy that describes how the information flow is to be regulated is a **flow control policy**. The following discussions of security policies, models, and implementations are based on these two different views of security.

8.1.1 Security Policies, Models, and Mechanisms

The goals of achieving secrecy, integrity, and availability in a secure computer system rely on protection mechanisms against threats to the objects in the system. Objects that are susceptible to security threats are data, hardware, software, and communication links. There are four categories of common security threats to these objects: **interruption, interception, modification,** and **fabrication**. Loss of data and denial of service are examples of interruption. Interception is related to secrecy, while modification and fabrication are violations of system integrity. Security threats may come from external intruders, internal intruders, or unintentional system or user faults. Typically, external intruders can be excluded by user authentication verification, internal intruders may be controlled by authorization validation, and unintentional faults can be prevented or recovered from by some fault-tolerant mechanisms. This scenario is simple. However, it demonstrates three fundamental approaches, **authentication, authorization,** and **fault-tolerance**, in dealing with computer security problems.

There are two other important approaches that are implicit in the scenario for protecting a system from intrusion, namely, **encryption** of data and **auditing** of accesses and information flow. Encryption prevents the exposure of information and maintains privacy. Auditing is a passive form of protection against security threats but is often very effective in deterring them. Auditing of an activity log may be used to catch security breaches and to improve security measures. Figure 8.1 summarizes the security threats and the associated protection methods for data access and information flow.

Security policies are user requirements. Security models are formal representation methods for security policies. Protections are mechanisms for enforcing security policies based on the security models. Naturally, it is desirable to choose a security model that can represent a wide variety of security policies. Most operating system implementations separate policy and decision making from the mechanisms of enforcing the policies. For example, a resource manager is responsible for scheduling resource usage while the kernel implements the mechanism, but it makes no decision about how the resource is managed. Separation of higher-level services from the kernel to facilitate simple system integration is an important characteristic in a distributed system. Security management is part of resource management. Therefore, a security server that specifies the policies should be placed on top of the kernel that enforces those policies.

FIGURE 8.1   Security threats and protection methods.

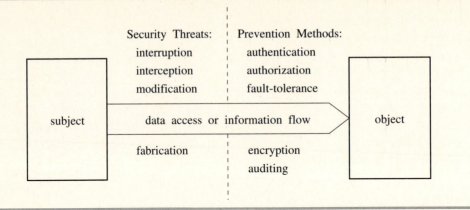

A security model is classified as either **discretionary** or **mandatory**. A discretionary security model provides separation of users and data. It enforces access limitations on an *individual basis*. The conventional **access control matrix** enforcement mechanism is an example of discretionary access. Users are allowed to specify the control of shared objects by individuals or groups of individuals, but the propagation of access rights is limited. The control of access to an object belongs to the owner of the object. Contrary to the discretionary access model, a mandatory security model requires access control of all subjects and objects under its control on a *systemwide basis*. Only the system security manager manages the control of accesses. The military **multilevel security** model is an example of mandatory access control. In this model, all subjects and objects in the system are assigned a sensitivity label, which may be a combination of hierarchical classification and nonhierarchical categories (see Section 8.3). These labels are used as the basis for mandatory access control decisions. Discretionary and mandatory accesses are two of the main criteria used by the DoD National Computer Security Center in evaluating Trusted Computer Systems (TCS). The official security document is commonly known as the *Orange* book in the *Rainbow* series.

8.1.2 Security Issues in Distributed Systems

We are interested in the unique security issues that arise from the requirements of two fundamental goals, *interoperability* and *transparency*, for computer networks and distributed systems. Interoperability refers to the ability to have effective information exchange between hosts and between processes in systems that have heterogeneous components. The effectiveness of information exchange must be augmented with security attributes. Transparency refers to the uniform view of a system that has transparent distribution of computation and resources. It is worthwhile to find out the effect of transparency on the design of a secure distributed system and whether the transparency concept should be extended to include security. To address these issues, let us first consider the system architecture with embedded security features.

System Architecture

Generally, there are only two basic approaches to implementing new services that have a significant impact on the operating system. The first is to add an additional layer of software that runs on top of the existing system to provide the new services. Modification of the original system is either unnecessary or very minimal. The second is to redesign the system (including the kernel) so that the new services can be executed more effectively in the kernel mode. The difference between the two approaches is a trade-off between cost and efficiency. We have seen a similar example in the implementation of the *threads* concept. Threads can be implemented either as a user package or in the system kernel. Likewise, integrating security control in a distributed system can use either approach, but it requires more thought.

Distributed operating systems typically use the client/server paradigm. Most system services are moved out of the kernel, and the kernel is kept to a minimum to facilitate portability. If we prefer separation of policies and mechanisms, it is natural to implement security policies in servers and protection mechanisms in the kernel. Policies in security servers can vary, but the protection mechanism for enforcing security policies remains unchanged. This strategy offers a more uniform and flexible platform for implementing security policies. The small size of the kernel also makes it easier to ensure that the kernel is safe and can be trusted. This is an important property since all security services will have to rely on a secure kernel.

The use of client/server model for structuring systems fits very well with the *object-oriented* programming paradigm. Objects to be protected are associated with servers managing the objects. Each object has a set of allowable *well-formed* operations that can be invoked by the client processes. An object can be better safe-guarded by allowing only indirect accesses through well-formed operations. In this model, security attributes can be assigned to an object as well as to each well-formed operation. A client initiates an access to an object through the kernel. The kernel authenticates the client and then invokes the object server, which authorizes the access, performs the operation, and returns the results to the client through the kernel. To maintain the spirit of the client/server model, the authentication and the authorization parts of the process can be implemented as separate servers: *authentication* and *authorization* servers. Figure 8.2 shows such an architecture in which security resides in various security servers, and the kernel only grants or denies an access request based on the decision made by the security servers, without interpreting either the request or the response. Examples of other security servers in the figure include *audit* and *encryption* servers.

Besides the structure of security services, there is the issue of the placement of security servers. Most operating systems and communication network architectures are either hierarchical or layered. Security is concerned with the protection of objects and thus should be associated with the resource managers. Security servers are responsible for access control, which must rely on secure communication in a distributed system. In such systems, remote security servers interact with each other through their peer-to-peer protocols using Interprocess Communication (IPC) implemented at the transport layer in the network architecture. This end-to-end communication, in turn, must be supported by a secure host-to-host communication at the network layer and a secure

FIGURE 8.2   Client/server distributed security architecture.

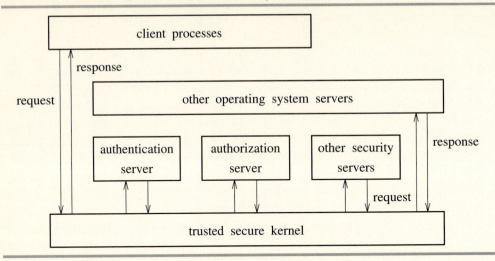

node-to-node communication at the link layer. Security at the three network layers (transport, network, and link) are concerned with information flow control and the secrecy and integrity of the messages that flow in the network. Message security is usually achieved by using cryptography and routing to avoid analysis of and tampering with the message traffic. These are the functions of a secure gateway. A secure distributed system consists of communicating security servers using trusted gateways to ensure access and communication security.

The above paragraph shows the need for a layered security system architecture that is similar to the standard OSI for network system architectures.

Interoperability and Transparency

Interoperability and transparency are very desirable characteristics in a computer system. In fact, they are so unique that we use them to define network and distributed operating systems. These characteristics provide flexibility and uniformity for the users of the system. However, when security is a concern, the issue of interoperability and transparency become complicated. In an environment with heterogeneous systems under different domains and administrative authorities, it is difficult to come to an agreement about security models and protection mechanisms. On the one hand, users enjoy the freedom of communication and resource sharing. On the other hand, users need to restrict the freedom, perhaps because of possible competing interest or potential security threats. To balance these two conflicting interests, a solution is to give users a convenient option to simulate a secure private network over the public network, without losing too much interoperability and transparency. To achieve this objective we must address three fundamental problems:

- Interdomain authentication
- Secure message transfer between domains
- Interdomain access control

When a service is requested at a remote host in a different domain, the interdomain access control is responsible for the authorization of accesses and the interoperability between two domains that possibly have different access control models. Successful interdomain accesses depend on the system's ability to transmit request/reply messages securely in the network. Secure message transfer, in turn, depends on the successful interdomain authentication of the client and server. Secure message transfer utilizing cryptographic techniques is a well-understood subject. The problems of interdomain authentication and authorization are still wide open. This chapter discusses only some of the emerging techniques for authentication and authorization in distributed systems.

To achieve security transparency, a standard security system architecture with a well-defined Trusted Application Program Interface (TAPI) must be developed. Several standards have been developed toward this goal. One notable example is the Generic Security Service Application Program Interface (GSS-API), which was developed at DEC and has been widely accepted by the industry. GSS-API allows users to call on security services of a supporting security mechanism in a generic manner. The API is independent of the underlying security mechanism and communication protocol. The security services available to application users include mutual authentication, data confidentiality and integrity, transfer of security attributes, and delegation. TAPI is expected to continue to evolve with the increasing demand for security in distributed systems.

The discussion in the following sections looks at access control (authorization), message security (cryptography), then authentication.

8.2 DISCRETIONARY ACCESS CONTROL MODELS

Discretionary security models provide access control on an individual basis. The *Access Control Matrix* (ACM) model is perhaps the most fundamental and widely used discretionary access control model for enforcing *simple* security policies. A simple security policy is a statement that specifies what privileges and limitations a certain subject has on an object, without any other special constraints. A security policy such as subject *s* can access object *x* if it has not already accessed object *y*, is considered a *complex* security policy. Complex security policies are security requirements that are dependent on how and when other accesses are being performed. Many complex security policies are more relevant in distributed systems and will be discussed in Section 8.6. Access control matrices are data structures that represent privileges that subjects have on objects for simple security policies.

8.2.1 Access Control Matrix

Formally stated, an access control is a function that given a subject and object pair, (s,o), and a requested operation, r from s to o, returns a true value if the request is permitted and a false value otherwise. For simple security policies, this function can be represented in a matrix form, where the indices are subjects and objects, and the entries in the matrix are the permissible access rights or privileges. We use P to denote the matrix and $R = P(s, o)$ to represent each entry, where R is a set of allowable access operations. An access operation r is granted if $r \in R$. Conceptually this process of access validation can be performed by a centralized *reference monitor* with a large and sparse access control matrix for all subjects and objects in the system. Practically, it is preferable to have separate reference monitors for different categories of subjects and objects for apparent reasons. For instance, resource and process protection can use separate access control matrices. We will show some examples of useful access control matrices.

For resource protection, we can assume that subjects are users and objects are protected resources such as data files. The access rights in this case may include *read, write, execute,* and *append.* Figure 8.3(a) shows a typical resource protection access control matrix. Access control matrices must first be created, then maintained as the system progresses. A special privilege, *owner,* may be assigned to the creator of an object. In the case of a file object, the file is created through a request to the file sever. In addition to the normal access rights, the owner of a file has the privilege of deleting the file and transferring subset of its normal access rights to other users. If transferring a transferred right is desired, a copy bit may be associated with a particular right for repeated passing of the access right. Naturally the owner of an object can revoke any access right that it has given to others. An access control matrix itself is a special object and requires a secure managing mechanism to ensure its integrity.

For process protection, the subjects and the objects are both processes. Process interactions are either communication or synchronization. Common privileges for processes include *send* and *receive* for process communication and *block* and *unblock* for process synchronization. Figure 8.3(b) is an example of a process protection access control matrix. Process A can send messages to processes B and C. Processes B and C can block each other, while process A can unblock B and C.

The notion of a subject can be generalized beyond simple users and processes. Users and processes have attributes and state information. Those that share common attributes and state information are said to be in the same domain. In the context of security, we can define a domain as a set of objects associated with some access rights. Processes in the same domain have the same access rights to some common objects. The domain concept is useful in a structured system where processes are assigned in a certain domain to execute and can move from one domain to the other with different privileges in each domain. To regulate the movement between domains, a domain protection access control may be used as shown in Figure 8.3(c), where *enter* is the privilege that a process in a domain must possess in order to move into another domain. The domain concept is important in a layered operating system where layers can be interpreted as domains such that access protection between layers can be enforced. Using domains as subjects in a domain access control matrix not only enforces domain access control but also changes the process' access rights as a process moves between domains. Using domains for access control is a complicated issue since domains may be disjoint, overlapped,

FIGURE 8.3   Access control matrices.

subj. \ obj.	file a	file b	file c	file d
user A	owner	read / write	execute	owner
user B	copy read	owner		
user C		read	owner	append

(a) Resource ACM

subj. \ obj.	process A	process B	process C
process A		send / unblock	send / unblock
process B	receive		block
process C	receive	block	

(b) Process ACM

subj. \ obj.	domain A	domain B	domain C
domain A		enter	
domain B			enter
domain C	enter		

(c) Domain ACM

or subsets/supersets of one another. It is up to the applications to carefully choose the structure of the domains.

Reducing the Size of the Access Control Matrix

It is clear that the access control matrix should be categorized with respect to applications, as is illustrated in Figure 8.3. Even with only a resource access control matrix, the size of the matrix can still be very large and sparse. The user subjects are generally related and could have similar access rights to some common objects. That is, some subject rows in the matrix have identical entries. These rows can be merged as a single *group* of users just as in the previous discussion of domains. A user is first identified with a group name and the enforcement of the access control is based on the group rather than the user name. If a user belongs to more than one group, its access right is the union of all access rights of the groups to which it belongs. The group concept is convenient since it coincides with a user's view of class organization in real life. Similarly, object columns with the same entries can be merged to reduce the size of the matrix. These merged objects are call a *category*. Categories are different from user groups in the sense that grouping is based on the information contents in the objects rather than the attributes of the users. With subject groups and object categories, the access control matrix can be significantly simplified.

Distributed Compartments

The concept of grouping subjects and objects is of particular importance for implementing access control in distributed systems. Suppose that each autonomous node in a distributed system uses the access control matrix model to manage its own local resources. A distributed application with collaborating processes may consist of subject users and object resources crossing the physical boundaries of distributed nodes. It is neither feasible nor desirable to have a global access control matrix that encompasses all subjects and objects in the entire system. Instead, a logical access control matrix that regulates accesses among the collaborating users would serve a better purpose. Figure 8.4 shows the logical grouping, called a **distributed compartment**, of subjects and objects in a distributed system. Although a distributed compartment is designed to manage distributed resources, it can be used as a security model, including the access control matrix model.

A distributed compartment is a logical group composed of objects from physically distributed nodes. It has users called members, or subjects. Members have privileges and objects have associated access rights. The relationship between subjects and objects can be modeled by an access control matrix. Each distributed compartment has at least one member called an *owner*. Owners have the maximum privileges for the distributed compartment they own. Distributed compartments may be hierarchically structured with the root as the supreme distributed compartment. Accesses to distributed compartments are based on *distributed handles* rather than user ids. Distributed handles are application oriented and independent of the underlying operating system. They provide a protective wall around an application and are authenticated by the particular application. This

FIGURE 8.4   A distributed compartment model.

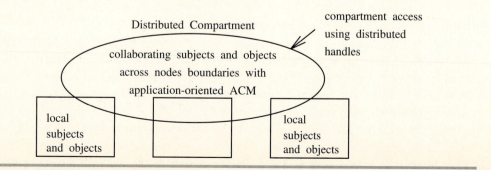

approach has several advantages. The grouping of subjects and objects is logical and application specific. The accesses are made more transparent since they are not dependent on operating systems and administrative units. Management of distributed handles is part of the applications, which allows different security policies to be implemented. A user can have multiple distributed handles with different privileges to different applications without any intervention from the system administrator. The distributed compartment model and the distributed handles for accessing compartments offer a very clean way to deal with the complex issues of managing distributed security.

8.2.2 Implementations of ACM

For efficiency and organizational purposes, access control matrices need to be partitioned and implemented independently. The privileges in the large sparse access control matrix can be collected with respect to an object (column) or a subject (row). The linked list structure that contains all nonempty entries in a column for a particular object is called an **Access Control List** (ACL) for the object. Likewise, the linked list structure that contains all entries in a row for a subject is called a **Capability List** (CL) for the subject. An ACL is analogous to the reservation book in a restaurant (object) where a customer (subject) is allowed seating in the reservation-only restaurant if his or her name appears in the reservation book. An ACL specifies the permissible rights that various subjects have on the object. A CL is analogous to a ticket for a concert. Whoever (subject) has the ticket is allowed to enter the concert hall (object). A CL specifies privileges to various objects held by a subject.

It may appear that ACL and CL are equivalent since both are derived from the same access control matrix. However, due to implementations, there are many significant differences. First of all, for the implementation of access control lists, the identification of a subject (e.g., the driver's license of the restaurant patron) must be authenticated, whereas in the implementation of capability lists, it is the capability (ticket for the concert) that must be authenticated. The authenticity of the ticket holder is secondary and may not be required. Secondly, the access control list of an object resides in the object server and contains pairs of subject and the corresponding privileges, (s_i, R_{si}). The capability list of a subject, in the form of object and privilege pairs, (o_i, R_{oi}), is a part of the subject (i.e., client process).

ACL and CL are contrasted in Figure 8.5(a) and (b). For ACL implementation, a subject client (s) presents an access request (s, r) to an object server. Upon authentication of the subject, the object server validates the request against its ACL to see whether s is an authorized user and the requested privilege r is a member of R_s. In the case of CL implementation, the object server compares the access request (o, r) against the CL in the subject to authenticate the capability and to determine that the requested privilege is one that is allowed for the object.

Most centralized operating systems use the access control list approach or its variations (such as the rwx file protection in Unix) for resource access control. Since it is difficult to determine the set of potential subject users for an object in a distributed system, the capability list approach is more widely used in modern distributed systems. Enforcing access control using capability lists is simple if the capability can be authenticated. A

FIGURE 8.5   Implementations of access control matrices.

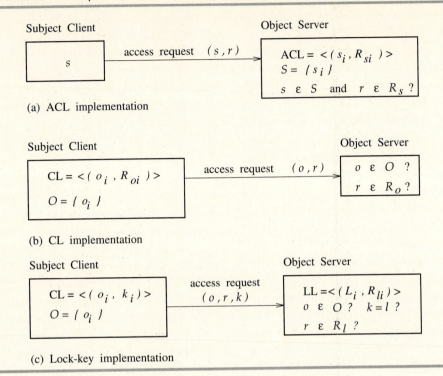

(a) ACL implementation

(b) CL implementation

(c) Lock-key implementation

five-dollar bill (capability list) is much easier to use than five dollars in the bank (access control list). However, the five-dollar bill must be easily authenticated to be useful. For example, the blue and red threads hidden in the bill serve the authentication purpose. Similarly, in a capability list we want the privileges to be readable and associated with some hidden secret (or verifiable) information to avoid forgery.

The **lock-key** is one such method that provides capability with some safety. It is actually a combination of CL and ACL. Each CL is a list of object and key (o, k) pairs in the subject. The object server maintains a *lock list* (LL) of (l_i, R_{li}), which is similar to an ACL with subjects replaced by locks. Each lock l_i corresponds to a set of privileges R_{li} for the object. For each access request (o, r, k), the object server searches for the key (k) in the subject's CL and attempts to match it with a lock (l) in the object's LL. If it is successful and the requested operation (r) is in R_l, the access is granted. In the implementation, the keys are encrypted for secrecy and authentication. Figure 8.5(c) depicts the lock-key method.

This approach is used and extended in the Amoeba system. In this system, a capability is associated with two fields: *rights* and *check*. The *check* field is generated at the object creation time. It serves as a key in the capability and a lock in the object. The key and lock are compared for each access to the object. When a subset of the rights is passed to another subject, a capability with a secret *check* field is given to the subject. This new secret *check* field is computed through a one-way mapping function with the exclusive-or operation of the *rights* (subset of the owner's rights) field and the object owner's original *check* bits as the inputs to the function. The one-way function ensures that the subset of the *rights* is strictly enforced because it is not possible to modify the *rights* field and generate the correct secret *check* field without knowing the original check field. Note that in the scheme, the capability with check bits prevents tampering with the *rights* field but not eavesdropping on the capability.

8.2.3 Comparison of ACL and CL

The previous section described the internal structures of access control and capability lists and outlined a combined approach, the lock-key method. In this section we will summarize the different ways ACL and CL are used. The comparisons are discussed in terms of the ways that they are managed. The managing functions include authentication; reviewing, propagation, and revocation of access rights; and conversion between ACL and CL.

Authentication

Subject identities must be verified before each access to the ACL. Subjects are usually users or processes. Authentication of users and processes is a basic function that each system must provide, so there is no added overhead for authentication in the ACL approach. For the CL, the authentication is performed with respect to the capability, so the object server must assume the responsibility. However, unlike users and processes, the capabilities are known to the objects. It is easier to authenticate capabilities. This is also one of the reasons that many distributed system implementations favor the capability list approach. It is much easier to issue tickets than to use reservations when dealing with a large crowd (subjects).

Review of Access Rights

It is sometimes desirable to know which subjects are authorized to use a certain object. This *reviewing* process is useful to the system administrator. The reviewing of access rights is trivial for the ACL since it contains the exact information in the list. For storage efficiency, we can use subject grouping to avoid enumerating all subjects that have common access rights. We can also use the *wild card* and *prohibitive right* to indicate cases such as an access right is open to all except users X and Y.

It is difficult to review access rights with the CL approach unless some type of activity log is kept for all subjects that are given the capability.

Propagation of Access Rights

Access rights must be replicatable to facilitate sharing. Propagation of access rights is normally referred to as the duplication of all or part of the privileges from one subject to the others. It is not a transfer of rights; the rights of the original subject are not removed after being propagated. Propagation of rights in ACL is explicitly initiated by a request to the object server, which modifies or adds an entry to its ACL. Subjects may be users or processes. Propagation of rights is infrequent between users but more likely among processes since subprocesses are often created to perform subtasks that require sharing of privileges. Propagation of rights must adhere to the principle of *least privileges*. That is, only the minimum privileges that are necessary to perform the subtasks are given when propagating the rights. For the CL, theoretically, it is possible to propagate rights freely from subject to subject without the intervention of the object server. This may result in a competely uncontrollable system. Therefore, we would like to avoid it by requiring the propagation to go through the object server, particularly when locks and keys are used as in the Amoeba system.

Revocation of Access Rights

Allowing propagation of access rights means that there must exist some mechanism to revoke rights that were given to subjects. Revocation is trivial for ACL since subject entries can be deleted from an ACL easily, but it is difficult for CL to revoke access rights selectively. In a computer system, once keys (or tickets) are given, the only way to reclaim them is to invalidate them. This can be done by changing the locks in the object server and distributing the new keys to those subjects that are not supposed to have been affected, if they can be located easily. Otherwise we can wait until a subject finds out that its access rights have been denied and subsequently makes a request for the new key. Another alternative is to maintain a list of the prohibited subjects. A lock is changed only when the prohibited subject list grows to a certain size. However, this approach carries the flavor of the ACL.

Conversion between ACL and CL

Interactions among processes in a distributed system that consists of nodes using different access control models requires a gateway for access control protocol conversion. Processes in a capability-list-based system may access remote objects in access-control-list-based system, and vice versa. The former case is straightforward to implement. The gateway authenticates the process identifier and verifies the operation in the capability list. The request is then converted into the ACL form and presented to the remote host using ACL. The remote host grants the access request if its ACL contains the process as a subject and the requested operation is within the authorized range. The gateway is assumed to be trusted. The latter case is slightly more complex. To convert an ACL request to a CL request, there must be a database with resource capabilities for the interacting processes. The gateway first validates the ACL request and obtains the resource capability from the database server. This capability is then presented to the capability-based object server.

A system utilizing both ACL and CL suffers the drawbacks of both approaches. Furthermore, the need for conversion between ACL and CL causes additional security hazards.

8.3 MANDATORY FLOW CONTROL MODELS

Traditional operating systems use discretionary access control methods for controlling accesses to resources. With the advances in networks and distributed systems, it is necessary to broaden the scope to include the control of information flow between distributed nodes. Information flow control on a *systemwide* basis is mandatory as opposed to discretionary. For example, driving to the university involves both discretionary and mandatory control. Our parking decal for the parking garage is a *capability* given to us on a discretionary basis for accessing the university resource. On the way to the university, we have to obey the mandatory traffic regulations, which are applied to everybody on the roads. Exceptions are some of the emergency vehicles or police cars that may be allowed to *occasionally* violate the rules because they are *trusted* subjects. This section describes some of the basic mandatory flow control models.

8.3.1 Information Flow Control

The access control matrix model is effective in providing a basic framework for enforcing security requirements and is easy to implement in practice. However, using either ACL or CL, it has inherent disadvantages that limit how a protection system can meet some security requirements. In particular, some questions pertaining to the security of using an access control matrix cannot be decided theoretically. An example is the *confinement problem* cited by Lampson, which is to determine whether there is any mechanism by which a subject authorized to access an object may leak information contained in that object to some other subjects not authorized to access that object. It has been shown that the confinement problem is *undecidable* due to the characteristic of discretionary transfer of access rights between subjects in the access control matrix model. To confine the leak of information, security control should be applied to the information in addition to the subject holding the information. If a security system can be verified such that no such mechanisms exist, that system is not vulnerable to the attack of a *Trojan horse*, which is usually interpreted as a piece of hidden code intentionally placed in a program to perform nefarious functions in addition to the normal goals of the program. Another disadvantage of the access control matrix model is that no semantics of information in the objects are considered; thus the security sensitivity of an object is hardly expressed by that model.

To alleviate these problems in the access control matrix model, the concept of *information flow control* is needed to provide additional security. Information flow control is different from regulating accesses of objects by subjects, as in the access control model. It is concerned with how information is disseminated or propagated from one object to another. A security system employing information flow control usually categorizes all the system entities in different *security classes*, and all the valid channels along which information may flow between classes are regulated. The concept of classification matches the security requirement of many real-world applications. Labeling a classification on every subject and object and controlling accesses according to the classifications of interacting entities (instead of according to the identities of subjects and objects as in the access control model) can considerably reduce both implementation and operation overhead of the enforcement mechanisms. An information flow control is normally mandatory. The security classes of all entities (subjects and objects) must be specified explicitly and the class of an entity seldom changes after it has been created (changes are sometimes made by the system security administration). All permissible information flow paths among different classes are regulated using unambiguous security rules that must be strictly obeyed by any access of a subject to an object. Information flow control can be applied to very fine-grained objects such as variables in a program, although access controls are usually used to govern accesses of larger objects such as files or processes.

8.3.2 Lattice Model

The lattice model introduced by Denning is the best-known information flow model. It employs a mathematical structure for formulating the requirements of secure information flow among classes of a secure system. Since all information flow is regulated precisely by the mathematical properties of the structure rather than by a set of descriptive axioms, the security of the system can be easily verified. The central component of Denning's model is a lattice whose mathematical meaning is a structure consisting of a finite partially ordered set together with a least upper bound and a greatest lower bound operator on the set. A lattice is a Directed Acyclic Graph (DAG) with a single source and sink.

To restrict information flow by a lattice in a security system, each subject or object is associated with a security class, and all security classes form a partially ordered set. The least upper bound and greatest lower bound operators are defined clearly and precisely such that the security class of the result of the operation between two operand classes can be uniquely determined. Information can only flow in the direction that matches the partial ordering. That is, information is permitted to flow from a lower class to a higher class (upward flow) but not to a lower class (downward flow) or to a unrelated class.

Formally stated, a lattice model of secure information flow for a particular system FM^5 can be defined as

$$FM = \ <S, O, SC, F, \oplus, \otimes, \rightarrow>$$

where

- S is the set of subjects that are active agents responsible for all information flow.

- O is the set of objects that are logical or physical information resources such as files, segments, or program variables.

- SC is the finite set of security classes corresponding to disjoint classes of information. All security classes form a partial ordering.

- F is a mapping function from S or O to SC, which is called *binding* by Denning. Each object o is bound to a security class, commonly called security *classification*, which specifies the security class with the information stored in o. Each subject s is also bound to a security class, often called security *clearance*, which is usually determined by the security clearance of the user or another subject creating s.

- $\oplus$ is the least upper bound operator on SC. For any two classes A and B, the class of $A \oplus B$ is uniquely defined.

---

[5] The model stated here is slightly different from the model proposed by Denning.

- $\otimes$ is the greatest lower bound operator on SC. For any two classes A and B, the class of $A \otimes B$ is uniquely defined.

- $\rightarrow$ is a flow relation defined on pairs of security classes. For classes A and B in a lattice, $A \rightarrow B$ means information in class A is permitted to flow into class B, and it exists only if B is a higher class than A in the partial ordering. Information is said to flow from class A to class B whenever information associated with A affects the value of information associated with B.

Using the definitions above, an FM is secure only if the execution of a sequence of operations cannot give rise to an information flow that violates the relation $\rightarrow$. Therefore, to verify whether a system is secure, we need to examine all access operations to identify all possible information flow in the system and to check to see if they are all permitted by the flow relation.

Examples

A lattice model that consists of a simple linear ordering on a set of security classes is shown in Figure 8.6. Information can only flow upward, and once it reaches to a class C_i, it cannot flow down to any class below C_i, unless a *sanitization* process declassifies the security class of the information. This structure is suitable for any system in which all security classes need to be totally ordered. One prominent example is the military security system in which all data storage is classified as *unclassified*, *confidential*, *secret*, and *top secret*, and all personnel are also similarly classified according to rank or mission.

Another lattice model is derived from a nonlinear ordering on the set of all subsets of a given finite set X. Figure 8.7 illustrates such an example for $X = \{x, y, z\}$. It satisfies the definition of a lattice. There is a single source and sink. The least upper bound and the greatest lower bound of all security classes are uniquely defined. For example, the least upper bound of the security classes $\{x\}$ and $\{z\}$ is $\{x, z\}$, and the greatest lower bound of the security classes $\{x, y\}$ and $\{y, z\}$ is $\{y\}$. In such a model, each security class consists of a set of categories, and a class A has a lower ordering than B iff A is contained by B. For example, class $\{x\}$ has a lower ordering than class $\{x, y\}$ (or $\{x, y\}$ *dominates* $\{x\}$). This structure is suitable for an environment in which X is regarded as a set of properties, and a class is a combination of some properties from X. For instance, if each document in a company has a class consisting of a set of categories according to the contents of the document and each employee working in a department also has a class comprised of a set of categories depending on the characteristic of that department, a document d can only be accessible to an employee e (thus information flows from d to e) if the class of e contains the class of d.

FIGURE 8.6 A linear ordered lattice, in which $SC = \{C_1, ..., C_n\}$, $C_i \rightarrow C_j$ iff $i \leq j$, $C_i \oplus C_j = C_{max(i,j)}$, and $C_i \otimes C_j = C_{min(i,j)}$.

$$C_1 \longrightarrow C_2 \longrightarrow \cdots \cdots \longrightarrow C_{n-1} \longrightarrow C_n$$

FIGURE 8.7 A lattice of subsets of $X = \{x, y, z\}$, in which $SC = powerset(X)$, $C_i \rightarrow C_j$ iff $C_i \subseteq C_j$, $C_i \oplus C_j = C_i \cup C_j$, and $C_i \otimes C_j = C_i \cap C_j$.

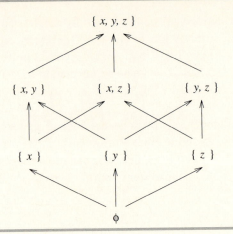

A more general example is a richer structure formed by the (Cartesian) product of these two lattices, where both a hierarchical order and a nonhierarchical category set are associated with each entity and each flow must be regulated by the original information flow relations of the two composing lattices.

Flow Properties of a Lattice

The flow relations $\rightarrow$ in the information flow model based on a lattice of security classes has some important properties that are useful in the design and certification of secure systems. The relation $\rightarrow$ is reflexive, transitive, and antisymmetric; that is, for all $A, B, C \in SC$:

- **Reflexive:** $A \rightarrow A$
  The statement $a = a$ in a program is trivially secure, and information flow from an object to another at the same class certainly does not violate security.
- **Transitive:** $A \rightarrow B$ and $B \rightarrow C$ implies $A \rightarrow C$
  This indicates that a valid flow does not necessarily occur between two classes adjacent to each other in the partial ordering.
- **Antisymmetric:** $A \rightarrow B$ and $B \rightarrow A$ implies $A = B$
  If information can flow back and forth between two objects, they must have the same security classes.

With no additional restrictions on information flow, the other two inherent flow properties of a lattice model result from the stateless characteristic of the model:

- **Aggregation:** $A \to C$ and $B \to C$ implies $A \cup B \to C$
  If information can flow from both A and B to C, the information aggregate of A and B can flow to C.
- **Separation:** $A \cup B \to C$ implies $A \to C$ and $B \to C$
  If the information aggregate of A and B can flow to C, information can flow from either A or B to C.

These flow properties are directly deduced from the basic properties of a lattice. There are some multilevel applications whose security policies require exceptions to these properties. The exception to the first property, called an *aggregation exception*, is that after C sinks information from either A or B, it cannot sink information from the other class. The exception to the second property, called a *separation exception*, is that C must sink information from both A and B. It cannot just sink information from only one of the two classes. Handling these more complex security requirements is discussed in Section 8.6.

8.3.3 Multilevel Security

Strictly speaking, multilevel security is a special case of the lattice-based information flow model, although its concept has been practiced in the government and military for a long time. With a specific security goal predetermined, information flow in a multilevel security system is regulated in order not to violate the "security" as determined by the security goal. Two well-known and fully established multilevel security models, the Bell–LaPadula model for information confidentiality and the Biba model for information integrity, are briefly discussed below.

The Bell–LaPadula Model

With all system entities in a computer system classified, the Bell–LaPadula model provides a formal description of all access operations that any subject can perform on any object, such that the confidentiality of information can be preserved. It has been implemented in many computer systems where the confidentiality of information flow is the primary security concern.

The security class assigned to a subject or an object includes two components: a hierarchical *security level* and a nonhierarchical *security category*. The security level, commonly called *clearance* if applied to subjects and *classification* if applied to objects, is a linear ordering that determines the degree of sensitivity of information a subject can view or an object can contain. The security category, consisting a set of *compartments* that represents natural or artificial characteristics of subjects and objects, is used to enforce the *need-to-know* principle. A subject is given access only to the objects that it requires to performs its jobs. The security category itself forms a lattice with subset containment as the basis of the dominance relation. Therefore, the security classes form a lattice determined by the Cartesian product of the linear lattice of security levels and the subset lattice of security categories. A security class A is said to dominate a security class B if A's level is higher than B's and B's category is a subset of A's category. Security with respect to confidentiality in the model is described by two fundamental axioms:

- **The simple security property**: Reading information from an object o by a subject s requires that $SC(s)$ dominates $SC(o)$ ("no read up").
- **The ⋆-property**: Writing information to an object o by a subject s requires that $SC(o)$ dominates $SC(s)$ ("no write down").

The simple security property ensures that a subject cannot view information contained in an object unless the security class of the subject is as least as high as the class of the object, which is a conventional view of confidentiality in military. The ⋆-property prevents a subject from modifying an object unless the security class of the object is greater than or equal to the class of the subject. It prevents indirect viewing of objects because an illicit subject is forbidden to leak information contained in a higher-class object to a lower-class object. With the ⋆-property, information cannot be compromised by exercising a Trojan horse program, because a subject cannot pass information in an object to another subject that does not have a proper security level and category.

The Biba Model

For many business applications, system integrity is more important than information confidentiality. Their primary security goal is to prevent unintentional and malicious modifications to data by unauthorized users. The Biba model, which is a dual of the Bell–Lapadula model, is a multilevel access control model for information integrity. To preserve data integrity, an *integrity class*, analogous to the security class in the Bell–LaPadula model, is defined for each subject and object. Contrary to the Bell–LaPadula model, the Biba model regulates all access operations of subjects to objects such that information can only flow from a higher integrity class to a lower one.

The integrity class also may include a hierarchical *integrity level* and a nonhierarchical *integrity category*. All integrity levels form a linear lattice in which each level represents the classification of integrity of information an object can contain or the clearance of a subject for modifying an object. All integrity categories that form a subset lattice are also used to enforce the *need-to-have* principle, similar to the role of security categories in the Bell–LaPadula model. A security class A is said to dominate a security class B if A's level is higher than B's and B's category is a subset of A's category.

Similar to those of the Bell–LaPadula model, the two fundamental axioms regarding access of subjects to objects of the Biba model are:

- **The simple integrity property**: Writing information to an object o by a subject s requires that $SC(s)$ dominates $SC(o)$ ("no write up").
- **The ⋆-property**: Reading information from an object o by a subject s requires that $SC(o)$ dominates $SC(s)$ ("no read down").

The simple integrity property ensures that a subject cannot modify information contained in an object unless the integrity class of the subject is as least as high as the class of the object. The integrity of an object is preserved by preventing a low-integrity-class subject from making any modifications to it. The ⋆-property prevents a subject from reading an object unless the integrity class of the object is greater than or equal to the class of the subject. It prevents indirect modification of objects. Otherwise, a high-integrity-class subject s_1 could contaminate a high-integrity-class object o_1 (thus destroying its integrity) by reading information from a low-integrity-class object o_2 (which may have been written earlier by a low-integrity-class subject s_2) and then writing into o_1.

Comparisons of Two Multilevel Models

The Bell–LaPadula model is concerned with how to prevent information leakage (i.e., how to prevent disclosure of information to a subject at a lower security class). Any subject reading an object must possess a security class that is equal to or higher than that of the object to preserve the confidentiality of high-class objects. In a security system enforced by the Bell–LaPadula model, information can only flow from an entity with a lower level and a smaller category to an entity with a higher level and a larger category. Any downward information flow is viewed as violation of information confidentiality.

The Biba model emphasizes how to protect information from corruption (i.e., how to prevent unauthorized modifications to information contained in a object at a higher integrity class). Any object modified or written by a subject must have an integrity class that is equal to or lower than that of the subject; thus integrity of high-class objects can be preserved. In a security system enforced by the Biba model, information can only flow from an entity with a higher level and a larger category to an entity with a lower level and a smaller category. Any upward information flow is viewed as violation of information integrity.

8.4 Cryptography

The discretionary access control and mandatory flow control are concerned with *authorizations*. Authorizations are preconditioned on authentications. Before an access can be authorized, the subject identity or its credential must be authenticated. We have seen the need for authentications for subject identifications in ACL, capabilities in CL, and labels in the flow control models. In the most abstract sense, we can describe a distributed system as a collection of clients and servers communicating by exchange of messages. Identities of clients and servers are called **principals** in the context of computer security. Authentication of principals and messages is the major issue in secure distributed systems. In Section 4.4, we described how entities can be named using their unique attribute(s). An authenticated principal can be thought of as a subject entity that is given a secret key (a unique attribute) for access to and communication with another principal. Possession of a unique (nonreproducible) or secret key infers the true identity of the principal if the key can be securely protected. An authenticated message is a data unit that carries a *digital signature* so that the message cannot be forged or repudiated. Cryptography has long been used for the protection of information confidentiality. This section presents two common cryptographic systems and their applications for authentication of principals and messages in distributed systems.

8.4.1 Private-key Cryptographic Systems

To prevent disclosure of information, we can encrypt the information so that it will not be understood even if it is intercepted. An encryption algorithm E maps a plaintext M into a ciphertext C by $C = E(M)$. Inversely, a ciphertext C is decrypted by applying a decryption algorithm D, an inverse function of E, to recover the plaintext M by $M = D(C)$. Confidentiality of the message M is preserved if the encryption and decryption algorithms are kept secret. The scheme seems simple, but it is not practical since different sets of E and D are required for different pairs of communicating principals. It is hard for each principal to keep track of a large number of algorithms. This problem can be solved by decomposing an algorithm into two parts: a *function* and a *key*. The function (also called the algorithm) is public, but the key is secret. A message is encrypted using a common encryption algorithm with respect to a secret encryption key Ke and can only be decrypted with the corresponding inverse decryption algorithm and secret decryption key Kd. That is, $M = D_{Kd}(E_{Ke}(M))$. The combination of a common function and variable number of keys is equivalent to a class of algorithms indexed by the keys. The function must have the properties that different messages with the same key and a same message with different keys will result in distinct ciphertext, and it is impossible to infer the key with some given plaintexts and their corresponding ciphertexts. Mathematically speaking, the encryption function is a one-to-one *injective* mapping and *one-way* function, meaning that it is easy to compute the ciphertext from the plaintext but difficult the other way even if the encryption algorithm is known. The keys Ke and Kd are different, but it is convenient to choose a pair of encryption and decryption algorithms such that a same key K can be applied to both. The secrecy of communication hinges on K rather than on the algorithms. The key should be of sufficient length in bits that it is computationally infeasible to exhaust all key combinations to decipher a ciphertext.

The cryptographic system discussed above is a **private-key** cryptographic system in which a single secret key is used to maintain a secret conversation between principals. It is also referred to as a *symmetric cryptography* since both encryption and decryption use the same key. There have been several attempts to standardize private-key systems. The U.S. government adopted the Data Encryption Standard (DES), which was originally developed by IBM. The DES is a private-key based encryption/decryption mechanism. In the DES, a plaintext is split into blocks of 64 bits. Each block is encrypted with respect to a 56-bit secret key. The encryption consists of 3 stages of transposition and 16 stages of substitution of bits. Transpositions use fixed rules and are key independent. The substitution stages are performed using 16 subkeys (48 bits in length) derived from the 56-bit key. The 56-bit key is considered sufficient since $2^{56} = 7.2 * 10^{16}$, a number too large to enumerate even with the speed of modern computers. Since the DES algorithm involves only simple transpositions and substitutions, it can be implemented easily in very large-scale integration (VLSI) and embedded in hardware. The basic DES algorithm is a **block cipher**, meaning that blocks are in fixed size and encrypted individually and independently with the same key. Such an approach has some drawbacks. If the plaintext contains repetition of identical blocks, the ciphertext will also appear repetitive. This will give a significant clue to the eavesdroppers. Furthermore, a correctly encrypted block can be inserted or can replace any block in a ciphertext without being detected by the receiver. Thus, an intruder with the knowledge of the secret key can spoof and inject spurious data into the system without being detected. To remedy this weakness, ciphered blocks can be made to be dependent on each other. This is the concept of **cipher block chaining** (CBC). Using the basic DES with the extended *chaining* mode, each block of 64 bits is exclusive-ORed with the previous encrypted block before it passes through the DES encryption algorithm. The first block of data is exclusive-ORed with an *initialization vector* that is part of the input to the combined DES-CBC algorithm. Finally, a checksum is attached to the ciphertext to add additional protection for integrity.

8.4.2 Public-key Cryptographic Systems

Using the private-key system for communication among n principals requires a total of $[n * (n - 1)]/2$ keys in the system, one for each conversation channel between a pair of principals. On top of this, the conversation key, which is secret information, must be agreed upon before secure communication can commence. The secret conversation key can be negotiated between two principals or distributed by a centralized key server. In either case, it needs a separate communication channel or some kind of key distribution protocol for secure transmission of secret keys. Managing keys is a function of the **key distribution server** (KDS). The dual-key public-key cryptographic system presented in the following paragraphs reduces the key requirement to two per principal and a total of $2n$ for the system. It also eliminates the need to transmit a secret key before secret communication can proceed.

The concept of public-key cryptographic system was first introduced by Diffie and Hellman. In the public-key systems, each principal maintains a pair of encryption and decryption keys, Ke and Kd. The encryption algorithm E and its key Ke are known to public. The decryption algorithm D and its key Kd are secret information and belong to a principal. Any principal wishing to communicate encrypts the messages using the receiver's public encryption key. The receiver recovers the messages by applying its decryption algorithm and secret decryption key. That is, $M = D_{Kd}(E_{Ke}(M))$. The secrecy of communication is achieved since only the receiver has possession of the decryption algorithm and key. The dual-key public-key approach is called *asymmetric cryptography* since encryption and decryption use different keys. Like general encryptions and decryptions, the encryption algorithm must be a one-to-one, one-way, and invertible function, and given an E, it is unfeasible to derive D from E. Alternatively, both E and D can be made public and shared provided that Ke and Kd are chosen such that it is impossible to infer Kd from Ke.

The widely used Rivest–Shamir–Adleman (RSA) algorithm is an ingenious implementation of public-key cryptographic systems. In this algorithm, both E and D are known and have an additional property that they are inverse functions of each other and $M = D_{Kd}(E_{Ke}(M)) = D_{Ke}(E_{Kd}(M))$. Since the keys are used both for encryption and decryption, it is more convenient to refer to the public encryption key Ke simply as public key Kp and the secret decryption key Kd as secret key Ks. Thus $M = D_{Ks}(E_{Kp}(M)) = D_{Kp}(E_{Ks}(M))$. The robustness of the algorithm relies on the computational complexity in factoring a large number upon which the keys are based.

Plaintext messages are limited to a size of k bits. The integer value k is chosen such that 2^k is less than N, which is a product of two large prime numbers p and q. This means the numeric value of message M is less than N. Kp and Ks are derived from p and q. The significance of p and q will be discussed later. For now we assume that it is impossible to infer Ks from Kp. The encryption algorithm E to obtain the ciphertext C is

$$E : C = M^{Kp} \bmod N$$

and the decryption algorithm D to recover the plaintext M is

$$D : M = C^{Ks} \bmod N.$$

To compute Kp and Ks for a given $N = p \times q$, any large integer can be chosen for Kp as long as it is relatively prime to $(p - 1)(q - 1)$; that is, Kp and $(p - 1)(q - 1)$ have no common factor except 1. With Kp chosen, Ks is decided by finding the smallest integer that satisfies the following relation:

$$(Kp \times Ks) \bmod (p - 1)(q - 1) = 1$$

So, Kp and Ks are distributed by the key server. To infer Ks from the knowledge of Kp and N, one must first obtain p and q, which requires factoring of N, a task that is computationally expensive. The algorithm was proven to work and no security flaw has been found. Since the two algorithms E and D are symmetrical, the keys are interchangeable. A message encrypted in Kp can be decrypted by Ks, and vice versa. Therefore, the RSA algorithm has the property of $M = D_{Ks}(E_{Kp}(M)) = D_{Kp}(E_{Ks}(M))$. Assume that principal A with public and secret keys AKp and AKs wants to send a message M to principal B with public and secret keys BKp and BKs. $E_{BKp}(M)$ will guarantee the secrecy of the message since only principal B has the secret key BKs to decrypt it. $E_{AKs}(M)$ implies the authenticity of the message from principal A. Any principal can decrypt the message using principal A's public key AKp. However, only principal A could have produced such a message with its secret key Aks. $E_{BKp}(E_{AKs}(M))$ provides both secrecy of the message and authenticity of the sender. Only principal B can decrypt the message, which must have come from principal A.

8.4.3 Comparison of Cryptographic Systems

Table 8.1 summarizes the fundamental differences in assumptions for the cryptographic systems discussed in the previous sections. It is worthwhile to add that the private-key DES is computationally efficient, while the public-key RSA is computationally expensive. The RSA algorithm is elegant but must deal with the computation of enormous integer numbers. It seems a combined private-key and public-key approach should yield the best results. For instance, the RSA can be used for encrypting short but important data such as secret keys and the DES can be used to encrypt long but less critical messages. The Privacy Enhanced Mail (PEM) system being developed by the Internet community is one such example.

TABLE 8.1   Comparison of encryption/decryption algorithms.

non-key-based $M = D(E(M))$	secret E and D invertible E
private-key $M = D_K(E_K(M))$	public E and D secret K invertible and one-way E
public-key $M = D_{Kd}(E_{Ke}(M))$	public E and Ke secret D and Kd invertible and one-way E E cannot infer D, Ke cannot infer Kd
RSA $M = D_{Ks}(E_{Kp}(M))$ $= D_{Kp}(E_{Ks}(M))$	public E, D, and Kp secret Ks E and D are mutually invertible Kp cannot infer Ks

PEM is designed to work with a variety of existing mail systems for privacy enhancement. It is documented in a series of Request For Comments (RFCs) from the Privacy and Security Research Group of IRTF and the PEM Working Group of IETF. The system provides mechanisms for mail users to specify the cryptographic algorithm and parameters to be used for mail messages and how this information can be transmitted securely. We will demonstrate the concepts by showing an example in which the private-key DES algorithm is used to encrypt data and the public-key RSA algorithm is used to manage the keys. Three of the most essential data fields in PEM mail are:

- DEK: The Data Encryption Key is the private key for encrypting a mail message. It is an *one-shot* key generated either by the sender's local PEM server or distributed by a centralized key distribution server for a chosen private-key encryption algorithm such as DES. The secrecy of the message is achieved by $E_{DEK}(M)$.
- IK: The Interchange Key has a public and a secret component of a public-key encryption algorithm such as RSA. It is used for authentication and secure transmission of keys and algorithm parameters (e.g., algorithm type, initial vector of DES).
- MIC: The Message Integrity Check is similar to a checksum and is used to detect message tampering. It is computed from a *one-way* function using M and DEK. Essentially, an MIC is a **message digest** that serves as a *fingerprint* of the message.

The sender (A) and the receiver (B) of a mail transfer first obtain a pair of public key and secret keys, the IKs, from their local PEM servers. Let us assume they are ($AIKp$, $AIKs$) and ($BIKp$, $BIKs$), respectively. $AIKp$ and $BIKp$ are registered public information. The sender then obtains an one-shot private key DEK and uses it to encrypt the message M. The encryption key DEK and algorithm type must be conveyed to the receiver for decryption. This information is encrypted with the receiver's public key $BIKp$ and attached to the encrypted message for transmission to the receiver. Only the receiver B, who has the secret key $BIKs$, can decrypt this data field to uncover the private key DEK. The MIC is a message digest computed from the Message Digest algorithm number 5 (MD5) in this example. It is encrypted with the sender's secret key $AIKs$ and also appended to the transmitted message. After receiving and decrypting the message M, the receiver computes an MIC using the same message digest algorithm MD5. The result is compared to the decrypted $E_{AIKs}(MIC)$ using the sender's public key $AIKp$. A match ensures that the message has not been tampered with and indeed came from sender A since only A could have produced $E_{AIKs}(MIC)$ with its own secret key even if the encrypted message M is intercepted and the MD5 algorithm is known. The major data fields of the PEM message example are:

$E_{BIKp}(DEK)$	$E_{DEK}(M)$	$E_{AIKs}(MIC)$
RSA	DES	MD5

PEM services are to be included in the X400 Mail Handling System (MHS) under the Simple Mail Transfer Protocol (SMTP). PEM uses cryptographic techniques to provide confidentiality, authentication, message integrity, nonrepudiation of origin, and key management. Interested readers are encouraged to read [RFC 1421-1424].

8.5 AUTHENTICATION AND KEY DISTRIBUTION

Authentication is the process of verifying the identity of an object entity. Traditional password verification is a simple example of user authentication. It is a one-way verification of user identification by the system, assuming that the system is trusted and the users are not trustworthy. There is a greater need for authentication in distributed systems. In an open distributed environment, the authenticity of the machine to which a user is connected must be assured as well as that of the user. This type of *mutual authentication* is even more crucial for communication between peer processes and between clients and servers in distributed systems where the communicating principals are autonomous and under different administrative authorities. The potential threat of imposters in an open environment is real and cannot be ignored. In addition, messages being exchanged in the system must also be authenticated such that they are free of forgery, counterfeiting, and repudiation. These authentication-related security threats are illustrated in Figure 8.8. Forgery could occur when a communication key is compromised. A counterfeit in the context of communication is the replay of a secret message. Repudiation is the denial of sending what seems to be an authenticated message.

In real life, authentication is often achieved by using some unique physical characteristics that can be verified by a third party such as the fingerprint of a person or the seal on a document. Unfortunately, physical identifications are not feasible in a computer system. Nevertheless, a unique identification can be represented by a piece of secret information. If the secret information is secure, possession of it should imply the authenticity of the possessor. For message authenticity, an irreproducible secret message digest can be used

FIGURE 8.8   Authentication-related security threats.

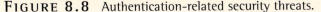

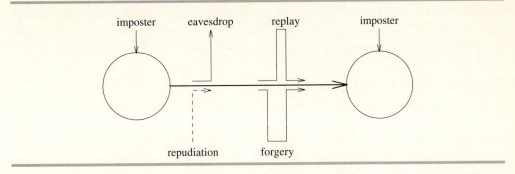

to *sign* the messages. In both cases, the secrecy of information can be accomplished by encryption using secret keys. Thus authentication protocols are concerned with the distribution and management of secret keys for communication. Key distribution in a distributed environment is an implementation of distributed authentication protocols.

The design of distributed authentication protocols depends on the underlying assumptions of communication services. The types of communication services may be either connection-oriented or connectionless between peer processes or client/server. Figure 8.9 shows four typical communication services for authentication.

For the interactive connection-oriented service between peer processes, the final goal of the authentication protocol is to achieve a mutually trusted session (or conversation) key for the communicating processes. Many such protocols have been proposed. The protocols vary depending on their security goals, the encryption system used, and whether an authentication server exists or not. We have already seen an example (Secure Socket Layer) in Chapter 4. A full discussion of these mutual authentication protocols is given in the next section.

For one-way connectionless services, the authentication and the protection of secrecy and integrity are combined into a one-shot message. This is best illustrated by the PEM secure mail system described in the previous section. The example relies on the public-key system to transmit a private secret key in the same message. The protocol assumes a trusted directory service that can distribute public keys securely.

Most distributed applications follow the client/server programming paradigm. The interaction between client and server is viewed as a request/reply communication. Although session keys can be used as well for client/server communication, it is

FIGURE 8.9   Communication services for authentication.

	Connection	Connectionless
Peer Processes	interactive	one-way
Clinet and Server	session	resquest / response

conceptually simpler to use the notion of **tickets**. A ticket is a signed certificate that contains information for authenticating the client that presents the ticket for a service request. We will revisit the use of tickets for authentication protocols shortly when we discuss the Kerberos protocol.

8.5.1 Design of Authentication Protocols

Many authentication protocols have been proposed for distributed systems. In the following sections, we summarize some representative protocols and show how they have evolved for practical use in distributed systems. All protocols assume that some secret information is held initially by each principal, and authentication is achieved by one principal demonstrating to another that it really holds that secret information. Although the final *beliefs* (conclusions) guaranteed by these authentication protocols are not identical, they all achieve the very basic goals of authentication (i.e., one principal can assure the identity of the other and believes that a secure session key is shared and used for their subsequent communication).

The system environment that most authentication protocols assume is very insecure. Any machine could be occupied by a malicious user who may try to impersonate another user. So, every principal is suspicious of any remote principal that is trying to communicate with it. The network links are also extremely vulnerable. An intruder can intercept any message transmitted on the network, can change or copy part of a message, can replay old messages, or can just emit false messages. So, any message received by a principal must have its origin authenticity, integrity, and freshness[6] verified. To achieve authentication effectively, most protocols presume the existence of an *authentication server* that is both *capable* and *trustworthy*. The authentication server is capable in that it can generate good-quality session keys on request and distribute them to the requesting principals securely. The authentication server is trustworthy in that it usually shares some secret information with each principal and must be entrusted not to reveal any secrets to others and to faithfully provide the service.

Confidentiality, integrity, and origin authenticity of a message can be effectively achieved with cryptography. A more critical problem is the simple security attack of an intruder replaying a message. An intruder can record some confidential messages of a genuine user from the network in an authentication session and then replay those messages in another session to impersonate the genuine user. Therefore, most protocol designers concentrate on the protocol's ability to verify the freshness of a message and to prevent a replay attack. As a result, all existing authentication protocols can be roughly divided into two categories according to how the freshness of messages is guaranteed. One category of protocols uses a nonce (defined in Chapter 4) and a challenge/response handshake to verify that the response to a request is fresh. Since it is easy to demonstrate that replay attacks can be effectively prevented by this technique, most proposed protocols are nonce-based. The other category of protocols uses timestamps to ensure the freshness of messages and must rely on the assumption that all machines of a distributed system are properly clock-synchronized so that an intruder cannot possibly play any tricks within

---

[6] That a message is fresh means it is generated and used for current session only.

a short interval between the discrepancy of local clocks on different machines. Because of the advantage of protocol efficiency and new clock synchronization techniques, in practice many authentication protocols use timestamps to guarantees freshness.

8.5.2 Evolution of Authentication Protocols

Many authentication protocols have been proposed in the literature and implemented in real systems. In the next two sections, we will discuss the two most widely used protocols: Kerberos and X.509. But first we will show a brief history of how encryption techniques have been applied to authentication protocols. To uniformly describe and compare the authentication protocols, we will use the following notations. Other notations will be noted when they are used in the description of a protocol.

A	principal A on one machine.
B	principal B on another machine.
S	the authentication server.
K_{as}	the secret key shared only by A and S.
K_{bs}	the secret key shared only by B and S.
K_{ab}	the session key to be shared by A and B after authentication.
K_a	the public key of A in a public-key cryptosystem.
K_a^{-1}	the private key of A in a public-key cryptosystem.
$A \rightarrow B : M$	A sends a message M to B.
$\{M\}_K$	a message M encrypted by a key K.
	K could be a secret key, a private or public key, or a session key.
N_a	a nonce (a random number "used only once") issued by A.
N_b	a nonce issued by B.
T_s	a timestamp of the machine S resides in.

Needham–Schroeder Protocol

Needham and Schroeder were the first to propose the use of encryption techniques for authentication and key distribution in computer networks and distributed systems. Their classical paper has stimulated a great deal of interest in the development of authentication protocols. This original work introduces protocols for establishing interactive connections between two principals A and B, protocols for one-way communication such as e-mail, and protocols for providing digital signatures, with both secret-key and public-key cryptosystems. We will use only the protocol for authenticating interactive communication with a secret-key cryptosystem to demonstrate the authentication concept. The protocol consists of five steps:

1. $A \rightarrow S :$ A, B, N_a
2. $S \rightarrow A :$ $\{N_a, B, K_{ab}, \{A, K_{ab}\}_{K_{bs}}\}_{K_{as}}$
3. $A \rightarrow B :$ $\{A, K_{ab}\}_{K_{bs}}$
4. $B \rightarrow A :$ $\{N_b\}_{K_{ab}}$
5. $A \rightarrow B :$ $\{N_b - 1\}_{K_{ab}}$

The basic idea is that initially A contacts S, which returns to A a session key and a certificate encrypted with K_{bs} to convey the session key and A's identity to B. Since the certificate is unrecognizable to A, A cannot do anything useful but forward it to B. B decrypts this certificate and carries out a nonce handshake with A to assure that A is present currently and both the request and the certificate are fresh. Subtracting 1 from N_b in the last message ensures that the message is not a replay of the previous one from B to A. Any other function that allows B to differentiate these two messages could also be used.

This protocol is neat and intuitive but has a drawback, as pointed out by Denning and Sacco. That is, if the session key between A and B is compromised, and the certificate to B containing it is recorded, an intruder can impersonate A by carrying out the last three steps of the protocol to trick B to use the compromised session key and to think it was communicating with A. Needham and Schroeder responded to this criticism in another paper and modified their original protocol by requiring A to obtain another nonce from B before it contacts with S and requiring S to place this nonce into the certificate to be forwarded to B. On receipt of the certificate, B is able to check whether this certificate is a replay or not by checking the presence of the nonce it has just issued.

Denning–Sacco Protocol

Denning and Sacco proposed their own protocol to overcome the potential disadvantage of the Needham–Schroeder protocol. Their protocol actually takes an approach similar to the Needham–Schroeder protocol in that A requests, from S, a session key and a certificate containing the session key and A's identity to be forwarded to B. Message freshness is guaranteed by including a timestamp in an encrypted message instead of using a nonce handshake.

1. $A \rightarrow S :$ A, B
2. $S \rightarrow A :$ $\{B, K_{ab}, T_s, \{A, K_{ab}, T_s\}_{K_{bs}}\}_{K_{as}}$
3. $A \rightarrow B :$ $\{A, K_{ab}, T_s\}_{K_{bs}}$

A and B can verify that their messages are not replays by checking that

$$Clock - T < \Delta t 1 + \Delta t 2$$

where $Clock$ is the local clock time, $\Delta t 1$ is the interval representing the normal discrepancy between the server's clock and the local clock, and $\Delta t 2$ is the interval representing the expected network delay time. As long as $\Delta t 1 + \Delta t 2$ is less than the interval between two contiguous authentication sessions, this protocol can protect against replay attacks. Timestamps eliminate message handshake and corresponding encryption/decryption operations; thus they enhance protocol performance, but the requirement of a small $\Delta t 1$ demands that the clock of each machine is well synchronized with that of the authentication server. This synchronization is feasible in today's distributed systems.

Otway-Rees Protocol

The authentication protocol from Otway and Rees is based on a belief that for timely authentication any suspicious principal should generate its own nonce challenge. The Otway-Rees protocol attempts to provide timely authentication in a small number of messages without synchronized clocks.

1. $A \rightarrow B$: $M, A, B, \{M, A, N_a, B\}_{K_{as}}$
2. $B \rightarrow S$: $M, A, B, \{M, A, N_a, B\}_{K_{as}}, \{M, A, B, N_b\}_{K_{bs}}$
3. $S \rightarrow B$: $M, \{N_a, K_{ab}\}_{K_{as}}, \{N_b, K_{ab}\}_{K_{bs}}$
4. $B \rightarrow A$: $M, \{N_a, K_{ab}\}_{K_{as}}$

A sends to B some encrypted information that is only useful to S and also some clear information that lets B make a similar encrypted message. A and B issue their own nonces, N_a and N_b, and a common nonce challenge M (M is a special message for challenge/response purpose) is issued by A and must be included in both encrypted messages. After S receives the messages from B, it decrypts them and checks to see if A, B, and M appear in both encrypted messages. If so, S generates K_{ab} and embeds it in two encrypted messages, one for A and the other for B, accompanied by their own nonces. S sends these two encrypted messages back to B, which then forwards the part encrypted by A's key to A.

In addition to the feature of symmetrical authentication request and replies, this protocol uses fewer messages to achieve authentication and key distribution without clock synchronization. The most attractive property of this protocol is that it can be implemented as two nested remote procedure calls. However, a major disadvantage is that principal B has no way to check that the request from A is genuine and fresh, because A does not need to verify to B it already has the session key.

8.5.3 The Kerberos Protocol

As a part of Project Athena at MIT, Kerberos is one of the most promising implementations of the authentication service. It is based on the Needham–Schroeder protocol and uses the timestamps suggested by Denning and Sacco to prevent replays and to reduce the total number of messages required. Because of its simplicity and reliability, Kerberos has now been adopted by a number of organizations for their distributed systems.

Kerberos was designed for the client-server model; thus it provides authentication service between a client and a server when the former requests a service from the latter. Relying upon a secret-key cryptosystem (DES), Kerberos actually places the authentication service on two kinds of servers: *Kerberos* server and *Ticket Granting Server* (*TGS*). While the *Kerberos* server authenticates the user at login time and issues a ticket for a *TGS*, the *TGS* issues tickets for individual servers to a client. A simplified version of the Kerberos protocol that treats *Kerberos* and *TGS* as a single entity S is shown as follows.

1. $A \rightarrow S$: A, B
2. $S \rightarrow A$: $\{K_{ab}, Ticket_{ab}\}_{K_{as}}$, where $Ticket_{ab} = \{B, A, addr, T_s, L, K_{ab}\}_{K_{bs}}$
3. $A \rightarrow B$: $Authenticator_{ab}, Ticket_{ab}$, where $Authenticator_{ab} = \{A, addr, T_a\}_{K_{ab}}$
4. $B \rightarrow A$: $\{T_a + 1\}_{K_{ab}}$

The idea of Kerberos is quite straightforward. When principal A (a client) tries to connect to principal B (a server), it first sends a request to S with its own identity and that of the server. S responds with a session key K_{ab} to be used between A and B and a ticket for B, both encrypted by A's secret key. The ticket itself is confidential to anybody but B and thus is encrypted by B's secret key. A ticket containing the identities of B and A, the IP address of A's machine, a timestamp T_s, a lifetime L, and a session key is used to pass the identity of the principal to whom the ticket was issued securely between the authentication server and the end server. After A gets the session key and a ticket to B, it needs to build its own authenticator that contains A's identity, the IP address of A's machine, and a timestamp, all encrypted by the session key just obtained. A then sends the authenticator along with the ticket to B. The purpose of the authenticator is to prove that the principal representing the ticket is the same one to which the ticket was issued. So after B receives the authenticator and ticket, it decrypts the ticket, uses the session key included in the ticket to decrypt the authenticator, and compares the information in the ticket with that in the authenticator. If they match, B allows the service request to proceed. (This does not mean the service request is allowed; it could be denied for authorization reasons.) There are two things to be examined by the server B after receiving the authenticator and ticket. The first is that their identity and address information match. The second is the discrepancy between the time in the authenticator and the current local time. It is assumed that clocks are properly synchronized; if the time discrepancy is larger than a predetermined value, B treats the request as an attempt to replay a previous request. Finally, if mutual authentication is desired, B adds 1 to the timestamp in the authenticator sent by A, encrypts the result by the session key, and sends it back to A.

The limitations and weaknesses of the Kerberos system were elaborated by Bellovin and Merritt. They include the difficulty of adapting Kerberos to an environment other than that for which Kerberos was originally designed, the deficiencies of the protocol itself, and the need for special-purpose hardware. Subsequently, Kerberos has been upgraded to Version V, in which many environmental shortcomings and technical deficiencies have been resolved.

The terms *ticket* and *authenticator* are a very convenient way to express message exchanges between a client and a server, particularly when the service requests are cascaded. An authenticator and ticket pair is called a **credential**. When making a service request, the client presents the request along with the credential. The credential authenticates the client and its right to access the server. Figure 8.10 illustrates use of the ticket and authenticator in the following Kerberos Version V protocol. In the protocol, K denotes the Kerberos authentication server, G is the ticket granting server, N is the nonce, and C and S are client and server, respectively.

FIGURE 8.10   Kerberos *V* authentication protocol.

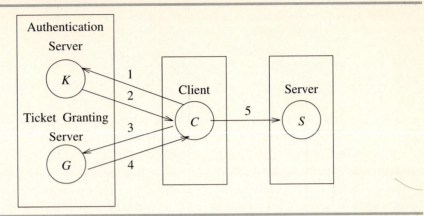

1. $C \rightarrow K$: C, G, N
2. $K \rightarrow C$: $\{K_{cg}, N\}_{K_c}, Ticket_{cg}$
3. $C \rightarrow G$: $Authenticator_{cg}, Ticket_{cg}$
4. $G \rightarrow C$: $\{K_{cs}, N\}_{K_{cg}}, Ticket_{cs}$
5. $C \rightarrow S$: $Authenticator_{cs}, Ticket_{cs}$

The protocol is slightly different from the simplified Kerberos protocol. The Kerberos server is separated into two components, the authentication server for login and the ticket-granting server for issuing ticket to the requested server. The login authentication is proved by the client's ability to derive K_c from its password. Once the client is able to do that, it can build the authenticator using K_{cg} to prove itself to the ticket granting server in message 3. Messages 4 and 5 are similar to messages 2 and 3. The same exchange of messages can be repeated if there are more servers (e.g., privilege servers) in the request/reply chain.

Kerberos *V* has been widely installed. It is also implemented in the DCE security service and used in SESAME.

8.5.4 CCITT X.509 Protocol

The protocols discussed thus far assume a separate authentication server for authentication service. X.509 recommendations by CCITT define a framework for the provision of authentication services by the X.500 Directory to its users. It specifies how authentication information is formed and held by the directory server, describes how user authentication information can be obtained from the directory, and also defines methods in which OSI applications may use the authentication information to perform authentication. Based upon public-key cryptosystems, X.509 assumes that user certificates that contain a user's public key information may be held within the Directory as an attribute of the user and may be obtained from the Directory in the same manners as other attributes. The *three-way strong authentication* [7] between two users A and B follows:

1. $A \rightarrow B$: $A, \{T_a, N_a, B, sgnData, \{encData\}_{K_b}\}_{K_a^{-1}}$
2. $B \rightarrow A$: $B, \{T_b, N_b, A, N_a, sgnData, \{encData\}_{K_a}\}_{K_b^{-1}}$
3. $A \rightarrow B$: $A, \{N_b\}_{K_a^{-1}}$

In the protocol above, *sgnData* means the data whose data origin authentication and integrity need to be provided, and *encData* stands for data whose confidentiality needs to be protected during transmission (e.g., a shared session key). In the three-way (i.e., three message) authentication protocol, timestamps are not checked because replay is detected by the use of nonces (this releases the requirement of clock synchronization). However, timestamps are used and checked in the one- or two-way authentication protocols, which definitely need well-synchronized clocks. The digital signature to *sgnData* is provided by encrypting it using the private key of the sending principal, and the confidentiality required by *encData* is implemented by encrypting it using the public key of the receiving principal. Nonces N_a and N_b are used to detect any replay attacks.

However, X.509 has a serious security defect, originally discovered by Burrows, Abadi, and Needham and further described by I'Anson and Mitchell. A malicious principal C could intercept the first message from A to B, decrypt it using A's public key, extract the parts of $sgnData$ and $\{encData\}_{K_b}$, form a new message, $C, \{T_c, N_c, B, sgnData, \{encData\}_{K_b}\}_{K_c^{-1}}$, and then send the new message to B. When B receives this new message, B decrypts it using C's public key, and believes that it came from C originally. Then B constructs an appropriate reply and sends it back to C. Now C can work out what A's original request was. A possible simple solution is to include the identity of A with *encData* to be encrypted by B's public key.

8.5.5 KSL Protocol for Multiple Authentication

The existence of a centralized authentication server in a distributed system implies a performance and security bottleneck. However, in a system operating in a relatively benign environment with good quality session keys (i.e., ones that cannot be compromised easily), it is possible to reduce the workload of the authentication server and the communication overhead of contacting the server each time an authentication session is initiated, by duplicating the use of a session key. This is achieved by protocols for multiple authentication, by which some credential information (called *tickets* by most research) will be kept by a principal during the initial authentication session and used to verify its identity and to convey the session key to the other principal for subsequent sessions without contacting the authentication server again. For example, during the initial authentication B can give A a ticket that contains the corresponding identity and session key information. This ticket is encrypted with a secret key generated by B. For later authentication sessions, A can present the ticket directly to B for handshaking

---

[7] X.509 describes two levels of authentication: simple authentication, using a password as a verification of claimed identity, and strong authentication, involving credentials formed using cryptographic techniques.

without the need to contact the authentication server S. We use the KSL protocol here to demonstrate this idea.

Initial Authentication

1. $A \rightarrow B$: A, N_a
2. $B \rightarrow S$: A, N_a, B, N_b
3. $S \rightarrow B$: $\{A, N_b, K_{ab}\}_{K_{bs}}, \{B, N_a, K_{ab}\}_{K_{as}}$
4. $B \rightarrow A$: $\{B, N_a, K_{ab}\}_{K_{as}}, \{A, T_B, K_{ab}\}_{K_{bb}}, \{N_a\}_{K_{ab}}, N_c$
5. $A \rightarrow B$: $\{N_c\}_{K_{ab}}$

The initial authentication part of the KSL protocol is similar to the Otway-Rees protocol. A generates a nonce challenge N_a and requests B to forward this nonce and the nonce challenge N_b generated by B to S, both in clear form. (The Otway-Rees protocol sends the nonce challenge in encrypted forms, although it is not really required.) Then S returns to B two encrypted components, one for A and the other for B, notifying them of the session key chosen. When B returns the encrypted part from S to A, it also sends several other strings. One of them is a ticket, encrypted by a *ticket key* (K_{bb}) known only to B itself, which contains a generalized timestamp T_B,[8] the identity of A, and the session key K_{ab}. B also sends a response to the nonce challenge N_a to convince A that B has agreed to share the session key K_{ab} with A. Furthermore, B also sends A a new nonce N_c; if A can successfully respond to this challenge using K_{ab}, B is convinced of A's possession of the session key.

Principal A, knowing the session key K_{ab} and possessing a valid ticket, can repeat the authentication with B as follows.

Repeated Authentication

1. $A \rightarrow B$: $N_a', \{A, T_b, K_{ab}\}_{K_{bb}}$
2. $B \rightarrow A$: $N_b', \{N_a\}_{K_{ab}}$
3. $A \rightarrow B$: $\{N_b', \}_{K_{ab}}$

It is basically a nonce handshake with a ticket presented to B in the first message, which gives B the same knowledge as A has. Because the ticket is encrypted by a ticket key only accessible to B, its confidentiality is guaranteed, and it is impossible for other principals to fabricate a counterfeit ticket.

The authors of the KSL protocol claim that their protocol achieves a strong set of formalized authentication goals with a minimum number of messages. However, Neuman and Stubberbine proposed another protocol for multiple authentication that needs one less message in the initial authentication than the KSL protocol, yet achieves a set of weaker but acceptable formalized goals.

---

[8] A generalized timestamp contains three parts: a current local clock timestamp, a lifetime that limits the validity of the ticket, and a time identifier to prevent replay attacks.

8.6 ISSUES RELEVANT TO DISTRIBUTED SECURITY

Protection methods for guarding a computer system against security threats generally fall into three categories: Authentication, Authorization, and Auditing (AAA). Authentication of communicating principals and messages is the first line of defense for a secure computer system. In the previous section, we saw how cryptosystems can be applied to the design of authentication protocols. Once processes have been authenticated, the second line of defense is authorization, which allows an object access only to authorized subjects. We have discussed two fundamental approaches for authorization in this chapter: discretionary access control and mandatory access control. This section presents some additional issues related to authentication and authorization in distributed systems.

The last line of defense for security is auditing. If access activities are maintained in an audit log, security attacks can be traced by analyzing the audit log. Although auditing is a passive protection method, it has been practiced in every system and shown to be effective in deterring security threats, particularly against internal intrusion. Security auditing is quite different from authentication and authorization. Auditing is an important protection mechanism for security. We conclude the chapter with a brief discussion of network traffic analysis and auditing.

8.6.1 Complex Security Policies

The security policies that can be modeled by the previously described access control models such as the access control list (ACL) or the capability list (CL) are stateless. In these models the security attributes maintained by the authorization server remain fixed unless explicitly changed by the server. Complex access control policies are distinguished as those with state-dependent security requirements. Some complex access control policies may require that the authorization of access to objects by a subject depends on the subject's past access history and its interaction with other subjects and objects. For example, a subject S is not allowed to access object O_1 if it has already read object O_2, or subject S_1 or subject S_2 can write object O_3, but they together cannot write O_3.

There are too many state-dependent security policies to enumerate. For illustration, we will only categorize a class of state-dependent access control control policies in terms of exceptions to normal information flow. Information flow policy is a different view of authorization control. Since information flow is caused by read or write accesses, information flow policies can be modeled as access control policies.

Multilevel Information Flow Exceptions

An information flow model (Section 8.3) usually characterizes all system entities with different security classes and governs how information can flow between classes. Traditional information flow models are built on a structure of a lattice with components comprising all the security classes, and information can only flow between components of the lattice in the direction the properties used to construct the lattice permit. However, there are some applications whose security-related or non-security-related (e.g., for procedural purposes) requirements do need information flow, which violates some properties of lattice. We will elaborate these *information flow exceptions*.

Information flow in a lattice-based model is transitive (i.e., if information is allowed to flow from class A to class B and from B to class C, it is allowed to flow from A to C directly). However, in some applications this transitive property is not desirable. If we define the information flow relation $\rightarrow$ for each pair of security classes to represent the allowable direction of flow and use $\not\rightarrow$ to represent the prohibited direction of flow, the **transitivity exception** is formalized as $A \rightarrow B$ and $B \rightarrow C$, but $A \not\rightarrow C$.

Another exception to information flow that may be desired by some applications is the **aggregation exception**. In a lattice-based model, if $A \rightarrow C$ and $B \rightarrow C$, then the aggregate of information from A and B, represented as $A \cup B$, can flow to C. If this property is not desired, then we have an aggregation exception, which is formalized as $A \rightarrow C$ and $B \rightarrow C$, but $A \cup B \not\rightarrow C$. This exception can be interpreted in two ways. One is that C cannot sink information from the aggregate of A and B (e.g., information from A and B is combined and mixed by sharing a common *pipe* or *FIFO* with C), and the other is that after C sinks information from either A or B, it cannot sink any information from the other class.

The dual problem of aggregation exception is the separation exception. Separation of duty is one of the most important ingredients in security policies and models concerning data integrity. With respect to information flow, it can be described as follows: Information cannot flow from a single class, either A or B, to another class C; only the aggregate of information from A and B can flow. In practice this requirement means that once information transfers from either A or B to C, the other must also transfer information to C. The information flowed to C from the first entity will not be valid or meaningful to C until information flow from the second entity also occurs. This requirement cannot be satisfied by a lattice-based information flow model alone, so we call it **separation exception**, formalized as $A \cup B \rightarrow C$, but $A \not\rightarrow C$ and $B \not\rightarrow C$.

These exceptions place more constraints on information flow among different classes than are permitted by a lattice-based multilevel model. Since we are more familiar with the concept of access control than flow control, let us define flow exceptions in terms of access control.

Redefining Flow Exceptions in Terms of Access Control

Although the three exceptions mentioned above originate from information flow policies, they can be redefined in terms of access control. In access control, the main operations for information transfer between entities are read and write. So $A \rightarrow B$ means subject A writes information to object B or subject B reads information from object A. Furthermore, an access control model is usually chosen for either data confidentiality or data integrity purposes. Therefore, these information flow exceptions are classified according to how subjects and objects interact and the security purpose in the context of access control, as shown in Figure 8.11. The following details each exception and justifies its significance with possible applications.

Let us first look at what transitivity exception looks like in access control. Transitivity exception in formation flow ($A \rightarrow B$ and $B \rightarrow C$, but $A \not\rightarrow C$) can be described in access control as a relation among two subjects and two objects in two different ways. The first way, concerning integrity, shown in Figure 8.11(a), is that subject S_1 can write to object

FIGURE 8.11 A taxonomy of information flow exceptions refined in terms of access control. R = read, W = write, $\oplus$ = exclusive or, and $*$ = and.

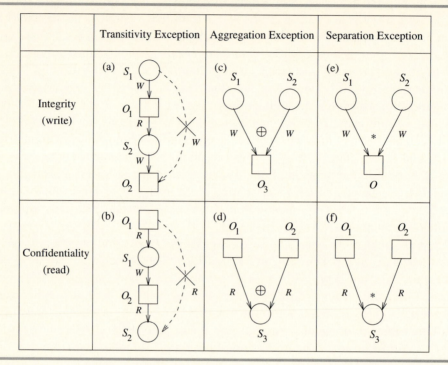

O_1, O_1 can be read by subject S_2, and S_2 can write to object O_2, but S_1 cannot write to O_2 directly. This exception simulates the concept of a *well-formed transaction* for the commercial integrity policy. For example, a bank transaction cannot manipulate account data directly unless the operation is a well-formed *deposit* or *withdraw* transaction. The second, which concerns confidentiality, shown in Figure 8.11(b), is that object O_1 can be read by subject S_1, S_1 can write to object O_2, and O_2 can be read by subject S_2, but O_1 cannot be read by S_2 directly. An example of this exception is that raw data (O_1) cannot be read by some user (S_2) directly without being converted to a specific format (O_2) by some formatting software (S_1), perhaps stripping out confidential information.

Aggregation exception can also be redefined in terms of access control according to whether the security concern is data integrity or data confidentiality. If data integrity is the concern, as in Figure 8.11(c), either subject S_1 or subject S_2 can write to object O_3, but they together cannot write to O_3. The interpretation is that after O_3 is written to by S_1, it can no longer be written to by S_2, and vice versa. Any application that requires an object to be written to by only one subject, but not a specific one, falls into this category of exception. For example, an electronic check can only be prepared by one accountant, and after it is prepared, no other accountants can change it, to prevent malicious modification. If data confidentiality is the concern, as in Figure 8.11(d), subject S_3 can read either object O_1 or object O_2, but S_3 cannot read the aggregate of both objects. This can be interpreted as after S_3 reads O_1, it can no longer read O_2, and vice versa. A well-known example that generalizes this exception is the Chinese Wall security policy in which a market analyst cannot access information from more than one company within the same class to avoid a conflict of interest.

Since the original concern of separation exception is data integrity, many practical examples can be found in the literature that discuss integrity policies (a simple one is that a check must be prepared and signed by two different accountants, to achieve separation of duty) and models. It is described, as shown in Figure 8.11(e), as two subjects S_1 and S_2 accessing object O_3. After a subject (e.g., S_1) writes to O_3, only the other (S_2) is allowed to write to that object. If data confidentiality is the concern, as in Figure 8.11(f), separation exception means that initially subject S_3 is allowed to read both objects O_1 and O_2, but once S_3 has read one object (e.g., O_1), it can only read the other object (O_2). An example is that after a user of a dial-up database service has accessed some data, he or she may only read service charge information before being allowed to continue to use the database services.

Complex access control policies are quite common in our daily life. For example, consider a computer automated bank loan application. A loan application document (object O) must be first prepared by a bank clerk (subject S_1), who has the write permission to the document. Once the document has been prepared, it must be reviewed by one of two bank officers: the bank manager (subject S_2) and the bank accountant (subject S_3). Both bank officers only have an *append* permission (to add comments and signature) to the application document. Finally the approved application is appended with an electronic check that must be signed by the manager and the bank cashier (subject S_4). This electronic distributed information processing procedure illustrates several interesting security issues:

- The electronic document must be tamper-resistant. Only subjects with write permission can modify the object.

- The digital signatures on the document must be authenticatable.

- The transitivity exception, Figure 8.11 [i], of the write accesses to the document must be enforced. That is, the bank clerk cannot modify the document once it has been signed by either of the two bank officers.

- The sequential order of the write (and append) operations to the document must be observed. That is, the document must be processed by the clerk, followed by either the bank manager or the bank account, and then by the bank cashier.

- The application can only carry one signature (approval or disapproval) of the manager or the accountant, but not both. (An application approved by one authorized person cannot be disapproved by another.) This requirement is an aggregation exception, as shown in Figure 8.11(c).

- The electronic check must carry two authorized signatures. This is the common separation of duty, the separation exception shown in Figure 8.11(e), required for many applications.

FIGURE 8.12   Example of a complex security information flow.

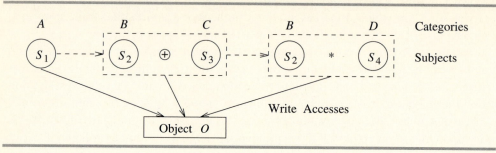

The information flow of this commercial bank application is illustrated in Figure 8.12. The first two problems in the above list are simple to solve. Data integrity in a document can be protected by the use of an encrypted message digest. Authenticity of signatures can be accomplished by encryption with secret keys. The remaining four requirements (access sequence, transitivity exception, aggregation exception, separation exception) are new and intriguing for security in distributed systems. The modeling and enforcement of complex security policies are still open issues. No elegant solution to the problems exists. However, we can discuss some of the implementation difficulties in the context of distributed systems.

The challenges are to develop a simple model that can be used to specify a large class of complex security policies and an efficient mechanism that can be used to enforce the policies. We can always use a finite state machine (FSM) to specify any access rule. The authorization server executes the finite state machine for each object access and moves the FSMs from one steady state to another. But, the solution is not acceptable since it is neither simple to use nor efficient to implement. Looking at the example in Figure 8.12, it seems that we should be able to represent some of the requirements by using Boolean expressions since the requirements involve Boolean operators: XOR $\oplus$ (for aggregation exception) and AND $*$ (for separation exception).

Let us assume that the four subjects (S_1, S_2, S_3, and S_4) have the capabilities of A, B, C, and D, respectively. Each capability is a category that represents a privilege in accessing an object. The object O is associated with a Boolean access control expression

$$ACE_w(O) = < A + B \oplus C + B * D >$$

for writing to the object. When a subject accesses an object, it presents its capabilities as Boolean variables to the object's ACE. These variables carry a *true* value, while the other undefined variables in the access control expression are initialized to *false*. The access is granted if the ACE is evaluated to true. The second term of the Boolean expression $ACE_w(O)$ shows that the expression will have a true value if only one of B (by S_2) and C (by S_3) is presented. The third term shows that both B (by S_2) and D (by S_4) must be presented to have a true value.

Before we discuss the inadequacy of Boolean expressions to represent state information, let us point out some of the advantages of this Boolean access control model. First of all, the model employs two familiar mechanisms: ACL and CL. In fact, the model is a lock-key approach that combines ACL and CL. The categories that each subject possesses are keys. And the *ACEs* are *sophisticated* combination locks maintained by the object servers. Second, since the access decision is not based on subject identities, the access control lists represented by *ACEs* for each object are greatly simplified. Third, the Boolean expressions are intuitive for specifying access control rules and can represent a large class of policies.

The $ACE_w(O)$ expression is not sufficient to represent the access control rules for the banking example. The expression is *memoryless* (in switching theory, the expression is a combinatorial circuit that does not have state information). To enforce the access sequence, evaluation of the second term $B \oplus C$ must be preconditioned by the previous evaluation of the first term A. Furthermore, subject $S1$ must be prohibited from accessing object O once it has the $ACE_w(O)$ evaluated to true with category A. Similarly, the enforcement of the exceptions (in the second and third terms) also requires knowledge of access history.

It is clear that we must have an efficient way to represent state information in order to model state-dependent access rules. The next question is whether the state information should be kept at the subject client or at the object server. We have encountered such a question in the discussion of distributed file systems (i.e., whether a file server should be *stateless* or *stateful*). If the state information on object accesses is maintained at the server site, the access control expressions will have to be changed dynamically upon every object access. Alternatively, the state information can be kept at the client sites (i.e., the client's capabilities, categories, are changed every time it accesses an object). The latter approach is less desirable. First, changing a client's capabilities may affect the client's ability to access other objects. Second, the effect of the client's access cannot be easily propagated to other client subjects. Therefore, it seems appropriate to embed state information in the access control expressions at the server site. Moreover, the access control expressions for related objects can be collected centrally at an authorization server to reduce the burden of the object server.

We conclude the discussion of complex access control policies by briefly mentioning an approach[9] to embedding state information in ACE. State information necessary for controlling access sequence and enforcing exceptions are implemented by using special Boolean variables. These variables are different from the clients' capabilities and are transparent to the clients. They are generated automatically and placed in the ACE according to the specific access rules. The details are beyond the scope of this book.

8.6.2 Proxy

The complex security policies described in the above section are motivated by commercial applications. Another requirement of some commercial applications, which is relevant to security in distributed systems, is the concept of a **proxy**. A proxy in the business world is the delegation of authorities for decision making. In the context of computer security, a proxy is a *certificate* used to verify that a principal truly delegates a subset of

---

[9] This approach was proposed in a Ph.D. dissertation at the University of Florida by I-Lung Kao, who is currently at IBM. I-Lung contributed the materials for this section.

its rights to another principal for performing some tasks on its behalf. Although a proxy is concerned with the authorization of access rights, the implementation of a proxy is primarily concerned with the authentication of the proxy. A proxy is a good example of the interrelationship between authorization and authentication.

Why is a proxy useful in distributed systems? Consider the following example in which a client process makes a request to a print server to print a file (for which the client has a read-access right). One implementation for this print operation is for the client to copy the file from the file server and then pass the file to the print server for printing. Another implementation is for the client to pass its read-access right to the print server and let the print server access the file directly from the file server. The latter approach requires that a proxy be issued by the client to the print server and that the proxy must be verifiable by the file server. An immediate advantage of the proxy approach is that the amount of file transfer in the network is reduced. In addition, the client has no need to wait for the printer server even if the print server does not have sufficient buffer space for the file at the time of the request. In general, delegation of responsibilities improves the efficiency of processing.

Basic System Assumptions

We assume that the underlying system is a collection of autonomous, mutually suspicious computer systems connected by a network. Each computer system has its own reference monitor to enforce its own security policies for access to the objects under its control. The security threats come from the network. The network links can be tapped so that an intruder can view the messages transmitted in the network. In addition, an intruder may be able to modify the contents of individual messages or reorder a stream of messages and inject them back into the network. The proxy protocols may assume the existence of a trusted authentication/directory server using either a private- or public-key cryptographic algorithm.

Figure 8.13 shows an example of cascaded delegation involving four principals: A, B, C, and D. The proxy originator A is the principal from which a proxy originates. A is also a proxy granter, who grants a proxy to the proxy grantee B. B in turn grants the granted proxy to the grantee C. Finally, C makes a request to the end server D, on behalf of its proxy granter.

FIGURE 8.13 Proxy protocols using public/private key cryptographic algorithms.

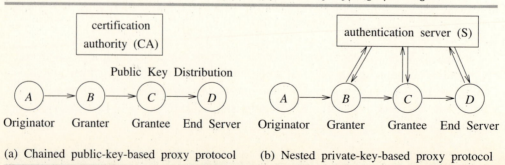

Public Key Distribution

Originator   Granter   Grantee   End Server   Originator   Granter   Grantee   End Server

(a) Chained public-key-based proxy protocol   (b) Nested private-key-based proxy protocol

A proxy protocol should exhibit the following basic properties:

- **Authenticity and integrity:** The proxy granter and grantee must be able to authenticate each other. The information on the proxy cannot be forged and must be verifiable.
- **Additivity and sufficiency:** Although the information shown on a proxy is generally nonremovable, more information can be added to indicate additional restrictions (e.g., privileges or the lifetime of the proxy) on making requests. However, the information on a proxy must be sufficient for the end server to make access decisions.
- **Revocability and lifetime:** A proxy should be revocable immediately upon an explicit request from the granter or an implicit termination of the granter. Optionally, a proxy granter can place a time-out to limit the lifetime of the proxy.

Proxy Protocols

A proxy protocol may utilize a symmetric private-key or an asymmetric public-key system. Since a proxy may be cascaded with more constraints added by the intermediate principals, the compound proxy (called a token) can be *chained* or *nested*. Using the principals in Figure 8.13, we will show two of the four combinations of proxy protocols: a chained public-key based proxy protocol and a nested private-key based proxy protocol.

Chained Public-Key-Based Proxy Protocol

In a public-key-based system, there is a trusted certification authority (which could be implemented in the directory server) that serves as a depository of registered public keys. The authenticity of the public keys is assured since the public keys are encrypted with the secret key of the certification authority (CA). The certification authority, shown in Figure 8.13(a) is responsible for the secure distribution of public keys but not the authentication of a proxy. The message sequence of the chained public-key-based proxy protocol is explained as follows.

1. $A \rightarrow B :$ $\{A, T_a\}$

    where $T_a = \{A, B, R_a, N_a, L_a\}_{K_a}$ is the proxy token issued by principal A to principal B. R_a is a subset of A's access rights to be delegated to B. N_a is a nonce generated by A to uniquely identify the proxy. L_a is the lifetime of the proxy assigned by A. The proxy token can be authenticated since it is encrypted with the secret key of A. B can obtain A's public key from the certification authority for decrypting T_a. For B to make a request to the end server D, the following message is sent along with the request to D:

2. $B \rightarrow D :$ $B, \{B, D, N_b\}_{K_b}, \{A, T_a\}$

    where N_b is an unique identifier for the request. Using B's public key, the end server D can decrypt B's request and verify it with the proxy issued by A to B. If B chooses to further delegate access rights to C, it appends an addendum proxy and sends the chain of proxy tokens to C:

3. $B \rightarrow C$: $\{B, T_b\}, \{A, T_a\}$

where $T_b = \{B, C, R_b, N_b, L_b\}_{K_b}$ has a format and meaning that are similar to those of T_a. The set (R_b) of privileges passed on by B is a union set of B's own privileges and the privileges delegated from A to B. Finally, the access request from C to D takes the following message format:

4. $C \rightarrow D$: $C, \{C, D, N_c\}_{K_c}, \{B, T_b\}, \{A, T_a\}$

By checking the token chain, the end server D will be able to verify that the access request identified by N_c satisfies the proxy chain from A to B and from B to C. It is not difficult to see that the chained proxy token has some flaws. We leave the discussion of the weakness of the chained proxy token approach for an exercise.

Nested Private-Key-Based Proxy Protocol

The weakness of chained proxy tokens can be alleviated if proxy tokens are nested. In the following proxy protocol, we also assume that the symmetric private-key system is used. In a private-key-based system, there is a trusted authentication server (S) that shares a secret key with every registered principal. Contrary to the certification authority, the authentication server authenticates the proxy but does not distribute keys.

As shown in Figure 8.13(b), when principal A sends a proxy to principal B, the proxy token is encrypted with the secret key K_{as}, which is shared only between A and S. For B to verify the proxy, B needs to forward the proxy to S since only the authentication server knows A's secret key. The authentication server needs to know and verify the proxy token. So the plaintext version (T_A) of T_a (encrypted with K_{as}) is sent along with T_a. The first two messages are:

1. $A \rightarrow B$: $\{A, \{T_A, T_a\}\}$
2. $B \rightarrow S$: $\{B, \{B, S, N_b\}_{K_{bs}}\}, \{T_A, T_a\}$

In message 2, B sends a challenge (N_b) to S to ensure that the acknowledgment returned from S is authentic. S proves the challenge by message 3, showing that S knows B's secret key and is capable of finding N_b. Thus the corresponding request and reply messages are matched and fresh.

3. $S \rightarrow B$: $\{S, \{S, B, ACK, N_b\}_{K_{bs}}\}$

Principal B continues the proxy delegation by sending message 4 to C:

4. $B \rightarrow C$: $\{B, \{T_B, \{T_B, T_a\}_{K_{bs}}\}, A\}$

The compound token in message 4 is nested rather than chained. That is, plaintext T_B and the encrypted T_a are combined and encrypted again with the secret key of B. The last component A in the message identifies the principal that initiated the previous delegation. Finally in message 5, C can pass the nested token when making a request to end server D:

5. $C \rightarrow D :$ $\{C, \{\{C, D, N_c\}, \{T_B, \{T_B, T_a\}_{K_{bs}}\}_{K_{cs}}, B, A\}$

After verifying the nested proxy token with authentication server S, end server D will have the nonce N_c to reply to C.

Discussion

A proxy is similar to a capability list (CL). The delegated privileges in a proxy can directly represent the capabilities. However, there are many significant differences. First of all, proxy protocols are identity based. Therefore, proxy protocols are equally applicable to end servers with access control lists (ACL). In this case an end server can grant temporary access to a delegated request without actually changing the ACL. Secondly, a proxy is created so that rights delegation can be verified and a capability can be duplicated and propagated freely to achieve object sharing. A proxy can be passed only between a granter and a grantee and is valid temporarily. Both a proxy and a capability are used as a certificate to indicate the privileges for accessing objects. Besides rights delegation, a proxy has an additional function of authentication. As a result, the end server of a proxy system is more complex than that of a capability-based object server.

A proxy and a capability share a common drawback in that it is difficult to revoke delegated/propagated access rights. Several approaches, for the revocation of proxy have been proposed:

- The proxy granter can send a revocation message to the proxy grantee and trust the grantee to terminate its own proxy and to propagate the revocation to the successive proxy grantee. This approach is not acceptable if the reason for revocation is that the grantee is no longer trustworthy.

- The proxy granter can contact the end server directly to invalidate all proxies issued by the granter. This approach requires the end server to maintain a list of invalid proxies.

- With a private-key system, the proxy granter can request the authentication server to change, delete, or withdraw the key used in the proxy verification process. This approach is difficult to implement in the public-key system since the certification authority does not perform authentication.

- The proxy granter does not really grant a proxy but sends a "read" capability to the delegated principal. The end server, on the presentation of a read capability, may read the proxy from the originator and verify the delegation. This approach is simple and effective, except that the communication overhead between the end server and the originator may be high.

It can be seen that instant privilege revocation is difficult for both a proxy and a capability, although a proxy seems to have more traceability.

8.6.3 Covert Channel, Traffic Analysis, and Audit

There are many security problems that cannot be dealt with adequately either by an authentication or an authorization scheme. **Covert channel** is one such problem. A covert channel is a communication path that conveys information illegitimately by seemingly legitimate use of computer resources. For example, an authenticated and authorized user may access or process data in a certain way that signals (leaks) information to an outside collaborator. A covert channel may be intentional or unintentional. Even an unintentional covert channel can cause a significant security threat. For example, ordering 250 pizzas for delivery to the Pentagon the night before the Gulf war was an unintentional covert channel of great value to Iraq. Similarly, by not knocking out all Iraqi communication command posts completely, the UN task force intentionally preserved the unintentional covert channels of the Iraqi military, which are more valuable than the communication facilities.

Theoretically, a covert channel exists in a system as long as events in the system can be observed (but not necessarily understood). The question is: How effective is a covert channel and how much information (bandwidth) can one carry? Therefore, the research on covert channels has been focused on limiting the bandwidth of covert channels. Traditionally, covert channels are classified in two categories: storage channels and timing channels. For network and distributed systems, we are more interested in a new type of covert channel: the **network covert channel**.

Covert storage channels convey information through the observation of direct or indirect changes in data storage. If the data is a file, the observable changes can be the name, size, and the lock status of the file. If the storage is a disk, a simple way to convey information is to vary the size of the free space. These examples show that a covert storage channel typically involves sharing a storage resource between two collaborating subjects at different security levels. Illegitimate information flow between the two subjects is possible even when they are explicitly prohibited by the security level to communicate directly.

Covert timing channels convey information through the observation of timing behavior of processes and events. The processing time of an operation can be modulated (by adding redundant computation) in such a way that the elapsed time carries some meaningful information. Similarly, events can be scheduled such that the ordering of events and inter-event time also reveal information.

Network Covert Channels

Covert channels are a more serious problem in a network system. It is easy to tap into a network and perform a traffic analysis of the information flow in the network. A network covert channel can be based either on *spatial* or *temporal* information of the traffic pattern. Using spatial information, covert data can be coded by varying the destination and size of the packets. Using temporal information, a covert channel can be represented by the frequency and burstiness of packet generation. Since the interceptor's attack is passive and does not require access to the system resources, the detection of a network covert channel is extremely difficult. However, some preventive measures can be used to prevent traffic analysis.

Traffic Analysis Prevention (TAP)

The key to traffic analysis prevention is to regulate information flow in the network such that the spatial and temporal imparity of the network traffic pattern is reduced. TAP methods should be transparent to the network users and ideally should not impose too much additional load to the network. The common TAP approaches are:

- **Encryption:** Messages to be transmitted in a network can be encrypted to prevent unauthorized disclosure of the contents of the messages. However, messages are often packetized with clear (unencrypted) header information to facilitate transport of packets in the network. The addresses and other attributes contained in the headers are potential sources of a covert channel. The strongest protection against eavesdropping is to encrypt all information (including headers) at the link level. This approach requires that all network nodes participate in the security policy. Data encryption and decryption are necessary for every packet at every link node. The overhead can be high, and all nodes must be trusted. If the encryption is moved to the network level, all packets need to be broadcast since the destination addresses are also encrypted. Requiring every node in the network to broadcast every packet is not a desirable solution. A reasonable compromise should be an end-to-end encryption system in which only the participating nodes pay for the cost of security.

- **Padding:** Packets transmitted in a network are limited in size according to the protocol used for communication. Small packets can be padded with redundant bytes such that all packets appear to be the same size. With all packets the same size, an interceptor cannot infer packet type from packet size. Padding can also be done at the network level. To hide the source and destination of an intended communication, the network can randomly generate spurious packets between pairs of nodes. In addition, padding of spurious packets can be selective for some network routes in some instances such that the network traffic appears to be uniform in every part of the network at all times. Spurious packets are decoys (artificial noises) padded to the network to deceive the interceptors. The major drawback of padding is the extra traffic load generated by the padding algorithm. Furthermore, each network node must be capable of recognizing the spurious packets to ignore them. However, if spurious packets are recognizable, the camouflaged real network traffic also can be exposed. These problems can be alleviated by packet routing and scheduling as follows.

- **Routing:** Most routers are designed to route packets via the shortest available route. Sometimes, a router may choose a less desirable route to avoid potential congestion in the preferred route. The routing algorithm can be further modified to route packets so that every link in the network has a similar traffic load. A packet may travel through more nodes than necessary and does not need to end at the destination node. The approach is similar to padding, but without adding spurious packets. It is not necessary to detect spurious packets and requires less traffic overhead than padding.

- **Scheduling**: The packet rate that each network node generates has a very different characteristics. Some applications generate bursty data; others generates steady stream of data. To prevent inferring an application from the frequency of packet generation, a network node can buffer packets and delay packet transmission. This approach is commonly used to avoid network congestion caused by bursty traffic. It has the side effect of hiding temporal information. Scheduling and routing are easy to implement for traffic analysis prevention.

Covert channels are difficult to detect. The traffic analysis prevention methods are used to prevent network covert channels from occurring. The complementary problem of traffic analysis prevention is the traffic analysis for detecting network intrusions (a positive use of traffic analysis). In this case, we must first *audit* the traffic so that network activities can be traced to catch security breaches.

Auditing

Auditing is the last resort when other more formal mechanisms (e.g. authentication protocol and authorization model) are not sufficient to protect the security of the system. Although the problem of covert channels falls into the category of security problems that lack of formal solutions, covert channels cannot be easily detected by auditing. The network traffic can be audited and analyzed to estimate the bandwidth of the network covert channel. However, a nonzero covert channel bandwidth does not imply that a covert channel attack has actually occurred. Fortunately, some preventive measures can be used to avoid network covert channels.

Another critical security problem that does not have a strong underlying theory is the denial of service (DoS) attack. At the beginning of the chapter we described the DoS as an availability issue, the third security goal besides secrecy and integrity. Contrary to covert channels, the denial of service attacks are easy to detect but difficult to prevent. Consequently, the DoS attack is a good candidate problem to solve by using an audit.

The denial of services attacks in local computer systems typically use the techniques of resource exhaustion and viruses. An attacker can use excessive logins or process forking to exhaust the process table and slow down the computation. This type of attack is targeted at the computational resources. File storage is another vulnerable resource for the DoS attacks. Excessive file creation can exhaust i-nodes and disk storage. Viruses, as we know, can create all kinds of damage to data. Denial of services is the least malignant problem caused by viruses.

In network systems, the denial of service attacks are also generally caused by resource exhaustion and viruses (or **worms**). The most likely targets for resource exhaustion are the communication ports. An attacker can easily flood a communication port with excessive service or connection requests. Network worms are segments or multiple copies of the same program traveling from one machine to another on the network. Once a worm program resides in one machine, it can perform DoS attacks on the local machine.

Besides resource exhaustion and worms, network systems suffer another critical DoS threat called **spoofing**. Because of the openness of network communications, it is easy to inject or replay messages in a network. With respect to DoS, the most likely targets are the routers. An attacker can spoof a Routing Information Protocol (RIP) packet to cause an erroneous update to the routing table or an Address Resoultion Protocol (ARP) packet to confuse the address resolution. These attacks disrupt the normal communication services. Other services are also vulnerable to spoofing. For example, a spoofed message can deregister a service in the portmapper, making the service unreachable.

Fortunately, most DoS attacks leave a trace (or signature) that can be used to detect the intrusions. For example, port flooding is characterized by service requests on successive ports, and RIP spoofing can be identified by RIP packets sent from nonrouter machines. The questions to be considered are how much information needs to be logged and when an audit should be performed. An audit can be performed *on-line* in the **firewalls** for early detection of potential threats, or *off-line* when problems have already occurred. The former is only a threat predictor based on quick analysis of simple signatures. The latter is a complete threat analysis (which may be computationally expensive) using detailed audit logs.

Many approaches for intrusion detection using audit information have been studied and implemented. They are classified in three categories:

- **Statistical analysis**: This approach is used when there is no clear signature of attack. It requires large log files and is computationally intensive. Therefore, it is normally done off-line. The statistical analysis may be useful since the results give a profile of the system.

- **Artificial intelligence**: The AI approach has great potential since it is based on knowledge of the system. Like any knowledge-based system, the challenge lies in the formulation of knowledge and rules. Moreover, the approach also tends to be computationally expensive and therefore less applicable to real-time reactive systems.

- **Formal language**: The main idea of this approach is that attack signatures can be thought of as valid sentences in a formal language. Using the well-known principles of lexical analysis and parsing in compiler/interpreter technologies, event streams can be parsed to determine if there is an attack pattern embedded within the event stream. The approach is attractive since the analysis is both sensitive to data and inexpensive to compute. It lends itself not only to easy extension but also to formal treatment of a well-developed area of theoretical computer science.

Auditing analysis is like mining data. Its applications are not limited to traffic and security threat analysis. An audit log is like a box of chocolates. You never know what you are going to get.

8.7 SUMMARY

Computer security has become an increasingly important subject for the implementation of a network-based distributed system. The desirable properties of the openness in a computer network and the automicity in a distributed system can be justified only if security and safety measures can be adequately supported in the system. This chapter begins with a discussion of security goals, policies, models, and mechanisms. We identify three unique security issues in distributed systems: access authorization, message security, and mutual (communicating principals) authentication.

The issue of access authorization is demonstrated by using two broad categories of access control models: the *discretionary access control* and the *mandatory access control*. The discretionary access control is a familiar access model. We use the *access control matrix* as an example and show how it can be implemented using either *access control lists* or *capability lists* or a combination of both. The pros and cons of each implementation approach are compared.

Access authorization in the discretionary access control model is based on the privileges that a subject possesses in respect to an object. The privileges are given to the subject on a discretionary basis. The mandatory access control model assumes an opposite view. In this case, all communicating principals are peer entities. Access control is represented as information flow among communicating entities. Regulation of information flow is enforced uniformly across the system on a mandatory basis. We use the *lattice* models to show how information flow can be controlled by labeling communication entities with security *levels* or *categories*. Two common lattice models, the Bell–Lapadula model for confidentiality and the Biba model for integrity, are introduced.

Cryptographic techniques are traditionally used for protecting the secrecy of information. We discuss the fundmentals of cryptography and show two basic cryptographic systems: the *private-* and the *public-key systems*. Both systems can use secret keys to provide integrity and authenticity of messages in addition to secrecy. Also, by sharing secret information, mutual authentication between two communicating principals can be established. We show the development of mutual authentication protocols in distributed systems. These protocols are characterized by whether a third-party authentication server is assumed and by how the *freshness* of messages is guaranteed. The freshness of messages to prevent message replay attacks can be implemented by using either *nonces* or *timestamps*. We show two prevailing authentication protocol standards: Kerberos and X.509.

Many other interesting issues for computer security in distributed systems still remain open problems. The complex security policies require the inclusion of state information in the access control mechanism. A *proxy* is considered a key mechanism for the delegation of access rights in distributed systems. The proxy protocols are described in the context of authentication and management of proxies. Finally, we emphasize the importance of *network traffic analysis* and *auditing* as complementary solutions to security problems in distributed systems.

ANNOTATED BIBLIOGRAPHY

This chapter addresses three major security issues in distributed systems: access authorization, message security, and mutual authentication. Access authorization security models are classified by NCSC as either discretionary or mandatory according to the Orange Book [NCS85]. Message security and authentication rely heavily on cryptography. We give an introduction on cryptography to provide a background for the discussion of its applications in authentication. We show how the development of authentication protocols has evolved and led to the design of Kerberos [SNS88, KNT91] and X.509 [IT88].

For discretionary access control, we illustrate the authorization concept by using the access control matrix model, which was first presented by Lampson [Lam71] and later refined by Graham and Denning [GD72], and Harrison, Ruzzo, Ullman [HRU76]. Three conventional implementations of access control matrix are discussed: ACL, CL, and lock-key. We show the simplicity of ACL and the suitability of CL for access control in distributed systems. Since lock-key is a combination of ACL and CL, it has great potential for modeling complex security policies. Reference to the lock-key approach in Amoeba is due to Tanenbaum [Tan95]. The distributed compartment model, which can be used for access control for logical domain, was introduced by Greenwald [Gre94].

For the mandatory access control, we illustrate the authorization concept by using the information flow model [Den76, Den83, Lan81, Kar78]. Mandatory information flow control is a solution to the confinement problem cited in [Lam73]. The lattice information flow model was first presented by Denning [Den76]. The two special cases of the lattice model discussed are the Bell–LaPadula [BL75] and the Biba [Bib77] models. Although these basic multilevel flow models are very restricted, the importance of mandatory information flow control requires further research.

Cryptography is a subject that is older than computers. The significance of its applications for communication security and authentication cannot be understated. We use the Privacy Enhanced Mail [PEM93] to show the application of three important international cryptographic standards: the private-key system DES [NBS77, DH77], the public-key system RSA [RSA78, DH76], and the message digest algorithm MD5 [Riv92].

Needham and Schroeder were the first to propose the use of encryption techniques for authentication and key distribution in networks and distributed systems [NS78]. Many authentication protocols have been proposed since. We show the evolution of authentication protocols with examples from [DS81, OR87]. The research on authentication protocols led to two popular standards: the private-key-based Kerberos and the public-key-based X.509 three-way authentication protocol. These are protocols for initial authentication. For repeated multiple authentication we show the protocol by Kehne, Schonwalder, Langendorfer [KSL92] and cite [NS93, Syv93]. Most researchers use the BAN logic [BAN90] to prove the correctness of the authentication protocols.

Finally, we conclude the chapter by showing three interesting problems for security in distributed systems: complex security policy, proxy, and covert channel and traffic auditing. The research in complex security policies is primarily stimulated by the well-known Clark–Wilson [CW87] model for commercial security. The model is the first to address nondiscretionary access control, privilege separation, and least privilege.

We describe a class of complex security policies using the notion of flow exceptions [KC95, Lun89, Mea90, Bad89, Kar89, NP90, San88, Fol91]. Some examples of security applications are given for each of the exceptions. Proxy is another example of a business concept applied to computer security. It is concerned with the delegation of access rights in distributed systems. Proxy implementation also relies on authentication by cryptography. The examples we use are due to Varadharajan, Allen, and Black [VAB91] and work in [Neu91, GM90]. The criteria for covert channel analysis are specified in the Pink Book [NCS85] by NCSC. The discussion of TAP, DoS, and auditing is due to [NWV91].

EXERCISES

1. How are the following attacks different from each other: masquerading, replay, and repudiation? How are they dealt with?

2. Interdomain access control is similar to international travel where passport and visa are required. Using the analogy, outline a scheme for interdomain access control by showing the necessary agent processes in each domain and the protocols between domains.

3. Discuss the implementation issues for the authentication, review, propagation, and revocation of access rights for the lock-key method.

4. Discuss the strength and weakness of the Unix *rwx* file protection scheme.

5. Why is the *prohibitive* access right not used in most of the ACL systems?

6. Groups are formed explicitly by users. Show possible ambiguities in assigning access rights when a user may belong to multiple groups. If we set a limit of one group per user, suggest a way for a user to participate in more than one group.

7. The *set-user-id* in UNIX allows a program to be executed with the permission of the user who owns the program. Relate this capability to the relevant subjects discussed in the chapter. Why is *set-user-id* useful, but also a source of security threat?

8. Show the lattice structure for the security class of a system with two nonhierarchical categories (A,B) and two hierarchical security levels (X,Y, where X dominates Y).

9. A security policy that is represented by a nonacyclic information flow graph cannot be enforced by a lattice-based access control model. Show an application in which the information graph is cyclic.

10. Summarize the advantages and disadvantages of the symmetric private-key and the asymmetric public-key systems.

11. Why is end-to-end encryption considered more advantageous than link encryption?

12. Compare the use of nonces and timestamps with respect to their ability to guard against replay attacks and the required message count.

13. The three authentication protocols presented in Section 8.5.2 assume an authentication server (S) and two communicating principals (A, B). Draw a diagram showing the message sequence of each protocol. Suggest another plausible message sequence using the same diagram.

14. Why does Kerberos separate the authentication service into two servers: the authentication server (K) and the ticket granting server (G)?

15. Describe the differences among the following: capability, certificate, proxy, ticket, authenticator, and credential.

16. In real life we have combination locks and locks that remain open once they are unlocked. Show possible applications of these types of lock for access control in a computer system.

17. In real life we have master keys and keys that are for one-time use only (e.g., a one-time ticket). Show possible applications of these types of key for access control in a computer system.

18. Give some examples showing the advantages (or necessity) of using a proxy in distributed systems.

19. Why is a nested proxy considered more secure than the chained proxy?

20. The bandwidth of a network covert channel is considered much higher than the bandwidth of a storage or timing channel in a local computer system. Why?

21. Access audit log and intrusion detection can be implemented at different network layers (transport, network, datalink). Discuss the pros and cons of the implementation at each layer.

P A R T

II

Distributed Algorithms

Models of Distributed Computation

In the second part of this book, we discuss some fundamental distributed algorithms and their correctness. A proof of correctness requires a model of computation; such models are the subject of this chapter.

Serial programs have a fairly simple model of computation, since the system has a global state and one step is carried out after another. The model of computation for a distributed system is more complex for three reasons. First, the system is composed of concurrently executing components. Second, there is no global time in a distributed system and thus no global state. Third, the model of computation must capture the effects of possible failures of system components.

We will present three approaches to modeling a distributed computation: causality, consistent states, and global states. It turns out that the three approaches to modeling a distributed computation are closely related. By understanding the models, their similarities, and their differences, one can develop a better understanding of how a distributed algorithm works.

9.1 PRELIMINARIES

Because we specify many algorithms in the second part of the book, we need a consistent notation for clarity. The pseudocode is similar to C, although we take liberties where convenient. All variables referenced by a program are stored on the processor on which the program executes. If the same program is executed on two different machines, the programs access different sets of variables even though the names of the variables in both processors are the same. If we want to specify the value of a variable at a particular processor, we subscript the variable with the processor name. For example, x_p is the value of variable x at processor p. The distributed programs need mechanisms for sending messages and receiving external input. In this section, we will discuss our standard notation.

When we discuss distributed protocols, we will assume that each instance of the protocol executes on a separate processor. In general, we will discuss communication in terms of one processor sending a message to another. Of course, a single processor executes many tasks simultaneously and perhaps even executes several instances of the same protocol. The address of a communicating entity is a combination of a machine name and the port number on the machine (i.e., a socket address). However, our discussion will bypass these details and use the abstraction of processors communicating with each other.

The protocols we discuss usually send *control* messages to each other. A control message will specify the *action* that the sending processor wishes the receiver to take and also a set of parameters. A processor can send a message of type action to processor destination with parameters parameters by executing the following statement:

    send(destination,action; parameters)

We will usually make the assumption that message sending is nonblocking and reliable (i.e., semantics similar to those of TCP sockets). We will sometimes prefer to make use of a weaker message passing layer (i.e., equivalent to UDP), so we will specify the assumptions about the message passing layer when we present the algorithms.

In addition to sending messages, processors need to be able to receive messages as part of the protocols that they execute. The protocols will need to respond to internal interrupts and timeouts as well as external messages. We will generalize the receipt of a message to the receipt of an **event**, which can be an external message, a timeout, or an internal interrupt. An event cannot be handled until a thread declares that it will process the event, and the event is buffered until it is handled. If the processor must be able to handle the event at any time, it must execute a thread dedicated to handling the event. A processor declares that it is waiting for events A1, A2, . . ., An by executing the following code:

```
wait for A1, A2, . . ., An
      A1 (source; parameters)
            code to handle A1

.....
      An (source; parameters)
            code to handle An
```

When processor p executes send(q,A1; parameters) and processor q executes the above code, q will eventually process the message sent by p. The variable source will contain the processor name p, and the parameters that p sent will be unpacked by q. The semantics of this construction are similar to the select system call used with Berkeley sockets.

The protocols we discuss will often need to take an action if they suspect that a remote processor has failed. Failures are usually detected with timeouts. We use the following construction to specify that the protocol must wait for a message of type event from P for up to T seconds and to take the specified timeout action if no such message is received:

```
wait until P sends (event; parameters), timeout=T
      on timeout
            timeout action
```

Often, we will want to take an action only if we received a response, and to take no action on a timeout. In this case, we will use the following construction to specify the action to take if a return message is received:

```
wait until P sends (event; parameters), timeout=T
      on timeout ;
If no timeout occurred
      (Successful response actions)
```

Other times, the algorithm does not need to wait for the response from a particular processor but must wait for responses from a set of processors. In the following construction, the processor waits for up to T seconds for the responses. That is, if the processor finds that there are no responses to be processed at a time T seconds after the waiting started, the waiting will end and the protocol will continue. As a shortcut, the protocol can stop waiting when all expected responses arrive.

```
wait up to T seconds for (event; parameter) messages
    Event: < message handling code >
```

Some protocols are best described by using several threads of control on a processor, each thread performing a different function. We will often use this construction. Since the concurrent threads will usually access the same set of variables, we need to describe some sort of concurrency control among the threads. Instead of using many complex lock and unlock statements in the code, we will assume that once a thread gains control of the CPU, it does not release control (to a thread of the same family) until it is blocked. This semantics of thread execution is similar to that provided by most user-level threads packages.

The distributed protocols will often need to store information about the state of other processors in a table. We perform this by indexing an array by the processor's name (i.e., state[q] contains q's state). In actual implementations, processor names are too sparse to directly reference tables, so a level of indirection must be used. We index the tables directly to simplify the presentation. Finally, a processor might need to refer to its own state. We assume that a special global variable, self, that contains the processor's name is available for use.

9.2 CAUSALITY

A fundamental property of a distributed system is the lack of a global system state. There are several factors that prevent an observer from determining the global state of a distributed system.

1. **Noninstantaneous communication:** Suppose that two professors, Joe and Sharon, stand on nearby mountain tops, mountains A and B. Both professors have their hand on a buzzer that is loud enough to be heard on the other mountain. A third professor, Calvin, stands on mountain C, which is equidistant from mountains A and B, and signals Joe and Sharon to press their buzzers by lighting a flare. Calvin then hears that the buzzers from the other two professors go off at the same time. However, Joe hears his own buzzer go off well before Sharon's. Similarly, Sharon thinks that her buzzer sounded first. Thus, the observer's view of the global state of the system depends on the observation point.

   In a distributed system, communications are not instantaneous for many reasons, including propagation delays, contention for network resources, and lost messages that require retransmission. Your view of the state of the system depends on your observation point.

2. **Relativistic effects:** Suppose that Joe and Sharon, discouraged by their mountaintop experiment, decide to observe a global state by using synchronized clocks. They both agree to meet at a restaurant at 5 p.m. Joe takes a nap until 5, while Sharon enjoys an excursion around the solar system at close to the speed of light. Joe arrives at the

restaurant at 5, then leaves after waiting for Sharon for an hour. Sharon arrives at the restaurant when her watch reads 5 p.m., but finds that Joe never shows up.

While most computers do not travel at relativistic speeds, clock synchronization is nevertheless a problem, since real clocks tend to drift apart in their readings. Thus, synchronizing by time is not a reliable mechanism.

3. **Interruptions:** Joe and Sharon decide to run a race. They wait side by side and watch for a flag to drop. Now, communication is almost instantaneous and relativistic effects are negligible. However, Joe suddenly notices that his shoe is untied. While Joe ties his shoe, the flag drops and Sharon gains a considerable lead before Joe starts running.

   Even when other effects are negligible, one cannot count on simultaneous reactions from different machines. A modern computer system is very complex, and execution times are made unpredictable due to CPU contention, interrupts, page faults, cache line misses, garbage collection, and so on.

Since one cannot count on simultaneous observations of global states in a distributed system (that is, in an **asynchronous system**), we need to find properties on which we can depend. If we exclude the possibility of traveling backward in time, distributed systems are **causal**; the cause precedes the effect. In particular, we assume that the sending of a message precedes the receipt of a message.

Suppose that the distributed system is composed of the set of processors $P = \{p_1, \ldots, p_M\}$.[10] We want to look at the **events** that occur on the processors. We consider every sending and receipt of a message to be an event. In addition, some actions that are internal to a processor are considered to be events. For example, one might want to consider the receipt of user input, the raising of a signal, the creation of output, the decision on a commit point, etc., to be events. We define $\mathcal{E}$ to be the set of all events in our system and $\mathcal{E}_p$ to be all events in $\mathcal{E}$ that occur at processor p.

We are interested in defining *orders* between different events (recall the discussion and uses of logical clocks in Chapter 3). If we know that event e_1 occurred before event e_2, we write $e_1 < e_2$.[11] In a distributed system, it can be difficult to deduce which event came first. Typically, one needs to combine information from different sources to determine the ordering. Because there is the possibility of confusion, we will often specify how we came to know the ordering. So, if information source I tells us that e_1 comes before e_2, we write $e_1 <_I e_2$.

There are some orders between the events in $\mathcal{E}$ that we can immediately discern. First, events that occur on the same processor are totally ordered. So, if $e_1 \in \mathcal{E}_p$ and $e_2 \in \mathcal{E}_p$, either $e_1 <_p e_2$ or $e_2 <_p e_1$.[12] Second, let e_1 be the sending of message m, and let e_2 be the receipt of message m. Then $e_1 <_m e_2$.

---

[10] Equivalently, there are M cooperating processes that we are interested in. These processes are spread throughout the system and might even reside on the same processor.

[11] A notation that is popular in the literature is to write $e_1 \rightarrow e_2$ (as is used in Chapter 3) However, we feel that the notation $e_1 < e_2$ better expresses the comparison between events.

[12] Here, we are following Lamport in assuming that the events on a processor have a total order. On a complex system, the events on a single processor might be better modeled as a partial order.

FIGURE 9.1   The happens-before relation (happens-before DAG).

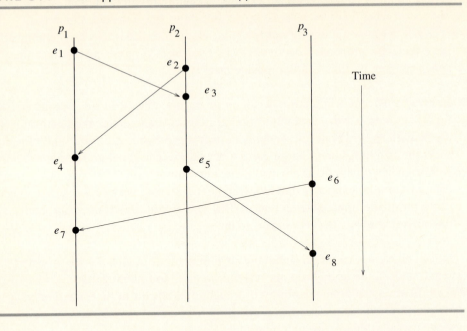

We define the **happened-before** relation to be the transitive closure of the processor orderings and the message passing orderings:

1. If $e_1 <_p e_2$ then $e_1 <_H e_2$.
2. If $e_1 <_m e_2$ then $e_1 <_H e_2$.
3. If $e_1 <_H e_2$ and $e_2 <_H e_3$, then $e_1 <_H e_3$.

That is, event e_1 happened before e_2 ($e_1 <_H e_2$) if there is causally linked chain of events leading from e_1 to e_2. We note that the happened-before relationship is a partial order but (usually) not a total order, since it is possible to have events e and e' such that neither $e <_H e'$ nor $e' <_H e$. If two events are not ordered by the happens-before relation, then the events are **concurrent** (or **disjoint**).

Consider the example in Figure 9.1. Events e_1, e_4, and e_7 all occur on processor p_1, so we can deduce that $e_1 <_{p_1} e_4 <_{p_1} e_7$. Event e_1 is the sending of a message and e_3 is the reception of the message, so $e_1 <_m e_3$. Similarly, $e_5 <_m e_8$. By applying rules 1 and 2, we deduce $e_1 <_H e_4 <_H e_7$, $e_1 <_H e_3$, $e_5 <_H e_8$, and so on. By applying the transitive closure property of $<_H$, we can deduce that $e_1 <_H e_8$. Since there is no path between e_1 and e_6, neither event is ordered against the other, so they are concurrent.

It is sometimes useful to describe the happens-before relationship as a directed acyclic graph. That way, we can execute graph algorithms on it. The vertices V_H of a *happens-before DAG*, or H-DAG, are the events in $\mathcal{E}$. The directed edge (e_1, e_2) is in the edge set, E_H if and only if $e_1 <_p e_2$ or $e_1 <_m e_2$. Figure 9.1 illustrates an H-DAG as well as the happens-before relationship.

9.2.1 Lamport Timestamps

While we have argued that global time does not exist in a distributed system, it would nevertheless be nice to have a global clock. Such a global clock will assign a total order to the events in the distributed system. Furthermore, the total order that the global clock imposes on the events should be consistent with the partial order imposed by the happened-before relation. If we have such a clock, we can use it to arbitrate requests for resources in a fair manner, because the global clock will tell us who asked for what first.

Since the happened-before relation is a partial order, we can see that it is possible to create a consistent total order by performing a topological sort on $<_H$. However, we would like to be able to create the total order on the fly so that it can be used immediately. Lamport provided just such an algorithm, and one which is surprisingly simple.

Each event e has a timestamp attached to it, $e.TS$. Each processor p maintains a local timestamp, my_TS. When the processor executes an event, it assigns the timestamp to the event. In addition, the processor attaches its timestamp to all messages that it sends. The timestamp assignment is shown in Algorithm Listing 9.1.

The timestamps that are assigned by Algorithm Listing 9.1 are causal, in the sense that if $e_1 <_H e_2$, then $e_1.TS < e_2.TS$. This is true because every time that $e_1 <_p e_2$ or $e_1 <_m e_2$, e_2 is assigned a higher timestamp than e_1. Thus, every event on a causal chain of events linking e and e' has a larger timestamp than its predecessor, so that $e.TS < e'.TS$. However, these timestamps do not assign a total order to the events in the system, since two events might receive the same timestamp. Since events with identical timestamps must be concurrent, we can break the ties arbitrarily. Lamport suggests using the processor address for the lowest order bits of the timestamp.

An example of the Lamport timestamps is shown in Figure 9.2. The events are labeled by their assigned timestamp, which has the form (timestamp, processor id). Event e_7 must be labeled 3.1 because it follows an event labeled 2.1. Similarly, event e_8 must be labeled 4.3 because it follows event 3.2.

Lamport's algorithm for generating timestamps is an interesting example of a distributed protocol, since it is completely distributed, is fault tolerant, and imposes a

ALGORITHM LISTING 9.1

Lamport's timestamp algorithm.

```
Initially,
    my_TS=0

On event e,
    if e is the receipt of message m,
        my_TS=max(m.TS,my_TS)
    my_TS++
    e.TS=my_TS
    if e is the sending of message m,
        m.TS=my_TS
```

FIGURE 9.2   Lamport timestamps.

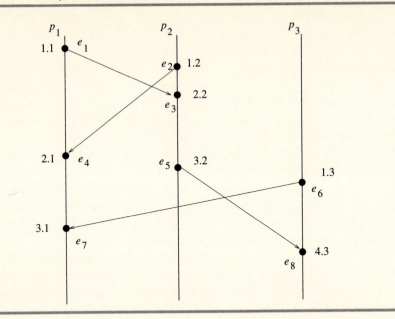

minimal overhead on the system. In the subsequent chapters, we will see many applications of Lamport timestamps.

9.2.2 Vector Timestamps

The Lamport timestamp algorithm provides the guarantee that if $e <_H e'$, then $e.TS < e'.TS$. However, there is no guarantee that if $e.TS < e'.TS$, then $e <_H e'$. In fact, Lamport's algorithm is simple because it orders concurrent events arbitrarily.

However, there are occasions when we want to look at two events and determine whether they are causally related. For example, we might want to be able to detect a causality violation. Suppose that we have a distributed object system, and the objects are mobile. That is, an object (an encapsulated collection of data, procedures, and a thread of control) can move between the processors in a distributed system. One might want to move an object for load balancing so that the object is close to the calling process, or so that the object is close to some resource (data, other objects, etc.) that it needs.

Consider the example in Figure 9.3. Suppose that processor p_1 holds object O but decides to migrate O to processor p_2 so that O will be close to the resources on p_2 that it needs. Processor p_1 marshals O into message $M1$ and sends $M1$ to p_2. Shortly thereafter, p_1 receives a request from processor p_3 asking for access to O. Processor p_1 informs p_3 of O's new location in message $M2$. Next, p_3 asks p_2 for access to O in message $M3$. Unfortunately, when message $M3$ arrives at p_2, O is not available, so p_2 responds with an error message. When you debug the system, you find that O really does reside at p_2, and you are baffled about what can be the source of the error.

FIGURE 9.3   An example of a causality violation.

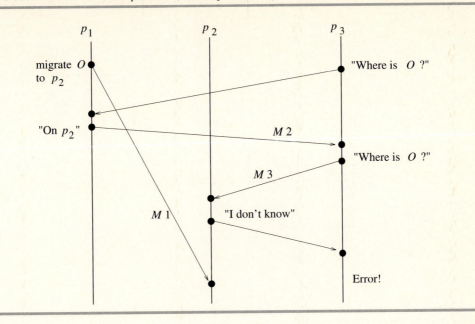

The source of the problem is a **causality violation**. p_3's request for O causally follows the transfer of O from p_1 to p_2 but is processed before the transfer at p_2. More formally, let $s(m)$ be the event of the sending of message m, and let $r(m)$ be the event of the receipt of message m. We will say that message m_1 *causally precedes* message m_2 (written as $m_1 <_c m_2$) if $s(m_1) <_H s(m_2)$. Then, a causality violation occurs if $m_1 <_c m_2$, but $r(m_2) <_p r(m_1)$. That is, a causality violation occurs if message m_1 is sent before message m_2 is sent, and m_2 is received before m_1 is received.

If we had a timestamp VT with comparison function $<_V$ such that $e <_H e'$ if and only if $e.VT <_V e'.VT$, we would be able to detect the causality violation in the distributed object system. We can make some observations about the properties of VT. First, $<_V$ must be a partial order, since $<_H$ is. Second, we must be able to tell which events of every processor an event e causally follows, and therefore $e.VT$ must contain information about the state of every other processor in the system. These two considerations lead us to the idea of a **vector timestamp**.

The timestamp VT is an array of integers, and we denote the ith entry by $VT[i]$. Intuitively, if $e.VT[i] = k$, then e causally follows the first k events that occurred at processor i.[13] This property is illustrated in Figure 9.4. So, $e'.VT \leq_V e.VT$ only if e follows every event that e' follows. More precisely, we define the ordering on vector timestamps as:

---

[13] We follow the standard practice of saying that an event follows itself. This practice is not necessary for the theory, and we can develop an equivalent and very similar theory by saying that an event does not follow itself.

FIGURE 9.4   An example of a vector timestamp.

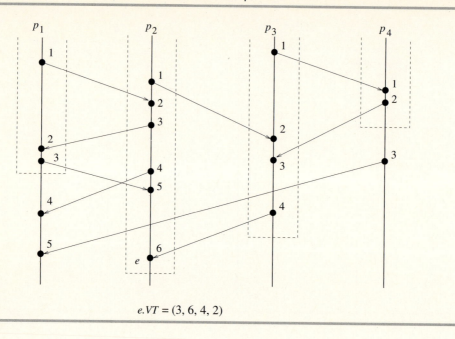

$$e.VT = (3, 6, 4, 2)$$

$$e.VT \leq_V e'.VT \quad \text{if and only if} \quad e.VT[i] \leq e'.VT[i] \text{ for every } i = 1, \dots, M$$

$$e.VT <_V e'.VT \quad \text{if and only if} \quad e.VT \leq_{VT} e'.VT \text{ and } e.VT \neq e'.VT$$

As in Lamport's algorithm, each processor p maintains a local timestamp my_VT. The vector timestamp associated with an event or message is stored in m.VT. When the processor executes an event, it assigns the timestamp to the event. In addition, the processor attaches its timestamp to all messages that it sends. The processing for a vector timestamp assignment is shown in Algorithm Listing 9.2.

It is easy to see that $e.VT <_{VT} e'.VT$ if $e <_H e'$, because the algorithm ensures that for every event such that $e <_p e'$ or $e <_m e'$, $e.VT <_{VT} e'.VT$. Next, suppose that $e \not<_H e'$. We need to show that $e.VT \not<_{VT} e'.VT$. Suppose that e' is the kth event on processor p and that $e.VT[p] = l > k$. Then, there is a path from the lth event on processor p to event e in the happens-before DAG (since there is no other way for $e.VT[p]$ to be as large as l). So, if $e \not<_H e'$, then $e.VT \not<_{VT} e'.VT$. If e and e' are concurrent, $e.VT \not<_{VT} e'.VT$ and $e'.VT \not<_{VT} e.VT$.

As an example, consider events e_1, e_2, and e_3 in Figure 9.5. Events e_1 and e_2 are concurrent, since there is not a path from e_1 to e_2, and vice versa. Notice that $e_1.VT[1] > e_2.VT[1]$, but $e_1.VT[2] < e_2.VT[2]$. Event e_1 follows event e_3, and $e_1.VT >_V e_3.VT$.

Returning to the distributed object example, we could determine the cause of the error by installing a causality violation detector at every processor. In Figure 9.6, we have attached vector timestamps to the events of Figure 9.3. The causality violation occurs

ALGORITHM LISTING 9.2

Vector timestamp algorithm.

Initially,
    my_VT=[0,...,0]

On event e,
    if e is the receipt of message m,
        for i = 1 to M
            my_VT[i]=max(m.VT[i],my_VT[i])
    my_VT[self]++
    e.VT=my_VT
    if e is the sending of message m,
        m.VT=my_VT

when message $M3$ with vector timestamp $(3, 0, 3)$ arrives at p_2, because p_2 will later receive a message that causally precedes message $(3, 0, 3)$ [i.e., message $M1$ with vector timestamp $(1, 0, 0)$, which delivers O]. The causality violation can be detected when message $M1$ arrives at p_2 because $(1, 0, 0) <_V (3, 2, 3)$, since $(3, 2, 3)$ is p_2's timestamp

FIGURE 9.5   Comparison of vector timestamps.

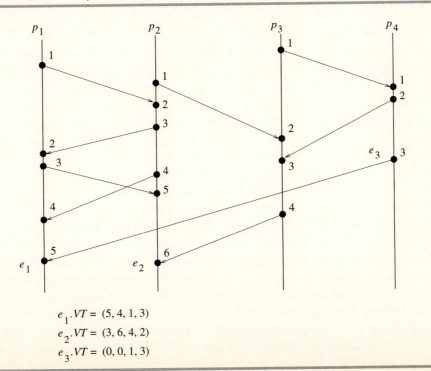

$$e_1.VT = (5, 4, 1, 3)$$
$$e_2.VT = (3, 6, 4, 2)$$
$$e_3.VT = (0, 0, 1, 3)$$

FIGURE 9.6   Detecting the causality violation.

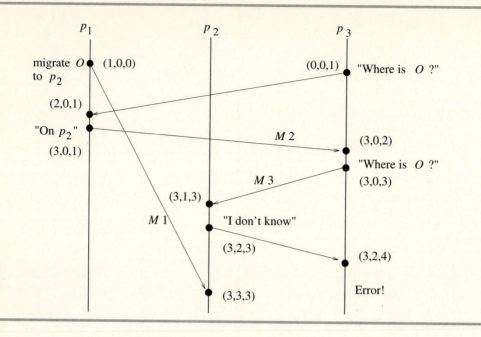

when message $M1$ arrives. Even though nothing can be done about the causality violation at run-time, logging the causality violations can aid debugging.

9.2.3 Causal Communication

Considering the problems that causality violations can cause, some researchers have proposed that the communications subsystems should ensure causal communications. That is, a processor never experiences a causality violation. A processor usually cannot choose the order in which messages arrive. However, it can change the order in which applications executing on the processor have messages delivered to them. The delivery order can be revised by holding back messages that arrived "too soon." We need to distinguish between when messages are *received* by the processor and when they are **delivered** to the applications that consume them. It is the responsibility of the communications subsystem to order the messages that are delivered to the applications.

The implementation of causal communication can be understood by using the example of how FIFO communication (i.e., TCP) is implemented. An example is illustrated in Figure 9.7. A layer in the message passing protocol stack is responsible for ensuring FIFO communications. The source processor sequentially numbers each message it sends over the communications channel. The destination processor knows that the messages it accepts should be sequentially numbered. If the destination receives a message with sequence number x but has never received a message with sequence number $x - 1$, it delays the delivery of the message numbered x until it can be delivered in sequence. A protocol layer that implements causal communication works in a similar way. The source attaches timestamps, and the destination delays the delivery of out-of-order messages.

FIGURE 9.7   Protocol for FIFO message delivery.

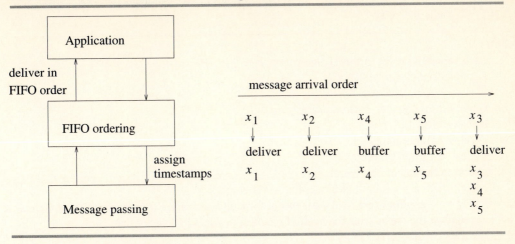

Since a causality violation can occur because messages come from different processors, the causal ordering layer in the protocol stack will need to buffer messages from a set of message channels and to make a global ordering comparison.

If we assume that all point-to-point messages are delivered and in the order sent (i.e., using TCP), we can use timestamps to ensure causal communication. The idea is to hold back a message m sent from processor p until we are assured that no message $m' <_H m$ will be delivered from any other processor. Each processor p keeps an array earliest[1 ... M], which stores a lower bound on the timestamps of the messages that can be delivered from the different processors. In addition, each processor maintains an array of blocked message queues blocked[1 ... M] and one FIFO queue for messages from each other processor. The algorithm for causal message delivery is shown in Algorithm Listing 9.3.

Either Lamport or vector timestamps can be used with the Algorithm Listing 9.3. Vector timestamps will give better performance because they do not introduce false orderings.

The timestamp of the earliest message that can be delivered from processor k is stored in earliest[k]. The variable earliest[k] is initialized to 1_k, which is the smallest timestamp that processor p_k can attach to one of its messages. If Lamport timestamps are used, $1_k = 1$. If vector timestamps are used, 1_k is a vector of length M that has the value 1 in its kth position and zeros elsewhere. When the processor (self) receives a message m from processor p, the message is put into a holding queue (blocked[p]) and held there until it is safe to deliver. If there are no messages in blocked[p], then earliest[p] is set to m.timestamp, because we now know that no earlier message can be delivered from p.

Since the arrival of m can move earliest[p] forward, several blocked messages might become unblocked. In addition, it might be safe to deliver m. Finally, the delivery of a message that becomes unblocked might unblock other messages. The protocol executes a loop that terminates only when no further messages can become unblocked.

A message is unblocked only if no message with an earlier timestamp can be delivered from another processor. That is, the message m at the head of blocked[k] is unblocked only if there is no earliest[i] that is smaller than m.timestamp=earliest[k]. Since m can be

ALGORITHM LISTING 9.3

Causal message delivery.

Initially,
    each earliest[k] is set to the 1_k timestamp, $k = 1 \ldots M$
    each blocked[k] is set to {}, $k = 1 \ldots M$

On the receipt of message m from processor p
    delivery_list = {}
    if (blocked[p] is empty)
        earliest[p]=m.timestamp
    Add m to the tail of blocked[p]
    while (there is a k such that blocked[k] is not empty,
                and for every i = 1 .. M, except for k and Self, not_earlier(earliest[i],earliest[k],i))
        remove the message at the head of blocked[k], put it in delivery_list
        if blocked[k] is not empty
           set earliest[k] to m'.timestamp, where m' is at the head of blocked[k]
        else
           increment earliest[k] by 1_k.
    Deliver the messages in delivery_list, in causal order

---

delivered, we need to update earliest[k]. If blocked[k] is not empty, the earliest message that can be delivered from k is the next message in blocked[k]. Otherwise, the earliest message that can arrive from processor k must have a timestamp at least 1_k greater than m.timestamp = earliest[k].

To complete the protocol, we need to specify the function not_earlier, which compares two timestamps and determines if the first is not earlier than the second. When we use vector timestamps, we can take advantage of the fact that a processor k's dependence on events at processor i is specified by the ith entry in k's vector timestamp. Suppose m is sent from processor k. Let $earliest[i][j]$ be the jth entry in the vector timestamp $earliest[i]$. If $m.timestamp[i] \geq earliest[i][i]$, then m depends on a message from i that is later than any that has been delivered. So, the function not_earlier is specified by Algorithm Listing 9.4.

The causal message delivery algorithm in Algorithm Listing 9.3 has several problems. If one processor does not send you messages for a long time, you will be blocked from

ALGORITHM LISTING 9.4

The not_earlier function for vector timestamps.

---

not_earlier(proc_i_vts,msg_vts,i)
    if msg_vts[i] < proc_i_vts[i]
           return TRUE
    else   return FALSE

---

receiving any messages. In fact, deadlock can occur (see the exercises). It is possible to obtain causal point-to-point communications without deadlock; this is in the exercises.

Because of the deadlock problem, causal communication is usually implemented as part of a multicast communication (discussed further in Section 12.2). Every processor in the multicast list receives the same set of messages. That way, if a processor p receives a message m_1 that causally follows a message m_2, p will eventually receive m_2, permitting the delivery of m_1.

For an example of how the causal message delivery algorithm executes, consider the execution illustrated in Figure 9.8. Processor p_2 multicasts message m_1. Processor p_1 receives m_1 and then multicasts m_2. Because the protocol is interested in causal ordering between sending events only, a processor increments its vector timestamp only when it sends a message. For this reason, the vector timestamp attached to m_2 is $(1, 1, 0)$. When processor p_3 receives m_2 from p_1, it puts m_2 in blocked[1] and updates earliest[1]. Since earliest[2] is less than head(blocked[1]).timestamp, p_2 might deliver an earlier message. The delivery of m_2 is blocked. When p_3 receives m_1, the message is put into blocked[2], and the queues are checked for unblocked messages. Message m_2 can be delivered, since it does not depend on any other events. Since blocked[2] is empty, the second component of earliest[2] is incremented. Now, message m_2 unblocks, because earliest[1][2]=1 < earliest[2][2]=2.

FIGURE 9.8   An example of causal multicast.

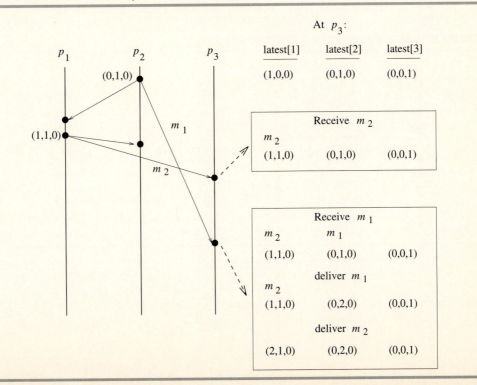

9.3 DISTRIBUTED SNAPSHOTS

In the previous section, we gave reasons why one cannot determine the global state of a distributed system. Nevertheless, we sometimes would like to summarize the state of the system. Instead of asking for the exact global state of the system, we can ask for a global view of the system that is consistent with causality. In a sense, we are asking for a **distributed snapshot** of the system that corresponds to a state that the system might have been in. We will soon make these statements precise.

There are many occasions when a distributed snapshot is useful. For example, distributed deadlock algorithms have often turned out to be incorrect because the state of the waits-for graph might be changing while the deadlock detection computation is executing [Tay91]. Consider the example in Figure 9.9. Two processes, p_1 and p_2 make use of resources r_1 and r_2. Process p_1 acquires r_1 and r_2, and then releases r_2. Process p_2 acquires r_2 and then requests r_1. The deadlock detector observes the processes and resources at the points marked 1 through 4. Based on the observations of the local state, the deadlock detector finds a cycle in the waits-for graph and decides that a deadlock exists. However, there is no deadlock (only a **phantom deadlock**). If we can take a distributed snapshot, we can gather the current state of the system and then look for cycles.

For another example, we might have a token-passing system, and we want to be able to detect if the token has been lost. As with deadlocks, detecting a lost token is tricky because the state of the system changes while the detection is taking place. For example,

FIGURE 9.9 Detection of a false deadlock.

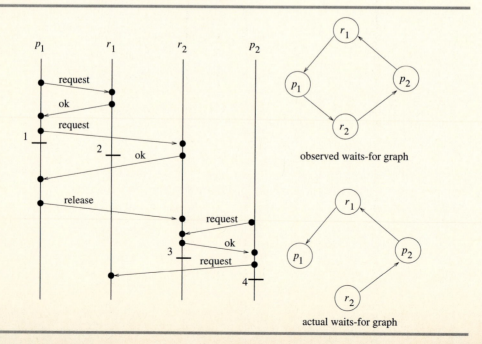

two processors p and q might pass token o between themselves. We might probe p's state and discover that p does not own the token. We proceed to probe q's state. However, before we probe q, q sends the token to p. So when we probe q, we find that q does not hold the token either. We falsely conclude that the token is lost. If we have a distributed snapshot, we can simply look at the system state and search for the token.

We first need to define what we mean by the state of the system. Let us again assume that there are M processors in the system $p_1, \ldots, p_M$. At a given point in time, processor p_i is in state s_i, where $s_i \in \mathcal{S}$. Formally, a processor is only allowed to be in one of the predefined states that are collected in $\mathcal{S}$, which can be an infinite set. Informally, the state of a processor is the values of the important variables of the protocol that we are interested in observing. We can even call the entire contents of the computer's memory its state. Let $S = (s_1, s_2, \ldots, s_M)$ be the global processor state (that is, the collection of the individual processor states).

Although we have captured the state of the processors, we still haven't captured the global system state because there might be undelivered messages in transit (the "missing" token, for example). Between every pair of processors p_i and p_j, there is a unidirectional communications **channel** $C_{i,j}$ (i.e., a TCP socket). We assume that the communications channels are reliable and that they deliver messages in the order sent. The contents of $C_{i,j}$ are an ordered list of messages $L_{i,j} = (m_1, m_2, \ldots, m_k)$, where each $m_i \in \mathcal{M}$. As with processor states, the messages in the channel are drawn from a predefined set of possible messages (the set of all 8196-byte strings, for example). The state of a channel consists of both the messages in the channel and the order of the messages. Message m_1 is at the *head* of the message channel and is the next message from p_i to be delivered to p_j. Message m_k is at the *tail* of $C_{i,j}$ and is the last message sent from p_i to p_j. The collection of all message channels is $C = \{C_{i,j} | i, j \in 1, \ldots, M\}$, and the collection of their contents is $L = \{L_{i,j} | i, j \in 1, \ldots, M\}$. Now we have the processor states and the message channel states, and combined they are the **global state** $G = (S, L)$.

For a global state to be meaningful, it must be one that could have occurred. Suppose that when we observe processor p_i (obtaining state s_i), it has received a message m from processor p_k. When we observe processor p_k (obtaining state s_k), it should have already sent m to p_i. Otherwise, we will be observing a state in which a message was received but never sent. In addition, L should contain the set of messages sent but not yet received. Let o_i be the event of observing the state s_i of processor p_i to collect the snapshot. Then, the state $S = (s_1, s_2, \ldots, s_M)$ is a **consistent cut** if for every pair of observations o_i and o_j, $i \neq j$, it is not the case that $o_i <_H o_j$. That is, the events $\{o_1, \ldots, o_M\}$ should be concurrent. Notice that in the example of Figure 9.9, the deadlock detector constructs a state in which $o_{p1} <_H o_{r2}$. The message by which p_1 releases r_2 is received but never sent. This inconsistency causes the deadlock detector to falsely declare a deadlock.

The requirement that the observations of the processor states be concurrent seems to be very hard to implement — how does a processor know when to make an observation? Obviously, some outside mechanism must invoke the state observations. The snapshot algorithm uses this trick. We can use some special messages, called *snapshot tokens*, that control the snapshot collection process. If the state observations are mutually concurrent with respect to the observed protocol (i.e., use only observed protocol messages in the

H-DAG), and the snapshot protocol does not interfere with the observed protocol, we will collect a consistent snapshot.

Our examples of how distributed snapshots can be used are similar in that both are examples of **stable properties**. Let global state G be a consistent cut. A property P is **stable** if $P(G)$ implies $P(G')$ for all G' that causally follow from G. So, if we detect P in consistent cut G, we will detect G in all future consistent cuts G'. That is the problem with, for example, deadlocks — they don't go away. But, we are guaranteed that if we detect a deadlock in consistent cut G, we know that the deadlock actually exists and is not an artifact of the method we used to collect the global state.

Let us consider how to design an algorithm to collect a consistent cut. First, we need to collect a set of local processor states s_i. There is a constraint on when we can collect a processor state. If we collect s_i at p_i, and the next message that p_i sends to p_j is m, we must collect s_j at p_j before p_j receives m. We must also collect the state $L_{i,j}$ of each channel $C_{i,j}$. $L_{i,j}$ consists of all messages that processor i sent in s_i which have not yet been received by processor j in s_j.

A distributed snapshot is started at the request of a particular processor p_i (for example, processor p_i might suspect a deadlock because of a long delay in accessing a resource). At this point, p_i can record its state s_i. Next, p_i must inform all of the other processors in the system about the snapshot. To do so, p_i sends a token t to every processor p_j that p_i communicates with (i.e, to every p_j such that $C_{i,j} \in C$). In fact, p_i must send the token to every p_j before sending any other message to p_j; otherwise p_j might record a state such that $o_i <_H o_j$.

When processor p_j receives a token t from p_i informing it of the snapshot, p_j must record its state before it receives the next message from p_i, or else the snapshot will not be a consistent cut. After recording its state, processor p_j should send the snapshot tokens t to every processor it communicates with before sending them any other messages. In general, the first time that processor p_k receives a snapshot token, it must record its state.

Notice that the state observations are not really concurrent. In particular, they all happen after o_i. However, the snapshot tokens do not affect the protocol that is being observed. If we delete the snapshot token messages from the H-DAG of the computation, the observations will be concurrent.

We still need to determine how to record the message channel states. Suppose that processor p sends a token to processor q, and when processor q receives the token, it is the first time it has ever received the snapshot token. Then, processor q immediately records its state s_q. Since messages are delivered in order, q has received every message sent from p before p sent the token. Therefore, the channel $C_{p,q}$ is empty (i.e., $L_{p,q} = \emptyset$).

Suppose that q receives a token from p, but q has already recorded its state. Let L' be the messages that q received from p between the time that q recorded its state and when q received a token from p. Then the messages in the message channel $C_{p,q}$ are L' (i.e., $L_{p,q} = L'$). Why? First, no message that q received from p when q recorded its state can be in the message channel, since the message has already been received. No message that p sends after the token can be in the message channel, or the message will appear in the channel without having been sent. All of the messages in L' must be in the channel, since p has sent them in S_p, but q has not received them in S_q. Therefore, $L_{p,q}$ is L'.

Since a processor makes the independent decision to take a snapshot, there might be several distributed snapshots being collected concurrently. Also, a processor might request a second snapshot while the first snapshot is still being collected. For this reason, we assign a processor number and a version number to each snapshot token. Tokens with different processor-version pairs belong to different snapshots and should be treated separately.

In the algorithm we present, every processor sets aside storage to compute its local position of the latest snapshot requested at every processor. The local variables used by a participant in the snapshot are shown in Algorithm Listing 9.5. The processor state for the snapshot requested by processor r is stored in S[r], and the state of the channel from q is stored in L[r][q] (note that L[r][q] will contain $L_{q,self}$ in the snapshot requested by r). The current version number of the snapshot for processor r is stored in current_snap[r]. When processor r requests a new snapshot, the old snapshot for r is discarded. The code we present runs at processor self and is symmetric at all processors. O_{self} is the set of processors that receive messages from self, and I_{self} is the set of processors that send messages to self. The algorithm for taking a distributed snapshot is shown in Algorithm Listing 9.6.

When each processor has recorded that a particular snapshot is finished the global snapshot is finished. The processor that requested the snapshot needs to be informed that the snapshot is finished, so that it can take an action (perhaps collecting the global snapshot).

In Figure 9.10 (on p.341), we illustrate an execution of the distributed snapshot algorithm. Two processors, p and q, repeatedly exchange a privilege token (represented by the black dot). The state of the processor (with respect to the token-passing protocol) is whether or not it is holding the privilege token. There are two message channels, $C_{p,q}$ and $C_{q,p}$. Processor p requests a snapshot because it has waited a long time for the privilege token. Processor p records its state, and sends the snapshot token (represented by t) to q. Concurrently, q releases the privilege token and sends it to p. When the snapshot token arrives at q, the local state and the state of $L_{p,q}$ is recorded (both empty). Since q has

ALGORITHM LISTING 9.5

Variables used in the snapshot algorithm.

Variables
        integer   my_version
        integer   current_snap[1 .. M]
        integer   tokens_received[1 .. M]
        processor_state S[1 .. M]
        channel_state   L[1 .. M][1 .. M]

Initially,
        my_version=0
        for each processor, p
                current_snap[p] = 0

ALGORITHM LISTING 9.6

Distributed snapshot algorithm.

```
execute_snapshot()
    Wait for a snapshot request or a token
        Snapshot_Request :
            my_version++
            put current state into S[self]
            current_snap[self]=my_version
            for each q in O_self,
                send(q,TOKEN; self,my_version)
            tokens_received[self]=0
        TOKEN (q; r,version)
            if current_snap[r] < version
                put the current state in S[r]
                current_snap[r]=version
                set L[r][q] to empty
                for every p in O_self,
                    send token(r,version) to p
                tokens_received[r]=1
            else if (current_snap[r] = version)
                tokens_received[r]++
                put all messages received from q since first receiving token(r,version) into L[r][q]
                if tokens_received[r]=|I_self|
                    the local snapshot for (r,version) is finished.
```

received tokens from all of its input channels, its local portion of the snapshot is finished. Processor q sends the snapshot token to p. Because the message channels are reliable, p receives the privilege token first. So, when p receives t from q, it records the state of $L_{q,p}$ as holding the privilege token. At this point, both p and q have computed their local snapshots. The observed global state is that the privilege token is on its way from p to q.

As in serial algorithms, there are some common themes running through the design of distributed algorithms. We would like to observe some techniques used in this algorithm.

- **Diffusing computation:** Some distributed algorithms naturally impose a tree structure on the processors in the system. In the distributed snapshot algorithm, the root of the tree is the processor that requested the snapshot, and processor q is the parent of processor p if p first learns of r's snapshot by a message from q. We can take advantage of the tree structure to design a **termination detection** algorithm. Processors send done messages to indicate that their local snapshot is finished. When the root process receives done messages from all of the processors it sent a token to, the snapshot has finished.

  - If you receive a token and you have received the token before, reply with a done message.

FIGURE 9.10   Taking a snapshot of a token passing system.

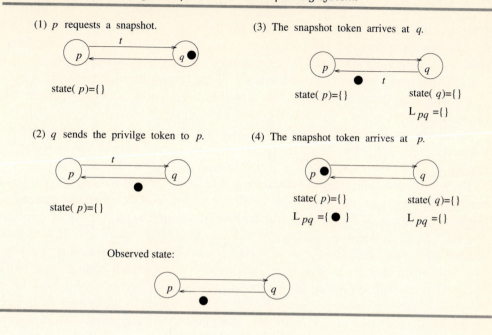

(1) p requests a snapshot.

state(p)={}

(2) q sends the privilge token to p.

state(p)={}

(3) The snapshot token arrives at q.

state(p)={}   state(q)={}

L_{pq} ={}

(4) The snapshot token arrives at p.

state(p)={}   state(q)={}

L_{pq} ={ ● } L_{pq} ={}

Observed state:

- When you receive done messages from all processors that you sent a token to, send a done message to the processor that first sent you the token.

- **Version numbers:** There are many occasions when we want to distinguish between objects that have the same name, but are actually different. One example is when we implement exactly-once semantics for RPC calls. The distributed snapshot algorithm is another example. All snapshot requests use the same algorithm. To distinguish between snapshots performed on behalf of different processors, we attach the name of the requesting processor to the snapshot tokens. In addition, we allow a processor to request a second snapshot before the first snapshot is finished. The processor might suspect a failure and reissue the request (as in an RPC call). However, the two snapshot requests from the same processor have the same name and might lead to an incorrect snapshot, so we distinguish them by version numbers. The version numbers do more than identify the different snapshots, they tell how the snapshots are related. In this case, we save space by performing only the new snapshot and throwing away the old one. Similarly, in exactly-once RPC, a request is performed only if its version number is newer than any previous request, which means that it is not a repeat.

- **Message channel flushing:** There are occasions when it is safe to proceed with an action only when a message channel has been cleared of all pending messages. In the case of the distributed snapshot, we know the state of a message channel only after it has been cleared. If the message channel delivers messages in order, we can flush the message channel by sending a token through it.

9.4 MODELING A DISTRIBUTED COMPUTATION

If we have a distributed protocol, we would like to be able to prove that it is correct or at least intuitively reason about its correctness using the right intuition. We need a formal model of a distributed computation that captures the idea of a distributed protocol and also captures how a computation can actually occur. It turns out that a *consistent cut* is a very good description of the states that a distributed protocol can be in and how they can evolve.

The distributed system has a state that is defined by $G = (S, L)$, as in previous section. For every process p_i, there is an **initial state** s_i^0. The initial state of the system G^0 is defined by $s_i = s_i^0$ for each processor $p_i \in P$ and by $L_{p,q} = \emptyset$ for each $C_{p,q} \in C$.

The global state changes when *events* occur. Intuitively, an event occurs at a particular processor and changes the state of the processor and at most one message channel (as do the events we consider for Lamport timestamps). We define an event to be a 5-tuple $e = (p, s, s', m, c)$, where $p \in P$, $s, s' \in S$, $m \in \mathcal{M} \cup \text{NULL}$, and $c \in C$ is a message channel that leads to or from p or is NULL. The interpretation of e is that it takes p from state s to s' and sends or receives message m on channel c. If m (and c) are NULL, the event is internal. We define the collection of all possible events to be E and the set of events that can occur at processor p to be E_p. The events in the system are defined by the protocol that the processes are executing (or equivalently, the events define the protocol).

The reader should not be intimidated by the seemingly unnatural formulation of an event. Describing a distributed protocol as the collection of events that can occur makes it easier for us to understand how the protocol executes. A dynamically executing protocol becomes a sequence of states that occur one after another, with the transition rules completely and conveniently defined by the events. Analyzing the protocol becomes a matter of analyzing the resulting combinatorial object. While one would not normally program a protocol as a collection of events, one can imagine a compiler that takes a distributed program written in a high-level language and creates an object code consisting of the events of the protocol.

More formally, let the global state be $G = (S, L)$. An event $e = (p, s, s', m, c)$ **can occur** in G if:

1. $s_p = s$, and
2. c is an incoming channel, $head(L_c) = m$.

If e can occur in G, the execution of e changes the global state to G'. We write this as $G' = next(G, e)$ or as $G \to_e G'$. Let the state of c be $L_c = (m_1, m_2, \ldots, m_k)$ in G. Then G' is defined by:

1. $s_p = s'$, and all other processor states remain the same.
2. If c is an outgoing channel from p, then $L_c = (m_1, m_2, \ldots, m_k, m)$, and all other channel states remain the same.

3. If c is an incoming channel to p, then $L_c = (m_2, \ldots, m_k)$, and all other channel states remain the same.
4. If c is NULL, all channel states remain the same.

As an example, let us define the events that can occur in the token-passing example of Figure 9.10. The states of the processors are $S = \{\text{tok}, \text{notok}\}$. The only possible message is $\mathcal{M} = \{\text{token}\}$. The two events that can occur in p are $E_p = \{(p, \text{notok}, \text{tok}, \text{token}, C_{q,p}), (p, \text{tok}, \text{notok}, \text{token}, C_{p,q})\}$. E_q is defined symmetrically.

Let $seq = (e_0, \ldots, e_j)$ be a sequence of events. Then, seq can occur in G if there is a sequence of global states $(G = G_0, \ldots, G_{j+1} = G')$ such that $G_{i+1} = next(G_i, e_i)$. If seq can occur in G, we write $G' = compute(G, seq)$ or $G \rightarrow_{seq} G'$. If G is the initial state (i.e., $G = G^0$), then seq is a *computation of the system*. If there is a sequence seq such that $G \rightarrow_{seq} G'$, then G' is **reachable from** G.

For example, suppose that the current state of the privilege token protocol is

$$G_1 = (s_p = \text{tok}, s_q = \text{notok}, C_{p,q} = C_{q,p} = \{\})$$

If we apply the sequence of events $seq = ((p, \text{tok}, \text{notok}, \text{token}, C_{p,q}), (q, \text{notok}, \text{tok}, \text{token}, C_{p,q}))$, we reach the state $G_2 = (s_p = \text{notok}, s_q = \text{tok}, C_{p,q} = C_{q,p} = \{\})$. That is, $G_1 \rightarrow_{seq} G_2$.

The advantage of this model of a distributed computation is that we now have global states and a linear chain of computation. However, events can occur at different processors, so in general the computation is nondeterministic. To show that a protocol is correct, we need to show that all states reachable from the initial state satisfy a correctness property.

To illustrate a proof of correctness, let us consider a slightly more complex example, the *double token* protocol. Processors p and q pass tokens t_1 and t_2 to each other. The protocol that p and q follow is that they can always receive a token, and they can send it only if they possess it. We would like to show that the protocol never "hangs up" and that the tokens are never lost. Figure 9.11 illustrates the double token protocol. Token t_1 is represented by an open dot, and token t_2 is represented by a black dot. A global state is specified by the locations of the tokens, whether on processors p and q or on the channels $C_{p,q}$ and $C_{q,p}$. In the initial state G_0, t_1 is at p and t_2 is at q. That is, $G_0 = (\{t_1\}, \{t_2\}, \{\}\{\})$. There are two possible events that can occur in G_0: p can send t_1 to q (e_1), or q can send t_2 to p (e_2). In state $G_1 = next(G_0, e1)$, event e_2 can occur; it is similar for $G_2 = next(G_0, e_2)$. If e_2 is applied to G_1 or e_1 applied to G_2, the result is the same, global state G_3. Proving the correctness of the double token protocol is a matter of enumerating all possible global states, showing that an event can occur in any state reachable from G_0 and that t_1 and t_2 are never lost.

The double token protocol is simple enough for its correctness to be proved by listing all possible global states. A more interesting protocol is likely to be complex enough that listing all possible states is infeasible or impossible. A proof of correctness for a more complex algorithm typically requires that one prove assertions about classes of states. Nevertheless, the principle is the same.

FIGURE 9.11   Double token protocol example.

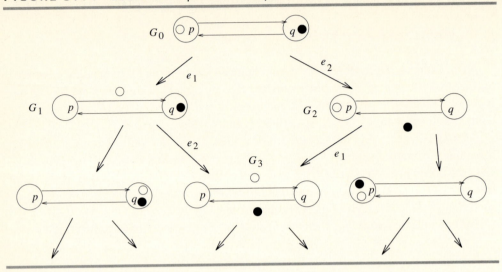

An unusual property of the global snapshot algorithm is that it can record a state that never occurred. Let us consider an example in which events occur slowly enough for us to be able to observe their real-time execution. For example, suppose that in state G_0 of the double token example, p requests a snapshot. Processor p records its state ($\{t_1\}$) and sends the snapshot token to q. Immediately after sending the snapshot token, p sends t_1 to q. Soon afterward, q sends t_2 to p. Next, the snapshot token arrives at q. q records its local state ($\{\}$) and sends the snapshot token to p. When p receives the snapshot token, it records the state of channel $C_{q,p}$ to be $\{t_2\}$. So, the snapshot algorithm records global state G_2, but the actual sequence of global states was $G_0, G_1, G_3, \ldots$

If the global snapshot algorithm does not necessarily capture a state that existed, it is natural to ask what relationship the snapshot has to the states that actually did occur in the computation. It turns out that a snapshot is a state that could have occurred, modulo concurrent events. It is possible to prove the following theorem (in the exercises, for example):

Theorem 1 Let $G^0 \rightarrow_{seq} G^f$, and let G^s be a snapshot taken during the computation seq. Then there is a permutation of seq, $seq' = seq'_1 | seq'_2$, such that $G^0 \rightarrow_{seq'_1} G^s \rightarrow_{seq'_2} G^f$.

Many of the models of distributed computation that one encounters in the literature are variants of the Chandy–Lamport model presented in this section. For example, one can model unordered messages delivery by removing the requirement that message channels are ordered. An event can occur if the message that triggers it is in the message channel. One can model a processor failure by permitting a processor to take a finite number of steps in an infinite computation sequence.

9.4.1 Relationships between Models

Thus far, we have seen three closely related models of an execution of a distributed protocol. The first model is based on events related by happens-before, and the second model is based on consistent cuts. Both of these models are observational − they give us a framework for interpreting what happened during an execution. The third model, of global states, is predictive. Given an initial state and a protocol, it tells us what might occur when the protocol executes.

The global states model contains both causal events and consistent states. An event is triggered only if it can causally occur and a new consistent state is created. However, the global states model is linear, since the execution follows the specified sequence of events. By contrast, the other two models explicitly account for concurrency. We next develop these models further and show the connections between them.

Recall the definition of $\mathcal{E}$ and $\mathcal{E}_p$. $\mathcal{E}$ is the collection of all events in the computation, and $\mathcal{E}_p$ is the collection of all events at processor p.

Since events at processor p (i.e., $\mathcal{E}_p$) are totally ordered, we can assign them index numbers. Given event e, let $index(e)$ be its index number in $\mathcal{E}_p$. Let $\mathcal{E}_p[i]$ be the first i events in $\mathcal{E}_p$. Let $\mathcal{E}_p[e] = \mathcal{E}_p[index(e)]$ (i.e., we use some shorthand).

Recall that a consistent cut c identifies a set of events (i.e., the observations) $(c_1, \ldots, c_M)$ at the M processors that are mutually concurrent. For shorthand, let us define $\mathcal{E}_p[c] = \mathcal{E}_p[c_p]$. Then, $\mathcal{E}_p[c]$ is a **history-oriented** view of a consistent cut.

We can define a consistent cut in this way. Let $Z = (z_1, \ldots, z_M)$ be a set of events at the M different processors. Then Z is a **consistent state** if for each $i = 1, \ldots, M$, if r is in $\mathcal{E}_i[Z]$ and r is the reception of message m from processor p_j, then s is in $\mathcal{E}_j[Z]$, where s is the sending of message m. Then, a consistent cut that the distributed snapshot algorithm can observe is one of the consistent states.

Given an execution $\mathcal{E}$, let $\mathcal{Z}$ be all of the consistent states that can be observed. Let $Z = (z_1, \ldots, z_M)$ and $Z' = (z'_1, \ldots, z'_M)$ be two consistent states in $\mathcal{Z}$.

Then $Z \leq_H Z'$ if

$$index(z_i) \leq \quad index(z'_i) \quad i = 1, \ldots, M$$

Further, Z' **immediately follows** Z if there is a j such that

$$index(z'_i) = \quad index(z_i) \quad i = 1, \ldots, M \text{ and } i \neq j$$
$$index(z'_j) = \quad index(z_j) + 1$$

The **execution DAG**, $\mathcal{G}(\mathcal{E})$ of execution $\mathcal{E}$, is built as follows. The vertex set V is the set of all consistent states $\mathcal{Z}(\mathcal{E})$. The (directed) edges E is the set of all pairs (Z_1, Z_2) such that Z_2 immediately follows Z_1.

For example, consider the execution $\mathcal{E}$ on processors p_1, p_2, and p_3 illustrated in Figure 9.12. The familiar happens-before description of the events in the execution is on the left-hand side, and the corresponding execution DAG is on the right-hand side. The events in the happens-before DAG are labeled by their index, and states in the execution DAG are labeled by the vector of the indices of the state of each processor. Notice the

FIGURE 9.12   Example of an execution DAG.

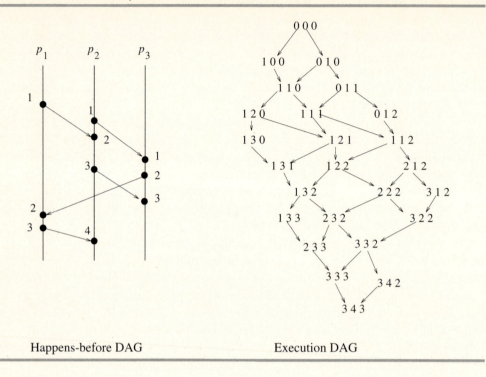

Happens-before DAG   Execution DAG

duality between the two representations of an execution. In the happens-before DAG, the vertices are the events, and the edges are the constraints on the order in which the events can occur. In the execution DAG, the vertices are the consistent states, while the edges are the events.

There is a great deal of similarity between the execution DAG in Figure 9.12 and the example of all possible executions of the double token protocol, in Figure 9.11. In both graphs, the vertices are states and the edges are events. Further, the subgraph of Figure 9.11 consisting of states $\{G_0, G_1, G_2, G_3\}$ can also represent an execution DAG. A given path through the protocol representation (i.e., a run) corresponds to an execution. That execution will contain a happens-before relationship that can be translated to an execution DAG. The execution DAG will be a subset of the protocol representation. However, the graph in Figure 9.11 represents all possible executions, and one state might contain events that never occur in a different state.

Another method for storing the H-DAG is to use a **direct dependence vector**. Let $e.DDV$ be the direct dependence vector attached to event e executed at p. Then $e.DDV[q]$ is the highest sequence number of a message sent from q that was received at p before e. It is easy to see that a set of events tagged with a direct dependence vector contains the same information that it does when the events are tagged with a vector timestamp (see the discussion in Section 13.7.3). But an advantage of direct dependence vectors is that only $O(1)$ space is needed to propagate timestamps (see the exercises in Chapter 13).

The definition of a consistent state is a vector that identifies which events have been executed at each processor. We can make use of this connection between events and states in the following definitions of causal history and causal cone. These ideas are useful in understanding algorithms and are used in Chapter 13 (on rollback and error recovery).

- **Causal history state:** Given event e at processor p_j, the **causal history state** of e, $CH(e)$, is the earliest consistent state containing e. More formally, let c be a consistent state, such that the last event in $\mathcal{E}_j(c)$ is e. For each $i = 1, \ldots, M$, $i \neq j$, let $k_i = index(c(i))$, and for each $i = 1, \ldots, M$, $i \neq j$, substitute $\mathcal{E}_i[k_i - 1]$ for $\mathcal{E}_i[k_i]$ in c to form c_i. Then $c = CH(e)$ if no c_i is a consistent state. For example, if e_h is the second event at processor 2 in Figure 9.12, then $CH(e_h) = (1\ 2\ 0)$. Note that the vector timestamp of an event is the index of its causal history.

- **Causal cone state:** Given event e at processor p_j, the **causal cone state** of e, $CC(e)$, is the earliest consistent state $c = CC(e)$ such that at every processor $j = 1, \ldots, M$, the causal history of c_j contains e. That is, $CC(e)$ is a lower bound on the set of all states such that all processors in the state know about event e. For example, if e_c is the first event at processor 2 in Figure 9.12, then $CC(e_c) = (2\ 1\ 2)$.

We can make similar definitions about the events in the causal cone and causal history of an event e. However, there is a subtlety. Notice that the causal cone for event e_c includes the second event at processor 3, but processor 3 learns of event e_c at its first event. We need to advance the number of events processed at p_3 to ensure that we get a consistent state. If we are interested in events, not states, our definitions are slightly different:

- **Causal history:** Given event e at processor p_j, the **causal history** of e, $ch(e)$, is the set of all events e' such that $e' \leq_H e$. Note that we can represent $ch(e)$ as a vector, in which case $ch(e) = CH(e)$.

- **Causal cone:** Given event e at processor p_j, the **causal cone** of e, $cc(e)$, is the set of all events e' such that $e \leq_H e'$. We can represent $cc(e)$ as a vector of event indices, one at each processor. Then, $cc(e)[j] = k_j$ if $e \in ch(\mathcal{E}_j(k_j))$, but $e \notin ch(\mathcal{E}_j(k_j - 1))$. For example, $cc(e_c) = (1\ 1\ 2)$.

9.4.2 Execution DAG Predicates

When we describe distributed algorithms, we often want to make statements like, "at most one processor is executing the critical section" or "the data are never inconsistent". These statements implicitly require a simultaneous observation of the state of every processor, that is, an observation of a global state. While we understand how to observe a global state, it is not clear how to evaluate a predicate (i.e., a formula that evaluates either true or false) on an execution. The problem is that there might be many vertex-disjoint paths between the source and the sink of an execution DAG (excluding the source and sink). In Figure 9.12, it is easy to find two such paths. We need to define in what sense a predicate can be true for an execution.

Let $G(\mathcal{E})$ be an execution DAG, and let $\Phi(g)$ be a predicate that can be evaluated on any state $g \in G(\mathcal{E})$. Let $Conc(g)$ be the set of all states $g' \in G(\mathcal{E})$ such that there is no path from g to g' or from g' to g (and also g). Then:

- $POSSIBLY(\Phi, G(\mathcal{E}))$ is true if there is a $g \in G(\mathcal{E})$ such that $\Phi(g)$ is true.
- $ALLPATH(\Phi, G(\mathcal{E}))$ is true if for every path P from the source to the sink of $G(\mathcal{E})$, there is a $g \in P$ such that $\Phi(g)$ is true.
- $DEFINITELY(\Phi, G(\mathcal{E}))$ is true if there is a $g \in \mathcal{E}$ such that $\Phi(g')$ is true for every $g' \in Conc(g)$.
- $ALWAYS(\Phi, G(\mathcal{E}))$ is true if $\Phi(g)$ is true for every $g \in G(\mathcal{E})$.

These four predicates (and other related predicates) are often used for **distributed debugging**. The predicates can be evaluated on-line or off-line. They can be used to set **distributed breakpoints**. These issues are explored in the exercises.

For an example, let us consider how we would phrase desirable properties of a mutual exclusion algorithm in terms of the execution DAG predicates. Suppose we want to determine if at most one processor entered the critical section at a time in execution $\mathcal{E}$. Then, make $\Phi_{mutex}(g)$ evaluate to true if zero or one processor is in the critical section. The predicate we need to evaluate is $ALWAYS(\Phi_{mutex}, G(\mathcal{E}))$. Suppose we want to ask if processor p_3 ever entered the critical section. Then, make Φ_3 evaluate to true if p_3 is in the critical section and evaluate $POSSIBLY(\Phi_3, G(\mathcal{E}))$. Note that we could also evaluate $DEFINITELY(\Phi_3, G(\mathcal{E}))$.

9.4.3 Summarizing Future Executions

When discussing the properties of a distributed protocol, we often want to make a statement along the lines of "Eventually, all processors converge". Such a statement is tied to notions of real time and therefore is not a precise statement of the property of a distributed algorithm. We need a way to describe the future state of a protocol given its current state.

Let r be a finite or infinite sequence of events, let $r[i]$ be the subsequence of r consisting of the first i events in r, and let $r(i)$ be the ith event in r (if $i > |r|$, then $r[i]$ and $r(i)$ are undefined). We define a **run** on initial state G_0 to be a finite or infinite sequence r such that for every $i = 1, \ldots, |r|$, $r(i)$ can occur in $compute(G_0, r[i-1])$. That is, r is a possible execution of a protocol starting in state G_0. We define $\mathcal{R}(G_0)$ to be the set of all possible runs on G_0.

We want to make a definition about the future properties of global states. The property must hold in any run that we deem permissible (for example, a property might eventually hold only if no new failures occur). This leads us to the following definitions.

- Property A is **eventually true** starting in state G_0 on runs with property Q:

$$eventually(A, G_0, Q) \quad \text{iff} \ \forall_{r \in \mathcal{R}(G_0)} \left(Q(r) \text{ is false, or } \exists_i A(compute(G_0, r[i])) \right)$$

- Property A is **always true** starting in state G_0 on runs with property Q:

$$always(A, G_0, Q) \quad \text{iff} \ \forall_{r \in \mathcal{R}(G_0)} \left(Q(r) \text{ is false, or } \forall_{i \leq |r|} A(compute(G_0, r[i])) \right)$$

The predicate $eventually(A, G_0, Q)$ means that in any future execution starting in state G_0, property A will hold in one of the states. The predicate $always(A, G_0, Q)$ is similar to the statement that A is a stable property. If A is stable, $A(G_0)$ implies $eventually(A, G_0, True)$. We note that the $eventually$ and $always$ predicates are often written as $\diamond$ and $\square$ in the literature. However, we prefer to make explicit the dependence on the run r having property Q for the statement to be meaningful.

We make use of these predicates to state temporal properties of protocols (whether formally or informally), especially in Chapters 10 and 12. For an example, suppose that we want to state that a protocol guarantees mutual exclusion. The execution DAG predicate is not appropriate, because the predicate must range over all possible executions. Instead, we use the $always$ predicate. We set G_0 to be an appropriate initial state (the protocol variables are initialized and no messages are in transit), and set Q to always evaluate to true. Our predicate is $always(\Phi_{mutex}, G_0, Q)$. Suppose we want to determine if p_3 is guaranteed to be able to enter the critical section. We set Q_3 to evaluate to true on runs in which p_3 requests the critical section and evaluate $eventually(\Phi_3, G_0, Q_3)$.

9.5 FAILURES IN A DISTRIBUTED SYSTEM

Reasoning about the correctness of distributed protocols is further complicated because one must often account for the possibility of failures. As one increases the number of components in a system, one increases the chance that at least one component has failed at any given time. In order to make a system robust, the distributed protocols must incorporate *fault tolerance*. To achieve this, we need an understanding of the types of failures that can occur. We divide the failures into two types: processor failures and network failures.

- **Processor failures**: A processor failure occurs when the processor acts in an unexpected manner. There are three fault models, in order of increasing difficulty.

  - **Fail-stop**: In the **fail-stop** model, either a processor is executing and can participate in a distributed protocol, or it has failed and will never respond to any requests. In addition, every working processor can detect the failed processor (presumably by a timeout mechanism), and no processor is incorrectly labeled as "failed".
  Many non fault-tolerant distributed protocols can be easily modified to handle some number of failed processors in a fail-stop model. Unfortunately, it is not a realistic

failure model. It depends on having a working processor that can always respond to a request within a predetermined amount of time. However, response times are in general unpredictable, so it is difficult to determine what timeout guarantees us that the nonresponding processor is actually failed.

- **Slowdown**: In the processor slowdown model, a processor might actually fail or it might execute slowly for a while. As a result, a processor might be incorrectly labeled as "failed". Since the "failed" processor doesn't know that it has failed, it can disrupt the distributed protocol when it tries to participate.

  It is generally difficult to write a distributed protocol that explicitly handles slowdown failures. However, it is possible to write algorithms that consistently track which processors are labeled as "failed" (and we discuss them in subsequent chapters), so a distributed protocol can be made fault tolerant by making use of these algorithms.

- **Byzantine**: In the Byzantine failure model (named for the Byzantine Generals problem, which we discuss later), a processor can fail, execute slowly for a while, or execute at the normal speed but actively try to make the computation fail. Therefore, every action made by the computation must be decided upon by a group of processors, since any single message might be corrupt.

  While algorithms to handle Byzantine failures exist (and are discussed in Chapter 11), they are extremely expensive to execute. As a result, the Byzantine failure model is often thought of as being unrealistic, and most pragmatic algorithms do not attempt to handle Byzantine failures. However, we are occasionally presented with evidence that Byzantine failures do occur. A recent example occurred when the telephone service to a large portion of the northeastern United States was cut off because a telephone switch began to send garbage requests.

- **Network Failures**: A network failure prevents processors from communicating with each other, even though the processors themselves are working properly. Networks are notoriously unreliable and often fail to deliver messages, or they deliver them out of order. We have already seen protocols that provide reliable links as long as some messages can be sent over a line. However, if a link fails entirely, it can cause new kinds of problems:

  - **One-way Links**: A network failure can cause an unusual topology to arise. For example, processor A might be able to send messages to processor B but not be able to receive messages from processor B. Processor C might be able to talk to both A and B. So, the processors can have an inconsistent view of which processors are labeled "failed". One-way links thus cause problems similar to those encountered due to processor slowdowns.

  - **Network Partitions**: A network partition occurs when one portion of the network is completely isolated from another. For example, processors A and B might be able to communicate with each other but not with processors C and D, while the reverse is true for processors C and D.

If processors A, B, C, and D are managing a piece or replicated data (a file, for example), A and B might perform update U1 on the data, and C and D might perform update U2 while the network is partitioned. When the partition is repaired, the data is inconsistent , and it is not clear how to make the data consistent again.

9.6 SUMMARY

This chapter is about understanding distributed computations. An analogy to consider is the debugging of a program. One can only debug a program if the semantics of each line of code are well understood. The difficulties encountered in the classical problems of concurrent process control can be seen as a problem in debugging concurrent processes – the value in a variable can change without any action by the process being debugged. Distributed computations are even harder to understand because the processes execute concurrently, and also because there is no (real) global state.

The first step to understanding a distributed computation is to understand the ordering of events. We can use *causality* to define a *partial order* on the events. We can *timestamp* the events in a way that expresses the partial order (*vector timestamps*) or in a way that expresses a total order consistent with the partial order (*Lamport timestamps*). The partial order on the events lets us model a distributed computation by using the *happens-before DAG*, or *H-DAG*. We can also keep track of the *causal history* of each event e, which is the set of events in the execution that can influence the processing of e. It turns out that a vector timestamp precisely expresses a causal history.

We can also try to model a distributed computation by observing *consistent cuts* (or *consistent states*), in which all observations are mutually concurrent. The collection of all possible consistent states is the *execution DAG*, or *E-DAG*. The H-DAG and E-DAG express the same information and are duals of each other.

The H-DAG and E-DAG models are *observational models*, which let us interpret what we have seen. A *predictive model* of a distributed computation views the set of processors as automata driven by well-defined state transitions. We can discuss *runs*, which are permissible executions. Then we can ask questions about the properties of runs. The set of all possible runs forms a lattice, and an E-DAG is a portion of this lattice.

There are other ways to model the execution of a distributed protocol, and the best model depends on the problem you are trying to solve. For example, the causal multicast algorithm considers that send events are important, while the rollback and recovery algorithms of Chapter 13 consider that receive events are important. The problem of assigning *sequence numbers* so that the important events of an execution can be reconstructed is an ongoing theme in this book.

ANNOTATED BIBLIOGRAPHY

The happens-before relation and Lamport timestamps are contained in the classic paper of Lamport [Lam78]. Vector timestamps are a common technique to precisely model the happens-before relation. Parker et al. [Par83] use *version vectors* to detect conflicting updates in a replicated file system. Fidge [Fid89] makes use of vector timestamps for parallel debugging. Gunaseelan and LeBlanc [GL93] show how to capture causality in a shared memory system. Good surveys of logical timestamps are [RS95, SM94a]. Charron-Bost [CB91] shows an execution with "good mixing" such that logical timestamps that capture causality require $O(M)$ space.

The causal message ordering algorithm in the text is based on the algorithm presented in by Schiper, Eggli and Sandoz [SES89]. The ISIS project uses vector timestamps to ensure causal multicast [BSS91]. Singhal and Kshemkalyani [SK92] show how to reduce the size of the vector timestamps attached to messages by sending only the modified fields of the timestamp. Meldal, Sankar, and Vera [MSV91] show how to reduce vector timestamp overhead by restricting communication patterns. Raynal, Schiper, and Toueg [RST91] give an algorithm for deadlock-free causal point-to-point communication. Soneoka and Ibaraki [SI94] define the "no message crossing" property, which is a point-to-point analog of totally ordered multicast and give an algorithm for enforcing the property. A technique for bounding the size of sequence numbers, based on a generalization of sliding windows, is given by Lloyd and Kearns [LK90].

The algorithm for distributed snapshots is due to Chandy and Lamport [CL85]. Groselj [Gro93] gives an algorithm for recording a shapshot with a bounded number of messages in each channel. A limitation of the Chandy and Lamport algorithm is that it depends on reliable FIFO communication channels. Lai and Yang [LY87] present a simple algorithm for taking a snapshot over non-FIFO channels by using piggyback information. After a processor p has taken a snapshot of its local state, it flags every message that it sends. If a processor q receives either a snapshot token or a flagged message, it records its local state also (see also [LRV87]). Spezialetti and Kearns [SK86] give an algorithm to disseminate the snapshot over the spanning tree it creates. These ideas are more elegantly captured by the *flush* primitives of Ahuja [Ahu90, Ahu91, Ahu93]. Mattern [Mat93] improves on the algorithm of Lai and Yang to efficiently capture messages in transit. Acharya and Badrinath [AB92] give an algorithm to record a snapshot using causal communications. This algorithm is improved on by Alagar and Venkatesan [AV94].

The discussion of consistent cuts is also primarily due to Chandy and Lamport [CL85]. The idea of a run appears in many works, notably that of Fischer, Lynch, and Paterson [FLP85]. Pratt [Pra86] discusses a mathematics of partial orders; the *eventually* and *always* predicates are adapted from this work. Mattern [Mat89] discusses some of the connections between models of distributed computations. Ahuja and Mishra [AM94] present a model of a distributed computation based on waves (consistent cuts in which all message channels are flushed) and wavefronts.

An alternative approach to proving the correctness of communicating protocols is the use of *I/O Automata*. I/O automata can be composed into larger automata, permitting hierarchical proofs. Unfortunately, this text does not have the space to devote to a discussion and use of I/O automata. We refer the interested reader to the book by Lynch, Merritt, Weihl, and Fekete [LMWF94]. We also refer the interested reader to the recent book by Lynch [Lyn96], which provides much more detail about proofs and proof techniques than this text has space for.

The *POSSIBLY* and *DEFINITELY* predicates were proposed by Cooper and Marzullo [CM91]. Venkatesan and Dathan [VD95] give algorithms to evaluate conjunctive form predicates on global states using the happens-before DAG. A related discussion is given by [GW94]. Several authors have given algorithms for setting global breakpoints based on evaluating global predicates [MI92, HW88, MC88, SG94b]. Garg and Chase [GC95] give fully distributed algorithms for detecting conjunctive predicates. Frometin, Jard, Jourdan, and Raynal [FJJR95] show how to compute global predicates that are accepting states of finite state automata (see also [JJJR94]). Chase and Garg [CG95] show that general predicate detection is NP-complete, and propose algorithms for efficient detection of linear predicates. Chiou and Korfhage [CK94] give a distributed algorithm for detecting composable global predicates. Spezialetti and Kearns [SK89] propose *simultaneous regions*, a technique for numbering periods of execution on processors that makes the reconstruction of simultaneous states easy after the execution is finished. Fromentin and Raynal [FR95] define inevitable global states and give an algorithm for finding them.

Instant replay debugging records the information about the happens-before DAG of an execution to permit a precise re-execution [CW82]. Netzer and Miller [NM92] show how the information required for a replay can be minimized by only collecting ordering information for race conditions. Wang [Wan95] gives algorithms to find consistent checkpoints from uncoordinated checkpoints near a desired point in an execution.

A good discussion of the types of failures in a distributed system can be found in [BMD93, Cri91c]. Liskov [Lis91] shows that synchronized clocks can often be used to improve the performance of distributed algorithm. One trick is to use "leases", which are granted to the last processor that touches an object and last for X seconds or until revoked. For example, leases can reduce cache invalidation traffic and can permit optimistic reads from the primary copy of replicated data.

EXERCISES

1. Why must the happens-before graph be acyclic?
2. Suppose that you implement causal communication on point-to-point communications using the algorithm listed in Section 9.2.3. Show an example of how deadlock can occur.
3. Modify the above algorithm for causal communications to use Lamport timestamps. Your algorithm should implement a totally ordered multicast.
4. Write a deadlock-free protocol that implements causal point-to-point communication using one message per unicast. *Hint*: Have each processor record the number of messages it has sent to every other processor, and use that information instead of the usual vector timestamp.
5. When processor p sends its vector timestamp to processor q, a great deal of redundant information might be sent, since many of the entries in the timestamp might have the same value as in the previous message sent to q. Write an algorithm that sends only compressed timestamps. You may use $O(M^2)$ space per processor.

6. Write an algorithm that sends compressed timestamps and uses $O(M)$ space per processor. *Hint*: You can track the times when the vector timestamp is updated or distributed by using the local clock.

7. Write an algorithm to use compressed timestamps for causal multicast.

8. Let us consider an application of causality to shared memory multiprocessor programs. A multiprocessor system contains a number of parallel threads, $t_1, t_2, \ldots, t_M$, that access shared variables $x_1, x_2, \ldots, x_n$. A *race condition* occurs if two threads access the same shared variable concurrently. If we assume sequential consistency, shared variables are accessed sequentially (although different shared variables are accessed in parallel), so "concurrent" access means that neither thread's access causally follows the other (just like the distributed system definition of causality).

    Write an algorithm to perform race condition detection in a shared memory multiprocessor on the fly (i.e., while the program executes). You should write a routine that executes on every shared variable access. That is, write routines to replace the read(x) and write(x) functions. Each shared variable will need to store information in addition to the value of the shared variable in order to detect the race conditions. The threads will need to communicate their timestamps to the shared variables and possibly update their timestamps after an access.

9. In a non-FIFO message channel $C_{p,q}$, if $m1$ is sent from p to q before $m2$, it is possible that $m2$ arrives at q before $m1$. A *flush* message m_f on a non-FIFO channel will have the following properties:

    a. If m_f is sent from p after m, then m_f will be delivered to q after m.
    b. If m_f is sent from p before m, then m_f will be delivered to q before m.
    Write an algorithm to implement flush messages.

10. A *backward flush* message is a message m_f over a non-FIFO channel that has only property **b** in Exercise 9 of flush messages. Write an algorithm to collect a consistent snapshot of processor states only (not channel states) using backward flush messages.

11. Write an algorithm to collect a snapshot of processor states only using non-FIFO (i.e., UDP) communications.

12. Suppose that a set of processors communicates using causal multicast only. Give an algorithm to collect a distributed snapshot of only the processor states.

13. Suppose that a set of processors communicates using causal multicast only. Give an algorithm to collect a distributed snapshot of both processor and channel states. *Hint*: Integrate the snapshot algorithm with the causal message delivery algorithm.

14. Prove Theorem 1 of Section 9.4.

15. In Theorem 1, what restrictions can you place on the permutation seq' such that the theorem still holds?

16. Give an algorithm to convert a happens-before DAG into an execution DAG.

17. Give an algorithm to convert an execution DAG into a happens-before DAG (you may assume that messages are delivered in FIFO order).

18. Give an algorithm that takes as input a happens-before DAG and an event e and returns $Conc(e)$.

19. Give an algorithm that takes as input an execution DAG and an event e and returns $Conc(e)$.

20. Give an algorithm that takes as input an execution DAG and a state g and returns $Conc(g)$.

21. Suppose that processors $p_1, \ldots, p_M$ execute a *deterministic* protocol, in the sense that their actions depend only on their initial input and the messages they receive. An *instant-replay debugger* records the message exchanges of an execution of a protocol and permits an exact replay of an execution $\mathcal{E}$. Give an algorithm for an instant replay debugger in which each processor stores only local information, and all messages are sent over reliable FIFO channels. What are the storage requirements of your algorithm?

22. Show that given an execution $\mathcal{E}$, evaluating $POSSIBLY(\Phi)$ is NP-complete, for an arbitrary Φ.

23. A *conjunctive form predicate* is a predicate $\Phi = \Phi_1 \wedge \cdots \wedge \Phi_M$, where Φ_p is evaluated using information about the state of processor p only. Let $G(\mathcal{E})$ be an execution DAG, and let us define $FIRST(\Phi, G(\mathcal{E}))$ to be the first state $g \in G(\mathcal{E})$ such that $\Phi(G)$ is true. Show that if Φ is a conjunctive form predicate, $FIRST(\Phi, G(\mathcal{E}))$ is well defined.

24. A *spectrum*, S_p, is a consecutive set of events on processor p.
    a. Spectrum S_1 *strongly precedes* spectrum S_2 if the last event in S_1 precedes the first event in S_2. Give an algorithm to determine if S_1 strongly precedes S_2.
    b. Spectrum S_1 *weakly precedes* spectrum S_2 if the first event in S_1 precedes the last event in S_2. Give an algorithm to determine if S_1 weakly precedes S_2.

25. The *projection* of spectrum S_p onto S_q is the set of events in S_q that can occur concurrently with an event in S_p.
    a. Show that the projection is also a spectrum.
    b. Write an algorithm that, given S_p, S_q, and the happens-before DAG of an execution, computes the projection of S_p on S_q.
    c. Let Φ be a conjunctive form predicate that evaluates to true on spectrum S_p on processor p. Write an algorithm that computes $POSSIBLY(\Phi, G(\mathcal{E}))$.

26. (Programming project) A *stateless* server does not maintain a connection to a client (NFS, for example). The client requests service by sending a message to the server. The server executes the requests and sends back a response. The request or the response might get lost. Both cases look the same to the client — it doesn't get an answer. If the client does not receive an answer within a timeout period, it reissues the request. Since the commands (read, write) are *idempotent*, reexecuting the request doesn't cause a problem.

    Some servers must remember the state of the client (for example, a lock server). Executing a request twice can have very bad results. For example, suppose a client requests a lock on file F. The server grants the lock, but the response is lost. The client times out and reissues the request. The server responds with a message saying that the file is currently locked. Now, the file is permanently blocked because the client will never send the unlock command.

    An exactly-once service [PS88] will ensure that a client's request is executed at most once and is executed at least once if the client does not fail. Implement an exactly-once service.

Algorithm: To implement exactly-once service, the server must remember the states of the clients. In particular, the server must remember the last request that the client made.

At every processor where a client for the service can reside, the processor assigns to each client a unique number. Each client numbers its requests to a server sequentially, starting at 0. Finally, each processor has an *incarnation number*, which is incremented after every restart (and must be recorded on stable storage). With every request for service, a client attaches the triple (incarnation number, client number, request number).

When a server receives a request from processor P, numbered with the triple (I, C, R), it searches the *client table* table to see if it has ever received a request from processor P, incarnation I, client C before. If not, the client is new, so the server adds an entry to the client table, tagged with the triple (P, I, C). Otherwise, the server takes one of the following three actions.

Let the last request sent by (P, I, C) be request number r.

a. If $R < r$, ignore the request.

b. If $R = r$, send the stored response to the client.

c. If $R > r$, perform the service, record the response in the client table, update the response number in the client table and send the response to the client.

In a real implementation, the server needs to be able to garbage-collect the client table. We will return to that issue later. The server should log updates to the client table so that it does not reexecute a request after a crash. However, handling this issue is complex. Proper implementation of logging is not necessary for this assignment.

Assignment: Write a server that performs the following service:

a. Maintains a five letter string, initially all blank.

b. Accepts a call from a client. The client passes in a character. The first four letters from the string are appended to the letter from the client, which becomes the new string. The new string is returned to the client.

For example, suppose that the server's string is "xyzwv". The client calls the server and passes in 'a'. The new string is "axyzw", and this is returned to the client. The idea behind this service to be simple and nonidempotent.

The client and server should communicate through sockets using UDP. The server should simulate failures. On one-third of the requests, the server should drop the request without performing the request. On one-third of the requests, the server should perform the request and then drop the response. You should be able to simulate the failure of the client's machine. Log what is happening onto the screen (both at the client and at the server).

Before a client can make a request, it must establish a connection to the server. The client should send requests until it gets a response. Don't worry about deleting connections for this project. The server should implement exactly-once semantics. You don't need to worry about server failures or about cleaning up the tables.

CHAPTER

10

Synchronization and Election

In this chapter, we present the basic distributed protocols of synchronization and election. These protocols are concerned with picking a unique processor that will perform an action, a fundamental type of distributed coordination. Distributed mutual exclusion algorithms are required for the implementation of transaction processing on replicated data and to ensure consistency in distributed shared memory. Election algorithms appear wherever a protocol coordinator might be useful (for example, in replicated data management, atomic commit, process monitoring, and recovery coordination). In this chapter, we will be concerned with the specification of practical algorithms. In Chapter 11, we will revisit the topic in the more general context of **distributed agreement algorithms** and examine the possibility or impossibility of distributed agreement under different failure models.

10.1 DISTRIBUTED MUTUAL EXCLUSION

In this section, we will examine several algorithms for distributed mutual exclusion. Mutual exclusion is necessary for activities such as accessing shared data and coordinating a distributed program. In addition, a study of mutual exclusion algorithms provides an opportunity to study distributed algorithm design techniques. The algorithms in this section are difficult to make fault tolerant, except in a limited sense (an exception is voting). Hence, we assume that no failures occur. The exercises explore isuses related to failure recovery.

10.1.1 Timestamp Algorithms

The timestamp-based algorithms make use of Lamport timestamps to ensure fair access to to the critical section. The idea is as follows: Suppose you want to enter the critical section (CS). You look at your watch and record the time when you request entry into the critical section. Then you ask everyone else if you are allowed to enter the critical section. A remote processor, Bob, will agree that you should enter the CS if you made your request earlier than Bob made his request (or if Bob is not requesting the critical section). Otherwise, Bob will deny your request. If everyone agrees with your request, you can enter. The protocol will work because there is a method by which the priority of the requests can be globally ranked. That way, there is always a processor that gets permission from the others to enter the critical section, and this processor will deny permission to all others.

The Lamport timestamp serves as the global clock. Since it is a total order, there is a global ranking among all processors that have requested the critical section. Since it is causal, a processor that hasn't requested the critical section is ranked lower than a processor that has. When you ask permission from a processor, Jane, that hasn't made a request, the receipt of your request advances Jane's clock. Therefore, Jane's future request is ranked lower than your current request.

One way to translate the intuitive algorithm into a protocol is to have each processor announce its desire to enter the critical section. Every other processor must reply, to flush out concurrent requests. These replies carry the timestamp at which the replier requested the critical section or a null value if the replier is not waiting for or using the critical section. When a processor exits the critical section, it informs every other processor. By examining this information, every processor can construct the same priority queue of processors waiting to enter the critical section. When a processor finds that it is at the head of the priority queue, it knows that no other processor will think that it is at the head of the priority queue, so it is safe to enter the critical section.

ALGORITHM LISTING 10.1

Variables used by Ricart and Agrawala's algorithm.

timestamp	current_time	The current Lamport time.
timestamp	my_timestamp	The timestamp of your request.
integer	reply_count	The number of permissions that you still need to collect before entering the CS.
boolean	is_requesting	True iff the you are requesting or using the CS.
boolean	reply_deferred[M]	reply_deferred[j] is true iff you have deferred replying to processor j's request.

A short consideration of the algorithm dynamics shows that the "priority queue" algorithm is inefficient, since we are distributing more information than is really necessary. Suppose that processor p sends its request to processor q. Processor p will be blocked at least until q's reply. If q has a higher-priority request than p, p will be further blocked until q releases the critical section. Processor q knows the relative priority of the requests; therefore one round of communication is redundant.

A two-round algorithm executes as follows: When a processor wants to enter the critical section, it records the current timestamp and sends a request to every other processor. When a processor receives a request that it should grant, it sends a reply to the requester. When a processor receives a request that is later than its own, it will deny the request. There is no need to send an explicit message stating that the request was denied; the processor only needs to delay sending a reply to the requester. When a processor has received replies to all of its requests, it knows that its request is earlier than everyone else's, so it enters the critical section. Upon leaving the critical section, it sends all of the replies that it deferred, since its next request will be later than any requester's.

The protocol that we have described is due to Ricart and Agrawala. The details of the algorithm are the accounting of the state of the protocol. The algorithm uses the variables shown in Algorithm Listing 10.1 (recall that M is the number of processors).

The algorithm for requesting the token is shown in Algorithm Listing 10.2. A critical section monitor, shown in Algorithm Listing 10.3, is responsible for handling the

ALGORITHM LISTING 10.2

Algorithm for requesting the critical section.

```
Request_CS()
    my_timestamp=current_timestamp
    is_requesting=TRUE
    reply_pending=M-1
    for every other processor j,
        send(j,REMOTE_REQUEST; my_timestamp)
    wait until reply_pending is 0
```

ALGORITHM LISTING 10.3

Algorithm for the critical section monitoring thread.

```
CS_Monitor()
    Wait until a REMOTE_REQUEST or a REPLY message is received
        REMOTE_REQUEST (sender; request_time) :
            let j be the sender of the REMOTE_REQUEST message.
            if(not is_requesting or my_timestamp>request_timestamp)
                send(j,REPLY)
            else
                reply_deferred[j]=TRUE
        REPLY (sender) :
            reply_pending=reply_pending-1
```

REMOTE_REQUEST messages. This monitor also handles REPLY messages generated from other processors.

To release the critical section, the processor processes all of its deferred replies. This algorithm is shown in Algorithm Listing 10.4.

Because a processor that wants to enter the critical section must contact every other processor, this algorithm requires $2(M-1)$ messages. Many other authors have made modifications and improvements to this basic scheme (some of which we explore in the exercises; see also Section 4.5), but all of the algorithms have an $O(M)$ message complexity. However, the algorithm has an elegant simplicity, and we can draw a distributed algorithm design lesson from it.

- **Symmetric information:** In a protocol that uses **symmetric information**, every processor receives the same information. If one processor makes a decision, it knows that every other processor will make the same decision. Therefore, the processor can make assumptions about the actions at the other processors, which can lead to a simpler or more efficient protocol.

    In the example of the Ricart and Agrawala algorithm, the symmetric information makes the algorithm simpler if not more efficient. If a processor j does not reply to your request, it is because j's request is earlier than your own. If j withheld its reply

ALGORITHM LISTING 10.4

Algorithm for releasing the critical section.

```
Release_CS()
    is_requesting=FALSE
    for j= 1 through M
        if reply_deferred[j] = TRUE
            send(j,REPLY)
            reply_deferred[j]=FALSE
```

because of information you didn't know about, you would be compelled to investigate further, requiring a more complex protocol (as we will see in the next section). Further, you are certain to reply to j's request so that j will enter the CS.

10.1.2 Voting

A different approach to distributed synchronization is to let the processors that want to enter the critical section compete for votes, in analogy to candidates for public office. Whenever you want to enter the critical section, you ask every other processor for its vote (which it can give to at most one processor). If you know that you have received more votes than any other processor, you can enter the critical section. If you don't receive enough votes, you must wait until the processor that is in the critical section exits, releasing its votes for other contenders.

In political elections, the results are publically announced so that the winners and losers know who they are. In a distributed system, that means that every vote must be broadcast to every other processor. To reduce the message complexity, votes are usually not broadcast. Instead, a candidate is told by the voter whether or not the candidate got the voter's vote. A candidate can be assured that it has won the election if it has received more than half of the votes. (Why?) A simple algorithm for voting-based synchronization is shown in Algorithm Listing 10.5.

An advantage of the naive voting protocol is its high degree of fault tolerance. Fully half of the processors must fail before the lock becomes unobtainable (unless the lock holder fails). However, there are two problems with the simple voting protocol. First, it is susceptible to deadlock (for example, three processors might each get about one-third of the votes). The protocol that we will examine in detail contains code to handle this type of deadlock. Second, the voting algorithm does not give us a substantial performance advantage over the timestamp-based algorithms, since it requires $O(M)$ messages per critical section entry.

We can observe that some votes are more important than others. If two candidates are competing for the election among $M = 2m + 1$ processors and both candidates have already received m votes, the vote of the last processor decides the election. The two candidates did not really need to obtain the votes of the $2m$ processors, it was only the vote of the last processor that mattered.

In a tight political election, a small special interest group can decide the election by casting its votes for a particular candidate. For this reason, politicians often spend

ALGORITHM LISTING 10.5

Naive voting algorithm.

```
Naive_Voting_Enter_CS()
    Send a vote request to all of the processors.
    When you receive at least ⌈(M + 1)/2⌉ votes,
        enter the critical section.
```

inordinate amounts of time catering to the special interests who cast swing votes. We can apply this lesson to distributed synchronization. Instead of asking the mass of processors for their vote, a candidate needs only to campaign among the **swing voters**.

Every processor p has a voting district S_p. The set $\{S_1, \ldots, S_M\}$ is called a **coterie**. Some voting algorithms allow S_p to be constructed dynamically, but for this discussion we will assume that S_p is fixed and that processor p must acquire the votes of all processors in S_p in order to enter the critical section.

The candidates' voting districts need to be carefully gerrymandered. First, the S_p should actually be a set of swing voters. That is,

Intersection Rule: $S_i \cap S_j \neq \emptyset$ for $1 \leq i, j \leq M$.

To be fair, every voting district should be of about the same size, and every processor should be in about the same number of voting districts. That is, $|S_i| = K$, and every processor is in D voting districts.

Maekawa considered the problem of how small one can make D and K and still preserve the fairness and intersection properties. A candidate's voting district contains K voters, each of which can be members of at most $D - 1$ other voting districts. So the maximum number of voting districts that can be constructed is $M = (D - 1)K + 1$ (i.e., there can be $(D - 1)K$ other voting districts, plus this voting district). Given M, K, and D, we can observe that the maximum number of voting districts is DM/K, since each processor can be in D districts, but each district requires K voters. If we use as many processors as voting districts, we find that $M = DM/K$, or that $D = K$. So,

$$
\begin{aligned}
M &= K(K - 1) + 1 \\
K &= O(\sqrt{M})
\end{aligned}
$$

Gerrymandering to achieve $M = K(K-1)+1$ is difficult (Maekawa presents a solution based on finite projective planes). Fortunately, it is easy to achieve $K = O(\sqrt{M})$. Let $M = n^2$, and label the processors (i, j) for $1 \leq i, j \leq n$. Then the voting district for the processor labeled (r, s) is $(\bigcup_{1 \leq i \leq n}(i, s)) \cup (\bigcup_{1 \leq j \leq n}(r, j))$. Figure 10.1 shows S_{14} in a 36 processor system. There are many other ways to organize voting districts, some of which are explored in the exercises. But, all algorithms of this type are essentially the same as Maekawa's algorithm.

The general voting algorithm is similar to the naive voting algorithm. When a processor wishes to enter the critical section, it sends a vote request to every member of its voting district. When the processor receives replies from all the members of the district, it can enter the critical section. When a processor receives a vote request, it responds with a "Yes" vote if it hasn't already cast its vote. When a processor exits the critical section, it informs its voting district, which can then vote for other candidates.

The above protocol is susceptible to deadlock. We present a mechanism for automatically resolving deadlocks that is attributed to Sanders. When a processor makes a request, it assigns a (Lamport) timestamp to the request. The voters will prefer to vote for the earliest candidates. If a processor V has cast its ballot for processor B and then processor

FIGURE 10.1   A *O(sqrt(M))* voting district.

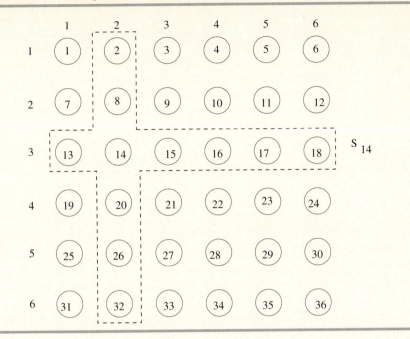

C, which has an earlier timestamp than B's, asks for V's vote, V will try to retrieve its vote from B with an INQUIRE message. If B has not yet received all the votes of its voting district, it will relinquish V's vote, which can then be given to C. Lamport timestamps impose a total order, so either the candidate with the lowest timestamp eventually gets all of the votes or the candidate with the lowest timestamp is blocked by a candidate that enters the critical section. In either case, some candidate enters the critical section, so deadlock is avoided.

There is one point at which we need to match up the messages with protocol invocations. Because the INQUIRE messages are generated by the voters asynchronously, a candidate might receive an INQUIRE message that was generated in response to a previous critical section request. The usual method for preventing ambiguous messages is to use sequence numbers. Since the candidate samples a timestamp for the algorithm, we use the timestamp as a sequence number to match INQUIRE messages with critical section requests.

The voting protocol uses the variables shown in Algorithm Listing 10.6, with a private set stored at each processor. The protocol for requesting entry to the critical section takes the actions we have described. The algorithm shown in Algorithm Listing 10.7 is straightforward, but the accounting needed to keep track of votes makes the protocol look complex.

The code to release the critical section sends a RELEASE message to all members of the processor's voting district and sets Incs to False (we don't show it to save space). Every processor runs a "voter" thread, which casts votes on the behalf of the processor. Note

ALGORITHM LISTING 10.6

Variables used for the voting based critical section algorithm.

S_{self}	The processor voting district.
LTS	The systemwide (Lamport) timestamp.
my_TS	The timestamp of your current critical section request.
yes_votes	The number of processors that voted "Yes".
have_voted	True iff you have already voted for a candidate (initially false).
candidate	The candidate that you voted for.
candidate_TS	The timestamp of the candidate that you voted for.
have_inquired	True if you have tried to recall a vote (initially false).
WaitingQ	The set of vote requests that you are deferring.

that this procedure never terminates, since it must always be available to cast votes. The code for a voter is shown in Algorithm Listing 10.8.

Figure 10.2 illustrates an example execution. Processors A, B, and C all decide to enter the critical section at roughly the same time. The request_TS of A, B, and C is 3, 5, and 7, respectively. First, let us suppose that C's request arrives at processors c, e, and f first. All of these processors will respond with a YES message, so C will enter the critical section. When processor A's REQUEST message arrives at e, e will attempt to retrieve its vote from C. Since C has entered the critical section, C will not relinquish e's vote until it exits the critical section. Therefore, A does not receive a YES vote from e until after C exits the critical section. Next, let us suppose that B's REQUEST message arrives at c before C's REQUEST. Then, C will not have received all of its votes when it receives an inquire message from e, so C will relinquish e's vote. Processor e will then send a YES vote to A. The processor that will be granted permission to enter the critical section is now the one (A or B) that delivered its REQUEST to b first.

ALGORITHM LISTING 10.7

Algorithm for requesting the critical section.

```
M_Voting_Entry()
    my_TS = LTS
    for every processor r in S_self,
        send(r,REQUEST; my_ts)

    while(yes_votes< |S_self|)
        Wait until a YES, NO, or INQUIRE message is received
        YES (sender) :
            yes_votes++
        INQUIRE (sender,inquire_TS) :
            if my_TS = inquire_TS)
                send(sender,RELINQUISH)
```

ALGORITHM LISTING 10.8

Algorithm executed by the thread that monitors the critical section.

```
M_Voter()
    while(1)
        Wait until a REQUEST, RELEASE, or RELINQUISH message is received.
        REQUEST (sender; request_ts):
            if have_voted is False
                send(sender,YES)
                candidate_TS=request_ts
                candidate=sender
                have_voted = True
            else
                add (sender, request_ts) to WaitingQ.
                if request_ts < candidate_TS and not have_inquired
                    send(candidate,INQUIRE; candidate_ts)
                    have_inquired=True
        RELINQUISH (sender):
            add (candidate, candidate_TS) to WaitingQ.
            remove the (s,rts) from WaitingQ such that rts is the minimum
            send(s,YES)
            candidate_TS=rts
            candidate=s
            have_inquired=False
        RELEASE (sender) :
            if WaitingQ is not empty
                remove the (s,rts) from WaitingQ such that rts is the minimum
                send(s,YES)
                candidate_TS=rts
                candidate=s
            else
                have_voted=False
            have_inquired=False
```

FIGURE 10.2   Voting example.

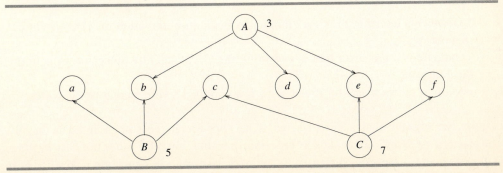

Maekawa's algorithm has two interesting aspects:

- **Voting:** Political bodies use voting so that their disparate components can come to a common decision. Distributed algorithms often make use of voting for the same reason. There are many ways in which an electorate can vote for a preferred candidate, majority voting being just one of the methods. In Maekawa's algorithm, we see that by manipulating the voting districts, processors can win elections with only a few well-chosen votes. The voting districts described by Maekawa are only one of many possible schemes, which possess various benefits. These schemes are explored in the exercises.

- **Handling deadlock:** In most voting schemes, processors must cast their votes before hearing about all possible candidates. So, a processor might cast the "wrong" vote. If the system can agree on the winner, casting the wrong vote does not cause a problem. If no candidate wins, the deadlock must be resolved. Political bodies can use pluralities instead of majorities or can use run-off elections. However, this can require a great deal of communication. We can instead rank the candidates on a total order (using Lamport timestamps). If a voter finds that it has cast the wrong vote, it can try to withdraw the vote. The total order guarantees that there is a winner eventually.

  We note that there is a simple alternative to handling deadlocks that is based on timeouts. If a processor does not acquire the lock within a timeout period, it releases the votes it holds and rerequests the lock. Typically, the timeout period and the time before rerequesting the lock are randomly chosen, to avoid livelock. A timeout-based deadlock resolution algorithm is simple and robust in actual implementation (e.g., resolving deadlock among heterogeneous software components) and so is often used in practice. However, it makes no guarantees, is difficult to analyze, and can require a careful choice of timeout periods.

Correctness

As the simple examples and Figure 10.2 have shown, determining exactly who will win an election has some subtleties. In this section, we present some machinery for proving that the voting algorithm is correct. As a side benefit, we can practice the use of the concepts presented in the previous chapter. We start with a few definitions.

- All statements referring to "time" implicitly mean an observation of a consistent cut or a global state.
- A **candidate** is a processor that is executing the M_Voting_Entry procedure or is in the critical section.
- Processor p *casts its vote* for processor q if q counts p's vote among its YES votes.

First, we observe that a processor casts its vote for at most one candidate in any consistent state. Why? Let us look at processor p's vote. Initially, p has not cast its vote. If no candidate q has p's vote, p can send a YES message to candidate r. But then, p has still cast its vote for at most one candidate. Processor p will cast another vote only after receiving a RELEASE or a RELINQUISH message from r. But then, there is a causally preceding event e' in which r loses p's vote. So, p will only send a YES vote if it exists in a consistent state in which no processor has its vote.

Second, we observe that the protocol ensures mutual exclusion. Why? Every pair of voting districts intersect. A processor must obtain all the votes in its voting district before entering the critical section. When a processor obtains all of its votes, it enters the critical section and does not release any votes until after it exits the critical section. We know that in any consistent cut, a processor will cast its vote for at most one candidate. So, in any consistent cut there can be at most one processor in the critical section.

Finally, we show that the algorithm always makes progress. That is, if G_0 is a global state such that candidates exist, but no processor is currently in the critical section, Q is the property that no failures occur and all messages are delivered during the run, and A is the property that a processor is in the critical section. Then $eventually(A, G_0, Q)$ (recall the definition of $eventually$ from Section 9.4.3).

Let r be an admissible run (i.e., no failures occur), and let $r[i]$ be the first i events in r. Let G_i be $compute(G_0, r[i])$. Let us assume for contradiction that no processor ever enters the critical section in any G_i. Eventually, the system is quiescent, since only a finite number of processors can become candidates (perhaps all of the processors become candidates or perhaps only a subset), and declaring a candidacy creates only a finite number of messages.

Let G_f be a quiescent system state. If candidate A is requesting a vote from voter v, and v has cast its vote for candidate B, we say that A is blocked by B through v. Let A be the candidate with the lowest timestamp in G_f. Since A is not entering the critical section, A must be blocked by another candidate B through voter v. Voter v must have received B's request before A's request. Because A's request has the lowest timestamp, v must have sent an INQUIRE message to B. Since B did not respond, B must be in the critical section. Since no processor is in the critical section in G_0, B must have entered the critical section during r. This contradicts our assumption that no processor entered the critical section during the execution of r. Therefore such a run cannot exist.

10.1.3 Fixed Logical Structure

A completely different approach to synchronization is to circulate a token among the processors. The token represents the synchronization permission. If a processor possesses the token, it is allowed to enter the critical section. The token must be able to reach every processor that participates in the synchronization in a reasonable time after a processor desires the token. One method for ensuring that the token can reach every processor is to impose a logical structure on the processors and require that the token follow the logical structure as it travels from processor to processor.

A simple logical structure is a ring with a circulating token. If a processor holds the token, it is allowed to enter the critical section. Afterward it passes the token along to the next processor in the ring. If a processor receives the token and does not wish to enter the critical section, it passes the token along immediately.

If the processors often want to enter the critical section when the token arrives, a token circulating in a ring is an efficient synchronization algorithm. Otherwise, the token can be passed considerably more than M times before a processor enters the CS. For this reason, we will look for a more efficient fixed logical structure algorithm. We note that if the critical section represents the permission to broadcast over a LAN, the problem of excessive token passing disappears (since the network is idle anyway). Several popular LAN access algorithms are based on Token Ring or Token Bus, and they have good performance, especially under a heavy load.

In order to reduce the number of messages that are passed, we want to impose a hierarchical structure on the processors. In particular, we can impose a tree structure on them. We next need to solve two problems: how to let a request navigate to the token and how to let the token navigate to the next processor to enter the CS.

Let us consider the situation of a processor that wants to issue a request for the token. It needs to determine to which of its neighbors it should send its request. In a tree, there is a unique path between any pair of processors. Therefore, there is only one neighbor that lies on a path to the token holder, and the request should be sent to that neighbor. This property holds true for every processor (the token holder sends a request to itself). To take advantage of this property, every processor stores a pointer current_dir, which holds the name of the neighbor that is closest to the token. If we think of this set of pointers as a directed graph, the set of processors forms a tree rooted at the token holder. This structure is illustrated in Figure 10.3.

When a processor requests permission to enter the CS, it sends a request in the direction of current_dir. When a processor (that doesn't hold the token) receives a request to enter the CS, it forwards the request in the direction of current_dir if it has not done so already. If the processor has already asked for the token, asking for the token again is not necessary since the token will arrive eventually. The processors on the path from the requester to the token must record a return path for the token. A processor that receives a

FIGURE 10.3 Tree structure.

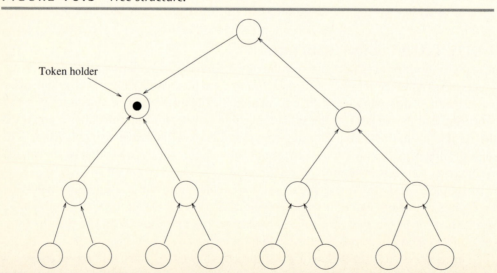

ALGORITHM LISTING 10.9

Variables used by the fixed structure algorithm.

Token_hldr	True iff the processor holds the token.
lncs	True iff the processor is using the critical section.
current_dir	The neighbor that is the root of the subtree that holds the token.
requestQ	A FIFO that stores the names of the neighboring processors.

request puts the request into a FIFO queue. Note that the heads of the FIFO queues define the return path.

When a processor releases the token, it checks to see if there are any pending requests for the token. These requests will be stored in the FIFO queue. If there is a pending request, the token is sent to the neighbor at the head of the FIFO. If there is another request in the FIFO, the processor sends off a request to satisfy the remaining pending request.

Every processor has the private storage shown in Algorithm Listing 10.9. In addition, every processor uses the operations on requestQ shown in Algorithm Listing 10.10.

The protocol consists of the following procedures. The request and release of the token are accomplished by executing the algorithms in Algorithm Listing 10.11. In addition, each processor executes a thread that responds to REQUEST and TOKEN messages. The thread's algorithm is shown in Algorithm Listing 10.12.

Figure 10.4 (on p.371) illustrates the execution of the fixed logical structure algorithm. When processor D requests the token, it places itself in requestQ$_D$ and forwards its request to B. When B receives the request, it stores D in requestQ$_B$ and forwards the request to A. Processor A takes a similar action. Note that A does not record the fact that D issues the request, only the fact that the request came from the direction of B. When C's request arrives at B, it is stored in requestQ$_B$. Since a request has already been issued, there is no need to send another request to A. Note that the return path for the token is stored in the heads of the requestQs. The final detail to note is that when B sends the token to D, it must follow up with another request, to ensure that C will eventually receive the token.

Raymond's algorithm (presented in this section) requires a very low message passing overhead, which is guaranteed to be $O(\log n)$ per critical section entry if the processors are organized into a d-ary tree. In addition, each processor needs to store at most $O(\log n)$ bits, because it needs to keep track of $O(1)$ neighbors. An interesting aspect of Raymond's algorithm is that as the demand for the critical section increases, the work required to

ALGORITHM LISTING 10.10

Operations on requestQ.

Nq(neighbor)	Add neighbor to requestQ.
Dq()	Remove and return the name at the head of requestQ.
ismt()	Returns True iff requestQ is empty.

ALGORITHM LISTING 10.11

Algorithms for requesting and releasing the critical section.

```
Request_CS()
    if not Token_hldr
        if ismt()
            send(current_dir, REQUEST)
        Nq(self)
        wait until Token_hldr is True
    Incs = True
Release_CS()
    Incs = False
    if not ismt()
        current_dir = Dq()
        send(current_dir,TOKEN)
        Token_hldr = False
        if not ismt()
            send(current_dir, REQUEST)
```

ALGORITHM LISTING 10.12

Algorithm executed by the thread monitoring the critical section.

```
Monitor_CS()
    while (True)
        wait for a REQUEST or a TOKEN message.
        REQUEST:
            if Token_hldr
                if Incs
                    Nq(sender)
                else
                    current_dir = sender
                    send(curent_dir,TOKEN)
                    Token_hldr = False
            else
                if ismt()
                    send(current_dir,REQUEST)
                Nq(sender)
        TOKEN:
            current_dir = Dq()
            if current_dir = self
                token_hldr = True
            else
                send(current_dir,TOKEN)
                if not ismt()
                    send(current_dir,REQUEST)
```

FIGURE 10.4 Example execution of Raymond's algorithm.

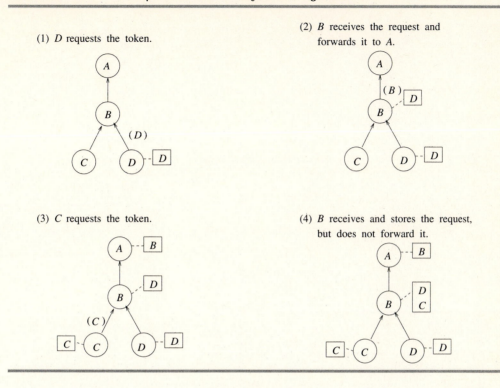

(1) D requests the token.

(2) B receives the request and forwards it to A.

(3) C requests the token.

(4) B receives and stores the request, but does not forward it.

pass the token decreases. One problem with the algorithm is that the token must travel a long distance before reaching its destination.

Raymond's algorithm is an example of imposing a logical structure on a distributed computation to achieve better performance. This type of trick is generally useful when designing distributed algorithms.

- **Logical process structures:** Algorithm efficiency can be improved by restricting the set of neighbors that a processor can communicate with. Since a processor only needs to communicate with a small set of nodes, it is easier to determine their state. The algorithm can make use of the properties of the logical structure. Raymond's algorithm makes use of the fact that there is a unique path between any pair of nodes in a tree. A ring algorithm lets the processors take an action in a round robin order.

10.1.4 Path Compression

Instead of requiring that processors have a fixed relation to one another, we can let the processors form a tree that takes an arbitrary shape. As in Raymond's algorithm, each processor stores a guess of who owns the token in the local variable current_dir. The algorithm will maintain the invariant that the paths formed by the current_dir pointers lead to a processor that is holding or is waiting for the token.

FIGURE 10.5   Example execution of path compression.

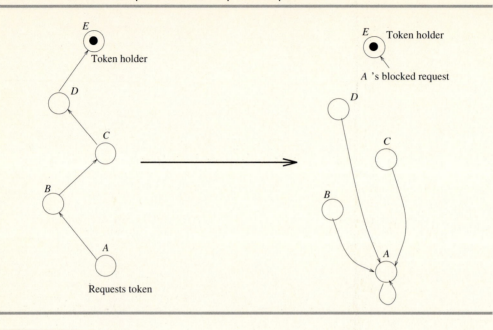

The original path compression algorithms were invented by Li and Hudak to support distributed shared memory. For every shared page p, every processor stores a guess in current_dir[p]. When a processor A traps an instruction to write to a shared page that is not resident, it must obtain the page from the current owner. Processor A sends a request to currentdir$_A$[p]. When a processor B receives a request for a page p, it returns the page if it holds the page, or it forwards the request to currentdir$_B$[p]. In either case, B sets currentdir$_B$[p] to A, since it knows that processor A will soon have the page. This process is illustrated in Figure 10.5.

The path compression is accomplished by setting the forwarding pointer for a page, currentdir[p], to the requesting processor. If one request for a page must make many hops to find the page, all processors that forwarded the request will point directly to the page owner. One can prove that path compression guarantees that k requests for a page shared by M processors will require $O(k \log(M))$ messages.

There is one problem with the algorithm of Li and Hudak. After a processor A sends a request for page p, its forwarding pointer currentdir$_A$[p] does not contain a meaningful value. If a request for p arrives from processor B before A receives p, then A must block B's request. While A is waiting, requests for p might arrive from many processors. In addition, if A holds p but cannot yet process requests for p, there might be several unserviced requests. The Li and Hudak algorithm requires each processor to store a map of the processors that have requested page p for each shared page p. When a processor A sends page p to a requester, it must attach the identities of all other processors that A knows have requested the page. When processor B receives p, it merges the attached list of processors with the set that B knows have requested p.

FIGURE 10.6   Structure of the processors in the path compression algorithm.

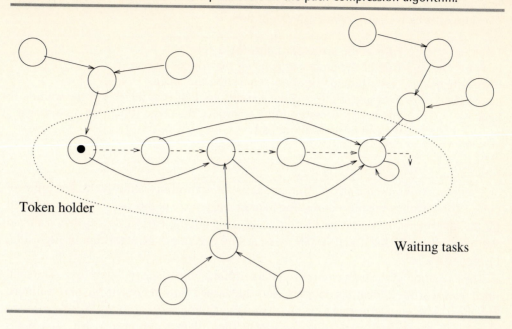

Token holder

Waiting tasks

The requirement that a processor remember all requests for a page means that each page carries an $O(M)$ bit overhead, where M is the number of processors that share the page. This map must also be transmitted with the page p. When we translate the Li and Hudak algorithm to distributed synchronization (replacing requests for the page with requests for the token), we find that it is not scalable.

Fortunately, the space overhead can be reduced without greatly increasing the message overhead or algorithm complexity. We can thread a list (using the pointer next) among the processors that are waiting for the token. When a processor requests the token, it sets its value of next to NIL and then follows the current_dir pointers to find the list of waiting processors. When the request reaches the token holder or a waiting processor, it tries to find the end of the list. If the processor has a NIL value in its next pointer, the processor is (effectively) at the end of the list. Every other processor on the waiting list tries to maintain its value of current_dir to point to the end of the waiting list (note that this is different in Raymond's algorithm). So, if a waiting processor receives a request, the request is forwarded to current_dir. Since the requester will soon be at the end of the list, the processor sets its value of current_dir to the name of the requester.

The structure of the processors involved in the synchronization is illustrated in Figure 10.6. The solid lines represent the current_dir pointers, and the dashed lines represent the next pointers. For the processors that are not waiting for the critical section, the current_dir pointers lead to a processor that either holds or is waiting for the critical section. Of the processors that hold or are waiting for the critical section, the current_dir pointers lead to the last processor to have requested the critical section.

ALGORITHM LISTING 10.13

Variables used by the path compression algorithm.

Token_hldr	True iff the processor holds the token.
Incs	True iff the processor is using the critical section.
IsRequesting	True iff the processor is requesting the token.
current_dir	The current guess about the process that is at the end of the waiting list.
next	The next processor in line to receive the token (NIL if the processor is at the end of the waiting list).

Every processor has the private storage shown in Algorithm Listing 10.13. The protocol consists of the following procedures. The request and release of the token are accomplished by the algorithms in Algorithm Listing 10.14. In addition, each processor has a thread that responds to REQUEST and TOKEN messages by executing the algorithm in Algorithm Listing 10.15.

The execution of the path compression algorithm is illustrated in Figure 10.7. The solid lines represent the current_dir pointers, and the dashed lines represent the next pointers. The processors marked with an 'r' are waiting for the critical section. When processor D requests the critical section, it sets IsRequesting to True and next to NIL, and sends its request in the direction of currentdir$_D$. When A receives D's request, it forwards the request to B and sets its currentdir variable to D. Note that unlike Raymond's algorithm, A tells B who the requester is. Processor B forwards the request to C and adjusts its value of currentdir. Processor C has a NIL value of next, so it sets next to D. Note that after D is added to the waiting list, processor B points directly to D with currentdir. Any

ALGORITHM LISTING 10.14

Algorithms for requesting and releasing the critical section.

```
Request_CS()
    IsRequesting = True
    if not Token_hldr
        send(current_dir,REQUEST; self)
        current_dir = self
        next = NIL
        wait until Token_hldr is True
    Incs = True
Release_CS()
    Incs = False
    IsRequesting = False
    if Next ≠ NIL
        token_hldr = False
        send(next,TOKEN)
        next=NIL
```

ALGORITHM LISTING 10.15

Algorithm executed by the thread monitoring the critical section.

```
Monitor_CS()
    while (True)
        wait for a REQUEST or a TOKEN message.
        REQUEST(requester):
            if IsRequesting = True
                if next = NIL
                    next = requester
                else
                    send(current_dir,REQUEST; requester)
            elseif token_hldr = True
                token_hldr = False
                send(requester,TOKEN; requester)
            else                    // the processor is not requesting the token
                send(current_dir,REQUEST; requester)
            current_dir = requester
        TOKEN()
            token_hldr = True
```

new requests that arrive at B are forwarded directly to D, bypassing C. Note also that while D was being added to the list, a request (say from E) could have arrived at D.

FIGURE 10.7   Execution of path compression mutual exclusion.

(1) Processor D sends its request to A.

(2) A forwards the request to B.

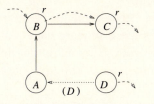

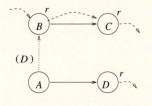

(3) B forwards the request to C.

(4) C's next pointer is nil, so it adds D to the end of the waiting list.

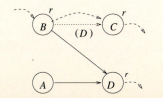

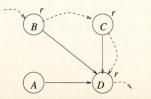

Then, D would point to E when it is added to the waiting list, and E would be the last processor on the list instead of D.

The interesting aspect of the path compression algorithm is the use of incomplete information.

- **Incomplete information:** A way to improve the performance of a distributed algorithm is to loosen the requirement that the state of all processors be consistent. Instead, a processor can be required to store only a "good guess" about the current global state. To make such a scheme work, a distributed operation must be able to recover from mistakes due to incomplete information, and processors must be able to update their state regularly.
- **Path compression:** The path compression algorithm is a very effective use of incomplete information. A processor does not know where the token is, but knows a processor that has more recent information about where the token is held. Recovery is automatic, by repeating the operation on processors that have better and better information. Information update is easy because the requesting processor represents a better guess about the future token holder than any current guess. In addition to being a good example of making effective use of incomplete information, the path compression algorithm is a useful algorithm structure in its own right.

10.2 ELECTION

We next turn our attention to the problem of **election**, which is broadly defined as getting a set of processors to agree on a leader. We often call the leader the **coordinator** and the other processors the **participants**. The leader typically knows the participants it leads. The coordinator and the participants are called the **group**.

Election is used when the distributed computation needs a unique, centralized coordinator. For example, some replicated data schemes use a primary copy and several secondary copies, where the data held by the primary copy is by definition the up-to-date data. A distributed computation might use a coordinator to assign subtasks to the participating processors.

The problem with assigning a unique and vital role to a single processor is the lack of fault tolerance. If the leader fails, the computation stops. The purpose of an election is to find another coordinator, which will determine the state of the system and restart the computation.

In some ways, election is similar to synchronization, since all processors must come to an agreement about who owns a token. However, in an election all participants must know who owns the token (i.e., who is the leader), while in synchronization the nontoken holders only need to know that they do not hold the token. Also, synchronization algorithms are designed to work well in the absence of failures, and failure handling is usually an afterthought. We explore the issue in the exercises. In contrast, election is usually performed only if there is a failure, so failure handling must be an integral part of the protocol.

We will examine the classic election algorithms of Garcia-Molina. Several variations of election have been proposed, but the Garcia-Molina algorithm best defines and handles the possible failures.

Garcia-Molina devised two algorithms, using two different failure models. The first algorithm works under the fail-stop model and makes use of the failure assumptions to achieve simplicity. The second algorithm works under a more general, and a much more realistic, failure assumption. Since the failure model is complex, even stating the correctness conditions of the second algorithm requires care. However, the second algorithm is applicable to systems that one generally encounters.

Both algorithms make assumptions about the environment in which they operate. The most significant assumption is that each node has access to some permanent storage that survives node failures. This storage is used to record version numbers and ensure that they are strictly increasing. Typically, the node will save its state to a hard disk drive, although another possibility is nonvolatile semiconductor memory. This assumption does not require that the node have a local disk drive; a remote file system can serve as well. In addition, the algorithms assume that when a processor fails, it halts all processing (i.e., failures will not cause a node to behave erratically).

10.2.1 The Bully Algorithm

The **bully algorithm** makes an additional two assumptions about the computing environment:

1. The message delivery subsystem delivers all messages within T_m seconds of the sending of the message (message propagation time).
2. A node responds to all messages within T_p seconds of their delivery (message handling time).

These two assumptions allow the bully algorithm to build a **reliable failure detector**: If a processor doesn't respond to a message within $T = 2T_m + T_p$ seconds, it must have failed. All processors that look for this failure will detect it, and the failed processor will know that it failed when it recovers. These assumptions let us simplify the description of what the election algorithm must accomplish, because it can establish a global property. Distributed systems with these tight timing constraints are called **synchronous systems**.

Each processor keeps track of the state information shown in Algorithm Listing 10.16. When a node recovers from a failure, it sets Status to Down and stays in that state until the node begins an election to determine the coordinator (possibly itself). Whenever a node starts the election, it sets Status to Election. When the election is finished, the processors need to reestablish a common state (i.e., ensure that nodes that have recovered from a failure learn of the changes to the system state, etc.), so the processors enter the Reorganization status. After receiving the new common state, the nodes enter the Normal status and are again ready to proceed with the computation.

ALGORITHM LISTING 10.16

State information for election.

Status	One of {Down,Election,Reorganization,Normal}.
Coordinator	The current coordinator of the node.
Definition	The state information for the task being performed.

We are now ready to state the correctness condition of the bully algorithm.

Correctness Assertion 1: Let G be a consistent state. Then, for any pair of nodes p_i and p_j, the following two conditions hold in G:

1. If $Status_i \in$ {Normal, Reorganization} and $Status_j \in$ {Normal, Reorganization} then $Coordinator_i = Coordinator_j$.
2. If $Status_i =$ Normal and $Status_j =$ Normal then $Definition_i = Definition_j$.

The correctness assertion for the bully algorithm states that if two nodes think that they are in working order, they agree on who is the coordinator and on the state of the system. So, the coordinator can direct the execution of the system, and the state of the system will not diverge in different processors. However, the coordinator cannot assume that all processors will obey its orders, since some of the processors might have failed. We will see algorithms that handle this problem in a later chapter.

We need another correctness assertion to guarantee that assertion 1 is not vacuously satisfied. For example, an algorithm that keeps all processors in the election state is "correct" according to assertion 1 but obviously is not an algorithm that we would want to use. So, we need to guarantee that the election algorithm makes progress (**liveness**).

Correctness Assertion 2: Let G be a consistent state. Then, the following two properties are eventually true in any run with no further failures starting in G:

1. There is a node i such that $State_i =$ Normal and $Coordinator_i = i$.
2. For every other nonfailed node j, $State_j =$ Normal and $Coordinator_j = i$.

The idea behind the bully algorithm is that we can preselect which processor should be the leader. That way, we avoid a lot of squabbling. We can assign a *priority* to each of the nodes so that the priority of a node is known to all other nodes. In an election, a node first checks to see if the higher-priority nodes are failed. If so, the node knows that it should be the leader; therefore the node "bullies" the other nodes into accepting its leadership. Since we have assumed that our failure detection is reliable, a low-priority node will not attempt to establish itself as the leader while a higher-priority node is still unfailed.

The bully algorithm makes use of two global variables, shown in Algorithm Listing 10.17 in addition to the ones used for the correctness assertion.

ALGORITHM LISTING 10.17

Additional variables used by the bully algorithm.

Up	A set containing names of processors known to be in the group.
halted	Identity of the processor that notified you of the current election.

An election is initiated by the Coordinator_Timeout procedure if a node does not hear from the coordinator for a suspiciously long time and by the Recovery procedure when the node recovers from a failure (Algorithm Listing 10.18). In addition, the coordinator periodically checks the state of other nodes (Algorithm Listing 10.19). If the coordinator detects that a failed processor has recovered, or that a processor in the group has failed, it will form the group again by calling an election. It might seem drastic to call an election when you learn of a recovered or failed processor, but the participants in the group will need to reorganize their computations when the recovered processor joins the group. We note that the coordinator might use a different mechanism to detect failures and recoveries (i.e., timeouts in the supported protocol or "let me join" messages). The important point is that there is some mechanism by which the coordinator learns of failed and recovered processors in a timely manner.

The election procedure, shown in Algorithm Listing 10.20 (on p.381), determines if a better leader (i.e., higher-priority node) exists. If so, the node waits for the higher-priority node to initiate the election. Otherwise the node attempts to establish itself as the coordinator by sending "enter-election" messages to the lower-priority processors. When the new coordinator establishes the new group, it will try to use an accurate picture of the processors that are nonfailed participants. If one of the participants in Up does not respond to the protocol messages, it must have failed. So, a new election is called to ensure an accurate group. This is not strictly necessary for correctness.

The election protocol makes use of several different types of queries about remote machines. The queries are handled by a thread that executes the algorithm in Algorithm Listing 10.21 (on p.382) and waits to answer the queries (and perhaps change the state of

ALGORITHM LISTING 10.18

Algorithms to initiate an election.

```
Coordinator_Timeout()
    if State = Normal or State = Reorganization
        send(Coordinator,AreYouUp), timeout=T
            wait until Coordinator sends (AYU_answer), timeout=T
            On timeout
                Election()

Recovery()
    State = Down
    Election()
```

ALGORITHM LISTING 10.19

Algorithm used by the coordinator to check the state of other processors.

```
Check()
    if State = Normal and Coordinator=Self
        for every other node j,
            send(j,AreYouNormal)
            wait until j sends (AYN_answer; status), timeout=T
                if (j ∈ Up and status=False) or j ∉ Up
                    Election()
                    return()
```

the protocol). One of the entries, Enter_Election, has the side effect of making the node enter the Election state. Since the coordinator is no longer well defined, the protocol must stop the computation that the node is performing, using the the procedure stop_processing(). For example, if the node was a copy of a replicated server, the node would stop accepting requests on the behalf of clients. In addition, the node must stop running its own election if it is executing one. The stop_processing() routine can be implemented in many ways (sending signals, setting flags in shared memory, etc.), and the systems issues must be carefully thought out.

Receiving an Enter_Election message means that a higher-priority processor is running its own election and should be elected as the leader. Although the node has already checked the higher-priority nodes and determined that they have failed, a higher-priority node might recover from its failure during the election.

Informally, the bully algorithm works because a node n makes certain that every other node has heard about its election before declaring itself the winner. It might seem that the Enter_Election messages can be combined with the Set_Coordinator messages to save a round of communication. But, to ensure that correctness assertion 1 is satisfied, no nonfailed processor can still be in the Normal state.

An execution of the bully algorithm is illustrated in Figure 10.8 (on p.382). In stage 1, p_3 tests all higher-priority nodes. After the timeout, p_3 knows that in consistent cut c_1 there is no higher-priority processor that is executing in the Normal state. In stage 2, p_3 tests all lower-priority nodes with an Enter_Election message. This message causes the recipient to enter the Election state. So, at cut c_2, p_3 knows that there is no processor in the Normal state, and there is no processor acting as a coordinator. Processor p_3 proposes itself as the coordinator and at cut c_3 it knows that all processors in Up are in the Reorganization state and believe that p_3 is the coordinator. Finally, at cut c_4, processor p_3 knows that all processors in Up are in the Normal state.

Correctness assertion 1 follows from the way that a processor that proposes itself as the coordinator first finds a consistent cut in which no processors is in the Reorganization or the Normal state. If two processors are concurrently trying to elect themselves the coordinator, one will have higher priority. Any progress toward election made by the lower-priority processor will be erased by the higher-priority processor when the higher-priority processor establishes cut c_2.

ALGORITHM LISTING 10.20

Bully election algorithm.

```
Election()
    highest = True
    For every higher-priority processor p
        send(p,AreYouUp)
        wait up to T seconds for (AYU_answer) messages
            AYU_answer (sender) :
                highest = False
        If highest = False
            return()

    State = Election
    halted = Self
    Up = {}
    For every lower-priority processor p
        send(p,Enter_Election)
        wait up to T seconds for (EE_answer) messages
            EE_answer (sender) :
                Up = Up ∪ {sender}

    num_answers = 0
    Coordinator = Self
    State = Reorganization
    for each p in Up
        send(p,Set_Coordinator; Self)
        wait up to T seconds for (SC_answer) messages
            SC_answer (sender):
                num_answers + +
        if num_answers < |Up|
            Election()
            return()

    num_answers = 0
    for each p in Up
        send(p,New_State; Definition)
        wait up to T seconds for (NS_answer) messages
            NS_answer (sender):
                num_answers + +
        if num_answers < |Up|
            Election()
            return()

    State = Normal
```

ALGORITHM LISTING 10.21

Algorithm executed by the thread that monitors the election.

```
Monitor_Election()
    while (True)
        wait for a message.
            case AreYouUp (sender):
                send(sender,AYU_answer)
            case AreYouNormal (sender):
                if State = Normal, send(sender,AYN_answer; True)
                    else send(sender,AYN_answer; False)
            case Enter_Election (sender) :
                State = Election
                stop_processing()
                stop the election procedure if it is executing
                halted = sender
                send(sender,EE_answer)
            case Set_Coordinator (sender, newleader) :
                if State = Election and halted = newleader
                    Coordinator = newleader
                    State = Reorganization
                send(sender,SC_answer)
            case New_State (sender, newdef):
                if Coordinator = sender and state = Reorganization
                    Definition = newdef
                    State = Normal
```

FIGURE 10.8   Execution of the bully algorithm.

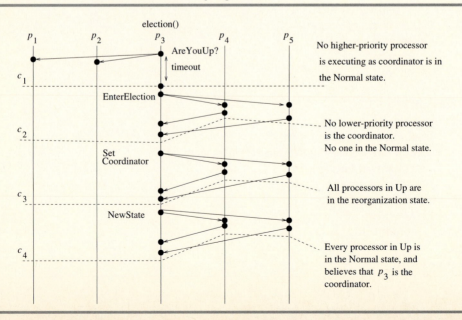

10.2.2 The Invitation Algorithm

The bully algorithm is simple, but it makes a strong use of the fact that timeouts can accurately detect failed processors. Through an arbitrary timing glitch (lost messages, overfull buffers, temporary overloads at the processors), the bully algorithm can elect two leaders. The timeouts T can be made so large that a failure to respond to a timeout almost certainly means that it is impossible to communicate with the processor in question. However, such large timeouts mean that the election algorithm can take a very long time to execute. Furthermore, the node that fails to respond might not have failed, because a network partition might have occurred.

If we admit the possibility that the network and the processors might experience arbitrary processing delays (i.e., delete assumptions 1 and 2), it no longer makes sense to talk about the global coordinator. If there is a network partition, a coordinator will (should?) appear in both partitions. Two processors in the same partition might not be able to communicate with each other and thus both declare themselves the coordinator. If one cannot make safe assumptions about the timing of system events, one is developing algorithms for an **asynchronous system**.

Since declaring a global leader is fraught with peril, we need to reconsider what we mean by "coordinator." A coordinator is needed to guide a group of processors through a distributed computation. Hence it makes sense to tie the coordinator to the group that it coordinates. In addition to leading the group, the coordinator needs to ensure that the participants in the group are working according to the same plan. A coordinator might form the same group twice but with a different plan the second time around (for an example, see the dynamic quorum change protocols in Chapter 12). For this reason, it is convenient to make unambiguous the group identity with a **group number** (i.e., a sequence number). All members of the group agree on the group number, and the same group number is never used twice. We include the group number as part of the defining state of a node, as shown in Algorithm Listing 10.22.

Next we need to revise the correctness assertions. The first assertion states that all members of the same group agree on the identity of the coordinator:

Correctness Assertion 3: Let G be a consistent state. Then, for any pair of nodes p_i and p_j, the following two conditions hold in G:

1. If $\text{Status}_i \in \{\text{Normal, Reorganization}\}$, $\text{Status}_j \in \{\text{Normal, Reorganization}\}$, and $\text{Group}_i = \text{Group}_j$, then $\text{Coordinator}_i = \text{Coordinator}_j$.
2. If $\text{Status}_i = \text{Normal}$, $\text{Status}_j = \text{Normal}$, and $\text{Group}_i = \text{Group}_j$, then $\text{Definition}_i = \text{Definition}_j$.

ALGORITHM LISTING 10.22

Additional state variable required for asynchronous election.

Group	Identifier of the group that the processor belongs to.

We also need a liveness property. Since we now allow for communication errors, we might need to restrict ourselves to the set of nodes that can actually communicate with each other.

Correctness Assertion 4: Let R be a maximal set of nodes that can communicate in consistent state G_0. Then, the following two conditions are eventually true in any run starting at G_0 such that R remains a maximal set of nodes that can communicate and no further failures occur:

1. There is a node $p_i \in R$ such that $\text{State}_i = \text{Normal}$ and $\text{Coordinator}_i = p_i$.
2. For every other nonfailed node $p_j \in R$, $\text{State}_j = \text{Normal}$ and $\text{Coordinator}_j = p_i$.

Correctness assertion 3 is actually very easy to satisfy. When processor p wishes to establish itself as the coordinator, it creates a unique group identifier and targets a set of potential participants (including itself). Next, p suggests to the potential participants that they join the new group, with p as the coordinator. To join the new group, the participants accept p's suggestion. Since the group identifier is unique, correctness assertion 3.1 is automatically satisfied. When the new group is formed, p distributes the new definition to the participants in the group. Correctness assertion 3.2 is automatically satisfied if the participant only accepts new definitions from its current group coordinator, and only in the Reorganization state.

The main difficulty in implementing an election algorithm is to ensure that correctness assertion 4 is satisfied. There are many possible ways to run the election. In this section, we will generally follow the procedure suggested by Garcia-Molina but will point out where modifications are possible.

Since it is possible that there is more than one coordinator, the bully algorithm might not be able to ensure correctness assertion 4. The problem is that if the coordinators compete for participants, they might repeatedly steal participants from each other and no progress will be made toward forming a new group. It might make more sense to try to get the competing coordinators to agree to merge their groups into a single group. This is the approach taken by the invitation algorithm — one coordinator invites the other to merge into one group. By repeatedly merging groups, eventually there will be a single global group.

Groups that can communicate need to coalesce into larger groups. Periodically, the group coordinator searches for other groups, using the Check procedure shown in Algorithm Listing 10.23, and the coordinators it finds are added to the Others set. If another coordinator is found, the node will try to merge the other coordinator's group into its own. The other coordinator will be doing the same thing. To avoid livelock, the node delays for a time between detecting a new coordinator and acting on the information. Note that unlike the case in the bully algorithm, not receiving a response within T seconds does not mean anything in particular. In fact, the node might receive messages from the last time it sent AreYouCoordinator messages. In the Check procedure, this will not cause a problem. However, in other procedures we will need to match replies with requests.

ALGORITHM LISTING 10.23

Algorithm used by a coordinator to find the coordinators of other groups.

```
Check()
    If State = Normal and Coordinator = Self
        Others = {}
        for every other node P,
            send(P,AreYouCoordinator)
            wait up to T seconds for (AYC_answer) messages
                AYC_answer (sender; is_coordinator)
                    if is_coordinator = True
                        Others = Others ∪ sender
        if Others = {}
            return()
        Wait for a time inversely proportional to your priority
        Merge(Others)
```

We note that many optimizations can be made to the Check procedure. For example, we can try to assign priorities to the coordinators. If a high-priority coordinator receives an AreYouCoordinator from a lower-priority coordinator, the high-priority coordinator can make a note of the low-priority coordinator and attempt to merge the lower-priority coordinator's group into its own in a short period of time. The low-priority coordinator will not add the high-priority coordinator to the Others set, and will delay executing the Merge procedure for a while. If a participant receives an AreYouCoordinator message, it can answer with the identity of its coordinator. However, all that is required is that a coordinator searches out and attempts to merge with other groups. The implementer can experiment with this part of the protocol to find the most effective techniques.

If a node does not hear from its coordinator for a long period of time, the coordinator might have failed. The algorithm for handling a suspected failure of the coordinator is shown in Algorithm Listing 10.24. If the node still cannot get a response, the node declares its own group. Declaring a new group is performed by the recovery algorithm (Algorithm Listing 10.25), which is also invoked when a processor recovers from a failure. We note that this strategy is simple and legal (single processor groups are permitted by correctness assertion 3) but perhaps can be improved on. When a participant p finds that its coordinator has failed, it knows the identities of many other potential participants — the other participants in the group. Processor p can then use this information to try to quickly form a new group by sending invitations to all of the other participants of the old group. However, all that is required is that the failure of the coordinator be detected so that a new group can be formed.

Most of the work of the invitation algorithm is done in the Merge procedure, shown in Algorithm Listing 10.26. This procedure accepts a list of potential coordinators from the Check procedure and attempts to merge the groups of all known coordinators into one group. The node starts by forming its own group, with a new group number. Note that the group number is made unique by attaching a version number to the node name. All other

ALGORITHM LISTING 10.24

Algorithm to handle a suspected failure of the coordinator.

```
Timeout()
    if Coordinator = Self
        Return()
    send(Coordinator,AreYouThere; Group)
    wait for AYC_answer, timeout is T
        On timeout,
            is_coordinator = False
        AYC_answer (sender; is_coordinator) :

    If is_coordinator = False
        Recovery()
```

---

known groups, and the members of the current group, are invited to join the new group. The code to handle acceptance messages is located in the Monitor_Election thread (which executes the algorithm shown in Algorithm Listing 10.28 on p.389) because the node must be able to respond to acceptance messages even while it is not merging groups. Finally, the new definition is distributed to the members of the new group. If a member of the group fails to acknowledge the new definition, the group needs to be formed again.

Since a node must be able to respond to Invitation messages at any time, these messages are handled by their own thread. The algorithm for this thread is shown in Algorithm Listing 10.27 (on p.388). A node will accept an invitation if it is in the normal state. If the node was the coordinator of its own group, it will extend the invitation to join the new group to the old group members. As in the bully algorithm, the election monitor responds to messages that can arrive at any time.

The execution of the invitation algorithm is illustrated in Figure 10.9 (on p.388). Processor p_1 executes the Merge procedure after collecting p_2 and p_3 as the processors to query. Processor p_2 accepts the invitation immediately. Processor p_3 was acting as a

ALGORITHM LISTING 10.25

Algorithm for recovery after a failure.

```
Recovery()
    State = Election
    stop_processing()
    Counter ++; Group = (Self | Counter)
    Coordinator = Self
    Up = {}
    State = Reorganization
    Description = (a single node task description)
    State = Normal
```

ALGORITHM LISTING **10.26**

Algorithm by which a coordinator merges other groups into one.

```
Merge(Coordinator_set)
    if Coordinator = self and state = Normal
        State = Election
        stop_processing()
        Counter ++; Group = (Self | Counter)
        Coordinator = Self
        UpSet = Up
        Up = {}
        For each p in Coordinator_set,
            send(p,Invitation; Self,Group)
        For each p in Upset,
            send(p,Invitation; Self,Group)
        Wait for T seconds  // Answers are collected by the Monitor_Election thread.
        State = Reorganization
        num_answer = 0
        For each p in Up
            send(p,Ready; Group,Definition)
            wait up to T seconds for Ready_answer messages
            Ready_answer (sender; ingroup, new_group):
                if ingroup = True and new_group = Group
                    num_answer + +
        If num_answer < |Up|
            invoke Recovery()
        else
            state = Normal
```

coordinator itself, so p_3 forwards the invitation to p_4 and p_5. After T seconds, p_1 uses the set of responses it collected as the Up set. Because these processors explicitly accepted the invitation, p_1 knows that they have entered the Reorganization state. Processor p_1 replies with a Ready message, taking the participant processors into the Normal state. When all answers are received (within T seconds), p_1 knows that every processor in Up has accepted the group and that normal processing can resume.

The similarities and differences between the bully and the invitation algorithms highlight some issues we have seen before and will see again.

■ **Logical structure:** The bully algorithm is simple and efficient because it imposes a logical structure on the processors. It might take a long time for groups to merge when using the invitation algorithm because there is no strongly defined structure on them.

■ **Synchronous versus asynchronous:** The bully algorithm uses the technique of flushing information from every other processor, so it feels similar to the distributed snapshot algorithm. It makes very strong use of its assumptions of bounded response time to

ALGORITHM LISTING 10.27

Algorithm executed by the thread that handles invitations.

```
Invitation()
    while True
        Wait for Invitation (new_coordinator; new_group):
        If State = Normal
            stop_processing()
            old_coordinator = Coordinator
            Upset = Up
            State = Election
            Coordinator = new_coordinator
            Group = new_group
            if old_coordinator = Self
                for each P in Upset
                    send(P,Invitation; Coordinator,Group)
            send(Coordinator,Accept; Group)
            wait up to T seconds for an Accept_answer(sender; accepted) message
                On timeout,
                    accepted = False
            if accepted is False invoke Recovery()
            State = Reorganization
```

FIGURE 10.9   Execution of the invitation algorithm.

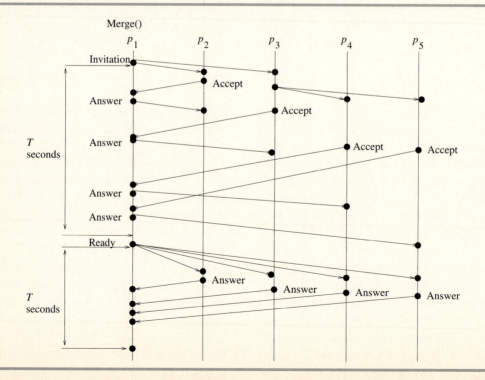

ALGORITHM LISTING 10.28

Algorithm executed by the thread that monitors the election.

```
Election_Monitor()
    while True
        wait for a message
        Ready (sender; new_group,new_description)
            if Group = new_group and State = Reorganization
                Description = new_description
                State = Normal
                send(Coordinator,Ready_answer; True,Group)
            else
                send(sender,Ready_answer; False)
        AreYouCoordinator (sender)
            if State = Normal and Coordinator = Self
                send(sender,AYC_answer; True)
            else
                send(sender,AYC_answer; False)
        AreYouThere (sender; old_group)
            if Group = old_group and Coordinator = Self and sender in Up
                send(sender,AYT_answer; True)
            else
                send(sender,AYT_answer; False)
        Accept (sender; new_group)
            if State = Election and Coordinator = self and Group = new_group
                Up = Up ∪ sender
                send(sender,accept_answer; True)
            else
                send(sender,accept_answer; False)
```

build a simple algorithm. Unfortunately, such assumptions are not realistic in most systems.

The invitation algorithm works correctly in the presence of timing failures and thus is a practical algorithm. Note that in the new environment, stating the correctness of the algorithm becomes a much more difficult task. We will run into this difference between synchronous and asynchronous algorithms again, and the next chapter examines a fundamental difference between algorithms for synchronous and for asynchronous systems. Stating correctness criteria for asynchronous systems generally requires elaborate and perhaps unsatisfying statements.

■ **Relative consistency:** In the synchronous system, correctness depends on *every* processor agreeing to a value. In the asynchronous system, correctness depends on getting a group of processors to agree to group membership and then to agree on a value. Since there may be several groups, consistency is relative to the group. Processors that do not communicate can be safely ignored.

To account for the lack of global knowledge, the invitation algorithm makes a strong use of sequence numbers. The algorithm is fundamentally simple — a coordinator asks other nodes to join its group. If they join, they satisfy the correctness criteria; if they do not join, they again satisfy the correctness criteria.

10.3 SUMMARY

In this chapter, we examine distributed coordination algorithms related to choosing a unique processor among a set of participants. The *mutual exclusion* problem is that of granting permission to execute a *critical section* to at most one processor at a time, while ensuring that progress is made. We examine two *permissions-based* and two *token-based* algorithms. *Voting*, a permission-based algorithm, can be made highly fault tolerant and is the basis of most replicated transaction processing algorithms. Token-based algorithms can be made very efficient. We examine two approaches, one that imposes a *fixed logical structure* on the processors and a second that uses *path compression*. The path compression algorithm has roots in techniques for implementing distributed shared memory.

The *election* problem is that of choosing a unique leader among a set of participants. Unlike mutual exclusion, we are not concerned with fairness, but we are required to inform all participants of the elected leader. We present the *bully* algorithm, which requires a synchronous system, and the *invitation* algorithm, which will execute correctly on an asynchronous system. A comparison of the two algorithms shows how a problem statement can be translated from a synchronous to an asynchronous system, requiring a change from total consistency to *relative* consistency. The bully algorithm has the advantage of being fast and efficient as long as timing errors do not occur. Good leader election algorithms use a combination of techniques from both approaches.

ANNOTATED BIBLIOGRAPHY

The first timestamp-based distributed mutual exclusion algorithm is attributed to Lamport [Lam78]. The algorithm presented in the text is that of Ricart and Agrawala [RA81]. Carvalho and Roucairol [CR83a] present an optimization that requires substantially fewer messages when only a few processors communicate. Suzuki and Kasami [SK85] show how to reduce the number of messages required to M by using a privilige token. Mizuno, Neilsen, and Rao [MNR91] improve on Suzuki and Kasami's algorithm by restricting a processor's requests to a quorum. Makki, Pissinou, and Yesha [MPY93] use Maekawa's coterie structure. Singhal [Sin89, Sin92] improves on Suzuki and Kasami by making a good guess about who holds the token to reduce the number of required messages. Raymond [Ray89a] generalizes the Ricart and Agrawala algorithm to allow K simultaneous entries to the critical section, while Srimani and Reddy [SR91] modify Suzuki and Kasami's algorithm. Baldoni and Ciciani [BC94] add priorities to the requests in Srimani and Reddy's algorithm to improve performance.

Thomas [Tho79] introduced the idea of **quorum consensus** for distributed synchronization. Garcia-Molina and Barbara [GMB85] formalized the idea of "voting districts" into coteries. The quorum construction technique for voting was developed by Maekawa [Mae85]. Maekawa also provided a voting technique that automatically resolves deadlock. However, Sanders [San87] showed that this algorithm has a bug that can lead to deadlock, and proposes a fix. Later, Sanders [San96] showed that even the fixed algorithm is susceptible to deadlock in some cases. A deadlock-free algorithm is provided and proved correct, and we use this algorithm in the text.

Subsequent authors have investigated other quorum structures that either have more fault tolerance or require fewer messages [AA91, AA92, CAA90a, CT94, WB92, PS92, TK91, TPK95, AJ92]. Kumar [Kum91] replaces the sites in Maekawa's algorithm with quorums to gain availability. Kumar and Cheung [KC91] propose a hierarchy of grids. More generally, Neilsen, Mizuno, and Raynal [NMR92] show how to create new coteries by composing construction methods. Ibaraki and Kameda [IK93] and Ng and Ravishankar [NR95] provide a theory of coterie design. Chang, Ahamad, and Ammar [CAA90b] show how to represent any voting district by a multidimensional vote assignment. Kakugawa, Fujita, Yamashita, and Ae [KFYA94], Baldoni [Bal94], and Huang, Jiang, and Kuo [HJK93] extend voting algorithms to handle K simultaneous entries to the critical section.

Circulating token algorithms are discussed in [Ray88]. The algorithm presented in the text is given by Raymond [Ray89b]. Neilsen and Mizuno [NM91] describe an algorithm similar to Raymond's, except that waiting processors are linked in a list. Chang, Singhal, and Liu [CSL90a] extend Raymond's algorithm to execute on a graph, the extra edges providing a measure of fault tolerance. The authors show how to ensure that the graph structure is a DAG whose sink is the token holder. Satyanarayanan and Muthukrishnan [SM92] give a method for improving the fairness of Raymond's algorithm. Helary, Plouzeau and Raynal [HPR88] discuss algorithms for mutual exclusion that uses flooding. Bulgannawar and Vaidya [BV95] give an algorithm for K-mutual exclusion that uses K tokens each with its own logical structure, and a technique for letting requests switch between logical structures. Makki [Mak94] gives a mutual exclusion algorithm in which a coordinator makes decisions about which processes receive the mutex token. The location of the coordinator changes as the algorithm executes, and participants send requests to their best guess of the current coordinator. In [MBB+92, MPP94] this approach is extended to handle K-mutual exclusion.

Li and Hudak [LH89b] present distributed path compression algorithms in the context of distributed shared virtual memory. Trehel and Naimi [TN87, TM87] describe algorithms that apply path compression to distributed mutual exclusion. The algorithm presented in the text is that given by Chang, Singhal and Liu [CSL90b]. Johnson [Joh95] shows that the Chang, Singhal and Liu algorithm has better performance than Raymond's algorithm. Helary, Mostefaoui and Raynal [HMR94] describe a mutual exclusion scheme that generalizes the work of Raymond and of Chang, Singhal and Liu. This generalization is applied by Helary and Mostefaoui [HM94] to give a fast hybrid mutual exclusion algorithm. Agrawal and El Abbadi [AA95] give algorithms for fixing broken paths after a processor failure. Johnson and Newman-Wolfe [JNW96] present prioritized mutual exclusion algorithms using techniques similar to those in [CSL90b].

The election algorithm is that given by Garcia-Molina [GM82]. Given the basic mechanism for election in an asynchronous system, many policies for conducting the election are possible. Several policies are analyzed by Singh and Kurose [SK94]. See [CC93] for research on election on a ring of processors.

EXERCISES

1. Use the execution DAG predicates of Section 9.4.2 to state the mutual exclusion property.
2. Use the *eventually* predicate of Section 9.4.3 to express the progress property of mutual exclusion algorithms
3. Use the *always* predicate of Section 9.4.3 to state that the Ricart and Agrawala algorithm of Section 10.1.1 satisfies the mutual exclusion property, and prove your statement.
4. Modify the Ricart and Agrawala algorithm to handle *read* and *write* locks.
5. Modify the Ricart and Agrawala algorithm to permit up to K simultaneous entries into the critical section.
6. The Ricart and Agrawala algorithm uses more messages than necessary because a processor that does not want to enter the critical section for a long time is still required to send REPLY messages to processors that do. Modify the Ricart and Agrawala algorithm to make q's REPLY apply to all of p's requests until q makes a request. Your algorithm should require only a few messages if only a few processors want to enter the critical section.
7. Modify the Ricart and Agrawal algorithm to pass a critical section token directly to a requesting processor. *Hint*: Try attaching a vector timestamp to the token.
8. Modify Maekawa's algorithm to grant a mutual exclusion lock in spite of a single processor failure. *Hint*: Think about composing coteries.
9. Modify Maekawa's algorithm to permit at most two processors to be in the critical section simultaneously, not just one. *Hint* : Think about the properties of the coteries.
10. Consider the following method of constructing a voting district for mutual exclusion. You have nine processors, p_1 through p_9. You organize the processors into three subdistricts, each with three processors. So, $D_1 = \{p_1, p_2, p_3\}$, $D_2 = \{p_4, p_5, p_6\}$, and $D_3 = \{p_7, p_8, p_9\}$. A candidate wins an election if the candidate gets at least two of the three votes in at least two of the three subdistricts. For example, getting the votes $\{p_1, p_2, p_4, p_5\}$ would win the election.
    a. Show that there is at least one swing vote in any pair of voting districts.
    b. Generalize the method to handle an arbitrary number of processors such that each voting district uses $O(n^{\log_3(2)})$ voters.
    c. Compare the algorithm to Maekawa's for efficiency and fault tolerance.
11. Give an algorithm that has $O(\log n)$ voters in a voting district (if no processor has failed) and can tolerate at least $O(\log n)$ processor failures and still permit critical section entries. *Hint*: Change the quorum if a processor has failed.

12. Modify Maekawa's algorithm so that the voting district is chosen dynamically on a grid.

13. Suppose that a processor in Raymond's algorithm fails. Give a protocol to repair the tree and if necessary regenerate the mututal exclusion token. You may assume that a processor knows the identities of its neighbors' neighbors and that only one processor has failed.

14. Modify Raymond's algorithm so that when a processor releases the critical section and another processor is waiting, the token is passed to the waiting processor directly. *Hint*: Use the techniques of the path compression algorithm.

15. Modify Raymond's algorithm to pass the token to the highest-priority waiting processor.

16. Suppose that in the path compression algorithm, a processor in the waiting chain (but not the token holder) fails. Give an algorithm to recover from this failure.

17. Suppose that in the path compression algorithm, a processor not in the waiting chain, and not holding the token, fails. Give an algorithm to recover from this failure.

18. Given a set of M processors, partition them into K domains, $D_1, \ldots, D_K$. Give a mutual exclusion algorithm that uses the path compression algorithm within a domain but Raymond's algorithm between domains.

19. Modify the invitation algorithm for election to use the leader-choosing policies of the bully algorithm.

20. (Programming project) Implement an election algorithm, and test it by simulating failures. Recall the important points:

    a. When a processor forms a new group, it samples a new group I.D.

    b. The processor proposes itself as the new coordinator to lead the group identified with the new group I.D.

    c. Participant processors join the group by accepting the new coordinator and the new group I.D.

    The implementation-specific issues:

    a. searching for potential participants,

    b. deciding whether to accept an invitation,

    c. incorporating new participants

    can be implementation specific. You can use the suggested algorithm in the book or do something that you think is reasonable.

    The recommended architecture is the following:

    a. Start a program control process.

    b. The program control process rexec's several processes on different machines. The rexec'ed processes will execute the election algorithm.

    c. The election processes obtain port numbers for connections and relay these port numbers to the control process.

    d. When the control process has collected all port numbers, it distributes the addresses of the processes running the election algorithm to these processes.

    e. The election processes then execute the election protocols, and attempt to maintain a single group.

    f. The control process accepts commands from the user (i.e., for a process participating in the election protocol to simulate a failure or recovery) and relays these commands to the appropriate process.

    g. Processes participating in the election protocol send status report messages to the control process, which prints them on the terminal.

At the processes which participate in the election protocol:

    a. Recall that these processes will need to listen for and respond to unsolicited messages, so fork processes (threads) to handle these requests.

    b. Using UDP to handle communications for the election protocol might make the coding easier (i.e., require less session management).

11

CHAPTER

Distributed Agreement

Most researchers feel that the most fundamental problem in distributed computing is the **distributed agreement** or the **distributed consensus** problem —how to get a set of processors to agree on a value. For example, Chapter 10 covers mutual exclusion and election algorithms. All of these algorithms are concerned with ensuring that a set of distributed processors come to an agreement about a value. Other important issues, such as maintaining replicated data, monitoring a distributed computation, and detecting failed processors, are all special cases of the distributed agreement problem.

The formal setting for a distributed agreement protocol is the following: There are M processors $P = p_1, \ldots, p_M$ that are trying to reach agreement. A subset F of the processors are faulty, and the remaining processors are nonfaulty. Each processor $p_i \in P$ stores a value V_i. During the agreement protocol, the processors calculate an agreement value A_i. After the protocol ends, the following two conditions should hold:

1. For every pair p_i and p_j of nonfaulty processors, $A_i = A_j$. This value is the **agreement value**.
2. The agreement value is a function of the initial values $\{V_i\}$ of the nonfaulty processors $(P - F)$.

In this chapter, we study the possibility or impossibility of distributed agreement under a variety of failure models. While the algorithms discussed in this section generally are not practical, a study of distributed agreement protocols is necessary for a good understanding of distributed systems. If we want to understand how to accomplish something, we need to understand what can and cannot be done.

11.1 ADVERSARIES

The material in this chapter uses **adversary** arguments. You are charged with writing a protocol that accomplishes some objective (e.g., consensus). An adversary is a demon that has a great deal of control over the environment in which your protocol executes and will try to make your protocol fail. We assume that the adversary has the power to examine the global state and to schedule the execution of the protocol (i.e., schedule message delivery and event execution). An adversary might have additional powers, such as the ability to destroy or modify messages and change the protocol that some of the processors execute. Your task is to foil the adversary.

An adversary is a concise and anthropomorphic way of finding a worst-case execution for a protocol. Given an initial state and a protocol, there are many possible runs. It might be the case that in most runs the protocol works correctly, but for one bad run the protocol fails (see Figure 11.1). Specifying all possible runs can be a difficult task, especially when some processors are permitted to execute unspecified protocols. Instead, we specify the powers that we give to our adversary.

When first shown an adversary argument, many people react by saying "But that is so unlikely." or "How can those processors act in collusion?". The point of an adversary argument is not to find executions that are likely to occur, but bad executions that might be very unlikely to occur. The adversary might need to make widely dispersed processors act in collusion, but this corresponds to one possible execution and an execution that can cause the protocol to fail. If our protocol foils the adversary, we can have a very good confidence in its correctness.

Still, the power that we give to the adversary is an issue worth pondering. The adversary arguments in some problems seem better suited to discussions of security

FIGURE 11.1   The adversary finds the execution that makes the protocol fail.

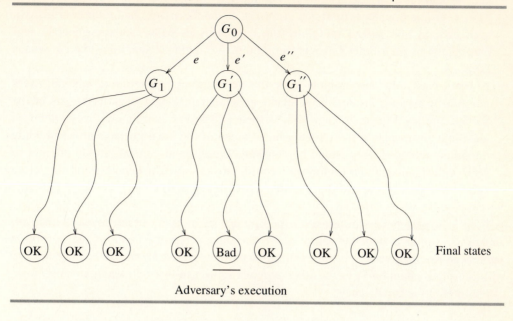

Adversary's execution

systems than to discussions of distributed computing. However, the adversaries that we discuss in this text correspond well to possible executions.

11.2 BYZANTINE AGREEMENT

Byzantine agreement generally refers to distributed agreement algorithms in which a failed processor can send arbitrary messages into the network. In particular, a failed processor can try to prevent the nonfailed processors from reaching an agreement.

We need to make an assumption about the nonfaulty processors, that they always respond to a message within T seconds. That is, the distributed system is **synchronous** (as in the bully algorithm for election). Faulty processors might require longer than T seconds to respond. In addition, we will assume that when a processor receives a message, it can reliably identify the sender.

The name *Byzantine agreement* comes from the story that is usually used to provide a setting for the problem. The **Byzantine generals** problem goes as follows:

■ One day in ancient times, the Turkish sultan led an invasion into Byzantium. The Emperor called out his armies to meet the invading Turks. Each of the armies was led by its own general.

The armies that marched out of Constantinople to meet the Turks were strong enough to resist the Sultan's army if their action was coordinated (either attack or retreat). After marching for several days, the Byzantine armies camped near to the Turkish armies. The Byzantine generals planned that night for an attack at dawn. Each general had his own appraisal of the strength of the Turkish army and had his own preference about whether to attack or retreat. Since the attacks had to be coordinated, each general had agreed to follow the consensus decision. So, the generals sent messengers to each other's camps throughout the night to determine the consensus decision.

There was only one problem with the generals' plan. Byzantine generals were notoriously treacherous, and some of the generals might have been in the pay of the Sultan. The loyal generals knew that if their attack was coordinated, they would be victorious (or escape to fight again), but if some of the loyal generals attacked while the others retreated, they would be defeated. The disloyal generals would attempt to deceive the loyal generals to prevent a coordinated attack. The loyal generals therefore agreed to follow a protocol that ensured a distributed agreement.

If each loyal general can agree on the opinion V_j of every other (loyal or disloyal) general p_j, the loyal generals will all reach the same decision. Therefore, the Byzantine armies can reach agreement if there is a protocol for a *reliable broadcast*. Each general p_i will transmit its opinion V_i to the other generals subject to the following two conditions, called **interactive consistency**:

1. If the sender p_s is loyal, the loyal generals will agree on V_s.
2. If the sender p_s is treacherous, the loyal processors will agree on the same value for V_s.

Since the processors can come to agreement if each can reliably broadcast its opinion to all of the other processors, we will focus on a single broadcast. The general who is broadcasting his order is the *commanding general*; the other generals are the *lieutenant generals*. Each loyal general must agree on the the value of the broadcast. Note that the set of disloyal generals can include the commanding general. To solve the Byzantine general's problem, each general takes his turn as commander and broadcasts his opinion. To develop the theory of Byzantine generals, we will first look at the smallest possible cases.

Question 1: Suppose there are three generals (one commanding general and two lieutenant generals), and one general is treacherous. Can the loyal generals reach agreement, and if so, by what protocol?

The answer is no. Why? Mainly because there are not enough generals to form a consensus opinion. The scenario is illustrated in Figure 11.2. Suppose that the commanding general C is treacherous. Then, C can tell the first lieutenant general L_1 "Attack" and tell L_2 "Retreat." The lieutenants can try to verify their orders by talking to each other. L_1 will learn that L_2 heard "Retreat", and L_2 will learn that L_1 heard "Attack." It would seem that the lieutenants could conclude that C is disloyal. However, let us consider a different scenario. Suppose that C is loyal and L_2 is disloyal. C tells L_1 and L_2 "Attack ". When L_1 asks L_2 about the orders, L_2 replies that he heard "Retreat." From L_1's view, both scenarios are the same. Further communication does not provide more

FIGURE 11.2   Three generals can not reach Byzantine agreement.

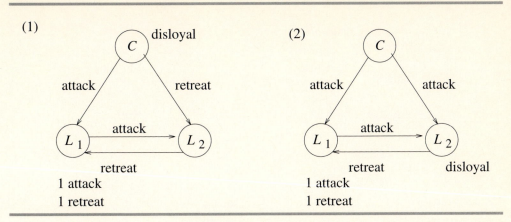

information, because the commander can only repeat his order and the lieutenants have already communicated their information. Lieutenant L_1 can't follow C's order, because if C is disloyal, L_1 and L_2 would obey different orders. L_1 can't disobey the order either, because C might be loyal. Therefore, L_1 can not make a decision.

Question 2: Suppose there are four generals (one commanding general and three lieutenant generals), and one general is treacherous. Can the loyal generals reach agreement and if so, by what protocol?

The answer is yes, because with a total of four generals there are enough generals to reach a consensus opinion. The scenario is illustrated in Figure 11.3. The protocol is the following. The commander C broadcasts his order to each of the lieutenants L_1, L_2, and L_3. Next, each lieutenant tells the other two lieutenants the order he received from C. The lieutenant then obeys the majority opinion to either attack or retreat.

To see that the protocol works, first suppose that C is disloyal. Then, all lieutenants are loyal and they will send their command to the other lieutenants. All three lieutenants learn the same set of commands, so they will choose the same course of action when they take the majority opinion. Second, suppose that C is loyal. Then C sends the same command to all three lieutenants, but one of the lieutenants is disloyal. A loyal lieutenant will hear from another loyal lieutenant and from the disloyal lieutenant. The command from C will agree with what the lieutenant hears from the other loyal lieutenant, so taking the majority opinion will ensure that the loyal lieutenants will make the same decision, and that decision will be the order that C sent.

These results can be extended to arbitrary numbers of processors or generals. Suppose that there are t traitors among M generals. Then we can prove:

Theorem 2 If $M \leq 3t$, the system cannot reach agreement.

We will not actually prove this theorem, but we instead give some insight about why it is true. Suppose there was an algorithm A that would solve the Byzantine generals problem with t traitors among $M = 3t$ generals. Then we could solve the three Byzantine

FIGURE 11.3   Four generals can reach Byzantine agreement.

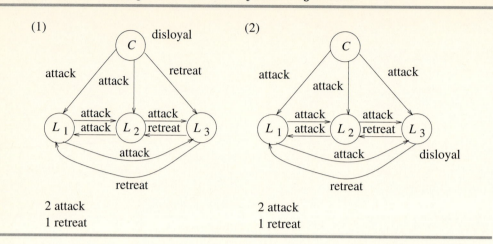

general agreement problem. Each of the generals would simulate the actions of t of the generals in algorithm A. Since we know the three Byzantine general agreement problem cannot be solved, A cannot work.

A more formal proof of the theorem requires a precise description of what information is sent, and how. The bibliography at the end of this chapter has some further references.

If there are t traitors and $M > 3t$, we can solve the Byzantine generals problem. The algorithm to solve the Byzantine generals problem is parameterized by k, the maximum number of traitors that can be tolerated. The k-traitor Byzantine general protocol $BG(k)$ will correctly find a consensus opinion if $M > 3k$ and $t \leq k$. The cost of the protocol grows rapidly with k, so it is desirable to use as small a value of k as is prudent.

The $BG(k)$ protocol has a number of similarities to the one-traitor, four-general example. First, decisions are made by majority consensus. If the processor must tabulate an even number of votes, there might be no majority. In that case, the processor decides on a default value ("Retreat", for example). Second, the processor must communicate with others to determine the majority decision. Note that in the four-general example, each lieutenant performed its own broadcast after receiving the commander's orders. The lieutenant's broadcast did not need to be reliable, because the opinions of a disloyal lieutenant can be discarded.

The $BG(k)$ protocol makes the use of the function in Algorithm Listing 11.1 to compute its decision after hearing the opinions of other processors.

ALGORITHM LISTING 11.1

Majority and default decisions.

majority(v1,v2,...,vn)
    Return the majority v among v1,v2,...,vn, or "Retreat" if no majority exists.

ALGORITHM LISTING 11.2

Base case for a Byzantine Generals broadcast.

BG_Send(0,v,l)
    The commander broadcasts v to every lieutenant in l.
BG_Receive(0)
    Return the value the sent to you, or "Retreat" if no message is received.

The $BG(k)$ protocol is recursive. Performing a broadcast that can tolerate k traitors requires that the lieutenants perform broadcasts that can tolerate $k - 1$ traitors. Why? Suppose that the commander is disloyal and sends to half of the loyal generals the command "Attack" and sends the command "Retreat" to the other half. If the disloyal lieutenants are in collusion with the commander, they can give the loyal lieutenants different versions of the command they received and make some of the loyal lieutenants attack while others retreat. So, the loyal lieutenants need to agree on the opinions of all lieutenants, including the disloyal ones. Since the commander is a traitor, there are only $k - 1$ traitors among the lieutenants, so $BG(k - 1)$ will suffice.

The protocols that we present do not explicitly account for the timing or which processor performs a broadcast and which processor waits to receive the message. Accounting for these details would greatly complicate an already complicated protocol (but we will illustrate the execution soon).

We first present the base case, $BG(0)$, shown in Algorithm Listing 11.2. This is a regular broadcast. Since there are no faulty processors, all messages are delivered within the timeout period.

The Byzantine General protocol for $k > 0$ is shown in Algorithm Listing 11.3. The recursive protocol $BG(k)$ uses two unusual constructions. First, the BG_Receive(k) protocol "knows" which lieutenants have broadcast or rebroadcast a message v. Second, every lieutenant will broadcast and then receive a message. Both are accomplished by careful scheduling. Each lieutenant will follow the same protocol, and will therefore know who has broadcast or rebroadcast the message and when one processor should be listening to

ALGORITHM LISTING 11.3

Byzantine General's broadcast.

BG_Send(k,v,l)
    send v to every lieutenant on l
BG_Receive(k)
    let v be the value sent to you, or "Retreat" if no value is sent.
    Let l be the set of lieutenants who have never broadcast v.
        (i.e., the delivery list for this message).
    BG_Send(k-1,v,l - Self)
    Use BG_Receive(k-1) to receive v(i) for every i in l - Self.
    return majority(v,v(1),...,v(|l|-1)).

---

another. A disloyal lieutenant can refuse to obey the protocol, but a message that is not received is treated as a "retreat" message.

Figure 11.3 shows an execution of $BG(1)$ on four generals. A more complex example with seven generals and two traitors is shown in Figure 11.4. The commander starts the protocol by sending his order to each of the six lieutenants. Each lieutenant then sends his order to the other five lieutenants. Since there may be a traitor among the lieutenants, the broadcast has to be executed using $BG(1)$. So, each lieutenant broadcasts to the others what he heard the other lieutenants say. For example, L_2 tells L_3, L_4, L_5, and L_6 what L_1 said his order is. Next L_3 tells L_2, L_4, L_5, and L_6 what L_1 said his order is, and so on. The execution of the protocol follows the tree structure of successive broadcasts (we show only one branch of the tree in Figure 11.3). All of the message passing is used to build consensus values. To help keep track of what messages are passed, we label them with their senders. O_i represents the command sent to L_i, and $L_i : O_i$ is L_i's rebroadcast of its command. $L_j : L_i : O_i$ is L_j's rebroadcast of what L_i said his order was.

At the end of a step of $BG(k)$, the processors have enough information to make a consensus decision. Consider what happens when L_1 finishes its rebroadcast of $L_1 : O_1$ using $BG(1)$. Each processor has a consensus opinion of what the other processors think that L_1 broadcast. So, L_2 has the messages ($L_3 : L_1 : O_1$, $L_4 : L_1 : O_1$, $L_5 : L_1 : O_1$, $L_6 : L_1 : O_1$). Similarly, L_3 has the messages ($L_2 : L_1 : O_1$, $L_4 : L_1 : O_1$, $L_5 : L_1 : O_1$, $L_6 : L_1 : O_1$). Each lieutenant other than L_1 uses this set of messages to compute its

FIGURE 11.4   An execution of $BG(2)$ on seven generals.

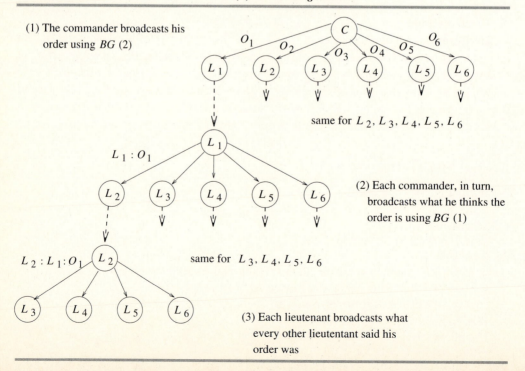

(1) The commander broadcasts his order using $BG(2)$

same for L_2, L_3, L_4, L_5, L_6

(2) Each commander, in turn, broadcasts what he thinks the order is using $BG(1)$

same for L_3, L_4, L_5, L_6

(3) Each lieutenant broadcasts what every other lieutenant said his order was

version of L_1's order using the majority function. This continues in turn for L_2 through L_6. When all of the $BG(1)$ steps are finished, each processor has a consensus opinion of what the other processors received for their commands. For example, L_1 has the opinions $(L_2 : O_2, L_3 : O_3, L_4 : O_4, L_5 : O_5, L_6 : O_6)$, and so on. Each processor decides on the commander's order by taking a majority opinion of the majority opinions.

The tree structure of the communication lets us perform the scheduling for the unusual constructions. Every processor knows which step of the algorithm is being executed, because the system is synchronous. So, every processor knows whether it should be broadcasting a message, listening for a message, or doing nothing. Every processor knows which other processors were on the delivery list for the message it received, so every processor that receives a message can compute l. Note that we cannot send l as part of the message — a disloyal general could send a corrupt delivery list.

The proof that the the BG protocol works is asymmetric — A disloyal commander causes more problems than a disloyal lieutenant. So, we consider these cases separately.

Lemma 1 For any t and k, if the commanding general is loyal, the $BG(k)$ protocol is correct if there are no more than t traitors and at least $2t + k$ generals.

Proof: The proof is by induction on k. First, its easy to see that the $BG(0)$ protocol works when the commander is loyal (all loyal lieutenants follow the commander's orders). For the induction, we will assume that the $BG(k - 1)$ protocol works for $M = 2t + k - 1$ generals and t traitors, $k > 0$. Let us consider the $BG(k)$ protocol with $M = 2t + k$ generals and t traitors. The commander broadcasts his order, and then each lieutenant broadcasts the order he received using the $BG(k - 1)$ protocol. Each loyal lieutenant can reliably broadcast his order, because there are $M = 2t + k - 1$ generals and t traitors when he applies $BG(k - 1)$. However, the disloyal generals might succeed in giving different loyal generals different versions of their own orders. When a loyal lieutenant collects the consensus opinion, he will have the commander's order and the orders of the $t + k - 1 \geq t$ loyal lieutenants, and they will all agree. So, by taking a majority opinion, the $t + k \geq t + 1$ opinions of the loyal generals will outweigh the t opinions of the disloyal generals. ∎

To finish showing that the BG protocol is correct, we need to account for the possibility that the commanding general is disloyal.

Theorem 3 For any k, the $BG(k)$ protocol is correct if there are more than $3k$ generals and no more than k traitors.

Proof: Again, the proof is inductive. The base case is $BG(0)$, and here the protocol is correct because there are no disloyal generals. We'll assume that the $BG(k - 1)$ protocol works if there are more than $M = 3(k - 1)$ generals and no more than $t = k - 1$ traitors. Let us consider the case when there are $M = 3k + 1$ generals and $t = k$ traitors, and the commander broadcasts an order using the $BG(k)$ protocol. If the commander is loyal, the lemma that we just proved tells us that the protocol will be correct (since there are more than $2t + k = 3k$ generals). If the commander is disloyal, every loyal lieutenant might receive a different order. But, when any lieutenant broadcasts its opinion, there will be at most $k - 1$ traitors and at least $3k$ generals. So, our inductive assumption that the $BG(k - 1)$ works applies, and every lieutenant receives a consistent description of the other lieutenant's version of the orders. Therefore, every loyal lieutenant computes a consistent value of the majority opinion. ■

Notice that executing the BG protocol is very expensive; the $BG(k)$ protocol on M processors requires $O(M^k)$ messages. The Byzantine general's problem has received wide attention in the literature, and there are many extensions of the problem. For example, one can greatly reduce the number of messages required if one can assume the use of unforgeable signatures (i.e., encrypted messages). We will explore some of these extensions in the exercises. However, we will not pursue the Byzantine general's problem further in this book.

While there have been cases where errant programs have caused very serious problems in distributed systems (i.e., the malfunctioning switch that caused outages in AT&T's long distance service in the northeast in 1990), the problems can be solved by simpler application-specific consistency checks. In engineering terms, the Byzantine general's problem is usually not worth solving. The model of the BG problem assumes that the malfunctioning processors are *adversarial* and will do everything in their power to make the protocol fail. Failed processors are usually not quite that smart, and the effort needed to make the system immune to Byzantine failures can be better applied to improving system components, testing of software, and applying software engineering techniques to distributed software development. Still, it is worth being familiar with the problem and its solution. In fact, there has been a great deal of work to investigate Byzantine general protocols that can be made efficient. We discuss several of these in the bibliography.

11.3 IMPOSSIBILITY OF CONSENSUS

The previous section gave algorithms for obtaining consensus in spite of a very difficult failure model. This section will show that distributed consensus is impossible, even when Byzantine failures are excluded. The natural question to ask is how to reconcile these two statements.

When we solved the Byzantine general's problem, we assumed that the system was synchronous. That is, all functioning processors will respond within a fixed amount of time. If the system is asynchronous, we have no such guarantee. It turns out that this change makes consensus an impossible problem. That is, there is no algorithm that can guarantee that all nonfailed processors agree on a value within a finite amount of time.

The impossibility result depends completely on the fact that the distributed system is asynchronous. While processors can fail, the system is otherwise reliable. There are no Byzantine failures, and every message that is sent is eventually received. The processors are required to solve the simple agreement problem of the Byzantine general's problem: Each processor p_i has a value V_i, and all nonfaulty processors are required to agree on a consensus value $f(V_1, \ldots, V_M)$.

In this section, we describe the formal proof of Fischer, Lynch, and Peterson (FLP). The proof uses a model which is similar to the global states model described in Chapter 9.

A **consensus protocol** R consists of N processors that communicate to achieve consensus. Each processor p has an **input register** V_p and an **output register** C_p. The input register contains the value that the processor contributes to the consensus, and the output register contains whatever consensus value is decided upon. In addition, each processor is in some state, which corresponds to its internal execution of the protocol. When the protocol starts, each processor is in an *initial state*, which is the same for all processors except for the value of the input register and the knowledge of the processor's identity. While the protocol executes, the contents of C_p are a NULL value, X. When a processor decides on a consensus value, it writes a 0 or a 1 into C_p. Once a processor writes a value into its output register, it is not allowed to change the value (you need to make up your mind at some point).

Processors communicate by sending messages. The model of message passing we use here is slightly different from that used for distributed snapshots, since we do not require that messages are received in the order sent. A message consists of a pair (p, m) where p is the destination of the message and m is the message content. The contents m must be drawn from a fixed set of possible messages $\mathcal{M}$ (for example, all 1024-byte strings). The *message system B* contains all messages that have been sent but not yet delivered. The two operations on the message buffer are:

- send(p, m): Add (p, m) to B.
- receive(): When executed at processor p, either delete a message (p, m) from B and return m or return NIL and leave B unchanged.

Observe that we are permitting the message passing system to act nondeterministically, by returning any message that has been sent or by not returning any message at all. We will require that messages are eventually delivered. In particular, receive() can return NIL only a finite number of times if a message has been placed in B.

The global state of the system consists of the local processor states and the current value of B. In the **initial global state** I, each processor is in its initial state and B is empty. A **step** of the protocol takes the system from one global state to another by executing the following at a processor p:

1. receive a message m.
2. Based on the local state s and the contents of m (possibly NIL), send an arbitrary but finite number of messages.
3. Based on the local state s and the contents of m, change the local state to s'.

A step corresponds to the receipt of a message, possibly a NIL message. We will assume that a processor can always handle the reception of a NIL message. If we know the current global state, the execution of a step can be fully described by the processor that executes the step p and the message m that is received. We will call the pair (p, m) an **event**. If G is a global state, an event e can be **applied** to G and cause a step to occur, putting the system into the state $e(G)$. A **schedule** is a (possibly infinite) sequence of events. When a schedule is applied to a global state G, it results in a sequence of steps that we will call a *run*. A global state G' is *reachable* from G if there is a schedule σ such that $\sigma(G) = G'$. If G' is reachable from the initial global state I, then G' is **accessible**.

A global state G has a **decision value** $d \neq X$ if there is a processor p such that $C_p = d$ in G. A consensus protocol is **partially correct** if it satisfies the following two conditions:

1. No accessible global state has more than one decision value.
2. There are initial global states I_0 and I_1 such that there is a global state accessible from I_0 that has decision value 0 and there is a global state accessible from I_1 that has decision value 1.

If processor p takes only a finite number of steps in run r, p is **faulty**; otherwise p is **nonfaulty**. A run r is **admissible** if at most one processor is faulty and all messages that are sent to the nonfaulty processors are eventually received. Run r is a **deciding run** if some processor reaches a decision state in r. Finally, a consensus protocol $\mathcal{P}$ is **totally correct in spite of one fault** if it is partially correct and every admissible run is a deciding run.

Before we proceed to state and prove the impossibility of distributed consensus, let us examine the framework we have just defined. The model of the distributed system is similar in most aspects to the model we presented for distributed snapshots or global states. The main differences are that we want to make special note of an aspect of the protocol (i.e., the input and output variables) and the fact that messages are not necessarily delivered in the order sent. Since we can attach sequence numbers to obtain ordered message passing, the models are essentially the same. Finally, several steps in the model of Chapter 9 are summarized as a single step in this model. The communication that can significantly change the state of the protocol is the receipt of a message. Similarly, steps correspond to message receipts. Steps are defined in this way to simplify the discussion of the protocol. A similar approach is taken in some of the message recovery models in Chapter 13.

Next, we need to distinguish between faulty and nonfaulty processors. Since processors can delay their responses arbitrarily, no finite execution can distinguish between faulty and nonfaulty processors without explicit "I have failed" messages being posted. We do not want "I have failed" messages, so we use infinite runs instead. A failed processor stops, so it can take only a finite number of steps. A nonfailed processor can always receive a NIL message, so it can take an infinite number of steps in an infinite run.

The definition of a correct protocol is somewhat indirect. First, we need the assurance that a decision will be a consensus — that at most one value will be decided upon. The second clause in the definition of *partially correct* ensures that the protocol P cannot be trivial (cannot always decide 0, for example). Next, we need an assurance that the protocol always makes a decision as long as too many faults do not occur. The definition of *totally correct* does this by requiring that admissible runs are deciding. Note that the definition of totally correct only requires that some processor make a decision, not that all processors make a decision. However, a processor that makes a decision can broadcast the decision to all other processors. The nonfaulty ones can make the same decision when they receive the message. (Why?) It is easier to focus on the single event of a single processor reaching a decision, so we will use it in the proof.

We now have the framework to state the theorem:

Theorem 4 No consensus protocol is totally correct in spite of one fault.

Proof: To prove the theorem, we will first need the following lemma.

Lemma 2 Let σ_1 and σ_2 be two schedules such that the set of processors that execute steps in σ_1 are disjoint from the set that execute steps in σ_2. Let $\sigma_1(G) = G_1$ and $\sigma_2(G) = G_2$. Then $\sigma_1(G_2) = \sigma_2(G_1) = G_3$.

Proof: Since both σ_1 and σ_2 can execute in G, the messages necessary to start both σ_1 and σ_2 must already be in the message buffer $B(G)$. Since σ_1 and σ_2 execute on different processors, executing σ_1 does not prevent the execution of σ_2, and vice versa (i.e., the messages that enable the schedules are not used up). Finally, the result of executing σ_1 and then σ_2 is the same as executing σ_2 and then σ_1 because the sequences involve different processors. Therefore, the execution sequences commute. ∎

The theorem is proved by showing that for any protocol, we can prevent it from making up its mind. So, we need to define the set of decision values that the protocol can reach. If the protocol can decide on either 0 or 1 from global state G, G is **bivalent**. If only one of the decision values can be reached, G is **univalent**. If only 1 (or 0) can be decided on, G is **1-valent** (or **0-valent**).

Let us assume that we have a protocol P that is totally correct in spite of one failure. Then, we will show that P must have a number of properties that are contradictory. We will conclude that there is no such P. To prove a key lemma, we will make another assumption to obtain a contradiction. The reader will need to keep track of which assumptions we are making; otherwise the arguments look a bit circular.

First, we observe that P has a bivalent initial state. Why? Let us assume that P has only univalent initial states. Since P is partially correct, P must have a 1-valent and a 0-valent initial state. We can move from one initial state to another by changing the value of V_p for one of the processors p. An example is illustrated in Figure 11.5. Eventually, we can move from the 0-valent state to the 1-valent state. Therefore there must be a 0-valent initial state I_0 that differs from a 1-valent initial state I_1 by the value of V_p for one processor p. Suppose there is a run σ on I_0 where p fails at the first step and all processors execute without failure. Since our protocol $\mathcal{P}$ is totally correct, we are assured that the run reaches a decision value. We can execute this run starting with I_1 and get the same results, because I_0 and I_1 differ only at V_p and p makes no steps. If the result of σ on I_0 is a 1, then I_0 is bivalent. Otherwise, I_1 is bivalent.

Since we know that we can start with a bivalent global state, we should next show that we can always stay with a bivalent global state.

Lemma 3 Let $\mathcal{P}$ be a protocol that is totally correct, let G be a bivalent global state, and let $e = (p, m)$ be an event that can occur in G. Let A_{no-e} be the set of global states reachable from G without applying e, and let A_e be the result of applying e to A_{no-e}.

FIGURE 11.5   Bivalent states must exist.

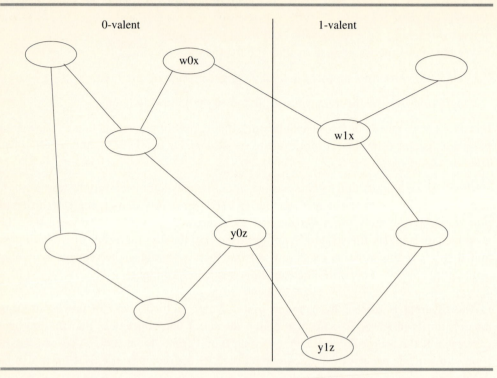

That is, $A_e = \{e(F)|F \in A_{no-e}$ and *e is applicable to* $F\}$. Then A_e contains a bivalent global state.

   Proof: First, note that $A_e = \{e(F)|F \in A_{no-e}\}$, because if e can be applied to G, the corresponding message m is in $B(G)$. Since we do not apply e, m is still in F for every F in A_{no-e}. Therefore, e can be applied to F. Figure 11.6 shows a schematic of the set A_{no-e}.

   Suppose for contradiction that A_e contains no bivalent states. (Note: This assumption is in addition to the one that P is totally correct in spite of 1 fault.) Let G_0 and G_1 be 0-valent and 1-valent states reachable from G (both must exist because G is bivalent). Furthermore, we can find G_0 and G_1 in A_e. Why? If G_0 is in A_e, the proof is complete. If G_0 is in A_{no-e}, we can use $e(G_0)$, which must also be 0-valent. If G_0 is not in A_{no-e} or A_e, e must have been applied in the sequence σ that led from G to G_0. Let σ_e be the prefix of σ that ends with e. Since $\sigma_e(G)$ is in A_e and A_e contains no bivalent states (by assumption), $\sigma_e(G)$ is 0-valent. Next, apply the same reasoning to G_1. This reasoning is illustrated in Figure 11.6.

   Finally, we can find G_0 and G_1 in A_e such that $G_0 = e(F_0)$, $G_1 = e(F_1)$, and F_1 and F_0 are *neighbors*. That is, there is an event d such that either $F_0 = d(F_1)$ or $F_1 = d(F_0)$. Why? Let G'_0 and G'_1 be the 0-valent and 1-valent states that we know must exist in A_e. Let σ_0 be the sequence that leads to G_0, and let σ_1 be the sequence that leads to G_1. Let $l_1 = |\sigma_1|$ and $l_2 = |\sigma_2|$. Let $\sigma_i[k]$ be the sequence consisting of the first k events in σ_i,

FIGURE 11.6 G_0 and G_1 must exist in A_e.

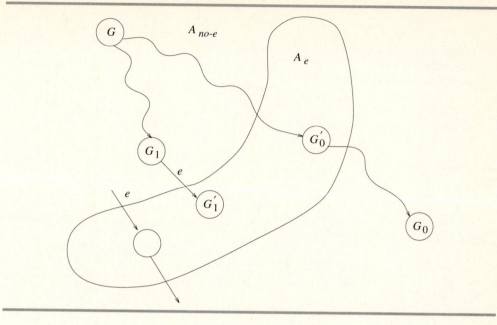

for $i = 1, 0$. The global state $e(\sigma_i[k](G))$ is in A_e for $k = 0 \ldots |l_i - 1|$, so it is univalent. Working from $k = l_i - 2$ to $k = 1$, compare whether $e(\sigma_i[k](G))$ and $e(\sigma_i[k+1](G))$ have different valency. If so, the proof is complete; otherwise continue. If we run through all k for both $i = 0, 1$ without finding acceptable states, we know that $e(\sigma_0[1](G))$ is 0-valent and $e(\sigma_1[1](G)$ is 1-valent. The state $e(G)$ is in A_e, so it is univalent (by assumption). If $e(G)$ is 1-valent, $F_1 = G$ and $F_0 = \sigma_0[1](G)$. The opposite applies if $e(G)$ is 0-valent. This reasoning is illustrated in Figure 11.7.

Let us assume that $F_1 = d(F_0)$ (the reasoning is the same if we assume the opposite). Since d is an event, it occurs at processor p_d. Then $p_d = p$, (i.e., e and d occur at the same processor). Why? If they occurred at different processors, e and d would commute. Therefore $d(G_1) = d(e(F_1)) = e(d(F_1)) = e(F_0) = G_0$. But, G_1 is univalent. So, e and d must occur at the same processor, p.

Let us consider a deciding run σ_{no-p} on F_0 in which p executes no steps (as in Figure 11.8). Note that the deciding run must exist because $\mathcal{P}$ is totally correct. That is, the state $A = \sigma_{no-p}(F_0)$ has a decision value. Since p executes no steps in σ_{no-p}, we know that

$$
\begin{aligned}
e(A) &= e(\sigma_{no-p}(F_0)) \\
&= \sigma_{no-p}(e(F_0)) \\
&= \sigma_{no-p}(G_0)
\end{aligned}
$$

FIGURE 11.7 F_0 and F_1 must be neighbors.

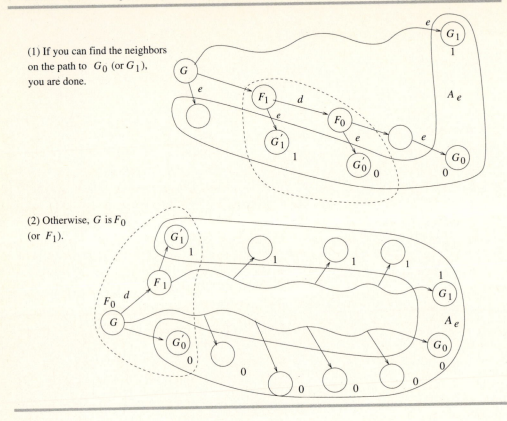

(1) If you can find the neighbors on the path to G_0 (or G_1), you are done.

(2) Otherwise, G is F_0 (or F_1).

and that

$$
\begin{aligned}
e(d(A)) &= e(d(\sigma_{no-p}(F_0))) \\
&= \sigma_{no-p}(e(d(F_0))) \\
&= \sigma_{no-p}(G_1)
\end{aligned}
$$

Since G_0 is 0-valent and G_1 is 1-valent, A must be bivalent. Therefore, σ_{no-p} cannot be a deciding run. Since P is totally correct in spite of one failure, the deciding run must exist. We resolve the contradiction by admitting that A_e contains a bivalent global state. ∎

Notice what we did in the lemma. We started with the assumption that P is totally correct in spite of one failure. Next, we assumed that all states in A_e are univalent. We found a contradiction. So, we concluded that *if P is totally correct in spite of one failure, A_e contains a bivalent state*. We still need to show that P cannot be totally correct in spite of one failure.

With the lemma, we can see that it is possible to prevent P from ever making a decision. If P is about to execute an event e that would change the state from a bivalent

FIGURE 11.8 State A must be bivalent.

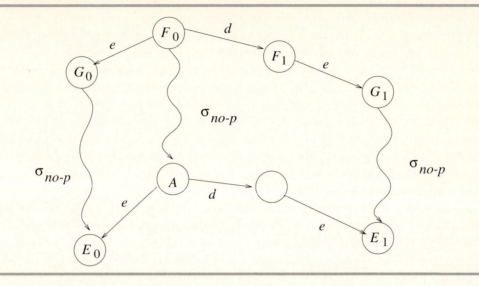

to a univalent one, we know that we can execute some other events until it is possible to execute e without making a decision.

We would like to do a little more. We can create an execution in which no failures occur and every message is eventually delivered but which prevents P from ever making a decision. That is, we need to deliver on the promise of constructing an admissible run. That way we can finish the contradiction that is central to the proof.

We let the processors execute in a round robin fashion. The processor p that is allowed to execute either reads a NIL from the message buffer B or is allowed to read the earliest message (p, m) in B. At this point we check to see if executing (p, m) results in a univalent state. If so, we execute a schedule σ to reach state G' such that $e(G')$ is bivalent. We can find G' by an exhaustive search on all possible schedules of length 1, of length 2, and so on. The lemma guarantees that eventually we will find the σ that we need. Then we execute e.

In the run, every processor executes an infinite number of steps and every message is eventually delivered. However, no decision is ever made. Therefore, we conclude that if P is totally correct, there is an admissible run in which P makes no decision. Therefore P is not totally correct. ∎

Discussion

The proof of the FLP theorem is in a sense the opposite of the proof that the BG algorithm is correct. To show that the BG protocol is correct, we showed how we can use majority voting to foil any possible adversary. To prove the FLP theorem, we played the part of the adversary and foiled the protocol.

The FLP result is considered to be a very negative result. Some researchers have used it to conclude that studying asynchronous distributed systems is futile because consensus is impossible. However, distributed systems are being used and depended on now, their use is increasing, and they are overwhelmingly asynchronous distributed systems. How can we connect the theoretical result to this reality?

A theorem of what is impossible must be studied very carefully. If one doesn't fully understand the result, one can become misled about the real meaning of the result. It would seem that many of the bases have been covered, since the system model is very general and no processor actually has to fail to produce the adversarial argument. However, there are three avenues of attack.

The first avenue observes that the theorem does not exclude the possibility of a partially correct protocol, and the adversary must be very clever to foil the agreement protocol P. This fact suggests that when we develop a distributed agreement protocol P, we take care to ensure that it will fail to reach agreement only in some very rare cases. When a failure does occur, we let humans sort the problems out.

Unfortunately, real-life circumstances might make the protocol that we devised in the lab fail often, because the assumed rare circumstances actually happen quite frequently. A second avenue of attack is to randomize the protocol. While the randomized protocol will occasionally fail for no good reason, it will fail rarely and will not consistently fail.

The third avenue of attack is to redefine what we mean by *distributed agreement*. Perhaps we do not need to insist on a completely consistent decision, but one that is only relatively consistent. We have already seen an example of this approach in the invitation algorithm for election. Instead of insisting on a global coordinator, we only need a coordinator for a group of processes that are willing to cooperate. In general, the *relatively consistent* approach lets a processor ignore messages from a different processor that is not responding quickly enough. (However, there are some subtleties; see the exercises.)

In the remainder of this chapter, we explore randomized consensus protocols. The chapter on managing replicated data will make extensive use of methods for achieving asynchronous distributed consensus, at least most of the time for most of the processors.

11.4 RANDOMIZED DISTRIBUTED AGREEMENT

The difficulty of reaching agreement depends on the strength of the adversary that is trying to prevent the processors from reaching agreement. In the Byzantine agreement problem, the adversary is allowed to choose t generals to be disloyal and have them send arbitrary messages. However, all loyal generals respond correctly and within specified time limits. In the FLP model, all processors work correctly and all messages are delivered, but the adversary is allowed to choose when processors can execute and when messages are delivered.

The FLP adversary is permitted knowledge of the state of execution of all processes in the system, but it is not allowed to interfere with the execution of any process that it chooses to execute. In particular, an adversary is generally not permitted to bias a sample of a random number (although it is allowed to learn the result of the "coin flip" and act accordingly).

Recent research has developed several **randomized consensus** protocols that halt after an expected polynomial number of steps. At first glance, it is not intuitively obvious that these protocols work, nor is it obvious how they are derived. As an aid to understanding, we will present a sequence of increasingly refined protocols, the last of which is a t-resilient protocol for randomized consensus that requires a polynomial number of messages to be sent. Our starting point is a **shared memory** randomized consensus protocol that requires an exponential number of messages be sent. These protocols were proposed over the course of a decade, in roughly the sequence presented in this section.

In a *shared memory* protocol, the system consists of a number of processors N, of which up to t can be faulty. Processors communicate by using *shared registers*. The shared registers are nonfaulty, and accesses to the shared registers are assumed to be sequentially consistent. The shared registers may be of fixed size (even 1 bit) or arbitrary size and may admit a variety of atomic operations. In this section, the registers can be of an arbitrary size, but the only permitted operations are atomic reads and writes of the contents of the registers.

Shared memory consensus protocols do not use a realistic processing model, because if the processors are unreliable, why should the registers be reliable? However, distributed protocols are often first described as shared memory protocols, because it is generally easier to develop such protocols. In this section, we will see an example of how to transfer results developed for the shared memory model to the distributed memory model.

11.4.1 Exponential Time Shared Memory Consensus

Let us consider the following simple-minded approach to writing a consensus protocol in a shared memory system. We initialize by choosing a value to prefer, V_p. Then, we look at the value preferred by every other processor $\{V_i\}$. If all other processors have the same value $V_i = V_p$, we decide on value V_p. Otherwise, we flip a coin and set V_p to the value of the coin flip. If everyone starts out with the same preference (V_p), everyone will agree immediately. Otherwise, after enough coin flips, everyone will flip the same value. Then, no one will notice that someone else has a dissenting value, so everyone will agree on the same value.

The problem with the naive protocol is that it implicitly assumes that the processors execute in rounds (i.e., are synchronous). However, our system is asynchronous, and incorrect executions are easy to devise. Since the protocol can work on a synchronous system, our first attempt to fix up the protocol adds execution rounds. In addition to storing its preferred decision value, every processor stores in a shared register the number of protocol rounds it has executed. If a processor reads the preferred decision number and round number of every other processor and sees that every processor is at the same round and prefers the same decision, it can decide on the preferred value.

Unfortunately, this scenario is not likely because up to t processors can fail (and thus not increase the number or rounds they have executed). Let us instead concentrate on the fastest processors — the ones that have executed the largest number of rounds. If all of the fastest processors agree, and we know that the slower processors will eventually agree with the fastest ones, we can decide on the agreed upon value. We will need to assure

ALGORITHM LISTING 11.4

Shared and local variables for the randomized consensus protocol.

V[M]	Shared array of decision values, one for each processor.
V[i].value	Preferred decision value for processor i.
V[i].round	Execution round of processor i.
local_V[M]	Local storage for a copy of V.
leaders	The processors that have the largest round values in local_V.

ourselves that the slower processors will eventually agree with the fastest ones. We can do that by making the slow processors prefer to accept the value of the fast processors.

With this motivation, we present the algorithm. Algorithm Listing 11.4 shows the array of records (V[M]) stored as shared variables that are used by the consensus protocol and the local variables (local_V[M], leaders) used by a processor.

The algorithm uses the two functions shown in Algorithm Listing 11.5. The consensus protocol is shown in Algorithm Listing 11.6. When the protocol starts, every register V[i] is initialized to a NIL value, and the round is initialized to 0. Note that this protocol assumes that a processor can write both fields of V[i] in an atomic step.

As usual, we present an outline of the correctness proof. Let us loosely define a *round* to be the contents of V.value for a particular value of V.round. The key idea is to consider what happens when all processors choose the same value on a particular round, the *deciding round*. The processors that reach the deciding round first either decide on a value, or continue to store the same value in V[i].value. After the leaders choose the same value, the processors that lag by more than 1 will, on their next round, notice that all leaders agree and set their preference to agree with the leaders. A subset of the processes that lag by 1 will not have read the round value of the leaders and will flip a coin. Since all processors agree on V.value in the deciding round, all of the coin flipping processors will flip the agreement value. In either case, all processors have the same value of V.value for all rounds past the deciding round, so each processor will soon decide on the agreement value.

The significance of requiring that all processors who disagree with the leaders lag by at least two rounds is now clear. Processors that lag by one round might flip a coin and prefer a value different from the one preferred by the current leaders. Processors that lag by two rounds will see that the leaders agree and set their preferences to agree with the leaders. This is illustrated in Figure 11.9.

ALGORITHM LISTING 11.5

Functions used by the randomized consensus algorithm.

leader_set(local_V)	Calculates the set of leaders.
Flip()	Randomly returns either 0 or 1.

ALGORITHM LISTING 11.6

A shared memory randomized consensus algorithm.

```
SM_Consensus(self,preference)
    V[self] = (preference, 1)
    While I have not made a decision
        read V into local_V
        leaders = leader_set(local_V)
        If self in leaders, and for each i such that local_V[i].value ≠ local_V[self].value,
            local_V[i].rounds < local_V[self].rounds - 1
            decide(V[self].value)
        else if i,j in leaders ⇒ local_V[i].value = local_V[j].value
            V[self] = (V[i].value, V[self].round+1) for an i in leaders
        else if V[self].prefer != NIL
            V[self] = (NIL, V[self].round)
        else
            V[self] = (Flip(), V[self].round+1)
```

If the processors do not initially agree on their preferred value, the protocol will execute rounds until all leaders flip the same decision value. In the worst case, all processors

FIGURE 11.9   Processors that lag by 2 will see the agreement.

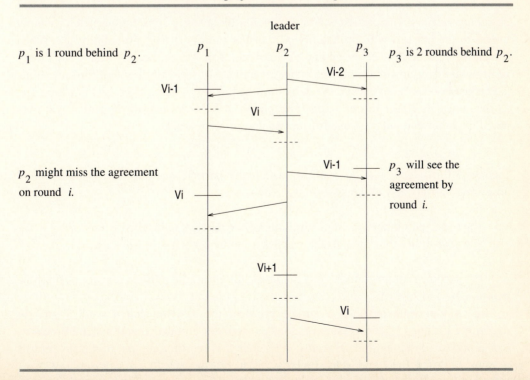

execute synchronously, so the probability that all leaders choose the same value is $O(2^{-N})$. The number of rounds before all leaders agree has a geometric distribution, so elementary probability theory tells us that the expected number of rounds is $O(2^N)$. An interesting aspect of the protocol is that it works better in the presence of asynchrony, because the set of leaders is smaller, so fewer rounds are required.

11.4.2 Polynomial Time Shared Memory Consensus

The SM_Consensus protocol requires an exponential number of steps, as written, because it is very unlikely that all processors will get the same value on their coin flip. Suppose we were to implement a protocol that makes it fairly likely that every processor obtains the same value on its Flip() on a given round r. If every processor obtains the same value for Flip() on an arbitrary round r with probability at least p_{same}, the SM_Consensus protocol will require $O(1/p_{same})$ rounds. If p_{same} is independent of N, only an expected constant number of rounds are required. So, it is worthwhile to spend a fair amount of effort to get every processor to flip the same coin.

We define a **weak shared coin** to be a protocol that returns a value v of either 0 or 1 such that the probability that every processor computes the same value of v is at least p_{same}, independent of the number of processors that participate. If we can execute a weak shared coin protocol in an expected polynomial number of steps, the SM_Consensus will also require only a polynomial number of steps.

The weak shared coin protocol was inspired by the mathematics of a stochastic random walk. In the mathematics of **Brownian motion**, a particle is contained in a line that contains $2M + 1$ positions, numbered $-M \cdots M$. The end points $-M$ and M are called *absorbing barriers*. The particle starts at position 0. At every step, the particle randomly moves to the left (-1) with probability 1/2, or the right (+1) with probability 1/2. When the particle reaches one of the end points (either $-M$ or M), the process stops. The theory of Brownian motion shows that the expected number of steps until one of the end points is reached is $O(M^2)$. (We leave the derivation of this result as an exercise.) Furthermore, as the coin gets closer to one of the end points, it becomes less likely that it will ever reach the other end point. A result from stochastic processes is:

Theorem 5 Consider a random walk in which the particle has starting position x and absorbing barriers at a and b, $a < x < b$. Then,

1. The expected number of steps until one of the barriers is reached is $(x - a)(b - x)$.
2. The probability that the particle reaches a before b is $(x - a)/(b - a)$.

If the particle is at position $M - x$, the probability that the particle reaches position M before $-M$ is $x/2M$.

The random walk suggests a simple protocol for a weak shared coin, shown in Algorithm Listing 11.7. Processors randomly increment and decrement a shared register. If a processor observes that the register reaches a value of KN, the processor returns a value of 1 for Flip() and acts similarly if the register reaches a value of $-KN$. A

ALGORITHM LISTING 11.7

A weak shared coin through shared memory.

```
Integer      counter
Flip()
    while True
        if Rand(0,1) = 1
            increment counter
        else
            decrement counter
        state = counter
        if state ≥ K*N
            return (1)
        if state ≤ -K*N
            return(0)
```

processor will return a value after the protocol has executed $O(K^2 N^2) = O(N^2)$ steps. If the counter reaches a value of $(K + 1)N$, every processor will return 1 (and similarly for $-(K + 1)N$). If the counter reaches a value of $-(K - 1)N$, some processor might return a 0. The probability of reaching $(K + 1)N$ before $-(K - 1)N$ is bounded by $(K + 1)/2K$.

11.4.3 Message Passing Randomized Consensus

If we examine the SM_Consensus protocol, we notice that the protocol is already very similar to a message passing protocol. The only shared variable is the V array. The element V[i] is written to by processor i only and is read by every other processor. So, array V makes shared memory look like a broadcast medium. A naive translation of the SM_consensus protocol to the MP_Consensus protocol is to broadcast all updates. Unfortunately, there is a consistency problem, because messages sent to a processor may be delayed for an arbitrarily long time. The SM_Consensus protocol makes use of the sequential consistency of the shared registers. A lagging process is guaranteed to see that the leaders agree, and change its preference accordingly. A clever adversary can block messages sent from the leaders to the lagging process, causing the lagging process to flip coins and disagree with the leaders.

One important property of the shared registers that we used in the SM_Consensus protocol is causality. If a processor reads my register, the processor reads information that is at least as up to date as the information that I read. In addition, if a processor issues a read following a write, the read must be delayed until the write is completed at all sites.

It would seem that the consistency problems could be solved by requiring that when a processor broadcasts the update to its register, it waits for all other processors to acknowledge the message. However, up to t processes can fail, so a single failure will cause the protocol to halt. Therefore, a processor can only wait for $n - t$ acknowledgments. However in this case, processors might execute their protocols using inconsistent data.

ALGORITHM LISTING 11.8

Variables used by the consistent broadcast module.

TS	Lamport timestamp.
Value[M]	One record for each processor.
.state	The most recent value written by p_i.
.ts	The time that p_i wrote .state.
is_sending	True if the processor is performing a consistent send.

We will make use of an **update propagation** technique to ensure consistency (see Chapter 12 for more material on update propogation). Suppose that every processor tells every other processor of the states of the registers that it knows about. Then, processor A can send its state to processor C even if C does not directly receive A's message, because the message can be propogated by an intermediate processor B. If $n > 2t$, then there must be always be an intermediate processor B that will forward the message.

Since processors are propogating the state of other processors, every processor must store its most recent knowledge of the state of every other processor. To ensure causality, each processor must store a vector timestamp. Finally, each processor must keep track of the number of processors that have acknowledged its update of its state. Therefore, the data structures required for the message passing module are those shown in Algorithm Listing 11.8. The algorithm to perform a consistent broadcast is shown in Algorithm Listing 11.9.

The algorithm to receive a consistent broadcast message is shown in Algorithm Listing 11.10. The equaltime() procedure tests the timestamps in NV and Value for equality. The precedes_eq() procedure tests to see if NV.ts $\leq_V$ Value.ts. If the processor receives a message NV with a vector timestamp that is not less than or equal to its own, the NV must contain at least one field that is more up to date than Value.

The Consistent_Send and Consistent_Receive provide a property that is even stronger than causality and sequential consistency. In fact they take an atomic snapshot of the values of Value[i] for $i = 1, \ldots, N$.

ALGORITHM LISTING 11.9

Consistent multicast algorithm — sending.

```
Consistent_Send(state)
    is_sending = True
    Value[self].state = state
    Value[self].ts = TS
    broadcast(Value)
    acks = 1
    wait until acks ≤ N-t
    copy Value into local_V
    is_sending = False;
```

ALGORITHM LISTING 11.10

Consistent multicast algorithm — receiving.

```
Consistent_Receive()
    while True
        receive(p,NV,remote_sending)
        if equaltime(NV,Value)
            acks ++
            if remote_sending = True
                send(p,NV,False)
        if not precedes_eq(NV,Value)
            Update V with the newer information in NV
            broadcast(Value)
            acks=1
```

Theorem 6 Let $Value_p$ and $Value_q$ be the contents of the Value array stored at processors p and q, respectively, immediately after executing the Consistent_Send routine. Then $Value_p \leq_H Value_q$ or $Value_q \leq_H Value_p$.

Proof: The theorem is proved by observing that between any pair of processors, there is at least one processor B that propogates information between them. It is B's acknowledgement that guarantees the ordering (i.e., acts as the swing voter). ∎

Returning to the randomized consensus protocol, the only translation that is needed is to combine the distribution of the new consensus opinion with taking a snapshot of Value. The consensus algorithm is shown in Algorithm Listing 11.11. Note that collecting the consistent snapshot of local_V is performed in Consistent_Send.

ALGORITHM LISTING 11.11

Message passing randomized consensus algorithm.

```
MP_Consensus(self,preference)
    mystate = (preference, 1)
    While I have not made a decision
        Consistent_Send(mystate)
        leaders = leader_set(local_V)
        If self in leaders, and for all i,
            local_V[i].value ≠ local_V[self].value ⇒ local_V[i].rounds < local_V[self].rounds - 1
            decide(mystate.value)
        else if i,j in leaders ⇒ local_V[i].value = local_V[j].value
            mystate = (local_V[i].value, local_V[self].round+1) for an i in leaders
        else if mystate.value ≠ NIL
            mystate = (NIL, mystate.round)
        else
            mystate = (Flip(), mystate.round+1)
```

ALGORITHM LISTING 11.12

Weak shared coin through message passing.

```
counter = 0                    // local counter value

Flip()
    while True
        if Rand(0,1) = 1
            increment counter
        else
            decrement counter
        Consistent_Send(counter)
        global_counter=0
        for i = 1 to N
            global_counter += local_V[i].value
        if global_counter ≥ K*N
            return (1)
        if global_counter ≤ -K*N
            return(0)
```

The communications behavior of the shared coin is more difficult than that of the consensus protocol, because the processors are operating on only one variable. We can make use of the commutative and associative properties of addition to let us use a broadcast. In particular, we can calculate the value of the shared coin by summing the contributions of each individual processor. The algorithm to flip the coin is shown in Algorithm Listing 11.12.

11.5 SUMMARY

In this chapter, we examine the problem of reaching distributed consensus under different failure models. First, we develop an algorithm for reaching consensus among the nonfaulty processors when the faulty processors may send arbitrary messages. By exchanging enough state information, an adversary that controls less than one-third of the processors cannot prevent the nonfaulty processors from correctly completing the protocol. The algorithm requires that the nonfaulty processors always meet timing constraints.

Next, we assume that a failed processor stops execution and does not transmit spurious messages. However, nonfaulty processors may experience arbitrary timing delays. In this case, we show that it is impossible to guarantee that all nonfailed processors reach consensus. Since the failed processors are well behaved, a comparison of these two results shows that asynchronous systems are very difficult to handle. This is the well-known FLP impossibility result (named after the initials of the authors).

Much of the applied distributed computing research is searching for a way to circumvent the FLP impossibility result. There are three approaches. First, we can observe that only the guarantee of termination is impossible. So, we can develop a protocol that will always reach consensus if it terminates, and we can then focus our efforts on ensuring that nontermination is rare. Second, we can redefine our goals and only require consensus among the processors that do not experience problems. For example, if we define a faulty processor to be one that has a message delivered late, we can use the Byzantine generals protocol for consensus. The difficulty is that it can be hard to identify the failed processors. Third, we can use a randomized consensus protocol. The chapter concludes with a discussion of this approach.

The FLP impossibility result is the reason why the mutual exclusion algorithms of Chapter 10 do not handle failures well. The invitation algorithm can terminate because it uses a form of relative consistency. The atomic commit algorithms of Chapter 12 guarantee consensus if they terminate but cannot be guaranteed to terminate. The group membership algorithms use unreliable failure detectors to achieve relative consistency.

ANNOTATED BIBLIOGRAPHY

The Byzantine generals problem was first described and solved by Lamport, Shostak, and Pease [LSP82, PSL80]. These authors also show that if messages can be encrypted, a much more efficient protocol can be used [LSP82]. Dolev et al. give an algorithm for solving the Byzantine generals problem without encryption and using only a polynomial number of messages. Dolev also describes and solves Byzantine agreement when the connectivity between generals is limited [Dol82]. Fischer, Lynch, and Merritt [FLM86] give a unifying framework for many variants of the Byzantine Generals problem. Barborak, Malek and Dahbura [BMD93] present a survey of fault detection and Byzantine agreement in a distributed system.

The impossibility of asynchronous consensus is given by Fischer, Lynch, and Patterson [FLP85]. The idea that asynchronous consensus is probably impossible had been known for several years. In [Gra78], it was informally shown that nonblocking consensus is impossible. The source of asynchrony can be due to slow processors or unreliable networks. Dolev, Dwork, and Stockmeyer [DDS87] show whether consensus is possible or impossible for models with a variety of failure assumptions. Chandra, Hadzilacos, and Toueg [CHT92] show that the weakest failure detector that can guarantee consensus is one that eventually stops giving false positives. Malki, Birman, Ricciardi, and Schiper [MBRS94] show that uniform actions (executed either by no processors or all nonfailed processors) can be implemented. Chandra, Hadzilacos, and Toueg and Charron-Bost [CHTCB95] show that a variant of group membership (thoroughly discussed in the next chapter) cannot be guaranteed to reach agreement. Herlihy [Her91] discusses consensus in the context of wait-free objects. A good survey of the field of impossibility results is [Lyn89].

The exponential time randomized asynchronous agreement protocol is given by Chor, Merritt, and Shmoys [CMS85]. Aspnes and Herlihy [AH90] use a "weak shared coin" to speed up the exponential randomized consensus. The results on random walks can be found in most textbooks on stochastic processes, such as [Ros83]. The algorithm for shared memory emulation is given by Bar-Noy and Dolev [BND89]. A more general algorithm for shared memory emulation that has the feel of quorum protocols is given in [ABND90]. Aspnes [Asp90] modified his shared coin algorithm to implement asynchronous agreement directly.

In this book, we have space for only a short coverage of distributed computing theory. We refer the interested reader to the recent book by Lynch [Lyn96] for more information.

EXERCISES

1. Suppose that the Byzantine generals only need to reach an *approximate* agreement. That is, the following two conditions must hold:
   a. All loyal generals attack within 10 minutes of each other.
   b. If the commander is loyal, all loyal generals attack within 10 minutes of the time given by the general's order.
   Show that approximate agreement cannot be guaranteed unless more than two thirds of the generals are loyal.

2. Suppose that the Byzantine generals send signed messages to each other. A loyal general's signature cannot be forged, any alteration of a signed document can be detected, and all signatures can be verified. However, one disloyal general can forge the signature of another disloyal general. Give an algorithm that guarantees interactive consistency for any number of traitors (if there are fewer than two loyal generals, interactive consistency is vacuously satisfied).

3. A *group membership* protocol ensures that every processor in a group has the same group membership list L. In the *weak group membership* (WGM) problem, every processor has an initial membership list L_{init}. A processor asks to leave the group, and a protocol is executed to install L_1 at every processor. Further,
   a. If p_1 or p_2, or both, ask to leave L_{init}, some processor eventually installs a new view and no processor installs a different view.
   b. If p_1 (or p_2) is the only processor that asks to leave L_{init}, there is a run in which only p_1 (or p_2) is removed from the group.
   Show that no protocol guarantees WGM. *Hint*: Cast WGM in terms of the decision problem of Section 11.3. The crucial problem is to show that an initial bivalent configuration exists.

4. A *failure detector* is a mechanism for detecting the failures of remote processors. A *weakly complete* failure detector eventually reports the failure of a processor at some nonfailed processor. A *strongly complete* failure detector reports the failure of a processor at all nonfailed processors. A *weakly accurate* failure detector can report that some nonfailed processors have failed, but there is at least one nonfailed processor that is never reported as having failed by any of the failure detectors. A *weak* failure detector is weakly complete and weakly accurate, while a *strong* failure detector is strongly complete and weakly accurate.

Give an algorithm to create a strong failure detector from a weak failure detector. *Hint*: Consider using an information propogation technique.

5. Suppose that you have a strong failure detector such that the processor that is never suspected of failure also never suspects that a nonfailed processor has failed. Give an algorithm for solving consensus.

6. A *uniform action* is an action executed either at all nonfailed processors or at none of them. Give an algorithm to implement uniform actions in an asynchronous environment where no messages are lost, failed processors do not recover, and no more than $M/2 - 1$ processors fail.

7. Modify the randomized consensus protocol to use only one call to the shared coin protocol. That is, all processors agree on the value of the shared coin. *Hint* : Modify the shared coin by using a bias when the observed value of the coin reaches a threshold value.

8. A *shared memory consensus* protocol is a protocol in which a set of M processors use shared registers to reach a consensus decision about their input values. The registers are assumed to be reliable and always respond to a processor's access. A shared memory consensus protocol is *wait-free* if a nonfailed processor is guaranteed to reach its consensus decision after executing a finite number of steps, regardless of the execution delays of the other processors.

Suppose that the only operations on the shared registers are atomic reads and atomic writes. Show that no protocol is guaranteed to reach consensus among all nonfailed processors if $M \geq 1$. *Hint*: Consider an execution where two processors p and q are about to reach different decision values and will commit to their decisions after an access to the shared registers. Then draw a diagram similar to the one in Figure 11.8.

9. Suppose that, in addition to atomic read and write operations on the shared registers, the agreement protocol also has the use of an atomic *fetch-and-add* operation. A fetch-and-add will increment the value of a register and return its value, in one atomic step. Give a wait-free decision protocol for two processors that uses fetch-and-add.

10. Show that there is no wait-free consensus protocol for three or more processors using atomic reads, writes, and fetch-and-add.

CHAPTER

12

Replicated Data
Management

In this chapter, we examine approaches to managing replicated data. Replicated data management is a fundamental building block for most distributed system activities. For example, distributed databases have the primary goal of managing data. Many system components, such as name servers or file servers, are designed to store and retrieve data consistently. The components of a distributed computation need to maintain a common idea of the current state of the computation.

Because the problem is so important, there has been much work done to develop techniques for managing distributed and replicated data. We will discuss three main methods: **database techniques**, **reliable broadcast**, and **update propagation**. At the time of this writing, it is not clear which method is the best. We feel that each of the approaches has merits and problems, and areas of best application. Certainly each method is worth studying, if only to examine the similarities and the differences.

The fundamental problem in managing replicated data is to maintain the consistency of the data. In a local sense, a query on the data should return the data value that was "most recently written". In a global sense, the interaction of a program with the collection of all global data should obey a global consistency constraint. For example, one might want the program to act like a transaction (i.e., appear to occur atomically), or one might want a program's interaction with the shared data to be causal. Different methods of managing replicated data give subtly different consistency guarantees. Depending on the application, these guarantees might be too weak to ensure correctness or too expensive to be justified.

A primary motivation for replicating data is *fault tolerance*. However, this term can have different meanings in different contexts. First, one might want to ensure that data is never corrupted or that the effects of a completed transaction are never lost. In this case, the database techniques of logging and commit points are necessary, but replication is not required. Second, one might want to ensure that a service is available in spite of failures. In this case, replication is necessary. Third, one might want to ensure that a distributed computation makes progress in spite of failures. In this case, the techniques of checkpointing and message logging, discussed in the next chapter, might be the most appropriate.

12.1 DATABASE TECHNIQUES

In this section, we study database techniques for managing replicated data. While we will not be examining the many subtle issues of implementing a database, we will examine the fundamental algorithms for maintaining data consistency in a distributed database.

The fundamental building block of a distributed database is a **transaction**, which is a program that appears to execute at an atomic point in time. Therefore, transactions should be **serializable** (i.e., appear to execute in some serial order), and only the effects of completed transactions should be visible to other transactions. More generally, a transaction should satisfy the ACID (atomicity, consistency, isolation, and durability) properties discussed in Section 4.3. See also Section 6.3 for a discussion of how transactions are used to build distributed system services.

Transactions were originally proposed for centralized multiuser databases to protect the integrity of the data. Researchers realized that building a distributed system out of transactions is a very attractive idea because it solves two difficult problems. The data consistency problem is solved because transactions appear to execute serially. If a person writes a program that is correct when it executes in isolation, it will still be correct when it executes as one of many concurrent programs executing in a distributed system. Because only the effects of completed transactions are visible to other transactions, a failed transaction has no effect on the shared data. Furthermore, the effects of a completed transaction are guaranteed to be visible in spite of failures. These properties make the system fault tolerant.

We can see that providing a distributed transaction facility can greatly facilitate the implementation of a distributed program. However, there are several issues to be addressed before a distributed transaction facility can be written. The two principle components of a distributed transaction facility are:

1. A mechanism to ensure that a distributed transaction occurs atomically at all sites.
2. A mechanism to ensure serializability, especially on replicated data.

A transaction processing facility must be **recoverable**, or able to restore a consistent state after a failure. A transaction processing facility implements fault tolerance by careful attention to recovery. We will briefly discuss recovery issues in this chapter to show the types of issues that must be addressed. We will discuss recovery further in the next chapter in the context of message recovery.

12.1.1 Database Logging and Recovery

A **transaction** is a program that accesses shared data. During its execution, a transaction tr will read a number of global data items (its **read set** R_{tr}) and write into a number of global data items (its **write set** W_{tr}). These data items are located at the **processor set** of the transaction P_{tr}. The set of processors that store data items in W_{tr} is called the **update set** U_{tr}. If the transaction fails before it completes, only some of the values in W_{tr} will be updated. Unless we take special actions, other transactions will be able to see the half-completed execution of the failed transaction.

To understand how recovery works, let us consider a scheme for implementing atomic transaction on a uniprocessor. The fundamental idea is the **commit point**. When a transaction tr asks the database system to update a data item w, the database system does not immediately update w but instead records the proposed update in tr's update set W_{tr}. When tr completes, it makes a decision to **commit** its execution. Before the transaction is allowed to commit, the contents of W_{tr} must be flushed to a special file called the **database log** in the **precommit** operation. After W_{tr} is flushed to the log file, a **commit record** for tr is written to the log file. Finally, the contents of W_{tr} are applied to the globally accessible database.

Writing the commit record to the database log is the commit point of tr. Suppose that a failure occurs before the tr's commit point. Since none of the tr's updates have been applied to the global database, the database system can restart in a state in which tr never executed. Suppose that a failure occurs after tr's commit record is written. Because W_{tr} is flushed to the log before the commit record is written, all updates that tr made can be applied to the database (if they haven't been applied already). Suppose that the system fails while the commit record is being written. Modern disk drives contain error-checking codes. So, either the commit record for the transaction is recorded in such a way that it can be read upon recovery, or it is garbage. If tr's commit record is garbage, tr is aborted; otherwise tr is committed. So, no matter when a failure occurs, either all updates that a transaction makes are recorded in the database, or none of the updates are recorded.

Notice that it is crucial for W_{tr} to be flushed to stable storage before tr's commit record can be written. A transaction will generally need to take actions to ensure recoverability before committing. These actions are referred to as the **precommit** of the transaction. A transaction may commit only after it has precommitted.

We note that there are other approaches to implementing recovery. The method we described is called **redo-only**, because it will update stale data after a failure. Another method for implementing atomicity is called **undo-only**. When tr performs an update on w, it performs the update immediately and also makes note of w's old value. If tr commits, the database system throws away the previous value of w. If tr aborts, the old value of w is restored. Recovery algorithms that are a hybrid between undo-only and redo-only are also possible. Although recovery is an important topic, a full discussion of recovery is beyond the scope of this book. This chapter's Annotated Bibliography has some pointers to better discussions.

In a distributed transaction, the atomic commit problem is to get all processors involved in the transaction to agree to either commit or abort the transaction. The set of processors in P_{tr} is called the **participants** in transaction tr. One of the participants executes the transaction program. This processor is called the **coordinator**. Each participant executes a logging protocol similar to the one describe above.

12.1.2 Two-phase Commit

Let us consider the problem that arises from a naive approach to distributed commit. Suppose that coordinator tr, executing on processor q, completes its execution and decides to commit. It commits the values it updated locally and then sends a commit message to every participant $p_i \in P_{tr}$. If one of the participants p_j has failed, it will not successfully commit the transaction. So, the transaction will not be atomic.

The problem with the naive commit protocol is that there is no coordination among the processors involved in the transaction. Before deciding to commit, the coordinator needs to poll the participants to see if they can commit the transaction locally. If so, the coordinator can make the decision to commit with the assurance that all sites will eventually commit their local updates.

More formally, an atomic commit protocol must satisfy the following conditions:

1. All processors reach the same decision (commit or abort).
2. A processor cannot reverse its decision once made.
3. The decision is "Commit" only if all processors can agree to commit the transaction.
4. If there are no failures and all processors can agree to commit the transaction, then the decision is "Commit."
5. If all processors can agree to commit the transaction, and all failures are repaired, then all processors eventually agree to commit the transaction. That is, if all processors have voted to commit the transaction in G_0, C is the property that all processors have committed the transaction, and Q is the property that all failures are repaired in the run, $eventually(C, G_0, Q)$.

Conditions 1 and 2 state that all processors must reach a consensus decision. Condition 3 states that any problem causes an abort. Conditions 4 and 5 require the protocol to commit its value if no problems occur.

The coordinator executes the protocol shown in Algorithm Listing 12.1, called **two-phase commit**, or 2PC. The first phase of the protocol is to obtain the votes from all participants, and the second phase to distribute the agreement to commit. A YES vote means that a participant wants to commit the transaction, while a NO vote means that the participant is aborting the transaction. Once a participant votes, it is not allowed to change its vote. Before a processor votes to commit a transaction, it is required to **precommit** the transaction (flush its updates to the log, etc.). The precommit ensures that the transaction is in a state to be committed.

A participant executes the protocol shown in Algorithm Listing 12.2. If a participant fails while executing the 2PC protocol, it must be able to recover enough state to finish the protocol. A transaction is in one of four states, *executing, uncertain, committed,* or *aborted* (abbreviated E, U, C, and A). The transaction is executing from its initiation point to its commit point and is committed or aborted after the commit or abort is finished (i.e., the commit or abort record is written to the log). A transaction is uncertain while the 2PC protocol is being executed. Note that these states are defined locally at each participant. A participant can recover the state of a transaction by examining its log. If there is a commit or abort record for the transaction, the transaction is in the C or A state, respectively. If there is no commit, abort, or voting record, the transaction was executing at the time of the failure. If there is a vote record, but no commit or abort record, the transaction is uncertain.

ALGORITHM LISTING 12.1

2PC algorithm for the coordinator.

```
2PC_Coordinator()
    precommit the transaction
    For every participant p,
        send(p,VOTE_REQ)
        wait up to T seconds for VOTE messages
            Vote (sender; vote_response):
                if vote_response = YES
                    increment the number of yes votes
        If each participant responded with a YES vote
            commit the transaction // write a YES vote and commit record to the log.
            for every participant p,
                send(p,COMMIT)
        else
            abort the transaction
            for every participant p,
                send(p,ABORT)
```

ALGORITHM LISTING 12.2

2PC algorithm for the participant.

```
2PC_Participant()
    while True
        wait for a message from the coordinator
            VOTE_REQ (coordinator):
                if I can commit the transaction
                    precommit the transaction
                    write a YES vote to the log
                    send(coordinator,YES)
                else
                    abort the transaction
                    send(coordinator,NO)
            COMMIT (coordinator):
                commit the transaction
            ABORT (coordinator):
                abort the transaction
```

So, a transaction must write a vote record when it initiates the 2PC protocol, for recovery. Writing the vote record can be done implicitly, but the protocol we present will explicitly write the YES vote.

The protocol as described will handle the failure of any processor prior to the vote request — by aborting the transaction. Failures after voting must be handled by a **recovery protocol**. The actions that a participant takes upon recovery depend on the state of the transaction at that participant at the time of the failure.

The idea behind the recovery protocol is illustrated in Figure 12.1. Every participant (including the coordinator) is required to vote, and once a processor votes it is not allowed to change its vote. The coordinator votes YES only if every participant votes YES, otherwise the participant votes NO. The purpose of the recovery protocol is to determine a stable property — whether or not every processor voted YES. Basing 2PC on detecting a stable property ensures that every participant will make the same decision about committing or aborting the transaction.

When a processor recovers from a failure, it aborts all transactions that have not yet precommitted (whether the processor is the coordinator or a participant of the transaction). This unilateral action is permissible because the processor is free to abort the transaction (i.e., vote NO) up to the time that the transaction is precommitted. Therefore, the stable property for the transaction is that a participant voted NO, and all processors will abort the transaction. If the coordinator fails after precommitting but before committing or aborting the transaction, it can unilaterally abort the transaction since the coordinator has again delayed its vote (in practice, the coordinator will attempt to commit the transaction). If a participant fails after precommitting but before committing or aborting the transaction, the transaction might have been committed or aborted during the failure

FIGURE 12.1   Stable properties in the 2PC protocol.

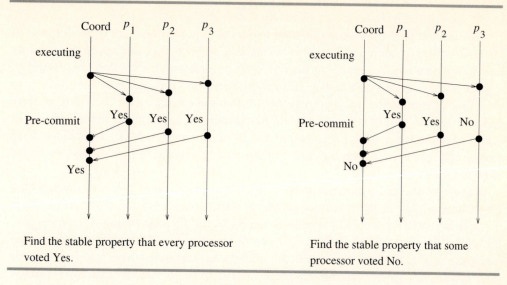

Find the stable property that every processor voted Yes.

Find the stable property that some processor voted No.

(depending on the votes of the other processors). Therefore, the recovered processor cannot take a unilateral action; instead it must contact the other processors to determine the decision (i.e., compute the stable property). Since the coordinator casts the final vote, recovery is a matter of learning whether some participant has committed or aborted the transaction.

The discussion of the recovery strategies makes the structure of the 2PC algorithm clear. Before the 2PC protocol starts, a transaction tr is in the executing state, and any participant can arbitrarily decide to abort tr (i.e., vote NO). The coordinator cannot decide to commit the transaction because one of the participants might have voted NO. Instead, the coordinator moves the transaction to the uncertain state, in which no participant can unilaterally decide to abort the transaction. Since the processors are not allowed to change their votes, the votes of the processors are a stable property. Once the coordinators hears all of the votes, it can compute the stable property and decide whether to commit or abort the transaction. That is, the YES vote flushes the state of the participants to the coordinator, as in the distributed snapshot protocol. The flush ensures that when the coordinator commits the transaction, it is in a global state such that no participant is in the E state.

The impossibility of asynchronous distributed consensus has the implication that all distributed commit protocols have the weakness that they are not guaranteed to complete. Any atomic commit protocol has an **uncertainty period**, during which time the protocol might not be able to complete if the wrong processors fail (hence the name of the uncertain state). If the protocol cannot complete, it is said to be **blocked**. The uncertainty period of a participant executing the 2PC protocol is the time during which it is in the uncertain state (hence the name). If the coordinator fails after each participant has voted YES, the coordinator might or might not have received all of the votes and decided to commit the transaction. The participants must wait until the coordinator recovers before committing or aborting their local transactions. During this time, the local data accessed by the transaction must be locked to ensure serializability.

The duration of the uncertainty period is typically small compared to the duration of the transaction. In addition, commit blocking is a problem that can always be fixed by human intervention (i.e., repairing the processor or replaying the commit log). However, a processor that is part of a high-performance transaction processing system is likely to be acting as coordinator for many transactions simultaneously and, therefore, is likely to be in the uncertainty period of several transactions at any random point in time. So, a processor failure is likely to cause several blocked commits. Many companies make money only when their databases are running, so any amount of blocking is considered to be too much.

Because of the great practical need, much research has been done on **nonblocking algorithms**, which are algorithms for parallel or distributed access to shared data that have the property that no processor can block access to the data by failing. Unsurprisingly, no algorithms that solve the atomic commit problem have been developed that do not make special assumptions about the underlying hardware. Other researchers have tried approaches where the commit problem is defined in such a way as to make a nonblocking commit algorithm possible. However, these approaches give only weak correctness guarantees. A discussion of their application is beyond the scope of this book, although we give a few references. An alternative approach is to minimize the duration of the blocking period, to make blocking unlikely to occur. A great deal can be done in the engineering of the system – 2PC executions are streamlined and given a high priority, 2PC execution logs are written on a special device that can be replayed while the host processor recovers, and so on. While small engineering considerations make the system work, they are beyond the scope of this chapter. Finally, the atomic commit protocol can be designed to reduce the uncertainty period. This is the goal of the **three-phase commit protocol**.

12.1.3 Three-phase Commit

The 2PC protocol has an uncertainty period because a processor must detect a stable predicate in order to commit or abort after voting YES. We would like to be able to remove this uncertainty period to as large a degree as possible. The **three-phase commit protocol** (3PC) will avoid blocking as long as a majority of processors can agree on the action to be taken, whether it is to commit or abort.

Since the participants will need to vote on committing or aborting a transaction, we will need to add some additional states that correspond to voting. The trick behind 3PC is to ensure that the property that a majority of the participants vote to commit (abort) is a stable property. Since a participant can vote for only one of the two options of commit or abort, every participant will make the same decision.

Given a processor that is executing transaction tr, we will label the execution of the tr on that processor by one of a number of states that depends on the local execution of the commit protocol. Before the commit protocol begins, tr is in an *executing*, or E state. When the protocol ends, tr is in a *committed* (C) or an *aborted* (A) state. When a processor is first contacted by the commit protocol and votes YES about tr, tr enters an *uncertain*

(U) state (if *tr* has not already aborted). The participant next enters a state in which it votes to commit *tr*, and we call this state *committable* (Ce). For the committable state to make sense, it must still be possible to abort a transaction in the Ce state (otherwise, the Ce state is the same as the C state). However, a processor cannot arbitrarily abort a Ce transaction; it must be required to come to a consensus with other processors to abort the transaction. Therefore, we will need an *abortable* (Ae) state to vote for an abort. Fortunately, no other states are needed, and we can proceed to derive the protocol.

If no failures occur, the 3PC protocol is the same as the 2PC protocol, but with an extra phase added. The coordinator's protocol is shown in Algorithm Listing 12.3 and the participant's protocol is shown in Algorithm Listing 12.4. The complications occur if there are failures. To make the discussion of failure handling clearer, the 3PC protocol is labeled with the states that the transaction enters at different points in the protocol. The labels can be interpreted as the points at which the participant writes a corresponding log record for later recovery.

As in the 2PC protocol, the 3PC protocol moves the transaction between states and uses intermediate states and the flush technique to ensure that certain states cannot coexist on any consistent state. Since there are so many states and there are complex transition rules, we show a table of the possible state coexistence in Table 12.1 (on p.435). If we restrict this table to states E, U, C, and A, we have a description of state coexistence in

ALGORITHM LISTING 12.3

3PC algorithm for the coordinator.

```
3PC_Coordinator()
State: E     precommit the transaction
State: U     For every participant p,
                     send(p,VOTE_REQ)
                     wait up to T seconds for VOTE messages
                         Vote (sender; vote_response):
                             if vote_response = YES
                                 increment the number of yes votes
                     If not every participant responded with a YES vote
State: A             abort the transaction
 (vote No)           for every participant p,
                             send(p,ABORT)
                     exit()
State: Ce    For every participant p,
 (vote Yes)          send(p,PRECOMMIT)
                     wait until a majority of participants has acknowledged the PRECOMMIT
                         ACK (sender):
                             increment the number of acknowledgments
State: C             commit the transaction
                     for every participant p,
                             send(p,COMMIT)
```

ALGORITHM LISTING 12.4

3PC algorithm for a participant.

```
3PC_Participant()
State: E    wait for a message from the coordinator
                VOTE_REQ (coordinator):
                    if I can commit the transaction
State: U            precommit the transaction
                    send(coordinator,YES)
                else
State: A            abort the transaction
                    send(coordinator,NO)
                    exit()
            ABORT (coordinator):
                abort the transaction
                exit()

            wait up to T seconds for a message from the coordinator
                PRECOMMIT (coordinator):
State: Ce           send(coordinator,ACK)
                ABORT (coordinator):
State: A            abort the transaction
                        exit()
                Timeout:
                    Execute the recovery protocol
                    exit()

            wait up to T seconds for a message from the coordinator
                COMMIT (coordinator):
State: C            commit the transaction
                Timeout:
                    Execute the recovery protocol
                    exit()
```

the 2PC algorithm. If we restrict our attention to the E, U, Ce and C states, then we have a description of normal 3PC execution. Handling the voting states requires some delicacy. If a participant is in the Ae state, it is voting to abort the transaction but suspects that the transaction can be committed. The Ae state can coexist with any other state, but only a minority of participants can be Ae if some processor has committed the transaction. If a participant is in the Ce state, it knows that every other participant can commit the transaction but does not yet know whether the transaction will be committed. So Ce cannot coexist with E. Also, if one participant has aborted, only a minority of processors can be in the Ce state.

The coordinator can detect a failure at one of two points, when waiting for votes and when waiting for acknowledgments of the PRECOMMIT message. If a participant does

TABLE 12.1   State compatibility.

	E	U	Ce	C	Ae	A
E	Yes	Yes	No	No	Yes	Yes
U		Yes	Yes	Majority are C or Ce	Yes	Yes
Ce			Yes	Yes	Yes	Majority are A or Ae
C				Yes	Majority are C or Ce	No
Ae					Yes	Yes
A						Yes

not respond to the vote request with a YES message within the timeout, the coordinator (which is in the U state) can unilaterally decide to abort (by voting NO, the coordinator ensures that no participant can move into the Ce state). After the coordinator sends the PRECOMMIT messages, the protocol enters the uncertainty period, and a decision can only be made by majority voting. However, the coordinator can decide to commit once a majority of participants respond with an ACK, because the stable property is ensured.

If the coordinator fails, the participants must communicate and reach a consistent decision. Furthermore, this decision must be consistent with any decision that could have been made in the past or could be made in the future (due to failures). To ensure a consistent decision, we base the decision to commit or abort on a stable property — that a majority of processors has voted to commit or abort. To ensure that this property is stable, we will not allow processors to change their vote (change from Ae to Ce, or vice versa). In the exercises, we explore variants of 2PC in which a participant can be persuaded to change its vote.

In the 3PC protocol, the participants elect a new coordinator when they suspect that the current coordinator has failed. The new coordinator asks each processor in its group for the state of the transaction and then makes a decision about moving toward committing or aborting. Based on the results of its poll, the coordinator decides on a course of action using one of the **majority termination rules:**

1. If a participant reports a C state, the coordinator decides to commit the transaction and sends a COMMIT message to all of its participants.
2. If a participant reports an A state, the coordinator decides to abort the transaction and sends an ABORT message to all of its participants.
3. If at least one participant reports a Ce state, and enough participants report U and Ce to be a majority of all processors involved in the transaction, then coordinator sends PRECOMMIT messages to all processors that did not report a Ce state. The coordinator

decides to commit and sends COMMIT messages when a majority of all processors have reported a **Ce** state.

4. If no participant reports a **Ce** state, and enough participants report **U** and **Ae** to be a majority of all processors involved in the transaction, the coordinator sends PRE-ABORT messages to all processors that did not report an **Ae** or **Ce** state. The coordinator decides to abort and sends ABORT messages when a majority of all processors have reported an **Ae** state.

5. If none of the above rules apply, block until enough participants join the group so that one of the above rules applies.

Rules 1 and 2 are obvious. For rule 3, if a processor reports a **Ce** state, all participants have voted YES and will abort only if persuaded to do so, so it is safe to attempt to commit the transaction. A majority of all participants should report non-**Ae** states, to help ensure that the protocol makes progress toward a decision. Similarly, for rule 4, if no processor reports a **Ce** state, some processor might have decided to abort. The only safe action in this case is to attempt to abort the transaction.

Note that since a processor never changes its vote from **Ae** to **Ce**, or vice versa, a participant might not react as expected. The coordinator might need to enlarge the group to get a sufficient number of votes to make a decision. We note that it is not really necessary to elect a leader to complete the 3PC protocol, since each participant can poll the other processors and reach its own decisions. However, this approach might create a very large overhead due to polling.

Figure 12.2 shows the state transitions in the 3PC protocol. The normal sequence of states is **E**, **U**, **Ce**, and finally **C**. If the coordinator fails, a participant executing the recovery protocol will try to find a consensus about whether to commit or abort the

FIGURE 12.2   State transitions in the 3PC protocol.

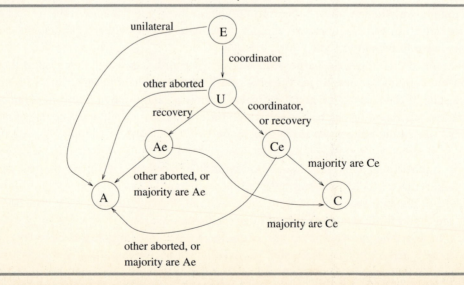

transaction. So, participants in the U state can be pulled into the **Ae** or **Ce** states. When a stable property is detected, participants can commit or abort.

Discussion
The 2PC and 3PC protocols use the following two techniques:

- **Stable properties:** The atomic commit protocols need to ensure that all participants reach the same decision in spite of failures of some of the protocol participants. This is done by tying the decision to the detection of a stable property. Processors that are trying to detect stable properties can make use of transitive information learned from other processors. For example, in the 2PC protocol if one processor has committed the transaction, every processor must have voted Yes.
- **Monotone algorithms:** The atomic commit protocols require that a processor never change its vote (i.e., from No to Yes, Ae to Ce, etc.). Since the vote counts are **monotone**, vote polling can be asynchronous. A processor can decide to commit as soon as it learns of a majority vote, because the majority will never become a minority in the future. If the participants can change their votes, then processors must take care to observe consistent states when changing votes to avoid breaking what should be a stable property.

12.1.4 Replicated Data Management
An atomic commit protocol can manage distributed data but is not sufficient to manage replicated data by itself. The atomic commit protocols require that all participants are available and able to commit the transaction. However, a primary motivation for replicating data is to make the data available in spite of failures. Thus, the failure of a single site should not prevent the other sites from committing the transaction.

Whenever data is replicated, the potential for inconsistent data exists. Consider the following examples:

1. Let data item d be stored at three processors A, B, and C (the copies denoted by d_A, d_B, and d_C). Suppose that when transaction tr_1 applies an update to d, processor C does not respond (because of network problems or a processing overload at C). So, tr_1 applies its update to d_A and d_B only and successfully commits its updates at these sites. When transaction tr_2 reads d, it reads the copy stored at C (which has in the meantime recovered from its previous problems). At this point, tr_2 has read an out-of-date version of d.

Whether or not tr_2 will experience problems (or cause problems) due to its reading an out-of-date version of d depends on the precise application semantics (generally, it will cause problems). In a transaction processing system, it can cause a **nonserializable execution** (we illustrate this with an example in Section 12.1.5). If d represents the state of a system service (for example, a name server), reading an out-of-date copy can cause a failure. For example, d might represent a name server, tr_1 deregisters a service, and tr_2 inquires about the availability and location of a service.

2. Let data item d be stored at four processors, A, B, C, and D (the copies denoted by d_A, d_B, d_C, and d_D). Suppose that two transactions tr_1 and tr_2 decide to update d concurrently. Due to network problems, tr_1 is only able to contact A and B, while tr_2 is only able to contact C and D. Both transactions commit their updates to d at the sites they can contact.

   The copies of d are now inconsistent (d_A and d_B are different from d_C and d_D), and there is no clear way to make the copies consistent again. When two transactions update different copies of a data item independently, we say that the copies have **diverged**. Most algorithms are designed to prevent copies from diverging, and the algorithms that allow divergence must specify how the copies of the data can be made consistent after all failures are repaired.

Serializability

In order to discuss what we mean by a "correct" algorithm for managing replicated data, we need to have a correctness criteria. The usual correctness criteria for a database system is **serializability**, which states that the execution of a set of concurrent transactions must be equivalent to some serial execution of the same transactions. This correctness condition is natural and is very widely accepted. Together with the all-or-nothing execution of a transaction (implemented by an atomic commit protocol), a transaction appears to execute in isolation. Therefore, it is easy to reason about the correctness of a program that executes as a transaction because there is no need to worry about the interactions between concurrent transactions. We will first define serializability for nonreplicated data, and then will develop the extensions for replicated data.

Let $T = \{tr_0, tr_1, \ldots, tr_m\}$ be a set of concurrent transactions. For each transaction tr_i, let R_i be the set of data items that tr_i reads (i.e., tr_i's **read set**), and let W_i be the set of data items that tr_i writes (the **write set**). For most transactions, $W_i \subseteq R_i$. An exception is tr_0, which writes the initial values of the data items.

In an execution $\mathcal{E}$ of the transaction set T, the transactions will access overlapping sets of data, and their data accesses will **conflict**. There are three types of conflicts, and these conflicts are used to establish how the transactions must be ordered in an equivalent serial execution. In order to detect which transactions conflict, we assume that we can determine which transaction wrote the value currently stored by a data item.

1. **Write-write**: If tr_i writes a value into data item d, and the current value of d was written by transaction tr_j, tr_i and tr_j have a *write-write* conflict, denoted by $tr_j \rightarrow_{ww} tr_i$. The arrow expresses the intuition that tr_j must precede tr_i in any equivalent serial execution. Since the updates are linearly ordered, we can assign a sequence of version numbers to the value of d. The initial of d is d_0. If tr_i updates d_k, then tr_i writes d_{k+1}. In this case, we define $tr(d_{k+1})$ to be tr_i.

2. **Write-read**: If tr_i reads d_k, $k \geq 0$, then tr_i must occur after $tr_j = tr(d_k)$ in any serial execution of the transactions. This is a *write-read* conflict, denoted by $tr_j \rightarrow_{wr} tr_i$.

3. Read-write: If tr_i reads d_k, tr_i must occur before $tr_j = tr(d_{k+1})$ in any serial execution of the transactions. This is a *write-read* conflict, denoted by $tr_i \rightarrow_{rw} tr_j$.

If for any reason $tr_i \rightarrow tr_j$, then tr_i must come before tr_j in any equivalent serial execution. So, the problem reduces to finding an ordering of the transactions in $\mathcal{T}$ that agrees with every conflict. To help us find such a serial ordering, we build a **serialization graph** SG. The vertices of SG are $\mathcal{T}$, and (tr_i, tr_j) is a directed edge in SG if and only if there is a conflict $tr_i \rightarrow tr_j$. We can now state the central theorem of serializability theory:

Theorem 7 If the serialization graph SG for execution $\mathcal{E}$ is acyclic, $\mathcal{E}$ is serializable.

Proof: The proof of the theorem is a statement of the obvious. If SG is acyclic (i.e., has no cycles), we can perform a topological sort of SG to find an equivalent serial execution. If SG has a cycle, we conclude that there is a set of transactions $T_{cycle} = \{tr'_1, \ldots, tr'_l\}$ each of which must execute before the other in any serial execution. Therefore, none of them can be executed. ∎

An example serialization graph is illustrated in Figure 12.3 (the initial transaction tr_0 is not shown). An example of a concurrent execution is illustrated at the top of the figure. Notice that the data accesses of the transactions are interleaved. The serialization graph for the execution is illustrated at the bottom of the figure. There is a read-write conflict between tr_1 and tr_2 on x, a write-read conflict between tr_2 and tr_3 on y, and a write-write conflict between tr_3 and tr_1 on z. So, the serialization graph contains a cycle, and the execution is not serializable.

Theorem 7 can only tell us whether or not an execution is serializable with a postmortem analysis. A **concurrency control protocol** is used to ensure that any execution

FIGURE 12.3 Example execution and serialization graph.

Sample execution of transactions
tr_1, tr_2, and tr_3.

$$tr_2 \qquad tr_3$$
$$tr_1$$
$$R_1(x)\, W_2(x)\, W_2(y) \quad R_3(y)\, W_3(z)\, W_1(z)$$

The serialization graph:

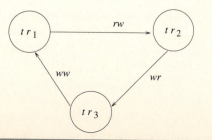

that follows the protocol is serializable. There are many ways to design a concurrency control protocol that enforces concurrency. The most widely used protocol is **two-phase locking (2PL)**. In 2PL, each data item is protected by a lock. Locks come in two modes: read locks and write locks. Many transactions can have a read lock on a data item, but if one transaction has a write lock on a data item, no other transaction may hold any other lock on that data. The rules that 2PL enforces are:

1. A transaction must obtain a read or write lock on data item d before reading d and must obtain a write lock on d before updating d.
2. After a transaction relinquishes a lock, it may not acquire any new locks.

The two phases of 2PL are the lock acquisition phase and the lock release phase. In addition to enforcing serializability, 2PL provides other consistency guarantees (as discussed in the exercises). We note that 2PL is susceptible to deadlock, but we do not pursue that issue here. For more material on 2PL, see Section 6.3.3.

A Quorum-based Protocol

If we can assure ourselves that any pair of conflicting accesses to the same data item access overlapping sites, we can apply a standard concurrency control protocol such as 2PL and ensure serializability. There are many ways to ensure this kind of overlapping, several of which were discussed in the section on quorum-based synchronization protocols (Section 10.1.2). In this section, we will discuss simple read/write quorums.

Here, we assume that the *logical* ordering of the transactions accesses that ensures serializability is externally supplied. We note that there are many possible techniques for obtaining this ordering, and we discuss some of them at the end of the section. The problem of replicated data management becomes one of ensuring that the transactions see a view of the data that is consistent with logical ordering.

A data item d is stored by a set of processors $P(d)$. Each processor $p \in P(d)$ has a **vote weight** $v_p(d)$. The vote weights generalize the idea of voting. One can assign a large vote weight to reliable processors and a small vote weight to unreliable processors. Also, it can help to break ties if an even number of processors manages the data. Every data item has a **read threshold** $R(d)$ and a **write threshold** $W(d)$. In order to read data item d, a processor must access a **read quorum** of d, which is a set of processors $P' \subseteq P(d)$ such that $\sum_{p \in P'} v_p(d) \geq R(d)$. Similarly, a **write quorum** for s is a set of processors $P' \subseteq P$ such that $\sum_{p \in P'} v_p(d) \geq W(d)$. The total number of votes that can be assigned for data item d is $V(d) = \sum_{p \in P} v_p(d)$.

To ensure overlapping access, read and write thresholds must satisfy two rules:

1. $2 * W(d) > V(d)$.
2. $R(d) + W(d) > V(d)$.

We next need to ensure that a reader reads the most recent update of data item d (i.e., ensure that the reader *reads from* the transaction indicated by the logical ordering). Recall that since all updates conflict, we can attach a sequence number to every update. In the discussion of serializability theory, the sequence number was conceptual and was used to simplify the proof. Here, we will make the sequence number explicit. So, every processor $p \in P(d)$ stores along with data item d the sequence number $n_p(d)$ of the version of d that it stores. By examining sequence numbers, a processor can determine which version of d is the most up to date. The rules for executing reads and updates on data items are:

1. *Update:* When a transaction t updates data item d, it locks d and reads the sequence numbers from a write quorum of d. Let $max\_n(d)$ be the largest sequence number read. Transaction t computes the update and then writes the new value of d to the write quorum, along with the sequence number $max\_n(d) + 1$.
2. *Read:* When a transaction t reads data item d, it locks d and reads the sequence numbers from a read quorum of d. Let p' be a processor in the read quorum such that $n_{p'}(d)$ is a maximum. Transaction t then reads the value of d stored at p'.

Because of the requirements for setting the read and write thresholds, any pair of conflicting accesses must access at least one processor in common. The rules for setting and interpreting sequence numbers let the transactions determine which data item in its quorum is the most up to date.

By following the rules for accessing quorums and using an atomic commit protocol, a transaction can use a standard concurrency control protocol over replicated data and have the same consistency guarantees as a nonreplicated database. Before we conclude, we should discuss the implementation of a few details.

- **Locking** For the quorum-based replication protocol to work properly, transactions that make conflicting accesses should not access the same data item concurrently. In the rules for accessing data, we specify that a transaction must obtain a lock before accessing the quorum. We need to specify how to obtain the lock. There are two main approaches:

  1. The transaction can obtain a lock on the data item using one of the methods discussed in Chapter 10. In particular, the transaction can use the quorum-based approach discussed in Maekawa's algorithm. When a processor accesses a copy of d to obtain the quorum, it locks d (in the appropriate mode). The quorum used to obtain the lock can be the same as the one used to access the data. If several transactions access d in conflicting modes concurrently, the transactions can deadlock in obtaining the lock (in addition to deadlocking after obtaining locks). Fortunately, these deadlocks can be resolved by using the method discussed in the context of Maekawa's algorithm.
  2. The transaction can ask a lock manager for permission to access d. In order to make the lock manager fault tolerant, the lock manager must also be replicated. This mostly corresponds to replicating the lock table, and the methods that we have been discussing must be applied. In particular, one must still obtain a lock on the lock table. However, the lock table is likely to be much smaller than the database, so the previous method might be easy to apply.

It is possible to develop quorum-based replicated database protocols that do not use locking and instead use **optimistic** or **timestamp-based** concurrency control. Because no locks are used, transactions can concurrently access data in conflicting modes. The conflicts are resolved at commit time — if a transaction that concurrently accessed an overlapping data item in a conflicting mode has already committed, the commit is refused and the transaction must reexecute. These algorithms have the advantage of not requiring the complexity of distributed locking. Unfortunately, they can also waste a great deal of processing resources. In this chapter, we have focused on locking-based methods because they are the most popular. Section 6.3.3 has a detailed discussion of the optimistic and timestamp-based techniques.

■ **Commit:** It is not enough to update a write quorum of a data item d; it is also necessary to commit the updates. The atomic commit protocols, such as 2PC and 3PC, are discussed under the assumption that all sites must agree to the commit for the commit to successfully occur. When naively applied to replicated data, this requirement is too strong. If every processor that stores a copy of a data item must agree to a commit, any site failure prevents the transaction from committing.

The atomic commit must ensure that any transaction that follows the committing transaction is able to see the updates. So, the requirement for a transaction t to commit is that for every data item d accessed by t, a quorum of the sites that store d must agree to the commit. If 2PL is used as the concurrency control algorithm, only the updates to the data items in the write set of t need to be committed. If a nonlocking algorithm is used, all accesses to the data items must be committed (to ensure serializability).

■ **Caching:** A common technique for obtaining high performance is to take advantage of the **locality of reference** and cache recently accessed data objects. (See Chapter 6 for a discussion of caching in distributed file systems.) The usual method for managing cached data is to use invalidations. (See the discussion in Chapter 7.) If the cached data object is also replicated, some additional care must be taken to ensure consistency.

When a processor reads an (uncached) data object, it creates a cached copy of the data object and of its version number. When a processor updates a data object, it uses the quorum protocol and sends invalidation messages to all of the cached copies. If a processor tries to read a data object, and a valid cached copy is available locally, the processor can use the cached copy for its operations. The transaction must also ensure that the cached copy is up to date by accessing a read quorum of the data object. If a more up-to-date copy of the data item is accessed, the transaction must be aborted. Since version numbers are typically much smaller than data objects, and since the consistency check can occur while the transaction executes, this technique can provide low-latency access to replicated data.

Replicated Servers

Many system services can be implemented using the **client/server** model (e.g., see the material in Chapter 3). A system resource (such as name tables, lock tables, file systems, etc.) is managed by a **server**. The server provides a well-defined interface to the resources it manages, (i.e., a set of **operations** on the resources that are managed). For example, files can be created, deleted, read from, and written to; entries in name tables can be inserted, deleted, read from, and updated. An application program (perhaps even another server) acts as a **client** by requesting the server to perform an operation on the resources it manages and to return the results of the operation. In order to make the server highly available, it must be replicated. If the resources managed by the server can be abstracted as a piece of data, the data replication techniques discussed in this chapter can be applied.

Often the operations provided to the client are independent of each other and are performed on only one logical data item. Examples include name tables, lock tables (perhaps to be used to maintain a replicated database), and file systems. In this case, we do not need to implement a replicated database to provide the replicated service and instead apply some special techniques.

Suppose that server S is replicated at processors $P(S) = \{p_1, \ldots, p_n\}$. When a client requests service from S, it contacts one of the replicas of S, say $S_{p'}$, $p' \in P(S)$. Server $S_{p'}$ can then provide the service by acting as the coordinator of a transaction and using the algorithms previously discussed in this section.

Alternatively, the server S can be implemented by using the **primary copy** method. One of the replicas of the servers, S', acts as the coordinator (i.e., the primary copy), and the participant servers accept commands only from their current coordinator. All operations are forwarded to S', which computes the updates and commits the operation (perhaps using 2PL). Since the execution of the operations is serialized at the coordinator, there is no need to maintain distributed locks. If the coordinator fails, a new coordinator is elected. The new coordinator polls the nonfailed servers to conclude any half-finished operations or commit protocols. After reconfiguring the servers, the new coordinator can execute new operations only if it is in contact with a write quorum of $P(S)$ (otherwise the state of S might diverge).

If a client submits an operation that doesn't modify the state of the server (i.e., submits a **query**), the operation might not need to be processed first at the coordinator. If it is not imperative for the client to receive the most up to date version of data (for example, when reading a block of a file), the query can be executed at any server that is a member of the current quorum group. Even the requirement that the server be a member of the current quorum group might not be necessary. Other optimizations are possible. For example, a client might lock the file through the coordinator and then read the file through the local server.

- **Witnesses:** Replicating a data object d requires that $|P(d)| \geq 3$ to ensure that if one site fails (or if the network partitions), the remaining sites can form a quorum. For most applications, replicating data three times is more than is needed because the most common failure is to have a single processor fail. If d requires a lot of storage (for example, d might be a file in a file system), storing d three times instead of twice is a large waste of space.

A trick that has been proposed is to actually store d at only two sites and add a third site as a **witness** to a quorum. The witness site does not store d but does store enough information about d to participate in the quorum and commit protocols.

12.1.5 Dynamic Quorum Changes

In practice, one needs to be able to change the quorum of sites that store an object. If all sites in the quorum are available, the quorum change can be committed just like any other update (we explore this issue further in the exercises). However, it would be convenient to dynamically change quorums to improve data availability. For example, many databases use a **read-one/write-all** approach to replication, under the assumption that reads are far more common than updates. If a single site fails, updates are blocked. If the quorum is updated after the failure, reads and writes can still occur, using read-one/write-all, while the failed site is being repaired. When the failed site is readmitted to the database, it is required to first obtain the most recent value of the database. The key idea is to treat the quorum of a data object as an object that can be updated by a transaction that obtains its quorum. The application of this type of trick requires a more sophisticated notion of serializability in a distributed system.

One-copy Serializability

The regular theory of serializability can be applied to the quorum-based protocol because the protocols are designed to ensure that every pair of conflicting accesses is performed at a minimum of one common site. A more aggressive protocol cannot necessarily make such a guarantee. For this reason, we cannot base a distributed serializability theory on conflicting accesses to data, but we must tie the accesses *to the sites at which they occur*.

Let us consider an execution $\mathcal{E}$ of a set of transactions $\mathcal{T}$ on the database D. As before, let $P(d) = \{p_{i_1}, p_{i_2}, \ldots, p_{i_k}\}$ be the set of sites at which d is stored during $\mathcal{E}$. We will denote the copy of d stored on processor j by d_j. Whenever transaction tr reads or writes data item d, it reads from or writes to a set of processors $\{p_i\} \in P(d)$. So, a *logical* read or write consists of a sequence of *physical* read and write operations.

A logical write by transaction tr_i on data item d is performed by a sequence of writes on $d_{i_1}, d_{i_2}, \ldots, d_{i_m}$. We denote these by $W_i[d_{i_1}], \ldots, W_i[d_{i_m}]$. A logical read is performed by accessing a set of copies of d, $d_{i_1}, \ldots, d_{i_l}$. After reading the sequence numbers, one of the copies, d_r, is selected and read by tr_i. Since a read consists of two different types of actions, we use different symbols to represent them. The accesses are represented by $A_i[d_{i_1}], \ldots, A_i[d_{i_l}]$, and the actual read is represented by $R_i[d_r]$.

In a replicated database, an execution $\mathcal{E}_i$ at a particular processor p_i is the interleaving of the data accesses of the transactions in $\mathcal{T}$ that occur at p_i. The execution $\mathcal{E}$ is the union of the execution $\mathcal{E}_i$ at all of the processors p_i. The conflicts that we can detect are the conflicting accesses that occur at a particular processor. So, we write $tr_i \rightarrow tr_j$ if tr_i accesses data item d before tr_j accesses data item d, both at some processor p and in a conflicting mode (i.e., ww, wr, or rw).

The fact that the serialization graph of an execution is acyclic does not mean that the execution is equivalent to a serial execution of the transactions on a single copy of the data. In Figure 12.4, transactions tr_1 and tr_2 access data items x (stored at A and B) and y (stored at C and D), and tr_0 is the initial transaction. The transactions use a read-one/write-all-available algorithm. Because sites A and D fail, the conflicts that should exist in the execution cannot be accounted for. So the SG is acyclic, even though there is no equivalent serial execution on a single copy of data.

Since serialization is not strong enough to express our intuitive notion of a correct execution in the presence of replicated data, we need a new definition. An execution $\mathcal{E}$ is **one-copy serializable** (1SR) if it is equivalent to a serial execution of the same transactions on nonreplicated data.

It would be nice to be able to use the serialization graph to determine if an execution $\mathcal{E}$ is 1SR. While $SG(\mathcal{E})$ alone is not strong enough to express the 1SR property, we can add some extra edges to SG that express the idea that replicated copies of a data item represent the same data item. In particular, a **replicated data serialization graph (RDSG)** for an execution $\mathcal{E}$ is $SG(\mathcal{E})$ with enough edges added so that

1. If tr_i and tr_j both write data item d, then $tr_i \rightarrow tr_j$ or $tr_j \rightarrow tr_i$.
2. If tr_j reads a value of d that was written by tr_i, tr_k writes d, and $tr_i \rightarrow tr_k$, then $tr_j \rightarrow tr_k$ (i.e., $tr_i \rightarrow_{wr} tr_j \rightarrow_{rw} tr_k$).

FIGURE 12.4   Example of a non-1SR execution.

X is stored at processors a and b. Y is stored at processors c and d.

Execution	Serialization graph

tr_1: $R_1(x_A)\ (y_D \text{ fails})\ W_1(y_C)$

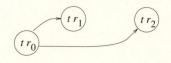

tr_2: $R_2(y_D)\ (x_A \text{ fails})\ W_2(x_B)$

But, tr_1 does not read tr_2's write to x, so $tr_1 \longrightarrow tr_2$

tr_2 does not read tr_1's write to y, so $tr_2 \longrightarrow tr_1$

So, the serialization graph of an equivalent execution with only a single copy of the data is:

The RDSG of the execution is:

Rule 1 states that transactions with overlapping write sets must be ordered. Rule 2 states that if tr_j does not read tr_k's write, and tr_k cannot precede tr_j, then tr_k must follow tr_j. These two rules have the effect of requiring that any pair of transactions that access a data item d in a conflicting manner must be ordered. Rule 1 handles ww conflicts and rule 2 handles rw conflicts. Since a transaction tr_j that reads d must read d from a particular transaction tr_i, immediate wr conflicts will be in $SG(\mathcal{E})$. Rule 2 extends the order to all rw conflicts.

For example, consider Figure 12.4. Both tr_1 and tr_2 have ww conflicts with tr_0 in SG, so we do not need to apply rule 1. Since tr_1 does not read x from tr_2, and $tr_0 \rightarrow tr_2$, we need to add the edge $tr_1 \rightarrow tr_2$. Similarly, we need to add the edge $tr_2 \rightarrow tr_1$. The RDSG for the example execution has a cycle between tr_1 and tr_2. We would like to conclude that the execution is not 1SR. In fact, we can do so.

Theorem 8 Given an execution $\mathcal{E}$, let $RDSG(\mathcal{E})$ be the set of all replicated data serialization graphs for $\mathcal{E}$. If there is an $R \in RDSG(\mathcal{E})$ such that R is acyclic, $\mathcal{E}$ is 1SR.

Proof: In light of Theorem 8, it is easy to prove that the quorum protocol is correct when 2PL is used. Why? Because $SG(\mathcal{E})$ is an RDSG. We can also see that there is room to improve on the quorum protocol. Theorem 8 does not require that the serialization graph be an RDSG, only that the necessary edges can be added. Furthermore, rule 1 gives us some leeway to set the edges (we can choose $tr_i \rightarrow_{ww} tr_j$ or $tr_i \rightarrow_{ww} tr_j$ if they are not already ordered). So, concurrent writes to a data item are allowable, as long as all subsequent transactions agree on which write was the last write. ∎

View-based Quorums

A data item d is stored at a set of sites $P(d)$, but some of these sites might be failed or not communicating with the main portion of the system. If we have a good reason to suspect that a site $p \in P(d)$ has failed, we can delete it from the set of processors from which d is accessible. The benefit we gain is that the failed sites do not have to be accounted for in any quorum used to access the data.

We define a **view** of a data item d to be the current notion of the sites that store d and the read and write quorums defined for d. The database will store a set of data items $d_1, d_2, \ldots, d_k$, and each data item will have its own quorum (there might be many uniquely accessible data objects in d that are grouped together for the purpose of quorum management). We assume that each view has a unique name v and the view names are totally ordered (i.e., a view name is a combination of a sequence number and a processor identifier). We denote the name of the current view of data item d by $v(d)$. If $v(d_1) = v(d_2)$, then d_1 and d_2 are *in the same view*. Normally, all data items stored at processor p are in the same view, but this is not required.

Each transaction tr executes in a single view $v(tr)$. That is, tr will only access data that is in view $v(tr)$. The idea behind view-based quorums is to ensure that if $v(tr_1) < v(tr_2)$, then tr_1 comes before tr_2 in an equivalent serial execution. That way, we can decompose the problem into two parts: ensuring serializability within a view and ensuring serializability between views.

The available sites that store d in view v is $P(d, v)$, and we define $n(d, v) = |P(d, v)|$. The read and write thresholds for d in view v are $R(d, v)$ and $W(d, v)$. For each d, we also define the read and write **accessibility** thresholds $A_r(d)$ and $A_w(d)$. A data item d can be read (or written to) in view v only if $n(d, v) \geq A_r(d)$ $(n(d, v) \geq A_w(d))$.

The thresholds must satisfy the following conditions:

1. $A_r(d) + A_w(d) > |P(d)|$
2. $R(d, v) + W(d, v) > n(d, v)$
3. $2 * W(d, v) > n(d, v)$
4. $1 \leq R(d, v) \leq n(d, v)$
5. $A_w(d) \leq W(d, v) \leq n(d, v)$

Conditions 2 and 3 are the usual read/write quorum conditions. Conditions 1 and 5 will ensure that updates made to d in one view are propagated to all subsequent views that can read d. Condition 4 simply states that the read threshold must make sense.

To perform a logical read or write, a transaction uses the same algorithm as the regular quorum algorithm but with the following modifications:

1. Only the sites in $P(d, v)$ can be accessed.
2. Version numbers consist of the view number and a sequence number within a view. Version numbers are compared on the basis of the view number first and the sequence number second.
3. If a processor p receives a request from transaction tr to access data item d and $v(tr) \neq v_p(d)$, the access is rejected.

A processor p that stores d can decide to update the view for d. Normally, a processor initiates a view change because it has detected that some sites in the quorum have failed or have been repaired. To update the view of d, p accesses at least $A_r(d)$ copies of d and determines their version numbers. p reads the copy with the largest version number, stores that value into its local copy, and increments the view number of its local copy. If p successfully installs the new view, all of the processors that it accessed will also initiate the protocol to install the new view.

Transactions are restricted to accessing data from a particular view, so all transactions execute within a particular view. Transactions within a view execute a quorum protocol that serializes their executions. So all that needs to be done is to ensure that transactions from different views are serialized by their view number. Recall that sequence numbers are ordered by the view number first, and the update within the view number second. In order to install a new view, the installer must read at least $A_r(d)$ copies of d. An examination of the rules (i.e., 1 and 5) for setting the thresholds shows that if p installs d in a new view, it must read the most up-to-date copy of d written in any previous view. So, transactions are serialized by the view number that they execute under. This is illustrated in Figure 12.5.

The protocol for changing views implements the strategy that we have discussed. The key observation is that a view change should be executed as a transaction. In the

FIGURE 12.5   Serialization within views and between views.

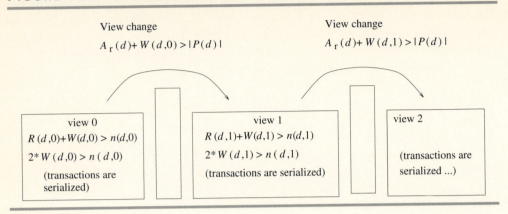

following protocol, the view of a data item is updated one site at a time. This is acceptable because a transaction is only permitted to access data items within a single view. Note that the transaction that updates the local view of d treats the replicas of d that it accesses as being unrelated data items. However, a commit to the transaction is still required. The protocol is simplified to update the view of only one data item; in practice the view would be updated for as many data items as possible. However, the installation of new views for different data items can be performed asynchronously.

The initiator of a view change executes the protocol in Algorithm Listing 12.5. A participant in the view change executes the algorithm in Algorithm Listing 12.6. If the participant sees a new view, it executes the protocol in Algorithm Listing 12.7. The protocols in Algorithm Listing 12.5 and Algorithm Listing 12.7 use the transaction in Algorithm Listing 12.8 (on p.450).

As an example of how view-based quorums can be used, consider a data item d that is replicated at five sites, A through E, with $A_r(d) = 2$ and $A_w(d) = 4$, as illustrated in Figure 12.6 (on p.450). Suppose that in the initial view v_0, $P(d, v_0) = \{P_1 \dots P_5\}$, $w(d, v_0) = 5$, and $r(d, v_0) = 1$ (i.e., read-one/write-all). Suppose that E is partitioned from the other processors. If we cannot change the view, no transaction can update d. But, by changing the view to v_1 with $P(d, v_1) = \{A, \dots, D\}$, d can still be read and

ALGORITHM LISTING 12.5

Initiating a new view.

```
initiate_new_view()
    While a new view is not yet installed
        new_view = a set of sites
        new_view_id = current_view_id + 1
        execute update_view(new_view,new_view_id)
    current_view = new_view
    current_view_id = new_view_id
```

ALGORITHM LISTING 12.6

View update algorithm of a participant.

```
view_access(d,proposed_view,proposed_view_id)
    if current_view_id < proposed_view_id
        access d and return the version number to the coordinator
        if the coordinator is not local
            signal the transaction manager to execute
            inherit_view(d,proposed_view,proposed_view_id)
    else if current_view_id = proposed_view_id
        access d and return the version number to the coordinator
    else
        abort the coordinator's transaction
```

written. The read and write thresholds can be set to $w(d, v_1) = 4$ and $r(d, v_1) = 1$, so the threshold policy is still read-one/write all. Data item d can still be read at site E even after the partition. In the execution illustrated in Figure 12.6, transaction tr_2 reads d at E after transaction tr_3 reads and writes d at A through D. The view-based quorum algorithm serializes tr_2 before tr_3. Note that tr_2 is not allowed to update d because there are not enough versions of d that still have view 0. Transaction tr_2 might update data item x, which transaction tr_3 would subsequently read. This is acceptable because tr_2 is serialized before tr_3 (of course, x would need to be brought into view 1 before tr_3 could access it). Transaction tr_3 might update data item y that tr_2 might try to read. However, tr_2 is only permitted to access data with view 0. So, either tr_2 accesses a copy of y in view 0, which tr_3 did not update, or tr_2 is forced to abort.

If another site (say D) fails, in any view v_2 that can be installed, $n(d, v_2) = 3 < A_w(d)$, so d cannot be written. However, as long as two sites are available, d can be read.

Notice that the settings of $A_r(d)$ and $A_w(d)$ determine the read and write availability of d. For example, if $A_r(d) = A_w(d) = 3$, d can be read and written as long as three sites are in the view, but d cannot be safely read when only two sites are available. So one penalty for increasing the write availability of a data object is the decrease in the read accessibility. In addition, at least $A_r(d)$ copies of d must be accessed to install a

ALGORITHM LISTING 12.7

Inheriting a new view.

```
inherit_view(proposed_view,proposed_view_id)
    if update_view(proposed_view,proposed_view_id) is not aborted
        current_view = new_view
        current_view_id = new_view_id
    else
        initiate_new_view()
```

ALGORITHM LISTING 12.8

View update transaction.

```
update_view(new_view,new_view_id)
    Begin Transaction
        Select a set S of at least A_r(d) copies of d, including the local copy.
        For every site s in S do
            execute view_access(d,new_view,new_view_id) at s.
        If no s in S aborted the view_access,
            choose a site s' that reported the largest version number
            read d at s' and store the value in the local copy of d.
        else
            abort the transaction
    End Transaction
```

---

new view. So, increasing the write availability of d increases the work required to install a new view of d.

If we set $A_r(d) = 4$ and $A_w(d) = 2$, it is possible to have two partitions that write d concurrently, in different views. If d is write accessible but not read accessible in a new

FIGURE 12.6 Example execution of the view-based quorum algorithm.

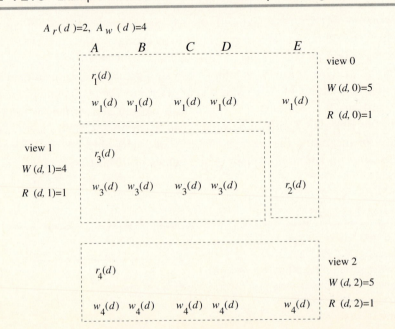

view, the new view of d can be installed without reading remote copies. We explore the issue of concurrent writes in the exercises.

The requirement that a transaction access only those data items in the same view can be weakened because a transaction can also use data items from previous views.

- **Relaxed write rule:** A transaction tr can use a data item d stored at processor p to form a write quorum if $v(tr) \geq v_p(d)$. After tr commits, all transactions that access d at p must have a view larger than or equal to $v(tr)$, and any view installed for d at p in the future must have a larger view number than $v(tr)$.
- **Relaxed read rule:** A transaction tr can use a data item d stored at processor p to form a read quorum if $v(tr) \geq v_p(d)$. After the access, all transactions that access d at p must have a view larger than or equal to $v(tr)$, and any view installed for d at p in the future must have a larger view number than $v(tr)$.

One way to enforce the post access requirements of the relaxed read/write rules is to have the processor install view $v(tr)$ immediately after the transaction commmit. After a relaxed write, d_p is likely to already contain the most up-to-date value of d.

Discussion

The algorithm presented in this section allows the read and write quorum threshold for a data item to change but requires that the availability thresholds and set of sites where the data is located ($P(d)$) to be permanently fixed. An alternative approach to changing quorums is to change $P(d)$ when the view is changed. If the protocol ensures that transactions that execute in an old view cannot commit updates to data in a new view, only a quorum of sites in $P(d)$ must commit the view change. This technique is explored further in the exercises.

A weakness of the dynamic quorum change algorithm presented in this section is that it interferes with the execution of regular transactions (although the relaxed read and relaxed write rule mitigate this problem). It is possible to change the quorum (i.e., change $P(d)$ and the associated vote weights) while transactions are accessing the data objects in d. The trick is to use a transitional view, in which transactions must acquire a quorum in both the old and the new views in order to access a data object. When no transaction is executing in the old view, transactions can start to use the new view.

The view-based quorum technique has two interesting aspects. First, it makes use of a relative consistency idea. When a transaction updates a data item, it creates the latest version (assuming that $A_w(d) > P(d)/2$). This version is not necessarily globally visible, because only transactions in the same view are guaranteed to see the latest update. So, data consistency is relative to the view in which updates are performed. Views and view changes are defined in such a way as to ensure global consistency.

The second interesting aspect of the algorithm is the way that it delays the effort needed for global consistency.

- **Optimistic design:** Distributed algorithms become complex and expensive when the components necessary to handle asynchrony and failures are added. Often a fast and simple algorithm can be designed to handle synchronous and/or failure-free environments. If one expects that the system is usually synchronous or that failures occur rarely, sometimes one can design an algorithm that works well under most circumstances and only slows down when the (rare) problems occur.

In the view-based quorum algorithm, the execution within a view can be optimized to expect no failures among the processors in the view (i.e., use a read-one/write-all quorum). When a failure does occur, installing a new view can require a significant amount of activity. For example, $A_r(d)$ must be larger by 1 than the number of failures than can be tolerated among the sites that store d. The two-level approach provides both fault tolerance and high performance in the normal case.

12.2 ATOMIC MULTICAST

Many researchers have observed that a reliable communications primitive can simplify the implementation of many distributed protocols (for example, consider the transformation of the shared memory randomized consensus protocol to the message passing randomized consensus protocol in Chapter 11). A particularly useful communications primitive is a reliable multicast — if one processor on the delivery list receives a reliable multicast message, every processor on the delivery list receives the message.

There are many different ways to define a reliable multicast, and much research has been done to explore alternative implementations. In this section, we will discuss one particular approach. Popular reliable broadcast systems (such as ISIS and Amoeba) use different algorithms, and we relate those algorithms to the material presented here. The approach we present provides a structure for implementing all aspects of atomic multicast. The approach used by systems such as ISIS is closely related, and we discuss it briefly.

As in the database approach to maintaining replicated data, the impossibility of distributed agreement requires that we carefully approach the definition of correctness. To motivate our definition of a reliable broadcast, we first present some naive approaches, and then discuss the problems that arise.

The simplest multicast algorithm is to send a message to every processor on an address list. If a reliable message passing layer, such as TCP, is used, every processor will receive the message. Unfortunately, this simple protocol does not handle processor failures. If a processor on the address list fails, or worse, the sending processor fails, the message will be delivered to a subset of processors on the address list.

We can fix the simple multicast algorithm by using a 2PC technique and treating a multicast as a transaction. Like a transaction, a multicast can succeed or fail. Therefore, we will distinguish between the **reception** of a message at a processor and the **delivery** of the message to the protocol that uses the message. A received message is only delivered after the receiver knows that the message will be delivered everywhere and is discarded if the requirement cannot be met. In the 2PC protocol, the sender sends the message to every process on the address list. When all acknowledgments are received, the sender delivers the message locally and tells all processors on the address list that it is safe to deliver the message.

The 2PC protocol will work, but it is not entirely appropriate for a message passing layer. Typically, a group of processes will communicate using a reliable multicast to perform a task, such as maintaining a replicated server or performing a distributed computation. If a member of the group fails, it will miss the progress of the computation. When the processor recovers, it will need to recover the current state of the computation. As a result, the correctness guarantees are stronger than necessary. Consider three possible consequences of a processor failure:

1. If a processor p fails after receiving a message m, p must be able to determine whether or not to deliver the m when it recovers. However, p will need to do more than recover message p when it recovers; p will need to be able to make its state consistent with that of the other processors, and this recovery subsumes the recovery of message m.
2. If the sending process s fails to obtain an acknowledgment from processor p, s must abort the delivery of message m. This is a more drastic action than seems necessary because p will recover a consistent state, including message m, when it recovers. So, there should be a way of deleting p from the delivery list on the fly, and proceeding with the multicast.
3. If s fails after delivering m to all processors on the waiting list, but before sending any "commit" messages, the delivery of m is blocked until s recovers.

The first two points show that the 2PC protocol is performing more work than is really necessary because the recovery of individual messages is subsumed by the recovery of the processor state. These points can be argued because individual message recovery might be a useful property (as we will explore in the next chapter). The third point is more critical. As in 2PC for distributed databases, the 2PC multicast algorithm is susceptible to a window of vulnerability. If a processor s is sending many messages, it is likely that there are several messages $\{m_i\}$ whose status cannot be determined until s recovers. If the messages $\{m_i\}$ are critical messages, delaying their delivery can bring all activity to a halt.

12.2.1 Virtual Synchrony

A better definition of reliable multicast is one that supports the recovery from failures. It is very difficult to define a distribution list and state that every nonfailed processor on that list receives the message. The difficulty lies in knowing which are the nonfailed processors. A more reasonable approach is to establish checkpoints and require that all processors that are non-failed between checkpoints receive the same set of messages between the checkpoints. After a checkpoint we can determine which processors have received all messages and which processors might need to be rolled forward to complete the computation.

Processes are organized into **groups**, corresponding to multicast delivery lists, that cooperate to perform a reliable multicast. The current list of processors to receive a multicast is called the **group view** (the terminology is reminiscent of the view-based quorum algorithm). The group view is consistent among all processes in the group. Processes are added to and deleted from the group via **view changes**.

A process group is a natural way to organize processes to perform reliable multicast. Multicast communication patterns are usually not arbitrary but instead are repeatedly confined to the same set of processes. Most activities, such as maintaining a replicated server, coordinating a distributed program, etc., require that all members of a group hear of an update to the global state. In addition, much of the work of performing a reliable multicast can be reduced to maintaining a consistent group view.

An algorithm for performing reliable multicast is **virtually synchronous** if:

1. There is a unique group view in any consistent state on which all members of the group agree.
2. If a message m is multicast in group view v before view change c, either no processor in v that executes c ever receives m, or every processor in v that executes c receives m before performing c.

Virtual synchrony gives a precise meaning to the notion of a delivery list. Between any two consecutive view changes, a set $\mathcal{G}$ of messages is multicast, and the senders are restricted to the processors in the view. So, if processor p is removed from the view, the processors remaining in the view can assume that p has failed. Virtual synchrony guarantees that no messages from p will be delivered in the future. In addition, virtual synchrony makes reliable message delivery easier (as is discussed in the next section).

Intuitively, all processors in a group view v that do not fail receive all messages in $\mathcal{G}$. A processor p that fails might not receive all of $\mathcal{G}$. But, since message delivery is

FIGURE 12.7 Lost messages in virtually synchronous multicast.

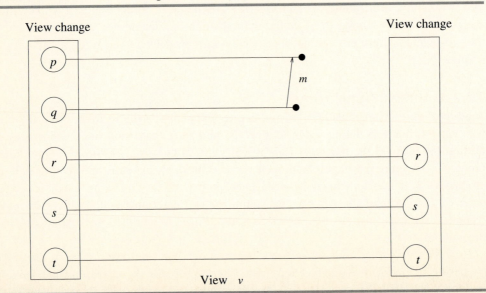

synchronized with view changes, we know what messages p must have received and therefore what actions to take to let p recover when it is repaired.

There is a subtlety in the definition of virtual synchrony. It is not necessarily the case that if a message m is delivered to a processor p in view v, then m is delivered to all processors in v. Why? The sender of the message might fail too (as shown in Figure 12.7). A stronger delivery criteria, **safe** message delivery, is explored in the exercises.

The issue of implementing virtually synchronous group membership contains several subtleties, and the algorithm requirements can be formally defined in several ways. We defer a discussion of group membership protocols until later in this section. In the meantime, we assume that a group view service that satisfies virtual synchrony is available for our use.

12.2.2 Ordered Multicasts

The virtual synchrony concept already has one order that the multicasts must obey: All messages must be delivered within the group view from which they are sent. There are several other orders that we might want the messages to obey. For example, messages should be delivered in the order sent by a processor, as in a regular reliable FIFO communications channel. A stronger ordering is **causality**: If p receives m_1 and then multicasts m_2, every processor that receives both messages should receive m_1 before m_2. The strongest ordering is a **total order**: If p receives m_1 before receiving m_2, all processors that receive both messages receive m_1 before m_2. A reliable multicast protocol that is virtually synchronous and delivers all messages in a total order is sometimes called an **atomic** multicast.

The advantage of an atomic multicast is clear, since it can be used to directly implement a shared state. The advantage of causal multicast is not immediately obvious. It turns out that causal communication simplifies the design of many algorithms because it removes the possibility that a processor will deliver a stale message that could confuse the protocol it is running. The atomic delivery and group membership protocols that we discuss make a strong use of causal message delivery.

More concretely, consider an example of opening a file. First, the process opens the file and obtains a file handle. Next, the process accesses the file through the file handle. Suppose that the server that serves the file handle is different from the server that serves the file. The file handle server tells the file server what access characteristics are defined on the file handles it has distributed. Suppose that the file handle server sends a message to the file server and then sends a message to the process. If communication is not causal, the process might ask to open a file and be given handle h. When the process attempts to access the file through h, it is returned an error message that indicates an unbound file handle. When the user applies the debugger, he or she sees that the file handle is valid and is annoyed by the bugginess of the operating system (consider also the example given in Chapter 9).

Atomic and causal multicast can work together if the atomic multicast is also causal (i.e., causally ordered with respect to the causal multicasts). For example, a processor can lock a shared variable using an atomic multicast and then access the data and release the lock using causal multicasts. The situation is analogous to using weak consistency instead of sequential consistency in shared memory multiprocessors. The atomic multicast defines a synchronization point, and the causal multicast ensures that all processors observe all causal accesses that precede (follow) the atomic multicast to come before (after) the atomic multicast.

One argument for using causal multicast is that it is "free" with most implementations of reliable multicast (there will be some additional message delivery delays). We will show why this is the case when we discuss the causal multicast algorithm used by ISIS.

We will first describe a reliable causal multicast that executes between two view changes. We will then build on the reliable causal multicast to build the total ordering and to implement the group view maintenance algorithm. Finally, we will present another approach to implementing reliable process groups that does not require a reliable causal multicast as a starting point.

12.2.3 Reliable and Causal Multicast

Let us consider an intelligent approach to designing a reliable multicast. The 2PC protocol is too restrictive because it does not take advantage of virtual synchrony — if a processor fails, it is not necessary to have the message delivered to it. An alternative naive approach is *flooding*: Whenever a processor receives a message that it has never received before, it relays the message to all other processors. Such a large volume of messages is sent that eventually all working processors receive the message. However, this algorithm is certainly not efficient.

A better approach combines ideas from 2PC and from flooding. When a processor p_{source} has a message m to multicast, it sends m to all of the processors on delivery list L. Processor p_{source} keeps m in a buffer until either every processor $p' \in L$ acknowledges the message or until p_{source} is informed that p' has failed (by the virtual synchrony layer). When processor $p_d \in L$ receives m, it sends an acknowledgment to p_{source} and stores m in a buffer until it knows that every $p' \in L$ has received m. If p_d is informed that p_{source} has failed (by the virtual synchrony mechanism), p_d sends m to every $p' \in L$ such that p_d does not know if p' received m. Therefore, if one processor p_d receives m, every processor that is still nonfaulty at the change in the group view will also receive m, making the multicast reliable.

One detail that needs to be addressed is how p_d can determine if a p' has received m. In general, processor p_d must acknowledge m not only to p_{source} but also to every $p' \in L$ (possibly by a different mechanism). Once p_d has received an acknowledgment of m from every $p' \in L$, p_d can discard m and reclaim the buffer space. The method for performing the direct and indirect acknowledgments determines the algorithm. For the moment, we can think about an algorithm in which a processor acknowledges every message it receives to every other processor in L.

One can observe that many of the acknowledgments sent in the above described protocol are unnecessary. Consider the following scenario, which is illustrated in Figure 12.8. The delivery list for a multicast is $L = \{A, B, C, D\}$. Processor A multicasts the first message a_1. Processor B multicasts the second message b_1 and attaches to b_1 an acknowledgment of a_1, $ack(a_1)$. Processor C receives messages a_1 and b_1, then multicasts message c_1 with $ack(b_1)$ attached. Now, consider what processor D can deduce about the

FIGURE 12.8   Transitive acknowledgments.

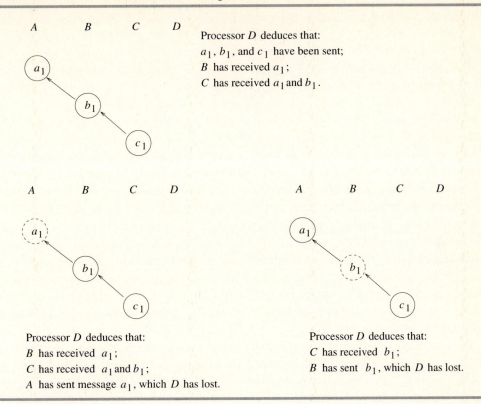

Processor D deduces that:
a_1, b_1, and c_1 have been sent;
B has received a_1;
C has received a_1 and b_1.

Processor D deduces that:
B has received a_1;
C has received a_1 and b_1;
A has sent message a_1, which D has lost.

Processor D deduces that:
C has received b_1;
B has sent b_1, which D has lost.

state of the system when it receives c_1. Since c_1 acknowledges b_1, D knows that b_1 has been sent and that C has received it. If D has not received b_1, it can broadcast a message asking for the retransmission of b_1. Otherwise, let us look at what can be deduced from b_1 which acknowledged a_1. D knows that a message a_1 has been sent and that B received it. In addition, D knows that C received a_1. Why? D knows that C received b_1, which has $ack(a_1)$ attached. Therefore C knows that a_1 was sent. Since C did not ask for a retransmission of a_1 in its message c_1, D concludes that C received a_1. So, if D has not received a_1, D will ask for a retransmission of a_1. Otherwise D now knows that all processors have received a_1, and therefore it is safe to discard a_1.

The reasoning in our example depends on the observation that if the broadcast protocols are well behaved, message acknowledgments are transitive. When D hears that C acknowledges the receipt of b_1, D knows that C knows about the existence of a_1, because $ack(a_1)$ is embedded in b_1. When D deduces that C must have received a_1, D is counting on the assumption that if C did not receive a_1, C would either not acknowledge b_1 or would prefer to state its nonreception of a_1. Since C acknowledges b_1 and is silent about a_1, D deduces that C received a_1.

Trans is a protocol (described here) for reliable and causal multicast that makes extensive use of transitive acknowledgments (hence the name).[14] The protocol maintains the following invariant: A processor p broadcasts an acknowledgment of message m only if p has received m and all messages that causally precede m. The consequence of the invariant is that when a processor acknowledges m, it does not need to acknowledge all unacknowledged messages that precede m.

The Trans protocol has three major components. The first component tracks the received acknowledgments to support the calculation of its own acknowledgments, support lost message detection, and detect when buffered messages are stable. The second component detects missing messages, based on the database maintained by the first component. When the protocol learns of a message that it did not receive, it broadcasts a negative acknowledgment of the missing message. The third component of the protocol buffers messages until they are known to be **stable** (i.e., received by every processor) so that they can be supplied to processors that negatively acknowledge them.

We assume that processors sequentially number their messages and the pair (*processor number, message number*) uniquely identifies a message. In addition, if a processor p receives messages a_i and a_j from processor A, and $i < j$, then p can deduce that a_i causally precedes a_j. We also assume that a message m has enough room to attach all the necessary positive and negative acknowledgments. The protocol uses the data structures shown in Algorithm Listing 12.9.

The causality DAG G maintains the state information for the protocol. At a particular processor p, the causality DAG G_p contains all messages m that p has received that are not yet stable. So, negatively acknowledged messages are served from G. If a message m acknowledges message m', G contains edge (m, m'). Since a message only acknowledges messages that it causally follows, G is actually a directed acyclic graph that expresses the causal relation between messages. Because the acknowledgments attached to a message are necessary for the proper functioning of a protocol, a rebroadcast message contains exactly the same positive acknowledgment list as the original message. Negative acknowledgments are only attached to the originally multicast message. We need several functions on the causality DAG, which we list in Algorithm Listing 12.10. We will discuss how to compute these functions shortly.

ALGORITHM LISTING 12.9

Variables used by the Trans protocol.

m		Message container.
	m.message	Application-level message.
	m.acks	List of acknowledgments and negative acknowledgments.
nack_list		List of messages to be negatively acknowledged.
ack_list		List of messages to be acknowledged.
G		The causality DAG, which also serves as the message buffer.

---

[14] The protocol we present is a simplification of the actual Trans protocol, suggested by Dolev, Malki, and Kramer, which in turn is a simplification of a protocol proposed by Melliar-Smith and Moser.

ALGORITHM LISTING 12.10

Causality DAG functions used by Trans.

add_to_DAG(m,G)	Inserts m (and its acknowledgments) into G.
not_duplicate(m,G)	Returns TRUE if m has never been received before.
causal(m,G)	Returns TRUE if all messages that m causally follows have been received.
stable(m,G)	Returns TRUE if all processors have acknowledged m.

The Trans_send protocol, shown in Algorithm Listing 12.11, composes a package to send m, by packing the application's message with the pending positive and negative acknowledgments. Pending positive acknowledgments can be immediately removed from the list, but negative acknowledgments can only be removed from nack_list when the nack'ed message arrives. When Trans_receive, shown in Algorithm Listing 12.12, receives a message, it first checks for any negative acknowledgments, and multicasts them if possible. Because the pattern of acknowledgments is needed to implement causal message delivery, a negatively acknowledged message m is rebroadcast with all of its original acknowledgments attached. If the message is not a duplicate, the acknowledgments are handled by noting if the new message acknowledges any missing messages and by noting if the message is on the nack_list. The message is then registered with G. When m is inserted into G, a number of messages (including m) can become causal and thus deliverable (compare this algorithm to the one presented in Chapter 9). A new ack_list of all causal messages that can not be transitively acknowledged is computed. Finally, all stable messages can be deleted from G to save space.

The execution of the protocol at processor E is illustrated in Figure 12.9. The first message to arrive is b_1, which acknowledges a_1. Message b_1 can not be delivered because a_1 must be delivered first. So, the acknowledgment list remains empty, and a_1 is put on the nack_list. Next, message c_1 arrives, acknowledging b_1 and d_1. Since d_1 has not been

ALGORITHM LISTING 12.11

Multicasting a message in Trans.

```
Trans_send(message)
    create m to contain the message
    m.message = message
    for every nack in nack_list
        attach nack to m.acks
    for every ack in ack_list
        remove ack from ack_list
        attach ack to m.acks
    put m in ack_list
    add_to_DAG(m,G)
    send m to every processor p on the delivery list L
```

ALGORITHM LISTING 12.12

Receiving a message in Trans.

Trans_receive(m)
    for every negative acknowledgment in m.acks
        multicast the nack'ed message if it is available.
    if not_duplicate(m,G)
        for every acknowledgment of m' in m.acks
            if not_duplicate(m',G)
                add m' to nack_list
        If m is in nack_list
            remove m from nack_list
        add m to undelivered_list
        remove negative acknowledgments from m.acks
        add_to_DAG(m,G)
        while there is an m' in undelivered_list such that causal(m',G)
            remove m' from undelivered_list
            deliver(m'.message)
        compute ack_list to be all m in G such that causal(m,G) is true, and
            there is no m' such that causal(m',G) is true and m acks m'.
        for every m' in G
            if stable(m',G)
                remove m' from G and reclaim the buffer space

---

FIGURE 12.9 Execution of the Trans protocol (at processor E).

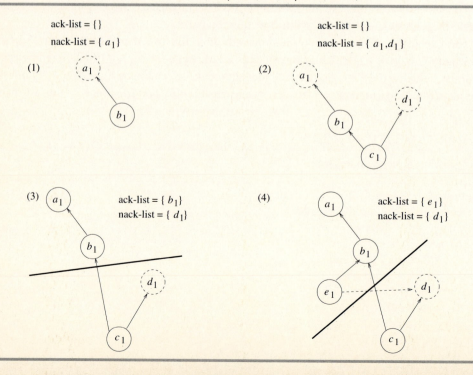

received, it is put on the nack_list, and the delivery of c_1 is blocked. When message a_1 arrives, messages a_1 and b_1 can be delivered. Message a_1 is removed from the nack_list, and b_1 is added to the ack list. Note that an acknowledgment of b_1 transitively acknowledges a_1. Finally, processor E multicasts its message e_1. An acknowledgment to b_1 is attached, and the ack list is modified to contain only e_1. Notice that e_1 causally follows a_1 and b_1 only, since c_1 has not yet been delivered (and is not causal). A negative acknowledgment for d_1 is also attached. A processor that receives e_1 and stores d_1 will remulticast d_1.

The execution of the protocol can be viewed as trying to advance the **causal line** (shown in Figure 12.9) and the **stable line** in G. A newly received message m is placed outside of the causal line. If all of the messages that m acknowledges are within the causal line (or if m does not acknowledge any messages), m is delivered and placed within the causal line. Messages that are acknowledged directly or indirectly by every other processor are moved within the stable line and deleted from G.

By examining the Trans protocol, one can see that:

1. If a message is delivered to a processor that does not fail, eventually every nonfailed processor receives the message.
2. Messages are delivered in causal order.
3. G forms a tight description of the causal ordering among messages.
4. Every processor delivers the same causality DAG G. However, the order in which nodes of G are delivered can differ from processor to processor.
5. If a processor fails, the storage requirement of the protocol grows without bounds.

The last point is the weakness of the protocol, namely, that a single failure will cause message delivery to eventually halt because the processors will run out of buffer space. The Trans protocol must be used with a group membership protocol so that failed processors can be quickly detected and removed from the membership list.

■ **Causality DAG:** The reliable causal multicast algorithm presented in this section provides a powerful tool for developing higher-level algorithms. Every working processor is guaranteed not only to receive the same messages, but to see the same data structure that the messages form (i.e., the causality DAG, of C-DAG). Furthermore, the C-DAG will not have any holes in the middle: If processor p has m placed in its DAG, p has all messages that precede m in its C-DAG. If processor q also has m in its C-DAG, q has all predecessors of m in its C-DAG. The only way in which processors disagree is the order in which the C-DAG is revealed to them. By using these synchronization guarantees, a complicated protocol can be reduced to a computation on the C-DAG.

12.2.4 Reliable Delivery in ISIS

In this section, we briefly discuss how ISIS and related reliable multicast systems provide reliable delivery. As has been noted, the method for acknowledging received messages is the main distinction between the various multicast algorithms.

When processor p multicasts a message m to delivery list L, processor p is responsible for ensuring that all processors in L receive m. Typically, this is done using TCP. If processor p fails, m might not have been delivered to all processors on L. Therefore, every processor on L is still responsible for buffering all messages until they are guaranteed to be **stable** (that is, received by all processors on L). If p fails, the group view must change. Before the group view changes, all nonfailed processors in L multicast the nonstable messages in their buffers. When these messages are flushed, the processors can install the new delivery list.

Every processor in L needs to keep every other processor in L informed about which messages it has received. A naive implementation requires $|L|^2$ acknowledgments per message. We can observe that the acknowledgments do not need to be sent out immediately; instead we can piggyback them onto regular messages (as Trans does).

Every processor p in L sequentially numbers the messages it sends. In addition, each processor keeps track of the number of messages it has received from every other processor in q in the array received. That is, when processor p receives the kth message from q, it executes received[q]=k.

If processor p knows received$_q$ for every q in L, processor p can calculate which messages are stable. So, whenever p multicasts a message m, it attaches received$_p$. Processor p keeps track of a lower bound on received$_q$ for every q in L in the matrix remote. That is, whenever p receives a message m from q, it strips off the attached vector m.received and executes the following:

```
for r = 1 to |L|
    remote[q][r]=m.received[r]
```

Note that remote[p][*] = received[*], so there is no need to keep a separate received array. After receiving a new message, p might find that some new messages are stable. The vector stable contains the highest sequence number of the messages known to be stable, from every processor on L. The vector is computed by Algorithm Listing 12.13.

We can make a couple of observations about this algorithm.

- **Matrix timestamp:** The remote[*][*] matrix is commonly called a **matrix timestamp**. A vector timestamp summarizes what a processor knows of the execution at all other processors, and a matrix timestamp summarizes what a processor knows about what all other processors know about the execution at all other processors. The usual application of matrix timestamps is to detect when special events have been detected by all processors.

ALGORITHM LISTING **12.13**

Computing stable messages.

```
for r = 1 to |L|
    stable[r]= min(remote[q][r] | q = 1 through L)
```

- **Comparison to Trans :** Although the Trans algorithm looks very different from the ISIS algorithm, in fact they differ only in some small details. A Trans message needs to acknowledge at most M other messages (one from each processor), and hence the acknowledgments can be represented by a vector timestamp. Causal multicast systems typically use timestamp compression (see the exercises in Chapter 9), and Trans can be viewed as an aggressive timestamp compression technique.
- **Causal multicast is free:** The received array that is attached to every message is equivalent to a vector timestamp. So, the causal message delivery algorithm of Chapter 9 can be applied. We note that the meaning of the timestamp here is slightly different than in Chapter 9; here it refers to the time of receipt by the reliable message delivery layer rather than to the time of receipt by the user application.
- **Optimistic design:** The use of virtual synchrony permits the optimistic assumption that when a processor multicasts a message, it survives long enough to deliver the message to all processors in L. If a failure occurs, many messages need to be exchanged to ensure reliable message delivery. However, we can expect that the group view changes rarely (compared to message passing).

12.2.5 Group Membership

A complete implementation of a reliable multicast requires a **group membership** facility to maintain the delivery list. As can be seen in the Trans protocol, the processors need to identify the failed processors to avoid unbounded storage requirements. Furthermore, the reliable multicast should observe virtual synchrony so that the application programs can be given guarantees about the delivery lists.

A reliable group membership facility will provide a delivery list L to the reliable multicast service. The versions of the delivery lists stored at different processors need to satisfy some consistency constraints, otherwise the reliable multicast protocols can become confused. The intuitive property that the lists must satisfy is that they be mutually consistent (i.e., if $p \in L_q$, $q \in L_p$).

A reliable group membership protocol can be used to solve the asynchronous agreement problem. Why? If the failed processors can be accurately identified, the nonfailed processors can disregard the opinions of the failed processors and agree among themselves. Therefore, a reliable group membership protocol must either achieve the impossible or (as in the case of 2PC and 3PC) achieve something less than accurate and nonblocking agreement among the nonfailed processors. The atomic commit protocols achieve an accurate agreement but are susceptible to blocking. The reliable group membership protocols that have been proposed typically sacrifice accuracy. In particular, they are designed to declare that a processor has failed if any processor suspects it of failing (the atomic commit protocols will unilaterally declare an abort if a failure is suspected before voting, but afterward they are required to reach agreement). A group membership protocol will not block but perhaps will collapse if bad failures occur.

In a protocol in which consistency is relative (such as the invitation algorithm for election), we need to define our correctness criteria carefully. The first complication is that our observations must be made along consistent states c. The second complication is that consistency is relative — all that is required is that the members of a group agree on what the group is.

In order to discuss consistency we will need to recall the idea of a run, which is execution of a protocol. We recall the definition of $\mathcal{R}(c)$, which is the set of all possible executions starting from consistent state c.

We start with some definitions about the global state. The predicates are defined in relation to a consistent state c, but we will drop the dependence on c in the notation if there is no ambiguity.

- P: the set of all processors.
- $crash_p[c]$: is *TRUE* if processor p has failed. We cannot access this variable, but it is convenient to assume its use for our discussion.
- $UP(c)$: the set of processors p for which $crash_p$ is *FALSE* in c.
- $DOWN(c)$: the set of processors p for which $crash_p$ is *TRUE* in c.

For a processor p, we will make use of some variables, predicates, and events that can be posted.

- $L_p(c)$: the current delivery list, or **view**, of processor p in consistent state c.
- L_p^x: the xth version of L_p. Since L_p evolves through a series of well-defined modifications, it is meaningful to discuss L_p's version number.
- $inlocal_p(q)[c]$: *TRUE* if $q \in L_p(c)$.
- $faulty_p(q)[c]$: posted by p when it is led to believe that processor q has failed (i.e., that $crash_q$ is *TRUE*).
- $operating_p(q)$: posted by p when it believes that q is operating and wants to join the group.
- $install_p(x)$: the event of the installation of L_p^x.

A group membership algorithm maintains a replicated data item — the membership list L. The membership list will go through a sequence of changes. So, we start with membership list L_0, change it into L_1, then L_2, and so on. The membership list has two special properties. First, the value of L_i is the same at all processors (i.e., at those that ever determine the value of L_i). Second, processors install new versions of the membership list in exactly the same sequence. If a processor currently holds L_i as its membership list, the next version it will install is L_{i+1}.

Intuitively, these two properties guarantee that processors in a virtually synchronous multicast system will receive the same sequence of messages, up to concurrent messages within a group view. All processors that view L_i and also the next k membership lists will receive all messages multicast in L_i, then L_{i+1}, and so on. It is easy to think about this definition of group membership algorithms because there is no reference to time or simultaneous actions. All that is required is that all processors follow the same sequence.

We can now define virtual synchrony in a more formal way. Let $deliver_p(m)$ be the event of the delivery of message m at processor p.

■ Suppose that processors p and q both install group views versions x and $x + 1$. Then,

$$install_p(x) <_H deliver_p(m) <_H install_p(x + 1) \Rightarrow$$
$$install_q(x) <_H deliver_q(m) <_H install_q(x + 1)$$

A more formal definition of a correct group membership algorithm must handle a number of details. We must ensure that the algorithm is not trivial, that the right processors are on the membership list, and that membership lists are installed in a timely fashion. The precise definition of a correct group membership algorithm is a matter of controversy at the time of this writing. We present a definition suggested by Ricciardi and Birman. However, the reader can skip this discussion as long as the informal correctness definition is understood.

A group view is determined by the set of processors that you ask. Let $S \subseteq P$ be a set of processors. The group view determined by S at consistent state c is:

$$GV_S(c) = \begin{cases} \mathsf{L}_p(c), & p \in S \bigcap UP(c) & S \bigcap UP(c) \neq \emptyset, \text{ and} \\ & & \forall_{p,q \in S \bigcap UP(c)} \mathsf{L}_p(c) = \mathsf{L}_q(c) \\ \text{undefined} & & \text{otherwise} \end{cases}$$

Note that a single processor can define a group view (i.e., $S = \{p\}$). However, the processors in L_p might have disagreeing membership lists (i.e., perhaps not all of L_p is in S). We define an **agreed group view at** c to be a $GV_S(c)$ such that $GV_S(c) = S$. We are now ready to state the correctness criteria for reliable group membership protocols. Intuitively, the criteria state that there is an initial agreed group view, that local views are formed based on observations of the real world, that there is a single agreed group view at any particular time, that all processors in the agreed group view see the same sequence of agreed group view versions, and that faulty processors are eventually removed from the agreed group view.

1. There is an initial agreed group view. That is, given an initial global state c_0,

$$\forall_{r \in \mathcal{R}(c_0)} \exists_{c' \in r} \exists_{S_0 \subseteq P} \; S_0 = GV_{S_0}(c')$$

2. Processors change their local views based on information about processor failures and new processors.
   a. If $c \to c'$ such that $q \in \mathsf{L}_p(c)$ and $q \notin \mathsf{L}_p(c')$, then $faulty_p(q)[c']$.
   b. If $c \to c'$ such that $q \notin \mathsf{L}_p(c)$ and $q \in \mathsf{L}_p(c')$, then $\exists_{\hat{c}}$ such that $c \to \hat{c} \to c'$ and $operational_p(q)[\hat{c}]$.

   The second part of the definition must be handled carefully because p might believe that q is faulty but has not yet removed q from L_p.
3. The agreed group view is unique. That is, if $\exists_{S, S' \subseteq P}$ such that $GV_S(c) = S$ and $GV_{S'}(c) = S'$, then $S = S'$. Since the agreed group view in a consistent state is unique, we denote it by $GV(c)$.

4. If two processors p and q are members of the agreed group view that goes through a series of changes, p and q see the same sequence of changes.

For every version number x, for each $p, q \in Proc$, and for each run $r \in \mathcal{R}(c_0)$, there is a $c \in r$ such that the following two conditions hold:

   a. If $q \in \mathsf{L}_p^x$, then $DOWN_q[c]$ is $TRUE$, or $\mathsf{L}_p[c] = \mathsf{L}_q[c] = \mathsf{L}_p^x$.

   b. If $q \notin \mathsf{L}_p^x$ but $q \in \mathsf{L}_p^y$ for every $y < x$, then L_q^x is not defined for every $\hat{c}$ such that $c \rightarrow \hat{c}$.

5. The protocol responds to notifications that processors are faulty or operating. That is,

   a. If $p \in GV[c]$ and $faulty_p(q)[c]$, then $\forall_{r \in \mathcal{R}(c)}$, $\exists_{c' \in r}$ such that $q \notin GV[c']$, or $p \notin GV[c']$.

   b. If $p \in GV[c]$ and $operating_p(q)[c]$, then $\forall_{r \in \mathcal{R}(c)}$, $\exists_{c' \in r}$ such that $q \in GV[c']$, $faulty_p(q)[c']$ or $p \notin GV[c']$.

   We need to include the possibility that p might fail or be cut off from the main group in both cases.

Some group membership algorithms allow a group to partition into smaller groups and then rejoin later. Such a group membership algorithm will allow processing to continue in spite of a network partition. In this case, group membership is no longer defined globally, as correctness requirements 3 and 4 state. Rather, consistent group membership is defined relative to the processors in the group. Therefore, requirement 4 is replaced with a requirement that if two processors both install view v_1 and v_2, they install the views in the same order.

We next discuss two group membership algorithms. The first algorithm is simple and elegant but is tightly integrated into the reliable multicast protocol. The second algorithm is more complex, but also rather more general. Although we do not discuss it here, a third algorithm worth noting is the Totem algorithm given by Amir, Moser, et al. Totem uses a token circulating in a logical ring to totally order multicasts and also to perform garbage collection. If the token is lost or the ring breaks, a membership protocol is invoked to establish a new ring. The membership protocol is similar to that of the Transis algorithm.

The Transis Algorithm

The Transis project developed algorithms for performing a reliable multicast, making a strong use of the causality DAG (the Trans protocol was developed as part of this project). In this section, we describe how the causality DAG can be used to help implement a reliable group membership protocol.

Asynchronous agreement protocols (such as reliable group membership protocols) have two usual characteristics. First, they are paranoid. If processor p suspects that processor q has failed, all processors in the group will remove q, even if they can still communicate with it. Second, they are unidirectional. Once a processor is suspected of being faulty, it will eventually be removed from the membership list (unless the suspecting processor fails) and never be readmitted.

These characteristics, in particular the unidirectional nature of the protocols, seem draconian and perhaps unnecessary. However, they greatly simplify the algorithms. If one recalls the impossibility of distributed consensus, the schedule that foils the agreement protocol delays a critical message until a decision is avoided and then delivers the message. If the agreement protocol is paranoid, the processor that sends the delayed message is declared failed. Since the protocol is unidirectional, the delayed processor cannot deliver its critical message. Instead, an agreement is reached among the processors that can communicate without problems. More pragmatically, it is easy to imagine that a slow processor is repeatedly suspected of failure by some processors but repeatedly restored to the group by others. Finally, if a processor learns that it has been removed from the group, it can rejoin as a "new" processor by attaching an incarnation number to its name.

The paranoid and one-way properties make the agreement problem **monotone**. Only the nonsuspect processors in L need to agree on which processors are suspect. Whenever processor p suspects that q has failed, q is removed from the group (by paranoia) and is never readmitted (because the protocol is one-way). An exception occurs if the group has previously suspected that p failed (in which case messages from p are ignored). The set of suspected processors monotonically increases at every nonsuspect processor. Eventually, all of the nonsuspect processors agree on the set of suspect processors, or everyone suspects everyone else and the group collapses.

The group membership protocol will need to handle virtual synchrony. Every processor must be able to agree on what the last message from every other processor was, even from failed processors.

The group membership protocol is built on top of the Trans reliable broadcast protocol. The separation of layers between the reliable multicast and the group membership protocols is not as clean as might be desired. In particular, the group membership protocol will need to query and modify the C-DAG G and will require the immediate sending and blocking of some messages. The messages in the C-DAG that can be used are the ones that Trans has delivered — that is, the causal messages.

The idea behind the fault detection protocol is quickly to create a consistent line in the C-DAG, across which all processors on the membership list state their agreement about the membership list. Messages preceding the line are in the old view (membership list L_x) and messages after the line are in the new view (L_{x+1}). For the line to be consistent, all regular messages should occur either before or after the line and should not "straddle" the line.

When processor p detects that processor q is faulty, p multicasts a FAULT(q) message that identifies q as a faulty processor. When processor r can receive this message (i.e., when it becomes causal), it immediately concludes that q is faulty and multicasts its new opinion. When all processors in the multicast list (q excluded) have multicast their opinion that q has failed, they have reached an agreement across a consistent line that q has failed. Furthermore, the consistent line at which all processors agree can be found by examining G, since all processors receive the same causal DAG. This execution is illustrated on the left-hand side of Figure 12.10. The consistent line that separates messages from different views is enclosed by a dotted line.

There are a few details to be handled. First, two processors may detect two different failures (say of p and q) concurrently. In this case, neither failure candidate alone can be removed from the delivery lists and still have the delivery lists be consistent. The

FIGURE 12.10   Agreeing on faulty processors.

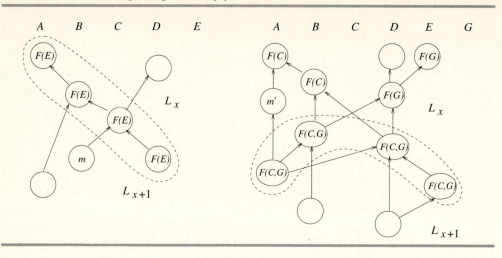

first processor that learns that both p and q have failed concurrently proposes that both processors be removed from the group. If there are no further failures, this change to the group view can be consistently accepted. Such an execution is illustrated in Figure 12.10, where processors C and G fail concurrently.

The delivery of some regular messages needs to be delayed until the new group view is computed. For example, message m from processor B (on the left-hand side of Figure 12.10) causally follows the group view agreement. Processor A might receive m before receiving the $F(E)$ message from D. Therefore, A must delay the delivery of m until after installing the new view. Notice that some of the delayed messages should be delivered before the group view change. For example, message m' from processor A (on the right-hand side of Figure 12.10) at first appears to belong in the new view (since it follows an $F(C)$ message). However, the agreement that changes the group view causally follows m'. A processor that is delaying the delivery of m' can deliver m' when the $F(C, G)$ message from A is received.

The intertwining of regular and group membership messages raises the issue of how to prevent regular messages from straddling the view change. That is, regular message m should not acknowledge message FAULT$_q$(...), which defines the consistent line at processor A and in turn is acknowledged by message FAULT$_p$(...), which defines the consistent line at processor B. The solution to this problem is to require that whenever a processor p receives notification FAULT$_q$(...) of a new faulty processor, it multicasts its agreement message "with high priority". That is, it will multicast no messages that acknowledge FAULT$_q$(...) before it multicasts its agreement message FAULT$_p$(...), which will acknowledge FAULT$_q$(...).

Finally, suppose that the failure of q is detected, but there are there are still undelivered messages from processor q. Recall that even though processor q is being removed from the group view, it might not have failed. So, a message m from q might causally precede or follow a FAULT(q) message, or might be concurrent with all FAULT(q) messages. Because

FIGURE 12.11   Messages from the faulty processor.

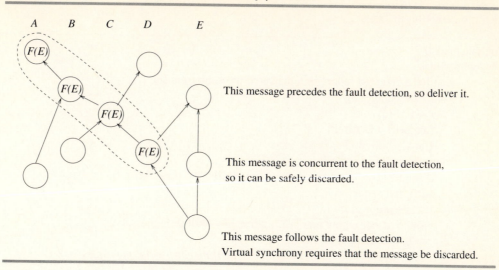

This message precedes the fault detection, so deliver it.

This message is concurrent to the fault detection, so it can be safely discarded.

This message follows the fault detection. Virtual synchrony requires that the message be discarded.

the consistent line of the FAULT(q) messages constitutes a view change, virtual synchrony requires that all messages from q that precede the first FAULT(q) message from any processor be delivered to all processors before the view change and any message from q that causally follows any FAULT(q) message not be delivered at any processor. For this reason, the view change protocol must ensure that no message from q can precede a FAULT(q) message from one processor and follow a FAULT(q) message from another processor. The messages from q that are concurrent to all FAULT(q) messages can be discarded. The three cases are illustrated in Figure 12.11.

The fault detection protocol uses the data structures listed in Algorithm Listing 12.14, in addition to those of the Trans protocol.

The protocol can detect an error due to timeouts (presumably after executing an "are-you-up" protocol) or after receiving a FAULT message. When every nonsuspect processor has broadcast its suspicion of the same set of faulty processors, they have reached agreement and can update their delivery lists. The protocol, shown in Algorithm Listing 12.15, detects the agreement by storing the last FAULT message from every nonsuspect processor (in the Last array). When all entries agree, the new group view is established.

ALGORITHM LISTING 12.14

Variables used by Transis.

L	The multicast list.
F	The set of processors suspected to be faulty.
Last[1 .. Nproc]	Last[i] is the set of processors that processor i last suspected to be faulty.
blocked	Holding area for messages blocked to satisfy virtual synchrony.

ALGORITHM LISTING 12.15

Failure detection in Transis.

```
detect_faults()
    while TRUE
        wait for a detected failure or a delivered message from the Trans layer.
        Failure Detection : (q)
            F = F ∪ {q}
            Last[self] = Last[self] ∪ F
            Trans_send(FAULTY; F)
        Trans_deliver : (msg; sender)
            if sender is in F, and msg follows any FAULTY(F') message in G
            such that sender in F',
                discard msg
            else if F is not empty and msg follows any FAULTY(F) message,
                put message in blocked
            else if message is a FAULT(fset) message // discard some messages in F
                Last[sender] = fset
                if fset - F is not empty
                    deliver all deliverable messages in blocked
                    F = F ∪ fset
                    Trans_send(FAULTY; F) // with high priority
                if Last[i] = Last[j] for every i and j in L - F
                    Deliver messages in blocked that precede every FAULT(F) message
                    L = L - F // Notify the application of the view change.
                    deliver all messages in blocked.
                    Perform garbage collection on G
                    F = ∅
                    for every i in L
                        Last[i] = ∅
            else
                deliver (message; sender)
```

One problem with a paranoid and unidirectional fault detector is that once a processor is suspected of being faulty, it will be removed from the group and will never be readmitted. By this logic, the group of processes performing the multicast will eventually shrink to nothing. We note that if a view change removes half or more of the processors from the group, the group must collapse (to ensure that there is at most one value of L_x). Therefore, we need a way to add processors to the group. If a nonfaulty processor gets removed from the group, it will not be allowed to rejoin. Instead, it must "fail" and rejoin as a new process. While this procedure seems cumbersome, it greatly simplifies the agreement protocol. In addition, it is the right action to take. If a processor was removed from the group, it is likely to have missed some of the communication and so must take action to recover the group state.

ALGORITHM LISTING 12.16

Variables used for adding new processes to the group.

J	The set of processors proposed to be the new group.
JLast[1 .. Nproc]	JLast[i] is the set of processors that p_i has proposed to join the group.

The joining protocol is similar to the fault detection protocol, but in reverse. A processor proposes that a set of new processors J join the group. Since several processors can propose new members simultaneously, the join set can grow and is never allowed to shrink. When all processors multicast the identical join set, we can identify a consistent line on which all processors admit the new members. At this point, the joining processors must receive enough information to start participating in the reliable multicast.

The group joining protocol uses the new variables shown in Algorithm Listing 12.16. The joining protocol, shown in Algorithm Listing 12.17, executes in the same layer as

ALGORITHM LISTING 12.17

Adding new processors to the group.

```
detect_new()
    while TRUE
        wait for a new processor, or a delivered message from the Trans layer.
        New processor : (q)
            J = J ∪ {q}
            JLast[self] = JLast[self] ∪ J
            Trans_send(JOIN; J)
        Trans_deliver : (message; sender)
            else if J is not empty and message follows any JOIN(J) message,
                put message in blocked
            else if message is a JOIN(jset) message
                JLast[sender] = jset
                if jset - J is not empty
                    deliver all messages in blocked
                    J = J ∪ jset
                    Trans_send(JOIN; J) // with high priority
                if JLast[i] = JLast[j] for every i and j in L
                    Deliver all messages in blocked that precede every JOIN(J) message
                    L = L ∪ J
                    Update G, inform processors in J of pending messages
                    deliver all messages in blocked
                    J = ∅
                    for every i in L
                        JLast[i] = ∅
            else
                deliver (message; sender)
```

the fault detection protocol. While both protocols should execute in cooperation, we are presenting them separately for clarity. If a member of the group is contacted by a processor that wishes to join, a New Member event is raised. This initiates the joining process.

The algorithms presented in this section illustrate the approach to building an algorithm for maintaining the group view by using the causality DAG. There are several issues that must still be addressed:

- **Hidden agreement:** The protocol for detecting when all processors agree on the new group view implicitly assumes that waves of failures are well separated in the causality DAG. If a new failure is detected concurrent to the execution of the fault agreement protocol, different processors might have seen different sequences of installed group views. Consider the example illustrated in Figure 12.12. Processor A announces its suspicion of processor C concurrent with the agreement on processor E's failure. Processor D will first remove processor E and then processor C from the group, because it will see agreement in its Last array when it multicasts its FAULT(E) message. Processor A declares that C has failed before receiving the FAULT(E) messages from C or E. Therefore, processor A will eventually remove both C and E from its group view simultaneously.

    The view change that deletes E from the group is a **hidden agreement** because it fits the definition of agreeing on a view change (i.e., it occurs on a consistent state), but it is not detected by all processors. While processors A, B, and D will eventually agree on the group view, the virtual synchrony property is lost. A correct group view maintenance algorithm will either detect or prevent hidden agreement. (We explore this issue in the exercises.)

- **Concurrent faults and joins:** Failures might occur while the join protocol is executing, and the lack of response from the failed processors might prevent the join protocol from completing. So, the join protocol must also collect an agreement about failures.

FIGURE 12.12   Hidden agreement.

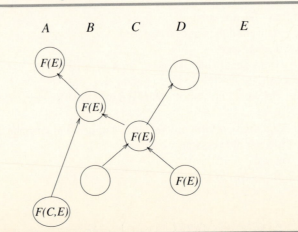

Discussion

The Transis group membership protocol illustrates the technique of propagating information between communicating processors. In this case, the information being propagated is the belief in whether processors have failed or wish to join the process group. Similar techniques can be used to propagate other types of information (e.g., distributed debugging) in both multicast and in unicast communications.

Group Management in ISIS

The Transis algorithm has the advantage of being elegant and very general (it can be modified to permit the merging of process groups, not just the addition of new members). However, there are a couple of drawbacks. First, it requires a multicast on the part of every member of the group. If a multicast is expensive, group maintenance is expensive. Second, it strongly depends on the Trans algorithm for support. Thus, the group membership algorithm can only be used to maintain multicast groups.

Ricciardi and Birman have proposed an alternative algorithm for the ISIS reliable multicast system that is based on point-to-point communication. There are two advantages to such an approach. First, if the multicast is implemented as a series of point-to-point messages, the ISIS algorithm is much more efficient. Second, the algorithm can be used in nonmulticast settings.[15] So, the protocol can be used to monitor the state of a set of processors that are cooperating to perform a distributed computation.

The ISIS algorithm is similar in many ways to a coordinating processor executing a 3PC to atomically install new group views. In normal execution, a centralized processor (the coordinator) repeatedly detects failures, computes new group views, and installs them. As long as the coordinator does not fail, the execution is simple. If the coordinator fails, however, a new coordinator is elected to establish the new group view. Since the old coordinator might have half-finished installing a group view, the new coordinator must poll the processors to learn of their opinions about what view should be installed (as in 3PC). It is also similar to 3PC in that other newly elected coordinators might be concurrently executing, or they might have half-executed and then failed. In spite of any sequence of failures and elections, all coordinators must reach the same decisions.

There are also some important differences between 3PC and the ISIS protocol. One difference is that the failure of a noncoordinator processor does prevent a new group view from being committed. The failed processor is removed on the next view change. Another difference is that 3PC commit only needs to reach a Commit/Abort decision, while the group membership protocol must reach agreement on which processors belong to the group. The nature of the data to be agreed on makes it difficult to define a stable predicate for determining the agreement value. A final difference is that 3PC is executed once, while the group membership protocol is continually executed. As a result, some processors might be waiting to decide about committing a fairly old group view.

In normal execution, the coordinator monitors the process group until it learns of a failure or of a processor that wants to join the group. The coordinator can perform the monitoring directly or can rely on the members of the group to report suspected failures.

---

[15] Interestingly, Ricciardi's algorithm was developed for the ISIS system to provide reliable multicast.

ALGORITHM LISTING 12.18

Variables used by the ISIS group management algorithm.

L	Current group view.
version	The version number of L.
change	Last proposed change to L.
rank	The rank of the coordinator who proposed change.
faulty	The list of processors in L suspected of having failed.
remote_state[1..M]	The state reported by a participant during reconfiguration.
remote_state[i].L	Participant i's current group view.
remote_state[i].version	Participant i's view version.
remote_state[i].rank	Rank of the coordinator that installed i's current group view.
remote_state[i].change	Participant i's proposed change.

Once the coordinator learns of the failure, it computes a new group view and commits it with a two-phase algorithm. Two phases are needed to establish a separation between a consistent state where some processor might not know of the proposed new group view and any state where a processor has committed the new group view. Thus, no processor can commit a new group view until every processor has learned of the new proposal.

The ISIS protocol uses the variables shown in Algorithm Listing 12.18.

As with the Transis algorithm, the ISIS algorithm is paranoid and one-way. In addition, the ISIS algorithm is gossipy. Every processor maintains a list of processors that are suspected of having failed in faulty. This list of suspected processors is attached to every message of the protocol. When a processor receives a message, it merges the gossiped list of suspected processors with its own faulty list. To simplify the presentation of the algorithm, we will not explicitly show the gossiping of the faulty lists. Instead, we will write

```
send(destination, action; parameters)
```

in place of

```
send(destination, action; parameters, faulty)
```

and

```
action(sender, parameters)
    code to handle action
```

in place of

```
action(sender, parameters, remote_faulty)
    faulty = faulty ∪ remote_faulty
    code to handle action
```

An important aspect of the protocol is the handling of messages sent from processors in faulty. In particular, these messages are discarded. This action greatly simplifies the protocol when two coordinators are competing to install a new group view.

The protocol consists of a coordinator sending messages to the participants and waiting for their responses. The coordinator will wait up to T seconds to receive the participant's responses. If a participant does not respond within this timeout period, it is presumed to be faulty. If only a minority of the processors respond, the group has failed and the protocol cannot continue. To simplify the presentation, we provide a macro that accomplishes all of these tasks:

```
distribute (action; parameters)
    return_action (sender; parameters)
        code to handle return_action
```

It expands to

```
for every p in L - faulty,
    send(p,action; parameters)
wait up to T seconds for return_action messages
    return_action (sender; parameters)
        code to handle return_action
For every p in L - faulty that did not respond,
    faulty = faulty ∪ {p}
If a minority of the processors in L responded
    crash()
```

Note that send and return_action are also macros. We assume that point-to-point communications are reliable and FIFO, although these requirements can be relaxed by carefully matching queries with responses.

Under normal conditions, the coordinator executes the protocol shown in Algorithm Listing 12.19. Note that the coordinator might detect some failed participants in the distribute macro. These suspected failures are not committed to L on this round. Instead, they are used to compute change on the next round.

Note that the coordinator must receive an acknowledgment from a majority of the participants in order to commit the view change. (Otherwise, the coordinator decides that the group has collapsed.) This property ensures that any replacement coordinator will learn about the proposed view change and take a consistent action. Each participant executes the protocol shown in Algorithm Listing 12.20.

If the coordinator crashes, a new coordinator (a **reconfigurer**) is elected to take the job. The reconfiguration executes in three phases. First the reconfigurer polls all of the processors in its group view for their opinion about what the current view is and what new views, if any, have been submitted. If the reconfigurer can obtain responses from a majority of the processors (in its group view), it chooses a new value for the view. Choosing the new value is delicate because its decision must be the same as any other

ALGORITHM LISTING 12.19

Coordinator's protocol.

```
Group_Coordinator()
    While True
        wait until an update to the group view is computed in change.
            distribute (COORD_UPDATE; change,version+1)
                CU_ACK (sender; version)
            version ++
            commit the change to L
            distribute (CU_COMMIT)
                CC_ACK (sender)
```

decision that was committed by a previous reconfigurer (in fact, the reconfigurer might learn of a more recently committed view). Second, after choosing the new view, the reconfigurer submits the updated view to the processors remaining in its view. If a majority of the processors respond, the reconfigurer can enter its third phase and commit the view change. The requirement of a majority response ensures that a reconfigurer distributes its opinion of the view update widely enough that any subsequent reconfigurer that can commit a view update will learn of its submission (as in the regular execution).

Every processor has a globally known **rank**, which is accessible through the rank(...) function. The rank of a processor is used to implement a variant of the bully election algorithm — the processor in L - faulty with the highest rank is the coordinator. A processor elects itself coordinator if it determines that it has the highest rank of any nonfailed processor. This election will occur after a fault detection. When a processor elects itself, it executes the reconfigure() protocol, shown in Algorithm Listing 12.21.

ALGORITHM LISTING 12.20

Participant's protocol.

```
Group_Participant()
    while True
        wait for a message from the coordinator
            COORD_UPDATE (coordinator; change,version):
                next_change = change
                next_version = version
                rank = rank(coordinator)
                send(coordinator,CU_ACK)
            CU_COMMIT (coordinator):
                commit next_change to L
                version = next_version
                next_change = {}
                send(coordinator,CC_ACK)
```

ALGORITHM LISTING 12.21

Reconfiguration algorithm for a coordinator.

```
reconfigure()
    mystate = (L, version, rank, {})
    distribute (INTERROGATE; mystate)
        INT_RESPONSE (sender; rstate)
            remote_state[sender] = rstate

    Let Ahead = {p|p ∈ L and remote_state[p].version > version}
    Let Current = {p|p ∈ L and remote_state[p].version = version}
    if Ahead is not empty
            // A more up to date view has been committed, you must propose it.
        change = remote_state[p].L for a p in Ahead
        next_version = version+1
        future_proposal = remote_state[p].change for a p in Ahead
        such that remote_state[p].rank is minimal
    else if remote_state[p].change is empty for every p in Current
            // No proposed changes; you are up to date.
        change = faulty // At least removes the old coordinator.
        next_version = version + 1
        future_proposal = faulty
    else if there is only one nonempty value of remote_state[p].change for p in Current
            // A proposal has been made; it might have been committed.
            // So, you must propose it.
        change = remote_state[p].change for a p in Current
        such that remote_state[p].change is not empty
        next_version = version + 1
        future_proposal = faulty
    else
            // There are competing proposals for a change.
            // The proposal from the lowest ranked reconfigurer
            // is the only one that might have committed.
        change = remote_state[p].change for a p in Current
        such that remote_state[p].rank is minimal
        next_version = version + 1
        future_proposal = faulty

    distribute (REORD_UPDATE; change, next_version)
        RU_ACK : (sender)
    update L with change
    distribute (REORD_COMMIT)
        RC_ACK (sender)
    coordinator = self
    change = future_proposal
    execute the Group_Coordinator protocol
```

ALGORITHM LISTING 12.22

Reconfiguration algorithm for a participant.

```
Reconfigure_Participant()
    wait for an INTERROGATE message
        INTERROGATE : (sender; (sender_L,sender_version,sender_rank,sender_change))
            if rank(self) > sender_rank
                crash()
            if version < sender_version // A new version was committed, so accept it.
                L = sender_L
                version = sender_version
                rank = sender_rank
                next_change = {}
            send(sender,INT_RESPONSE; (L,version,rank,next_change) )
            wait up to T seconds for REORD_UPDATE
                REORD_UPDATE : (sender, next_change,next_version)
            If there was no response
                add sender to faulty
                exit()
            change = next_change
            rank = rank(sender)
            send(sender, RU_ACK)
            wait up to T seconds for REORD_COMMIT
                REORD_COMMIT :
            If there was no response
                add sender to faulty
                exit()
            if next_version > version
                commit change to L
            version = next_version
            coordinator = sender
            send(coordinator,RC_ACK)
```

The participants execute the protocol shown in Algorithm Listing 12.22, which is integrated into the normal participant protocol. If the reconfigurer has a more recent group view, the participant accepts and commits the view. Then, the participant responds with its state, which includes any uncommitted changes of which it has been informed. The remainder of the protocol is similar to the regular participant protocol.

A processor will run the reconfiguration protocol after the failure of the coordinator is detected and the processor elects itself to be the reconfigurer. It is much easier to reason about the algorithm's execution if we know that only one reconfigurer will be executing at any time. Although we cannot obtain that guarantee, we can design the election such that only one reconfigurer should be executing at any given time. If there are two concurrent reconfigurers, one of them will have the lower rank. The lower-ranked reconfigurer must believe that higher-ranked reconfigurer is faulty (i.e., is in the faulty set) and will gossip this belief when it executes the reconfiguration.

As in the Transis algorithm, the membership protocol during the reorganization phase is paranoid and one-way. These properties enable us to deduce enough information about what group views can be committed to ensure that only unique views are committed. For example, it will help us deduce which reconfigurer a participant should listen to. If a participant is contacted by two reconfigurers, r_1 and r_2, one of the reconfigurers will have a lower rank, say r_1. Reconfigurer r_1 elects itself only if it believes r_2 to be faulty, and this belief is communicated to the participant. So, the participant will ignore r_2 after being contacted by r_1.

A reconfigurer r starts its execution because it believes that the coordinator has failed. The previous coordinator might have been in the process of committing a view change when it failed. The previous coordinator might even have committed the view change to some of the participants. Along with view changes committed by other reconfigurers, r might find that the participants it coordinates have views ahead of it or behind it (i.e., with larger or smaller version numbers). However, we can make a couple of observations that simplify the situation.

1. If r's version of L is x, r will never see a version larger than $x + 1$. Why? Because before a view with version $x + 2$ can be committed, an UPDATE message for version $x + 2$ must be sent and responded to. Since r never installed version $x + 1$, it could not have responded to the COMMIT message for version $x + 1$ and therefore was presumed faulty by the reconfigurer (or coordinator). The belief that r is faulty is transmitted with the UPDATE message, so any participant that has committed version $x + 2$ believes that r is faulty and will ignore r's messages. This scenario is illustrated in Figure 12.13.

2. Before the coordinator failed, it might or might not have committed version $x + 1$. If the reconfigurer learns of a proposal for version $x + 1$, it will commit that version. Since the coordinator needed a majority response in its UPDATE message, and the reconfigurer needs a majority response to its INTERROGATE message, if the coordinator committed a version $x + 1$, the reconfigurer will learn about and commit the same view with the same version number. It might be the case that the coordinator did not succeed in committing version $x + 1$, or even in getting a majority response. However, committing the proposed change is safe.

Let us consider what can happen after the coordinator fails. If only one reconfigurer executes, it will commit any previous proposal and become the coordinator (assuming it can reach a majority of L). So, let us consider what can happen if several reconfigurers start execution.

Let us start by assuming that the pending change proposed by the coordinator before it failed was to remove the processors in F from L. Suppose that r (with version x of L) receives acknowledgments from its INTERROGATE message from a majority of L, and it learns that some of the participants have committed version $x + 1$ already. Then, no coordinator or reconfigurer p that sent the COMMIT message for version $x + 1$ will ever be able to install a version $x + 2$. Why? First note that processor p must have a higher rank

FIGURE 12.13   A reconfigurer will see at most version $x+1$ already committed.

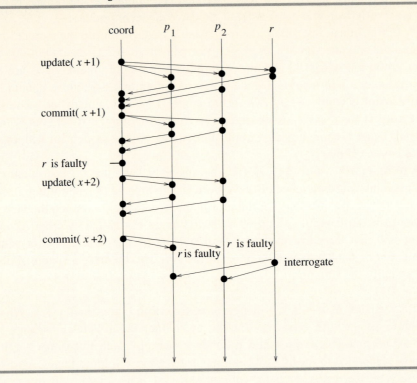

than r and must have believed that r is alive. Otherwise, the participants that committed version $x + 1$ would have believed that r is faulty, so they would not have responded to the INTERROGATE messages. Therefore, r is executing because it believes that p is faulty, and this belief is transmitted along with its INTERROGATE message. Since r received a majority response from version x of L, and version $x + 1$ of L is smaller than version x, a majority of the processors in view $x + 1$ believe that p is faulty, so p will never be able to obtain a majority response to its next UPDATE. This scenario is illustrated in Figure 12.14.

Next, let us suppose that the pending change proposed by the coordinator was to add the processors in J to L. The new processors change the meaning of majority, because the new processors are given a vote in view $x + 1$ on the view change $x + 2$. Let us again consider the case when r learns that some participants who acknowledged r's INTERROGATE message have installed version $x + 1$. Processor r will attempt to commit version $x + 1$ among the processors that responded. A processor p that sent the COMMIT message for version $x + 1$ might still be active, but r is taking a consistent action. Suppose next that both r and p attempt to install version $x + 2$ (and their versions are likely to be different). Since r did not respond to p's COMMIT message, p believes that r is faulty. So, both r's and p's SUBMIT messages convey the belief of the other's faultiness. The new members $n \in J$ will respond to only one of p or r, depending on whose SUBMIT message arrives first. Therefore, at most one of p and r can get a majority response from version $x + 1$ of L. This scenario is illustrated in Figure 12.15.

FIGURE 12.14   Competing reconfigurers when install($x+1$) removes processors.

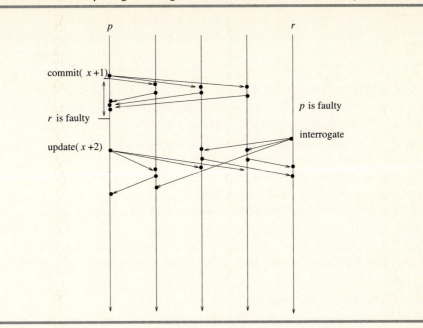

A final detail is that a reconfigurer might learn of several different proposals submitted for version $x + 1$. A little reflection shows that the safest choice is to use the proposal

FIGURE 12.15   Competing reconfigurers when install($x+1$) adds processors.

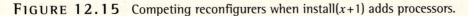
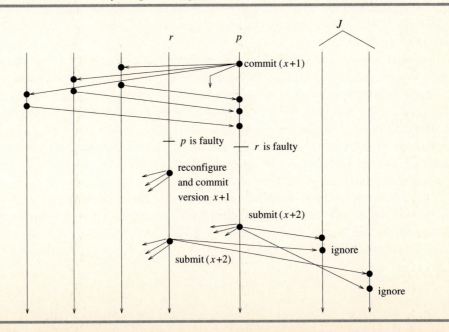

submitted by the lowest-ranking reconfigurer. If a higher-ranking reconfigurer managed to commit a view change, the lower-ranking reconfigurer would have learned about it and proposed the same change. Otherwise, the lowest-ranking reconfigurer will be the winner of any contest.

12.2.6 Atomic Group Multicast

In this section, we describe a protocol that uses a reliable, virtually synchronous causal multicast to build a totally ordered multicast. The protocol is implemented as a layer on top of the causal multicast and the group membership layers. The idea behind the protocol we present is to examine the C-DAG and determine a total ordering that every other processor will determine also. We investigate some other approaches to creating a total order on the messages in the exercises.

The nice property of the algorithm presented in this section is that no additional messages need to be sent to impose a total order on a causally ordered message stream. Section 4.1.5 discusses some other approaches to totally ordered multicast. Notice the similarity of this protocol to the causal message delivery protocol of Section 9.2.3.

Sketch of the Total Ordering Protocol

The flow of the protocol can be described as follows: The total ordering protocol is layered on top of the causal delivery and group membership protocols. Whenever a message is causally delivered ($m_{i,j}$ is the jth message from p_i), the protocol inserts the message in the C-DAG, G (perhaps reusing the C-DAG of the Trans protocol). Next, the protocol looks for a set of messages that can be delivered. It loops indefinitely, delivering one set of messages at a time. All sites deliver the same group of messages S_0, then group S_1, and so on. The delivery of each set S_i corresponds to an **activation** (or **wave**) of the protocol. Since the sequence $S_0, S_1, S_2, \ldots$, is unique, each wave i clearly defines a set of messages S_i, referred to as **source** messages. Messages in S_i are then delivered deterministically (ordered by processor id, for example).

A **pending** message is defined as a message submitted to the protocol that has not yet been delivered. A pending message being considered for insertion in the set of sources is called a **candidate** message, and the set of current candidate messages is denoted by C. A wave is complete when the set of sources S cannot change, even if more messages are received. Since messages are eventually received by all sites, they all agree on the composition of S. In other words, when the set of sources S is **stable**, a **consensus** is reached, and S can be safely delivered (Algorithm Listing 12.23). Here, A represents the set of messages that have so far been totally ordered.

In the following sections, we define more formally the candidates, the sources, the consensus decision, and also the deterministic order used in each wave to deliver sources messages to the application.

The candidates are defined as follows:

Definition 1 *Candidate message*

$$m \in C_p \Leftrightarrow m \text{ follows only delivered messages in } G \Leftrightarrow m \text{ is a root of } G$$

ALGORITHM LISTING 12.23

Sketch of a total ordering protocol for causal multicasts.

```
G = (Ø, Ø)           // Causality DAG
A = Ø         // Totally ordered messages
wave = 1
forever
    When causal-deliver(m_{i,j}), insert m_{i,j} in G. // Messages enter G in causal order.
    loop until exit
        compute C(G)              // Candidates
        compute S(G)              // Sources
        if Consensus(G)
            deliver S(G) in a deterministic order;
            A = A ∪ S
            wave++
        else exit
```

A simple algorithm for totally ordered delivery is to wait until there is a message from each machine in the causality DAG (**Consensus**) and to deliver the roots (**Sources**) of the DAG in a deterministic order. This approach is very similar to Lamport's proposal of putting a timestamp on messages and delivering messages in timestamp order. While this algorithm provides total ordering at no additional cost in messages or acknowledgments, it delays delivery until every processor has sent a message. The latency can be large, and it forces the system to operate at the speed of the slowest processor. Using the causality information already carried by the messages, we can give priority to the first messages acknowledged by a *majority* of processors.

The relationship between the C-DAG maintained by Trans and the C-DAG maintined by the total ordering algorithm is illustrated in Figure 12.16. Every processor that installs two successive group views receives the same set of messages, which form C-DAG $\hat{G}$. As discussed in Section 12.2.3, we can draw several lines in $\hat{G}$. The **received line** is the boundary of the set of messages that have been received. The **stable line** is the boundary of stable (received everywhere) messages. The reliable and causal multicast algorithms maintain the portion of $\hat{G}$ that lies between the stable and the received lines, while trying to advance the **causal line** by delivering causal messages. The **total ordering** line is the boundary of the set of messages that have been totally ordered. The protocols discussed in this section maintain the set of messages between the totally ordered line and the causal line as the C-DAG G. The causal line is advanced when a message is causally delivered, and the total ordering line is advanced on the completion of an activation.

Early Delivery

We characterize below sufficient conditions for any protocol $\mathcal{D}$ to deliver messages in a unique order.

Delivery is triggered when a *consensus* predicate is satisfied. At this point some number of candidate messages, the **sources**, can be delivered if the protocol can guarantee that

FIGURE 12.16   Multicast message status in a C-DAG.

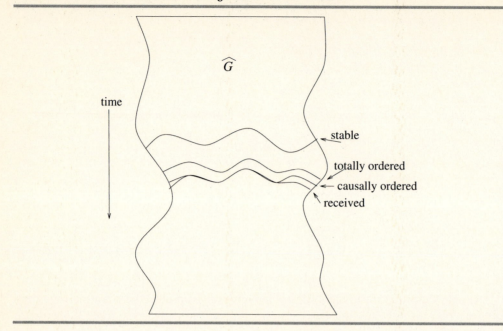

every other processor will deliver the same set of messages. Thus, the set of source messages must be **ordering-stable** (i.e., the set remains the same in every possible extension G' of the current DAG G). Ordering-stability is a form of safety condition: Nothing bad will ever happen if the sources are delivered as soon as they are ordering-stable.

We note that G' extends G if and only if $G \subseteq G'$. We define

$$Future(G) = \{G' | G' \text{ extends } G\}$$

That is, $Future(G)$ represents the remainder of $\hat{G}$, which the protocol does not yet have information about. These remaining messages in $\hat{G}$ are called *unseen messages*. In addition, we define the set of processors that have a message in G as:

$$tail(G) = \{p_i | \exists m_{i,j} \ s.t. \ m_{i,j} \in G\}$$

The set of sources is ordering-stable if for all possible extensions G' of G (when more messages are received) (1) every nonsource candidate message in G cannot become a source in G', (2) every source message in G is also a source in G', and (3) unseen messages cannot become sources in G'.

Definition 2 *Stability conditions (Safety)*

1. **Candidate stability:** If $m \in C_G \setminus S_G$, then $m \in C_{G'} \setminus S_{G'}$ for all $G' \in Future(G)$.

2. **Source stability:** If $m \in S_G$, then $m \in S_{G'}$ for all $G' \in Future(G)$.
3. **External stability:** If $i \notin tail(G)$, then for all j, $m_{i,j} \notin S_{G'}$ for all $G' \in Future(G)$.

The idea of **early delivery** is to devise a stability rule that works without requiring that a message be delivered from every processor. If G satisfies candidate, source, and external stability, G is said to be **stable**. While the stability conditions guarantee that every processor will deliver the same set of messages, we still need to guarantee that eventually some messages are delivered (something good will eventually happen). Thus, we need the following progress conditions:

Definition 3 *Liveness condition*

1. If $|tail(G)| = M$, then $S_G \neq \emptyset$.
2. If $|tail(G)| = M$, then G is stable.

Lemma 4 Suppose that messages are delivered at processor p only when the delivery protocol $\mathcal{D}$ applied to G_p satisfies the three stability conditions. Let S_p^1 be the first set of sources delivered by processor p. Then $S_p^1 = S_q^1$ for every $p, q \in P$.

Proof: Suppose that there exists $p, q \in P$ such that $S_p^1 \neq S_q^1$. Then there is a message m such that $m \in S_p^1$ and $m \notin S_q^1$. Let G_p (respectively G_q) be the causality DAG that is first stable at p (respectively q). The fact that G is the same at all processors in the group and the virtual synchrony property of the membership service guarantee that there is a common extension of G_p and G_q, which includes $\mathcal{G} = G_p \cup G_q$. Suppose that m is a candidate message in G_q. By candidate stability, m is not a source message in every extension of G_q, including $\mathcal{G}$, so m is not a source message in $\mathcal{G}$. By source stability, m is a source message in every extension of G_p, including $\mathcal{G}$. Therefore, m both is and is not a source message in $\mathcal{G}$, a contradiction. Therefore, m cannot be a candidate message in G_q and thus has not yet been delivered to q (m is a root of G_p). But then, by external stability, m is not a source message in every extension of G_q, including $\mathcal{G}$, leading to another contradiction. Therefore $S_p^1 = S_q^1$. ∎

Each wave of this protocol considers only the messages in G that have not been totally ordered (yet). In fact, the total ordering protocol $\mathcal{D}$ maintains only the most recent portion G^* of the DAG G.

Definition 4 $G^* = (E^*, V^*)$ is the most recent portion of G if given A, the set of messages delivered in all previous waves, it satisfies:

$$G^* \subseteq G \wedge E^* = E \setminus A \wedge \forall (a, b) \in E^*, \ (a, b) \in V \Rightarrow (a, b) \in V^*$$

To support multiple waves, the consensus decision does not consider messages already agreed to (present in A). It is therefore defined on G^* — the messages between the causal line and the total ordering line. In the following sections, we assume without loss of generality that all messages from previous waves have been removed from $G (G = G^*)$. Note that if $ntail(G) = n$ $(G \neq \emptyset)$, the set of candidates is nonempty.

Theorem 9 Suppose that the early delivery protocol $\mathcal{D}$ satisfies the three stability conditions and the two progress conditions. Then $\mathcal{D}$ delivers all messages in the same order at all working processors.

Proof: The liveness of the agreed multicast service ensures that every G_p contains within a finite amount of time a message from each processor. Condition (Definition 3) then guarantees that every G_p is eventually stable and has a nonempty set of source messages. Therefore, every working processor eventually delivers the same set $S^1 \neq \emptyset$. Then, apply Lemma 4 inductively to G^*. ∎

The TOP Protocol

In the following discussion, we define some functions used by the early delivery protocol. The functions are evaluated on the current causality DAG G at processor p. If there can be confusion about which causality DAG on which processor the functions are evaluated, we annotate the functions. Otherwise, we suppress the extra notation for simplicity.

Definition 5 *Processor vote*

The first message $m_{i,j}$ from processor p_i in G votes for the candidate messages of the DAG it causally follows. In addition, a candidate message votes for itself.

Message $m_{i,j}$ gives one vote to each candidate message it causally follows (the ones it approves of) or one to itself if $m_{i,j}$ is a candidate message.

Each candidate message m tracks the processors that voted for it in its **vote vector** $VV(m)$. The ith component of the vote vector, $VV(m)[i]$, is the vote that processor i casts for m and is defined by:

$$VV(m)[i] = \begin{array}{ll} 1 & \text{if processor } i \text{ votes for } m. \\ 0 & \text{if processor } i \text{ votes but not for } m. \\ * & \text{if processor } i \text{ has not cast a vote.} \end{array}$$

We define the **tail** of a candidate message m to be the set of processors that sent a message that causally follows m. Then, $ntail(m) = |tail(m)|$. The tail of the causality DAG G is the set of all processors that have a message in G, and $ntail(G) = |tail(G)|$. Let u be the number of processors that have not voted yet (unseen votes):

$$u = |P - ntail(G)| = |\{j : VV(m1)[j] = *\}| = M - ntail(G)$$

We denote the number of votes that a candidate message m receives to be

$$nvt(m) = |\{i : VV(m)[i] = 1\}|$$

Candidate messages are compared on the basis of the votes they receive. Let $\Phi \geq M/2$ be a threshold parameter. Let $m1$ and $m2$ be two candidate messages. We define a function *votes* by

$$votes(m1, m2) = \quad |\{j \; : \; VV(m1)[j] = 1 \wedge VV(m2)[j] = 0\}|$$

Candidate message $m1$ wins over candidate message $m2$ if it beats $m2$ in more than Φ votes. We define a function *Win* as

$$
\begin{aligned}
Win(m1, m2) = \quad &1 \quad \text{If } votes(m1, m2) > \Phi. \\
&0 \quad \text{If } votes(m2, m1) > \Phi. \\
&X \quad \text{Otherwise.}
\end{aligned}
$$

The value of *Win* is defined on the current causality DAG G. We need a function that tells us about all possible future extensions of G, G'. Thus, we use *Future*, which is all possible future values of *Win*:

$$Future_G(m1, m2) = \{Win_{G'}(m1, m2) \text{ in } G' \text{ extending } G\}$$

The only interesting way that G' can extend G is by specifying the votes of the processors that have no message in G. Thus, $1 \in Future(m1, m2)$ if and only if the number of processors that vote for $m1$ but not $m2$, plus the number of unseen votes ("*" votes), is greater than Φ. That is,

$$
\begin{aligned}
1 \in Future(m1, m2) \quad &\text{if} \quad votes(m1, m2) + u > \Phi. \\
X \in Future(m1, m2) \quad &\text{if} \quad X \in Win(m1, m2). \\
0 \in Future(m1, m2) \quad &\text{if} \quad 1 \in Future(m2, m1).
\end{aligned}
$$

Note that

$$1 \notin Future(m1, m2) \quad \Leftrightarrow \quad votes(m1, m2) + u \leq \Phi \Leftrightarrow votes(m1, m2) \leq \Phi + ntail(G) - M$$
$$Future(m1, m2) = \{1\} \quad \Leftrightarrow \quad Win(m1, m2) = 1$$

Let M_G be the set of candidate messages in the causality DAG G. The set of **source** messages S_G is defined as

$$i \in S_G \Leftrightarrow i \in M_G \wedge \forall j \in M_G, \; 1 \notin Future(j, i)$$

A message i is a source if it will never lose against any other candidate message j already in G. (j cannot *beat* i in more than Φ votes in any possible extension of G.)

Since configuration changes are reported in a consistent order by the group membership service, the TOP protocol accommodates failures as follows: A failed process votes,

ALGORITHM LISTING 12.24

Delivery rules for the total ordering protocol.

---

1) (early delivery rule)
    if   a) (internal stability)
               $\forall m \in M_G \setminus S_G, \ \exists m' \in S_G, \ Future(m', m) = \{1\}.$
    and b) (external stability)
              $\exists s \in S_G, \ nvt(s) > \Phi,$
                  Then deliver S_G.
2) (default delivery rule)
    Else, if $ntail(G) = M$,
            Then deliver M_G.

---

but for no particular candidate message ($VV(m)[i] = 0$ if i has failed). The TOP protocol is then specified by its delivery rules in Algorithm Listing 12.24.

S_G is stable when (1) all nonsource candidate messages will not become sources in the current activation (if they lose once) and (2) all unseen messages will not become sources (if a source message gets more than Φ votes, they will lose against it). The observation is that the first part of rule (1b) already guarantees external stability.

Theorem 10 The S-Top protocol is correct.

Proof: As messages are inserted in a causal order, a processor p that already has a message in the graph will not vote for an unseen message. The first message from p, m_p, votes for the candidate messages it causally follows that are already in G (or itself if it is a candidate message).

Suppose that the early delivery rule is satisfied. Then there is a source s with at least $\Phi + 1$ votes. s can share these votes with other candidate messages in G, but all $\Phi + 1$ processors that have voted for s will not vote for an unseen message s'. When G is extended by inserting s', if s' is a candidate message, s' will not become a source message. Indeed, s' will lose against s, since a majority of processors will still vote for s and not for s': $votes(s, s') > \Phi$. If s' gathers all unseen votes, $nvt(s) + nvt(s') = M \implies nvt(s') < M - \Phi$. Since $\Phi \geq M/2$, $nvt(s') < \Phi$. Therefore, $\forall i \in S_G, votes(s', i) < \Phi$ (s' will not take any source message i out of S_G), and the S-Top protocol satisfies external stability and source stability.

The internal stability rule then guarantees that every process delivers the same set of messages on every activation. A nonsource candidate message i will not become a source message if i loses against one candidate message j (if $win(j, i) = 1$ in G, $win(j, i) = 1$ in any extension of G). Thus S-Top satisfies candidate stability.

Finally, the S-Top protocol satisfies the progress conditions since if $ntail(G) = M$, either the early deliver rule is satisfied or all candidate messages are delivered. ∎

FIGURE 12.17   The sources $\{B, F\}$ are stable and can be delivered.

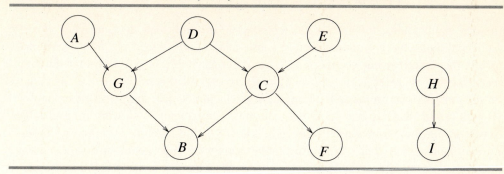

Example: The example in Figure 12.17 presents an activation of the protocol. Only the first message from a particular processor is shown. The causality DAG is depicted after the insertion of message J.

$M = 10$ processors, $\Phi = 5$ majority threshold
$ntail(G) = 10$ number of processors that have voted
$u = M - ntail(G) = 1$ unseen votes, $M_G = \{B, F, I\}$ roots of the DAG

m_i	B	F	I
$nvt(m_i)$	$|\{B, C, D, E, G\}| = 5$	$|\{C, D, E, F\}| = 4$	$|\{H, I\}| = 1$

$votes(row, col)$	B	F	I
B	$-$	$|\{B, G\}| = 2$	$|\{B, C, D, E, G\}| = 5$
F	$|\{F\}| = 1$	$-$	$|\{C, D, E, F\}| = 4$
I	$|\{H, I\}| = 2$	2	$-$

$S_G = \{B, F\}$ is computed as follows:

- $B \in S_G$ as $nvt(B) > \Phi$
- $F \in S_G$ as $votes(B, F) + u = 4 \leq \Phi$ and
  $votes(I, F) + u = 4 \leq \Phi$
- $I \notin S_G$ as $nvt(I) = 2 \leq \Phi \wedge \exists B \in M_G, votes(B, I) + u = 6 + 1 > \Phi$

S_p is stable and can be delivered:

1. $M_G \backslash S_G = \{I\}$
   $nvt(I) + u = 3 \leq \Phi \wedge \exists B \in S_G, \ votes(B, I) = 6$
2. $ntail(G) = 9 \geq n - \Phi \wedge \exists B \in S_G, \ nvt(B) > \Phi$

12.3 UPDATE PROPAGATION

In some applications, the consistency constraints on replicated data are very loose. A replicated data object is shared among a number of sites, which use and occasionally update the data. It is not necessary to support serializability or a notion that the "most recent" value of the object is returned on an access. All that is required is for updates on data items to be propagated among all replicas in a timely manner. One example of an application that has very loose data sharing requirements is network routing tables. New sites and new routes need to become known to the network at large, but there is no requirement that copies of routing tables always be consistent. Automatic software distribution is another example. An application with more consistency constraints is groupware bulletin board applications. The Lotus Notes groupware system makes use of update propagation to replicate the databases it manages. Updates (new postings) need to be propagated to all sites. The postings should obey a causality constraint so that a thread of conversation can be followed.

In this section, we describe several replication algorithms that are based on **gossip**. That is, when a data item is updated at a server, the update is recorded locally. The server occasionally contacts another server to see if one knows of updates that the other doesn't. The servers make themselves equally up to date by exchanging the updates that the other hasn't seen. Eventually, an update spreads to all servers.

We will examine gossip-type algorithms with two notions of what "new updates" are. In the simpler algorithms, an update overwrites the old value of an object. A more powerful algorithm allows updates to modify the old value of an object (i.e., increment a counter). In this case, the **history** of all updates must be recorded and distributed. Since the value of a data object depends on all of the updates performed on it, techniques similar to reliable multicast are used to ensure that every update is propagated to every site.

12.3.1 Epidemic Algorithms

We first examine the problem of choosing a method for gossiping updates to replicated data. In this section, we will assume that an update to a data item overwrites the older value. Let D be the shared database. When a server p_s computes an update to a data item $d \in D$, it assigns a timestamp to d. This timestamp can be a sample from a real-time clock, or it can be a causal timestamp. When two sites communicate to gossip updates, they compare the timestamps of the data items in D. If one server has a newer version of a data item d (i.e., it has a larger timestamp), d is sent to bring the other server up to date.

The challenge in designing **epidemic** algorithms lies not in maintaining consistency but in spreading news of an update without sending too many messages. The information distribution algorithms we discuss in this section are designed for application to hundreds or thousands of replicated servers. At such a scale, reliable multicast algorithms become untenable.

The simplest method for distributing the news of a new update is to use **direct mail**. When a server performs an update on d, it sends a message to all servers that also maintain a copy of d. However, there are two problems with direct mail. First, some of the destination sites might be unavailable. Since we do not want to support the overhead of a reliable multicast, some sites will not hear of the update. Second, contacting the remote processors and informing them of the update places a large communication burden on the updater. However, direct mail will require only $M - 1$ messages to support replication among M servers.

If we abandon the idea of direct mail (or reliable multicast), we have to accept that communication is limited. So, an updater will send its update to a few neighboring sites. These sites will communicate the update to other neighboring sites, and so on, until the message is fully distributed. Unfortunately, this type of message distribution means that many processors will attempt to distribute the message to each other when both are already up to date. So, the number of messages required to distribute the update can be many times greater than $M - 1$. In addition, there still might not be any guarantee that the update is propagated to all sites.

Epidemics

When a server updates a data item d, it should start the process of distributing the update. Similarly, when a server learns of an update, it should activate the process of distributing the update. However, if a server s_1 contacts server s_2 about the update to d and finds that s_2 is already up to date, then s_1 should detect that the update is well known and become less enthusiastic about distributing the update.

Given an update $u(d)$ to d, we can categorize the M servers in the system:

1. **Susceptible**: A server is susceptible if it has never heard of $u(d)$.
2. **Infectious**: A server is infectious if it has heard of $u(d)$ and is actively propagating $u(d)$.
3. **Removed**: A server is removed if it knows of $u(d)$ but is no longer actively propagating $u(d)$.

Given these definitions, the epidemic algorithm is as follows:

1. When a susceptible server learns of $u(d)$, it becomes infectious.
2. An infectious server repeatedly contacts a random server and tells the destination server about $u(d)$.
3. If an infectious server contacts an infectious or a removed server, with probability $1/k$, it becomes removed.

The parameter k controls how persistently the epidemic spreads. Let In be the fraction of servers that are infectous and s be the fraction of servers that are susceptible. Suppose that on every time unit, every infectuous server contacts another server. Then, In and s are modeled by the following differential equations:

$$\frac{ds}{dt} = -sIn$$
$$\frac{dIn}{dt} = sIn - \frac{(1-s)In}{k}$$

The first equation arises from the fact that a susceptible server becomes infectous if an infectous server contacts it. In the second equation, susceptible servers become infectous, and infectous servers become removed with probability $1/k$ if they contact a nonsusceptible server. To solve this system of equations, we take their ratio to get:

$$\frac{dIn}{ds} = \frac{1}{ks} - \frac{k+1}{k}$$

This differential equation has the solution:

$$In(s) = \frac{k+1}{k}(1-s) + \frac{\log(s)}{k} \tag{12.6}$$

The effectiveness of the epidemic is measured by the number of uninfected sites when the epidemic is over (i.e., when $In = 0$) and the total number of messages sent. We can find the **residue** s_0, or the fraction of sites that do not hear about the update, by solving Equation 12.6 for $In = 0$, to get:

$$\begin{aligned} s_0(k) &= e^{-(k+1)(1-s)} \\ &\approx e^{-(k+1)} \end{aligned} \tag{12.7}$$

Each processor that becomes infected will send infection messages until it contacts a sufficient number of already-infected sites. Since a processor will become *removed* with probability $1/k$ whenever it contacts an infected site, it becomes removed after contacting i infected sites with probability $(1 - 1/k)^{i-1}(1/k)$. So the expected number of messages m_{tot} is:

$$\begin{aligned} m_{tot} &= M(1-s)\left[1 + \sum_{i=1}^{\infty} i\left(1 - \tfrac{1}{k}\right)^{i-1}\tfrac{1}{k}\right] \\ &= Mk(1-s) \end{aligned}$$

In summary, the coverage of the epidemic improves exponentially with k, but the cost increases linearly with k. This may seem like a good trade-off but consider the improvement in coverage obtained by changing the parameter of the epidemic from k to $k+1$. The residue is approximately e^{k+1}, so the number of new sites infected by increasing k is:

$$\begin{aligned} M\{[1 - s_0(k)] - [1 - s_0(k+1)]\} &\approx M\left[\left(1 - e^{-(k+1)}\right) - \left(1 - e^{-(k+2)}\right)\right] \\ &= M(1-e)e^{-(k+1)} \end{aligned}$$

Thus, the number of messages required to infect new sites increases exponentially with the number of additional sites. Epidemics are good for initial distribution (setting $k = 2$ gives a 96 percent coverage) but are terrible at distributing the update to the last few sites. Therefore, we need a backup mechanism.

ALGORITHM LISTING **12.25**

Gossip algorithm.

Gossip()
  Pick a random processor, s
    exchange(s)

12.3.2 Antientropy

A different strategy for distributing updates is to have one site contact another to exchange recent updates (i.e., **antientropy**). A processor initiates contact by using the algorithm in Algorithm Listing 12.25.

  The exchange can be accomplished using one of three methods. First, the initiating processor can **pull** the more recent updates from s. Second, the initiating processor can **push** its more recent updates to s. Third, the initiator can **push-pull**, that is, do both. In either case, s sends its list of timestamps to the initiator, who determines which data items are to be transmitted. We present the pull algorithm in Algorithm Listing 12.26. The other two algorithms are similar.

  If most sites are infected (i.e., have heard of the most recent update of d), intuitively the pull algorithm is better than the push algorithm. Why? Push makes progress only if an infected initiator contacts an uninfected processor, which is unlikely. Pull makes progress only if an uninfected initiator contacts an infected processor, which is likely.

  More precisely, let p_i be the probability that a random processor has not heard of the most recent update of data item d after i communication rounds (i.e., it is uninfected). On the $(i + 1)$th round, an uninfected processor will remain uninfected with respect to d only if it contacts another uninfected processor, which happens with probability p_i. Therefore,

$$p_{i+1} = p_i^2$$

The corresponding formula for the push algorithm is (recalling Equation 12.7):

$$p_{i+1} \approx \frac{p_i}{e} 1$$

ALGORITHM LISTING **12.26**

Pull algorithm.

exchange(s)
  get T_s, the list of timestamps from s.
  for every d such that $T_s[d] > T_{\text{self}}[d]$,
    get d from s.

So, the push algorithm does not produce a convergence that is faster than that of the epidemic, while the pull algorithm gives a doubly exponential convergence. So, gossiping using the pull (or push-pull) algorithm is an effective supplement for an epidemic.

12.3.3 Update Logs

Often an update on a data item doesn't replace the data item but instead only modifies it. For example, the update might increment a counter, or modify an entry in a table. Both of these examples of updates have a nature that is different from an overwriting update. The value of an increment counter should reflect the values of many concurrent updates, so overwriting an old value can place too strong of a serialization constraint on the computation. The description of a modification of a table entry is likely to be much smaller than the table itself, so it is more efficient to distribute the update rather than the table.

In the discussion of epidemic algorithms, we assumed that an update completely overwrites a data object d. This simplifies the problem of distributing updates because it is permissible to miss some of the updates to d. In particular, if update $u_2(d)$ overwrites $u_1(d)$, then a processor p does not need to receive $u_1(d)$ after it receives $u_2(d)$. If the updates only modify the data object, and if $u_2(d)$ is initially performed in the context of $u_1(d)$, then $u_1(d)$ must be performed on d before $u_2(d)$ at all sites that store d.

The value of an object can be thought of as the combination of its initial value and the **history** of the updates applied to the object. For example, we can think of the state of a processor as the combination of its initial state and the sequence of events up to the state. In this discussion, we will apply the same technique to describing the state of a data object.

In order for all copies of a data object to become consistent, the entire history of the updates must be applied to all copies. The epidemic algorithms give only probabilistic guarantees that all updates are propagated to all sites. Clearly, this is not a sufficient correctness guarantee for update log propagation. The algorithm presented here guarantees that an update is propagated to all sites. As with reliable multicast, the information necessary to guarantee **reliable update propagation** gives causal update propagation "for free".

Every processor p keeps a **log** L of the updates that it has processed. The log is an (ordered) listing of **event records**, where each event corresponds to an update. Each event record e contains the fields shown in Algorithm Listing 12.27.

Algorithm Listing 12.27

Event record for causal event propagation.

e.op	The operation and its parameters.
e.p	The processor that first executed the operation.
e.VTS	A timestamp attached to the event.

Processors distribute information by exchanging their logs. As we have mentioned, the updates that are propagated throughout the system must maintain a consistency property of executing at a remote processor in the "same" environment as at the original processor. In particular, events must be added to the log in a causally consistent order.

We need some notation. Given a log L, the first i events of L are denoted by $L[i]$. If event e is in L, its position is denoted by $index(i)$. We will use $L[e]$ as a shorthand notation for $L[index(e)]$.

Consistent log property: Let e be an event that is first executed at processor p. Then for every processor $j = 1, \ldots, M$ and every event f,

$$f \in L_p[e] \quad \Leftrightarrow \quad f \in L_j[e]$$

With a little reflection, and the help of Figure 12.18, we see that causal log propagation has many similarities to causal multicasting. In Figure 12.18, we show the events (black dots) that are in p_1's log when the sixth event occurs at p_1. We assume that when one processor propagates its log to another processor (indicated by an arrow between time lines), it propagates all events in its log, including events that were propagated to it. So event propagation is transitive. Some of the events at processors p_2 through p_4 were propagated to p_1 when p_1's event six was executed. These events are enclosed in the dashed-line boxes.

Even though message passing (i.e., log propagation) is not considered to be the important activity (event execution is), log propagation still transmits context from one processor to another. The context of an event can be described by a vector timestamp.

FIGURE 12.18   Causal log propagation.

When event 6 is performed
at p_1, the first

5 events from p_1,
2 events from p_2,
3 events from p_3,
3 events from p_4
are in p_1's log.

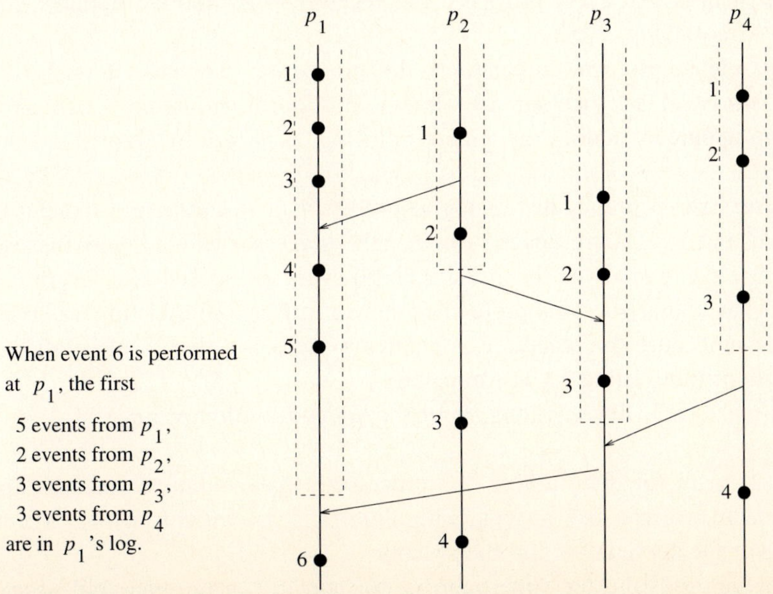

For example, the context of event 6 on processor p_1 is (5, 2, 3, 3). When one processor propagates its log to another, the context of the recipient can be computed by the usual timestamp merging algorithm. For example, before p_1 receives p_3's log, its context is (5, 1, 0, 0), while the context of p_3 is (0, 2, 3, 3). Events can be compared using vector timestamp comparison. So, given that event e first executed at p, we know that $f \in L_p[e]$ if $f.VT <_{VT} e.VT$.

We can see that maintaining the consistent log property is not difficult. Let us consider an event e that is first executed at processor p. When e is first propagated from p (say to q), all events that causally precede e are in p's log. So, they can all be propagated to q. The next time e is propagated, it might be from p or q. In either case, all events that precede e are in the log, so they can be propagated. The full argument proceeds inductively.

The final matter to address is efficiency. First, the logs must be garbage collected at some point. If processor p knows that every other processor has heard of an event e, then p can delete e from L_p. Second, p does not need to send its entire log to q. If p knows that q has heard of event e, then p does not send e to q.

The efficiency considerations require a processor p to know, for every other processor q, a lower bound on the set of events that must be in L_q. This lower bound is expressed as a vector of vector timestamps, one for every other processor q. Exactly the same problem must be solved for reliable and causal multicast, and the technique used mirrors that described in Section 12.2.4. In particular, we perform **garbage collection** by using a **matrix timestamp**

An example is illustrated in Figure 12.19. Before processor p_1 receives a log propagation from p_3, p_1 has only received information about p_2's events and timestamps. When p_4 propagates its log, it has learned about the timestamps of p_2 (transitively) and p_3 (directly). After p_1 receives p_3's log, it updates its timestamp estimate. By examining the estimate, p_1 learns that every processor has received p_2's first two updates, so they can be deleted from the log.

The log update protocol implements the procedures we have described. The data structures stored at a processor are shown in Algorithm Listing 12.28. A processor performs an update by adding the update to its log, as shown in Algorithm Listing 12.29 (on p.498).

When processor p propagates its log to processor q, p only needs to send the events that q might not have. Given event e in L_p, the processor where e was first executed is processor $r = e.p$, and e was the $k = e.TS[r]$th event originated at r. Event e should be sent to q if min_TS[q][r]<k. This protocol is shown in Algorithm Listing 12.30 (on p.498). Finally, the procedure for receiving and integrating a log that is distributed to you is shown in Algorithm Listing 12.31 (on p.498).

We can make some observations about the log distribution protocol:

- The mechanism for determining the processors that communicate their logs is not specified. So, we can use an epidemic algorithm, an antientropy algorithm, or one devised for the application and the system.
- Sending the log L and the timestamp vector min_TS can be separated, since they are used for different functions.

FIGURE 12.19   Propagating lower bounds on timestamps.

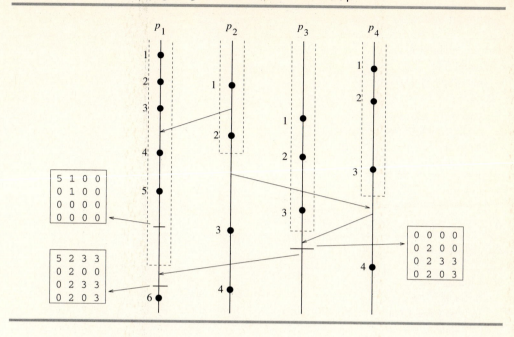

- Distributing the matrix timestamp can be expensive because its size grows as M^2. The space and message passing overhead can be reduced by keeping and distributing looser estimates of min_TS.

- The timestamps attached to the events act like vector timestamps. The log distribution algorithm can be used to build replicated servers that provide a causally consistent view of the managed data to their clients. Each client specifies the minimum timestamp of the environment in which its request can be executed. The execution of the request is blocked until the server is sufficiently up to date. In addition, when the server replies, it attaches the timestamp of the environment in which the reply was computed. The client can use this timestamp to ensure that it receives a causally consistent view of the data.

ALGORITHM LISTING 12.28

Variables used for causal update propagation.

count	The number of events originated at self.
L	The log of events that have been received.
min_TS[1 .. M]	min_TS[q] is a lower bound on the maximum timestamp of an event known to exist in L_q.
stable[1 .. M]	stable[q] is the highest numbered event originated by q that every processor has received.

ALGORITHM LISTING 12.29

Adding an update to the log.

```
perform_update(u)
    count ++
    min_TS[self][self]=count
    new e
    e.op = u
    e.VTS = min_TS[self]
    e.p = self
    append e to L
```

ALGORITHM LISTING 12.30

Propagating an update log.

```
send_log(q)
    initialize L' to ∅
    for every e ∈ L such that min_TS[q][e.p] < e.TS[e.p]
        append e to L'
    send L' to q
    send min_TS to q
```

ALGORITHM LISTING 12.31

Receiving an update log.

```
receive_log(p)
    receive L' from p
    receive min_TS' from p

    for every e in L'
        if e ∉ L
            append e to L (in causal order)
    for j = 1 to m // Update your timestamp.
        min_TS[self][j] = max(min_TS[self][j],min_TS[p][j])
    for i = 1 to M, i ≠ self // Update your timestamp lower-bound array.
        for j = 1 to M
            min_TS[i][j] = max(min_TS[i][j],min_TS'[i][j])
    for i = 1 to M // Compute the stable updates.
        stable[i] = min(min_TS[1][i], ..., min_TS[M][i])
    for every e in L
        if e.VTS[e.p] ≤ stable[e.p]
            remove e from L
```

12.4 SUMMARY

The best method for implementing a fault-tolerant distributed system is the subject of much controversy. This is best exemplified by a paper in a recent *SIGOPS*, which claims that reliable multicast is not a good basis for implementing reliable systems [CS93]. Although this paper makes several good arguments, another recent paper [Bir93b] makes good arguments that reliable multicast is a good basis for implementing reliable systems. In this chapter, we have presented several approaches. It is likely that the best method for implementing replication depends on the application and the system constraints. For example, Birman [Bir94] argues that reliable multicast techniques should be used to manage replicated transient data, while database techniques are used to manage replicated persistent data. We note that a different method for implementing a highly available service (recovery) is discussed in the next chapter. A discussion of techniques for implementing replicated servers can be found in [Coo85].

We first examine techniques for implementing transactions on distributed and replicated data. Transactions are made fault tolerant by *logging* enough information to ensure that any failure *recovery* is consistent with the execution of the transactions that have *committed*. Implementing transactions on distributed data requires the use of *atomic commit* protocols. Examples of these protocols are *two-phase commit* (2PC) and *three-phase commit* (3PC). These algorithms ensure recoverability by establishing a *stable property* and by basing the decision to commit or abort on the detection of the stable property.

The standard definition of the correct execution of transactions is *serializability*. If the transactions use replicated data, we must use *one-copy serializability* (1SR) as the definition of correctness. The standard method for ensuring one-copy serializability is to use *quorums* – a transaction must be able to commit its updates at a write quorum of the data set to atomically commit. For flexibility and availability, a database must be able to change the quorums defined for its data items. *Dynamic quorum change* protocols treat quorums as replicated data objects and apply replicated data management techniques on them.

Second, we examine *reliable multicast* techniques. The idea of reliable multicast only makes sense if the delivery list is well defined in spite of failures. *Virtual synchrony* defines group membership and view-change events. A multicast is reliable under virtual synchrony if every processor that performs two consecutive view-change events receives the same set of messages. We present a technique for reliable and virtually synchronous multicast that makes use of *transitive acknowledgments*. The transitive acknowledgments form a *causality DAG*, which contains information equivalent to that contained in the *vector timestamps* used by the ISIS reliable multicast mechanism. These algorithms also provide *casual* message delivery.

Next, we study two algorithms for performing group view maintenance, with the goal of providing virtual synchrony. Both algorithms use an *unreliable failure detector* (i.e., timeouts) and provide a consistent view of the nonfailed processors in a group. The first algorithm uses the causality DAG; the second algorithm uses a three-phase commit. To avoid the FLP impossibility result, the algorithms are *paranoid* and *gossipy*, providing a *monotone* view of the nonfailed processors. Finally, we study a method for totally ordering the multicast messages. A totally ordered, virtually synchronous, and reliable multicast is an *atomic* multicast, which can be used to manage replicated data.

A third technique for maintaining replicated data is to use *update propagation*. These techniques give only weak consistency guarantees but permit very large scale replication. If the application requires only that the most recent value of a data object be propagated, then the objects can be tagged with a sample from a real-time clock. If updates to the object are propagated, the propagation algorithm must ensure that the update reaches every site. The problem is similar to those of reliable multicast, and it is easy to ensure causal as well as reliable update propagation. Both reliable update propagation and reliable multicast make use of a *matrix clock*, which is used for *garbage collection*.

ANNOTATED BIBLIOGRAPHY

The 2PC protocol was proposed by Gray [Gra78] and by Lampson and Sturgis [LS76]. Some variants to reduce the message passing overhead are discussed in [Gra78, RSL78, Ske82b]. Ancilotti, Lazzarini, Prete, Sacchi [ALPS90] give a variant of 2PC suitable for nested transactions. Rothermel and Pappe [RP93] discuss 2PC on an open network with trusted and nontrusted nodes. Standards on 2PC include [ISO89a, ISO89b, IBM85]. The 3PC protocol for synchronous systems was proposed by Skeen [Ske82b, Ske82c, Ske82a]. The 3PC protocol for asynchronous systems was proposed in [Ske82a, CK85, CR83b]. The version discussed in the text is similar to the "nonblocking" commit proposed by Duchamp [Duc89]. Monotone predicates are discussed in [Spe91]. An alternative to 3PC for a nonblocking commit algorithm that uses process groups is proposed by Guerraoui, Larrea and Schiper [GLS95]. Some works that analyze the non-blocking properties of 3PC are [Coo82, DS83, Ram85]. Levy, Korth, and Silberschatz [LKS91] present an optimistic commit protocol that uses compensating transactions to undo the effects of mistakenly committed transactions.

The notion of serializability in database accesses is discussed in [BSW79, Pap79, SLR76]. One-copy serializability is discussed by Attar, Bernstein, and Goodman [BG86b, BG86a]. The paper [ABG84] discusses simple algorithms for initializing and recovering a replica. The two-phase locking protocol was first described by Esweran et al. [EGLT76]. The discussion of serializability, database recovery, concurrency control follows that of the book by Bernstein, Hadzilacos, and Goodman [BHG87], which provides a much more complete description of the issues and algorithms than this chapter has scope for. Another book that contains an in-depth coverage of transaction processing issues is by Gray and Reuter [GR93]. King, Halim, Garcia-Molina, and Polyzois [KHGMP91, PGM94] give a set of techniques for maintaining remote backup sites.

An early protocol for maintaining replicated data is the primary copy approach [AD76, Sto79]. Two sites are used to store the data, the primary and a backup. If the primary fails, the backup is used to serve the data. Unfortunately, communications failures can lead to an inconsistent database. A primary copy algorithm that accounts for communication failures is described by Oki and Liskov [OL88]. The majority consensus protocol was proposed by Thomas [Tho79], and was generalized to voting by Gifford

[Gif79]. The algorithm for view-based quorums is given by El-Abbadi and Toueg [AT89]. A related approach for dynamic quorum adjustment was proposed by Davcev [Dav89], Herlihy [Her87], Barbara,Garcia-Molina, and Spauster [BGMS86], and Jajodia and Mutchler [JM90]. Rabinovitch and Lazowska [RL93] show how to change the quorum for a data item by using a transitional view in which transactions must acquire quorums in both the old and the new views. Davidson, Garcia-Molina, and Skeen [DGMS85] present a survey of database-related replication management algorithms. Herlihy [Her90] shows that different transaction execution models give a trade-off between concurrency and availability. Barbara, Garcia-Molina, and Spauster [BGMS89] give an algorithm in which sites can independently but safely change their vote weight without requiring a 2PC.

A different approach for maintaining high availability is the **missing writes** algorithm of Eager and Sevcik [ES83]. The missing writes algorithm uses a read-one/write-all quorum if there are no failures but makes a transition to requiring a larger read quorum if a failure occurs (which is detected at commit time). To force the transition from read-one to read-quorum, a transaction that detects a failure posts "missing write" information at the sites that it updates. The missing write posting is deleted after the failures are repaired.

Pu, Noe, and Proudfoot [PNP88] introduce regeneration-based replica control protocols, in which new replicas can be made available to a site. Long, Carroll, and Stewart [LCS89] present techniques for integrating regeneration-based algorithms with other techniques, such as the available copies algorithm, and present a reliability model. Additional works relevant to regeneration-based algorithms include [NA87, CLP87, Par88].

Bernstein, Shipman, and Rothnie used 2PL and timestamp ordering to ensure serializability in the SDD-1 distributed database [BSR80]. Davidson [Dav84] uses a cycle-breaking approach to resolve possible inconsistent accesses to replicated data. A transaction execution that can lead to a non-1SR execution is aborted. Triantafillou and Taylor [TT94, TT95] give a nice discussion of how a high-performance replicated server can be built, by testing for conflicts at commit time. Temporary replicas can be cached at sites where they are often accessed, and servers can respond to requests without first obtaining a quorum. Cabrera et al. discuss the use of the ARIES logging and recovery algorithm for implementing fault-tolerant services [CMSW93].

If a data item is widely replicated (say, to dozens or hundreds of copies), executing a quorum protocol can be prohibitively expensive. An active field of research has been to find small but failure resilient quorums. This work has a feel similar to the gerrymandered voting districts of Maekawa's mutual exclusion algorithm [Mae85, AJ92]. Voting districts in this context are often called **coteries** [GMB85]. Agrawal and El-Abbadi [AA91, AA92] have proposed the tree quorum protocol. The processors that maintain a copy of a data item are logically structured in a tree. Once a tree structure is imposed, various strategies for defining quorums can be defined, each with different performance characteristics. For example, a write quorum can be a majority of the processors at every level of the tree, while a read quorum is a majority of the processors at any level of the tree. Alternatively a read or write quorum can be a path from the root to a leaf. If a processor on the path has failed, it can be replaced by a path from all of its children to a leaf. A related strategy that uses a hierarchical idea, but without a root bottleneck, is the hierarchical quorum consensus algorithm [Kum91]. Strategies that are a dynamic version of Maekawa's voting districts include the grid protocol [CAA90a], the triangular lattice protocol [WB92] the dynamic group protocol [PS92], the triangular net structure protocol [CT94], and generalizations [TPK95]. Rangarajan, Setia, Tripathi [RST92] propose a protocol that uses Maekawa's fixed structure, but replaces individual voters by quorums. Rabinovitch and Lazowska [RL92] show how to apply quorum change techniques to structured coteries. The idea is to base the structure of the coterie on the set of processors in the current view so that agreement on the current view is agreement on the coterie structure.

The idea of using transactions to build reliable distributed systems [TGGL82] has motivated the investigation of concurrency control on data objects. Papers that establish conditions for commutativity of operations on objects include [BR88, Wei88]. Birman et al. [BJRA85] discuss the implementation of exactly-once RPC on replicated objects. A nice discussion of an implementation of an atomic persistent object system is given in [SM94b].

Herlihy [Her86] shows how to generalize the idea of read/write quorums to abstract data type operations. Jing, Bukhresm and Elmagarmid [JBE95] use a similar trick to manage read locks for mobile transactions. Pu and Leff [PL91b] propose ϵ-serializability, in which reads can span several transactions during execution, but all writes are performed in the same order at all sites. Bloch, Daniels, and Spector [BDS87] give a practical algorithm for maintaining replicated directories. Sarin, Floyd, and Phadnis [SFP89] improve on the replicated directory by showing how key ranges can be independently replicated.

The technique of using **witnesses** to reduce the cost of replication algorithms was proposed by Paris [Par86, PL88, Par94]. A similar idea, voting with **ghosts**, was proposed by Van Renesse and Tanenbaum [RT88]. A ghost is a processor that takes the place of a failed processor, and can vote in write quorums but not read quorums. Paris and Long [PL91a] propose regenerable volatile witnesses — Adam and Tewari [AT93] propose a scheme to turn ghosts into actual replicas, to improve availability. Since witnesses record only state information, they can be stored in memory and therefore can be regenerated quickly in case of a failure. Tong and Kain [TK88] give an algorithm to compute the vote assignment that gives optimal availability. Spasojevic and Berman [SB94] extend this work to handle coteries also.

Atomic multicast has been the subject of much research because an atomic multicast algorithm permits the simple specification of many difficult synchronization problems [CASD84]. A system built on synchronous atomic multicast is the Advanced Automation System [Cri91a]. Active replication in Delta-4 [CPR+92] uses asynchronous atomic multicast. Server replication is supported by group communication [CASD84, Cri90], group membership changes [Cri91b], and clock synchronization [CAS92].

The practical utility of distributed process groups has long been recognized. The V kernel [CZ85] is the first operating system to provide the notion of group communication, but without reliability or ordering guarantees. Current extensions of the IP layer provide similar services [Dee89]. Murata, Shionozaki and Tokoro [MST94] discuss an implementation of reliable multicast over the IP services. Jalote [Jal95] gives a technique for implementing resilient objects with nested invocations using an atomic multicast. Bal,

Kaashoek, and Tanenbaum [BKT92] use atomic multicast to implement a sequentially consistent distributed shared memory in the ORCA parallel programming language.

Chang and Maxemchuck [CM84] describe the first algorithm for group membership and atomic multicast. The messages are ordered by a site that holds a token, which is passed among the processors in the system. A message needs to be multicast two or three times before it can be ordered, and the token must be passed L times before the messages it orders can be delivered.

Luan and Gligor [LG90] build an atomic multicast on the 3PC algorithm. However, four multicasts are required per atomic multicast. Birman and Joseph [JB86] give an algorithm for building an atomic multicast on top of a causal multicast for the ISIS system. The algorithm is distributed, and is based on computing the maximum timestamp at which all recipients first received the multicast. This timestamp is used for the total ordering. In a later work, Birman, Schiper, and Stephenson [BSS91] present an updated atomic multicast algorithm for ISIS. This algorithm uses a centralized ordering site as in Chang and Maxemchuck's algorithm. However, since a reliable group view mechanism is available, multicast ordering information can be quickly distributed. The idea of a matrix timestamp [RS95] first appears in [WB84, SL87] for use in discarding safe updates. Garcia-Molina and Spauster [GMS89] propose implementing total ordered multicasts by multicasting through a logical tree. An advantage of this scheme is the easy integration of multiple multicast groups. A related approach is suggested by Ng [Ng91]. Wilhelm and Schiper [WS95] analyze a subtlety in the semantics of atomic multicast, depending on whether the implementing algorithm is symmetric or asymmetric.

The algorithm for reliable multicast is based on the Trans algorithm first proposed by Melliar-Smith, Moser, and Agrawala [MSMA90]. This algorithm was simplified by Amir, Dolev, Kramer, and Malki [ADKM92b] for the Transis project. An advantage of Transis over Trans is that Transis provides causal multicast and access to a causality DAG. (The Transis algorithm is presented in this chapter.) Melliar-Smith, Moser, and Agrawala also provided a total ordering protocol, Total, that works on top of Trans. The attractive feature of the Total protocol is that no additional messages are required for atomic multicast beyond those required for reliable multicast. This algorithm was improved on by Dolev, Kramer, and Malki [DKM93]. The ToTo protocol was improved and simplified by Maugis and Johnson [MJ94]. A version of the Maugis and Johnson algorithm is presented in this chapter. Rodrigues and Verissimo [RV95] use transitive acknowledgments to enforce causal communications for point-to-point and multicast communications. Elnozahy and Zwaenepoel [EZ92b] use the *antecedence graph* maintained by Manetho (see Chapter 13) to enforce ordered message delivery among replicas of a server.

A protocol related to the Total family of protocols is that of Psynch [PBS89]. However, the Psynch protocol requires that a message be received from every processor in the group before any messages can be delivered, while the Total algorithm and its derivatives permit early delivery. An interesting aspect of the Psynch protocol is that it supports **semantic** message delivery as well as totally ordered message delivery [MPS89, MPS91a, MPS91b]. For example, messages corresponding to queries can be delivered with less delay than messages corresponding to writes. The idea of semantic delivery is improved on and applied to early delivery multicast by Maugis and Johnson [MJ94].

Moser and Melliar-Smith have developed an alternative method for implementing atomic multicast, based on token passing [AMMS+93, MMSA93, AMMS+95]. While this algorithm has good performance in a token passing LAN, space constraints prevent us from discussing it in this book.

The reliable and atomic multicast algorithms need to have well-defined delivery lists. So, they need group membership algorithms. In addition, virtual synchrony [JB87] is generally recognized as necessary to provide the proper semantics to the application programmer. Our discussion of virtual synchrony is similar to that of Schiper and Sandoz [SS93], who define a *view-atomic multicast*. Chang and Maxemchuck [CM84] provided a membership protocol for their atomic broadcast protocol. Bruso [Bru85] discussed algorithms for performing failure notification, but did not attempt to provide a consensus view. Mishra, Peterson, and Schlicting [MPS91b] discuss a protocol that uses the partial ordering of messages to help compute the consensus. Kaashoek and Tanenbaum [KT91] propose an algorithm similar to that of Chang and Maxemchuck for group membership in the Amoeba distributed operating system. Moser, Melliar-Smith, and Agrawala [MMSA94] present a group membership algorithm that uses the total order placed on messages. Jahanian et al. [JM92, JFR93] define weak, strong, and hybrid group membership, and provide 3PC-like algorithms to implement them.

The first algorithm for group membership discussed in the text is based on the algorithm of Amir, Dolev, Kramer, and Malki [ADKM92a]. This algorithm was subsequently extended to handle multiple process groups [DMS94]. Moser, Amir, Melliar-Smith, and Agarwal [MAMSA94] present a formal definition of correctness with multiple process groups. The second membership algorithm discussed in the text is from Ricciardi and Birman [RB93], and was proposed for use in the ISIS distributed computing system.

Epidemic algorithms were proposed by Demer et al. [DGH+87]. Rabinovitch, Gehani, and Kononov [RGK96] discuss efficient implementations of value propagation by epidemics. Additional work on the message diffusion algorithms includes work by Moses and Roth [MR89]. Bagchi and Hakimi [BH94] give algorithms for fast gossiping. The idea of a replicated and causally consistent log is due to Wuu and Bernstein [WB84]. The presentation in the text follows that of Agrawal and Malpani [AM91] and Heddaya, Hsu, and Weihl [HHW89]. Ruget [Rug94] discusses techniques for reducing the storage and transmission costs of matrix timestamps. Ladin, Liskov, Shrira, and Ghemawat [LLSG92] discuss a method for building a reliable server using replicated logs. Kawell et al. [KBH+88] discuss the update propagation algorithm used in Lotus Notes. Downing, Greenberg, and Peha [DGP90] discuss the use of update propagation to implement a weakly consistent database. Black and Artsy [BA90] discuss a replicated name service built in part by using update propagation. Ladin and Liskov [LL92] build a garbage collector for a distributed object system by using a server maintained by causal update propagation. Liskov, Scheifler, Walker, and Weihl [LSWW87] detect orphans by propagating information about the failures of parent processes.

EXERCISES

1. What techniques can be used to minimize the uncertainty period of 2PC without changing the algorithm into 3PC or changing the algorithm semantics?

2. Modify the 3PC algorithm to let the coordinator decide to abort a transaction if it times out before receiving ACK messages from a majority of the participants.

3. Suppose that there are m processors in a group. Give an algorithm that the coordinator of the group can use to take a snapshot of the states of the group participants.

4. Modify the 3PC protocol to allow a participant that votes Ae to be persuaded to change its vote to Ce. *Hint*: The coordinator must collect a consistent snapshot to verify stable properties.

5. Modify the 3PC protocol to allow a participant that votes Ae to be persuaded to change its vote to Ce and also to allow a participant that votes Ce to be persuaded to change its vote to Ae.

6. Suppose that in the 3PC protocol in which participants can change their vote, the coordinator is not required to verify that a majority of processors vote Ae in a consistent snapshot. Give an execution where one coordinator decides to commit and another coordinator decides to abort.

7. An *optimistic commit* protocol tentatively commits a transaction at a participant as soon as the participant votes Yes and cleans up its state if the transaction actually aborts. Give an algorithm that maintains serializability using an optimistic commit.

8. Develop a fault-tolerant version of Maekawa's algorithm for coterie assignment by replacing individual processor votes by quorums.

9. Modify the 2PC algorithm to commit a transaction if a quorum of the participants vote Yes.

10. Give an execution of the view-based quorum algorithm in which a data item is written to by transactions in two concurrent partitions and show that the execution is 1SR.

11. A *regeneration-based* replica control algorithm creates new replicas to ensure availability in the event of site failures. Develop a regeneration-based algorithm to manage a replicated database that ensures serializability and does not lock up the database. *Hint*: Apply the ideas used in the view-based quorum algorithm and use a two-phase commit.

12. A high-performance replicated server should respond to client requests immediately. Develop a protocol for replicated data management that answers requests immediately and permits the use of temporary cached replicas. *Hint*: Test for conflicts at commit time.

13. Give an algorithm in which processors can independently increase their vote weights, without requiring a 2PC. *Hint*: First incorporate the new vote weight into quorum thresholds and then increase the vote weight.

14. A *semi-queue* is a data structure with two operations: *enqueue* an object into the semi-queue and *dequeue* an object from the semi-queue. The enqueue operation is always successful. The dequeue operation returns one of the objects from the semi-queue if the semi-queue is not empty (not necessarily the first object in the queue)

and returns nil if the semiqueue is empty. What quorum threshold assignments can be made for enqueue and dequeue operations on a replicated semi-queue? *Hint*: Use operation logging instead of value logging.

15. Suppose that replicated data is managed by read-one/write-all. Show how a transaction that queries a data item can set its read lock at one site and release it at another. (This is useful for transactions issued by mobile computers.)

16. A *dictionary* is an abstract data type that associates keys with values (e.g., a name server). The operations on the directory are to add a key-value pair, delete a key-value pair, and to look up the value associated with a key. Write an algorithm for maintaining a replicated dictionary and which can permit concurrent operations on individual keys. *Hint*: The delete operations can cause problems for a naive approach. Think about using key ranges as the replicated objects.

17. Suppose that you associate a sequence of quorums with each replicated data object. A transaction that fails to obtain the current quorum, number x in the sequence, can attempt to obtain quorum $x + 1$. Develop this idea into a quorum adjustment protocol. (Do not worry about returning to a lower numbered quorum.)

18. Let us define *safe* message delivery as follows. A processor will deliver a safe message only if every processor in the process group has received the message. Modify the ISIS reliable multicast algorithm to provide safe message delivery.

19. Suppose that two causal multicast groups have overlapping members. Modify the ISIS causal multicast algorithm to ensure causal message delivery in spite of overlapping multicast groups.

20. Give an algorithm to build a C-DAG on the messages received using the ISIS reliable multicast algorithm.

21. Modify the Transis group membership protocol to detect all hidden agreements.

22. Modify the Transis group membership protocol to handle failures when joining new group members.

23. Suppose that you have the use of a service that places a total order on multicasts and reliably delivers messages in spite of processor failures. You want to implement a group membership protocol.
    a. Give an algorithm for removing a failed processor from the group.
    b. Give an algorithm for adding a new member to the group.
    Hint: Use the atomic multicast as ticks of a clock.

24. Let Φ_1 and Φ_2 be two thresholds such that $\Phi_1 > \Phi_2$. Modify the S-TOP protocol so that if a message cannot be delivered using the Φ_1 rule, it can be delivered using the Φ_2 rule.

25. Give an algorithm that places a total order on the updates propagated using the algorithm of Section 12.3.3.

26. Modify the update propagation algorithm to use *hierarchical matrix timestamps*. The processors are partitioned into domains. Each processor keeps a regular matrix timestamp on the processors in the same domain. For a remote domain, the processor stores a summary that is a safe description of the progress of all processors in the remote domain.

27. (Programming project) Implement the 2PC algorithm, and test it by simulating failures. Recall the important points:

    a. Recovery is based on logging. Keep a log in-memory. The log state persists between simulated failures.

    b. You need a recovery protocol as well as the regular commit protocol. This means that you need timers to detect possible failures. Note that the text does not specify the recovery algorithm in detail; you will need to supply these details.

    Architecture: Use the implementation framework developed for the programming project of Chapter 10. Perhaps a convenient coordinator would be the program control process (the one that starts up all of the other processes). Execute a single transaction at a time and make the execution of successive transactions completely separate (for ease of grading).

    Make certain that the user can specify failures and recoveries. The participant failures can occur:

    a. After the start of the transaction but before voting.

    b. After voting, before committing.

    c. After committing.

    The coordinator failures can occur

    a. After the start of the transaction but before submitting a vote request (you can omit this if you run out of time).

    b. After submitting a vote request and before committing locally.

    c. After committing locally and before sending out any commit messages.

    d. After sending some, but not all, commit messages.

28. (Programming project) Implement a replicated server and test it by simulating failures. In particular, replicate a set of five registers. There are three operations:

    a. Increment one of the registers by 1.

    b. Swap the value of two of the registers.

    c. Dump the register contents.

    Approach: You have the freedom to pick your approach. Here are two suggested strategies.

    a. Primary copy: The servers elect a coordinator. All operations are performed by the coordinator. Updates are committed to at least a quorum of the participants. If the primary fails, a new coordinator is elected. The new coordinator first brings itself up to date by accessing a read quorum of all data objects. Then, the coordinator resumes normal processing.

    b. Quorum access: A client submits its request to one of the servers. The server locks a quorum of the sites. After all locks are obtained, the operation is performed and then committed. Then the response is sent to the client. To obtain locks, you will need to use a variant of the locking and deadlock recovery protocol presented with Maekawa's algorithm in Chapter 10.

    Note that with both algorithms, you need to think about logging and recovery. Use main memory for logging (just an array). Perhaps candidates should poll voters about the vote status? For method **a**, you will need to implement election. For method **b**, you will need to think through the failure and recovery issues associated with lock management. For example, a voter should log its votes, a candidate might need to relinquish all of its votes and try again, etc.

Alternatively you can:

a. Use optimistic concurrency control.

b. Implement atomic multicast.

c. Use update propagation.

Option **b** can be difficult; you can punt on group view management if you wish (i.e., make the group coordinator/message sequencer reliable). Option **c** is easy, but it only provides weak consistency. You will need to justify and/or augment this approach.

You may assume that the clients are reliable and that if a server commits an operation, it reliably transmits the results to the client. That way, you can avoid the issue of exactly-once. If you are ambitious, implement exactly-once RPC, let the clients fail, and let the servers drop responses.

Architecture: It is a good idea to reuse the framework that you built for the previous projects. Here is one suggestion. The program control process starts up the clients and servers. During execution, the control process accepts user input to:

a. Direct a client to request service.

b. Specify the failures and recoveries that will occur during the execution of the service.

13

CHAPTER

Checkpointing and Recovery

If a processor fails and then is repaired, it will need to **recover** its state of the computation. To be recoverable, a processor will need to **checkpoint** (i.e., record on stable storage) its state from time to time and perhaps also **log** (i.e., also on stable storage) the messages that it receives. During recovery, the processor uses its last checkpoint and the message log to obtain the most up-to-date state possible. Because the recovering processor will generally not be able to restore its state to that immediately preceding its failure, the other processors in the system might observe an inconsistent state after the recovery — they might have received messages that the recovered processor never sent. Other processors might need to **rollback** to ensure consistency.

Checkpoint and recovery are useful when a set of processors is engaged in a long-term and large-scale computation. Several researchers have experimented with using idle cycles on networked processors to perform various computations such as finding very large prime numbers. The techniques discussed in this chapter can also be applied to developing highly available distributed services.

In the previous chapter, we discussed methods of managing replicated data. These approaches can be thought of as a proactive approach to fault tolerance — the shared state of a processor is explicitly replicated, so a hot spare can immediately take the place of a failed server. Recovery can be thought of as a reactive approach to fault tolerance, in the following sense. If a processor's checkpoint and message log information is placed in a publically available location (such as at a hot-spare processor), a spare processor can take the place of a failed processor by recovering the failed processor's state. The advantage of a recovery-based approach is that a processor does not need to wait until it is informed that a previous update is globally committed before proceeding to the next update (if an optimistic checkpointing algorithm is used). The disadvantage is that the failure of one processor can cause many processors to rollback their state.

13.1 PROBLEMS IN ROLLBACK

After a failure occurs, the processors must restart the computation in a **consistent state**. That is, the restarting state of one processor should not causally follow the restarting state of another processor (i.e., use the definition of *consistent state* as defined in Section 9.4.1). A set of consistent restarting states is called a **recovery line**. The problem of checkpointing and recovery is to ensure that a recovery line exists and to find the best recovery line after a failure.

Let us assume that M processors periodically take checkpoints of their state. We label the jth checkpoint recorded by processor p_i as $C_{i,j}$. Suppose that processor p_i fails and then recovers by restoring its state to its last checkpoint $C_{i,j}$. If there is no further coordination among the processors, they might observe **orphan** messages, which are received without having been sent. This possibility is illustrated in Figure 13.1. If the system were to roll back to the checkpoint defined by C_1, C_2, and C_3, message m_1 would have been received without having been sent. That is, the checkpoints C_1, C_2, and C_3 are not consistent.

If p_2 executes a **deterministic** program, p_2 will resend m_1 shortly after restarting the execution from C_2. In the restored state, processor p_1 will receive message m_1 twice. One way to handle the problem of orphan messages is to execute p_2 until it has sent m_1 and then establish a consistent state. Another way to handle the problem is to roll back the execution at other processors until a consistent global checkpoint is found (i.e., no checkpoint at one processor causally follows a checkpoint at a different processor). Rollbacks might be required if the programs cannot be guaranteed to be deterministic.

FIGURE 13.1   An inconsistent checkpoint.

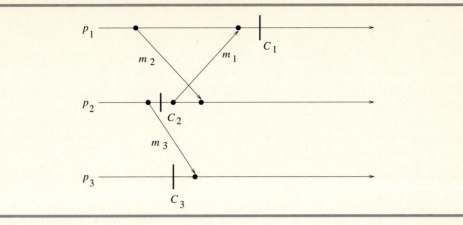

Message m_3 illustrates a different problem, for it was sent without being received (the same problem occurs with m_2). When p_2 and p_3 reexecute from C_2 and C_3, message m_3 will be lost. Message m_3 can be regenerated by rolling back p_2 to an earlier checkpoint. However, reliable communications protocols track the messages that have been sent but not yet delivered. So, an alternative to rolling back p_2 is to include in the checkpoint the information about the message passing protocol. In this method, p_2 and p_3 can detect the lost message after the rollback and cause p_2 to retransmit m_3. In some cases, it is necessary to capture the messages in transit as part of the consistent checkpoint (as in the consistent snapshot algorithm of Chapter 9). In this chapter, we assume that the channel states can be ignored or reconstructed, and the bibliography contains references to techniques for efficiently capturing the channel state.

A recovery algorithm based on repeatedly rolling back processors to earlier checkpoints can have **cascading rollbacks**. Suppose that processor p_i fails and then rolls back to $C_{i,j}$ upon recovery. To ensure consistency, all of the other processors $\{p_k\}$ must roll back their state to one that does not causally follow a message sent after $C_{i,j}$ was collected. Unfortunately, when p_k rolls back its state, another processor p_l might be forced to roll back also, and so on. This effect might snowball all the way back to the start of the computation, as is illustrated in Figure 13.2. The checkpoint defined by $C_{1,2}$ and $C_{2,3}$ is not consistent because m_7 has been received without being sent. We can try to roll back one more step and use the checkpoint defined by $C_{1,2}$ and $C_{2,2}$, but this checkpoint is not consistent because message m_5 has been received without being sent. In fact, no rollback state except for the initial state is consistent. So, a single processor failure effectively becomes a total failure.

A distributed computation might be expected to communicate with the "outside world" (e.g., the user's terminal, the file system, robotics, etc.). A computation that is made fault resilient by checkpointing and recovery might exhibit **stuttering** – asking for the same input twice or producing the same output twice. Stuttering will occur if a process performs I/O with the outside world and then rolls back to a point before the I/O occurred. Stuttering can be avoided by using special techniques for I/O with the

FIGURE 13.2   Cascading rollbacks.

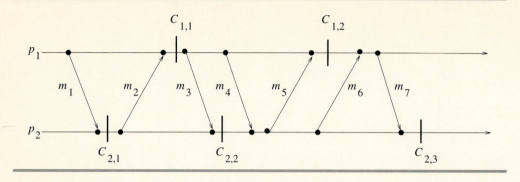

outside world. For example, input should be logged. Avoiding output stuttering requires an **output commit**, or a guarantee that the process will not roll back to a point before the output event before releasing the output to the outside world.

A final problem involves messages in transit from failed or rolled-back processors (**duplicate messages**). Suppose that p_1 sends m_1 to p_2 and then rolls back to a state where it has yet to send m_1. If p_2 learns of the rollback before receiving m_1, then p_2 will not need to roll back itself. But when p_2 receives m_1, it should recognize that m_1 is a duplicate message and refuse to deliver it to the application layer. Figure 13.3 illustrates an example of this problem. Notice the difference between this problem involving m_1 here and the problem involving m_1 illustrated in Figure 13.1. A orphan message is one that has been received before rollback, while an duplicate message is one received after rollback.

FIGURE 13.3   Duplicate messages from previous incarnations.

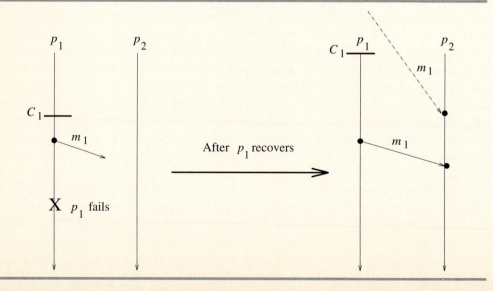

ALGORITHM LISTING 13.1

Variables used to detect duplicate messages.

| incarnation[i] | Current guess of p_i's incarnation number, | $i \neq self$. |
| | The incarnation number | $i = self$. |

13.2 INCARNATION NUMBERS

An issue common to all recovery algorithms is the handling of **duplicate** messages, or messages sent by a processor that has failed or rolled back, as in Figure 13.3. Since duplicate messages are handled in the same way among all of the recovery algorithms, we discuss it here.

Each processor keeps an **incarnation number**, which it uses to distinguish between different periods of execution. On every recovery from a failure or rollback, a processor increments its incarnation number. (Note that incarnation numbers require the use of stable storage.) In addition, the processor attaches its incarnation number to every message that it sends. In order to detect duplicate messages, a processor keeps a current guess of the incarnation number of every processor in the array incarnation. The value of this array is defined in Algorithm Listing 13.1.

When a processor p receives a message m sent from p_i, p takes one of the following three actions, depending on the incarnation number attached to m, m.incarnation:

1. m.incarnation < incarnation[i]: m is a duplicate message, so discard it.
2. m.incarnation = incarnation[i]: Deliver m.
3. m.incarnation > incarnation[i]: m belongs to an incarnation that p has not yet been informed of, so block the delivery of m until m.incarnation = incarnation[i].

13.3 TAXONOMY OF SOLUTION TECHNIQUES

There are two main choices to be made in implementing a failure recovery scheme. The first choice is whether or not to log the messages that a processor receives. The advantage of message logging is the greatly increased flexibility obtained during recovery. However, message logging presents two problems. First, logging every message might be expensive in terms of storage and I/O demand. Second, all message logging-based recovery schemes require that the process being recovered be **deterministic**. That is, the state of the process must be completely determined by its initial state and the sequence of messages that it has received.

Most operating systems give the processes that execute in them many opportunities to be nondeterministic, by catching signals, obtaining the current time, exchanging information through shared memory, receiving error conditions from system calls, and so on. For a process to be deterministic, and hence recoverable by message logging, all communication to the process must take the form of loggable messages. Achieving this property requires either a special kernel or an insulating layer to perform the logging. Some events, such as catching a signal, might be extremely difficult to wrap into a loggable message. In this case, message logging does not help until another checkpoint is taken.

The second choice in the recovery scheme is whether or not to coordinate the state recording. If the state is recorded with checkpoints only, the decision is whether or not the checkpoint recording occurs on a consistent cut. If message logging is used, the decision is whether or not a message must be logged before it can be delivered.

Corresponding to the four options for implementing recovery, we will discuss four algorithms. We also discuss a fifth technique, **adaptive logging**, that has similarities to several of the four basic options.

13.4 UNCOORDINATED CHECKPOINTING

In this scheme, we assume that the processors occasionally checkpoint their state, and do not log their messages and that checkpointing is not coordinated between processors. Because the checkpointing is not coordinated, there is no guarantee that the most recent collection of checkpoints is **consistent**. When uncoordinated checkpointing is used, the issue is to find a **maximal recovery line** (i.e., a recovery line that happens after every other possible recovery line).

Given processor p_i, we denote by $I_{i,j}$ the **checkpoint interval** of processing at p_i between checkpoints $C_{i,j}$ and $C_{i,j+1}$. If the last checkpoint taken by p_i is $C_{i,j}$, then $I_{i,j}$ consists of all work performed since $C_{i,j}$. A checkpoint interval $I_{k,l}$ **depends on** checkpoint interval $I_{i,j}$ if there is a message m that was received in $I_{k,l}$ and sent in $I_{i,j}$. Interval dependence is illustrated in Figure 13.4. If p_i rolls back to $C_{i,1}$, then p_k must roll back to $C_{k,2}$ to ensure consistency.

When a processor p_i fails and then is repaired, it starts the recovery procedure by restoring the state of its last checkpoint $C_{i,j}$. Next, every other processor in a state that

FIGURE 13.4   The depends-on relation.

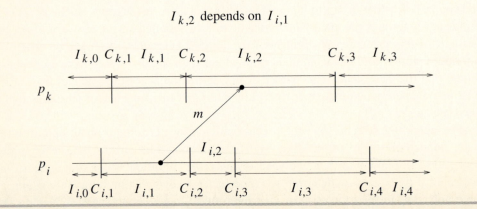

depends on $I_{i,j}$ must be rolled back. Furthermore, this rollback is transitive. If p_k rolls back to $C_{k,l}$, and $I_{m,n}$ depends on $I_{k,l+\delta}$, $\delta \geq 0$, then p_m must also roll back its state.

To conveniently capture the rollback requirements, we can build the **interval dependence graph** G_I. The vertices V_I are the checkpoint intervals $I_{*,*}$ that exist when the rollback procedure is initiated. For every pair of intervals $I_{i,j}$, $I_{i,j+1}$, we add the directed edge $(I_{i,j}, I_{i,j+1})$ to E_I. In addition, if $I_{k,l}$ depends on $I_{i,j}$, we add the directed edge $(I_{i,j}, I_{k,l})$ to E_I.

These two sets of edges precisely capture the rollback requirements. The edge $(I_{i,j}, I_{k,l})$ expresses the fact that if p_i rolls back from $C_{i,j+1}$ to $C_{i,j}$, then p_k must roll back to $C_{k,l}$. The edges $(I_{i,j}, I_{i,j+1})$ represent the fact that dependencies noted in subsequent intervals must be accounted for also.

The definition of interval dependences might not seem to account for lost messages. Consider the interval $I_{k,2}$ in Figure 13.4. If p_k rolls back to $C_{k,2}$, it will need to obtain message m sent in $I_{i,1}$. It would seem that p_i should roll back to $C_{i,1}$ in order to supply p_k with the missing message. However, we can treat any acknowledgment of m from p_k as a message that adds a dependence in the interval dependence graph. So, either the protocols use unreliable message passing and tolerate dropped messages, or p_i rolls back to a state preceding the acknowledgment of m and attempts to redeliver m when the execution restarts (see the chapter bibliography for techniques to capture the messages in transit).

A recovery line corresponds to a **maximum-sized antichain** in the interval dependence graph, that is, a set of M vertices such that there is no path from one vertex in the antichain to another. An interval dependence graph might have many maximum-sized antichains. Because of the way that we have constructed the interval dependence graph, all of the maximum-sized antichains are ordered (i.e., by the usual vector time ordering). We want to find the last maximum-sized antichain.

When a recovering processor p_r starts the execution of its recovery procedure, it takes the following steps:

1. Compute G_I. This requires that every processor mark its messages with its checkpoint number, that each processor store its own local portion of G_I, and that these pieces be combined at p_r.
2. Let $C_{r,j}$ be the last checkpoint recorded by p_r.
3. Mark $I_{r,j}$.
4. Mark all intervals reachable by some path from $I_{r,j}$ (using depth-first search, for example).
5. For each processor p_k, let I'_{k,l_k} be the marked interval such that l_k is a minimum.
6. Each processor p_k rolls back to C_{k,l_k}.

An example is illustrated in Figure 13.5. Processors p_1, p_2, and p_3 exchange messages and take uncoordinated snapshots. The corresponding interval dependence graph is shown at the bottom of the figure. If p_2 were to fail, it would be forced to roll back to the beginning of interval $I_{2,3}$. This would require rollbacks of p_1 and p_3 to the start of $I_{1,4}$ and $I_{3,3}$, respectively. The rollback of p_3 to the beginning of $I_{3,3}$ requires that p_2 roll

FIGURE 13.5   The depends-on relation.

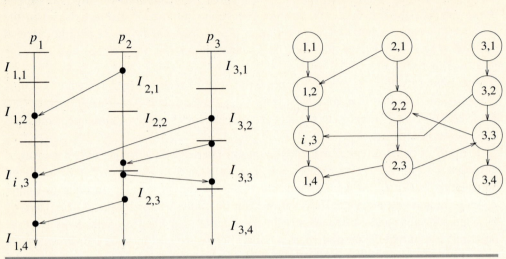

Message Passing and Checkpointing Activity   Interval Dependence Graph

back to the beginning of $I_{2,2}$. Now, we have found a consistent state. Notice that this state can be found by performing a depth-first search on the interval dependence graph starting at $I_{2,3}$.

There are two issues to note before concluding this section. First, there is no guarantee that the computation will not be rolled back all the way back to its initiation. The optimistic hope is that rollback is infrequent and limited. Second, the algorithm we present in this section is a centralized algorithm. One can implement the algorithm on a recovery manager that directs all participants to restart from a consistent checkpoint (if required). However, it is possible to write a distributed algorithm that also finds the maximum recovery line. This issue is explored in the exercises.

13.5 COORDINATED CHECKPOINTING

In a coordinated checkpoint, the processors $\{p_i\}$ take checkpoints $\{C_i\}$ that are guaranteed to form a recovery line. That is, a coordinated snapshot is a distributed snapshot saved on stable storage. Collecting a consistent snapshot is in fact the core of all coordinated checkpoint algorithms. However, there are several subtleties:

1. Only processor states need to be collected. The states of the message channels are captured by the states of the message passing protocols (the channel states can be captured as discussed in Chapter 9).
2. Checkpoints are taken to permit recovery in case of a failure. In particular, a failure might occur while the checkpoint is being collected. When recovery is initiated, the set of checkpoints that forms the maximum recovery line must be computed.

ALGORITHM LISTING 13.2

Variables used to track messaging.

last_rec[1 ... M]	last_rec[i] stores the sequence number of the last message received from p_i since the last checkpoint was taken.
first_sent[1 ... M]	first_sent[i] stores the sequence number of the first message sent to p_i since the last checkpoint was taken.

3. Because checkpoints are large, it is desirable to store the smallest number of them. Checkpoints superseded by a more recent recovery line need to be garbage collected.

4. Because taking a checkpoint of a processor can be an expensive operation, it is desirable to require the minimum number of processors to checkpoint their state. This goal is accomplished by limiting the propagation of the checkpoint token. In particular, a processor p needs to take a checkpoint only if there is a processor q that has taken a checkpoint of a state that includes the receipt of message m from p, and p has not recorded the sending of m in its snapshot.

The issues of taking the snapshot, finding the recovery line, and performing garbage collection can be handled by using techniques that we have discussed in other parts of the text (e.g., see Sections 9.3, 9.4.2, 12.2.4, 12.2.6, 12.3.3, and 13.4). We explore these issues in the exercises.

To limit the number of processors that are involved in taking a snapshot, we need to use an **incremental snapshot** algorithm. In the remainder of this section, we present a simplified algorithm for taking an incremental snapshot. This algorithm assumes that only one snapshot is taken at a time and does not support the version numbering needed for garbage collection and for finding a maximum recovery line. Like the snapshot algorithm of Chapter 9, this algorithm requires FIFO message channels.

To support the incremental snapshot, processors keep track of the communication over their message channels since their last checkpoint. The messages sent over a message channel are sequentially numbered. Each processor stores the two arrays as shown in Algorithm Listing 13.2. In addition, the checkpoint protocol uses the variables in Algorithm Listing 13.3.

Entry i in the arrays last_rec and first_sent is nil if no message was received from (sent to) p_i since the last checkpoint was taken. When a message is sent to processor p_i, first_sent[i] is updated using Algorithm Listing 13.4. When a message m is received

ALGORITHM LISTING 13.3

Variables used for consistent checkpointing.

checkpoint	Storage for the checkpoint.
seq_number[1 ... M]	seq_number[i] stores the sequence number of the last message sent to p_i.

ALGORITHM LISTING 13.4

Updating the state on a message send.

```
seq_number[i]++
if first_sent[i] = nil
    first_sent[i] = seq_number[i]
(attach seq_number[i] to the message sent to p_i)
```

from p_i, last_rec[i] is updated using Algorithm Listing 13.5. The processors take consistent checkpoints by executing Algorithm Listing 13.6.

An execution of the incremental snapshot algorithm is illustrated in Figure 13.6. When processor p_3 takes its second checkpoint, it consults the last_rec vector and learns that it has received a message from p_2 but not p_1 since its last checkpoint. Processor p_3 sends a TAKE_CHK message to p_2, which checkpoints its state on delivery of the message. Since p_2 has not received any messages since its last checkpoint, it takes no further action. Notice that the first checkpoint at p_1 and the second checkpoints at p_2 and p_3 form a recovery line.

When p_3 takes its third checkpoint, it has received another message from p_2, which in turn has received a message from p_1. So, all processors take a checkpoint. Since p_1 has received messages from p_2 and p_3 since its last checkpoint, it sends a TAKE_CHK message to them. However, p_2 and p_3 can detect that they have already taken a consistent checkpoint, since their values of first_sent[p_1] are nil and 2, respectively.

Notice how the first_sent array automatically terminates the snapshot. If processor p receives a TAKE_CHK from q for a snapshot that p has already taken, either first_sent$_p$[q] = nil or first_sent$_p$[q] > last. (Why?) By contrast, the snapshot algorithm in Chapter 9 requires that every processor record the state of every distinct snapshot. If we are trying to find recovery lines, it is desirable for concurrently requested snapshots to blend together and reduce the checkpointing activity. The incremental snapshot algorithm achieves this property.

An alternative method for coordinated checkpointing is to make use of synchronized clocks. Every processor takes a checkpoint every T seconds. Since the clocks might not be perfectly synchronized, there is no guarantee that the checkpoints are consistent. To solve this problem, we augment the synchronized clocks with a backup approach similar to that used for taking snapshots over non-FIFO message channels. Every processor

ALGORITHM LISTING 13.5

Updating the state on a message receive.

```
last_rec[i] = m.seq_number
```

ALGORITHM LISTING 13.6

Algorithm to take a consistent checkpoint.

```
monitor_checkpoint()
    wait until a TAKE_CHK or START_CHK event occurs
        START_CHK :
            Record the local state into checkpoint
            for each p_i such that last_rec[i] is not nil
                send(p_i,TAKE_CHK; last_rec[i])
            for each i = 1 to M,
                first_sent[i]=last_rec[i]=nil
        TAKE_CHK (sender; last) :
            if first_sent[sender] ≠ nil and first_sent[sender] ≤ last
                Record the local state into checkpoint
                for each p_i such that last_rec[i] is not nil
                    send(p_i,TAKE_CHK; last_rec[i])
                for each i = 1 to M,
                    first_sent[i]=last_rec[i]=nil
```

records the number of checkpoints it has taken and attaches this count to every message that it sends. If a processor receives a message sent in the context of checkpoint $k + 1$ while having taken only k checkpoints locally, the processor takes its $k + 1$ checkpoint before delivering the message to the application. Other modifications of the basic strategy are possible.

FIGURE 13.6   Computing an incremental snapshot.

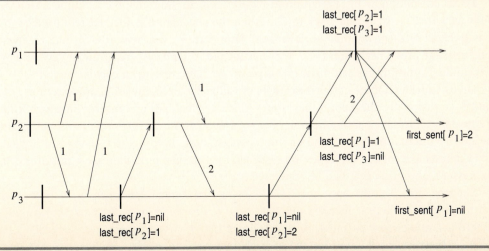

13.6 SYNCHRONOUS LOGGING

The invariant of synchronous logging is simple: A message must be logged before it can be delivered. Recovery is also simple, since the logged messages are replayed until the recovering process is up to date (recall that we assume that the programs are deterministic). However, the synchronization delays required to implement synchronous logging may reduce performance to an unacceptably low level.

13.7 ASYNCHRONOUS LOGGING

When asynchronous logging is used, every processor logs all messages, although not necessarily before using them. Asynchronous logging of messages helps performance in several ways. First, a message can be processed immediately upon reception, and the logging of the message can occur during an otherwise idle period. Second, several messages can be gathered together and logged simultaneously, permitting a more efficient use of the I/O device. We assume that processors occasionally checkpoint their state also.

The advantage gained by using logging in conjunction with uncoordinated check-pointing is that, if the logging is done properly, the rollback after a failure is limited. Consider the example illustrated in Figure 13.2. If the messages in the checkpoint intervals are logged, they can be replayed after a checkpoint is restored to reach a state where no orphan messages are received, but all required messages have been sent.

When a processor p recovers, it can recover a state based on the messages it has logged. So, if the first k messages have been logged, the state of p immediately before receiving message $k + 1$ can be recovered. The recovery needs to be consistent. If the current state of processor q depends on a message that p sends only after receiving its $k + 1$th message, q must be rolled back. Therefore, processor p should mark the message it sends by the number of messages it has received. That way, if q knows that p has rolled back to the state immediately before it has received its $k + 1$th message, q knows to roll back to a point where it has received no messages from p numbered larger than k.

Let us consider how the execution in Figure 13.2 can be rolled back. Suppose that p_1 rolls back to $C_{1,2}$. If p_2 rolls back to $C_{2,3}$, then the checkpoint is inconsistent because p_2 has received message m_7 that p_1 never sent. However, m_7 was sent after p_1 had received one message after checkpoint $C_{1,2}$. If p_1 has logged m_6, we can create a recovery line by executing p_1 until it has sent m_7. At this point, we have reached a consistent state.

Let us consider a more detailed example of rollbacks. In Figure 13.7, processors p_1, p_2, and p_3 occasionally checkpoint their states (thick vertical bar) and receive messages (thin vertical bar). Message passing between p_1, p_2, and p_3 is shown (the other messages might be due to internal events). Some of the messages that the process receives are logged. Checkpoints and logged messages are enclosed by a dashed box, indicating portions of a processor's execution that can be recovered.

Suppose that p_3 rolls back to $C_{3,2}$. By using the logged messages, p_3 can recover up to the point where it receives message $k_3 + 1$. Processor p_1 can rollback to a point where it has received no message that follows the $(k_3 + 1)$th message received by p_1 (at r_1). However, p_2 has not logged enough messages to reach a recovery line that is

FIGURE 13.7   Consistent states and rollbacks with asynchronous logging.

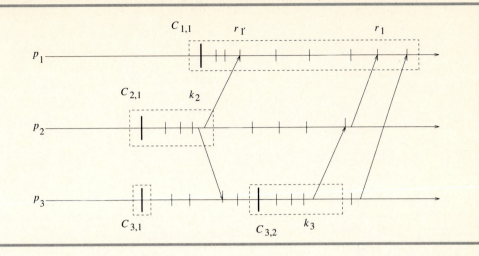

consistent with p_1 and p_3. Processor p_2 must roll back to checkpoint $C_{2,1}$ and then can use its logged messages to reach a state immediately before receiving message $k_2 + 1$. Processor p_1 can reach the consistent state r_1', but p_3 has not logged enough messages to be consistent with p_2 and must roll back to checkpoint $C_{3,1}$. The rollback of p_3 might force further rollbacks, depending on whether p_1 and p_2 can recover a consistent state.

13.7.1 Vector Interval Indices

At a given processor p, the time between receiving two consecutive messages is called an **interval**. Each interval is consecutively numbered with an **interval index**, starting from zero. Each message sent during an interval is labeled with the processor's interval index.

We note that the rollbacks can be transitive. If p sends message m to processor r in interval $k + 1$ and then r sends message m' to q, then if p rolls back to the end of interval k, q must roll back to a point before it received message m' (because r must roll back to a point before it has sent m'). In Figure 13.7, rolling back p_3 to a state before it received message k_3 will force p_1 to roll back to a state earlier than r_1. (Note the similarities to uncoordinated checkpointing.)

The usual method for precisely capturing transitive dependencies is to use vector timestamps. While a vector timestamp approach is possible, in this section we will use **direct dependencies** (the use of transitive dependences is discussed in the exercises). A **direct dependence vector** is a timestamp attached to each event, defined as follows: Let $e.DDV$ be the direct dependence vector attached to event e executed at p. Then $e.DDV[q]$ is the highest sequence number of a message sent from q and which was received at p before e. The advantage of using direct dependencies instead of transitive dependencies is that direct dependence information can be transmitted by attaching $O(1)$ information to each message. Transitive dependencies can be computed from a set of direct dependencies, so no information is lost. (See the exercises.) However, some work is

FIGURE 13.8   Intervals and vector interval timestamps.

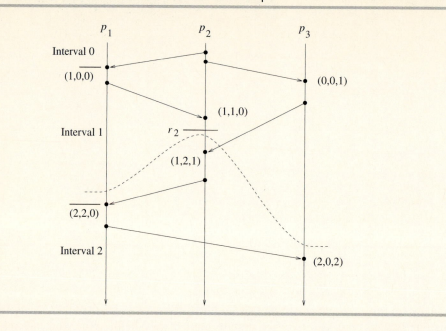

required. Using direct dependencies reduces the cost of normal execution at the expense of increasing the cost of recovery.

Direct dependence vectors are illustrated in Figure 13.8. Processors p_1, p_2, and p_3 exchange message. Every time a processor receives a message, its direct dependence vector increases. The direct dependence vector describes the intervals on all processors that the current state directly depends on. In the execution illustrated in Figure 13.8, suppose that p_2 rolls back to state r_2. Then, p_1 and p_3 must roll back to states that precede the receipt of any message following interval 2 of processor p_2. A consistent recovery line is shown as a dashed line (and this is a maximum recovery line).

13.7.2 An Algorithm

Given the framework for detecting rollback dependencies, there are two questions to be addressed. First, given that p rolls back to the end of interval k, what is the minimum distance that the other processors need to roll back (i.e., find a maximum recovery line)? Second, if a processor occasionally takes checkpoints, when is it safe to discard old messages in the log, and old checkpoints?

We need to develop some definitions. Suppose that we are told the current state of each processor in the system. Each system state can be represented by its direct dependence vector DDV_p. We define the **global system state** to be the collection of these states, and can be represented by the **global state matrix** GDV, the collection of the processor timestamps. That is,

$$GDV(p) = DDV_p$$

Note the similarities and differences between the global state matrix and a matrix timestamp (discussed in Sections 12.2.4 and 12.3.3). Both are composed of an array of timestamps. However, while the matrix timestamp is used to establish a lower bound on the knowledge that other processors have about the global state, a global state matrix is intended to represent the actual global state. The global state matrix GDV is **consistent** if no processor depends on a message that has not yet been sent. That is, if

$$GDV(p)[q] \le GDV(q)[q] \qquad 1 \le p, q \le M$$

An example of a consistent and an inconsistent global state, and the value of the corresponding GDV is shown in Figure 13.9. The top recovery line is not consistent because p_1 receives a message that p_2 has not sent. In the global state matrix, $GDV(p_1)[p_2] > GDV(p_2)[p_2]$.

At a processor p, a message is **logged** if it has been received by the application protocol and written to stable storage. If the message that starts interval i has been logged, we can assert that $logged(i)$ is True. In addition to logging messages, the processor also takes checkpoints on occasion. If the interval immediately following the receipt of message k was checkpointed, we can assert that $check(k)$ is True. We can assert that state interval

FIGURE 13.9   Detecting consistent states.

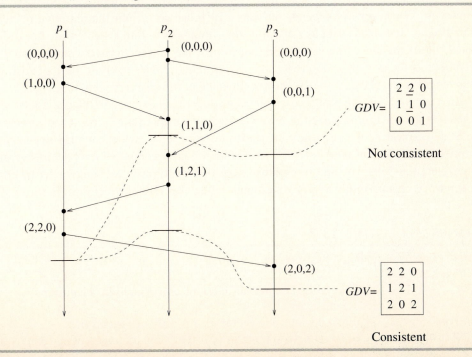

j at processor p is **stable** if we can reconstruct it from checkpointed states and logged messages. That is,

$$stable_p(j) \quad iff \quad \exists_{k \leq j} check(k) \text{ and } \forall_{k < i \leq j} logged(i)$$

For example, the processor states enclosed by dashed lines in Figure 13.7 represent stable states. A global state is **recoverable** if it is consistent and every component processor state is stable. That is, if for each $i = 1, \ldots, M$, $stable_{p_i}(GDV(i)[i])$.

If we know that a global state is recoverable, we can perform garbage collection. In particular, suppose that $GDV(i)[i] = k$ for the recoverable global state represented by GDV. Let j be the largest integer such that $j \leq k$ and $check(j)$ is True. Then all checkpoints of intervals with an index less than j can be discarded. In addition, all logged messages that started intervals with an index less than j can be discarded.

Finally, we need to compute a recoverable state. We give an algorithm that can be used by a centralized recovery manager to advance the current recoverable state RV; it is informed whenever interval k of processor p becomes stable. The vector RV is the diagonal of the matrix GDV and is equivalent to a vector timestamp.

The algorithm uses the variables in Algorithm Listing 13.7. The find_recoverable procedure, shown in Algorithm Listing 13.8 is called with the current recoverable state and is asked to find a new recoverable that includes interval k of processor p. The procedure has access to DDV(p,i) for every p and i. Presumably, the processors continually send updated information about their dependency vectors to the recovery manager.

The algorithm constructs a new tentative recovery state TRV from the current recovery state RV by advancing RV to k at processor p. Next, the algorithm tries to make TRV consistent. Whenever TRV depends on state t of processor q, but the tentative recovery state has not advanced as far as t at q, the algorithm tries to find a stable state l of q such that $l \geq t$. If the algorithm cannot find such an l, the current recovery state cannot be advanced as far as k at p. Otherwise, the algorithm continues to try to find a consistent recoverable state, taking into account the advance in the recovery state to l at q.

An execution of the find_recoverable algorithm is illustrated in Figure 13.10. The algorithm is called to advance the recovery state to include state interval k of processor p. State interval k of p depends on state interval l of q, which in turn depends on interval i of r. If all of these intervals are stable, we have computed the new recoverable state. Note that what the find_recoverable algorithm really does is change a set of direct dependence vectors into a vector timestamp, while checking for recoverable states. The

ALGORITHM LISTING 13.7

Variables used for finding a recovery line.

RV	RV[p] contains the interval index of processor p in the current recoverable state.
DDV(p,i)	The direct dependence vector of interval i of processor p.
DDV(p,i)[q]	The maximum state interval of q that state interval i of p depends on.

ALGORITHM LISTING 13.8

Finding a recovery line from direct dependence vectors.

```
find_recoverable(RV,p,k)
    TRV = RV
    TRV[p]=k
    for q = 1 to M
        Max[q] = max(TRV[q],DDV(p,k)[q])
    While there is a q such that Max[q] > TRV[q]
        Let l be the minimum index such that l ≥ Max[q] and stable_q(l)
        If no such l exists
            return(fail)
        TRV[q] = l
        for r = 1 to M
            Max[r] = max(Max[r],DDV(q,l)[r])
    RV = TRV
    return(success)
```

algorithm can handle sets of states such as those pictured in Figure 13.7, where there are holes in the set of stable states at a processor. These holes might be due to a failure to log messages or to unmaskable nondeterministic events.

Using this algorithm to implement garbage collection and recovery after a failure requires the specification of some details. The algorithm is not complete, since it works to advance the index in the recoverable state of only one processor (advancing the index

FIGURE 13.10   Executing the find_recoverable procedure.

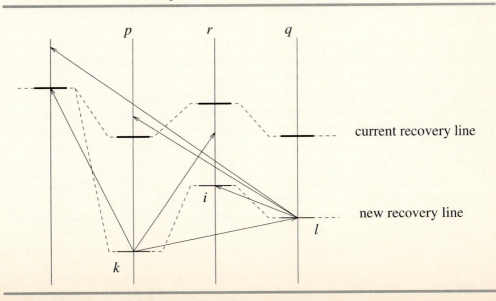

of other processors is a side effect). It might be the case that the index of other processors in the recoverable state vector can also be advanced. If the implementor is not careful, many calls to find_recoverable might be required, and these calls are expensive. The range of the state space in the search can be limited by the following observation. Suppose that the maximum recoverable interval state index of processor p is index k. Then, no state interval of processor p that depends on interval $k + 1$ of p is recoverable.

Further issues regarding the implementation of the algorithm to advance the recovery line include whether the algorithm uses a centralized recovery manager or is made into a distributed algorithm, whether recovery is done on-line or off-line, and whether or not transitive dependence vectors (vector timestamps) should be used instead of direct dependence vectors. We explore these issues further in the exercises and the chapter bibliography.

13.7.3 Sender-based Logging

The logging protocols presented thus far use **receiver-based** logging — the receiver of a message eventually logs it. Another option is to use **sender-based** logging. Here, it is the sender of a message that logs the message. If a processor fails, it can recover up to its failure point by using the messages it received before failure that are logged at the senders. Thus, sender-based logging can provide rollback-free recovery as long as "neighboring" processors do not fail simultaneously.

There are two issues to address in sender-based logging. The first issue is the policy for logging *message content*. One option is to log messages in the volatile memory of the sender only. In this case, the system in general will be resilient to only one failure at a time. (Why?)[16] Alternatively, the messages in the sender's volatile storage might be checkpointed along with the processor state. For example, if processor p_3 fails and then restarts from checkpoint C_3, processors p_1 and p_2 can supply messages to p_3 from their volatile message logs and from the message logs stored with checkpoints C_2 and C_3. We leave as an exercise the problem of determining when a checkpoint can be garbage collected.

The second issue is the policy for logging *message ordering*. In the example above, processor p_3 can be supplied with messages m_4, m_5, m_6, and m_8, but the precise order in which the messages should be consumed is not clear. Since the sender is logging message content, we can require the sender to also log message orders. When a sender adds a message m to its log, the message is **partially logged**. The message m is **fully logged** when the sender also logs the receive order of m. A simple protocol for propagating message receive orders to the senders is the following. A receiver tags each message that it receives with a **receive sequence number**. The receiver acknowledges message m to m's sender and attaches m's receive sequence number to the acknowledgment.

To avoid rollbacks in the presence of a single processor failure, the receiver must wait for a return acknowledgment from the sender before the receiver can send any new messages. The second acknowledgment is required for the following reason. Suppose that p receives a message m from q and then sends a message m' to r. Process p then fails,

---

[16] One is able to reconstruct lost messages by reexecuting the failed processors, but we do not consider this approach here.

FIGURE 13.11 Volatile and checkpointed sender logs. Messages m4 and m5 must be supplied from the checkpointed information.

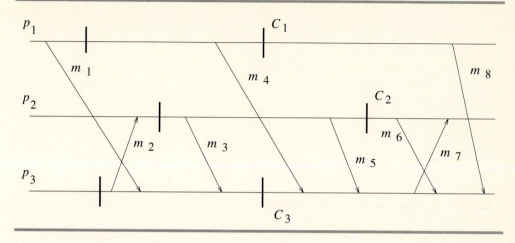

and its acknowledgment to q (with m's receive sequence number attached) is lost. The order in which p should receive m on recovery is not clear, so m' is an orphan message, forcing the rollback of r.

We can observe that logging receive sequence numbers at the sender can be overly pessimistic. Consider the example of process p_3 in Figure 13.11. Suppose that p_3 fails after receiving m_8. For a consistent recovery, it is not necessary for the receive order of m_6 and m_8 to have been logged, because p_3 takes no external action after sending these messages. It is only necessary for the message receive order of m_4 and m_5 to have been logged because m_7 is sent in the context of p_3 having received m_4 and m_5. To enforce this logging, we can attach the receive sequence numbers of m_4 and m_5 to m_7 and can have p_2 log the message receive orders. This way, m_4 and m_5 are fully logged before m_7 is delivered to the application running on p_2.

In the above protocol, message content and message ordering are likely to be logged at two different locations. During recovery, the failed processor must poll all the other processors to reconstruct both message content and ordering.

13.8 ADAPTIVE LOGGING

It is easy to observe that not every message needs to be logged; only the messages that are needed to ensure a recovery line must be logged. A simple example is shown in Figure 13.12. In this example, every processor takes a checkpoint of its local state every T seconds. The intended recovery line is the set of the last checkpoints taken at each processor. However, the collection of checkpoints is not synchronized between processors (i.e., they are **weakly coordinated**). Since the clocks on the processors might drift (or checkpointing might be delayed until an idle period), the set of the kth checkpoints from each processor might not form a consistent state.

FIGURE 13.12   Logging for weakly coordinated checkpointing.

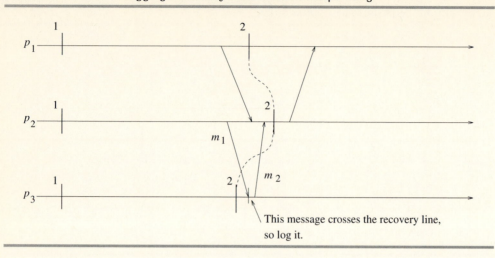

This message crosses the recovery line,
so log it.

The problem is that a processor p might receive a message from checkpoint interval k on processor q while p is still in interval $k - 1$ (for example, message m_2 in Figure 13.12). The coordinated checkpoint solution is to checkpoint p_2 before delivering m_2. However, we do not want to force checkpoints. Instead we will log message m_1.

If processor p in interval k receives a message m from processor q in interval $k - 1$ (or lower), p might send a message m' that is delivered to q before q takes its kth snapshot. Note also that a message that causally depends on m' might be delivered to q. In either case, a rollback of p to checkpoint k will cause a rollback of q to checkpoint $k - 1$. Therefore, p needs to log m so that it can execute past its kth checkpoint and up to the sending of m' to q.

In the more general case, processors take checkpoints in a completely uncoordinated fashion. Therefore, it is more difficult to determine the global recovery line. Instead, each processor has its own version of which checkpoints form the recovery line. A processor logs messages that it thinks have crossed the recovery line.

Each processor numbers its checkpoints sequentially. A recovery line is identified by a vector of checkpoint numbers, one for each processor. The protocol uses the two arrays shown in Algorithm Listing 13.9.

The CRL vector represents the processor's **current recovery line**. When a processor fails and then recovers, it will roll back no further than the current recovery line associated with the checkpoint. When a processor takes a checkpoint, it increments NRL[self] and

ALGORITHM LISTING 13.9

Variables used for adaptive logging.

CRL[1 .. M]:	The processor's recovery line for the current checkpoint interval.
NRL[1 .. M]:	The processor's recovery line for the next checkpoint interval.

ALGORITHM LISTING 13.10

Algorithm for adaptive logging.

```
for i from 1 to M do
    NRL[i] = max(NRL[i],m.CRL[i])
if m.CRL[self] < CRL[self]
    log m
```

then sets CRL=NRL. The idea is to advance the recovery line as far as possible whenever a checkpoint is taken. NRL accomplishes this by tracking the highest-numbered checkpoint at each processor of which it is informed.

Initially, CRL and NRL are initialized to a vector of zeros at all processors. When a processor sends a message, it attaches CRL to the message. When a processor receives a message, it updates NRL and optionally logs the message by executing Algorithm Listing 13.10.

Suppose that processor p in checkpoint interval k receives a message m from processor q, and processor q's current recovery line uses a checkpoint of p numbered less than k. If p sends a message to q, the message might be delivered to q before q takes a checkpoint C_q that includes checkpoint k of processor p. If q rolls back to the recovery line CRL_q of checkpoint interval C_q, the checkpoint will be inconsistent. Processor p needs to execute starting from its kth checkpoint until it has sent all messages to q that q has received by C_q. Therefore, p needs to log m (e.g., just as m_1 must be logged in the example in Figure 13.12).

FIGURE 13.13 Reducing message logging. Black dots indicate logged messages.

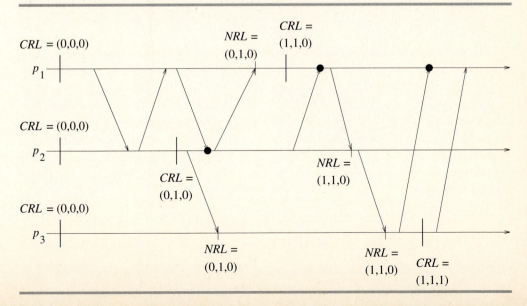

An execution of the protocol is illustrated in Figure 13.13. The logged messages are indicated by the black dots. After processor p_2 takes checkpoint 1, it receives a message from p_1. Since p_1's current recovery line does not include checkpoint 1 at p_2, p_2 might send a message to p_1 before p_1 takes its next checkpoint (which in fact happens). But then, p_2 can execute to the point where it has sent the required message to p_1.

The algorithm in this section has an advantage over the one presented in Section 13.7 in that information about a recovery line is computed on the fly (in CRL and NRL). Note that a recovery line reported by NRL cannot be made into a consistent state until some messages have been logged. (Consider the example in Figure 13.12.) So, either synchronous logging must be used, or stable recovery lines must be detected on the fly. This issue is explored in the exercises.

13.9 SUMMARY

In this chapter, we have seen techniques for recovering the state of a computation after a failure. The processors take *checkpoints* and restart their computations from a checkpoint after a failure. After a failure, the processors must find a *recovery line* (a previously recorded consistent state) from which to restart the computation. It is possible that no recovery line can be found and a *cascading rollback* occurs. The processors can *log* messages to increase flexibility during recovery and avoid cascading rollbacks.

The method used for recovery depends on what information is recorded during execution and how it is recorded. Processors can take coordinated or uncoordinated checkpoints and can optionally log messages. If the processors log messages, the message logging can be synchronous or asynchronous. The message logging can occur at the sender or at the receiver of a message.

If the processors take uncoordinated checkpoints and do not log messages, the problem is to find a recovery line among the checkpoints. If the processors take coordinated checkpoints, the problem is similar to the distributed snapshot problem, discussed in Chapter 9.

If the processors take uncoordinated snapshots and also log their messages, the problem is to find a maximum recovery line defined by the most advanced states reachable by applying the logged messages to a checkpointed state. For the case when the receiver logs the messages, we present a method for determining the maximum recovery line. The algorithm uses *direct dependence vectors*, which do not record transitive dependences. The advantage of using direct dependence vectors is that only $O(1)$ timestamp information must be attached to the messages. If the sender logs messages, the problem is to log both the message contents and the message receive order. Finally, we present an adaptive logging technique.

ANNOTATED BIBLIOGRAPHY

The algorithm for computing a consistent checkpoint when checkpoints are uncoordinated and no logging is performed was presented by Bhargava and Lian [BL88]. Wang, Lowry, and Fuchs [WLF94] show that a consistent recovery line can be computed from direct dependency information only. Fowler and Zwaenepoel [FZ90] give an algorithm that converts a set of events labeled a direct dependence vector into a vector timestamp. Wang and Fuchs [WF92b] argue that delaying the delivery of a message that follows a new checkpoint reduces rollback propagation. Netzer and Xu [NX95] show that rollback dependencies can be summarized as **zigzag paths**. Wang, Chung, Lin, and Fuchs [WCLF95] show how to aggressively garbage collect uncoordinated checkpoints. They propose an *extended checkpoint graph*, which is an interval dependence graph extended with potential future checkpoints. Wang and Fuchs [WF92a] propose that channel states be collected during uncoordinated checkpointing and give an algorithm to avoid logging messages that will not be a part of any consistent checkpoint.

The algorithm for incremental checkpointing is due to Koo and Toueg. [KT87]. An alternative algorithm for collecting an incremental snapshot is due to Venkatesan [Ven89]. This algorithm has been optimized to reduce the message passing overhead of taking the consistent checkpoints [KP93]. Ahamad and Lin [AL89] present an algorithm to minimize rollback recovery in a checkpointed server. Elnozahy, Johnson, and Zwaenepoel [EJZ92] find that consistent checkpointing imposes only a small overhead on the checkpointed programs. These authors also discuss implementation techniques to reduce checkpointing overhead. Elnozahy and Zwaenepoel [EZ94] find that consistent checkpointing imposes less overhead than message logging and suggest combining consistent checkpointing with sender-based logging to reduce delays for output commit. Wang et al. [WHV+95] also discuss checkpointing implementation. Wang and Fuchs [WF93] propose *lazy* checkpoint coordination, in which the kth checkpoints are coordinated, and the other checkpoints are uncoordinated. Venkatesh, Radhakrishnan, and Li [VRL87] show an efficient method for capturing the channel states during a coordinated checkpoint. Cristian and Jahanian [CJ91] propose scheme for consistent checkpointing in which participants trigger new checkpoints based on a time interval or on learning that some participant has initiated the new checkpoint.

Systems based on synchronized logging include those described in [PP83, BBG83]. The paper by Borg et al. [BBG+89] provides a nice description of the systems issues of synchronized logging. Goldberg et al. [GGLS91] discuss how to hide nondeterministic events. Juang and Venkatesan [JV91] roll back the state to the causal cone of the failed event, and give distributed algorithms to compute the causal cone. Ruffin [Ruf92] discusses a general purpose logging service.

Strom and Yemeni [SY85] introduced the idea of using message logs and checkpoints to implement recovery. Lowry, Russel, and Goldberg [LRG91] suggest that for large-scale systems, communication within a domain is asynchronously logged, while communication between domains is routed through a gateway that uses synchronous logging. The discussion of recovery using checkpoints and logging is from Johnson and Zwaenepoel [JZ90]. These authors present an algorithm for finding an maximal recoverable state. Sistla and Welch [SW89] present a distributed version of the algorithms in [JZ90]. Paterson and Kearns [PK93] show how to compute the recovery line after a failure by making use of vector timestamps attached to each event. Smith, Johnson, and Tygar [SJT95] make this algorithm execute on-line, which requires careful attention to the correspondence of actual and useful execution. Johnson [Joh93] gives an algorithm to commit an output message, by ensuring that all messages in the causal history of the output message are logged. Wang, Hunag, and Fuchs [WHF93] propose that software errors in distributed systems can be avoided by replaying message logs in a different sequence than the one which led to the error.

Johnson and Zwaenepoel [JZ87] suggest logging messages at the sender as well as the receiver to get fast recovery in the case of a single failure. Strom, Bacon, and Yemeni [SBY88] show how sender-based logging can handle multiple failures by checkpointing message logs as well as processor states. In addition, they propose techniques to compress logs by fitting the dependences to regular communications patterns. Elnozahy and Zwaenepoel [EZ92a] discuss *Manetho*, which uses sender-based logging and propagates a H-DAG to reconstruct execution sequences of nondeterministic events. Young and Chiu [YC94] give an algorithm to reconstruct the message reception sequence for recovery in a sender-based logging system. Alvisi, Hoppe, and Marzullo [AHM93] analyze when information about a message must be logged to avoid orphan states after a failure. Alvisi and Marzullo [AM95] classify message logging protocols based on whether the actions they take to avoid orphan messages.

The "weakly coordinated checkpoints" is similar to an idea proposed in [FZ90]. The discussion of adaptive message logging is a modification of the work of Netzer and Xu [NX93b, NX93a, NSX94] and Wang and Fuchs [WF92a]. Leong and Agrawal [LA94] give a technique to detect when message exchanges do not effect processor states, and thus can be ignored for the purposes of rollback and recovery.

EXERCISES

1. Let $GC = \{C_p \mid 1 \leq p \leq M\}$ and $GC' = \{C'_p \mid 1 \leq p \leq M\}$ be a pair of consistent checkpoints. If C_p and C'_p occur on the same processor, let $\max(C_p, C'_p)$ return the checkpoint that was collected later. Let us define $max(GC, GC') = \{\max(C_p, C'_p) \mid 1 \leq p \leq M\}$
   a. Show that $max(GC, GC')$ is a consistent checkpoint.
   b. Show that a maximum checkpoint always exists.

2. In uncoordinated checkpointing, we define checkpoint C' at processor q to be *rollback dependent* on checkpoint C at p if a rollback to C on p causes a rollback to a checkpoint earlier than C' on q. Show that C' can be rollback dependent on C even if the events of collecting C and C' are concurrent.

3. Characterize the path in the happens-before DAG that causes C' to be rollback dependent on C.

4. Give a distributed algorithm for finding the optimal consistent checkpoint when uncoordinated checkpointing is used. The algorithm should be initiated when the failed processor recovers. Show that your algorithm finds the maximum recovery line.

5. Give an algorithm to garbage collect checkpoints when uncoordinated checkpointing is used. Hint: Checkpoints that follow the maximum recovery line can be garbage collected if they cannot form any future recovery line.

6. Show an interval dependence graph with $O(M^2)$ nongarbage checkpoints.

7. Give an algorithm for garbage collecting old checkpoints when coordinated checkpointing is used.

8. Give an algorithm for garbage collecting old checkpoints and logged messages when weakly coordinated checkpointing is used with asynchronous logging.

9. A *direct dependence vector* is a timestamp attached to each event, defined as follows: Let $e.DDV$ be the direct dependence vector attached to event e executed at p. Then $e.DDV[q]$ is the highest sequence number of a message sent from q and that was received at p before e.

   Give an algorithm that maintains direct dependence vectors using $O(1)$ space in each message for attaching timestamp information.

10. Suppose that asynchronous logging and uncoordinated checkpointing are used, and each event is tagged with its transitive dependence vector (i.e., a vector timestamp). Give an algorithm to find the maximum recovery line.

11. A process can *commit* its output when the process is assured that it will never roll back to a point preceding the output event. Give an algorithm to force an output commit when asynchronous logging is used with uncoordinated checkpointing.

12. Suppose that the logging and recovery subsystem can identify messages that correspond to queries (i.e., read the value of a variable). Give an algorithm that uses this semantic information to obtain a better recovery line after a failure.

13. Give an algorithm to garbage collect checkpoints when sender-based logging is used, where the checkpoints include the sender's logs.

14. Give an algorithm to compute the recovery line after a failure when sender-based logging is used and receive sequence numbers are attached to the messages that the receiver sends.

15. Characterize when a message must be fully logged to avoid rollbacks of nonfailed processors after a failure.

16. Give a distributed algorithm for garbage collecting old checkpoints and logged messages when adaptive logging (with asynchronous writes to the log) is used.

17. Give an algorithm to compute the recovery line after a failure when adaptive logging (with asynchronous writes to the log) is used.

BIBLIOGRAPHY

[AA91] D. Agrawal and A. El Abbadi. An efficient and fault-tolerant solution for distributed mutual exclusion. *ACM Trans. on Computer Systems*, 9(1):1–20, 1991.

[AA92] D. Agrawal and A. El Abbadi. The generalized tree quorum protocol: An efficient approach for managing replicated data. *ACM Trans. on Database Systems*, 17(4):689–717, 1992.

[AA95] D. Agrawal and A. El Abbadi. A token-based fault-tolerant distributed mutual exclusion algorithm. *J. of Parallel and Distributed Computing*, 24:164–176, 1995.

[AB86] J. R. Archibald and J. L. Baer. Cache coherence protocols: Evaluation using a multiprocessor simulation model. *ACM Trans. on Computer Systems*, 4(4):273–298, 1986.

[AB92] S. Acharya and B. R. Badrinath. Recording distributed snapshots based on causal order of message delivery. *Information Processing Letters*, 44:317–321, 1992.

[ABC+95] A. Agarwal, R. Bianchini, D. Chaiken, K. Johnson, D. Kranz, K. Kubiatowicz, B. Lim, K. Mackenzie, and D. Yeung. The MIT Alewife machine: Architecture and performance. *Proc. 22nd Annual Int'l Symp. on Computer Architecture*, 1995. Also available at http://cag-www.lcs.mit.edu/alewife/.

[ABG84] R. Attar, P. A. Bernstein, and N. Goodman. Site initialization, recovery, and backup in a distributed databse system. *IEEE Trans. on Software Engineering*, SE-10(6):645–650, 1984.

[ABND90] H. Attiya, A. Bar-Noy, and D. Dolev. Sharing memory robustly in message-passing systems. *Proc. Principles of Distributed Computing*, pages 363–375, 1990.

[AD76] P. A. Alsberg and J. D. Day. A principle for resilient sharing of distributed resources. *Proc. 2nd Int'l Conf. on Software Engineering*, 1976.

[ADKM92a] Y. Amir, D. Dolev, S. Kramer, and D. Malki. Membership algorithms for multicast communication groups. *6th Int'l Workshop on Distributed Algorithms,* Springer-Verlag, pages 292–312, November 1992.

[ADKM92b] Y. Amir, D. Dolev, S. Kramer, and D. Malki. Transis: A communication subsystem for high availability. *Proc. 22nd Annual Int'l Symp. on Fault-Tolerant Computing*, pages 76–84, July 1992.

[AF89] Y. Artsy and R. Finkel. Designing a process migration facility: The Charlotte experience. *IEEE Computer*, 22(9):47–56, 1989.

[AG96] K. Arnold and J. Gosling. *The Java Programming Language*. Addison-Wesley, 1996. Also available at http://java.sun.com/.

[AH90] J. Aspnes and M. Herlihy. Fast randomized consensus using shared memory. *J. of Algorithms*, 11:441–461, 1990.

[AHM93] L. Alvisi, B. Hoppe, and K. Marzullo. Nonblocking and orphan-free message logging protocols. *IEEE Symp. on Fault Tolerant Computing*, pages 145–154, 1993.

[Ahu90] M. Ahuja. Flush primitives for asynchronous distributed systems. *Information Processing Letters*, 34:5–12, 1990.

[Ahu91] M. Ahuja. An implementation of F-channels, a preferable alternative to FIFO channels. *Proc. Int'l on Conf. on Distributed Computing Systems*, pages 180–187, 1991.

[Ahu93] M. Ahuja. Assertions about past and future in *highways*: Global flush broadcast and flush-vector-time. *Information Processing Letters*, 48:21–28, 1993.

[AJ92] G. Agrawal and P. Jalote. An efficient protocol for voting in distributed systems. *Proc. Int'l Conf. on Distributed Computing Systems*, pages 640–647, 1992.

[AL89] M. Ahamad and L. Lin. Using checkpoints to localize the effects of faults in distributed systems. *Proc. 8th Symp. on Reliable Distributed Systems*, pages 2–11, 1989.

[ALPS90] P. Ancilotti, B. Lazzarini, C. A. Prete, and M. Sacchi. A distributed commit protocol for a multicomputer system. *IEEE Trans. on Computers*, 39(5):718–724, 1990.

[AM91] D. Agrawal and A. Malpani. Efficient dissemination of information in computer networks. *The Computer J.*, 34(6):534–541, 1991.

[AM94] M. Ahuja and S. Mishra. Units of computation in fault-tolerant distributed systems. *Int'l Conf. on Distributed Computing Systems*, pages 626–633, 1994.

[AM95] L. Alvisi and K. Marzullo. Message logging: Pessimistic, optimistic, and causal. *Proc. Int'l Conf. on Distributed Computing Systems*, pages 229–236, 1995.

[AMMS$^+$93] Y. Amir, L. E. Moser, P. M. Melliar-Smith, V. Agrawala, and P. Ciarfella. Fast message ordering and membership using a logical token passing ring. *Int'l Conf. on Distributed Computing Systems*, May 1993.

[AMMS$^+$95] Y. Amir, L. E. Moser, P. M. Melliar-Smith, D. A. Agarwal, and P. Ciarfella. The totem single-ring ordering and membership protocol. *ACM Trans. on Computer Systems*, 13(4):311–342, 1995.

[And79] S. Andler. Predicate path expression. *Proc. 6th ACM Symp. on Principles of Programming Languages*, pages 226–236, 1979.

[And81] G. R. Andrews. Synchronizing resources. *ACM Trans. on Programming Languages and Systems*, 3(4):405–430, 1981.

[And82] G. R. Andrews. The distributed programming language SR – mechanisms, design, and implementation. *Software Practice and Experience*, 12(8):719–754, 1982.

[And91] G. R. Andrews. *Concurrent Programming – Principles and Practice*. Benjamin/Cummings, 1991.

[Arc88] J. K. Archibald. A cache coherence approach for large multiprocessor systems. *Proc. ACM Int'l Conf. on Supercomputing*, pages 337–345, 1988.

[AS83] G. R. Andrews and F. B. Schneider. Concepts and notations for concurrent programming. *ACM Computing Surveys*, 15(1):3–43, 1983.

[Asp90] J. Aspnes. Time and space efficient randomized consensus. *Proc. Principles of Distributed Computing*, pages 325–331, 1990.

[AT89] A. El Abbadi and S. Toueg. Maintaining availability in partitioned replicated databases. *ACM Trans. on Database Systems*, 24(2):264–290, 1989.

[AT93] N. R. Adam and R. Tewari. Regeneration with virtual copies for distributed computing systems. *IEEE Trans. on Software Engineering*, 19(6):594–602, 1993.

[AV94] S. Alagar and S. Venkatesan. An optimal algorithm for distributed snapshots with causal message ordering. *Information Processing Letters*, 50:311–316, 1994.

[BA90] A. P. Black and Y. Artsy. Implementing location independent invocation. *IEEE Trans. on Parallel and Distributed Computing*, 1(1):107–119, 1990.

[Bac93] J. Bacon. *Concurrent Systems*. Addison-Wesley, 1993.

[Bad89] L. Badger. A model for specifying multi-granularity integrity policies. *Proc. IEEE Symp. on Security and Privacy*, pages 269–277, 1989.

[Bak90] T. P. Baker. A stack-based resource allocation policy for real time processes. *Real Time Systems Symp.*, pages 191–200, 1990.

[Bal94] R. Baldoni. An $O(N^{M/(M+1)})$ distributed algorithm for the k-out-of-M resources allocation problem. *Int'l Conf. on Distributed Computing Systems*, pages 81–88, 1994.

[BAN90] M. Burrows, M. Abadi, and R. Needham. A logic of authentication. Technical Report SRC RR-39, Digital Equipment Corporation, 1990.

[BBG83] A. Borg, J. Baumbach, and S. Glazer. A message system supporting fault tolerance. *ACM SIGOPS Symp. on Operating System Principles*, pages 90–99, 1983.

[BBG+89] A. Borg, W. Blau, W. Graetsch, F. Herrmann, and W. Oberle. Fault tolerance under UNIX. *ACM Trans. on Computer Systems*, 7(1):1–24, 1989.

[BC94] R. Baldoni and B. Ciciani. Distributed algorithms for multiple entries to a critical section with priority. *Information Processing Letters*, 50:165–170, 1994.

[BDLM95] M. Blumrich, C. Dubnicki, K. Li, and M. Mesrina. Virtual memory mapped network interface. *IEEE Micro*, 15(1):21–28, 1995.

[BDS87] J. J. Bloch, D. S. Daniels, and A. Z. Spector. A weighted voting algorithm for replicated directories. *J. of the ACM*, 34(4):859–909, 1987.

[BF88] R. Bisiani and A. Forin. Multilanguage parallel programming of heterogeneous machines. *IEEE Trans. on Computers*, 37(8):930–945, 1988.

[BG81] P. A. Bernstein and N. Goodman. Concurrency control in distributed database systems. *ACM Computing Surveys*, 13(2):185–221, 1981.

[BG86a] P. A. Bernstein and N. Goodman. A proof technique for concurrency control and recovery algorithms for replicated databases. *Distributed Computing*, 1, 1986.

[BG86b] P. A. Bernstein and N. Goodman. Serializability theory for replicated databases. *J. of Computer and System Sciences*, 31(3):355–374, 1986.

[BGMS86] D. Barbara, H. Garcia-Molina, and A. Spauster. Protocols for dynamic vote reassignment. *Proc. 5th ACM SIGACT-SIGOPS Symp. on Principles of Distributed Computing*, pages 195–205, 1986.

[BGMS89] D. Barbara, H. Garcia-Molina, and A. Spauster. Increasing availability under mutual exclusion constraints with dynamic vote reassignment. *ACM Trans. on Computer Systems*, 7(4):394–426, 1989.

[BH73] P. Brinch-Hansen. *Operating System Principles*. Prentice-Hall, 1973.

[BH77] P. Brinch-Hansen. *The Architecture of Concurrent Programs*. Prentice-Hall, 1977.

[BH78] P. Brinch-Hansen. Distributed processes: A concurrent programming concept. *Communications of the ACM*, 21(11):934–941, 1978.

[BH94] A. Bagchi and S. L. Hakimi. Information dissemination in distributed systems with faulty units. *IEEE Trans. on Computers*, 43(6):698–710, 1994.

[Bha87] B. Bhargava. *Concurrency Control and Reliability in Distributed Systems*. Van Nostrand Reinhold, 1987.

[BHG87] P. A. Bernstein, V. Hadzilacos, and N. Goodman. *Concurrency Control and Recovery in Database Systems*. Addison-Wesley, 1987.

[Bib77] K. J. Biba. *Integrity Consideration for Secure Computer Systems*. MITRE Corporation, 1977.

[Bir93a] K. P. Birman. The process group approach to reliable distributed computing. *Communications of the ACM*, 36(12):36–53, 1993.

[Bir93b] K. P. Birman. A response to Cheriton and Skeen's criticism of causal and totally ordered multicast. *ACM SIGOPS Operating Systems Review*, 28(1):11–21, 1993.

[Bir94] K. P. Birman. Integrating runtime consistency models for distributed computing. *J. of Parallel and Distributed Computing*, 23:158–176, 1994.

[BJ87] K. P. Birman and T. A. Joseph. Reliable communication in the presence of failures. *ACM Trans. on Computer Systems*, 5(1):47–76, 1987.

[BJRA85] K. P. Birman, T. A. Joseph, T. Raeuchle, and A. El Abbadi. Implementing fault tolerant distributed objects. *IEEE Trans. on Software Engineering*, 11(6):502–508, 1985.

[BK91] N. S. Barghouti and G. E. Kaiser. Concurrency control in advanced database applications. *ACM Computing Surveys*, 23(3):269–317, 1991.

[BKT92] H. E. Bal, M. F. Kaashoek, and A. S. Tanenbaum. Orca: A language for parallel programming of distributed systems. *IEEE Trans. on Software Engineering*, 18(3):190–205, 1992.

[BL75] D. E. Bell and L. J. LaPadula. *Computer Security Model: Unified Exposition and Multics Interpretation.* MITRE Corporation, 1975.

[BL88] B. Bhargava and S. Lian. Independent checkpointing and concurrent rollback for recovery in distributed systems – an optimistic approach. *Proc. 7th IEEE Symp. on Reliability in Distributed Systems*, pages 3–12, 1988.

[Bla89] U. Black. *Data Network: Concepts, Theory, and Practice.* Prentice-Hall, 1989.

[BLA+94] M. Blumrich, K. Li, R. Albert, C. Dubnicki, E. Felten, and J. Sandberg. Virtual memory mapped network interface for the SHRIMP multicomputer. *Proc. 21st Int'l Symp. on Computer Architecture*, pages 142–153, 1994. Also available at http://www.cs.princeton.edu/shrimp/.

[BMD93] M. Barborak, M. Malek, and A. Dahbura. The consensus problem in fault-tolerant computing. *ACM Computing Surveys*, 25(2):171–220, 1993.

[BN84] A. D. Birrell and B. J. Nelson. Implementing remote procedure calls. *ACM Trans. on Computer Systems*, 2(1):39–59, 1984.

[BND89] A. Bar-Noy and D. Dolev. Shared-memory vs. message-passing in an asynchronous distributed environment. *Proc. Principles of Distributed Computing*, pages 307–318, 1989.

[BNG92] N. S. Bowen, C. N. Nikolaou, and A. Ghafoor. On the assignment problem of arbitrary process systems to heterogeneous distributed computer systems. *IEEE Trans. on Computers*, 41(3):257–273, 1992.

[Bok79] S. H. Bokhari. Dual processor scheduling with dynamic reassignment. *IEEE Trans. on Software Engineering*, SE-5(6):326–334, 1979.

[Bok81] S. H. Bokhari. On the mapping problems. *IEEE Trans. on Computers*, C-30:207–214, 1981.

[BR88] B. R. Badrinath and K. Ramamritham. Synchronizing transactions on objects. *IEEE Trans. on Computers*, 37(5):541–547, 1988.

[BR90] R. Bisiani and M. Ravishankar. Plus: A distributed shared memory system. *Proc. 17th Int'l Symp. on Computer Architecture*, pages 115–124, 1990.

[Bru85] S. A. Bruso. A failure detection and notification protocol for distributed computing systems. *Proc. IEEE 5th Int'l Conf. on Distributed Computing Systems*, pages 116–123, 1985.

[BS84] F. Berman and L. Snyder. On mapping parallel algorithms into parallel architectures. *Proc. Int'l Conf. on Parallel Processing*, pages 307–309, 1984.

[BSR80] P. A. Bernstein, D. W. Shipman, and J. B. Rothnie. Concurrency control in a system for distributed databases (SDD-1). *ACM Trans. on Database Systems*, 5(1):18–51, 1980.

[BSS91] K. P. Birman, A. Schiper, and P. Stephenson. Lightweight causal and atomic group multicast. *ACM Trans. on Computer Systems*, 9(3):272–314, 1991.

[BST89] H. E. Bal, J. G. Steiner, and A. S. Tanenbaum. Programming languages for distributed computing systems. *ACM Computing Surveys*, 21(3):261–322, 1989.

[BSW79] P. A. Bernstein, D. W. Shipman, and W. S. Wong. Formal aspects of serializability in database concurrency control. *ACM Trans. on Software Engineering*, 5(3):203–216, 1979.

[BV95] S. Bulgannawar and N. H. Vaidya. A distributed k-mutual exclusion problem. *Proc. Int'l Conf. on Distributed Computing Systems*, pages 153–160, 1995.

[BZ91] B. N. Bershad and M. J. Zekauskas. Midway: Shared memory parallel programming with entry consistency for distributed memory processors. Technical Report CMU-CS-91-170, Carnegie Mellon University, 1991.

[BZS93] B. N. Bershad, M. J. Zekauskas, and W. A. Sawdon. The Midway distributed shared memory system. *Digest of Papers COMPCON*, pages 528–537, 1993. Also available at http://www.cs.cmu.edu /afs/cs.cmu.edu /project/midway/.

[CAA90a] S. Y. Cheung, M. Ahamad, and M. H. Ammar. The grid protocol: A high performance scheme for managing replicated data. *Proc. 6th Int'l Conf. on Management of Data*, pages 438–445, 1990.

[CAA90b] S. Y. Cheung, M. Ahamad, and M. H. Ammar. Multi-dimensional voting: A general method for implementing synchronization in distributed systems. *IEEE Int'l Conf. on Distributed Computing Systems*, pages 362–369, 1990.

[CAL$^+$89] J. Chase, F. Amador, E. Lazowska, H. Levy, and R. Littlefield. The Amber system: Parallel programming on a network of multiprocessors. *Proc. 12th Symp. on Operating Systems Principles*, pages 147–158, 1989.

[CAS92] F. Cristian, H. Aghili, and R. Strong. Clock synchronization in the presence of omission and performance failures, and processor joins. Technical Report, IBM Almaden Research Center, 1992.

[CASD84] F. Cristian, H. Aghili, R. Strong, and D. Dolev. Atomic broadcast: From simple message diffusion to Byzantine agreement. Research Report RJ 4540, IBM Research Laboratory, December 1984.

[CB91] B. Charron-Bost. Concerning the size of logical clocks in distributed systems. *Information Processing Letters*, 39:11–16, 1991.

[CBZ91] J. Carter, J. Bennett, and W. Zwaenepoel. Implementation and performance of Munin. *Proc. 13th Symp. on Operating System Principles*, pages 152–164, 1991.

[CC93] M. Y. Chan and F. Y. L. Chin. Optimal resilient distributed algorithms for ring election. *IEEE Trans. on Parallel and Distributed Systems*, 4(4):475–480, 1993.

[CCI88] CCITT. *Recommendation X.500*, 1988. Also ISO/IEC 9594.

[CDK94] G. Coulouris, J. Dollimore, and T. Kindberg. *Distributed Systems: Concepts and Design*. Addison-Wesley, 1994.

[CF78] L. M. Censier and P. Feautrier. A new solution to the coherence problems in multicache systems. *IEEE Trans. on Computers*, C-27(12):1112–1118, 1978.

[CG95] C. M. Chase and V. K. Garg. Efficient detection of restricted classes of global predicates. *Proc. Workshop on Distributed Algorithms*, pages 303–316, 1995.

[CH74] R. H. Campbell and A. N. Habermann. The specification of process synchronization by Path expression. *Lecture Notes in Computer Science*, volume 16. Springer-Verlag, 1974.

[CHT92] T. D. Chandra, V. Hadzilacos, and S. Toueg. The weakest failure detector for solving consensus. *ACM Symp. on Principles of Distributed Computing*, pages 147–158, 1992.

[CHTCB95] T. D. Chandra, V. Hadzilacos, S. Toueg, and B. Charron-Bost. On the impossibility of group membership. Technical Report 95-1533, Dept. of Computer Science, Cornell University, 1995. Available at ftp.cs.cornell.edu.

[CJ91] F. Cristian and F. Jahanian. A timestamp-based checkpoint protocol for long-lived distributed computations. *Proc. Symp. on Reliable Distributed Systems*, pages 12–20, 1991.

[CK79] R. H. Campbell and R. B. Kolstad. Path expressions in Pascal. *Proc. 4th Int'l Conf. on Software Engineering*, pages 212–219, 1979.

[CK85] D. Cheung and T. Kameda. Site-optimal termination protocols for network partitioning. *Proc. 4th ACM SIGACT-SIGOPS Symp. on Principles of Distributed Computing*, pages 111–121, 1985.

[CK88] T. L. Casavant and J. G. Kuhl. A taxonomy of scheduling in general purpose distributed computing systems. *IEEE Trans. on Software Engineering*, SE-14(2):141−154, 1988.

[CK94] H.-K. Chiou and W. Korfhage. Efficient global event predicate detection. *Int'l Conf. on Distributed Computing Systems*, pages 642−649, 1994.

[CL75] N. F. Chen and C. L. Liu. T.-Y Feng ed., *Lecture Notes in Computer Science*, pages 1−16. Springer, 1975.

[CL83] V. Cerf and R. Lyons. Military requirements for packet-switched networks and their implications for protocol standardization. *Computer Networks*, October 1983.

[CL85] K. M. Chandy and L. Lamport. Distributed snapshots: Determining global states of distributed systems. *ACM Trans. on Computer Systems*, 3(1):63−75, 1985.

[CL90] M. I. Chen and K. J. Lin. A priority ceiling protocol for multiple-instance resources. *Real Time Systems Symp.*, pages 140−149, 1990.

[CL96] H. Cordova and Y. H. Lee. Multicast trees to provide message ordering in mesh networks. *Int'l J. of Computer Systems*, 11(1):3−13, 1996.

[CLNW92] R. Chow, K. Luo, and R. Newman-Wolfe. An optimal distributed algorithm for failure-driven leader election in bounded-degree networks. *Proc. IEEE Workshop on Future Trends of Distributed Computing Systems*, pages 136−141, 1992.

[CLP87] J. L. Carroll, D. D. E. Long, and J.-F. Paris. Block-level consistency of replicated files. *Proc. 7th Int'l Conf. on Distributed Computing Systems*, pages 146−153, 1987.

[CM84] J. M. Chang and N. F. Maxemchuk. Reliable broadcast protocols. *ACM Trans. on Computer Systems*, 2(3):251−273, August 1984.

[CM88] K. M. Chandy and J. Misra. *Parallel Program Design − A Foundation*. Addison-Wesley, 1988.

[CM91] R. Cooper and K. Marzullo. Consistent detection of global predicates. *Proc. ACM/ONR Workshop on Parallel and Distributed Debugging*, pages 167−174, 1991.

[CMS85] B. Chor, M. Merritt, and D.B. Shmoys. Simple constant-time consensus protocols in realistic failure models. *Proc. Principles of Distributed Computing*, pages 152−160, 1985.

[CMSW93] L.-P. Cabrera, J. A. McPherson, P. M. Schwarz, and J. C. Wyllie. Implementing atomicity in two systems: Techniques, tradeoffs, and experience. *IEEE Trans. on Software Engineering*, 19(10):950−960, 1993.

[Cof76] E. G. Coffman Jr. *Computer and Job-Shop Scheduling Theory*. Wiley, 1976.

[Coo82] E. C. Cooper. Analysis of distributed commit protocols. *Proc. ACM SIGMOD Conf. on Management of Data*, pages 175−183, 1982.

[Coo85] E. C. Cooper. Replicated distributed programs. *Proc. ACM Symp. on Operating Systems Principles*, pages 63−78, 1985.

[CPR+92] M. Chereque, D. Powell, P. Reynier, J.-L. Richier, and J. Voiron. Active replication in Delta-4. *Proc. Int'l Symp. on Fault Tolerant Computing*, pages 28−37, 1992.

[CR79] E. J. Chang and R. Roberts. An improved algorithm for decentralized extrema-finding in circular configurations of processes. *Communications of the ACM*, 22(5):281−283, 1979.

[CR83a] O. S. F. Carvalho and G. Roucairol. On mutual exclusion in computer networks. *Communications of the ACM*, 26(2):146−147, 1983.

[CR83b] F. Chin and K. V. S. Ramarao. Optimal termination protocols for network partitioning. *Proc. 2nd ACM SIGACT-SIGMOD Symp. on Principles of Database Systems*, pages 25−35, 1983.

[Cri90] F. Cristian. Synchronous atomic broadcast for redundant broadcast channels. *J. of Real-Time Systems*, 2(1):57−94, 1990.

[Cri91a] F. Cristian. Fault-tolerance in the advanced automation system. *ACM SIGOPS Operating Systems Review*, 25(2):117, April 1991.

[Cri91b] F. Cristian. Reaching agreement on processor-group membership in synchronous distributed systems. *Distributed Computing*, 4(4):175–188, 1991.

[Cri91c] F. Cristian. Understanding fault-tolerant distributed systems. *Communications of the ACM*, 34(2):56–78, 1991.

[CS91] D. E. Comer and D. L. Stevens. *Internetworking with TCP/IP: volume I and II*. Prentice-Hall, 1991.

[CS93] D. R. Cheriton and D. Skeen. Understanding the limitations of causally and totally ordered communication. *14th ACM SIGOPS Symp. on Operating Systems Principles*, pages 44–57, 1993.

[CSL90a] Y. I. Chang, M. Singhal, and M. T. Liu. A fault tolerant algorithm for distributed mutual exclusion. *IEEE Symp. on Reliable Distributed Systems*, pages 146–154, 1990.

[CSL90b] Y. I. Chang, M. Singhal, and M. T. Liu. An improved $O(\log(n))$ mutual exclusion algorithm for distributed systems. *Int'l Conf. on Parallel Processing*, pages 295–302, 1990.

[CT85] F. Chin and H. F. Ting. An almost linear time and $O(n\log n + e)$ messages distributed algorithm for minimum weight spanning trees. *Proc. Foundations of Computer Science Conf.*, pages 257–266, 1985.

[CT94] H. Chen and J. Tang. An efficient method for mutual exclusion in truly distributed systems. *Int'l Conf. on Distributed Computing Systems*, pages 97–104, 1994.

[Cus93] H. Custer. *Inside Windows NT*. Microsoft Press, 1993.

[CW82] R. Curtis and L. Wittie. Bugnet: A debugging system for parallel programming environments. *Proc. 3rd Int'l Conf. on Distributed Computing Systems*, pages 394–399, 1982.

[CW87] D. D. Clark and D. R. Wilson. A comparison of commercial and military computer security policies. *Proc. IEEE Symp. on Security and Privacy*, pages 184–194, 1987.

[Cyp91] R. J. Cypser. *Communications for Cooperating Systems: OSI, SNA, and TCP/IP*. Addison-Wesley, 1991.

[CZ85] D. R. Cheriton and W. Zwaenepoel. Distributed process groups in the V kernel. *ACM Trans. on Computer Systems*, 3(2):77, May 1985.

[Dav84] S. B. Davidson. Optimism and consistency in partitioned database systems. *ACM Trans. on Database Systems*, 9(3):456–481, 1984.

[Dav89] D. Davcev. A dynamic voting scheme in distributed systems. *IEEE Trans. on Software Engineering*, 15(1):93–97, 1989.

[DDS87] D. Dolev, C. Dwork, and L. Stockmeyer. On the minimal synchronism needed for consensus. *J. of the ACM*, 34(1):77–97, 1987.

[Dee89] S. Deering. Host extensions for IP multicasting. Technical Report RFC 1112, Stanford University, August 1989.

[Dei90] H. M. Deitel. *Operating Systems*. Addison-Wesley, 1990.

[Den76] D. E. Denning. A lattice model of secure information flow. *Communications of the ACM*, 19(5):236–243, 1976.

[Den83] D. E. Denning. *Cryptography and Data Security*. Addison-Wesley, 1983.

[DGH+87] A. Demers, D. Greene, C. Hauser, W. J. Larson, S. Shenker, H. Sturgis, D. Swinehart, and D. Terry. Epidemic algorithms for replicated database maintenance. *Proc. 6th Annual ACM Symp. on Principles of Distributed Computing*, pages 1–12. ACM, August 1987.

[DGMS85] S. B. Davidson, H. Garcia-Molina, and D. Skeen. Consistency in partitioned networks. *Computing Surveys*, 17(3):342–370, 1985.

[DGP90] A. R. Downing, I. G. Greenberg, and J. M. Peha. OSCAR: A system for weak-consistency replication. *IEEE Workshop on Management of Replicated Data*, November 1990.

[DH76] W. Diffie and M. Hellman. New directions in cryptography. *IEEE Trans. on Information Theory*, IT-22(6):644−654, 1976.

[DH77] W. Diffie and M. Hellman. Exhaustive cryptanalysis of the NBS data encryption standard. *Computer*, 10(6):74−84, 1977.

[Dij68] E. W. Dijkstra. Cooperating sequential processes. F. Geunys, editor, *Programming Languages*, pages 43−112. Academic Press, 1968.

[DJT89] R. P. Draves, M. B. Jones, and M. R. Thompson. MIG − the mach interface generator. Technical Report, Computer Science Dept., Carnegie Mellon University, 1989.

[DKM93] D. Dolev, S. Kramer, and D. Malki. Early delivery totally ordered broadcast in asynchronous environments. *Proc. 23rd Annual Int'l Symp. on Fault-Tolerant Computing*, pages 544−553, June 1993.

[DKR82] D. Dolev, M. Klawe, and M. Rodeh. An $O(n\log n)$ unidirectional distributed algorithm for extrema-finding in a circle. *J. of Algorithms*, 3:245−260, 1982.

[DLA88] P. Dasgupta, R. J. LeBlanc, and W. F. Appelbe. The Clouds distributed operating system. *Proc. 8th Int'l Conf. on Distributed Computing Systems*, pages 2−9, 1988.

[DMS94] D. Dolev, D. Malki, and R. Strong. An asynchronous membership protocol that tolerates partitions. Technical Report TR94-6, Institute of Computer Science, The Hebrew University of Jerusalem, 1994. Also available at http://www.cs.huji.ac.il/papers/transis /transis.html.

[Dol82] D. Dolev. Byzantine generals strike again. *J. of Algorithms*, 3:14−30, 1982.

[DS81] D. E. Denning and G. M. Sacco. Time-stamps in key distribution protocols. *Communications of the ACM*, 24(8):533−536, 1981.

[DS83] D. Dwork and D. Skeen. The inherent cost of nonblocking commitment. *Proc. 2nd ACM SIGACT-SIGOPS Symp. on Principles of Distributed Computing*, pages 1−11, 1983.

[DSB86] M. Dubois, C. Scheurich, and F. Briggs. Memory access buffering in multiprocessors. *Proc. 13th ISCA Conf.*, pages 434−442, 1986.

[Duc89] D. Duchamp. Analysis of transaction management performance. *Proc. Symp. on Operating Systems Principles*, pages 177−190, 1989.

[DZ83] J. Day and H. Zimmerman. The OSI reference model. *Proc. of the IEEE*, December 1983.

[EGLT76] K. P. Esweran, J. N. Gray, R. A. Lorie, and I. L. Traiger. The notions of consistency and predicate locks in a database system. *Communications of the ACM*, 19(11):624−633, 1976.

[EJZ92] E. N. Elnozahy, D. B. Johnson, and W. Zwaenepoel. The performance of consistent checkpointing. *Proc. IEEE Symp. on Reliable Distributed Computing Systems*, pages 39−47, 1992.

[EK72] J. Edmonds and R. M. Karp. Theoretical improvements in algorithm efficiency for network flow problems. *JACM*, 19(2):248−264, 1972.

[EKB$^+$92] J. Eykholt, S. Kleiman, S. Barton, S. Faulkner, A. Shivalingiah, M. Smith, D. Stein, J. Voll, M. Weeks, and D. Williams. Beyond multiprocessing: Multithreading the SunOS kernel. *Proc. Summer USENIX Conf.*, pages 11−18, 1992.

[ELZ86] D. L. Eager, E. D. Lazowska, and J. Zahorjan. Adaptive load sharing in homogeneous distributed systems. *IEEE Trans. on Software Engineering*, SE-12(5):662−675, 1986.

[Enn83] G. Ennis. Development of the DOD protocol reference model. *Proc. of the SIGCOMM'83 Symp.*, 1983.

[ES83] D. L. Eager and K. C. Sevcik. Achieving robustness in distributed database systems. *ACM Trans. on Database Systems*, 8(3):354–381, 1983.

[Esk89] M. R. Eskicioglu. Design issues of process migration facilities in distributed systems. *IEEE Technical Committee on Operating Systems Newsletter*, 4(2):3–13, 1989.

[Esk96] M. R. Eskicioglu. A comprehensive bibliography of distributed shared memory. *IEEE Operating Systems Review*, January 1996. Also available at http://www.cs.uno.edu /rasit/dsmbiblio.html.

[EZ92a] E. N. Elnozahy and W. Zwaenepoel. Manetho: Transparent rollback-recovery with low overhead, limited rollback, and fast output commit. *IEEE Trans. on Computers*, 41(5):526–531, 1992.

[EZ92b] E. N. Elnozahy and W. Zwaenepoel. Replicated distributed processes in manetho. *IEEE Symp. on Fault Tolerant Computing*, pages 18–27, 1992.

[EZ94] E. N. Elnozahy and W. Zwaenepoel. On the use and implementation of message logging. *IEEE Symp. on Fault Tolerant Computing*, pages 298–307, 1994.

[FB89] D. Fernandez-Baca. Allocating modules to processors in a distributed system. *IEEE Trans. on Software Engineering*, 15(11):1427–1436, 1989.

[Fel79] J. A. Feldman. High level programming for distributed computing. *Communications of the ACM*, 22(6):353–368, 1979.

[FF62] L. R. Ford, Jr. and D. R. Fulkerson. *Flows in Networks*. Princeton University Press, 1962.

[Fid88] J. Fidge. Time-stamps in message passing systems that preserve the partial ordering. *Proc. 11th Australian Computer Science Conf.*, pages 56–66, 1988.

[Fid89] C. J. Fidge. Partial orders for parallel debugging. *ACM SIGPLAN Notices*, 24(1):183–194, 1989.

[FJJR95] E. Fromentin, C. Jard, G. V. Jourdan, and M. Raynal. On-the-fly analysis of distributed computations. *Information Processing Letters*, 54:267–274, 1995.

[FLM86] M. Fischer, N. Lynch, and M. Merritt. Easy impossibility proofs for distributed consensus problems. *Distributed Computing*, 1:26–39, 1986.

[FLP85] M. J. Fischer, N. A. Lynch, and M. S. Patterson. Impossibility of distributed consensus with one faulty processor. *J. of the ACM*, 32(2):374–382, 1985.

[FM82] M. J. Fischer and A. Michael. Sacrificing serializability to attain high availability of data in an unreliable network. *Proc. ACM Symp. on Principles of Database Systems*, pages 70–75, 1982.

[Fol91] S. Foley. A taxonomy for information flow policies and models. *Proc. IEEE Symp. on Research in Security and Privacy*, pages 98–108, 1991.

[FP88] S. R. Faulk and D. L. Parnas. On synchronization in hard real-time systems. *Communications of the ACM*, 31(3):274–287, 1988.

[FR95] E. Fromentin and M. Raynal. Characterizing and detecting the set of global states seen by all observers of a distributed computation. *Proc. Int'l Conf. on Distributed Computing Systems*, pages 431–438, 1995.

[Fra82] W. R. Franklin. On an improved algorithm for decentralized extrema-finding in circular configurations of processes. *Communications of the ACM*, 25(5):336–337, 1982.

[FZ90] J. Fowler and W. Zwaenepoel. Causal distributed breakpoints. *Proc. Int'l Conf. on Distributed Computing Systems*, pages 134–141, 1990.

[Gaf85] E. Gafni. Improvement in time complexity of two message-optimal algorithms. *Proc. Principles of Distributed Computing Conf.*, pages 175–185, 1985.

[Gas92] D. Gastavson. The scalable coherent interface and related standards projects. *IEEE Micro*, pages 10–22, 1992. Also available at http://sunrise.scu.edu.

[GC95] V. K. Garg and C. M. Chase. Distributed algorithms for detecting conjunctive predicates. *Proc. Int'l Conf. on Distributed Computing Systems*, pages 423–430, 1995.

[GCK79] D. I. Good, R. M. Cohen, and J. Keeton-Williams. Principles of proving concurrent programs in Gypsy. *Proc. 6th ACM Symp. on Principles of Programming Languages*, pages 42–52, 1979.

[GD72] G. S. Graham and P. J. Denning. Protection – principles and practice. *Proc. AFIPS Spring Joint Computer Conf.*, 1972.

[Gel85] D. Gelernter. Generative communication in Linda. *ACM Trans. on Programming Languages and Systems*, 7(1):80–112, 1985.

[GGH91] K. Gharachorloo, A. Gupta, and J. Hennessy. Performance evaluation of memory consistency models for shared memory multiprocessors. *ACM SIGPLAN Notices*, 264(4):245–257, 1991.

[GGLS91] A. P. Goldberg, A. Gopal, A. Lowry, and R. Strom. Restoring consistent global states of distributed computations. *Proc. ACM/ONR Workshop on Parallel and Distributed Debugging*, pages 144–154, 1991.

[GHS83] R. Gallager, P. Humblet, and P. Spira. A distributed algorithm for minimum-weight spanning trees. *ACM Trans. on Programming Languages and Systems*, 5(1):66–77, 1983.

[Gif79] D. K. Gifford. Weighted voting for replicated data. *Proc. 7th Annual ACM Symp. on Operating System Principles*, pages 150–162. ACM, 1979.

[GL93] L. Gunaseelan and R. J. LeBlanc, Jr. Event ordering in a shared memory distributed system. *Proc. Int'l Conf. on Distributed Computing Systems*, pages 256–263, 1993.

[GLL+90] K. Gharachorloo, D. Lenoski, J. Laudon, P. Gibbons, A. Gupta, and J. Hennessy. Memory consistency and event ordering in scalable shared memory multiprocessors. *Computer Architecture News*, 18(2):15–26, 1990.

[GLS95] R. Guerraoui, M. Larrea, and A. Schiper. Non blocking atomic commitment with an unreliable failure detector. *IEEE Symp. on Reliable Distributed Systems*, pages 41–50, 1995.

[GM82] H. Garcia-Molina. Elections in a distributed computer system. *IEEE Trans. on Computers*, C-31(2):48–59, 1982.

[GM90] M. Gasser and E. McDermott. An architecture for practical delegation in a distributed system. *Proc. IEEE Symp. on Security and Privacy*, pages 20–30, 1990.

[GMB85] H. Garcia-Molina and D. Barbara. How to assign votes in a distributed system. *J. of the ACM*, 34(4):841–860, October 1985.

[GMS89] H. Garcia-Molina and A. Spauster. Message ordering in a multicast environment. *Proc. Int'l Conf. on Distributed Computing Systems*, pages 354–361, 1989.

[Gos91] A. Goscinski. *Distributed Operating Systems: The Logical Design*. Addison-Wesley, 1991.

[GR93] J. Gray and A. Reuter. *Transaction Processing: Concepts and Techniques*. Morgan Kaufmann, 1993.

[Gra78] J. Gray. Notes on data base operating systems. *Operating Systems: An Advanced Course. Lecture Notes in Computer Science #60*. Springer-Verlag, 1978.

[Gre94] S. Greenwald. *The Distributed Compartment Model for Resource Management and Access Control*. Dissertation, CISE Dept., University of Florida, 1994.

[Gro93] B. Groselj. Bounded and minimum global snapshots. *IEEE Trans. on Parallel and Distributed Technology*, 1(4):72–83, 1993.

[GW88] J. R. Goodman and P. J. Woest. The Wisconsin Multicube: A large scale cache-coherent multiprocessor. *Proc. Int'l Symp. on Computer Architecture*, pages 422–431, 1988.

[GW94] V. K. Garg and B. Waldecker. Detection of weak unstable predicates in distributed programs. *IEEE Trans. on Parallel and Distributed Systems*, 5(3):299–307, 1994.

[HA79] C. E. Hewitt and R. R. Atkinson. Specification and proof techniques for serializers. *IEEE Trans. on Software Engineering*, 5(1):10–23, 1979.

[HA90] P. W. Hutto and M. Ahmad. Weakening consistency to enhance concurrency in distributed systems. *Proc. 10th Int'l Conf. on Distributed Computing Systems*, pages 302–311, 1990.

[Hal92] F. Halsall. *Data Communications, Computer Networks and Open Systems*. Addison-Wesley, 1992.

[HC88] R. C. Holt and J. R. Cordy. The Turing programming language. *Communications of the ACM*, 31(12):1410–1423, 1988.

[HCA88] J. Hwang, R. Chow, and F. Anger. An analysis of multiprocessing speedup with emphasis on the effect of scheduling methods. *Proc. 8th Int'l Conf. on Distributed Computer Systems*, pages 242–248, 1988.

[HCAL89] J. Hwang, R. Chow, F. Anger, and C. Lee. Scheduling precedence graphs in systems with interprocessor communication times. *SIAM J. of Computing*, 18(2):990–1013, 1989.

[Her86] M. Herlihy. A quorum-consensus replication method for abstract data types. *ACM Trans. on Computer Systems*, 4(1):32–53, 1986.

[Her87] M. Herlihy. Dynamic quorum adjustments for partitioned data. *ACM Trans. on Database Systems*, 12(2):170–194, 1987.

[Her90] M. Herlihy. Concurrency and availability as dual properties of replicated atomic data. *J. of the ACM*, 37(2):257–278, 1990.

[Her91] M. Herlihy. Wait-free synchronization. *ACM Trans. on Programming Languages and Systems*, 11(1):124–149, 1991.

[HHW89] A. Heddaya, M. Hsu, and W. Weihl. Two phase gossip: Managing distributed event histories. *Information Sciences*, 49:35–57, 1989.

[Hil86] M. Hill. Design decisions in SPUR. *IEEE Computer*, 19(11):8–22, 1986.

[HJK93] S-T. Huang, J-R. Jiang, and Y-C. Kuo. K-coteries for fault tolerant K-entries to a critical section. *Proc. Int'l Conf. on Distributed Computing Systems*, pages 74–81, 1993.

[HKM$^+$88] J. H. Howard, M. L. Kazar, H. G. Menees, D. A. Nichols, M. Satyanarayanan, and R. N. Sidebotham. Scale and performance in a distributed file system. *ACM Trans. on Computer Systems*, 6(1):55–81, 1988.

[HM94] J. M. Helary and A. Mostefaoui. An $O(\log n)$ fault-tolerant distributed mutual exclusion algorithm based on open-cube structure. *Int'l Conf. on Distributed Computing Systems*, pages 89–96, 1994.

[HMR94] M. Helary, A. Mostefaoui, and M. Raynal. A general scheme for token and tree based distributed mutual exclusion algorithms. *IEEE Trans. on Parallel and Distributed Systems*, 5(11):1185–1196, 1994.

[Hoa72] C. A. R. Hoare. Towards a theory of parallel programming. R.H. Perrott, editor, *Operating Systems Techniques*, pages 61–71. Academic Press, 1972.

[Hoa74] C. A. R. Hoare. Monitors: An operating system structuring concepts. *Communications of the ACM*, 17(10):549–557, 1974.

[Hoa78] C. A. R. Hoare. Communicating sequential processes. *Communications of the ACM*, 21(8):666–677, 1978.

[HPR88] M. Helary, N. Plouzeau, and M. Raynal. A distributed algorithm for mutual exclusion in an arbitrary network. *The Computer Journal*, 31(4):289–295, 1988.

[HRU76] M. A. Harrison, W. L. Ruzzo, and J. D. Ullman. Protection in operating systems. *Communications of the ACM*, 19(8):461–471, 1976.

[HS80] D. S. Hirshberg and J. B. Sinclair. Decentralized extrema-finding in circular configurations of processors. *Communications of the ACM*, 23(11):627–628, 1980.

[Hu70] T. C. Hu. *Integer Programming and Network Flows*. Addison-Wesley, 1970.

[HW88] D. Haban and W. Weigel. Global events and global breakpoints in distributed systems. *21st Hawaii Int'l Conf. on Systems Science*, pages 288–289, 1988.

[HW90] M. Herlihy and J. Wing. Linearizability: A correctness condition for concurrent objects. *ACM Trans. on Programming Languages and Systems*, 12(3):463–492, 1990.

[IBM85] IBM Corporation. *Systems Network Architecture, Format and Protocol Reference Manual: Architectural Logic for LU Type 6.2*, 1985. GC30-3269.

[IK93] T. Ibaraki and T. Kameda. A theory of coteries: Mutual exclusion in distributed systems. *IEEE Trans. on Parallel and Distributed Systems*, 4(7):779–794, 1993.

[Int96] Internet Engineering Task Force. *Secure Socket Layer*, 1996. Available at http://www.ietf.org/.

[ISO89a] ISO. *Information Processing Systems – Open Systems Interconnection – Definition of Common Application Service Elements – Commitment, Concurrency and Recovery. Draft Int'l Standards ISO 9804/2.*, 1989.

[ISO89b] ISO. *Information Processing Systems – Open Systems Interconnection – Distributed Transaction Processing – Part 1: Model, Part 2: Service Definition, Part 3: Protocol Specification. Draft Int'l Standards ISO 10026/1-3, 1989.*, 1989.

[IT88] ITU-T. *X.509, The Directory – Authentication Framework*. CCITT, ITU-T, 1988.

[Jal95] P. Jalote. Resilient objects in broadcast networks. *IEEE Trans. on Software Engineering*, 15(1):68–72, 1995.

[JB86] T. A. Joseph and K. P. Birman. Low cost management of replicated data in fault-tolerant distributed systems. *ACM Trans. on Computer Systems*, 4(1):54–70, 1986.

[JB87] T. A. Joseph and K. P. Birman. Exploiting virtual synchrony in distributed systems. *Proc. ACM SIGOPS Symp. on Operating System Principles*, pages 123–138, 1987.

[JBE95] J. Jing, O. Bukhres, and A. Elmagarmid. Distributed lock management for mobile transactions. *Proc. Int'l Conf. on Distributed Computing Systems*, pages 118–125, 1995.

[JFR93] F. Jahanian, S. Fakhouri, and R. Rajkumar. Processor group membership protocols: Specification, design, and implementation. *IEEE Symp. on Reliable Distributed Systems*, pages 2–11, 1993.

[JJJR94] C. Jard, T. Jeron, G.-V. Jourdan, and J.-X. Rampon. A general approach to trace-checking in distributed computing systems. *Int'l Conf. on Distributed Computing Systems*, pages 396–403, 1994.

[JM90] S. Jajodia and D. Mutchler. Dynamic voting algorithms for maintaining the consistency of a replicated database. *ACM Trans. on Database Systems*, 15(2):230–253, June 1990.

[JM92] F. Jahanian and W. L. Moran. Strong, weak, and hybrid group membership. *Workshop on Replicated Data Management II*, pages 34–38, 1992.

[JNW96] T. Johnson and R. E. Newman-Wolfe. A comparison of fast and low overhead distributed priority locks. *J. of Parallel and Distributed Computing*, 32:74–89, 1996.

[Joh93] D. B. Johnson. Efficient transparent optimistic rollback recovery for distributed application programs. *Proc. Symp. on Reliable Distributed Systems*, pages 86–95, 1993.

[Joh95] T. Johnson. A performance comparison of fast distributed synchronization algorithms. *Int'l Parallel Processing Symp.*, pages 258–264, 1995.

[JP86] M. Joseph and P. Pandya. Finding response times in a real time system. *BCS Computer J.*, 29(5):390–395, 1986.

[JV91] T. T.-Y. Juang and S. Venkatesan. Crash recovery with little overhead. *Proc. Int'l Conf. on Distributed Computing Systems*, pages 454–461, 1991.

[JZ87] D. B. Johnson and W. Zwaenepoel. Sender-based message logging. *IEEE Symp. on Fault Tolerant Computing*, pages 14–19, 1987.

[JZ90] D. B. Johnson and W. Zwaenepoel. Recovery in distributed systems using optimistic message logging and checkpointing. *J. of Algorithms*, 11:462–491, 1990.

[Kan92] K. Kant. *Introduction to Computer System Performance Evaluation.* McGraw-Hill, 1992.

[Kar78] P. A. Karger. The lattice security model in a public computing network. *Proc. 1978 ACM Annual Conf.*, pages 453–459, 1978.

[Kar89] P. A. Karger. Implementing commercial data integrity with secure capabilities. *Proc. IEEE Symp. on Security and Privacy*, pages 130–139, 1889.

[KBH+88] L. Kawell, Jr., S. Beckhardt, T. Halvorsen, R. Ozzie, and I. Grief. Replicated document management in a group communication system. *Proc. 2nd Conf. on Computer-supported Cooperative Work*, 1988.

[KC91] A. Kumar and S. Y. Cheung. A high availability sqrt(n) hierarchical grid algorithm for replicated data. *Information Processing Letters*, 40:311–316, 1991.

[KC95] I. Kao and R. Chow. Enforcement of complex security policies with beac. *Proc. 18th National Information Systems Security Conf.*, pages 1–10, 1995.

[KFYA94] H. Kakugawa, S. Fujita, M. Yamashita, and T. Ae. A distributed K-mutual exclusion algorithm using K-coterie. *Information Processing Letters*, 49:213–218, 1994.

[KHGMP91] R. P. King, H. Halim, H. Garcia-Molina, and C. A. Polyzios. Management of a remote backup copy for disaster recovery. *ACM Trans. on Database Systems*, 16(2):338–368, 1991.

[Kle75] L. Kleinrock. *Queuing Systems, Volume 1: Theory.* Wiley, 1975.

[KNT91] J. T. Kohl, B. C. Neuman, and T. Y. Tso. The evolution of the kerberos authentication service. *Proc. EurOpen Spring'91 Conf.*, pages 295–313, 1991.

[KOH+94] J. Kuslin, D. Ofelt, M. Heinrich, J. Heinlein, R. Simoni, K. Gharachorloo, J. Chapin, D. Nakahira, J. Baxter, M. Horowitz, A. Gupta, M. Rosenblum, and J. Hennessy. The Stanford FLASH multiprocessor. *Proc. 21st Annual Int'l Symp. on Computer Architecture*, pages 302–313, 1994. Also available at http://www-flash.stanford.edu/index.html.

[KP93] J. L. Kim and T. Park. An efficient protocol or checkpointing recovery in distributed systems. *IEEE Trans. on Parallel and Distributed Systems*, 4(8):955–960, 1993.

[KSL92] A. Kehne, J. Schonwalder, and H. Langendorfer. A nonce-based protocol for multiple authentication. *Operating Systems Review*, 26(4):84–89, 1992.

[KT87] R. Koo and S. Toueg. Checkpointing and rollback-recovery for distributed systems. *IEEE Trans. on Software Engineering*, SE-13(1):23–31, 1987.

[KT91] M. F. Kaashoek and A. S. Tanenbaum. Group communication in the Amoeba distributed operating system. *Proc. 11th Int'l Conf. on Distributed Computing Systems*, pages 222–230, 1991.

[Kum91] A. Kumar. Hierarchical quorum consensus: A new algorithm for managing replicated data. *IEEE Trans. on Computers*, 40(9):994–1004, 1991.

[LA94] H. V. Leong and D. Agrawal. Using message semantics to reduce rollback in optimistic message logging recovery schemes. *Int'l Conf. on Distributed Computing Systems*, pages 227–234, 1994.

[Lam71] B. W. Lampson. Protection. *Proc. 5th Princeton Symp. on Information Sciences and Systems*, pages 437–443, 1971.

[Lam73] B. W. Lampson. A note on the confinement problem. *Communications of the ACM*, 16(10):613–615, 1973.

[Lam78] L. Lamport. Time, clocks, and the ordering of events in a distributed system. *Communications of the ACM*, 21(7):558–564, 1978.

[Lam79] L. Lamport. How to make a multiprocessor computer that correctly executes multiprocess programs. *IEEE Trans. on Computers*, C-28(9):241–248, 1979.

[Lan81] C. E. Landwehr. Formal models for computer security. *Computing Surveys*, 13(3):247–278, 1981.

[LCS89] D. D. E. Long, J. L. Carroll, and K. Stewart. Estimating the reliability of regeneration-based replica control protocols. *IEEE Trans. on Computers*, 38(12):1691–1702, 1989.

[LE91] R. P. LaRowe and C. S. Ellis. Experiment comparison of memory management policies for NUMA multiprocessors. *ACM Trans. on Computer Systems*, 9(4):319–363, 1991.

[LEH92] R. P. LaRowe, C. S. Ellis, and M. A. Holliday. Evaluation of NUMA memory management through modeling and measurements. *IEEE Trans. on Parallel and Distributed Systems*, 3(6):686–701, 1992.

[LG90] S. Luan and V. Gligor. A fault-tolerant protocol for atomic broadcast. *IEEE Trans. on Parallel and Distributed Systems*, 1(3):271–285, 1990.

[LH89a] K. Li and P. Hudak. Memory coherence in shared virtual memory systems. *ACM Trans. on Computer Systems*, 7(4):321–359, 1989.

[LH89b] K. Li and P. Hudak. Memory coherence in shared virtual memory systems. *ACM Trans. on Computer Systems*, 7(4):321–359, 1989.

[LHCA88] C. Lee, J. Hwang, R. Chow, and F. Anger. Multiprocessor scheduling with interprocessor communication delays. *Operation Research Letters*, 7(3):141–147, 1988.

[Li88] K. Li. Ivy: A shared virtual memory system for parallel computing. *Proc. Int'l Conf. on Parallel Processing*, pages 94–101, 1988.

[Lil93] D. J. Lilja. Cache coherence in large-scale shared-memory multiprocessors: Issues and comparisons. *ACM Computing Surveys*, 25(3):303–338, 1993.

[Lis88] B. Liskov. Distributed programming in Argus. *Communications of the ACM*, 31(3):300–312, 1988.

[Lis91] B. Liskov. Practical uses of synchronized clocks in distributed systems. *Principles of Distributed Computing*, pages 1–9, 1991.

[LK90] W. S. Lloyd and P. Kearns. Bounding sequence numbers in distributed systems : A general approach. *Proc. Int'l Conf. on Distributed Computing Systems*, pages 312–319, 1990.

[LKS91] E. Levy, H. F. Korth, and A. Silberschatz. An optimistic commit protocol for distributed transaction management. *ACM SIGMOD*, pages 88–97, 1991.

[LL72] C. L. Liu and J. W. Layland. Scheduling algorithms for multiprogramming in a hard real-time environment. *J. of the ACM*, 20(1):46–61, 1972.

[LL92] R. Ladin and B. Liskov. Garbage collection of a distributed heap. *Proc. Int'l Conf. on Distributed Computing Systems*, pages 708–715, 1992.

[LLG+92] D. Lenoski, J. Laudon, K. Gharachorloo, W. Weber, A. Gupta, J. Hennessy, M. Horowitz, and M. Lam. The Stanford DASH multiprocessor. *IEEE Computer*, 25(3):63–79, 1992.

[LLSG92] R. Ladin, B. Liskov, L. Shrira, and S. Ghemawat. Providing high availability using lazy replication. *ACM Trans. on Computer Systems*, 10(4):360, November 1992.

[LMKQ89] S. J. Leffler, M. K. McKusick, M. J. Karels, and J. S. Quarterman. *The Design and Implementation of the 4.3BSD UNIX Operating System*. Addison-Wesley, 1989.

[LMWF94] N. Lynch, M. Merritt, W. Weihl, and A. Fekete. *Atomic Transactions*. Morgan Kaufmann, 1994.

[Lo88] V. M. Lo. Heuristic algorithms for task assignment in distributed systems. *IEEE Trans. on Computers*, 37(11):1384–1397, 1988.

[Loh85] E. Lohse. The role of the ISO in telecommunication and information systems standardization. *IEEE Communications Magazine*, 23(1):18–24, January 1985.

[LRG91] A. Lowry, J. R. Russell, and A. P. Goldberg. Optimistic failure recovery for very large networks. *IEEE Symp. on Reliable Distributed Systems*, pages 66–75, 1991.

[LRV87] H. F. Li, T. Radhakrishnan, and K. Ventatesh. Global state detection in non-FIFO networks. *Proc. Int'l Conf. on Distributed Computing Systems*, pages 364–370, 1987.

[LS76] B. Lampson and H. Sturgis. Crash recovery in a distributed data storage system. Technical Report, Xerox PARC, 1976.

[LS83] B. Liskov and R. Scheifler. Guardians and actions: Linguistic support for robust, distributed programs. *ACM Trans. on Programming Languages and Systems*, 5(3):381–404, 1983.

[LS90] E. Levy and A. Silberschatz. Distributed file systems: Concepts and examples. *ACM Computing Surveys*, 22(4):321–374, 1990.

[LSP82] L. Lamport, R. Shostak, and M. Pease. The Byzantine generals problem. *ACM Trans. on Programming Languages*, 4(3):382–401, 1982.

[LSWW87] B. Liskov, R. Scheifler, E. Walker, and W. Weihl. Orphan detection. *IEEE Symp. on Fault Tolerant Computing*, pages 2–7, 1987.

[Lun89] T. F. Lunt. Aggregation and inference: Facts and fallacies. *Proc. IEEE Symp. on Security and Privacy*, pages 102–109, 1989.

[LW82] J. Y. T. Leung and J. Whitehead. On the complexity of fixed-priority scheduling of periodic real-time tasks. *Performance Evaluation*, 2:237–250, 1982.

[LY87] T. Lai and T. Yang. On distributed snapshots. *Information Processing Letters*, 25:153–158, 1987.

[Lyn89] N. Lynch. A hundred impossibility proofs for distributed computing. *Principles of Distributed Computing*, pages 1–27, 1989.

[Lyn96] N. Lynch. *Distributed Algorithms*. Morgan Kaufmann, 1996.

[Mae85] M. Maekawa. A sqrt(n) algorithm for mutual exlcusion in decentralized systems. *ACM Trans. on Computer Systems*, 3(2):145–159, 1985.

[Mak94] K. Makki. An efficient token-based distributed mutual exclusion algorithm. *J. of Computer and Software Engineering*, 2(4):401–416, 1994.

[MAMSA94] L. E. Moser, Y. Amir, P. M. Melliar-Smith, and D. A. Agarwal. Extended virtual synchrony. *Int'l Conf. on Distributed Computing Systems*, pages 56–65, 1994.

[Mat89] F. Mattern. *Virtual Time and Global States of Distributed Systems*, pages 215–226. Elsevier Science Publishers, 1989.

[Mat93] F. Mattern. Efficient algorithms for distributed snapshots and global virtual time approximation. *J. of Parallel and Distributed Computing*, 18(4):423–434, 1993.

[May83] D. May. Occam. *ACM SIGPLAN Notices*, 18(4):69–79, 1983.

[MBB+92] K. Makki, P. Banta, K. Been, N. Pissinou, and E. K. Park. A token based distributed K mutual exclusion algorithm. *Proc. IEEE Symp. on Parallel and Distributed Processing*, pages 408–411, 1992.

[MBRS94] D. Malki, K. P. Birman, A. Ricciardi, and A. Schiper. Uniform actions in distributed systems. *Proc. Symp. on Principles of Distributed Computing*, pages 128–135, 1994.

[MC88] B. P. Miller and J. D. Choi. Breakpoints and halting in distributed programs. *8th Int'l Conf. on Distributed Computing Systems*, pages 316–323, 1988.

[Mea90] C. Meadows. Extending the brewer-nash model to a multilevel context. *Proc. IEEE Symp. on Research in Security and Privacy*, pages 95–102, 1990.

[MI92] Y. Manabe and M. Imase. Global conditions in debugging distributed programs. *J. of Parallel and Distributed Computing*, 15:62–29, 1992.

[MJ94] L. Maugis and T. Johnson. Two approaches for high concurrency in multicast-based object replication. Technical Report TR94-041, University of Florida, Dept. of CIS, 1994. Available at ftp.cis.ufl.edu:cis/tech-reports/tr94/tr94-041.ps.Z.

[MMS79] J. G. Mitchell, W. Maybury, and R. Sweet. Mesa language reference manual (version 5.0). Technical Report CSL-79-3, Xerox PARC, 1979.

[MMSA93] L. E. Moser, P. M. Melliar-Smith, and V. Agrawala. Asynchronous fault-tolerant total ordering algorithms. *SIAM J. on Computing*, 22(4):727–750, 1993.

[MMSA94] L. E. Moser, P. M. Melliar-Smith, and V. Agrawala. Processor membership in asynchronous distributed systems. *IEEE Trans. on Parallel and Distributed Systems*, 5(5):459–473, 1994.

[MNR91] M. Mizuno, M. L. Neilsen, and R. Rao. A token-based distributed mutual exclusion algorithm based on quorum agreements. *IEEE Int'l Conf. on Distributed Computing Systems*, pages 361–368, 1991.

[Moc87] P. Mockapetris. Domain names: Concepts and facilities. Technical Report RFC 1034, Internet Network Information Center, 1987. Available at /usr/pub/RFC/ at nic.ddn.mil.

[MOO87] M. Maekawa, A. E. Oldehoeft, and R. R. Oldehoeft. *Operating Systems: Advanced Concepts*. Benjamin/Cummings, 1987.

[Mos93] D. Mosberger. Memory consistency models. *Operating System Notices*, pages 18–25, June 1993.

[MPP94] K. Makki, N. Pissinou, and E. K. Park. An efficient solution to the critical section problem. *Proc. Int'l Parallel Processing Symp.*, pages II:77–80, 1994.

[MPS89] S. Mishra, L. L. Peterson, and R. D. Schlichting. Implementing fault-tolerant replicated objects using psync. *Proc. 8th Symp. on Reliable Distributed Systems*, pages 42–52, October 1989.

[MPS91a] S. Mishra, L. L. Peterson, and R. D. Schlichting. Consul: A communication substrate for fault-tolerant distributed programs. Technical Report TR 91-32, University of Arizona, 1991.

[MPS91b] S. Mishra, L. L. Peterson, and R. D. Schlichting. A membership protocol based on a partial order. *Proc. Int'l Working Conf. on Dependable Computing for Critical Applications*, May 1991.

[MPY93] K. Makki, N. Pissinou, and Y. Yesha. An $O(\sqrt{N})$ token based distributed mutual exclusion algorithm. *Informatica*, 17:221–231, 1993.

[MR89] Y. Moses and G. Roth. On reliable message diffusion. *Proc. 9th ACM SIGACT-SIGOPS Symp. on Principles of Distributed Computing*, pages 119–127, 1989.

[MSC⁺86] J. H. Morris, M. Satyanarayanan, M. H. Conner, J. H. Howard, D.S. Rosenthal, and F.D. Smith. Andrew: A distributed computing environment. *Communications of the ACM*, 29(3):184–201, 1986.

[MSMA90] P. M. Melliar-Smith, L. Moser, and V. Agrawala. Broadcast protocols for distributed systems. *IEEE Trans. on Parallel and Distributed Systems*, 1(1):17–25, 1990.

[MST94] S. Murata, A. Shionozaki, and M. Tokoro. A network architecture for reliable process group communication. *Int'l Conf. on Distributed Computing Systems*, pages 66–73, 1994.

[MSV91] S. Meldal, S. Sankar, and J. Vera. Exploiting locality in maintaining potential causality. *ACM Symp. on Principles of Distributed Computing*, pages 231–239, 1991.

[Mul93] S. Mullender. *Distributed Systems*. Addison-Wesley, 1993.

[NA87] J. D. Noe and A. Andreassian. Effectiveness of replication in distributed computing networks. *Proc. 7th Int'l Conf. on Distributed Computing Systems*, pages 508–513, 1987.

[NAB+95] A. Nowatzyk, G. Aybay, M. Browne, E. Kelly, M. Parkin, B. Radke, and S. Vishin. The S3.mp scalable shared memory multiprocessor. *Proc. 24th Int'l Conf. on Parallel Processing*, pages I:1–10, 1995. Also available at http://playground.sun.com /pub/S3.mp/s3mp.html.

[NBS77] NBS. *DES, Data Encryption Standard*. National Bureau of Standards, 1977.

[NCS85] NCSC. *Trusted Computing System Evaluation Criteria*. National Computer Security Center, 1985.

[Neu91] B. C. Neuman. Proxy-based authorization and accounting for distributed systems. Technical Report TR-91-02-01, CSE Dept., University of Washington, 1991.

[Ng91] T. P. Ng. Ordered broadcasts for large applications. *IEEE Symp. on Reliable Distributed Systems*, pages 188–197, 1991.

[NL91] B. Nitzberg and V. Lo. Distributed shared memory: A survey of issues and algorithms. *IEEE Computer*, 24(8):52–60, 1991.

[NM91] M. L. Neilsen and M. Mizuno. A DAG-based algorithm for distributed mutual exclusion. *Int'l Conf. on Distributed Computer Systems*, pages 354–360, 1991.

[NM92] R. H. B. Netzer and B. P. Miller. Optimal tracing and replay for debugging message-passing parallel programs. *Supercomputing '92*, pages 502–511, 1992.

[NMR92] M. L. Neilsen, M. Mizuno, and M. Raynal. A general method to define quorums. *Int'l Conf. on Distributed Computer Systems*, pages 657–664, 1992.

[NP90] M. Nash and K. Poland. Some conundrums concerning separation of duty. *Proc. IEEE Symp. on Research in Security and Privacy*, pages 201–207, 1990.

[NR95] W. K. Ng and C. V. Ravishankar. Coterie templates: A new quorum construction method. *Proc. Int'l Conf. on Distributed Computing Systems*, pages 92–99, 1995.

[NS78] R. M. Needham and M. D. Schroeder. Using encryption for authentication in large network of computers. *Communications of the ACM*, 21(12):993–999, 1978.

[NS93] B. C. Neuman and S. G. Stubblebine. A note on the use of time-stamps as nonces. *Operating Systems Review*, 27(2):10–14, 1993.

[NSX94] R. H. B. Netzer, S. Subramanian, and J. Xu. Critical-path based message logging for incremental replay of message passing programs. *Proc. Int'l Conf. on Distributed Computer Systems*, pages 404–413, 1994.

[NWV91] R. E. Newman-Wolfe and B. R. Venkatraman. High level prevention of traffic analysis. *Proc. 7th Annual Computer Security Applications Conf.*, pages 102–109, 1991.

[NX93a] R. H. B. Netzer and J. Xu. Adaptive message logging for incremental replay. *IEEE Trans. on Parallel and Distributed Technology*, 1(4):32–40, 1993.

[NX93b] R. H. B. Netzer and J. Xu. Adaptive message logging for incremental replay of message-passing programs. *Supercomputing '93*, pages 840–849, 1993.

[NX95] R. H. B. Netzer and J. Xu. Necessary and sufficient conditions for consistent global snapshots. *IEEE Trans. on Parallel and Distributed Systems*, 6(2):165–169, 1995.

[OCD⁺88] J. K. Ousterhout, A. R. Cherenson, F. Douglis, M. N. Nelson, and B. B. Welch. The Sprite network operating system. *IEEE Computer*, 21(2):23–36, 1988.

[ODP93] ODP. *Reference Model: Open Distributed Processing – ISO/IEC DIS 10746*. ISO and ITU-T, 1993. Available at http://www.dstc.edu.au/.

[OL88] B. M. Oki and B. Liskov. Viewstamped replication: A general primary copy method to support highly-available distributed systems. *Proc. 7th ACM SIGACT-SIGOPS Symp. on Principles of Distributed Computing*, August 1988.

[OMG91] OMG. *The Common Object Request Broker – Architecture and specification, No. 91.12.1*. OMG, 1991. Available at http://www.omg.org/.

[OR87] D. Otway and O. Rees. Efficient and timely mutual authentication. *Operating Systems Review*, 21(1):8–10, 1987.

[OSF92] OSF. *Introduction to OSF DCE*. Prentice-Hall, 1992.

[OV91] M. T. Ozsu and P. Valduriez. *Principles of Distributed Database Systems*. Prentice-Hall, 1991.

[Pap79] C. H. Papadimitriou. Serializability of concurrent database updates. *J. of the ACM*, 26(4):631–653, 1979.

[Par83] D. S. Parker, et al. Detection of mutual inconsistency in distributed systems. *IEEE Trans. on Software Engineering*, 9(3):240–246, 1983.

[Par86] J.-F. Paris. Voting with witnesses: A consistency scheme for replicated files. *Proc. 6th Int'l Conf. on Distributed Computing Systems*, page 36. IEEE Computer Society, 1986.

[Par88] J.-F. Paris. Efficient management of replicated data. *Proc. Int. Conf. on Database Theory*, 1988.

[Par94] J.-F. Paris. A highly available replication control protocol using volatile witnesses. *Int'l Conf. on Distributed Computing Systems*, pages 536–543, 1994.

[PBS89] L. L. Peterson, N. C. Buchholz, and R. D. Schlichting. Preserving and using context information in interprocess communication. *ACM Trans. on Computer Systems*, 7(3):217–246, August 1989.

[Pea92] K. Peacock. File system multithreading in System V Release 4 MP. *Proc. Summer USENIX Conf.*, pages 19–29, 1992.

[PEM93] PEM. *PEM, Privacy Enhanced Mail, RFC 1421-1423*. IRTF and IETF, 1993. Available at /rfc/rfc1421.txt at www.internic.net.

[Pet82] G. L. Peterson. An $O(n\log n)$ unidirectional algorithm for the circular extrema problem. *ACM Trans. on Programming Languages and Systems*, 4:758–762, 1982.

[PGM94] C. A. Polyzois and H. Garcia-Molina. Evaluation of remote backup algorithms for transaction processing systems. *ACM Trans. on Database Systems*, 19(3):423–449, 1994.

[PK93] S. L. Peterson and P. Kearns. Rollback based on vector time. *Proc. Symp. on Reliable Distributed Systems*, pages 68–77, 1993.

[PL88] J.-F. Paris and D. E. Long. Efficient dynamic voting algorithms. *Proc. IEEE Int'l Conf. on Data Engineering*, page 268, February 1988.

[PL91a] J.-F. Paris and D. E. Long. Voting with regenerable volatile witnesses. *Proc. Int'l Conf. on Data Engineering*, pages 112–119, 1991.

[PL91b] C. Pu and A. Leff. Replica control in distributed systems: An asynchronous approach. *ACM SIGMOD*, pages 377–286, 1991.

[PM83] M. L. Power and B. P. Miller. Process migration in DEMOS/MP. *Proc. 9th ACM Symp. on Operating Systems Principles*, pages 110–119, 1983.

[PNP88] C. Pu, J. D. Noe, and A. Proudfoot. Regeneration of replicated objects: A technique and its Eden implementation. *IEEE Trans. on Software Engineering*, 14(7):936–945, 1988.

[PP83] M. L. Powell and D. L. Presotto. Publishing: A reliable broadcast communication mechanism. *Proc. ACM SIGOPS Symp. on Operating System Principles*, pages 100–109, 1983.

[Pra86] V. Pratt. Modeling concurrency with partial orders. *Int'l J. of Parallel Programming*, 15(1):33–72, 1986.

[PS88] F. Panzieri and S. K. Shrivastava. Rajdoot: A remote procedure call mechanism supporting orphan detection and killing. *IEEE Trans. on Software Engineering*, 14(1):30–37, 1988.

[PS92] J. F. Paris and P. K. Sloope. Dynamic management of highly replicated data. *IEEE 11th Symp. on Reliable Distributed Systems*, pages 20–27, 1992.

[PSL80] M. Pease, R. Shostak, and L. Lamport. Reaching agreement in the presence of faults. *J. of the ACM*, 27(2):228–234, 1980.

[PTM95] J. Protic, M. Tomasevic, and V. Multinovic. A survey of distributed shared memory systems. *Proc. 28th Annual Hawaii Int'l Conf. on System Sciences*, pages 74–84, 1995.

[PW85] G. Popek and B. Walker. *The LOCUS Distributed System Architecture*. MIT Press, 1985.

[RA81] G. Ricart and A. K. Agrawala. An optimal algorithm for mutual exclusion in computer networks. *Communications of the ACM*, 24(1):9–17, 1981.

[Raj90] R. Rajkumar. Real-time synchronization protocols for shared memory multiprocesors. *Proc. IEEE 10th Int'l Conf. on Distributed Computing Systems*, pages 116–123, 1990.

[RAK88] U. Ramachandran, M. Ahamad, and Y. Khalidi. Unifying synchronization and data transfer in maintaining coherence of distributed shared memory. Technical Report GIT-CS-88-23, Georgia Institute of Technology, 1988.

[Ram72] C. V. Ramamoorthy, et al. Optimal scheduling strategies in a multiprocessor system. *IEEE Trans. on Computers*, C-21(2):137–146, 1972.

[Ram85] K. V. S. Ramarao. On the complexity of commit protocols. *Proc. ACM SIGACT-SIGMOD Symp. on Principles of Database Systems*, pages 235–244, 1985.

[Ray88] M. Raynal. *Distributed Algorithms and Protocols*. Wiley, 1988.

[Ray89a] K. Raymond. A distributed algorithm for multiple entries to a critical section. *Information Processing Letters*, 27:189–193, 1989.

[Ray89b] K. Raymond. A tree-based algorithm for distributed mutual exclusion. *ACM Trans. on Computer Systems*, 7(1):61–77, 1989.

[RB93] A. Ricciardi and K. P. Birman. Process membership in asynchronous environments. Technical Report TR 93-1328, Dept. of Computer Science, Cornell University, 1993.

[RGK96] M. Rabinovitch, N. Gehani, and A. Kononov. Scalable update propogation in epidemic replicated databases. *Proc. 5th Conf. on Extended Database Technologies*, pages 207–222, 1996.

[Ric94] J. Richter. *Advanced Windows NT*. Microsoft Press, 1994.

[Riv92] R. L. Rivest. *RFC 1321, The MD5 Message-Digest Algorithm*. Internet Network Information Center, 1992. Available at ftp://nic.ddn.mil/rfc /rfc1321.txt.

[RKF92] W. Rosenberry, D. Kenney, and G. Fisher. *Understanding DCE*. O'Reilly, 1992.

[RL92] M. Rabinovitch and E. D. Lazowska. Improving fault tolerance and supporting partial writes in structured coterie protocols for replicated objects. *Proc. ACM SIGMOD*, pages 226–235, 1992.

[RL93] M. Rabinovitch and E. D. Lazowska. Asynchronous epoch management in replicated databases. *Proc. Workshop on Distributed Algorithms*, pages 115–128, 1993.

[RN91] J. Ramanathan and L. M. Ni. Critical factors in NUMA memory management. *Proc. 11th Int'l Conf. on Distributed Systems*, pages 500–507, 1991.

[Rom91] C. G. Rommel. The probability of load balancing success in a homogeneous network. *IEEE Trans. on Software Engineering*, SE-17(9):922–933, 1991.

[Ros83] S. M. Ross. *Stochastic Processes*. Wiley, 1983.

[RP93] K. Rothermel and S. Pappe. Open commit protocols tolerating commission failures. *ACM Trans. on Database Systems*, 18(2):289–332, 1993.

[RS87] V. J. Rayward-Smith. UET scheduling with unit interprocessor communication delays. *Discrete Applied Mathematics*, 18:55–71, 1987.

[RS95] M. Raynal and M. Singhal. Logical time: A way to capture causality in distributed systems. Technical Report 900, IRISA, 1995.

[RSA78] R. Rivest, A. Shamir, and L. Adelman. A method of obtaining digital signatures and public-key crypto-systems. *Communications of the ACM*, 21(2):120–126, 1978.

[RSL78] D. J. Rosenkrantz, R. E Stearns, and P. M. Lewis. System level concurrency control for distributed database systems. *ACM Trans. on Database Systems*, 3(2):178–198, 1978.

[RST91] M. Raynal, A. Schiper, and S. Toueg. The causal ordering abstraction and a simple way to implement it. *Information Processing Letters*, 39:343–350, 1991.

[RST92] S. Rangarajan, S. Setia, and S. K. Tripathi. A fault-tolerant algorithm for replicated data management. *Int'l Conf. on Data Engineering*, pages 230–237, 1992.

[RT88] R. Van Renesse and A. S. Tanenbaum. Voting with ghosts. *8th Int'l Conf. on Distributed Computing Systems*, pages 456–462. IEEE, June 1988.

[Ruf92] M. Ruffin. KITLOG: A generic logging service. *Proc. Symp. on Reliable Distributed Systems*, pages 139–146, 1992.

[Rug94] F. Ruget. Cheaper matrix clocks. *Proc. Workshop on Distributed Algorithms*, pages 355–369, 1994.

[RV95] L. E. T. Rodrigues and P. Verissimo. Causal separators for large-scale multicast communication. *Proc. Int'l Conf. on Distributed Computing Systems*, pages 83–91, 1995.

[San87] B. Sanders. The information structure of distributed mutual exlcusion algorithms. *ACM Trans. on Computer Systems*, 5(3):284–299, 1987.

[San88] R. Sandhu. Transaction control expressions for separation of duties. *Proc. 4th Aerospace Computer Security Application Conf.*, pages 282–286, 1988.

[San91] M. Santifaller. *TCP/IP and NFS, Internetworking in a UNIX Environment*. Addison-Wesley, 1991.

[San96] B. Sanders. Data refinement of mixed specifications: A generalization of UNITY. Technical Report 96-010, Dept. of CISE, University of Florida, 1996. Available at ftp.cis.ufl.edu.

[SB94] M. Spasojevic and P. Berman. Voting as the optimal static pessimistic scheme for managing replicated data. *IEEE Trans. on Parallel and Distributed Systems*, 5(1):64–73, 1994.

[SBY88] R. E. Strom, D. F. Bacon, and S. Yemini. Volatile logging in n-fault-tolerant distributed systems. *Proc. Int'l Symp. on Fault Tolerant Systems*, pages 44–49, 1988.

[SES89] A. Schiper, J. Eggli, and A. Sandoz. A new algorithm to implement causal ordering. *Proc. 3rd Int'l Workshop on Distributed Algorithms*, pages 219–232, 1989.

[SFP89] S. Sarin, R. Floyd, and N. Phadnis. A flexible algorithm for replicated directory management. *Proc. Int'l Conf. on Distributed Computing Systems*, pages 456–464, 1989.

[SG94a] A. Silberschatz and P. B. Galvin. *Operating System Concepts*. Addison-Wesley, 1994.

[SG94b] M. Spezialetti and R. Gupta. Debugging distributed programs through the detection of simultaneous events. *Int'l Conf. on Distributed Computing Systems*, pages 634–641, 1994.

[SGK+85] R. Sandberg, D. Goldberg, S. Kleiman, D. Walsh, and B. Lyon. Design and implementation of Sun Network Filesystem. *Proc. Summer USENIX Conf.*, pages 119–130, 1985.

[SH86] V. Sarkar and J. Hennessy. Compile-time partitioning and scheduling of parallel programs. *Proc. SIGPLAN Symp. on Compiler Construction*, pages 17–26, 1986.

[SH92] B. A. Shirazi and A. R. Hurson. Scheduling and load balancing. *J. of Parallel and Distributed Computing*, 16(4):271–275, 1992.

[SHK95] B. A. Shirazi, A. R. Hurson, and K. M. Kavi. *Scheduling and Load Balancing in Parallel and Distributed Systems*. IEEE Computer Society Press, 1995.

[SI94] T. Soneoka and T. Ibaraki. Logically instantaneous message passing in asynchronous distributed systems. *IEEE Trans. on Computers*, 43(5):513–527, 1994.

[Sin89] M. Singhal. A heuristically-aided algorithm for mutual exclusion in distributed systems. *IEEE Trans. on Computers*, 38(8):651–661, 1989.

[Sin92] M. Singhal. A dynamic information-structure mutual exclusion algorithm for distributed systems. *IEEE Trans. on Parallel and Distributed Systems*, 3(1):121–125, 1992.

[SJT95] S. W. Smith, D. B. Johnson, and J. D. Tygar. Completely asynchronous optimistic recovery with minimal rollbacks. *IEEE Symp. on Fault Tolerant Computing*, pages 361–370, 1995.

[SK85] I. Suzuki and T. Kasami. A distributed mutual exclusion algorithm. *ACM Trans. on Computer Systems*, 3(4):344–349, 1985.

[SK86] M. Spezialetti and J. P. Kearns. Efficient distributed snapshots. *Proc. Int'l Conf. on Distributed Computing Systems*, pages 382–388, 1986.

[SK89] M. Spezialetti and J. P. Kearns. Simultaneous regions : A framework for the consistent monitoring of distributed systems. *Proc. Int'l Conf. on Distributed Computing Systems*, pages 61–68, 1989.

[SK92] M. Singhal and A. Kshemkalyani. An efficient implementation of vector clocks. *Information Processing Letters*, 43, 1992.

[SK94] S. Singh and J. Kurose. Electing "good" leaders. *J. of Parallel and Distributed Computing*, 21:184–201, 1994.

[Ske82a] D. Skeen. Crash recovery in a distributed database system. Technical Report UCB/ERL M82/45, Electronics Research Laboratory, University of California at Berkeley, 1982.

[Ske82b] D. Skeen. Nonblocking commit protocols. *Proc. ACM SIGMOD Conf. on Management of Data*, pages 133–147, 1982.

[Ske82c] D. Skeen. A quorum based commit protocol. *Proc. 6th Berkeley Workshop on Distributed Data Management and Computer Networks*, pages 69–80, 1982.

[SKK+90] M. Satyanarayanan, J. J. Kistler, P. Kumar, M. E. Okasaki, E. H. Siegel, and D. C. Steere. Coda: A highly available file system for a distributed workstation environment. *IEEE Trans. on Computers*, 39(4):447–459, 1990.

[SKS92] N. G. Shivaratri, P. Krueger, and M. Singhal. Load distributing for locally distributed systems. *IEEE Computer*, 25(12):33–44, 1992.

[SL87] S. K. Sarin and N. Lynch. Discarding obsolete information in a replicated database. *IEEE Trans. on Software Engineering*, 13(1):39–46, 1987.

[SLR76] R. E. Stearns, P. M. Lewis, and D. J Rosenkrantz. Concurrency controls for database systems. *Proc. 17th Symp. on Foundations of Computer Science*, pages 19–32, 1976.

[SM92] R. Satyanarayanan and D. R. Muthukrishnan. A note on Raymond's tree based algorithm for distributed mutual exclusion. *Information Processing Letters*, 43:249–255, 1992.

[SM94a] R. Schwarz and F. Mattern. Detecting causal relationships in distributed computations: search of the holy grail. *Distributed Computing*, 7(3):149–174, 1994.

[SM94b] S. K. Shrivasta and D. L. McCue. Structuring fault-tolerant object systems for modularity in a distributed environment. *IEEE Trans. on Parallel and Distributed Systems*, 5(4):421–432, 1994.

[SNS88] J. G. Steiner, B. C. Neuman, and J. I. Schiller. Kerberos: An authentication service for open network systems. *Proc. Winter 1988 USENIX Conf.*, pages 191–202, 1988.

[SP86] A. B. Sheltzer and G. J. Popek. Internet Locus: Extending transparency to an Internet environment. *IEEE Trans. on Software Engineering*, SE-12(11):1067–1975, 1986.

[Spe91] M. Spezialetti. An approach to reducing delays in recognizing distributed event ocurrences. *ACM/ONR SIGPLAN Workshop on Parallel and Distributed Debugging*, pages 155–166, 1991.

[SR91] P. K. Srimani and R. L. N Reddy. Another distributed algorithm for multiple entries to a critical section. *Information Processing Letters*, 41:51–57, 1991.

[SRL90] L. Sha, R. Rajkumar, and J. P. Lehoczky. Priority inheritance protocols: An approach to real-time synchronization. *IEEE Trans. on Computers*, 39(9):1175–1185, 1990.

[SS92] D. Stein and D. Shaw. Implementing light weight threads. *Proc. Summer USENIX Conf.*, pages 1–9, 1992.

[SS93] A. Schiper and A. Sandoz. Uniform reliable multicast in a virtually synchronous environment. *Proc. Int'l Conf. on Distributed Computing Systems*, pages 561–568, 1993.

[SS94] M. Singhal and N. G. Shivaratri. *Advanced Concepts in Operating Systems*. McGraw Hill, 1994.

[Sta92] W. Stallings. *Operating Systems*. Macmillan, 1992.

[Sta94] W. Stallings. *Data and Computer Communications*. Macmillan, 1994.

[Ste91] W. R. Stevens. *UNIX Network Programming*. Prentice-Hall, 1991.

[Sto77] H. S. Stone. Multiprocessor scheduling with the aid of network flow algorithms. *IEEE Trans. on Software Engineering*, SE-3(1):85–93, 1977.

[Sto79] M. Stonebraker. Concurrency control and consistency of multiple copies of data in distributed INGRES. *Communications of the ACM*, 3(3):188–194, 1979.

[SW89] A. P. Sistla and J. L. Welch. Efficient distributed recovery using message logging. *Proc. Symp. on Principles of Distributed Computing*, pages 223–238, 1989.

[SWP90] B. A. Shirazi, M. Wang, and G. Pathak. Analysis and evaluation of heuristic methods for static task scheduling. *J. of Parallel and Distributed Computing*, 10:222–232, 1990.

[SY85] R. E. Strom and S. Yemini. Optimistic recovery in distributed systems. *ACM Trans. on Computer Systems*, 3(3):204–226, 1985.

[Syv93] P. Syverson. On key distribution protocols for repeated authentication. *Operating Systems Review*, 27(4):24–30, 1993.

[SZ90] M. Stumm and S. Zhou. Algorithms implementing distributed shared memory. *IEEE Computer*, 23(5):54–64, 1990.

[Tan90] A. S. Tanenbaum. *Computer Networks*. Prentice-Hall, 1990.

[Tan92] A. S. Tanenbaum. *Modern Operating Systems*. Prentice Hall, 1992.

[Tan95] A. S. Tanenbaum. *Distributed Operating Systems*. Prentice-Hall, 1995.

[Tay91] Y. C. Tay. A theory for deadlocks. Technical Report Research Report No. 459, Dept. of Mathematics, National University of Singapore, 1991.

[TBW94] K. W. Tindell, A. Burns, and A. J. Wellings. An extendible approach for analyzing fixed priority hard real-time tasks. *Real Time Systems*, 6:133–151, 1994.

[TGGL82] I. L. Traiger, J. Gray, C. A. Galteri, and B. G. Lindsay. Transactions and consistency in distributed database systems. *ACM Trans. on Database Systems*, 7(3):323–342, 1982.

[Tho79] R. H. Thomas. A majority consensus approach to concurrency control for multiple copy databases. *ACM Trans. on Database Systems*, 4(2):180–209, 1979.

[TK88] Z. Tong and R. Y. Kain. Vote assignments in weighted voting mechanisms. *Proc. 7th Symp. on Reliable Distributed Systems*, pages 138–143, 1988.

[TK91] Z. Tong and R. Y. Kain. Vote assignments in weighted voting mechanisms. *IEEE Trans. on Computers*, 40(5):664–667, 1991.

[TLC85] M. M. Theimer, K. A. Lantz, and D. R. Cheriton. Preemptable remote execution facilities for the V-System. *Proc. 10th ACM Symp. on Operating Systems Principles*, pages 2–12, 1985.

[TM87] M. Trehel and M. Maimi. An improvement of the log(n) distributed algorithm for mutual exclusion. *Proc. 7th Int'l Conf. on Distributed Computing Systems*, pages 371–375, 1987.

[TN87] M. Trehel and M. Naimi. A distributed algorithm for mutual exclusion based on data structures and fault tolerance. *IEEE Phoenix Conf. on Computers and Communication*, pages 35–39, 1987.

[TN91] S. K. Tripathi and V. Nirkhe. Pre-scheduling for synchronization in hard real-time systems. *Operating Systems of the '90s and Beyond, Int'l Workshop*, pages 102–108, 1991. Appears as Springer-Verlag Computer Science Lecture Note No. 563.

[Tow86] D. Towsley. Allocating programs containing branches and loops within a multiprocessor system. *IEEE Trans. on Software Engineering*, SE-12(10):1018–1024, 1986.

[TPK95] O. Theel and H. Pagnia-Koch. General design of grid-based data replication schemes using graphs and a few rules. *Proc. Int'l Conf. on Distributed Computing Systems*, pages 395–403, 1995.

[TS92] A. Tang and S. Scoggins. *Open Networking with OSI*. Prentice-Hall, 1992.

[TT94] P. Triantafillou and D. J. Taylor. Multiclass replicated data management: Exploiting replication to improve efficiency. *IEEE Trans. on Parallel and Distributed Systems*, 5(2):121–138, 1994.

[TT95] P. Triantafillou and D. J. Taylor. The location-based paradigm for replication: Achieving efficiency and availability in distributed systems. *IEEE Trans. on Software Engineering*, 21(1):1–17, 1995.

[Ull75] J. D. Ullman. NP-complete scheduling problems. *J. of Computing System Science*, 10:384–393, 1975.

[VAB91] V. Varadharajan, P. Allen, and S. Black. An analysis of the proxy problem in distributed systems. *Proc. IEEE Symp. on Research in Security and Privacy*, pages 255–275, 1991.

[VD95] S. Venkatesan and B. Dathan. Testing and debugging distributed programs using global predicates. *IEEE Trans. on Parallel and Distributed Systems*, 21(2):163–176, 1995.

[Ven89] S. Venkatesan. Message-optimal incremental snapshots. *Int'l Conf. on Distributed Computing Systems*, pages 53–60, 1989.

[VLL90] B. Veltman, B. J. Lageweg, and J. K. Lenstra. Multiprocessor scheduling with communication delays. *Parallel Computing, North-Holland*, 16:173–182, 1990.

[VRL87] V. Venkatesh, T. Radhakrishnan, and H. F. Li. Optimal checkpointing and local recording for domino-free rollback recovery. *Information Processing Letters*, 25:295–303, 1987.

[Wan95] Y.-M. Wang. Maximum and minimum consistent global checkpoints and their applications. *IEEE Symp. on Reliable Distributed Systems*, pages 86–95, 1995.

[WB84] G. T. J. Wuu and A. J. Bernstein. Efficient solutions to the replicated log and dictionary problems. *Proc. 3rd. Symp. on Principles of Distributed Computing*, pages 233–242, 1984.

[WB92] C. Wu and G. G. Belford. The triangular lattice protocol: A highly fault tolerant and highly efficient protocol for replicated data. *IEEE 11th Symp. on Reliable Distributed Systems*, pages 66–73, 1992.

[WCLF95] Y.-M. Wang, P.-Y. Chung, I.-J. Lin, and W. K. Fuchs. Checkpoint space reclamation for uncoordinated checkpointing in message passing systems. *IEEE Trans. on Parallel and Distributed Systems*, 6(5):546–554, 1995.

[Wei88] W. E. Weihl. Commutivity-based concurrency control for abstract data types. *IEEE Trans. on Computers*, 37(12):1488–1505, 1988.

[WF92a] Y.-M. Wang and W. K. Fuchs. Optimistic message logging for independent checkpointing in message-passing systems. *IEEE Symp. on Reliable Distributed Systems*, pages 147–154, 1992.

[WF92b] Y.-M. Wang and W. K. Fuchs. Scheduling message processing for reducing rollback propagation. *Proc. Int'l Symp. on Fault Tolerant Computing*, pages 204–211, 1992.

[WF93] Y.-M. Wang and W. K. Fuchs. Lazy checkpoint coordination for bounding rollback propogation. *Proc. Symp. on Reliable Distributed Systems*, pages 78–85, 1993.

[WHF93] Y.-M. Wang, Y. Huang, and W. K. Fuchs. Progressive retry for software error recovery in distributed systems. *Proc. Int'l Symp. on Fault Tolerant Computing*, pages 138–143, 1993.

[WHV$^+$95] Y.-M. Wang, Y. Huang, K.-P. Vo, P.-Y. Chung, and C. Kintala. Checkpointing and its applications. *Proc. Int'l Symp. on Fault Tolerant Computing*, pages 22–31, 1995.

[Win96] WinSock Standard Group. *WinSock*, 1996. Available at http://www.stardust.com /wsresource/.

[Wir77] N. Wirth. Modula: A language for modular programming. *Software Practice and Experience*, 7(1):3–65, 1977.

[WLF94] Y.-M. Wang, A. Lowry, and W. K. Fuchs. Consistent global checkpoints based on direct dependency tracking. *Information Processing Letters*, 50:223–230, 1994.

[WM85] Y. T. Wang and R. J. Morris. Load sharing in distributed systems. *IEEE Trans. on Computers*, 34(3):204–217, 1985.

[WS95] U. Wilhelm and A. Schiper. A hierarchy of totally ordered multicasts. *IEEE Symp. on Reliable Distributed Systems*, pages 106–115, 1995.

[Xer81] Xerox Corporation. *Courier: The Remote Procedure Call Protocol. Xerox System Integration Standards 038112*, 1981.

[YC94] C.-R. Young and G.-M. Chiu. A crash recovery technique in distributed computing systems. *Int'l Conf. on Distributed Computing Systems*, pages 235–242, 1994.

[Zay87] E. R. Zayas. Attacking the process migration bottleneck. *Proc. 11th ACM Symp. on Operating Systems Principles*, pages 13–24, 1987.

INDEX